COMPREHENSIVE APPLIED SPORT PSYCHOLOGY

Edited by Jim Taylor

Routledge
Taylor & Francis Group

NEW YORK AND LONDON

First published 2020
by Routledge
52 Vanderbilt Avenue, New York, NY 10017

and by Routledge
2 Park Square, Milton Park, Abingdon, Oxon, OX14 4RN

Routledge is an imprint of the Taylor & Francis Group, an informa business

© 2020 Taylor & Francis

The right of Jim Taylor to be identified as the author of the editorial material, and of the authors for their individual chapters, has been asserted in accordance with sections 77 and 78 of the Copyright, Designs and Patents Act 1988.

Library of Congress Cataloging-in-Publication Data
Names: Taylor, Jim, 1958- editor.
Title: Comprehensive applied sport psychology / edited by Jim Taylor.
Description: New York : Routledge, 2019.
Identifiers: LCCN 2019010068| ISBN 9781138587359 (hardback) | ISBN
     9781138587885 (paperback) | ISBN 9780429503689 (ebook)
Subjects: LCSH: Sports—Psychological aspects. | Coaching (Athletics) |
     Psychology, Applied.
Classification: LCC GV706.4 .C65 2019 | DDC 796.01/9—dc23
LC record available at https://lccn.loc.gov/2019010068

ISBN: 978-1-138-58735-9 (hbk)
ISBN: 978-1-138-58788-5 (pbk)
ISBN: 978-0-429-50368-9 (ebk)

Typeset in Bembo
by Swales & Willis Ltd, Exeter, Devon, UK

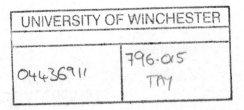

MIX
Paper from
responsible sources
FSC   FSC™ C013985   Printed in the United Kingdom
www.fsc.org   by Henry Ling Limited

COMPREHENSIVE APPLIED SPORT PSYCHOLOGY

The aim of Comp ... beyond its
current status and ... broad and
multi-layered exar ... community
contends with in p ... heir professional capacities.

Comprehensive ... pansive and
deep exploration c ... ainers do in
their work.

CASP plumbs ... al obstacles,
mental "muscles" ... s, and other
areas that are esser ... consultants
impact athletes, bu ... oups such as
sports medicine te ...

The book is gr ... duate training in applied spo ... ith athletes,
coaches, teams, an ... the field, is
to create the defin ...

Jim Taylor, Ph.I ... ort and parenting. He has co ... ck and field,
swimming, footba ... Taylor is the
author of eight be ... orld-ranked
alpine ski racer, 2 ...

CONTENTS

INTRODUCTION

The fields of applied sport psychology and mental training have grown significantly over the last several decades. Graduate programs all over the world are attracting students with a passion for helping athletes achieve their sports goals. Professionals in psychology and the sport sciences are drawn to the opportunities for career advancement and fulfillment our field has made available. Professional and Olympic athletes and teams in most sports employ consultants on a regular basis, and, more and more, high school and youth sports organizations are leveraging the resources that sport psychologists and mental coaches (termed "consultants" from this point forward to avoid licensing and title conflicts) have to offer.

As part of that growth, many outstanding applied sport psychology books have been published for graduate student and professional audiences, including *Handbook of Sport Psychology* (Tennebaum & Eklund, 2007), *The Oxford Handbook of Sport and Performance Psychology* (Murphy, 2012), *Foundations of Exploring Sport and Exercise Psychology* (Van Raalte & Brewer, 2013), *Sport and Exercise Psychology* (Weinberg & Gould, 2014), and *Applied Sport Psychology: Personal Growth to Peak Performance* (Williams & Krane, 2014).

Comprehensive Applied Sport Psychology (*CASP*) builds on the tradition of these seminal books and goes further in offering consultants value by:

- addressing the needs, interests, and goals of students in applied sport psychology graduate programs and professionals who want to continue to grow;
- providing rigorous theory and research for each of the topics explored;
- offering both an evidence-based and "boots on the ground" resource to consultants for their work in sports;
- creating an easily recognizable and intuitive chapter and sentence structure; and
- delivering an accessible and compelling writing style.

CASP is aimed at offering a truly expansive and deep exploration of what consultants do, "from attitude to athletic success and most everything in between," you could say. It plumbs the depths of the athletic mind, first, with the widely discussed topics found in the quivers of every consultant to help maximize mental preparation for athletic performance and then to other topics rarely talked about that, nonetheless, play a vital role in athletic performance including:

- essential attitudes for athletic success;
- psychological and emotional obstacles to athletic success;
- mental "muscles" and mental "tools";
- quality sport training; and
- special challenges that every athlete faces.

CASP also does a "deep dive" into other areas that impact athletes both within their sporting lives and in their personal lives including overall health and well-being, as well as mental health issues that affect athletes both on and off the field of play. *CASP* doesn't stop at the athlete though. Instead, it explores the work that consultants do in the entire sport "solar system" including:

- conditioning and sport coaches;
- teams;
- parents;
- sports medicine staff; and
- a sports organization's management.

A More Precise Vocabulary

The fields of applied sport psychology and mental training have a long history of helping athletes in many sports and around the world. A part of that history is a shared vocabulary that is commonly used to label mental areas that impact athletic performance and the techniques to develop those areas. These labels, titles, words, and phrases have become the accepted nomenclature for most consultants in our field. Yet, an essential aspect of my vision in developing *CASP* is to challenge our field in ways that will encourage its growth and relevance to the sports community that we hope to serve and support.

With that in mind, my intention is introduce a new vocabulary for many of the most frequently used terms in our field. I do this not just for the sake of being different. In fact, one could argue that the language I will be introducing offers only semantic differences and it doesn't really matter what words are use. However, as a "wordsmith" (i.e., someone whose work revolves around their use), I would suggest that words matter because they act as the lens through which we come to interpret and understand ideas. Moreover, words provide the intended meaning behind those ideas which becomes the foundation for all subsequent thinking, feeling, and action around them. Given the complexity of the work we do, I believe that we must choose the words we use thoughtfully and intentionally.

I have several goals in offering a more precise vocabulary. First, to cause our field to question its many tenets as a means of "disrupting" (in the best sense of the word) the status quo and to push it to innovate and evolve in ways that will better support its members and the sports in which we engage. Second, to deepen and broaden our understanding of what applied sport psychology and mental training are and how to offer more and better to the athletes and others we are all committed to helping. Third, to use a vocabulary that more accurately reflects what those mental areas mean and represent to those in our field. Finally, the sports community will more easily grasp what we do because it will speak to them in their own language, thus making our work more welcoming, accessible, and meaningful to those in sports we are so dedicated to assisting.

A Natural Structure and Progression

Another way in which I hope to disrupt our field is to provide more structure to a wide swath of content that isn't always cohesive or integrated. This framework is so important because athletes and others don't seek out professionals in our field for specific methods, strategies, or techniques that we offer; the internet can provide those with ease and at no cost. The various members of a sports community (i.e., athletes, coaches, parents, teams) reach out to us to provide a structured program and progression that will lead them toward their goals (just as they do with conditioning coaches).

I believe that every body of knowledge has a natural structure and progression, where the disparate parts join together to create a unified whole that is orderly, sensible, understandable, and enables readers to say, "Yeah, I get it." As part of the construction of this "house," there is a clearly defined order for putting the building blocks in place and an inherent flow from one building block to the next (e.g., you can't put on the roof before the foundation is laid and the walls have been built). I have applied this perspective to *CASP* such that each part, chapter, and section emerges out of and builds on its predecessor and each feels like it is an integrated part of the book and an organic extension of that which came before it.

This structure has several benefits. First, an essential part of *CASP* is not just the many ideas we share with you, but the structure itself that you can use to scaffold your own approach to consulting in applied sport psychology and mental training. Second, it enables you to create a structure in your own mind in which to organize and synthesize the information you garner from *CASP*. Third, this structure allows you to more readily wrap your arms around the many ideas we share in *CASP* and to apply them to your work within the sports community.

Comprehensive, but not Exhaustive

As the title suggests, *CASP* provides a comprehensive, but, not exhaustive, exploration of essential issues in applied sport psychology and mental training. Due to limits placed on its length, I had to make some tough decisions about what topics to include and those to omit. I based my decisions on two criteria. First, was the topic of direct and practical value to students and professionals in applied sport psychology and mental training in their work with the sports community? Second, were there more thorough explorations of the topics in other resources such as books? For example, ethics lie at the heart of effective consulting, yet a thorough accounting of the topic has been wonderfully rendered by my colleagues Drs. Ed Etzel and Jack Watson in their book, *Ethical Issues in Sport, Exercise, and Performance Psychology* (Fit Publishing, 2013). Similarly, though assessment is a fundamental tool in every consultant's toolbox, it has been examined in great detail in *Assessment in Applied Sport Psychology* (Human Kinetics, 2017), a book for which I am the editor.

What Lies Ahead

CASP is scientifically rigorous, grounded in the latest applied sport psychology and mental training theory and research. At the same time, it is intended to be more than an academic tome that is used as a scholarly reference. An essential goal of the book is that it will take the theoretical and empirical foundations of our field and translate this scholarly body of knowledge into practical insights, information, and approaches that consultants can use directly in their work with athletes, coaches, parents, and teams. The goal of *CASP* is to define and explain what applied sport psychology and mental training is and can be in the most broad, deep, and sophisticated way possible and, yet, also to make it useable in consultants' daily work lives. Moreover, I have two bigger ambitions in creating *CASP*. First, for *CASP* to be the definitive resource for graduate programs and professionals of what applied sport psychology and mental training is and does. Second, and more importantly, for *CASP* to provide impetus for our field to progress beyond its current place in the sports world and have applied sport psychology and mental training become what we all know it is capable of being, that is, an essential and truly transformative force for everyone in the sports community to be and do their best.

PART I

Mental Training

1

ATTITUDES

Introduction

Jim Taylor

Attitudes play a foundational role in sports performance because they establish how athletes perceive, think about, interpret, and evaluate their sports experiences. Attitudes also influence the emotions athletes feel, their behavior in training and competitive situations, and, ultimately, the quality of their competitive performances. Additionally, although attitudes normally carry a positive connotation, they can be either positive or negative and have a beneficial or harmful impact on athletes. The attitudes that will be discussed in this chapter demonstrate the power that positive attitudes have on athletes.

What makes attitudes so complex is they can arise from either conscious or unconscious sources. Conscious attitudes are ones in which athletes are aware of how they developed, athletes can easily access them, and they are easy to modify if they prove themselves to be unhelpful. Conversely, attitudes that are embedded in athletes' unconscious minds are difficult to recognize, identify their origins, gain access to, and alter. Attitudes typically develop in athletes from life and sports experiences and through modeling during childhood. Because of this early entrenchment in the psyches of athletes, they rarely make a conscious choice about which attitudes to adopt, but rather accept those attitudes that are most present in their lives, for good or for ill. Thus, they are not able to make deliberate choices about their attitudes until much later in their lives and, as will be discussed in Chapter 2, some attitudes can have an unhealthy influence not only on athletes' sports efforts, but also on the quality of their lives in general.

Though the "attitude is everything" axiom is used frequently in the sports community, there has been little in-depth discussion or explanation about what specific attitudes impact sports performance, why they are important, why some attitudes can be positive and others negative, or how athletes can foster attitudes that support their sports lives and jettison those that don't.

Chapter 1 focuses on attitudes that are essential for athletic success. The six attitudes that will be explored are:

- Ownership
- Growth Mindset
- Challenge
- Risk-taking
- Process
- Long Term

Consultants have several goals in helping athletes to develop healthy attitudes. First, they can assess the attitudes athletes possess. Second, consultants can evaluate the degree to which those attitudes help or hurt athletes. Third, they can show athletes how to strengthen the positive attitudes that they hold.

OWNERSHIP

Tim Herzog and Jim Taylor

A fundamental building block of athletic success is for athletes to take ownership of their training and performance in appropriately increasing increments over the course of their development. Macmillan Dictionary (n.d.) defines ownership as: "An attitude of accepting responsibility for something and taking control of how it develops." When athletes feel a sense of ownership over their sports lives, they believe that they are capable of influencing all of its aspects and effecting change when necessary. This sense that athletes possess control over their own sport training, development, and performance contributes to a positive environment, an overall feeling that their sport is enjoyable, and is motivating in its own right.

Cultivating a sense of ownership does not have to happen all at once. As Dawes and Larson (2011) put it, "Encouragement from parents, incentives, and the desire to affiliate with peers may be valuable means to get some youth in the door; but these extrinsic incentives do not preclude youth from developing deeper, more sustained engagement in program activities" (p. 266). Ultimately, a shift is most likely to occur if: (1) participation connects in some way to young athletes' earnest and serious side; (2) participation becomes an increasingly integral component of identity and/or of some bigger purpose; and (3) there is some kind of "hook" that connects with personal values or goals (Dawes & Larson, 2011). Thus, ownership over sport participation appears to be closely related to athletes' engagement, which evolves as their involvement in their sports lives deepen rather than all at once.

On a practical level, consultants can facilitate cultivation of athlete ownership over their sports participation by asking them several questions:

- Do you take responsibility for everything that impacts your sports performances?
- Do you give your fullest effort regularly in training and competitions?
- Do you hold yourself accountable for your efforts?
- Do you make excuses or blame others when you perform poorly?
- Do you ease up or quit readily when struggling in training or competition?

If athletes respond "yes" to the first three questions and "no" to the last two, they are taking significant ownership of their sports lives. If athletes are ready to hear it, consultants can convey that, if their aspirations in their sport are high and they want to give themselves the opportunity to experience success, ownership of their sport is essential (Prochaska, DiClemente, & Norcross, 1992). In line with a motivational interviewing approach, if athletes express any ambivalence regarding their investment, helping them to explore both sides of their thinking (without imposing bias) can help athletes to arrive at decisions that they truly "own" (Markland, Ryan, Tobin, & Rollnick, 2005).

Theory and Research

Ownership is a vital part of athlete development and fundamental to helping athletes achieve their sports goals. However, ownership is not something that athletes can just assume (particularly younger athletes) because, often, there are many stakeholders who want to gain or maintain ownership as well. As a result, athletes can experience a tug of war for ownership, potentially defaulting to stakeholders' desires or rebelling against those desires in an effort to experience autonomy.

Every sport has its own unique set of stakeholders including parents, coaches, and team administrators. At the highest level of sport, the list of stakeholders grows to include agents, sponsors, media, and assorted hangers-on. Every stakeholder has a vested interest in athletes' careers, there is a risk that athletes could either never gain or lose their sense of ownership as other stakeholders assert themselves into their lives within and outside of their sport. Particularly in youth sports where young athletes are often not yet capable of assuming full ownership of their sports participation, stakeholders must be sensitive to what they should and shouldn't appropriately take responsibility for. For example, parents' ownership of their young athlete's participation might include paying relevant fees, providing necessary equipment, knowing the practice and competition schedules, and ensuring that their children arrive on time for team activities. Conversely, overstepping those parental responsibilities could involve coaching their children (when not a coach), setting outcome goals, and carrying their kids' gear to games. As a foundation of preparing athletes for ownership, adult stakeholders can communicate effectively and with transparency, facilitate harmony, and cultivate an optimal development experience for youth athletes to prevent this co-opting from occurring. Identifying what is in one's control, what is influenceable, and what must be accepted, is an empowering process for athletes that can encourage ownership (Herzog, Zavilla, Dupee, & Stephenson, 2018). Specifically in the context of navigating dynamics with other stakeholders, athletes can be mentored at any age to hone effective communication skills, asking for what they want and need, and developing awareness of when and how to effectively set boundaries.

Four Obstacles to Ownership

In addition to knowing what aspects of athletes' lives should be owned by whom and helping athletes to gain age-appropriate ownership, it behooves consultants and athletes to identify potential obstacles to athletes' ownership. There are four primary obstacles: (1) Ill-advised agendas; (2) overinvolved parents; (3) extrinsic motivation; and (4) triangulation.

Ill-advised Agendas

While primary stakeholders in athletes' lives, most notably their parents, are often well-intentioned, those good intentions are sometimes not realized with good action. For instance, parents could be unknowingly living vicariously through their children, while also weighing whether the family is getting return on their financial investment. In turn, athletes can feel immense pressure to succeed. Relatedly, a coach could fear losing status and power if parents or other stakeholders intervene in their athletes' development. Thus, each stakeholder's best intentions can get inverted by complicated relationship dynamics and their own unconscious needs.

Over-involved Parents

The current era of sport parenting is characterized by over-involvement. Known by many names, including helicopter parents, Little League parents, and stage parents, these parents control their children's sports lives (and lives in general), "swoop in" to rescue their children, even adult children, rather than letting them have autonomy thereby learning how to handle adversity on their own (Shiffrin et al., 2014; Padilla-Walker & Nelson, 2012). "Tiger parenting" is the stereotype that Asian-Americans manage their children's lives to ensure their success in academics and other performance domains via strict regimens with little ownership or leeway to make choices. Tiger parenting styles are not confined to Asian-Americans; it is a parenting trend among many families and incorporates demanding, pushing, pulling, threatening, cajoling, directing, bribing, instructing, scheduling, and monitoring of children in a well-intentioned but misguided effort to drive them to succeed. Hudson and Rapee (2002) demonstrated that over-involvement often backfires because as athletes lose ownership over their sport, they become more susceptible to anxiety, feel an increased perception of "threat," lose self-efficacy in their coping, and, ultimately, quit their sport because it has become so aversive.

Extrinsic Motivation

Extrinsic rewards meted out to athletes, whether tangible (e.g., money, gifts) or intangible (e.g., attention, praise), can initially act as motivators for athletes to work hard and find success. At the same time, using rewards has the potential to undermine intrinsic motivation, weaken athletes' motivation and ownership over the long run (Deci, Koestner, & Ryan, 1999). Essentially, athletes who already love their sport and then receive extrinsic reinforcers to participate or perform can experience a shift from participating for internal reasons (e.g., love of the sport) to external reasons (e.g., to please their parents). If the rewards are big enough (e.g., love of a parent, a full college scholarship, admiration of fans), athletes may believe that they only engage in their sport for those rewards. Moreover, with a shift from intrinsic to extrinsic motivation, athletes may lose their sense of ownership of sports involvement.

Triangulation

A concept from family systems, known as "triangulation," can be useful in understanding relationships in sport and its impact on athlete ownership. When triangulation occurs, two people (a "dyad") use a third party to mediate rather than communicating directly (Turman, 2007). Triangulation often occurs in an attempt to exert more control over the other member of the dyad. This negative pattern can also be seen with coaches and other stakeholders in athletes' lives who may inadvertently undermine the healthy involvement of athletes to satisfy their own needs and goals. It prevents direct communication aimed at sorting through tensions (Herzog, 2014). Moreover, when different stakeholders' agendas conflict, a battle for control may ensue in which the ultimate loser is the athlete, who may experience a lost (or non-existent) sense of control over domains that should be under their control. With this loss of ownership, athletes can feel confused about what they value, feel out of touch with what truly motivates them, and lose track of the process goals that could be focal points under their control (Herzog, 2014).

Practical Implications

Consultants can play a valuable role in athletes' development of a strong sense of ownership. Moreover, this impact doesn't just come from working with athletes. Equally important, consultants provide insights and perspectives to other stakeholders about how to maintain a healthy investment (and partial ownership) of their athletes' lives while progressively ceding ownership to the athletes themselves over time.

Parents and Other Stakeholders

Ownership isn't something that young athletes can just take for themselves. The reality is that they aren't ready to gain ownership early in their sports careers. Instead, ownership is progressively given to them by their parents, coaches and others as they demonstrate both commitment and responsibility in their sports efforts.

Be a Partner, Not a Boss

Taming the tiger or grounding the "helicopter parent," parking the "snowplow parent," or popping the "bubble-wrapper" can occur by following these guidelines stemming from an empirically based Human Performance Resource Center (www.hprc-online.org) resource:

- ask your children how they would like you to act in their sport;
- encourage your children to have direct conversations with other stakeholders such as coaches;
- provide guidance on aspects of their athletic lives in which they lack experience (e.g., scheduling, packing gear);
- focus on the process, not the outcome; and
- help your children set their own goals.

Listen More, Talk Less

Listening in a way where athletes truly feel heard is vital to their feelings of ownership over their sports lives, and, ultimately, their enjoyment and success in their sport. Consultants can educate parents and other stakeholders on how to help athletes feel listened to (de-emphasizing the content of what is said, and illuminating their thoughts and emotions). For example, can a parent hear and sense athletes' feelings of disappointment and frustration after a painful defeat and respond empathically, rather than being consumed by the details? These are the kinds of skills that consultants can help train in parents, optimizing the athlete's environment.

Let the Athletes Decide

Parents can further encourage ownership in their young athletes by allowing them to make age appropriate decisions. For example, as children mature, they can have input on what team to join, how often to practice, and their overall level of commitment. As children mature and become more experienced in their sport, parents can incrementally cede decision making. As their decision-making increases, so will their sense of ownership. An additional benefit is that the greater decision making and ownership boosts athletes' self-esteem because they will feel more capable and in control of their lives which, in turn, adds to their sense of ownership even further.

Everyone Does Their Job

One practical way for parents to help their children gain ownership of their sports lives is to ensure that every stakeholder does their job and no one else's. There are three key stakeholders in youth sports: parents, coaches, and athletes. Each member of these groups has specific responsibilities to fulfill for the sake of the athletes. Parents enroll their young athletes in the sports program of best fit, cover the cost of their participation, provide transportation to practices and competitions, and offer their children the support and encouragement. Coaches are responsible for guiding physical, technical, and tactical development and to prepare them for success in competitions. The job of young athletes is to give their fullest effort, pay attention to their coaches, and express gratitude to the other stakeholders for the opportunities they have been given.

When parents (and coaches) take on the responsibilities outside of their job description, athletes feel that their ownership has been taken away from them. This often occurs when parents go beyond the appropriate management of their children and begin to micromanage aspects of their sport in which athletes are perfectly capable of taking care of themselves. Athletes' responses may include loss of interest and motivation, lack of enjoyment, anger toward parents, less success, and may drop out of their sport. Children can gradually assume full ownership of their sport when stakeholders do their own jobs, respect boundaries of different roles, and expect athletes to do their job. When this happens, athletes reap more benefits that sports participation offers them.

Athletes

Giving athletes the opportunity to embrace ownership of their sport does not matter unless athletes accept ownership. Consultants can assist athletes in understanding what ownership means, and how to embrace it within their sport.

Clarify Values

When athletes have a clear idea of why they participate in sports, they are more likely to feel highly connected to and feel ownership of it. Unfortunately, the current youth sports culture doesn't necessarily provide athletes (or other stakeholders) with values that are affirming or that foster ownership. Unfortunate examples of values that are sometimes promoted in sports include:

- winning is the number-one goal;
- winning at any cost;
- early specialization is necessary;
- early success is essential for later success;
- selfishness is acceptable;
- wealth and fame define success; and
- success means being "better than" your opponent.

None of these values are intentionally embraced by athletes, parents, or coaches, yet constant exposure, often through televised sports, leads to assimilation into a culture that *does* emphasize these values. Conversely, athletes behaving in congruence with their values can perform while feeling a deeper degree of ownership (Gardner & Moore, 2017). Consultants can take athletes through a process of value clarification as a means of elucidating their values and connecting those values with concrete efforts associated with their sports involvement. This process can involve two steps. First, consultants can ask athletes why they participate in sports. Hopefully, the reasons include, for example, love of sport, enjoyment in learning, being a member of a team, and the challenge of competing. Second, they can ask athletes what they hope to gain from their sports involvement. Hopefully, athletes say, for example, to develop a life-long love of sports, being physically healthy, develop resilience in the face of adversity, and learning essential life lessons. Embracing these kinds of values can contribute to a strong sense of ownership.

Own Their Sport

Ownership isn't just a state of mind or an approach that athletes take to their sport. It is also expressed by what athletes do in their training and competitive efforts. Consultants can help athletes to make this leap from attitude to action. Through techniques such as motivational interviewing or Socratic questioning, they can help athletes determine that if they don't take ownership of and give their fullest effort in every contributor to athletic performance, they are unlikely to achieve their sports goals (Markland, Ryan, Tobin, & Rollnick, 2005; Corlett, 1996). Consultants can then assist athletes in identifying all of the important aspects of sports performance (e.g., conditioning, technique, tactics, mind, equipment, nutrition, sleep), asking athletes if they are owning every one of those areas, and helping them determine how to maximize ownership and get the most out of their sports efforts.

Own Their Mind

Mental training is often the last component of sports development that athletes take ownership of. Because of this disconnect, consultants can work with athletes to help them to assume this ownership. Consultants can educate athletes about what it takes to achieve their sports goals, explore of their sports performance history, and assess of mental strengths and weaknesses (see Chapter 3 for more) to create initial buy-in and foster greater ownership. Consultants can also solicit athletes' perspectives on their ownership and ask probing questions that will help them to identify areas in which they can increase their ownership.

Own the Details

As athletes develop and progress up the competitive ladder in their sport, it is safe to assume that most of them do most things well. They're fit, technically and tactically skilled, and prepare the best they can to perform their best in competition. If everyone is engaging in the more-or-less the same training and preparation, success goes to those who own and pay attention to the seemingly little details that can make the difference between goals achieved and goals missed. If consultants can help athletes determine for themselves that the details *do* matter, they can also help them to identify and capitalize upon these small details. These minutiae can exist within and outside of sports. In sports, athletes can be extra conscious of their nutrition to ensure adequate energy in training. They can hang out with teammates who are positive and motivating. Athletes can even stay away from their social media before competitions to prevent distractions. Outside of sports, they can stay on top of their workload at school, get to bed early in the days leading up to a competition, and keep stress to a minimum in their lives.

Summary

- A fundamental building block of athletic success is for athletes to take ownership of their training and performance in appropriately increasing increments over the course of their development.
- The dictionary defines ownership as: "An attitude of accepting responsibility for something and taking control of how it develops."
- Consultants can help athletes to determine the degree of ownership they have of their sports participation.
- Ownership is not something that athletes can just assume because, often, there are many stakeholders whose "needs" have to be managed.
- Every sport has its own unique set of stakeholders including parents, coaches, and team administrators and there is a risk that athletes could either never gain or lose their sense of ownership as stakeholders assert themselves into the lives of athletes.

- There are four obstacles that can prevent athletes from taking full ownership of their sports lives: ill-advised agenda of stakeholders, overly involved parents, extrinsic motivation, and triangulation.
- As athletes develop in their sport and in their lives, they progress through stages of athletic development that include phases of sampling, selection, investment, and maintenance.
- Consultants can play an important role in athletes' development of ownership by working with athletes directly *and* with other stakeholders including parents and coaches.
- Consultants can provide insights and perspectives to other stakeholders about how to maintain a healthy investment and clear boundaries/roles in their athletes' lives while progressively ceding ownership to the athletes themselves.
- Parents and other stakeholders can work to be partners not bosses with athletes, listening more and talking less, giving athletes more power in their decision making, ensuring that every stakeholder knows, and doing their own job and no one else's.
- Parents and other stakeholders can offer athletes the opportunity to embrace ownership of their sport, and athletes themselves must be willing to accept that ownership.
- Consultants can help athletes to gain ownership of their sports lives by helping them to clarify their values, own every aspect of their sport, owning their minds, and owning the details.

References

Corlett, J. (1996). Sophistry, Socrates, and sport psychology. *The Sport Psychologist, 10*(1), 84–94.

Dawes, N. P., & Larson, R. W. (2011). How youth get engaged: Grounded-theory research on motivational development in organized youth programs. *Developmental Psychology, 47*(1), 259–269.

Deci, E. L., Koestner, R., & Ryan, R. M. (1999). The undermining effect is a reality after all—Extrinsic rewards, task interest, and self-determination: Reply to Eisenberger, Pierce, and Cameron (1999) and Lepper, Henderlong, and Gingras (1999). *Psychological Bulletin, 125*(6), 692–700.

Herzog, T. (2014). To communicate, don't triangulate! Retrieved from https://reachingahead.com/to-communicate-dont-triangulate

Herzog, T., Zavilla, S., Dupee, M., & Stephenson, M. (2018). The psychophysiology of self-regulation. In G. Cremades & A. Mugford (Eds.), *Sport, Exercise, and Performance Psychology: Theories and Applications* (ch. 15). New York, NY: Routledge/ Psychology Press.

Hudson, J. L. & Rapee, R. M. (2002). Parent–child interactions in clinically anxious children and their siblings. *Journal of Clinical Child & Adolescent Psychology, 31*, 548–555.

Macmillan Dictionary (n.d.). Ownership. Retrieved from www.macmillandictionary.com/us/dictionary/american/ownership

Markland, D., Ryan, R. M., Tobin, V. J., & Rollnick, S. (2005). Motivational interviewing and self-determination theory. *Journal of Social and Clinical Psychology, 24*(6), 811–831.

Padilla-Walker, L. M., & Nelson, L. J. (2012). Black Hawk down? Establishing helicopter parenting as a distinct construct from other forms of parental control during emerging adulthood. *Journal of Adolescence, 35*(5), 1177–1190.

Prochaska, J. O., DiClemente, C. C., & Norcross, J. C. (1992). In search of how people change: Applications to addictive behaviors. *American Psychologist, 47*(9), 1102–1114.

Schiffrin, H. H., Liss, M., Miles-McLean, H., Geary, K. A., Erchull, M. J., & Tashner, T. (2014). Helping or hovering? The effects of helicopter parenting on college students' well-being. *Journal of Child and Family Studies, 23*(3), 548–557.

Turman, P. D. (2007). Parental sport involvement: Parental influence to encourage young athlete continued sport participation. *Journal of Family Communication, 7*(3), 151–175.

GROWTH MINDSET

Sheryl Smith and Nicole Gabana

Cultivating a positive mindset is an essential process for athletes to achieve their sports goals. It is also a topic commonly discussed among athletes, coaches, and consultants alike because they all know that how athletes perceive various aspects of their sport impacts their experience, enjoyment, and performance. A *mindset* is a set of beliefs that people hold that guide their thinking, emotions, and behavior (Dweck, 1999). Dweck described two types of mindsets that have dramatically different effects on how people approach achievement-oriented activities such as sports. A *fixed* mindset involves the belief that a person's abilities are permanent and unalterable. It also includes the belief that talent or innate ability is the primary cause of success. A fixed mindset leads to a focus on outcome goals and motivates behaviors aimed at demonstrating competence, particularly in comparison to others (Sarrazin et al., 1996). Those with a fixed mindset often exhibit a fear of failure because they don't believe they can turn that failure in later success.

In contrast, a *growth* mindset is defined as the belief that a person's ability is developed through dedication and hard work rather than a stable attribute. From this perspective, success is believed to be determined primarily by effort, which includes trying new strategies and seeking input when stuck (Dweck, 2015). Those with a growth mindset have little fear of failure because they believe that they can learn from these setbacks and improve their performance in the future. They see failure as an opportunity for growth. A growth mindset leads to a focus on process and mastery, and motivates learning behaviors in which mastering a skill takes priority over appearing competent relative to others. Originally, the concept of growth versus fixed mindset pertained primarily to beliefs about intelligence; however, recent research has extended its application to other domains such as beliefs about athletic ability (Gardner, Vella, & Magee, 2015).

Theory and Research

The body of research on mindsets, both outside and within sport, suggests that a growth mindset has facilitating effects of performance through increased persistence, feedback-seeking, and attention to errors; whereas fixed mindsets have benefit when social comparison favors the athlete, but can have debilitating effects during adversity.

Adaptive vs. Maladaptive Behaviors

Mindset is important to consider because of the adaptive and maladaptive behaviors that stem from them. Growth-minded individuals tend to select learning or mastery goals over performance or outcome goals (Sarrazin et al., 1996). Mindset can also impact the way people respond to failure. Failure can either motivate or undermine individuals depending on their belief about what failure represents: a potential challenge (growth mindset) or a painful confirmation of inadequacy (fixed mindset). In her research regarding perspectives on the nature of intelligence, Dweck and her colleagues demonstrated that students with a growth mindset are more likely to persist in the face of failure than those with a fixed mindset (Blackwell, Trzesniewski, & Dweck, 2007; Dweck, 2006). Additionally, individuals with mastery goals (growth mindset) are more likely to persist in the face of failure, pursue challenging tasks, and view negative feedback as useful to learning (Dweck, 1996; Nicholls, 1984, 1989; Sideridis & Kaplan, 2011). In contrast, outcome-focused individuals (fixed mindset) tend to perceive negative feedback as threatening, select easier problems to avoid "being wrong," and are more likely to engage in self-handicapping (Lee & Kim, 2014; Ommundsen, 2001a; Yeager et al., 2016).

Enhanced Performance

Neuroscientific research on the effects of mindset on resilience after failure provides support for the benefits of a growth mindset on attention allocation. Examination of brain activity revealed that children with growth mindsets showed greater attention to mistakes and higher accuracy after mistakes (Schroder et al., 2017; Tirri & Kujal, 2016) than those possessing a fixed mindset. Using fMRI assessments, Lee and Kim (2014) demonstrated that mastery-oriented college students focus more on the constructive, task-relevant elements of negative feedback, whereas outcome-oriented individuals focus more on the feedback valence. These results suggest that there are neural dynamics which facilitate people's ability to recover from failure, and that these differ between growth- and fixed-minded individuals.

Sport Experience

Within sports, beliefs and goals associated with a growth mindset have been correlated with greater levels of enjoyment (Biddle, Wang, Chatzisarantis, & Spray, 2003; Biddle, Wang, Kavussanu, & Spray, 2010; Botswick,

Collie, Martin, & Durksen, 2017; Gardner, Vella, & Magee, 2018; Ommundsen, 2003; Vella, Cliff, Okely, Weintraub, & Robinson, 2014), continued participation in youth sports (Gardner, Vella, & Magee, 2017), and motives of skill development and team membership (Biddle et al., 2010). In contrast, fixed-mindset beliefs have been associated with motives of status, recognition, and competition, as well as unsportsmanlike attitudes (Biddle et al., 2010). Interestingly, growth and fixed mindsets are not opposite ends of one continuum, but can co-exist (Roberts, Treasure, & Balague, 2008). This finding means an individual can possess implicit beliefs of both types; which mindset influences them depends on the related domain (e.g., intelligence, athletic ability). Although mindsets have some stability over time, they are capable of changing as information is processed (Roberts, Treasure, & Conroy, 2007). This means that athletes can learn to shift into a growth mindset from a fixed mindset.

Motivational Climate

A motivational climate refers to the psychological and social environment that is created in a family or team that impacts self-esteem, enjoyment, perceived competence, and how athletes think about skill development and feedback (Mageau & Vallerand, 2003). A mastery climate is an environment designed and perceived to foster mastery goals that are reflective of a growth mindset. In their systematic review of 104 studies of motivational climates in sport and physical activity, Harwood, Keegan, Smith, and Raine (2015) found a positive association between mastery goals and adaptive strategies such as persistence, help-seeking, cooperation, and feelings of interpersonal relatedness. In contrast, performance climates that are indicative of a fixed mindset and characterized by interpersonal comparison and punishment of mistakes are more often associated with maladaptive strategies such as self-handicapping and avoidance.

Skill Development in Sports

A growth mindset has been shown to facilitate a number of precursors to skill development in sport. Feedback about accuracy, including error feedback, is necessary for athletic skill development, and accurate attention allocation is necessary for error detection. The ability to tolerate mistakes and derive important information from errors enhances learning. Furthermore, qualities such as persistence, commitment, and enjoyment lead to prolonged deliberate practice.

Researchers have suggested that young people may be more likely to exhibit a growth mindset toward athletic ability as compared to academics, since effort tends to be more emphasized in a sport environment (Atwood et al., 2010). Athletes with a greater growth mindset have been shown to have a more positive reaction to both success and failure (Potgieter & Steyn, 2010). A growth-minded approach can help athletes recover from mistakes, whereas those with a fixed view may attempt to conceal their shortcomings by making excuses or placing blame on others. Moreover, with a growth mindset that emphasizes learning, athletes are more likely to be focused on the process than the outcome. Dweck (2009) explained that the more athletes believed their athletic ability was a result of effort and practice (as compared to natural talent), the better they performed the following season. Furthermore, these athletes were more likely to have a superior season if they felt their coaches valued effort and practice over natural ability. Consequently, the importance of coaches, parents, and consultants fostering a growth mindset in athletes is essential to athletes' developing such a mindset.

Practical Implications

As evidenced above, how athletes with fixed vs. growth mindsets react to different aspects of their sport experience varies greatly and will have a significant impact on their participation, enjoyment, and performance in their sport. Consultants can have a powerful influence on athletes by showing them how to develop or strengthen a growth mindset toward their sports lives.

Athletes' mindsets can be altered by the motivational climate created by important people in their sports including parents, coaches, and teammates. A learning environment that emphasizes effort, progress, and support is more likely to promote a growth mindset, whereas a climate encouraging a focus on results and comparison of others can lead to a fixed mindset (Ommundsen, 2001b). Interventions designed to foster a growth mindset can promote challenge-seeking behaviors and enhance performance in both high and low achievers (Yeager et al., 2016). A motivational climate that nurtures a growth mindset can be cultivated in several ways.

Mindsets are developed and reinforced by the way athletes are praised. Dweck (2009) suggested that coaches and parents should focus on praising effort over talent and setbacks and failures be treated as opportunities for growth (Sarkar et al., 2015). Based on the evidence supporting the adaptive effects of implicit beliefs, Vella et al. (2014) describe strategies for coaches to use in promoting a growth mindset in their athletes:

- focus on, reward, and promote effort and persistence;
- recognize and reinforce attempts at challenging tasks and pushing beyond comfort zones;
- explore the value of setbacks (e.g., by facilitating reflection and problem solving);
- define success as giving best efforts;
- emphasize process over outcome;
- avoid comparisons with others;
- promote learning; and
- provide high expectations and encouragement of improvement.

For example, during a performance review, coaches can connect current successes back to previous setbacks and ongoing persistence. Coaches who focus on encouraging task improvement and mastery endorse the separation between self-worth and performance (Watson, Connole, & Kadushin, 2011) and promote a growth mindset.

Because of the impact that coaches have on athletes, coaches should be aware of fixed-minded tendencies and should strive to develop a growth mindset (Chase, 2010; Dweck, 2009). Coaches are first encouraged to explore their own implicit beliefs about the influence of talent vs. hard work on success; then, they can model a growth mindset by seeking and using feedback, persisting through their own challenges, and speaking about their own setbacks and failures (Chase, 2010). Consultants can help coaches through the process of becoming aware of their implicit beliefs and challenge those that are fixed. Then, consultants can guide coaches toward developing a growth mindset that will benefit both themselves and their athletes.

Parents can also play a significant role in the development and maintenance of a growth mindset in their young athletes by the motivational climate they create at home (Dweck, 2006). Like coaches, parents should consider not only what they say, but also what they do. In a series of studies on intelligence, Haimovitz and Dweck (2016) found that parents' attitudes toward failure most strongly shaped their children's fixed or growth mindsets. Parents who see failure as debilitating tend to focus on their children's ability and results rather than on their effort and progress. Treatment of failure is an integral piece of this equation, both in terms of their children's mistakes and their own. Parents who develop a tolerance for failure and can effectively manage the emotions that often accompany it can model a growth mindset in their children at a visceral level. At a verbal level, parents can acknowledge and empathize with the discomfort that arises when their children risk failure when they push themselves outside of their comfort zone. In this way, parents can use their influence to emphasize and strengthen their children's growth mindset as both athletes and as people.

Consultants can also help athletes to shift away from a fixed mindset and toward a growth mindset. Consultants can start by educating athletes about what a mindset is, what fixed vs. growth mindsets are, and how each can impact their experience, enjoyment, and performance in their sport (Dweck, 2009). Then, they can assess the mindset that athletes currently possess. Signs of a fixed mindset can include:

- athletes' belief that their efforts will not make a difference in how successful they become;
- preoccupation with results;
- negative and self-critical thinking;
- excessive concern for how others perform;
- rumination about past performances;
- worry about future performances;
- setting outcome expectations;
- view an upcoming competition as a threat to avoid;
- pre-competitive anxiety;

- strong negative emotional reactions to failure; and
- seeing teammates as threats.

If a fixed mindset is evident in athletes, consultants can show them how these beliefs may hurt their athletic development, performance, and sport experience. They can also teach athletes that a fixed mindset can be changed with practice over time, in order to move toward a healthier, more facilitative growth mindset.

Finally, consultants can show athletes how to alter their beliefs and foster a growth mindset:

- adopt the belief that their efforts matter;
- focus on self, process, present, and progress;
- encourage positive and supportive thinking;
- cultivate acceptance of past performances;
- establish process and mastery goals;
- acknowledge some pre-competitive anxiety as normal;
- understand failure as necessary for success;
- develop appropriate emotional reactions to failure;
- view an upcoming competition as a challenge to pursue; and
- seek support from teammates.

In both individual and team sessions, consultants can encourage a growth mindset in several ways:

- clarify the values that drive athletes' sports participation;
- highlight athletes' efforts when facing challenges, persistence after failure, and creative responses to setbacks;
- develop effective coping tools to buffer disappointing performances and negative feedback, stay positive, maintain a constructive focus, manage competitive stress, and manage emotions; and
- encourage mental training geared toward the value of effort, openness to challenge and growth, and building resilience.

Furthermore, in the spirit of a growth mindset, consultants can frame mental training as a developable commodity which can be improved through hard work and practice just like with physical and sport skill development. Evans and Slater (2014) recommended promoting a growth mindset toward mental training by emphasizing the malleability of psychological attributes, exercises, and tools, to increase athletes' understanding and engagement during mental training sessions. Lastly, having a growth mindset has been shown to promote help-seeking behavior, since fixed-minded individuals tend to doubt the usefulness of assistance (Ommundsen, 2003). If athletes believe that their mental and physical abilities can be developed and improved (i.e., growth mindset), they may be more amenable to using available support resources.

Summary

- A mindset is a set of beliefs that people hold that guide their thinking, emotions, and behavior.
- A fixed mindset involves the belief that a person's abilities are permanent and unalterable.
- Individuals with a fixed mindset tend to perceive negative feedback as threatening, select easier problems to avoid "being wrong," and are more likely to engage in self-handicapping.
- A growth mindset is defined as the belief that a person's ability is malleable and can be developed through hard work.
- Research has shown that students with a growth mindset are more likely to persist in the face of failure, pursue challenging tasks, and view negative feedback as useful to learning.
- A growth mindset is associated with more adaptive behaviors, enhanced performance, and greater enjoyment as compared to a fixed mindset.
- A motivational climate that fosters a growth mindset encourages self-esteem, perceived competence, and positive perceptions of skill development and feedback.

- A growth mindset in sports has been found to be correlated to more positive reactions to failure, seeing failure as a learning opportunity, learning from mistakes, and greater resilience.
- Consultants can help athletes to develop a growth mindset by cultivating a supportive motivational climate, giving praise for effort and persistence, emphasizing process over outcome, avoiding comparison with others, and encouraging athletes to push beyond their comfort zone.
- Coaches and parents can reinforce a growth mindset in athletes by being good role models and encouraging growth-minded thoughts and behaviors.
- Consultants can frame mental training in terms of a growth mindset, thus increasing buy-in toward both.

References

Atwood, J. (2010). Mindset, motivation and metaphor in school and sport: Bifurcated beliefs and behavior in two different achievement domains. Paper presented at the Annual Meeting of the American Educational Research Association (Denver, CO, April 30 to May 4).

Biddle, S. J. H., Wang, C. K. J., Chatzisarantis, N. L. D., & Spray, C. M. (2003). Motivation for physical activity in young people: Entity and incremental beliefs about athletic ability. *Journal of Sports Sciences*, 21, 973–989. doi: 10.1080/02640410310001641377

Biddle, S., Wang, C. K. J., Kavussanu, M., & Spray, C. (2010). Correlates of achievement goal orientations in physical activity: A systematic review of research. *European Journal of Sport Science*, 3(5), 1–20. doi: 10.1080/17461390300073504

Blackwell, L. S., Trzesniewski, K. H., & Dweck, C. S. (2007). Implicit theories of intelligence predict achievement across an adolescent transition: A longitudinal study and an intervention. *Child Development*, 78, 246–263.

Botswick, K. C. P., Collie, R. J., Martin, A. J., & Durksen, T. L. (2017). Students' growth mindsets, goals, and academic outcomes in mathematics. *Zeitschrift für Psychologie*, 225(2), 107–116.

Chase, M. A. (2010). Should coaches believe in innate ability? The importance of leadership mindset. *Quest*, 62(3), 296–307. doi: 10.1080/00336297.2010.10483650

Dweck, C. S. (1996). Implicit theories as organizers of goals and behavior. In P. M. Gollwitzer & J. A. Bargh (Eds.), *The psychology of action: Linking cognition and motivation to behavior* (pp. 69–90). New York, NY: Guilford Press.

Dweck, C. S. (1999). *Self-theories: Their role in motivation, personality and development*. Philadelphia, PA: Psychology Press.

Dweck, C. S. (2006). *Mindset: The new psychology of success*. New York, NY: Random House.

Dweck, C. S. (2009). Mindsets: Developing talent through a growth mindset. *Olympic Coach*, 21, 4–7.

Dweck, C. S. (2015). Growth mindset, revisited. Retrieved from www.edweek.org/ew/articles/2015/09/23/carol-dweck-revisits-the-growth-mindset.html

Dweck, C. S., & Leggett, E. L. (1988). A social-cognitive approach to motivation and personality. *Psychological Review*, 95, 256–273. doi: 10.1037/0033-295X.95.2.256

Evans, A., & Slater, M. (2014). Getting down with the kids: Doing sport psychology with Gifted and Talented youth athletes. *Sport & Exercise Psychology Review*, 10(3), 58–67.

Gardner, L. A., Vella, S. A., & Magee, C. A. (2015). The relationship between implicit beliefs, anxiety, and attributional style in high-level soccer players. *Journal of Applied Sport Psychology*, 27(4), 398–411.

Gardner, L. A., Vella, S. A., & Magee, C. A. (2017). Continued participation in youth sports: The role of achievement motivation. *Journal of Applied Sport Psychology*, 29, 17–31. doi: 10.1080/10413200.2016.1173744

Gardner, L. A., Vella, S. A., & Magee, C. A. (2018) The role of implicit beliefs and achievement goals as protective factors in youth sport. *Journal of Applied Sport Psychology*, 30, 83–95. doi: 10.1080/10413200.2017.1334160

Haimovitz, K., & Dweck, C. S. (2016). What predicts children's fixed and growth intelligence mind-sets? Not their parents' views of intelligence but their parents' views of failure. *Psychological Science*, 27(6), 859–869. doi: 10.1177/0956797616639727

Harwood, C. G., Keegan, R. J., Smith, J. M., & Raine, A. S. (2015). A systematic review of the intrapersonal correlates of motivational climate perceptions in sport and physical activity. *Psychology of Sport and Exercise*, 18, 9–25. doi: 10.1016/j.psychsport.2014.11.005

Lee, W., & Kim, S. (2014). Effects of achievement goals on challenge seeking and feedback processing: Behavioral and fMRI evidence. *PLoS One*, 9(9), e107254. doi: 10.1371/journal.pone.0107254 PMID: 25251396

Mageau, G.A., & Vallerand, R.J. (2003). The coach-athlete relationship: A motivational model. *Journal of Sports Sciences*, 21, 883–904.

Nicholls, J. G. (1984). Achievement motivation: Conceptions of ability, subjective experience, task choice, and performance. *Psychological Review*, 91, 328–346.

Nicholls, J. G. (1989). *The competitive ethos and democratic education*. Cambridge, MA: Harvard University Press.

Ommundsen, Y. (2001a). Self-handicapping strategies in physical education classes: The influence of implicit theories of the nature of ability and achievement goal orientations. *Psychology of Sport and Exercise*, 2, 139–156.

Ommundsen, Y. (2001b). Students' implicit theories of ability in physical education classes: The influence of motivational aspects of the learning environment. *Learning Environments Research, 4*, 139–158.

Ommundsen, Y. (2003). Implicit theories of ability and self-regulation strategies in physical education classes. *Educational Psychology, 23*(2), 141–157. doi: 10.1080/01443410303224

Potgieter, R. D., & Steyn, B. J. M. (2010). Goal orientation, self-theories and reactions to success and failure in competitive sport. *African Journal for Physical, Health Education, Recreation and Dance, 16*(4), 635–647.

Roberts, G. C., Treasure, D. C., & Balague, G. (2008) Achievement goals in sport: The development and validation of the Perception of Success Questionnaire. *Journal of Sports Sciences, 16*(4), 337–347. doi: 10.1080/02640419808559362

Roberts, G. C., Treasure, D. C., & Conroy, D. (2007). Understanding the dynamics of motivation in sport and physical activity: An achievement goal interpretation. In G. Tenenbaum & R. Eklund (Eds.), *Handbook of research in sport psychology* (pp. 3–30). New York, NY: Wiley.

Sarrazin, B., Biddle, S. J. H., Famose, J. P., Curry, F., Fox, K. R., & Durand, M. (1996). Goal orientations and conceptions of sport ability in children: A social cognitive approach. *British Journal of Social Psychology, 35*, 399–414. doi: 10.1111/j.2044-8309.1996.tb01104.x

Schroder, H. S., Fisher, M. E., Lin, Y., Lo, S. L., Danovitch, J. H., & Moser, J. S. (2017). Neural evidence for enhanced attention to mistakes among school-aged children with a growth mindset. *Developmental Cognitive Neuroscience, 24*, 42–50.

Sideridis, G. D., & Kaplan, A. (2011). Achievement goals and persistence across tasks: The roles of failure. *The Journal of Experimental Education, 79*(4), 429–451. Doi: 10.1080/00220973.2010.539634

Tirri, K., & Kujala, T. (2016). Students' mindsets for learning and their neural underpinnings. *Psychology, 7*, 1231–1239.

Vella, S. A., Cliff, D. P., Okely, A. D., Weintraub, D. L., & Robinson, T. N. (2014). Instructional strategies to promote incremental beliefs in youth sport. *Quest, 66*, 357–370. doi: 10.1080/00336297.2014.950757

Watson II, J. C., Connole, I., & Kadushin, P. (2011). Developing young athletes: A sport psychology based approach to coaching youth sports. *Journal of Sport Psychology in Action, 2*(2), 113–122. doi: 10.1080/21520704.2011.586452

Yeager, D. S., Romero, C., Paunesku, D., Hulleman, C. S., Schneider, B., Hinojosa, C., . . . & Trott, J. (2016). Using design thinking to improve psychological interventions: The case of the growth mindset during the transition to high school. *Journal of Educational Psychology, 108*(3), 374–391.

CHALLENGE

Jim Taylor and Shawn Powell

How athletes perceive their sports experience produces a variety of thoughts, feelings, and behaviors that then positively or negatively impact their performances in training and competitions (Li, Zhang, & Zhang, 2013). One basic perception that plays a vital role in athletes performing up to their capabilities is whether they view the situation as a threat or a challenge. Whether athletes see a sport situation as a threat or challenge catalyzes in them strikingly different reactions including how they think, the emotions they experience, their physiology, their goals, and, ultimately, how they perform in training and competitions (Taylor, 2017).

Theory and Research

When a situation is perceived by athletes as a threat, athletic performance usually suffers. Conversely, situations that athletes see as challenges typically result in enhanced performance. As a result, how athletes come to perceive training and competitive situations should be a focus of consultants to ensure that those perceptions support rather than undermine their efforts (Cumming, Turner, & Jones, 2017).

Threat

There are three fundamental questions that must be asked about why athletes have a threat attitude in their sports participation:

1. What is the cause of the threat attitude?
2. How does the threat attitude impact athletes?
3. How can athletes mitigate or remove their threat attitude? (This question will be addressed in Practical Implications below.)

Cause

At the heart of a threat attitude is a fear of failure. Fear of failure is caused by athletes' belief that failure will lead to some dire consequences such as shame, loss of parental love, diminished respect from others, or the death of cherished goals (Amjad, Irshad, & Gul, 2018; see more on fear of failure in Chapter 2). The irony is that the fear of failure and the resulting threat attitude actually increases the chances that what athletes fear the most will be realized.

Secondary contributors to a threat attitude include athletes' overly narrow self-identity grounded in their sports lives and the accompanying overinvestment in their performances (Weinberg & Gould, 2015; see more on overinvestment in Chapter 2). With these two conditions, athletes' sports involvement assumes too great a role in their self-identity (i.e., how they define themselves). The result is that their self-esteem (i.e., how athletes feel about and value themselves) becomes overly reliant on their sports achievements. Additionally, that overinvestment creates immense pressure to fulfill the goals that athletes set for themselves. With so much of their self-worth on the line when they compete in their sport, the threat of failure can be debilitating. By putting their self-identity, self-esteem, and goals at risk, athletes carry a crushing burden that often leads to a self-fulfilling prophecy of failure.

Reactions

A threat attitude produces cascade of psychological, emotional, physiological, and performance reactions that significantly impede athletes' ability to perform their best. Cognitively, athletes engage in negative self-talk, lose confidence, and believe themselves incapable of achieving their sports goals (Renfrew, Howle, & Eklund, 2017). Additionally, motivation to compete declines and athletes are so overwhelmed with the many responses to the threat that they lose the ability to focus effectively on performing well.

A threat attitude also triggers a variety of interfering emotions. The perception of threat causes athletes to experience fear in a powerful and visceral way. Other emotions that can arise include anger, frustration, sadness, and despair, all of which cause athletes to want to avoid the sports situation, usually a competition, in which they find themselves.

Dramatic changes in physiology occur when athletes assume a threat attitude (Williams, Veldhuijzen van Zanten, Trotman, Quinton, & Ginty, 2017). Muscles tense, heart rate increases, breathing becomes rapid and shallow, and adrenaline is shot into the blood stream, These autonomic reactions can produce shaking, sweating, nausea, and dizziness. All of these responses create a physiological state that is largely incapable of meeting the demands imposed on athletes by sports.

The "perfect storm" that is created by these changes in response to a perceived threat has a significant impact on athletes' ability to perform at a high level. The result is efforts that are lacking in full commitment, confidence, intensity, and focus, the outcome of which are performances that are subpar and disappointing.

Challenge

Not surprisingly, a challenge attitude has a diametrically opposed effect on athletes as compared to a threat attitude. It starts with athletes' belief that sports situations they are confronted with are opportunities to pursue rather than a threat to avoid (Dixon, Turner, & Gillman, 2016). This opportunity allows athletes to push themselves outside of their comfort zone, stretch their limits, accomplish their goals, attain a new level of performance, and experience the satisfaction that comes with it. When athletes perceive competitions as challenges, they are more likely to strive toward and accomplish their goals and establish of new goals (Kavussanu, Dewar, & Boardley, 2014). Athletes who see their sports participation as challenges also perform better than those who possess a threat attitude (Williams, Veldhuijzen van Zanten, Trotman, Quinton, & Ginty, 2017). As with the threat attitude, there are causes of and reactions to a challenge attitude that are worth exploring.

Causes

The foundation of a challenge attitude is athletes' desire to see what they are capable of and enjoyment in the full experience of their sport. With this attitude toward their sports participation, athletes can embrace their training and competitive efforts with total commitment, trust, abandon, and, unlike a threat attitude, without hesitation, apprehension, or dread. A challenge attitude is connected with their valuing the process of their sport instead of being afraid of the results of their efforts.

Expectedly, a challenge attitude produces an entirely different set of psychological, emotional, physiological, physical, and performance reactions. Mentally, athletes who embrace a challenge attitude are highly motivated to train and compete. They are also confident in their capabilities and believe they can achieve the goals they set for themselves. Because athletes aren't overwhelmed with the many burdens that a threat attitude places on them, they are able to focus intently on what they need to do to perform their best, free of mental clutter or distraction.

Athletes' emotional experience that is grounded in the challenge attitude is also supportive of high performances. They feel beneficial emotions including pride, inspiration, excitement, and satisfaction, all of which act as fuel to and validation of their efforts. These emotions, considered to be "approach" emotions, further propel athletes toward their goals.

When athletes view a sports situation as a challenge, physiological changes occur that produce increased performance (Kavussanu, Dewar, & Boardley, 2014). Though athletes react in similar ways to a threat attitude (as described above), their responses to a challenge attitude can vary. For example, some athletes react with a physiologically calming effect (e.g., deep breathing, calm muscles, slow heart rate), while others respond with physiological excitation (e.g., more rapid breathing, greater muscle activity, racing heart). What both types of athletes have in common is that they interpret these diverse physiological experiences as positive and comfortable.

Perhaps the most interesting aspect of this distinction between a threat attitude and a challenge attitude is that both originate in the minds of athletes, that is, how they perceive a sports situation rather than in the objective reality of the experience. For example, two golfers of equal ability arrive at a course on which they will be playing in the first round of an important tournament that both hope to play well in. Additionally, it rained the previous night, so the fairways are soaked and the greens are slick. To make matters worse, a strong wind is blowing. The two golfers are in the same group so they will be faced with identical conditions. The most significant difference is in the attitude they bring to the round of golf. One has a threat attitude, so her first thoughts are: "What horrible conditions! This is not going to be fun. I don't even want to be here." The other possesses a challenge attitude and thinks, "This a great opportunity for me. I played in these conditions just last week. Let's see how well I can play." Everything else being equal, the latter golfer is more likely to have a good round. When athletes adopt a challenge attitude, they position themselves to enter training and competitions with the psychological and physiological states that will allow them to perform their best and achieve their sports goals.

Practical Implications

Because attitudes develop through experience and modeling from an early age, they can become entrenched and habitual, thus changing attitudes is difficult. If athletes have developed a threat attitude, consultants can play an essential role in showing these athletes how to replace it with a challenge attitude.

Understanding

This change process begins by consultants educating athletes about how a threat attitude hurts their sports efforts. Consultants can draw from athletes the interfering perceptions, thoughts, emotions, and behaviors that are triggered by a threat attitude. Athletes are also encouraged to identify those situations in which a threat attitude imposes itself on athletes. This delineation helps athletes to gain clarity on the harmful impact that a threat attitude has on them and also girds their determination to overcome it and replace it with a challenge attitude.

Insight

Once athletes have a deep understanding of the threat attitude and how it affects them, consultants can dig deeper into the relationship that athletes have with it. This step involves helping athletes to recognize the causes of their threat attitude (see Chapter 2 for several causes). As discussed above, the primary contributors to a threat attitude are:

- overly developed athletic identity;
- overinvestment;
- perfectionism;
- fear of failure;
- expectations; and
- emotions.

A part of this "deep dive" involves consultants also encouraging athletes to explore how these contributors came into existence in their lives. Most often, these obstacles arise from messages that athletes received from parents, other significant people in their lives, and popular culture (Taylor, 2011). Underlying all of these negative influences is a deeply felt belief that some dire consequences will result if athletes fail, however irrational and unlikely those perceived consequences are. Research indicates that the most common consequences associated with failure are:

- losing parents' love;
- disappointing significant others;
- being rejected by peers;
- experiencing embarrassment, shame, or humiliation;
- indicative of a lack of ability;
- end to athletes' dreams; and
- all their efforts will have been a waste of time.

Debunk

Once the causes of athletes' threat attitude have been identified, consultants can challenge their perceptions and debunk the consequences associated with those perceptions. Consultants can literally talk athletes through their list and demonstrate how the identified consequences are not going to happen. Consultants can bring parents into the conversation, use examples of other athletes who have failed, but still survived, and draw on athletes' own past experiences to help them recognize that the fears that have caused the threat attitude are unwarranted.

Clarify

With the threat attitude well understood by athletes, consultants can then make the transition to a focus on a challenge attitude. This process begins with consultants educating athletes about what the challenge attitude is and how it will positively impact not only sports performance, but also sports enjoyment. The next step involves consultants sharing with athletes the thinking, emotions, and actions associated with a challenge attitude. This information is aimed at providing athletes with the incentive to commit to the change from threat attitude to challenge attitude.

Shift

The final and most difficult step in this process is for athletes to make the shift to a challenge attitude when a situation triggers a threat attitude. There are a number of shifts that consultants can help athletes make based on issues that are discussed throughout Part I of *CASP*:

- fixed to growth mindset;
- overinvestment to balance;
- outcome to process focus;

- fear to courage;
- doubt to confidence;
- tension to relaxation;
- avoidance to pursuit; and
- caution to risk.

One shift that isn't formally addressed in other parts of this book yet warrants more in-depth exploration is that from "what if" to "when. When athletes are overcome by a threat attitude, they are myopically focused on everything that can go wrong in their sports lives. They ruminate on the worst-case scenarios, the "what ifs", which only further intensifies the perception and experience of threat. Examples of "what if" statements include:

- What if I do terribly?
- What if my friend beats me?
- What if I let my parents down?
- What if I look bad?
- What if I don't get any better?

These "what if" statements are so damaging because each is followed by an implicit, yet deeply threatening, consequence such as ". . . people will think I'm a real loser", ". . . my parents will be angry"; or ". . . I'll never be successful at anything." What is ironic is that these "what ifs" that are representative of this threat attitude produces psychological, emotional, and physical states that almost guarantee athletes will have to face the experience that is most threatening to them—failure—which they so actively avoid.

To combat the "what ifs," consultants can offer athletes a replacement that can mitigate the threat attitude and foster a challenge attitude. This alternative involves swapping "what ifs" with "whens." Examples of "when" statements include:

- When I try my hardest . . .
- When I leave it all out there . . .
- When I do everything I can . . .
- When I have fun . . .

The tone of "when" statements triggers a challenge attitude in several ways. They eliminate the threat by doing away with the dire consequences that underlie the "what if" statements. "When" statements redirect athletes from a negative to a positive orientation, where good things rather than bad things are likely to occur. For instance, "When I give it my all . . . I often get the results I want"; "When I'm well prepared . . . I'm confident and determined"; and "When I am focused on performing my best . . . I usually feel good after no matter how I did."

Summary

- How athletes perceive their sports experience produce a variety of thoughts, feelings, and behaviors that then positively or negatively impact their performances in training and competitions.
- One basic perception that plays a vital role in whether athletes perform up to their capabilities is whether they view the situation as a threat or a challenge.
- Whether athletes see a sport situation as a threat or challenge catalyzes in them strikingly different reactions including how they think, the emotions they experience, their physiology, their goals, and, ultimately, how they perform in training and competitions.
- The three primary causes of a threat attitude is a fear of failure, an overly influential athletic identity, and overinvestment of self-esteem.
- A threat attitude produces cascade of psychological, emotional, physiological, and performance responses that significantly impede athletes' ability to perform their best.
- A challenge attitude has a diametrically opposed effect on athletes as compared to a threat attitude.

- At the heart of a challenge attitude is athletes' desire to see what they are capable of and enjoyment in the full experience of their sport.
- A challenge attitude pushes athletes outside of their comfort zone, strive to stretch their limits, accomplish their goals, attain a new level of performance, and experience the satisfaction that comes with it.
- Perhaps the most interesting aspect of this distinction between a threat attitude and a challenge attitude is that both originate in the minds of athletes, that is, how they perceive a sports situation, rather than in the objective reality of the experience.
- Consultants can help make the transition from a threat attitude to a challenge attitude through a process of understanding, insight, debunking, clarifying, and shifting.

References

Amjad, A., Irshad, E., & Gul, R. (2018). Relationship between completion anxiety and fear of failure among sportsmen and sportswomen. *Journal of Postgraduate Medical Institute, 32*(1), 65–69.

Cumming, S. J. D., Turner, M. J., & Jones, M. (2017). Longitudinal changes in elite rowers' challenge and threat appraisals of pressure situations: A season-long observational study. *The Sport Psychologist, 31*(3), 217–226.

Dixon, M., Turner, M. J., & Gillman, J. (2016). Examining the relationships between challenge and threat cognitive appraisals and coaching behaviours in football coaches. *Journal of Sports Sciences, 5*, 116–131. doi: 10.1080/02640414.2016.1273538.

Kavussanu, M., Dewar, A. J., & Boardley, I. D. (2014). Achievement goals and emotions in athletes: The mediating role of challenge and threat appraisals. *Motivation and Emotion, 38*(4), 589–599.

Li, Y., Zhang, L., & Zhang, L. (2013). The theory of challenge and threat stated in athletes and self-control in competition. *Advances in Psychological Science, 21*(9), 1696–1710.

Renfrew, J., Howle, T. C., & Eklund, R. C. (2017). Self-presentation concerns may contribute toward the understanding of athletes' affect when trialing for a new sports team, *Journal of Applied Sport Psychology, 29*(4), 484–492.

Taylor, J. (2011). *Your children are listening: 9 messages they need to hear from you.* New York, NY: The Experiment Publishing.

Taylor, J. (2017). *Train your mind for athletic success: Mental preparation to achieve your sports goals.* Lanham, MD: Rowman & Littlefield.

Weinberg, R. S., & Gould, D. (2015). *Foundations of sport and exercise psychology* (6th ed.). Champaign, IL: Human Kinetics.

Williams, S. E., Veldhuijzen van Zanten, J. C. S., Trotman, G. P., Quinton, M. L., & Ginty, A. T. (2017). Challenge and threat imagery manipulates heart rate and anxiety responses to stress. *International Journal of Psychophysiology, 117*, 111–118.

RISK-TAKING

Sherry Schweighardt and Jim Taylor

Elevating athletic performance requires taking risks involving uncertain outcomes and real or perceived dangers in pursuit of sport goals. All sports carry some prospect of physical injury that well-planned rigorous conditioning and a deliberate training regimen are intended to mitigate. At the same time, risks athletes take may also be psychological, emotional, or behavioral. Risks can be immediate, for example, athletes' efforts in conditioning or the execution of skills and tactics on the field of play. Risks may also involve longer-term decisions such as choosing to specialize in a sport or to change teams or coaches. All athletes striving to improve will be confronted with the opportunity to take risks. Each athlete must decide whether to "play it safe," which is comfortable, but may also lead to mediocre results—or choose to take a risk, which may result in spectacular success or crushing failure. Intellectually, the choice seems obvious for athletes with high aspirations in their sport, a variety of instinctual, psychological, emotional, and physiological influences can prevent athletes from taking appropriate risks as they strive toward their sports goals.

This discussion of risk should be prefaced with a clarification. In exploring risk-taking, the focus here is not on health, ethical, and behavioral risks that can cause great harm, such as drinking and driving; taking performance-enhancing drugs; or cheating, nor does it include athletes taking risks in which they have little chance of success. Rather, the focus is on adaptive responses to situational risk elements. Taking appropriate risk in sports means:

- identifying the costs and benefits of a particular risk;
- assessing the chances of advantageous or detrimental outcomes;
- evaluating athletes' readiness to take the risk;

- establishing their willingness to accept the consequences of failure; and
- committing to the behavior necessary to take the risk so as to ensure the best possible outcome.

Practically speaking, risk-taking involves athletes' willingness to move outside of their comfort zone, exceed their currently established limits and perform in their sport in a way that maximizes their chances of success.

Theory and Research

Risk-taking can be considered a form of novel behavior occurring in response to specific characteristics of the environment. In evolutionary terms, movement itself was one of the earliest forms of risk-taking in that it provided survival advantages by affording access to food, shelter, and reproduction (Catania, 2007; Pain & Pain, 2005). However, it also allowed exposure to predators and environmental conditions posing threats to survival. In light of unknown consequences, maintaining behavioral responses resulting in predictable outcomes minimized exposure to threats. Few people today face life-or-death threats; however, in the context of sports, the notion of survival shifts from physical survival to what it means to survive athletically. Survival in sports is defined in terms of athletes' ability to continue to progress and climb the competitive ladder. From this perspective, athletes' success ensures survival and their failure threatens survival in their sports lives (Jones, Milligan, Llewellyn, Gledhill, & Johnson, 2017; Taylor, 2017; Willig, 2008).

In this context, risk-taking has "survival" value for sport performance. Biologically, novel responses trigger the release of dopamine, which regulates cognitive and motor functioning and produces feelings of pleasure (Pain & Pain, 2005). At a behavioral level, deliberate, reflective risk-taking can be planned and managed, enabling athletes to learn to discount the probability of failure in relation to the probability of reward (Nigg, 2017) and to discern when the cost of taking a risk exceeds the benefit (Hughes & Coakley, 1991). Taking voluntary risks can also shape resilience, courage, and persistence. As a practice of self-actualization, risk-taking fosters the values of self-improvement, emotional engagement, and control over actions through preparation (Lupton & Tulloch, 2002).

Athletes' approach to risk and their perception of its magnitude are most likely to be impacted by factors relevant to the particular risk. Sandseter's (2009) study of children's outdoor active play determined that risk-taking behavior was influenced by both controllable physical skills and perceived self-efficacy while interacting with uncontrollable dimensions of the setting, such as weather, landscape, equipment, materials, and presence of other people. Wiese-Bjornstahl's Sport Injury Risk Profile (2010) elaborates on the factors affecting risk-taking in sports. Among the personal factors that are within athletes' control are their attitudes and beliefs about their sports participation, goals, motivation, confidence, intensity, and. Uncontrollable factors encompass social, cultural, and environmental elements such as sport rules, norms, and ethics; coaching and officiating; media; and social pressure. Taken together, Sandseter's (2009) and Wiese-Bjornstahl's (2010) work suggest that risk can be conceptualized as the discrepancy between perceived capability and perceived task difficulty, and that increasing athletes' perceived self-efficacy in managing uncontrollable environmental dimensions may be critical to successful risk-taking.

Athletes' willingness to test their skills against a standard is another factor related to risk-taking in sports. Setting clear goals is one effective method of specifying standards and doing so has been shown to increase the likelihood of risk-taking. Larrick, Heath, and Wu (2009) concluded that people who set challenging goals before attempting a series of tasks were more likely to take risks compared to people who were merely instructed to "do your best." Those who set goals typically used the goals as both a performance guide during the tasks and a benchmark for evaluating their performance, which tended toward high variability. It follows, then, that athletes who set realistically challenging goals are more likely to take appropriate risks.

Motivation orientation is another factor defining the set of cues to which athletes are most likely to attend and, as such, it is important to understand whether a particular athlete is approaching risks in anticipation of a productive outcome or avoiding the risks of expected failure (Elliott & Harackiewicz, 1996). Approach-motivated, action-oriented athletes are more inclined to focus on their goals and take risks than are athletes focused on preventing aversive consequences (Raab & Johnson, 2004). Although unrelenting pursuit of excellence is an integral part of the sport ethos (Hughes & Coakley, 1991), athletes' risk tolerance will differ across the physical, psychological, and social domains (Zou & Scholer, 2016); therefore, identifying athletes' motivational orientation is essential in devising appropriate plans for encouraging risk-taking.

The practice of risk-taking is associated with improved sport skills and increased self-efficacy, ultimately accelerating sport performance over time (Llewellyn & Sanchez, 2008; Sandseter, 2009). For example, studies of adventure-sports athletes show that those with higher skill levels also tend to be approach-motivated and action-oriented; they prepare more thoroughly for sport participation and are therefore more comfortable with the combination of novelty and unpredictability that characterizes risk-taking (Llewellyn, Sanchez, Asghar, & Jones, 2008; Lyng, 2008). Risk-taking also facilitates identify formation (Llewellyn & Sanchez, 2008; Lyng, 2008) and provides athletes with opportunities to overcome fear and anxiety, improve focus, achieve goals, and learn other behavior associated with personal growth.

Practical Implications

Given the necessity of taking risks to achieve success in sports, developing a repertoire of risk-taking responses would seem to be an obvious choice for athletes as they pursue their goals. Athletes would be expected to prefer to take risks and set themselves up for success rather than playing it safe and ensuring mediocrity (which is akin to failure in sports). Yet, choosing to take risks is not an easy choice because, although the chances of success increase with risk-taking, so do the chances of failure. Moreover, there are a variety of psychological and emotional factors that can prevent athletes from taking appropriate risks.

Initially, helping athletes move toward productive risk-taking involves working with them to explore attitudes toward risks and failure and to help them understand and appreciate the benefits of taking risks. Specifically, athletes must learn to focus on the advantages of taking risks while being willing to accept that doing so may not always pay off. If athletes can accept the possibility of failure in discrete situations, the threat to "survival" is mitigated and they will be more willing to take risks because they are focused on the benefits. Other key steps for consultants are to help athletes learn to recognize situations in which taking risks is appropriate; to engage in rigorous preparations prior to taking a risk, and to fully commit themselves to taking the risk so as to increase the chances of success.

Another facet of facilitating risk-taking is for consultants to guide athletes through a four-step process that will help them approach risks in a deliberate fashion. This structure provides the sense of control, confidence, and comfort that can make athletes more willing to take risks.

Assess Risks in Relation to Goals

An essential criterion that athletes should use in determining whether to take certain risks in their sport is the relationship of risks to their goals. Specifically, consultants can help athletes decide whether the risks they are considering will help them achieve a specific goal or set of goals they have established for themselves. Consultants can provide four guidelines that are useful when assisting athletes in assessing their risk-taking relative to their goals.

Define Goals

As will be discussed in Chapter 4, athletes can set a series of outcome and process goals that they want to strive toward in the near term and the long run. These goals can then be used as benchmarks for determining the specific risks athletes need to take to achieve them.

Identify Relevant Risks

Clearly stated sports goals enable athletes to identify the risks relevant to those goals. Consultants can then help athletes deconstruct the risks associated with their goals by assessing the athlete's perceived competence to take action relative to specific characteristics of the risk (adapted from Hineline, 1983). Does the athlete know:

- *Why* to take a risk?
- *Which* risk to take?

- *How* to take the risk?
- *When* to take the risk?
- *Where* to take the risk?
- *Who* can support the risk?

Analyzing these risk components affords athletes a clearer understanding of the perceived and objective magnitude of the risk which, if addressed, can increase the perceived and actual probability of success and decrease the probability of failure. This analysis may also change athletes' attitudes toward taking risks by delineating the most productive risks to take while also putting the potential liabilities of the risk in a realistic perspective.

Assess Risk Motivation

Determining athletes' motivation to take certain risks enables consultants to more accurately tailor strategies that will support appropriate risk-taking. Once risk components are identified, consultants can ask athletes to complete a decisional balance sheet (Janis & Mann, 1977) weighing costs and benefits of taking the risks vs. playing it safe. This exercise—shown in Table 1.1 below with frequently cited pros and cons—involves comparing the benefits of taking the risk with the costs of continuing the status quo.

Manage the Risk-taking Environment

After clarifying goals, relevant risks, and motivation to engage in risk-taking, consultants can help athletes successfully take risks by showing athletes how to intentionally approach risk-taking.

Planning

Risk planning is another strategy that consultants can use to increase the likelihood that athletes will take risks that pay off. Consultants can assist athletes in identifying specific risk-taking strategies based on their goals, the corresponding risks, and their risk motivations. They can then show athletes how to develop a risk-taking plan that takes into account the "why, which, how, when, where, and who" parameters detailed above. Once risk-taking strategies are formulated, consultants can assist athletes in developing an action plan consisting of smaller and more manageable actions that encourage them to progress toward taking appropriate risks in the highest-stakes situations.

TABLE 1.1 Benefits and Costs of Risk-taking.

Benefits of Taking These Risks	*Costs of Taking These Risks*
Pushing limits, moving to the next level	A lot of criticism
Achieve my dream	Too much time or effort
More wins	Failure
More awards and recognition	Make more mistakes, perform worse for awhile
Get out of rut/get unstuck	
Get stronger, more fit, better skills	
Better position on team/better ranking	
Learn to cope with mistakes	

Benefits of Playing it Safe	*Costs of Playing it Safe*
Easier	Stagnation
Safer (can't fail if they don't try)	Boredom
More comfortable	Frustration
	Won't reach the next level
	Regrets
	Damage to self-identity/self-esteem

Psychological Obstacles

In some cases, the source of athletes' reluctance to take risks comes from particular attitudes and beliefs they hold about themselves and their sports participation (see Chapter 2). Common psychological and emotional obstacles to risk-taking include:

- threat attitude;
- fixed mindset;
- lack of ownership;
- overinvestment;
- fear of failure;
- perfectionism;
- inaccurate assessment of the probabilities of success and failure;
- need to control;
- rigid adherence to rules;
- sensitivity to social consequences;
- overemphasis on results;
- comparison to others;
- lack of a long-term perspective; and
- unrealistic expectations about progress.

Consultants can use a variety of strategies, including those described throughout Part I of *CASP*, to help athletes transform unproductive attitudes and beliefs into productive ones:

- manage controllable environmental factors and accept those that are uncontrollable;
- adopt realistic perceptions about outcomes and progress;
- build confidence in their capabilities;
- use intensity control tools to manage fear and anxiety;
- engage in role play to rehearse productive responses to criticism;
- reframe fear as a normal part of performance; and
- reorient from an outcome focus to a process focus.

Environmental Obstacles

External factors beyond athletes' control can become significant barriers to gaining familiarity and comfort in taking risks including competition schedules, weather and venue conditions, spectators, media, opposing competitors or teams, and officials. Athletes' perceptions of these factors impact their willingness to take risks. Frequently, such uncontrollable elements may produce a threat reaction in which athletes experience a decline in confidence and motivation, an increase in intensity, a loss of focus, and a variety of debilitating emotions, all of which make it less likely that they will take risks. Consultants can help athletes to use various mental exercises and tools, including self-talk, imagery, breathing, and process focus to shift their reactions in a more productive direction, thus making them more open to taking appropriate risks.

Gaining Comfort with Risk-taking

Risk-taking is initially uncomfortable because of its inherent uncertainty. For athletes who do not regularly take risks, doing so places them in a position of unfamiliarity, unpredictability, and loss of immediate control. Consultants can assist athletes in becoming more comfortable with risk-taking by helping them to recognize and gain control over contributors to risks that are within their control and to eschew those they can't, including:

- People: Coaches, teammates, family, friends, opponents, officials, spectators, media.
- Places: Practice and competition venues, locker room, athletic training room, team gathering spots.

- Items: Sports equipment, measurement devices, clothing, water bottles and personal gear.
- Conditions: Lighting, room temperature, practice day and time, nutritional and sleep status.

Consultants can help athletes improve the probability of success and increase their comfort with risk-taking by encouraging them to identify the most controllable environmental factors and deciding how to eliminate or reduce those that are disadvantageous, alter existing stimuli to make them more beneficial, and add helpful supports that may be missing.

Risk-taking as a Habit

Taylor (2017) suggests that risk-taking should not be sport-specific, but rather a lifestyle choice that permeates all aspects of athletes' lives. In support of this approach, researchers have concluded that self-efficacy in taking risks in one domain carries over to other domains (Taniguchi, Bennion, Duerden, Widmer, & Ricks, 2017), thereby suggesting that taking unrelated low-stakes risks on a regular basis can have a measurable effect on risk-taking confidence in sport. With this perspective in mind, athletes can seek opportunities to take risks outside of sport. Examples of non-sport risk-taking might include:

- ordering a dish they've never tried at a restaurant;
- seeing a movie they know little about;
- listening to a new style of music;
- saying hello to people they pass on the street; and
- raising a hand in class or speaking up at a meeting.

Support Appropriate Risk-Taking

The inevitable uncertainty of risk-taking outcomes means that the ratio of success to failure will fluctuate. The resulting insecurity can cause additional discomfort for athletes; due to this instability, athletes can benefit from a strong social support system as they learn to become comfortable taking risks. Consultants are an integral part of this support network. They can actively reinforce athletes' commitment to and execution of risk-taking, regularly check to ensure there is sufficient acknowledgment of effort and progress from coaches, and they can encourage parents to support and cheer their athletes' healthy risk-taking efforts.

Consultants can also teach athletes self-support strategies that provide additional evidence of progress, opportunities to express and manage feelings, and reinforcement for effort invested in risk-taking.

- Self-reflection: journaling, affirmations, keeping records of attempts, successes, and perceived failures
- Stress management: breathing, relaxation training, mindfulness
- Recognize milestones: acknowledging and rewarding effort and successful outcomes

Evaluate Progress and Plan for Change

As athletes learn to grapple with and gain comfort with the uncertainty of risk-taking, they will seek to answer the questions "How am I doing?" and "What's next?" Consultants can help athletes bring stability to the uncertain process of risk-taking by using the following five strategies to evaluate progress and plan next steps.

First, consultants can build regular check-ins into athletes' risk-taking plan to bring stability to the process. During these periodic evaluations, consultants can use journal entries, performance records, coaches' feedback, and other relevant experiential and performance data to troubleshoot and fine-tune the risk-taking plan.

Second, using the gathered information, consultants can help athletes to determine whether the goals they set in their risk-taking plan are still relevant and realistic. Goals that may be too ambitious, not ambitious enough, or on an inaccurate timeline can be adjusted to better encourage athletes' risk-taking.

Third, consultants can help athletes assess the personal risk-management strategies being used by athletes for their ongoing appropriateness and effectiveness. Consultants can review each strategy in relation to athletes' goals to determine whether they are useful and necessary. They can then collaborate with athletes to modify suboptimal strategies, replace ineffective ones, and eliminate those that are no longer needed.

Fourth, to ensure continuing support until athletes fully embrace risk-taking, consultants can evaluate the effectiveness of the support system in place. With the information available about athletes' risk-taking efforts, they can identify and fill gaps in social support athletes receive as they immerse themselves in risk-taking.

Finally,, consultants can help to celebrate athletes' successes in taking risks. This recognition includes not only those times when risks are rewarded; additionally, athletes' commitment to the process, effort, and productive responses to risk-taking failures should also be highlighted and reinforced.

Take a Leap of Faith

Risk-taking can't always be deliberate and planned. Rather, there will be times when, during the course of training or competition, an opportunity arises in which taking a risk is warranted. In these situations, athletes don't have the luxury of stopping, analyzing, evaluating, and making a measured decision. Instead, they must immediately decide whether or not to take the risk. Although they may be unaware of it, the decision will be influenced by the athlete's history of reinforcement for taking risks in similar situations and by adaptive heuristics, or "mental shortcuts," enabling them to decide quickly and with incomplete information (Denrell, 2007; Gigerenzer & Selten, 2002). Taylor (2017) refers to this type of decision-making as "taking a leap of faith," and uses an analogy from the film *Indiana Jones and the Last Crusade* to illustrate. In the film, the protagonist archeologist, Indiana Jones, is following a map that will lead him to the Holy Grail. The film concludes with a scene in which Jones comes to a doorway beyond which is a bottomless chasm and, on the other side, a room where the Holy Grail will be found. There is no apparent way to cross the gulf, but the map depicts a man walking out into the abyss with the instructions to take a leap of faith that will allow him to reach the Holy Grail. Jones is faced with needing to make a spontaneous risk-taking decision in which there is no evidence that the risk will be rewarded and the likely consequences appear catastrophic, specifically, Jones will, with all probability, plunge to his death. Yet, gathering his courage, Jones jumps into the gap and discovers an invisible bridge across which he seizes the Holy Grail. In a similar fashion, athletes will, at times, need to take a leap of faith in their sport to achieve their goals (with comfort coming from the recognition that they will survive if the risk doesn't pay off).

For athletes to take this leap of faith, they must have an unwavering desire to strive toward their goals and a deep conviction that the only way they will find success is to get out of their comfort zones and push their limits. Consultants can help athletes to also recognize 100-percent confidence isn't possible with risks and that some doubt is normal. Finally, consultants can point out to athletes that this leap of faith is not blind; rather, it has been primed by the countless hours of preparation and, often, years of their lives athletes have spent. preparing for that leap. Therefore, athletes can be confident that the risks of failure are relatively smaller and the chances of success are substantially greater.

Summary

- Elevating athletic performance requires taking risks involving real or perceived dangers and uncertain outcomes in pursuit of sports goals.
- Each athlete must decide whether they want to "play it safe," which is comfortable, but may also lead to stagnation, or choose to take the risk, which may result in either spectacular success or crushing failure.
- Taking appropriate risk in sports involves identifying the costs and benefits of a particular risk, assessing the chances of desirable or undesirable outcomes, judging how ready athletes are to take the risk, and establishing their readiness to accept the consequences of failure.
- Our most powerful instinct is to survive and, in most situations, we are driven to seek familiarity, predictability, and comfort, all experiences that are run counter to risk-taking.
- Risk-taking has "survival" value for sport performance.
- Athletes' perception of risk, their desire to test their capabilities, and their motivation orientation contribute to their willingness to take risks.
- It would seem that athletes would prefer to take risks and set themselves up for success rather than playing it safe and ensure mediocrity, yet it's not an easy choice because, though the chances of success increase with risk-taking, so do the chances of failure.

- Consultants can help athletes to increase their risk-taking by exploring their attitudes toward risk and failure, aligning risks with goals, managing the risk environment, making risk-taking a habit, ensuring that athletes receive sufficient support for their risk-taking, and evaluating the effectiveness of their risk-taking.
- Ultimately, because risks are defined by their unpredictability, athletes must be willing to take a leap of faith and accept whatever happens.

References

Catania, A. C. (2007). *Learning* (4th interim ed.). Cornwall-on-Hudson, NY: Sloan.

Denrell, J. (2007). Adaptive learning and risk-taking. *Psychological Review*, *114*(1), 177.

Elliot, A. J., & Harackiewicz, J. M. (1996). Approach and avoidance achievement goals and intrinsic motivation: A mediational analysis. *Journal of Personality and Social Psychology*, *70*(3), 461.

Gigerenzer, G., & Selten, R. (Eds.). (2002). *Bounded rationality: The adaptive toolbox*. Cambridge, MA: MIT Press.

Hineline, P. N. (1983). When we speak of knowing. *The Behavior Analyst*, *6*(2), 183–186.

Hughes, R., & Coakley, J. (1991). Positive deviance among athletes: The implications of overconformity to the sport ethic. *Sociology of Sport Journal*, *8*(4), 307–325.

Janis, I. L., & Mann, L. (1977). *Decision making: A psychological analysis of conflict, choice, and commitment*. New York, NY: Free Press.

Jones, G., Milligan, J., Llewellyn, D., Gledhill, A., & Johnson, M. I. (2017). Motivational orientation and risk-taking in elite winter climbers: A qualitative study. *International Journal of Sport and Exercise Psychology*, *15*(1), 25–40.

Larrick, R. P., Heath, C., & Wu, G. (2009). Goal-induced risk-taking in negotiation and decision making. *Social Cognition*, *27*(3), 342–364.

Llewellyn, D. J., & Sanchez, X. (2008). Individual differences and risk-taking in rock climbing. *Psychology of Sport and Exercise*, *9*(4), 413–426.

Llewellyn, D. J., Sanchez, X., Asghar, A., & Jones, G. (2008). Self-efficacy, risk-taking and performance in rock climbing. *Personality and Individual Differences*, *45*(1), 75–81.

Lupton, D., & Tulloch, J. (2002). 'Life would be pretty dull without risk': voluntary risk-taking and its pleasures. *Health, Risk & Society*, *4*(2), 113–124.

Lyng, S. (2008). Risk-taking in sport: Edgework and reflexive community. In K. Young & M. Atkinson (Eds.), *Tribal play: Subcultural journeys through sport* (pp.83–109). Bingley: JAI Press.

Nigg, J. T. (2017). On the relations among self-regulation, self-control, executive functioning, effortful control, cognitive control, impulsivity, risk-taking, and inhibition for developmental psychopathology. *Journal of Child Psychology and Psychiatry*, *58*(4), 361–383.

Pain, M. T., & Pain, M. A. (2005). Essay: Risk-taking in sport. *The Lancet*, *366*, S33–S34.

Raab, M., & Johnson, J. G. (2004). Individual differences of action orientation for risk-taking in sports. *Research Quarterly for Exercise and Sport*, *75*(3), 326–336.

Sandseter, E. B. H. (2009). Characteristics of risky play. *Journal of Adventure Education & Outdoor Learning*, *9*(1), 3–21.

Taniguchi, S. T., Bennion, J., Duerden, M. D., Widmer, M. A., & Ricks, M. (2017). Self-efficacy of risk-taking in outdoor recreation as a predictor of the self-efficacy of risk-taking in essay writing. *Journal of Outdoor Recreation*, *9*(4), 425–438.

Taylor, J. (2017). *Train your mind for athletic success: Mental preparation to achieve your sports goals*. Lanham, MD: Rowman & Littlefield.

Wiese-Bjornstal, D. M. (2010). Psychology and socioculture affect injury risk, response, and recovery in high-intensity athletes: a consensus statement. *Scandinavian Journal of Medicine & Science in Sports*, *20*, 103–111.

Willig, C. (2008). A phenomenological investigation of the experience of taking part in extreme sports. *Journal of Health Psychology*, *13*(5), 690–702.

Zou, X., & Scholer, A. A. (2016). Motivational affordance and risk-taking across decision domains. *Personality and Social Psychology Bulletin*, *42*(3), 275–289.

PROCESS

Erin Ayala and Jim Taylor

Consider the athlete who delivers the best performance he has ever had but does not earn a medal due to the high level of competition. Then, consider the athlete who earns a place at the top of the podium, but knows she could have given more and pushed harder. It could be argued that the first athlete is worthy of more recognition for delivering a strong personal performance with the utmost effort, as opposed to the second athlete who could have tried harder but won due to their innate ability or competing against a weaker field. By focusing on the outcome of a competition, the importance of the process underlying such outcomes is often neglected.

Athletes, coaches, and parents hold many misconceptions about the importance of results in accomplishing sports goals. Although athletes need to get good results if they want to be successful, a key question remains regarding how athletes can achieve those results. Surprisingly, the answer conflicts with the conventional wisdom held by athletes, coaches, and parents.

An outcome attitude means that athletes are most focused on results, rankings, and outperforming others. A key aspect of an outcome attitude involves athletes paying attention to factors that are external to themselves and outside of their control. Conversely, a process attitude has athletes directing their attention toward their daily development (Botterill, 2005) and what they must do to perform as well as they can. Process examples include what athletes do to improve their conditioning, technique, and tactics. With a process attitude, athletes focus on themselves and on factors within their control.

A common question that consultants ask athletes, coaches, and parents is: "Which is better to have: an outcome attitude or a process attitude?" Based on an informal survey, many people indicate that they think an outcome attitude is best because it is important for athletes to focus on the results they want to achieve. Yet, as any experienced consultant will agree, surprisingly, an outcome attitude can do more harm than good in athletes' competitive efforts. Let's explain this paradoxical perspective.

Outcomes occur at the end of competitions, so if athletes are focused only on the outcome they want, they are not focused on what they need to do to perform their best from the start to the finish. In other words, the pressure of the outcome makes it extremely challenging to concentrate on the process of performing (Botterill, 2005). Focusing too much on the outcome can also increase stress and decrease focus, leading athletes to over-analyze rather than to trust themselves and their game. Also, as will be discussed in Chapter 3, it is common for athletes to experience anxiety before a competition, and it is this focus on the outcome that produces the nerves. This type of anxiety creates a threat attitude that comes from athletes' fear of failing to achieve their goals.

In contrast, when athletes embrace a process attitude, they bolster the odds of achieving the results they are striving for. Athletes who focus on what they need to do to perform at their highest level will experience fewer problems with competition and are more likely perform well (Botterill, 2005). In doing so, athletes put themselves in a position to get the results they want, and are more likely to accomplish their goals (Taylor, 2017).

The challenge for athletes, and the consultants that work with them, is that an outcome attitude—"Winning isn't everything; it's the only thing"—is embraced by most of our sports culture. From athletes, coaches, and parents to the teams, fans, and media, most are likely to value and promote outcome-oriented thinking (Burton & Raedeke, 2007; Weinberg, 2002). However, athletes can not only perform better, but can also experience more enjoyment in their sports participation, if they can resist the gravitational pull of these cultural and social forces and redirect the attention onto the process (Singer et al., 2001). Former UCLA basketball coach John Wooden demonstrated the importance of the process with his "Pyramid of Success," which outlined 15 characteristics to success (Wooden & Carty, 2005). Rather than telling athletes to look at the scoreboard, Wooden stressed that winning was a byproduct of preparation. Hence, his athletes were trained to focus on the process of preparation and how the game was played, rather than the outcome. Since Wooden's introduction of the pyramid in 1948, the field of sport psychology has seen both theory and research studies that support many of his principles (Perez, Van Horn, & Otten, 2014).

Theory and Research

A process attitude includes several aspects of sport performance: planning and organization, goal setting, proper preparation, mindfulness, and recognition of athletes' role or responsibility in their sport. While training or competing, athletes who adopt a process attitude appreciate the importance of planning and organization as it relates to their sport (Singer, Downs, Bouchard, & de la Pena, 2001). As Singer et al. (2001) state, "visualizing unrealistic goals and fantasizing success without the knowledge or plan of how to get there may lead to disappointment and hinder progress" (p. 215). For example, strong time-management skills are needed for athletes to prioritize and complete the training needed to prepare for competition. Without strong time-management skills, important tasks and responsibilities may not be completed for those with a busy schedule. Moreover, when unexpected changes occur to athletes' schedules, a process attitude allows athletes to adapt and respond effectively to challenges.

In addition to planning and organization, athletes with a process attitude develop an understanding of the factors needed to achieve an outcome goal, such as sport-specific skills and intentional practice (Singer et al., 2001). Process-oriented athletes recognize the importance of daily work and the stepping stones needed to reach outcome goals they set for their sport. They are also likely to create process goals for themselves that reflect personal growth or achievement in their own skill sets (Smrdu, 2015), ultimately leading to incremental and steady progress over time. This process gives athletes confidence and a perceived edge over their competitors because they know they have put in the work necessary to achieve their goals (Kingston & Hardy, 1997).

As athletes enhance their planning and goal setting by using a process attitude, they are more likely to focus on and engage in proper preparation for competitions. Athletes with a process attitude understand that proper preparation is an important component to producing the outcomes they want to accomplish. In addition to consistent training and engagement during practices, such process-oriented preparation includes proper rest, nutrition, hydration, and routines in training and before big events.

A final component of process orientation is mindfulness, which refers to athletes' abilities to maintain present moment awareness (Ludwig & Kabat-Zinn, 2008). Mindful athletes focus on the immediate experience of training and competition (e.g., thoughts, emotions, physical sensations, breathing, body position), rather than paying attention to the potential outcome of a competition and the emotions associated with it. Ultimately, the goal for mindfulness is to immerse athletes in the process of their sports experiences, which will lead to improved emotion regulation and well-being (Ludwig & Kabat-Zinn, 2008) as well as enhanced performance and better results. Athletes who engage in mindfulness are likely to see improved performance both within and outside of sport due to their abilities to stay focused on the process in the moment and to effectively navigate perceived distractions, obstacles, and difficulties that arise (Gardner & Moore, 2017). This type of mindset also increases the likelihood of finding the "flow" state that so many athletes strive for (Botterill, 2005).

Although our sports culture focuses on results, the research suggests that a focus on the process helps athletes achieve the outcomes they want (Burton & Raedeke, 2007). In golfers, process-oriented goals have been associated with higher levels of self-efficacy, concentration, and lower levels of anxiety (Kingston & Hardy, 1997). Process-oriented visualization and planning has been shown to improve performance in collegiate athletes when compared to those who possess an outcome attitude (Singer et al., 2001). Process attitudes also facilitate flow and positive mental states, allowing athletes to reach peak performance (Jackson & Roberts, 1992). In contrast, some studies have found that participants who focus on outcome performance (e.g., making a basketball shot) are more likely to perform poorly due to stress (Liao & Masters, 2002). Ultimately, to enhance performance, athletes, coaches, and parents need to recognize and commit to the process of sports excellence.

Practical Implications

As consultants well know, in an ideal world, they would convince athletes that results don't matter, and they should just trade their outcome attitude with a process attitude. Unfortunately, the reality is that results do matter in the sports world. Athletes don't progress in their sport because they work hard (though that helps); rather, they advance because they produce results. Furthermore, realistically, one reason why athletes participate in sports is because they enjoy competing, achieving results, and accomplishing the outcome goals they set for themselves.

That said, consultants can't expect athletes to expunge results from their minds. Instead, they should assume that athletes will focus on results a great deal, which can be beneficial in a few ways. For example, an outcome attitude can motivate athletes to get the results they want. It can also provide clarity on the direction athletes want to go in their development. At the same time, when athletes focus too much on results, it can become a distraction and the cause of pressure and anxiety. Thus, the goal for consultants is to show athletes how to use an outcome attitude for the benefits it can bring, and then shift to a process attitude in most aspects of athletes' training, preparation, and competitive efforts.

This shift from an outcome attitude to a process attitude involves athletes changing their relationship to results and how it affects their sports lives. This change then influences how athletes think about their sport, the emotions that emerge from their sport, and, ultimately, how they perform in competitions. Here is a framework that consultants can guide athletes through to ensure that a process attitude is predominant in their approach to their sport.

Understand Outcome and Process Attitudes

The first step in this shift involves consultants educating athletes about what the two attitudes are and how they influence them. An outcome attitude interferes with athletes' efforts and performances by how it demotivates, hurts confidence, creates stress and anxiety, and distracts them from what they need to focus on to perform their best. In contrast, a process attitude produces a very different effect on athletes by increasing motivation and confidence, engendering positive emotions and self-awareness, creating ideal intensity, and focusing athletes' efforts on what will help them perform at their highest level. If athletes can fully appreciate this difference and see the value in a process attitude, they will be more likely to embrace the need to make this change.

Recognize Outcome Attitude Moments

Because many athletes possess an outcome attitude, every reaction that comes from it will likely be their default response to training and competitive situations. The next step consultants can take is to help athletes to recognize those moments when it will cause the most problems. For example, outcome attitudes most impact athletes prior to important competitions in which they are heavily invested in the results. This awareness provides athletes with a "fork in the road" at which they can make this shift from outcome to process attitudes.

Pink Elephants and Blue Hippos

It is one thing for athletes to recognize situations in which an outcome attitude is hurting their efforts, but it is an entirely different and more difficult thing, in that moment, to make the change to a process attitude. In an ideal world, consultants would just tell athletes to stop using an outcome attitude, but the minds of athletes don't work that way. In fact, the more consultants tell athletes to avoid thinking about results, the more they will focus on them.

Here's an exercise that an experienced consultant uses to help athletes make this shift (Taylor, 2017). He tells them to not think about a pink elephant (anything that is distinctive will work). Of course, the more he suggests this, the more the pink elephant gets stuck in their minds. The lesson here is that it is extremely difficult for athletes to not think about something that is already deeply embedded in their psyches. The consultant's solution involves getting athletes to think about something else.

Once athletes learn how resistant old thinking habits can be, consultants can give them that something else that was just mentioned. The second part of this consultant's exercise is to ask to think about a blue hippo. With this cue, athletes, of course, think about a blue hippo and, in doing so, don't think about the pink elephant. Admittedly, it's more difficult to shift focus from an outcome attitude to a process attitude than from a pink elephant to a blue hippo, but the same principles apply; it simply takes more awareness and commitment. The key point that consultants can convey to athletes is that when they become aware that their outcome attitude is taking hold of their thinking, they can acknowledge it and then deliberately shift to a process attitude.

Navigating External Forces

One of the biggest challenges of making this transition is that athletes must often not only resist their own old thinking habits; they must also resist the pressure to focus on results from important people around them, as well as our results-obsessed sports culture. Consultants can help athletes identify the forces surrounding them that might be reinforcing an outcome attitude. Though parents, teams, and cultures can't be readily changed, there are a few suggestions that consultants can make to assist athletes.

Consultants and athletes can ask parents and coaches to reduce how much they talk about results, and can explain why an outcome attitude may hurt their athletes' performances. Consultants can also help athletes see the underlying and well-intentioned messages of support and encouragement from parents, coaches, siblings, friends, and others when they talk about results, however misguided they may be. Finally, in this day and age of technology, consultants can encourage athletes to remove themselves from social media pages or accounts that focus solely on results. If athletes can minimize the unhealthy outcome messages they are getting, they will find it easier to make the shift away from an outcome attitude and toward a process attitude.

Like change of any kind, athletes will be challenged to make this transition. Consultants would be wise to counsel commitment and patience in the change process. Similar to making technical changes that may be deeply ingrained in their muscle memory, this attitudinal shift will involve retraining years of "mental memory." Like an ineffective technical habit, as athletes practice the shift from outcome to process attitude, it will become easier until they get to a point where the process attitude will replace the outcome attitude and the latter will guide their thinking in their sport moving forward.

Stay in the Now

One of athletes' greatest challenges, especially in the days leading up to a big competition, involves staying focused on the present when they feel pulled back to the past or drawn to the future. There's an old adage, "You can't change the past, but you can ruin a perfectly good present by worrying about it." When athletes are struggling, their disappointing results can stick in their minds, causing them to ruminate on those poor performances. This past focus distracts them from focusing on what will help them perform their best in the present. Dwelling on past performances can lead to negative emotions such as sadness, frustration, and regret. These emotions not only make athletes feel bad, but they also hurt their motivation, confidence, intensity, and focus. When athletes become absorbed in the past, it creates a psychological and physiological state that leaves them unprepared to perform at their highest level. To help athletes makes this shift, consultants can ask athletes to watch for times when they get "stuck" in the past, invite them to identify one thing they learned from that performance, and return to a focus on the present.

Athletes don't do themselves any favors when they focus on the future either. When athletes direct their attention to what lies ahead, it usually leads to expectations about how they will perform and the results they will get. This future orientation causes athletes to worry about whether they will live up to those expectations and instills fear that they won't. A focus on the future can also contribute to stress, anxiety, and fear of failure. Like the past, it creates a psychological and physiological state that makes a successful future less likely.

A present focus that comes with a process attitude ensures that athletes focus on the present and what they need to do to be prepared to perform at a high level. Consultants can help athletes to gain this "in the now" orientations, particularly if they feel drawn to the past or future, by asking one question: "What do I need to do now?" This question impacts athletes in several positive ways. It directs athletes' minds away from the past or future and onto the present. In doing so, they focus on what precisely they need to do to be ready to perform their best. It also helps them identify what they have control over in the moment. By focusing on present and getting prepared, athletes also feel increased confidence and energy because they are paying attention to aspects of their sport over which they have control.

Mental Exercises and Tools for a Process Attitude

The above approaches are aimed at athletes creating and instilling a process attitude that is enduring and resilient. At the same time, because of the pervasive messages about results that athletes receive almost daily from parents, coaches, teammates, and the sports culture in general, itis not uncommon for them to be vulnerable to being pulled back into an outcome attitude. In these situations, there are specific exercises and tools they can use to keep their minds focused on a process attitude. All of these strategies are described in great detail in Chapters 3 and 4, so they will just be listed with a brief description here:

- process goals (creates standards related to specific aspects of performance);
- time management (establishes a schedule for what athletes need to do);
- routines (provides a method for getting prepared before a training or competitive performance);
- imagery (seeing and feeling themselves performing well is process focused);
- keywords (reminds athletes of what they need to focus on now);
- mindfulness (directs attention inward on self and focus on being in the moment);
- make a competition plan (details what athletes need to do when they compete); and
- focus on the competitive process after an event (directs attention on what athletes did, not how they did).

Summary

- Athletes need to get good results if they want to be successful, but a more important issue is how they can achieve those results.
- An outcome attitude means that athletes are most focused on results, rankings, and outperforming others, which means they are paying attention to things external to themselves and outside of their control.
- Many athletes, coaches, and parents believe that an outcome attitude is best because it's important for athletes to focus on the results they want to achieve.
- An outcome attitude can do more harm than good in athletes' competitive efforts because they are not focused on performing their best, and get anxious about not achieving the results they want.
- With a process attitude, when athletes concentrate on what they need to do to perform at their highest level, they will likely perform well and, in doing so, put themselves in a position to get the results and accomplish the goals they want.
- The challenge for athletes, and the consultants that work with them, is that an outcome attitude—"Winning isn't everything; it's the only thing"—is embraced by most of our sports culture.
- Research indicates that an outcome attitude interferes with performance and a process attitudes facilitates performance.
- The goal for consultants is to show athletes how to use an outcome attitude for the benefits it can bring, but then shift to a process attitude in most aspects of athletes' training, preparations, and competitive efforts.
- Consultants can guide athletes toward a process attitude by helping them understand how outcome and process attitudes impact them, recognize outcome attitude moments, shifting their focus from outcome to process, and staying in the now.
- Consultants can show athletes practical exercises and tools to enable them to embrace a process attitude including creating process goals, developing effective time management skills, using routines, imagery, and keywords to maintain a process focus, being mindful, making a competitive plan, and focusing on what athletes do, not how they did, after a competition.

References

Botterill, C. (2005). Competitive drive: Embracing positive rivalries. In S. Murphy (Ed.), *The sport psychology handbook* (pp. 215–238). Champaign, IL: Human Kinetics.

Burton, D. (1989). Winning isn't everything: Examining the impact of performance goals on collegiate swimmers' cognitions and performance. *The Sport Psychologist, 3*, 105–132.

Burton, D., & Raedeke, T. D. (2007). *Sport psychology for coaches*. Champaign, IL: Human Kinetics.

Gardner, F. L., & Moore, Z. E. (2017). Mindfulness-based and acceptance-based interventions in sport and performance contexts. *Current Opinion in Psychology, 16*, 180–184. doi: 10.1016/j.copsyc.2017.06.001

Jackson, S. A., & Roberts, G. C. (1992). Positive performance states of athletes: Toward a conceptual understanding of peak performance. *Sport Psychologist, 6*, 156–171.

Kingston, K., & Hardy, L. (1997). Effects of different types of goals on processes that support performance. *The Sport Psychologist, 11*, 277–293.

Liao, C., & Masters, R. S. W. (2002). Self-focused attention and performance failure under psychological stress. *Journal of Sport & Exercise Psychology, 24*, 289–305.

Ludwig, D. S., & Kabat-Zinn, J. (2008). Mindfulness in medicine. *Journal of American Medical Association, 11*, 1350–1352. doi: 101001/jama.300.11.1350

Perez, D., Van Horn, S., & Otten, M. P. (2014). Coach John Wooden's Pyramid of Success: A comparison to the sport psychology literature. *International Journal of Sports Science & Coaching, 9*, 85–101.

Singer, R., Downs, D. S., Bouchard, L., & de la Pena, D. (2001). The influence of a process versus an outcome orientation on tennis performance and knowledge. *Journal of Sport Behavior, 24*, 213–222.

Smrdu, M. (2015). First-person experience of optimal sport competition performance of elite team athletes. *Kinesiology, 47*, 169–178.

Taylor, J. (2017). *Train your mind for athletic success: Mental preparation to achieve your sports goals*. Lanham, MD: Rowman & Littlefield.

Weinberg, R. S. (2002). Goal setting. In J. S. Van Raalte & B. W. Brewer (Eds.), *Exploring sport and exercise psychology*, 2nd ed. (pp. 78–89). Washington, DC: American Psychological Association.

Wooden, J., & Carty, J. (2005). *Coach Wooden's Pyramid of Success: Building blocks for a better life*. Ventura, CA: Regal Books.

LONG TERM

Charlie Maher and Jim Taylor

A commitment to competitive sports offers athletes many lessons that they can take with them off the field of play and apply to many aspects of their lives. One of the most influential lessons is that anything of value takes deep engagement, hard work, and sustained effort over a long period of time. As much as athletes would like it to be otherwise, there are no magic pills, easy roads, or instant fixes on the way to success. All great athletes have experienced a journey filled with mistakes, setbacks, plateaus, and failures on their way to the pinnacle of their sport. To "make it," athletes must adopt a long-term attitude whereby they embrace this lengthy journey that lies before them. This attitude allows them to accept and react constructively to the inevitable challenges they will face as they strive toward their sports goals.

Unfortunately, our current sports culture sends a very different message to athletes: "You must be success-ful now or you won't be successful later." From a young age, athletes in the 21st century world of sports are expected to excel early if they want to have any chance of reaching the highest level of their sport. Athletes, parents, and coaches can fall prey to these messages and come to believe that early success is highly predictive of later success in your sport. Our athletic culture is obsessed with the "phenom" and the "can't miss kid" who show early dominance in a sport. Yet, though there have been phenoms who went on to great success later in their careers, this perception is as much fantasy as reality. For example, fewer than 60 Major League Baseball players were among the thousands who have played in the Little League World Series over the years. Though young superstars get a lot of attention, they are actually the exception and not the rule at the highest levels of most sports. Instead, the athletes who developed slowly but steadily and who pushed through the struggles and challenges are the ones who often make it to the top. Athletes can have a hard time withstand-ing these ever-present messages to be successful quickly. Sadly, this short-term attitude can lead athletes to feel frustrated and demoralized early in their sports lives which can lead to their giving up even though their journey has just begun.

A key aspect of athletes embracing a long-term attitude is that short-term results have little impact on their long-term goals. They understand that they are in their sport for the long haul and are more focused on where they want to go rather than where they are now. As such, athletes' efforts are best aimed at readying them for success years into the future instead of on achieving near-term success.

This long-term attitude not only enables athletes to be patient in their sports development, it also helps them deal with the many demands that are a part of participation in competitive sports. Because they are always seeing their efforts through a long lens, they are in a better position to approach those demands with a sense of confi-dence and calm rather than one of worry and stress. A long-term attitude also allows athletes the time to learn about themselves and gain an understanding of what knowledge, experience, and skills they will need to navigate their sports lives and the many demands that are an inherent part of it including:

- balancing their sport with other important aspects of their lives;
- managing their emotions in the face of setbacks and failures;
- experiencing and recovering from injuries;
- resolving conflicts with coaches, parents, and others;
- managing their performances in relation to the expectations of others; and
- being on the alert for people, places, and things that can derail their careers.

Theory and Research

As noted throughout this chapter, attitude can be considered as a mental domain as important to athletic perfor-mance as confidence, focus, or any other on which a set of attitudes, beliefs, and emotions are established (Folds, 2015; Maher, 2011). The mental domain of long-term attitude is informed by theory and research that have to do with values and perspective taking, as well as perseverance, balance, and self-control. Research conducted in the workplace reveals that having a long-term attitude, and the sense of purpose it provides, in relation to their work assists employees in being productive in both the short and long terms (Wrzesniewski, McCauley, Rozin, & Schwartz, 1997). In addition, research on commitment to long-term goals suggests that engagement and productivity is enhanced by workers being able to view their efforts beyond their immediate impact and in relation to future contributions (Sheldon, 2014). Moreover, the work of Duckworth (2016) on the notion of grit, the research of Dweck (2006) on mindset and the contributions of Grant (2008) and Taylor (2017) also inform the value that a long-term attitude brings to athletes.

Practical Implications

Consultants can play a central role in helping athletes to develop and maintain a healthy long-term attitude in their approach to their sports participation. This role is especially important when many people around athletes may be sending unhealthy messages that push a short-term attitude. The process of instilling a long-term attitude in athletes can be informed by a set of guidelines that consultants can use in assisting athletes in viewing their sports lives through a telescope rather than a microscope.

Clarify Values

Values involve how people judge what is important to them and which guide the decisions they make in their lives. The values that athletes hold can have a significant impact on whether they hold a short- or long-term attitude in relation to their sports participation. Specific values that directly impact a long-term attitude include:

- commitment;
- patience;
- diligence;
- follow-through;
- resilience;
- humility; and
- gratitude.

When consultants take the time to help athletes understand and shape their values in a healthy direction, they provide a reference point from which athletes can approach the demands of sports from a long-term attitude. In doing so, those demands seem more manageable because they don't need to be met all at once and completely. Rather, they can be addressed progressively over time. Consultants can assist athletes in clarifying their values with the intention of enabling them to place their sports participation in the context of both time and their broader lives by facilitating the following process:

1. Ask athletes to write down the values that they attach to their sports lives.
2. Have athletes express why these values are important and how they facilitate or interfere with a long-term attitude on their sport.
3. Have athletes place their values, in written form, in a location where they can review them on a regular basis.
4. Encourage athletes to ensure that their daily thoughts, emotions, and actions align with the above values.

Create an Athletic Mission Statement

An athletic mission statement reflects a declaration of values and goals held by athletes. This mission statement acts as the North Star, or the guiding purpose, in all of athletes' efforts in their sports lives. It also provides athletes with a reason for continuing to stay committed and work hard in the face of inevitable struggles of being involved in sports.

Here are two examples of actual athletic mission statements, written by two major league baseball players, one a pitcher and the other a position player, and which were written based on a consideration of their values:

- **Pitcher**: I am relentless in how I compete. I prepare for each outing in a systematic manner and am focused on delivering quality pitches. I leave all of this on the field and then spend time with my family.

- **Position Player**: Through my actions on the field, I have an effect on my opponent. I am honest with myself, when things are not going well and do not point fingers. I strive to make adjustments in my game and get better at it every day.

Consultants can have athletes post their athletic mission statement where they can see it regularly as a reminder of why they engage in sports. They can also encourage athletes to reflect on these statements every day to ensure that their thinking, emotions, and actions are grounded in its guidance.

Conduct an Athletic Self-assessment

Athletic mission statements can be thought of as coming from an altitude of 50,000 feet. An athletic self-assessment happens "boots on the ground" in athletes' everyday sports-related activities. It can support a long-term attitude by showing athletes where they are now and where they want to be with the goal of closing the gap that exists between their present and future states, The following are guidelines that consultants can use to help athletes conduct an athletic self-assessment:

1. Make a list of every area in their sports and general lives that impact their sports efforts (e.g., physical, technical, tactical, mental, equipment, sleep, nutrition, relationships, school work).
2. Rate themselves on a 1–10 scale (1 = poor; 10 = excellent) as a means of determining their strengths and areas in need of improvement.
3. Indicate how their strengths developed and why their areas in need of improvement haven't.
4. Establish SMARTER goals (see Chapter 4 for details) to further develop the strengths and alleviate the weaknesses.

Embrace Continuous Development

When athletes embrace a long-term attitude, they are implicitly adopting the belief in continuous development. This notion reflects the attitude that athletes never stop learning or growing as athletes and as people (Dweck, 2006; see "Growth Mindset" earlier in this chapter). Consultants can help athletes to embrace continuous development by using the following framework:

- **Name it**: Using the athletic self-assessment above, athletes can name the precise aspects of their sports development that they would like to improve on.
- **Claim it**: Identify and create a plan for how they will further develop those areas.
- **Tame it**: Commit to the above plan until they have developed the identified areas.
- **Same it**: Return to **Name it** and begin the process again on other areas that will ensure their continuous development.

Identify Athletic Threat Factors

Athletes don't exist in a vacuum; rather, they are part of a series of concentric circles that expand from self to family to team to sport to culture. Within each of these circles, there exist threat factors that have the potential to derail their sports efforts. There are four categories of threat factors that athletes must be cognizant of to ensure that they aren't overwhelmed with short-term attitude:

Self

As will be described in Chapter 2, athletes possess in themselves psychological and emotional obstacles that threaten their ability to see and commit to their sport with a long-term attitude. Those threat factors detailed in Chapter 2 include overinvestment, perfectionism, fear of failure, expectations from self and others, and emotions. Others involve impatience, lack of commitment, selfishness, and arrogance.

Decisions

In the high-stakes world of sports in which athletes now reside, they can feel pressure to do things that may be beneficial in the short run, yet are ultimately self-defeating. Well-known examples include taking performance-enhancing drugs, cheating, accepting money "under the table," gambling, or spending money profligately.

Others

From family and friends to fans, media, and team officials, not everyone has athletes' long-term best interests at heart. Whether for ego, power, money, or personal gain, other people may place their short-term concerns ahead of the long-term goals of the athletes they are associated with.

Places

Particular locations can harm athletes' long-term prospects. They can include particular teams that have a culture that isn't consistent with athletes' values, mission, and goals. Others might be gyms, bars, dorms, houses, or neighborhoods in which athletes may be tempted to act in ways that are inconsistent with a long-term attitude of their sport.

To develop and maintain a productive long-term attitude, consultants can help athletes identify these threat factors and make sure that these factors do not interfere with their efforts to commit to and pursue their sports goals.

Three Ps of a Long-term Attitude

How athletes approach their sports development is directly influenced by a long-term attitude. It begins with the realization and acceptance that the road that they have chosen is not a highway that is flat, wide, and smooth, with guard rails and clearly marked lane lines. Rather, it is a narrow dirt road filled with ruts, holes, and bumps, and with precipitous drop-offs on both sides. With this realistic attitude, when athletes get jostled around or get stuck, they accept it as a normal part of their journey rather than a destabilizing shock that slows or ends it. Consultants can help athletes to embrace this reality of sports by instilling in them what is called the three Ps (Taylor, 2017): patience, persistence, and perseverance.

Patience

Patience is characterized as the recognition that anything important in life takes time to achieve. Moreover, it is a commitment to the "long game" and the willingness on the part of athletes to give themselves the time to get where they want to go. Patience enables athletes to remain determined and positive when they struggle and to keep focused on their development during periods of plateaus or declines. Because athletes aren't expecting sudden or large jumps in improvement, patience allows them to focus on the small steps as they progress in their sport.

Persistence

The higher athletes climb the competitive ladder, the less innate talent matters. As athletes compete at increasingly higher levels, everyone has a substantial amount of natural ability, so that isn't what differentiates who continues to move closer to the top in their sport. This is where persistence begins to play a key role in which is most successful. Persistence involves athletes' willingness to keep plugging away in their development when their efforts get tiring, painful, and monotonous. Whether physical, technical, tactical, mental, equipment, or some other aspect of their sports or personal lives, persistent athletes are unwilling to give up.

Perseverance

The reality for athletes is that it's easy to become disheartened, lose faith, question their goals, and wonder whether their efforts will be rewarded when their sport isn't going their way. In response, many athletes simply give up. Perseverance involves another level of persistence that focuses on how athletes respond when they are faced with the many challenges of sports including illness, injury, technical difficulties, and competitive failures. The ability to persevere comes from a long-term attitude and an understanding of what it takes to achieve big sports goals. It also comes from athletes embracing patience and persistence.

Sports are Like the Stock Market

A helpful way for consultants to help athletes develop a long-term attitude and respond positively to the many challenges they will face is for them see their sports participation as being like the stock market. Like a demoralizing competitive defeat, the stock market can have its bad days where, for example, the Dow Jones Industrial Average plummets 500 points. If a person with little experience in investing saw only that day, they might conclude that the stock market wasn't a good place to put their money. If someone was already an active investor in the stock market, they may feel compelled to withdraw their money immediately to prevent further losses. Similarly, in sports, when athletes have a poor competitive performance (or have a string of them), they may feel that it's not worth the further investment of their time and energy in their sport. In both cases, investors and athletes, respectively, would be depending on a short-term attitude that doesn't offer them a balanced and realistic view of their investment.

A very different attitude arises when people examine the stock market over the past half century or more. When viewed in a graph, they would see an uneven line with many peaks and valleys, but the important trend they would notice is that the ragged line follows a continuous upward trajectory. With a long-term attitude, investing in the stock market and not pulling money out during financial slumps appears to be is a sound investment. A similar long-term attitude would indicate an ascending arc in sports development over time and would be seen as an equally sensible investment of athletes' time and energy. Consultants can help athletes from becoming unnerved on those bad days and encouraging them to remain patient and committed to their investment in their sport.

Consultants can assist athletes in maintaining this long-term attitude by directing their focus away from short-term results and developing a plan, similar to a financial plan, that will lead athletes to their long-term sports goals. An additional lesson related to maintaining a long-term attitude that consultants can help athletes to learn is that they shouldn't evaluate their progress based on their most latest training or competitive performances. That's akin to judging the benefits of the stock market on the day of a big decline. Rather, consultants can shift athletes' focus away from their immediate performances and onto the overall progress they have made over the past weeks and months. The long-term attitude that comes from having athletes see their sports development like the stock market will help them to stay motivated, confident, and relaxed even on bad days.

Summary

- One of the most influential lessons is that anything of value takes deep engagement, hard work, and sustained effort over a long period of time.
- To "make it," athletes must adopt a long-term attitude whereby they embrace this lengthy journey that lies before them and accept and react constructively to the inevitable challenges they will face as they strive toward their sports goals.
- Unfortunately, our current sports culture sends a very different message to athletes: "You must be successful now or you won't be later."
- Attitude can be considered as a mental domain as important to athletic performance as confidence, focus, or any other on which a set of attitudes, beliefs, and emotions are established.
- Consultants can play a central role in helping athletes to develop and maintain a healthy long-term attitude in their approach to their sports participation, particularly when many people around them may be sending unhealthy messages pushing a short-term attitude.

- Athletes can develop a long-term attitude by clarifying their values, creating an athletic mission statement, conducting an athletic self-assessment, embracing continuous development, identifying athletic threat factors, and adopting the "three Ps" of a long-term attitude (patience, persistence, perseverance, and progress.
- A helpful way for consultants to help athletes develop a long-term attitude, respond positively to the many challenges they will face, and accrue all of the benefits of sports is for them see their sports participation like the stock market in which there are many short-term ups and downs, but always a steady upward arc over the long-term.

References

Duckworth, A. (2016). *GRIT: The power of passion and perseverance*. New York, NY: Scribner.

Dweck, C. (2006). *Mindset*. New York, NY: HarperCollins.

Folds, D. (2015). Systems engineering perspective on human systems integration. In D. Boehm-Davis, F. T. Durso, & J. D. Lee (Eds.), *APA handbook of human systems integration* (pp. 21–35). Washington, DC: American Psychological Association.

Grant, A. (2008). Does intrinsic motivation fuel the prosocial fire? Motivational synergy in productivity, persistence, and productivity. *Journal of Applied Psychology, 93*, 179–201.

Maher, C. A. (2011). *The complete mental game: Taking charge of the process, on and off the field*. Bloomington, IN: Authorhouse.

Sheldon, K. M. (2014). Being oneself: The central role of self-concordant goal selection. *Personality and Social Psychology, 18*, 349–365.

Taylor J. (2017). *Train your mind for athletic success*. Lanham, MD: Rowman & Littlefield.

Wrzesniewski, A., McCauley, C., Rozin P., & Schwartz, J. (1997). Jobs, careers and ceilings: People's relations to their work. *Journal of Research in Personality, 31*, 25–43.

2
OBSTACLES

Introduction

Jim Taylor

As the authors of Part I of *Comprehensive Applied Sport Psychology* describe, there are many psychological factors that propel athletes toward their sports goals. Moreover, in their many years of working with a full spectrum of athletes, from youth to collegiate to Olympians and professionals, this mental "fuel" teamed up with physical talent, determination, and intelligence to drive athletes at every level of competition to success on the field of play. At the same time, there has also been a substantial subset of athletes who consistently underperformed and never realized the potential they exhibited early in their sports lives. These apparent failures have been a cause of consternation to consultants in applied sport psychology. A question that has often been asked is: "What prevented these athletes from performing up to their obvious capabilities?"

As this question was pondered in the study of the role that the mind plays in the psychology of athletic performance, a realization has emerged. To be sure, the mind has tremendous power to act as the "gas pedal" for athletes to perform their best. At the same time, the mind can act as the "brake" on those efforts. From this deep consideration, a robust explanation follows for why supposedly "can't miss" kids did, in fact, miss. From these explorations, five "obstacles" that can block athletes' path to their goals have been identified:

- Overinvestment
- Perfectionism
- Fear of Failure
- Expectations
- Emotions

These obstacles are counterproductive attitudes that athletes hold about themselves and how they think and feel about their sports lives. Paradoxically, these five obstacles start out by helping athletes find early success in their sports by creating a relentless focus, dogged determination to strive to be their very best, a deep aversion to failure, a compulsion to set and meet exceedingly high goals, and a need to protect themselves from unpleasant emotions, respectively.

However, at some point in their development, athletes who held these five attitudes saw them make a 180-degree turn and become obstacles that blocked their path toward their sports goals. Moreover, these obstacles create a lose–lose situation in which these athletes are not only unable to perform up to their capabilities and achieve their goals, but their sports participation becomes a truly aversive experience (e.g., stressful, no fun, negative feelings) that can drive them from their sport.

Chapter 2 will examine several key aspects of these obstacles:

- how these obstacles develop;
- who or what causes them;

- how they impact athletes psychologically, emotionally, athletically, and personally;
- what the consequences are of these harmful attitudes on athletes; and
- how parents, coaches, and others can help athletes tear down these obstacles and replace them with healthy attitudes to support their athletic efforts.

OVERINVESTMENT

Ashley Coker-Cranney and Jim Taylor

Self-identity refers to how people perceive themselves and the different roles they play in their lives. For example, different aspects of a self-identity can include athlete, student, friend, son/daughter, sister/brother, and many others. Self-identity can be thought of as a financial investment portfolio in which people deposit their earnings. Portfolios can be focused in a few investment vehicles (e.g., real estate, certain industries, stocks, or mutual funds) or highly diversified (e.g., many different types of stocks or funds). The number of investment vehicles in a portfolio is akin to the number of different elements that comprise a self-identity, and how important each of those elements are determines the degree of investment that a person has in any one aspect of themselves.

Overinvestment by athletes occurs when the athlete "investment" of their self-identity "portfolio is disproportionately large and of excessive importance to their sense of self-worth and well-being. Overinvestment is also the source from which the other four obstacles that are discussed in this chapter emerge.

Overinvestment becomes harmful when the athletic part of self-identity becomes the dominant source of validation to a person. It is most often expressed in the reactions that athletes have when their athletic identity is threatened by how they perform in their sport, in the form of mistakes, setbacks, and failure. Self-identity is also vulnerable when athletes believe that how important people in their sports lives, such as parents, coaches, teammates, fans, and media, perceive them is diminished due to disappointing competitive performance.

Though the research on overinvestment among athletes is limited, practical experience suggests that overinvestment impacts athletic performance in two ways. First, athletes' self-esteem becomes dependent on their athletic identity. With this overreliance on sports success, how athletes view and feel about themselves ("Am I valued? Am I worthy of respect?") becomes contingent on how they perform in their sport. Second, because athletes' perceptions of self-worth stem from successful attainment of the athlete role, their sport achievement is. Failure to accomplish their goals presents a significant threat to perceptions of themselves and to their future aspirations as athletes, leading sport to become a personal threat to their sense of self and well-being. Moreover, this perception can trigger the four additional obstacles discussed in this chapter, creating in athletes a "perfect storm" of obstacles blocking the path toward their sports goals. It also creates an athletic environment that is both hostile to and averse for athletes.

One measure of how invested athletes are in their sport is their emotional reactions in practice and at competitions. Athletes who are overly invested in their sport will likely perceive both practice and competition as threatening. Their thinking may be negative, doubting, and worried. They also experience high levels of anxiety and fear, accompanied by the requisite stress reactions. Their practice or competitive experience may produce a fight-or-flight-or-freeze reaction in overinvested athletes, any of which can have deleterious effects on performance. After a practice or competition, if these athletes manage to succeed, the dominant response is one of relief rather than excitement because they avoided the attack on your self-identity that comes with failure. If overinvested athletes perform below expectations, they are likely to feel devastated because the failure is perceived as an attack on their self-identity.

Theory and Research

A five-year-old defines herself as "strong" or a "big sister." A ten-year-old describes himself as "smart" or a "good friend." A college student introduces himself as "a baseball player." A middle-aged mom remembers fondly her youth as "a gymnast." All of these statements refer to perceptions of self-identity.

Despite its use in everyday language, self-identity is a complex concept. Erikson (1963) first introduced the notion of identity formation as part of his eight-stage theory of psychosocial development. According to Erikson, self-identity emerges in late adolescence and early adulthood. In this stage, people develop a cohesive sense of self grounded in the values they identify as important to them, the beliefs they have about themselves, and the goals they wish to accomplish in their lives. They then seek out roles that will support their values, beliefs, and goals. The priority they place on each role is dependent upon the sense of self they form in this process. In turn, each role may influence future values, beliefs and goals. This budding self-identity becomes the catalyst for how people think, feel, act, and react in their lives. For overinvested athletes, their athletic identity assumes a central role in their overall self-identity. In support of Erikson's (1963) model, athletic identity is highest in young adulthood until sport participation is terminated (Houle, Brewer, & Kluck, 2010).

Whereas Erikson saw self-identity as an entity that becomes fixed by early adulthood, McAdams (2001) offers a different perspective in which identity is a complex interaction of self-perceptions organized within the context an ever-evolving life story. The life story exists to assist people's understanding of their thoughts, feelings, or behaviors in various situations. This "life story" model suggests that individuals possess a self-identity that is fluid and changes over time based on their accumulating life experiences rather than one that is fixed and immutable once established. This conceptualization fits nicely in the sports context because evidence suggests that the degree to which athletes identify with the athlete role may change over time as their circumstances in their sports lives may change. For example, they may become injured, experience little progress, or be de-selected (Brewer, Selby, Linder, & Petitpas, 1999; Grove, Fish, & Eklund, 2004).

In addition, self-identity is not solely based in how people see or understand themselves. Rather, it also has a social component in which feedback from significant others and the groups they become a member of contributes to the formation of self-identity (Tajfel & Turner, 1979). For athletes, this influence can come from parents, coaches, teammates, fans, media, and others in their sports lives. The degree of importance on the athlete role, from a social-identity perspective, depends on the athlete's position within the group and the value they place on group membership (Tajfel & Turner, 1979).

Regardless of which approach to self-identity athletes embrace, self-identity and, by extension, investment, has important consequences in the lives of athletes, in terms of performance and enjoyment, as well as on and away from the field of play. One line of research that has significant relevance in this discussion is that of identity foreclosure in sports. According to Brewer and Petitpas (2017), identity foreclosure "refers to commitment to the athlete role in the absence of exploration of occupational or ideological alternatives" (p. 118). It occurs when a person is solely or primarily invested in the athlete role to the detriment of other life roles. In other words, identity foreclosure for athletes can lead to overinvestment in their sports lives and neglect of other aspects of the self-identities

The modern sports culture sends powerful messages to young athletes that reinforce the apparent value of overinvestment and increase the likelihood of identity foreclosure in sports. It offers athletes what appears to be a clear path to glory, fame, and wealth, all values venerated in our popular culture. Additionally, that sports are a way to get a better life, that hard work promises success, and that options for non-sport success are limited (Beamon, 2010; Coakley, 2009). Athletes also exist within a culture of risk which reinforces that struggles, injuries, and uncertainties are inherent in sport; that they should be expected and accepted by athletes.

Sports also present opportunities for athletes to gain self-esteem, validation, acceptance, and popularity through their efforts. Identity foreclosure, however unintentional, also enables athletes to avoid having to choose between conflicting roles (e.g., student vs. athlete; community volunteer vs. travel team member) by immersing themselves in an environment that discourages exploration of non-sport roles, activities, and rewards that conflict with the athlete role (Brewer & Petitpas, 2017).

There is a robust body of research examining identity foreclosure in sports. For example, identity foreclosure has been found to be highest among intercollegiate athletes compared to non-athletes and recreational athletes (Good, Brewer, Petitpas, Van Raalte, & Mahar, 1993). Moreover, Miller and Kerr (2003) indicate that "overidentification with the athlete role" (i.e., overinvestment) is the first and longest stage of role exploration for college athletes, persisting through the majority of their college athletic careers. Identity foreclosure, achieved prior to full exploration of other roles that might be fulfilling and have important long-term implications (e.g., broadening course selection and major options), has consequences for athletes because they may not pursue relationships, interests, or activities that are outside of their firmly established athletic identity, thus limiting potential opportunities after the conclusion of their athletic careers. Given that few athletes will establish professional careers in sports (Coakley, 2009), athletic identity foreclosure can present short-term obstacles both on and off the field, as well as unforeseen obstacles years into the future. For instance, the grandson who missed his last four family reunions in favor of voluntary summer workouts at the high school. Or the college athlete who chose not to pursue a pre-med degree, despite a strong interest in a medical career, because the course meeting times conflicted with her practice schedule.

Identity foreclosure has been linked to injury and career transition difficulties (Brewer & Petitpas, 2017). Athletes who overinvest in the athlete identity are at risk for burnout (Coakley, 1992), alcohol consumption, and using performance-enhancing drugs (Hale & Waalkes, 1994). Further, athletes who overcommit to the athlete role of their self-identity are at risk of overconforming to the sport ethic. Potentially, overconforming athletes may adopt a sport ethic that includes an overemphasis on winning, playing through pain/injury, sacrificing for the sport, and refusing to accept obstacles in the pursuit of excellence. Such over conformity may cause overinvested athletes to engage in disordered eating behaviors, overtraining, playing injured, taking performance-enhancing substances, or other unhealthy behaviors (Coker-Cranney, Watson, Bernstein, Voelker, & Coakley, 2017).

Practical Implications

Now let's return to the earlier introduction of the notion that self-identity is similar to a financial investment portfolio. Perhaps the most common advice given by financial planners is to create a diversified investment portfolio, meaning people should put their money into many different stocks and mutual funds. The reasoning behind this strategy is that, when there is a stock market decline, it is less likely that every investment will take a hit, thus minimizing the losses incurred. In contrast, if investors have a "put all your eggs in one basket" approach to investing, in which they put most or all of their money into one or two stocks, if those stocks crash, the losses could be catastrophic.

Related to self-identity, if athletes invest most or all of themselves in their sports lives and they become injured, have a bad season, are de-selected, or drop out of school to pursue their sport, the results could be equally devastating. However, if athletes have a "balanced portfolio" of life roles and their athletic role "loses value" due to one of the difficulties above, then their overall self-identity portfolio can absorb the athletic losses because they still have sources of validation from other roles they play in their lives.

Consultants who work with athletes who may be overly invested in their sports participation can help them reduce their investment to a healthy level. This shift will allow the athletes to perform better, enjoy their athletic experiences more, and develop more diversified self-identity that will better serve them in all aspects of their immediate and future lives. There are several strategies that consultants can use to facilitate this shift toward a more balance self-identity.

Assessing Self-identity in Athletes

The first step in addressing the challenges of an overly influential athletic identity and the accompanying over-investment in sport is to assess the extent to which athletes identify with the athlete role and the degree of investment they make in that role. One way to do that is with a symptom assessment in which athletes manifest certain signs associated with overinvestment. These "red flags" include:

- excessive pre-competitive anxiety;
- preoccupation with results;
- unrealistic expectations;
- extreme reactions to mistakes, setbacks, and failure;
- emotions that are out of proportion to the situation; and
- self-castigation following a disappointing performance.

Indications of any of these reactions can provide evidence of athletes' overinvestment in their sports lives. Evidence of these symptoms of overinvestment can be gathered through interviewing with athletes, observation of them in practice and competitions, and through triangulation in speaking with people who know the athlete well including parents and coaches. Additionally, there are two well-validated objective measures of athletic identity that can provide specific and objective data about the depth and breadth of athletic identity in the context of overall self-identity: the Athletic Identity Measurement Scale (Brewer & Cornelius, 2010) and the Social Identity Questionnaire for Sport (Bruner & Benson, 2018).

Consultants can then use these various assessment techniques to paint a detailed and accurate portrait of athletes from which an intervention plan can be developed. Continuing the financial investment metaphor, consultants can use interviews, observations, and self-report measures to assess the current self-identity portfolio and use that information to help athletes to create a self-identity portfolio that that is balanced, thus protecting them from significant losses and increasing the chances of a solid ROI (return on investment). This diversified self-identity portfolio provides more opportunities for success and more resources to handle setbacks in the present while also building a more holistic sense of self that ensures long-term well-being.

Strategies for Reducing Overinvestment

Once consultants have a clear understanding of the self-identity and causes of overinvestment in the athletes with whom they are working, they are in a position to help the athletes to actively redistribute their self-identity and reduce investment to a healthy level. Here are a number of strategies that have been shown to be effective.

Create a More Balanced Self-identity

There are several ways in which consultants can create a more balanced self-identity in the athletes with whom they work and, in doing so, reduce their overinvestment in their sport. One way is to increase the size of the investments in aspects of self-identity that are not related to their sports participation. For many athletes, it is not that they do not have other roles they play in their lives outside of sports, but rather that those other roles are not prominent and are overshadowed by athletic identity. In fact, some athletes may not even consider certain roles as part of their self-identity. So, the first step in expanding those roles is to have athletes recognize other areas of their self-identity that they may not pay much attention to, for example, family member or student, and gain appreciation for their role in their understanding of themselves. Athletes may begin to appreciate their role as a student more when they find subjects that interest them. They can also build skillsets that they can use when their sports careers end. As the nurture their "academic identity," athletes may learn that they enjoy school and are capable students, thus reinforcing this newly appreciated aspect of their self-identity and increasing its value with their overall self-identity portfolio. Simply through this acknowledgment, and then efforts on their part to assume those roles more often and in a more committed fashion, athletes affect their position within different groups and increase the value placed on those roles, which, in turn, increase the size of those roles in their overall self-identity and lives.

Second, athletes can actively create new self-identity "investment vehicles" by seeking out new roles in their lives. For example, they could take up a new hobby, re-enroll in school, improve a family relationship, or give back to their community. Assuming that self-identity is a zero-sum game, as more investments are added to their self-identity, their investment in their athletic identity will necessarily get smaller.

Third, a problem with athletes who suffer from identity foreclosure and overinvestment is that they create a social world that revolves around their sports lives and acts to reinforce this narrow conceptualization of themselves. They do this by having friends who are all athletes, living with athletes, and having most of their relationships related to activities that revolve around their sports lives. As such, another way to further expand athletes' self-identity and reduce overinvestment is to encourage them to meet and spend time with people who are not athletes. These diverse social opportunities might include a college athlete hanging out with dormmates who don't play sports, a high school athlete teaming up on a school project with classmates who aren't athletes, or an Olympic athlete who helps build a Habitat for Humanity house with strangers. As athletes' social identities begin to change, the story they construct to understand themselves changes, as does the level of investment in the athlete role.

By whatever means athletes establish a more balanced self-identity, they shrink the size of their investment in their sports lives and, as a result, lessen the impact that their sport has on their overall self-identity. As athletes commit themselves to and immerse themselves in these new roles, they will gain increasing competence and confidence in those roles. As these roles gain prominence in their self-identities, athletes' efforts at expanding them will be reinforced and they will be rewarded with higher self-esteem, greater comfort, and more resilience both within and outside of sport. Additionally, as they incorporate those new roles into their self-identities, athletes will find that they perform better and enjoy their sport more and that they find more success and happiness off the field of play as well.

Gain Perspective

When athletes care deeply about a sport and they invest time, effort, and energy into being the best they can be, it can turn into overinvestment. When athletes are overly invested in their sport, athletes can feel that they are putting their lives on the line every time they practice or compete. Of course, their physical lives aren't usually in jeopardy, but what can feel threatened are their self-identity "lives," which is too reliant on their athletic identity and goals. As such, their successes and failures in their sports can feel like life or death. Moreover, their "survival" as athletes depends on their continuing to improve, getting better results, and climbing the competitive ladder. So, if they perform well, they continue to "live" as athletes; if they perform poorly, they "die" as athletes. Given this approach to sports participation, it's not surprising that overinvestment leads to other significant obstacles in the path toward athletes' goals.

This unhealthy and unproductive attitude toward sports is caused by a loss of perspective, or the place that sports assume in the overall lives of athletes. So, to help athletes let go of this attitude and remove the obstacle of overinvestment, a key strategy that consultants can employ is to help the athletes with whom they work to regain perspective by putting sports in a beneficial context within their general lives.

The reality is that sports are rarely life or death to athletes, certainly not for young athletes who should be participating for the fun and the challenge. But it should also not be for college athletes, as well Olympians and professionals for whom the stakes get incrementally higher. Regardless of whether athletes win or lose, achieve their athletic goals or not, they will, in all likelihood, survive. No doubt, they will be disappointed if they aren't as successful as they want. And they may have to make adjustments in their goals and in their lives. They will certainly experience sadness, hurt, frustration, and anger from their unfulfilled goals. But, and here is where perspective comes in, athletes will survive. In time, they will get over their disappointment because they will come to realize that no matter what happens in their athletic lives, they will be okay. Their lives will continue, they will redirect their goals onto other life pursuits, they may go to or finish school, find a career, and perhaps get married and have children.

One of the most problematic aspects of identity foreclosure and overinvestment is that failure looms large and threatening to athletes. With a healthy level of investment, failure is disappointing, but also seen as a natural part of the athlete experience and offering essential lessons that have long-term benefits. In contrast, for athletes who are so invested in their athletic identity, failure is felt as direct attacks on their self-identity and their sports goals.

As such, another important way for athletes to gain a healthy perspective on their sports lives is to reframe failure. Rather than seeing failure as a measure of self-worth or as a marker of a lack of progress toward their goals, athletes can place setbacks and losses in the broader context of their overall athletic development. Failure is feedback. Feedback is necessary for change. Change is necessary for growth. Growth is necessary for greatness. Without failure, this progression cannot occur. When failure is seen by athletes through the lens of a healthy perspective and a balanced self-identity, the threat to the self is minimized. In doing so, athletes are freed from—or, at the very least, know how to handle—the negative thinking patterns, emotional reactions, and self-defeating behaviors that hurt both performance and enjoyment in their sports participation.

If consultants can help athletes to embrace this new perspective, they will also likely let go of their overinvestment. And, paradoxically, this shift will free them from the obstacles that come from overinvestment and allow them to pursue your sports goals with exuberance and without reluctance. As athletes approach competitions, they will feel more motivated, confident, relaxed, and focused. They will be excited, rather than afraid, of competing. Athletes will feel prepared psychologically, emotionally, and physically. And with this healthy investment in their sport, athletes set themselves up for success and, in doing so, have a better chance of achieving the goals they set for themselves.

Also, with a healthy perspective, athletes can look back on their sports careers with fondness and pride. They can remember the fun they had, the successes and failures they experienced, and the many life lessons they learned that prepared them to explore other aspects of their self-identity and pursue new dreams in other parts of their lives.

Summary

- Self-identity refers to how people perceive themselves and the different roles they play in their lives.
- Overinvestment by athletes occurs when, like a financial investment portfolio, their self-identity is overly invested in their sports lives and not sufficiently diversified such that their athletic identity is disproportionately large and of excessive importance to their sense of self-worth and well-being.
- One measure of how invested athletes are in their sport is their emotional reactions to training and competitions; athletes who are overly invested in their sport will likely perceive their sports efforts as threatening and experience a range of negative emotions.
- According to Erikson, self-identity emerges in late adolescence and early adulthood as people develop a cohesive sense of self grounded in the values they identify as important to them, the beliefs they have about themselves, and the goals they wish to accomplish in their lives.
- McAdams suggests that self-identity changes over time based on their accumulating life experiences rather than one that is fixed and immutable once established.
- Identity foreclosure refers to commitment to the athlete role in to the neglect of other aspects of the self.
- Overinvestment has been linked to injury, career transition difficulties, burnout, alcohol consumption, and the use of performance-enhancing drugs, disordered eating behaviors, overtraining, playing injured, taking performance-enhancing substances, and other unhealthy behaviors.
- It is recommended that athletes develop a balanced and diversified self-identity "portfolio" in which they find meaning and satisfaction from many roles in their lives.
- Consultants who work with athletes who may be overly invested in their sports participation can help them reduce their investment to a healthy level.
- Self-identity can be assessed with interviewing, observation, and objective assessments.
- Strategies to reduce identify foreclosure and overinvestment include highlighting other roles that athletes play in their lives, developing new roles, and putting into a healthier perspective how they view failure in their sport.

References

Beamon, K. K. (2010). Are sports overemphasized in the socialization process of African American males? A qualitative analysis of former collegiate athletes' perception of sport socialization. *Journal of Black Studies, 41*(2), 281–300.

Brewer, B. W. & Petitpas, A. J. (2017). Athletic identity foreclosure. *Current Opinion in Psychology, 16*, 118–122.

Brewer, B. W., Selby, C. L., Linder, D. E., & Petitpas, A. J. (1999). Distancing oneself from a poor season: Divestment of athlete identity. *Journal of Personal and Interpersonal Loss, 4*, 149–162.

Brewer, B. W., & Cornelius, A. E. (2010). Self-protective changes in athletic identity following anterior cruciate ligament reconstruction. *Psychology of Sport and Exercise, 11*(1): 1–5.

Bruner, M. W. & Benson, A. J. (2018). Evaluating the psychometric properties of the Social Identity Questionnaire for Sport (SIQS). *Psychology of Sport and Exercise, 35*, 181–188.

Coakley, J. (1992). Burnout among adolescent athletes: A personal failure or social problem. *Sociology of Sport Journal, 9*, 271–285.

Coakley, J. (2009). *Sports in society: Issues and controversies* (10th ed.). New York, NY: McGraw Hill.

Coker-Cranney, A. M., Watson, J. W., Bernstein, M., Voelker, D. & Coakley, J. (2017). How far is too far? Understanding identity and overconformity in collegiate wrestlers. *Qualitative Research in Sport, Exercise, & Health, 23*, 57–69.

Erikson, E. H. (1963). *Childhood and society* (2nd ed.). New York, NY: Norton.

Good, A. J., Brewer, B. W., Petitpas, A. J., Van Raalte, J. L., & Mahar, M. T. (1993). Identity foreclosure, athletic identity, and college sport participation. *The Academic Athletic Journal, 43*, 8–24.

Grove, J. R., Fish, M., & Eklund, R. C. (2004). Changes in athletic identity following team selection: Self-protection versus self-enhancement. *Journal of Applied Sport Psychology, 16*, 75–81.

Hale, B. D. & Waalkes, D. (1994). Athletic identity, gender, self-esteem, academic importance, and drug use: A further validation of the AIMS. *Journal of Sport & Exercise Psychology, 16*, S62.

Houle, J. L. W., Brewer, B. W., & Kluck, A. S. (2010). Developmental trends in athletic identity: A two-part retrospective study. *Journal of Sport Behavior, 33*(2), 146–159.

McAdams, D. P. (2001). The psychology of life stories. *Review of General Psychology, 5*(2), 100–122.

Miller, P. S. & Kerr, G. A. (2003). The role experimentation of intercollegiate student athletes. *The Sport Psychologist, 17*, 196–219.

Tajfel, H. & Turner, J. (1979). An integrative theory of intergroup conflict. In W. Austin (Ed.), *The social psychology of intergroup relations* (pp. 33–47). Monterey, CA: Brooks-Cole.

PERFECTIONISM

Jim Taylor

Perfectionism can be one of the most powerful obstacles that interfere with athletes' ability to perform their best, achieve their goals, and enjoy their sports participation. Unhealthy perfectionism involves people setting impossibly high standards for themselves and striving for goals that are unachievable (Flett & Hewitt, 2002). Additionally, these perfectionists believe that anything less than perfection is not only unacceptable, but a direct attack on their self-worth as people. As a result, when they fail to live up to the hopelessly high standards, they castigate themselves for failing to be perfect. Perfectionists are never satisfied with their efforts no matter how objectively well they perform, obsess over their mistakes, however minor they may be, and fail to enjoy the successes they experience. For example, a perfectionistic figure skater wins a prestigious event, but berated herself for making two mistakes in her long program and not getting the score she had wanted.

As will be discussed shortly, there can be benefits to one form of perfectionism. However, perfectionism usually presents itself as a hindrance to performance, goal attainment, and enjoyment in sports participation. At the heart of perfectionism lies a threat: If someone isn't perfect, bad things will happen to them, most commonly conceived as people see them as failures, they won't achieve their goals, and they will be unsuccessful in the future (Hill & Curran, 2016). This threat arises because perfectionistic athletes connect whether they are perfect with their self-worth; being perfect dictates whether they see themselves and others see them as successful people worthy of love and respect. The toll that perfectionism can take on these athletes is significant and can be truly destructive: depression, anxiety, eating disorders, substance abuse, and suicide.

Theory and Research

Perfectionism is largely defined in sport and performance psychology as a personality attribute characterized by an individual's alignment with extremely high standards and self-critique for performance marked by a striving for flawlessness (Flett & Hewitt, 2005; Gotwals, Stoeber, Dunn, & Stoll, 2012). Debate has centered on whether or not this trait is productive for athletes that can serve as a source of motivation to propel them toward their sports goals or if it is dysfunctional leading to self-doubt, worry, stress, and anxiety, resulting in strong negative emotional states and disappointing performances (Gotwals et al., 2012).

The more facilitative end of the spectrum for perfectionism is referred to as *perfectionistic strivings* and results in athletes' holding themselves to exceptionally high standards and determined efforts to achieve those standards. In contrast, the more debilitative end of the spectrum, referred to as *perfectionistic concerns*, is characterized by athletes setting impossibly high standards as a means of gaining approval from significant others (e.g., parents, coaches, peers) and, if those standards aren't reached, being highly self-critical (Stoeber, 2011; Weinberg & Gould, 2015). This delineation between perfectionistic strivings and concerns impacts an athletes' cognitions, emotions, behaviors, and performances in distinctly adaptive (healthy and functional) or maladaptive (unhealthy and dysfunctional), respectively, to performance and well-being (Flett & Hewitt, 2005; Gotwals et al., 2012; Hall 2006; Stoeber, 2011).

The research examining the above theoretical distinctions has not been entirely supportive of its assertions. For example, Stoeber (2011) reports a positive relationship between perfectionistic strivings and adaptive outcomes and perfectionistic concerns and maladaptive outcomes. However, other research has failed to find such a clear relationship. Much of this is due to difficulties surrounding the complexity of perfectionistic strivings in that it can manifest both adaptive and maladaptive outcomes. What is clear from the vast array of research on perfectionism, however, is that perfectionistic concerns consistently manifest maladaptive outcomes.

Perfectionism and Achievement Orientation

The health of any goal in sport is dictated by the thoughts, emotions, and behaviors that athletes express toward to that goal. Achievement motivation in sport has long been noted by two domains: process-orientation and ego-orientation (see Roberts, Treasure, & Conroy, 2012). Process orientation represents goal-directed behavior by athletes in which they evaluate themselves in terms of the development of relevant skills and competencies toward their goals. In contrast, ego orientation represents outcome-directed behavior by athletes which is evaluated in terms of comparison with others. Perfectionistic strivings is often association with a process orientation with particular emphasis on the focus of athletes on themselves and relative to their own path toward mastery. The behavior response by athletes to a process orientation and perfectionistic strivings is marked by resilience, determination, persistence, and resilience in the face of obstacles to their goals.

Conversely, perfectionistic concerns lead to athletes evaluating themselves through the same high standards, but they measure themselves based on their ability to deliver specific competitive results in relation to their opponents. Their reaction produces fear of failure, fear of disappointing others, and debilitative self-evaluation (for a full review, see Stoeber, Damien, & Madigan, 2018).

Adaptive vs. Maladaptive Coping to Perfectionism

As expressed in perfectionistic striving, the ability of athletes to cope effectively with mistakes, poor performances, failures, and setbacks depends on how well they are able to separate their sports efforts from their overall identity and sense of self-worth. This distinction between athlete and person allows them to adopt a perspective of "I failed" as opposed to "I am a failure" (Stoeber, Uphill, & Hotham, 2009; Stoeber & Otto, 2006). In contrast, perfectionistic concerns speaks to coping responses characterized by an excessive and obsessive worry about mistakes, being negatively evaluated by significant others, experiencing devastation and depression following poor performances, and the debilitating state of learned helplessness within the competition arena (Hall 2006; Dweck, 1980). Thus, any efforts or performances that fail to meet the unreachable standards that these perfectionists set for themselves is perceived as a direct attack on their value as people.

Practical Implications

Consultants can play a significant role in helping athletes to shift from perfectionistic concerns to perfectionistic strivings (Gustafsson, DeFreese, & Madigan, 2017). There are a number of strategies they can use to help athletes better understand the role that perfectionism plays in their athletic lives. Additionally, consultants can show these athletes how, if necessary, they can let go of their perfectionism and adopt healthier and more productive ways of thinking, feeling, and behaving in their sports lives.

Assessing Perfectionism

The first step involves assessing athletes' perfectionistic tendencies, particularly those who may have perfectionistic concerns. Research has identified a number of symptoms of perfectionistic concerns that can alert athletes to the type of perfectionism that they might have (Antony & Swinson, 2009):

- black-and-white thinking ("I either win or I lose!");
- catastrophic thinking ("If I lose today, my life will be over");
- must statements ("I must beat her today");
- negative emotions (e.g., depression, anxiety, frustration, angry, and despair);
- procrastination;
- tentative performances;
- preoccupation with mistakes;
- obsessing over minor details; and
- risk aversion.

Another important part of the assessment process involves athletes identifying the ways in which their perfectionism impacts their athletic efforts. Having identified the warning signs of perfectionistic concerns that were just described, athletes can connect those thinking patterns, emotions, and behaviors to their practice and competitive performances and recognize the harm they might be causing.

Strategies for Overcoming Perfectionism

In general, consultants can encourage perfectionistic athletes to focus on their own internally generated goals rather than those set by others such as parents or coaches. They can also assist athletes in identifying and focusing on what motivates them internally. These changes can reorient athletes away from perfectionistic concerns that interfere with their athletic efforts and onto perfectionistic strivings that can bolster their athletic performances.

Replace Perfectionism

Just using the word perfectionism carries a lot of psychological and emotional freight. One recommendation is to encourage athletes to remove any derivation of the word perfection from their vocabularies. As noted above, perfectionism might help in some situations, but, in general, it does more harm than good. Consultants should have athletes replace the standard of perfection with the goal of excellence. Excellence is generally viewed as still setting a high bar of performance. Additionally, excellence takes many of the best aspects of perfectionistic striving, such as intrinsic motivation, high standards, and sustained effort. At the same time, excellence leaves out the unhealthy parts of perfectionistic concerns including connecting success with self-esteem, impossibly high standards, unrealistic expectations, and risk aversion. Importantly, it never connects failure with athletes' perceptions of their ability in their sport or their self-worth as people (Taylor, 2017).

Gain Perspective

Similar to with overinvestment, perfectionistic athletes have lost perspective on what will happen if they aren't perfect. Though they may think it would be the end of the world as they know it, the reality is that they would survive and would be fine. Their family and friends would still love them, they would still be good people worthy of respect, and they could continue to strive toward their goals. Consultants can help perfectionistic athletes to gain perspective by offering this more grounded view of their sports lives (Adderholdt-Elliott & Goldberg, 1992).

Set Realistic Goals

A fear among perfectionistic athletes is that if they lower their goals at all, it is akin to embracing mediocrity or failure. Yet, paradoxically, by having them reduce their standards to levels that are actually attainable, these athletes are more motivated and confident, less fearful, and more likely to find success in their efforts. Consultants can assist athletes in establishing goals that will be challenging, yet also realistic and attainable (Basco, 2000).

Challenge Thinking

Athletes with perfectionistic concerns unwittingly normalize decidedly non-normal thinking. They come to embrace unrealistic standards, impossibly high goals, and self-criticism as just the way they think. Consultants can help these athletes to challenge their distorted and unproductive thinking ("I don't have a chance today!") and replace it will realistic and productive thinking ("I'm going to give my best effort!") (Antony & Swinson, 2009).

Act Differently

Perfectionistic athletes tend to be fairly rigid people who have deeply embedded habits, patterns, and rituals. Through repetition, they come to believe that certain behaviors are necessary to succeed. Moreover, if they don't engage in these behaviors, they will fail. Consultants can help these athletes to break free from these regimented behaviors by, first, identifying those behaviors that seem important, yet may not be so. Then, they can assist the athletes in recognizing and implementing healthier behaviors as replacements. Finally, consultants can encourage athletes to reality test the old behaviors to see if they are truly necessary or if other behaviors that are healthier will be equally or more effective (Taylor, 2017).

Summary

- Perfectionism that interferes with athletes' performances involves their setting impossibly high standards for themselves and striving for goals that unachievable.
- At the heart of unhealthy perfectionism lies a threat: If someone isn't perfect, bad things will happen to them, most commonly perceived as people see them as failures, they won't achieve their goals, and they will be unsuccessful in the future.
- The toll that perfectionism can take on these athletes is significant and can be truly destructive: depression, anxiety, eating disorders, substance abuse, and suicide.
- Research has identified two types of perfectionism, one beneficial, the other problematic: perfectionistic striving and perfectionistic concerns.
- Athletes with perfectionistic striving are conscientious, effective at coping with failure, and generally show positive emotions in their sport.
- Athletes with "perfectionistic concerns" tends to be maladaptive as it increases an athlete's likelihood to experience training distress, places intense focus on mistakes, leads to negative reactions to failure when performance expectations are not met, and injury.
- The first step in helping athletes to overcome their unhealthy perfectionistic tendencies is having them assess where on the continuum they lie and to what degree their perfectionism helps or hurts their sports efforts.
- Strategies for overcoming perfectionism including having athletes replace perfectionism with excellence as their primary goal, gain a realistic perspective on what would happen if athletes weren't perfect, set realistic goals, challenge their perfectionistic thinking, and change their perfectionistic behavior.

References

Adderholdt-Elliott, & Goldberg, J. (1992). *Perfectionism: What's bad about being too good.* Minneapolis, MN: Free Spirit.

Antony, M. M., & Swinson, R. P. (2009) *When Perfect Isn't Good Enough: Strategies for Coping with Perfectionism.* Oakland, CA: New Harbinger.

Basco, M. R. (2000). *Never good enough: How to perfectionism to your advantage without letting it ruin your life.* New York, NY: Free Press.

Dweck, C. (1980). Learned Helplessness in sport. In C. M. Nadeau, W. R. Halliwell, K. M. Newell, & G. C. Roberts (Eds.), *Psychology of motor behavior and sport—1979.* Champaign, IL: Human Kinetics.

Flett, G. L., & Hewitt, P. L. (2002). Perfectionism and maladjustment: an overview of theoretical, definitional, and treatment issues. In P. L. Hewitt & G. L. Flett (Eds.), *Perfectionism* (pp. 5–31). Washington, DC: American Psychological Association.

Flett, G. L., & Hewitt, P. L. (2005). The perils of perfectionism in sports and exercise: *Current Directions in Psychological Science, 14,* 14–18.

Gotwals, J. K., Stoeber, J., Dunn, J. G. H., & Stoll, O. (2012). Are perfectionistic strivings in sport adaptive? A systematic review of confirmatory, contradictory, and mixed evidence. *Canadian Psychology, 53*(4), 263–279.

Gustafsson, H., DeFreese, J. D., & Madigan, D. J. (2017). Athlete burnout: Review and recommendations. *Current Opinion in Psychology, 16,* 109–113.

Hall, H. K. (2006). Perfectionism: A hallmark quality of world class performers, or a psychological impediment to athletic development? In D. Hackfort & G. Tennenbaum (Eds.), *Perspectives in sport and exercise psychology, vol 1: Essential processes for attaining peak performance* (pp. 178–211). Oxford: Meyer & Meyer.

Hill, A. P., & Curran, T. (2016). Multidimensional perfectionism and burnout: a meta-analysis. *Personality and Social Psychology Review, 20,* 3, 269–288.

Roberts, G. C., Treasure, D. C., & Conroy, D. E. (2012). Understanding the dynamics of motivation in sport and physical activity: An achievement goal interpretation. In G. Tennenbaum & R.C. Ecklund (Eds.), *Handbook of sport psychology* (3rd ed.). Hoboken, NJ: John Wiley and Sons.

Stoeber, J. (2011). The dual nature of perfectionism in sports: Relationships with emotion, motivation, and performance. *International Review of Sport and Exercise Psychology, 4,* 128–145.

Stoeber, J., Damien, L. E., & Madigan, D. J. (2018). Perfectionism: A motivational perspective. In J. Stoeber (Ed.), *The psychology of perfectionism: Theory, research, and applications.* Abingdon: Routledge.

Stoeber, J., Uphill, M. A., & Hotham, S. (2009). Predicting race performance in triathlon: The role of perfectionism, achievement goals, and personal goal setting. *Journal of Sport & Exercise Psychology, 31*(2), 211–245.

Taylor, J. (2017). *Train your mind for athletic success: Mental preparation to achieve your sports goals.* Lanham, MD: Rowman & Littlefield.

Weinberg, R. S., & Gould, D. (2015). *Foundations of sport and exercise psychology* (6th ed.). Champaign, IL: Human Kinetics.

FEAR OF FAILURE

Christine Weinkauff Duranso and Jim Taylor

Most athletes are likely to report experiencing some anxiety about failing to meet their athletic goals, regardless of age, gender, ability or level of competition. That anxiety comes from the inherent risk of setting and pursuing goals because, when they enter the field of play, they are putting their self-identity, self-worth, hopes, and dreams, not to mention their time, money, and energy, on the line. In other words, they are risking failure. However, taking this risk doesn't have a deleterious effect on their sports efforts; rather, this "anticipatory arousal" acts to motivate athletes to perform their best.

For some athletes, however, the fear of failing, and the anticipated shame and negative evaluations that come from failing, impair their performance (Sagar, Lavallee & Spray, 2009) and can result in numerous psychological difficulties (Conroy, Willow, & Metzler, 2002). Whether they experience low confidence, pre-competitive anxiety, a preoccupation with results, or severe self-criticism, in most cases, when they dig deep enough, they discover a fear of failure at its root. Many athletes with a strong fear of failure experience heightened anxiety and increased risk of depression or eating disorders (Conroy et al., 2002; Conroy & Elliot, 2004; Elliot & McGregor, 2001). Other athletes increase their training intensity in an effort to avoid failure. Paradoxically, these efforts are often self-defeating because over-training increases their risk of burnout, injury, and loss of interest to continue in their sport (Conroy et al., 2002; Gustafsson, Hassmén, Kenttä & Johansson, 2008; Orlick, 1974; Sagar et al., 2009). Consultants in sport psychology are often recruited to help these athletes understand and let go of this fear so that they can train and compete unencumbered and, as a result, perform their best and fully enjoy their sports experience.

Theory and Research

Fear of failure is a motivation to avoid anticipated negative consequences when a goal is not met (Atkinson, 1957). According to Lazarus (1991), fear of failure involves two processes: anticipating that failure is possible, likely, or currently happening, and that failure in the current situation will bring about aversive consequences. Fear of failure is not limited to athletes. Many studies have uncovered this motivational tendency in other domains, such as academics (Elliot & Church, 1997; Monte & Fish, 1989) and relationships (Elliot, Gable, & Mapes, 2006). Individuals, athletes included, may experience this fear, and the negative consequences that follow across the lifespan.

Consequences of Fear of Failure

The deleterious consequences may include changes in the broad categories of unpleasant emotional states, motivational difficulties, and poorer than expected performance (Conroy et al., 2002; Conroy & Elliot, 2004; Elliot & McGregor, 2001; Gustafsson et al., 2008; Martin & Marsh, 2003; Orlick, 1974; Sagar et al., 2009). More specifically, they can be experienced as:

- embarrassment, humiliation, and shame;
- disappointment of self and others;
- loss of affection, respect, or interest from significant people;
- a loss of self-identity or self-worth; and
- expected loss of future opportunities within and outside of their sport (Conroy, Poczwardowski, & Henschen, 2001).

Many athletes with a strong fear of failure report high levels of anxiety (Conroy, 2001; Sagar, Lavallee & Spray, 2007; Sagar et al., 2009), depression (Conroy, 2001; Sagar et al., 2007), pessimism (Martin & Marsh, 2003), rumination over mistakes (Conroy & Elliot, 2004), worry (Conroy et al., 2002; Sagar et al., 2009), and low perceptions of control (Martin & Marsh, 2003). Additionally, many athletes with a fear of failure also report feeling less engaged (Gustafsson, Kenttä, & Hassmén, 2011), less intrinsic motivation (Sagar et al., 2009), and greater likelihood to drop out (Orlick, 1974).

Fear of Failure and Goals

Fear of failure often results in the adoption of avoidance goals instead of approach goals (Elliot & Church, 1997; McClelland, Atkinson, Clark, & Lowell, 1953). Approach goals are designed to view the challenges of sport as an opportunity for growth and improvement, while avoidance goals enable athletes to elude or reduce the risk of failure (Elliot & Church, 1997). Mitigating the risk of failure may occur through the adoption of *mastery-avoidance goals*, in which athletes persist toward skill improvement because they are worried about failing, or *performance-avoidance goals*, in which they try to avoid failure by outperforming competitors (which may be done by choosing less challenging competitions). Athletes who practice mastery-avoidance or performance-avoidance goals report high anxiety, low enjoyment and low intrinsic motivation, all of which impede performance (Conroy & Elliot, 2004; Elliot & McGregor, 2001). Finally, athletes who practice mastery-avoidance goals are at risk of burn out or injury from over training (Gustafsson, Sagar, & Stenling, 2017).

Causes of Fear of Failure

The antecedents to fear of failure are broadly categorized into three areas: parenting, personality, and experiences. Parents play a significant role in the socialization of fear of failure, and this socialization seems to be especially strong between 5 and 9 years of age (McClelland et al., 1953). Parental practices that contribute to the development of fear of failure include behavior that is controlling or punitive and high expectations for sport achievement (Sagar & Lavallee, 2010). Punitive strategies include criticizing their children's performance during and after practice or competitions, threatening withdrawal from future opportunities or competitions, or punishing their children by withdrawing love, affection, or attention after disappointing performances (Sagar & Lavallee, 2010). Parents also contribute to children's fear of failure by practicing over-controlling behaviors such as attending all practices or giving unsolicited instructions. Finally, parents increase the likelihood that young athletes will fear failure when they convey inappropriately high expectations or focus excessively on results over process and enjoyment. These unrealistic expectations and pressures, coupled with feelings of conditional love or acceptance, drastically increase the risk that young athletes will develop a fear of failure (Sagar & Lavallee, 2010).

In addition to parental influences, an athlete's inborn personality and temperament also influence their sensitivity to fear of failure. An *avoidance temperament* is characterized by high levels of negativity, anxiety and sensitivity to cues of punishment or aversive consequences, while an *approach temperament* is characterized by more positive than negative affect and a willingness to approach challenge (Carver & White, 1994; Elliot & Thrash, 2002; Gray, 1987a, 1987b). Fear of failure has been linked to avoidance temperament (Conroy & Elliot, 2004; Elliot & Thrash, 2002).

Research on personality suggests there are traits linked to this sensitivity, namely, perfectionism and neuroticism (Flett & Hewitt, 2002; Piedmont, 1995; Ross, Steward, Mugge & Fultz, 2001; Ryckman, Thornton & Gold, 2009). As discussed in the previous section, perfectionism is a multidimensional personality disposition typified by incredibly high performance standards, striving for flawlessness, and a tendency for overly critical evaluations of behavior or performance (Hewitt & Flett, 1991). Some elements of perfectionism are considered to be helpful in achieving one's potential (Flett & Hewitt, 2002). Others, such as the incredibly high standards and excessive self-criticism when the standards aren't met, are linked to fear of failure (Flett & Hewitt, 2002; Frost & Henderson, 1991). Some aspects of perfectionism are also found in fear of failure including being critical of performance, resulting in shame, embarrassment, or loss of interest or affection (Flett & Hewitt, 2002; Frost & Henderson, 1991; Hewitt & Flett, 1991).

Neuroticism, a dimension of personality characterized by persistent worry and anxiety, has also been associated with fear of failure. Several studies have found that individuals high on neuroticism also report a high fear of failure (Piedmont, 1995; Ross, Steward, Mugge & Fultz, 2001; Ryckman, Thornton & Gold, 2009). Neurotic tendencies in athletes are often self-fulfilling: these tendencies impair performance and increase the likelihood of failure (Barlow, Woodman, Gorgulu, & Voyzey, 2016).

Life experiences contribute to fear of failure by either further reinforcing or mitigating the fear of failure. Continued pressure from demanding parents (McClelland et al., 1953; Sagar & Lavallee, 2010) and coaches (Conroy, 2003; Conroy & Coatsworth, 2007) may encourage the maintenance of this disposition. Athletes' fear of failure may be heightened when they perceive the critical, demanding, or punitive interactions with their parents or coaches as a long-term and persistent dynamic (Sagar et al., 2007).

Ways Athletes Avoid Failure

Fear of failure can become so aversive and pervasive that athletes take active, though often unconscious, steps to relieve themselves of its psychological and emotional burden. There are three ways in which athletes avoid failure.

First, they can simply quit their sport; if they don't play, they can't fail. It's no surprise that, between the ages of nine and thirteen, 70 percent of children drop out of organized sports (Miner, 2016). The unrelenting pressure to succeed that they feel is certainly a contributing factor in this decision. Mysterious and persistent injury or illness, damaged equipment, apparent lack of interest or motivation, or just plain refusal to take part are common ways in which athletes can avoid failure and maintain your personal and social esteem. Yet, for these athletes, choosing not to participate is a painful decision because, despite their profound fear of failure that may drive them to quit, at a deep level, they may still love their sport and their decision to quit can make them feel even worse for not having the strength to continue (Taylor, 2017).

Second, athletes can avoid the perceived consequences of failure by failing, but protecting themselves from the failure by having an excuse—"I would have done well, but my ankle is killing me" or "I would have done just fine, but my opponent cheated." This is called self-defeating or self-handicapping behavior or self-sabotage (Martin & Marsh, 2003). Specifically, athletes may consciously or unconsciously construct a reason for the failure (outside of themselves) to relieve the pressure of failing (Chen, Wu, Kee, Lin, & Shui, 2009; Urdan & Midgley, 2001). Self-handicapping behaviors, for athletes, may include "forgetting" important gear, staying out late the night before a competition, or feigning injury or illness. In each case, athletes guarantee failure, but the excuse protects them because their failures are not seen as their fault; they can't be held responsible and their parents, coaches, and peers must continue to value and respect them (Chen, Wu, Kee, Lin, & Shui, 2009).

Third, another way that athletes can avoid failure is to get as far away from failure as possible by becoming successful. But, athletes who fear failure often get stuck in limbo between failure and real success, what Taylor (2017) refers to as the "safety zone." These athletes are far from failure, so no one can accuse them of being failures, for example, if they finish in the top 10 in their sport. At the same time, they are frustrated because a part of them knows that they can be truly successful. But, to find real success, they must be willing to take risks. And the problem with risks is that, by their very nature, they may not pay off and they may result in failure. If athletes are more concerned with avoiding failure than pursuing success, as those with a fear of failure are, they will focus on the downsides of risk and, as a result, will be unwilling to take those risks that are necessary to experience real success.

Practical Implications

All athletes fear failure to some degree. As the degrees of intensity increase, however, athletes may risk the emotional, motivational, and performance issues outlined above. There are significant and negative outcomes related to the fear of failure for these athletes both within their sport and in their overall personal development. Fortunately, consultants can help athletes to reduce their fear by, first, gaining an understanding of fear of failure and how it impacts them. Then, consultants can teach specific mental strategies that focus on reframing the risks and consequences of failure, adopting a growth mindset, and developing approach motivational tendencies.

Assessing and Understanding Fear of Failure

Fear of failure isn't difficult to diagnose because it manifests itself in a number of observable ways, some of which have been described earlier in this section:

- negative or critical self-talk;
- low or inconsistent motivation;
- pre-competitive anxiety;
- excessively negative emotions following poor performances;
- a preoccupation with results;
- unexplained injuries or illness;
- frequent excuses after disappointing performances; and
- cautious or tentative performances.

Consultants can identify these warning signs by interviewing athletes, observing them in practice or competitions, or from feedback from parents and coaches. Additionally, there is an objective measure that assess for fear of failure, The Performance Failure Appraisal Inventory, that can be a useful tool for consultants to use (Conroy, Willow, & Metzler, 2002).

The next step in the assessment process involves helping the athletes who suffer from a fear of failure to understand its causes. Once consultants understand where the athletes' fear of failure comes from, they are in a better position to develop an effective intervention plan to assist them in reducing or relieving their fear of failure.

Strategies for Alleviating Fear of Failure

At the heart of helping athletes to let go of their fear of failure is to change the way they think about failure and its perceived consequences. There are a variety of strategies that consultants can employ to reduce or alleviate athletes' fear of failure.

See Failure Realistically

The first step for consultants is to assist athletes in challenging their thoughts about failure and to disprove them. There are three particular perceptions that counter those held about athletes with a fear of failure that can enable them to adopt this "nothing to fear" perspective. First, none of the threatening consequences that athletes may attach to failure will likely come true. Admittedly, there are some parents who get angry and upset when their children perform poorly. However, all parents love their children no matter how they perform. Additionally, contrary to common perceptions that athletes with a fear of failure hold, their friends will still like them, they will not be rejected by their peers, and they will still be worthy of respect., Their time will still be well spent, and they will get over the fact that they may not achieve all of their sports goals. In other words, if they fail, athletes will be disappointed, but they will be okay in the long run.

Second, athletes' fear of failure is utterly self-defeating; it serves no worthwhile purpose in their sports lives. By falling victim to a fear of failure, athletes actually increase the chances that failure will result. It creates a "win"-lose scenario. Athletes "win" (in quotes because it is a hollow victory) by protecting themselves from those perceived painful consequences that they believe they will experience if they fail and are held responsible for it. At the same time, athletes lose in several powerful ways. They perform poorly, don't achieve their goals, don't enjoy their sports participation, feel regret for not giving their best effort, are continually frustrated because they know they can do better, and fear that failure will haunt them throughout their lives.

Third, when athletes let go of their fear of failure and perform in their sport with determination, confidence, and courage, the chances are that they will find some degree of success. How much success depends on many factors, some within athletes' control and others not. Athletes may not win an Olympic medal or compete professionally, but allowing themselves to be free of the fear of failure will result in some degree of success and, just as importantly, at the end of their athletic careers, the belief that they gave it everything they had.

Moreover, if athletes are willing to risk failure, contrary to being devastated by the negative consequences they believe they will experience, they would actually feel wonderful emotions, such as excitement, joy, pride, and inspiration, because they gave their fullest effort and "left it all out there". And, ultimately, that is all any athlete can do.

Get Support from Others

Fear of failure is a difficult obstacle for athletes to overcome on their own, so consultants can be a significant source of support in challenging that fear. Additionally, athletes can enlist family, friends, coaches, and teammates to help them break free from its grip. Athletes' support system can encourage them when they get down, challenge their thinking when they allow their fear of failure to take control, provide levity when the fear becomes intense, and give them hope when they feel hopeless to change. With many people behind the athletes, they will feel more confident, stronger, and better prepared to face their fears and pursue their sports goals without fear or hesitation.

Be Cautiously Optimistic

When athletes have a fear of failure, consultants cannot expect to readily turn them into eternal optimists ("Everything will turn out great!"). But, by encouraging them to be cautiously optimistic ("Good things could happen."), they are taking an important step toward letting go of their fear. Being cautiously optimistic involves athletes seeing a small ray of hope when they would otherwise see only the specter of those negative consequences of fear. It means being realistic by recognizing that failure is a possibility, while, at the same time, acknowledging that success is also a possibility. Cautious optimism means athletes give themselves a chance of being successful, which makes possible more hope, confidence, and motivation in their sports efforts.

Accept the Possibility of Failure

If athletes can accept the possibility of failure and realize that, even if it should occur, they will be okay, they remove any threat it might hold over them. When they feel that there is no more threat from the consequences of failure, then they will no longer live in fear of it. Releasing the fear of failure feels as if a great weight has been lifted athletes' shoulders and they will feel liberated to perform their best without reservation or hesitation. This will allow athletes throw themselves into their sport and pursue success with absolute abandon.

No Regrets

This shift will allow athletes to live by two cardinal rules. Rule #1 is that, at the end of a competition, season, or life, athletes won't have to ask: "I wonder what could have been?" That may be the saddest question athletes can pose to themselves because there are no "redos" in life. They want to look back and, win or lose, be able to say, "I left it all out there." And, as alluded to earlier in this chapter, only by leaving it all out there do athletes have any chance of fulfilling your goals.

Rule #2 involves athletes not having to experience one of the most painful and long-lasting emotions that can occur after a competition, season, or career: regret. Regret is defined as: "to feel sorry or disappointed about something that one wishes could be different; a sense of loss or longing for something gone," in other words, "Darn it, I wish I had left it all out there!" In the end, athletes want to be able to say: "I gave it everything I had," and experience two emotions: pride and fulfillment in having given it their all. If athletes can follow these two rules, they will likely find some success in their sport and experience a healthy, successful, and happy life.

Take Risks

As discussed earlier, fear of failure is really a fear of the consequences of failure. Yet risking failure is an essential part of finding success in sports. Athletes give themselves no chance of success unless they are willing to risk the possibility of failure. Yet, athletes who fear failure are more aware of the costs over the benefits of risks. With this attitude, they are less likely to take risks that will lead to success.

Consultants can encourage athletes with a fear of failure to take risks for three reasons. First, if they fail due to the risk, they see that they will survive and be okay. Second, athletes learn that when they take risks, they will experience success, at least some of the time. Third, they become more comfortable with taking risks, thus reducing their fear that the risks will lead to failure. Athletes should be emboldened to start small with their risk-taking, for example, in practice where the consequences of failure are minimal, and slowly intensify their risk-taking in increasingly more consequential situations.

Take Their Shot

When athletes with a fear of failure give their best effort and "take their shot," they are certainly risking failure. But, a key lesson to help them overcome their fear is that it is better to take their shot and fail than to never take their shot at all. The basketball great, Michael Jordan, once said, "I've missed more than 9000 shots in my career. I've lost almost 300 games. 26 times, I've been trusted to take the game-winning shot and missed. I've failed over and over and over again in my life. And that is why I succeed" (Greatist, 2012, p. 57). All of those misses didn't prevent him from continuing to take his shot and hitting far more buzzer beaters than he missed. And there is one simple fact here: If athletes don't take their shot, they ensure failure.

Establish Helpful Goals

Consultants can encourage risk-taking and help athletes develop a tendency for approach motivation through the adoption of mastery-approach goals (Yeager & Dweck, 2012; Wikman, Stelter, Melzer, Hauge, & Elbe, 2013). Adopting specific mastery-approach goals, such as learning a new soccer skill or improving a new swim stroke, provide athletes with specific, tangible opportunities to witness the power of risk and effort for improvement, generate positive emotions related to goal striving, distract them from the fear of failure that may impede their progress toward their goals, and encourage them to set and strive toward future mastery goals.

The great thing about all of these steps to overcome fear of failure is that they build on each other. The more athletes challenge their fear of failure with the above strategies, the more they see that their fear is unfounded, unhelpful, and unnecessary. And, as they let go of their fear of failure and gain a healthier perspective, they take away two valuable lessons. First, failure is fleeting and athletes will long outlive it. Second, when they free themselves of their fear of failure, they will perform better and find the success that they deserve.

Summary

- Fear of failure involves two processes: anticipating that failure is possible, likely, or currently happening, and that failure in the current situation will bring about aversive consequences.
- Some of the most common perceived consequences that athletes hold about fear of failure include embarrassment, humiliation, and shame; disappointing themselves and others; loss of affection, respect or interest from significant people, loss of self-identity or self-worth; and loss of future opportunities.
- Athletes who struggle with fear of failure may experience emotional, motivational, and performance difficulties.
- Some of the difficulties include depression, stress, anxiety, burnout, impaired performance, dropout, eating disorders, use of performance-enhancing drugs, and suicide.
- Athletes with fear of failure typically adopt avoidance rather than approach goals.
- The antecedents to fear of failure are broadly categorized into three areas: parenting, personality, and experiences.
- Parental practices that contribute to the development of fear of failure include punitive or controlling behavior and high expectations for sport achievement.
- An avoidant temperament and personality traits of perfectionism and neuroticism have been linked to fear of failure.
- Life experiences, such as continued pressure from demanding parents or coaches, can further contribute to fear of failure.
- Athletes can mitigate their fear of failure by quitting, engaging in self-defeating behavior, or achieving a minimal level of success that protects them from being perceived as a failure.
- Consultants can assist athletes to understand their fear of failure by identifying its warning signs including negative or critical self-talk, low or inconsistent motivation, pre-competitive anxiety, excessively negative emotions, a preoccupation with results, unexplained injuries or illness, frequent excuses, and tentative performances.
- Strategies that consultants can use to help athletes remove or reduce their fear of failure included seeing failure realistically, being cautiously optimistic, accepting the possibility of failure, learning to take risks, being willing to take their shot, and establishing approach goals.

References

Atkinson, J. W. (1957). Motivational determinant of risk-raking behavior. *Psychological Review, 64*, 359–372.

Barlow, M., Woodman, T., Gorgulu, R., & Voyzey, R. (2016). Ironic effects of performance are worse for neurotics. *Psychology of Sport and Exercise, 24*, 27–37. doi: 10.1016/j.psychsport.2015.12.005

Carver, C. S., & White, T. L. (1994). Behavioral inhibition, behavioral activation, and affective responses to impending reward and punishment: The BIS/BAS Scales. *Journal Of Personality And Social Psychology*, *67*(2), 319–333.

Chen, L. H., Wu, C., Kee, Y. H., Lin, M., & Shui, S. (2009). Fear of failure, 2 × 2 achievement goal and self-handicapping: An examination of the hierarchical model of achievement motivation in physical education. *Contemporary Educational Psychology*, *34*(4), 298–305.

Conroy, D. E. (2001). Fear of Failure: An exemplar for social development research in sport. *Quest*, *53*, 165–183.

Conroy, D. E. (2003). Representational models associated with fear of failure in adolescents and young adults. *Journal of Personality*, *71*, 757–783.

Conroy, D. E., & Coatsworth, J. D. (2007). Coaching behaviors associated with changes in fear of failure: Changes in self-talk and need satisfaction as potential mechanisms. *Journal of Personality*, *75*(2), 383–419.

Conroy, D. E., & Elliot, A. J. (2004). Fear of failure and achievement goals in sport: Addressing the issue of the chicken and the egg. *Anxiety Stress Coping*, *17*, 271–286.

Conroy, D. E., Willow, J. P., & Metzler, J. N. (2002). Multidimensional fear of failure measurement: The performance failure appraisal inventory. *Journal of Applied Psychology*, *14*, 76–90.

Elliot, A. J., & Church, M. A. (1997). A hierarchical model of approach and avoidance achievement motivation. *Journal of Personality and Social Psychology*, *72*, 218–232.

Elliot, A. J., Gable, S. L., & Mapes, R. R. (2006). Approach and avoidance motivation in the social domain. *Personality and Social Psychology Bulletin*, *32*(3), 378–391.

Elliot, A. J., & McGregor, H. A. (2001). A 2 × 2 achievement goal framework. *Journal of Personality and Social Psychology*, *80*(3), 501–519.

Elliot, A. J., & Thrash, T. M. (2004). The intergenerational transmission of fear of failure. *Personality and Social Psychology Bulletin*, *30*, 957–971.

Flett, G. L., & Hewitt, P. L. (2002). The perils of perfectionism in sports and exercise. *Current Directions in Psychological Science*, *14*(1), 14–18.

Frost, R. O., & Henderson, K. J. (1991). Perfectionism and reactions to athletic competition. *Journal of Sport and Exercise Psychology*, *13*, 323–335.

Gray, J. A. (1987a). Perspectives on anxiety and impulsivity: A commentary. *Journal of Research in Personality*, *21*, 493–509.

Gray, J. A. (1987b). *The psychology of fear and stress*. Cambridge: Cambridge University Press.

Greatist (2012). Quote: Michael Jordan on success through failure. Retrieved from https://greatist.com/fitness/quote-michael-jordan-success-through-failure

Gustafsson, H., & Hassmén, P., Kenttä, G., & Johansson, M. (2008). A qualitative analysis of burnout in elite Swedish athletes. *Psychology of Sport and Exercise*, *9*, 800–816.

Gustafsson, H., Kenttä, G., & Hassmén, P. (2011). Athlete burnout: An integrated model and future research directions. *International Review Sport Exercise Psychology*, *4*, 3–24.

Gustafsson, H., Sagar, S. S., & Stenling, A. (2017). Fear of failure, psychological stress, and burnout among adolescent athletes competing in high level sport. *Scandinavian Journal of Medicine & Science in Sports*, *27*, 2091–2102.

Hewitt, P. L., & Flett, G. L. (1991). Perfectionism in the self and social context: Conceptualization, assessment, and association with psychopathology. *Journal of Personality and Social Psychology*, *60*, 456–470.

Kamins, M.L., & Dweck, C. S. (1999). Person versus process praise and criticism: Implications for contingent self-worth and coping. *Developmental Psychology*, *35*, 835–847.

Lazarus, R. S. (1991). *Emotion and adaptation*. New York, NY: Oxford University Press.

Martin, A. J., & Marsh, H. W. (2003). Fear of failure: Friend or foe? *Australian Psychologist*, *38*, 31–38.

McClelland, D. C., Atkinson, J., Clark, R. A., & Lowell, E. L. (1953). *The achievement motive*. New York, NY: Appleton-Century-Crofts.

Miner, J. W. (2016) Why 70 percent of kids quit sports by age 13. *The Washington Post*. Retrieved from www.washingtonpost.com/news/parenting/wp/2016/06/01/why-70-percent-of-kids-quit-sports-by-age-13

Monte, C. F., & Fish, J. M. (1989). The fear of failure personality and academic cheating. In R. Schwarzer, H. M. Van der Ploeg, & C. D. Spielberger (Eds.), *Advances in test anxiety research*, vol. 6 (pp. 87–103). Amsterdam: Swets & Zeitlinger.

Orlick, T. D. (1974). The athletic dropout: A high price of inefficiency. *Canadian Association Health Physical Education Recreation Journal*, *41*, 21–27.

Piedmont, R. L. (1995). Another look at fear of success, fear of failure, and text anxiety: A motivational analysis using the five-factor model. *Sex Roles*, *32*, 139–158.

Ross, S. R., Steward, J., Mugge, M., & Fultz, B. (2001). The imposter phenomenon, achievement dispositions, and the five factor model. *Personality and Individual Differences*, *31*, 1347–1355.

Ryckman, R. M., Thornton, B., & Gold, J. A. (2009). Assessing competition avoidance as a basic personality dimension. *The Journal of Psychology*, *143*(2), 175–192.

Sagar, S. S., & Lavallee, D. (2010). The developmental origins of fear of failure in adolescent athletes: Examining parental practices. *Psychology of Sport and Exercise*, *11*, 177–187.

Sagar, S. S., Lavallee, D., & Spray, C. M. (2007). Why young elite athletes fear failure: Consequences of failure. *Journal of Sports Science, 25*, 1171–1184.

Sagar, S. S., Lavallee, D., & Spray, C. M. (2009). Coping with the effects of fear of failure: A preliminary investigation of young elite athletes. *Journal of Clinical Sport Psychology, 3*, 73–98.

Taylor, J. (2017). Train your mind for athletic success: Mental preparation to achieve your sports goals. Lanham, MD: Rowman & Littlefield.

Urdan, T., & Midgley, C. (2001). Academic self-handicapping: What we know, what more there is to learn? *Educational Psychology Review, 13*(2), 115–138.

Wikman, J. M., Stelter, R., Melzer, M., Hauge, M.-L. T., & Elbe, A.-M. (2013). Effects of goal setting on fear of failure in young elite athletes. *International Journal of Sport and Exercise Psychology, 12*(3), 185–205.

Yeager, D. S., & Dweck, C. S. (2012). Mindsets that promote resilience: When students believe that personal characteristics can be developed. *Educational Psychologist, 47*(4), 302–312.

EXPECTATIONS

Cory Shaffer and Jim Taylor

The *Oxford English Dictionary* defines expectations as "a strong belief that something will happen in the future . . . a belief that someone will or should achieve something" (Oxford Dictionaries, 2018). At first blush, an expectation seems like it's something that athletes should embrace. It appears to describe a positive scenario while expressing confidence of its realization. At the same time, considered from the perspective of athletes who must fulfill an expectation, it can feel more like an encumbrance that weighs them down rather than support that lifts them up. As such, expectations can actually thwart athletes' efforts to perform their best and achieve them.

A synonym for expectations is assumptions which carry with them an air of certainty that athletes will get a specific result. But, as all athletes know, sport is fraught with uncertainty in which other people (e.g., teammates, competitors, coaches, officials), environmental factors (e.g., field, course, or court conditions, weather), equipment failure (e.g., broken bat in baseball, snapped string in tennis), and the vagaries of luck (e.g., a bad bounce, a brief distraction), can cause what seemed certain to not be realized at all. That feeling of inexorableness can create a sense that the expectation has already been fulfilled even before athletes walk onto the field of play.

Additionally, expectations carry with them an implicit threat in which there is a hidden "or else" that precedes every expectation. For example, "I expect to beat her . . . or else my parents will be really mad at me." An expectation causes athletes to feel pressure to realize the expectation or else there will be some undesirable consequence. As a result, expectations can cause them to experience a fear of failure, debilitating anxiety, and a loss of confidence and motivation.

Lastly, expectations are dichotomous propositions with no shades of gray in between. Athletes either meet the expectation and find success or they do not and they must accept failure. This places them in an almost no-win situation in which there is a narrow window of success and a large window for failure.

Theory and Research

Lazarus (2000) posits that how a athletes *think* about performance can impact how they *feel*, and then subsequently how they *perform*. The danger of setting expectations is that they are held rigidly by athletes. Moreover, any deviation from the expectation, whether setbacks or outright failure to meet them, can cause athletes to appraise themselves negatively in relation to the thwarted expectation. In turn, that adverse appraisal leads to discouraging thinking and unproductive emotions such as frustration, anger or despair.

Considerable research has explored expectations in athlete populations and evidence supports Lazarus' theory. For example, Mellalieu, Neil, Hanton, and Fletcher (2009) found that expectations are a performance stressor for both elite and non-elite performers that hurt their appraisal, thinking, and emotions, suggesting that even seasoned athletes are vulnerable to expectations. Additionally, Uphill and Jacobs (2007) interviewed international-level athletes of various sports and found that athletes' expectations and self-pressure to perform well were associated with anxiety. Some athletes in the study even expressed shame for not reaching certain performance outcomes. Durand-Bush and Salmela (2002) provided similar insight in their study on Olympic athletes: "For most athletes, expectations from coaches, sport federations, family, and friends were high. This created pressure and stress that ultimately affected their performance. It was apparent that some athletes were scared of failing and letting others down" (p. 161). Hodge and Hermansson (2007) also acknowledged that stress stemming from a variety of variables, including public expectations, is a unique mental challenge facing Olympic athletes that can hinder performance.

Another line of research has focused on how expectations can lead to choking in competition. Williams et al. (2010) presented a model in which situations that lead to choking (i.e., anxiety or pressure stemming from expectations) influence physiological (e.g., increased muscle tension, heart rate, respiration) and attentional (e.g., narrowing of attention, internal focus) changes that can lead to performance problems (e.g., rushing, inability to attend to task-relevant cues). Gucciardi, Longbottom, Jackson, and Dimmock (2010) explored experienced golfers' choking experiences in focus groups and one-on-one interviews. They produced a model in which perfectionistic tendencies and perceived internal and external expectations and pressure were considered antecedents to a choking event. These antecedents led to a loss of attentional (e.g., shift to outcome from process) and emotional (e.g., sadness and anger) control, a departure from normal routine (e.g., stray typical shot processes and strategy) and physiological symptoms (e.g., muscle tension, racing heart). Even the New Zealand All Blacks national rugby team, one of the most successful sports franchises in history, attributed their 2007 World Cup loss to the pressure they felt from the expectation that they *had* to win (Hodge & Smith, 2014).

A final study of particular interest is that of Gould et al. (1999), in which the authors examined the comparison of teams that met or failed to meet performance expectations following the 1996 Olympics in Atlanta. Results indicated that one particular team did not meet performance expectations and reported feeling external expectations and pressure to perform.

Practical Implications

As the evidence mounts against athletes setting outcome expectations due to the mental and emotional toll that they take on them, consultants must look to how they can intervene to help athletes change this paradigm. Parents and coaches are also often the sources from which unhealthy expectations arise in athletes. As such, consultants are in a unique position to help athletes unburden themselves from expectations that interfere with both their sports performances and enjoyment in their participation, while also helping those around them who have an influence to make a shift in the messages they send athletes about expectations.

Six Phrases That Create Expectations (and Pressure)

Many athletes have so deeply internalized expectations that they don't even realize when they or others place expectations on them. There are six phrases that athletes unwittingly use or hear from others (with "I" replaced with "you") that are symptomatic of expectations and the pressure they place on them:

- "I must . . ."
- "I should . . ."
- "I need to . . ."
- "I have to . . ."
- "I better . . ."
- "I gotta . . ."

These phrases carry so much freight because, as just mentioned, they carry that inherent menace: for example, "I must do well today. . .or I will be so embarrassed." Every athlete who feels the weight of expectations has their own negative meaning that they connect to these phrases, usually associated with the meaning they attach to failure (as discussed in the previous session section on fear of failure).

Expectations take a significant emotional toll on athletes. Like the other obstacles discussed in Chapter 2, expectations produce emotional reactions that both feel bad and usually cause disappointing poor performances. Before a competition, expectations create in athletes pressure to fulfill the expectations and fear that they won't. This pressure creates physical (e.g., tension, choppy breathing, accelerated heart rate and respiration), psychological (e.g., doubt, worry), and emotional (e.g., fear, anxiety, frustration) changes that inhibit performance. During a competition, expectations can produce a cautious mindset fueled by fear, a lack of confidence, and an inability to focus, resulting in performances characterized by tension, tentativeness, and self-consciousness.

Athletes' emotional reactions to expectations after a competition can equally problematic. If they somehow produce a good result despite the burden of expectations, their strongest emotional reaction is often relief because they "dodged the bullet" of unmet expectations. In contrast, when they perform poorly and don't fulfill the expectation, they can experience devastation because failing to fulfill the expectation carries with it all sorts of perceived negative consequences.

From "Must" to "Would Like"

Consultants can be on the lookout for athletes' self-talk that includes the six phrases that were just described to see if expectations are the cause of their performance challenges. If they become aware that athletes are using any of the six phrases, they can encourage the athletes to replace them with the following more beneficial alternatives:

- "I would like to . . ."
- "I hope to . . ."
- "It is my goal to . . ."
- "I am working hard to . . ."
- "I am directing all of my energy to . . ."
- "I am excited to . . ."

Similarly, consultants can also be mindful of the messages that athletes are receiving from parents, family, coaches, friends, and the media. If unhealthy messages about expectations are evident, consultants can educate these people about how these types of expectations actually hurt and offer alternatives that will better support the athletes' efforts.

From Expectations to Goals

In discussing expectations, a role of consultants is to convince athletes that expectations, and the associated overemphasis on results, will do them no good as they pursue their sports goals. At the same time, the reality of sports is that results do matter and a focus on results can't simply be expunged from athletes' psyches. The challenge for consultants is to allow athletes to think about results, but enable them to replace expectations with another focus that will alleviate pressure and facilitate competitive performance. To that end, consultants can have athletes shift their attention from expectations to goals. Goals might seem little different than expectations, but, upon close examination, have a very different impact on the way athletes, think, feel, perform, and react to both victories and defeats.

There are several important distinctions that separate goals from expectations. Unlike the latter, goals have no air of *assumption or certainty* that they will be realized. At the heart of goals is the *possibility* that they could be realized. Along with that, the threat that exists with expectations isn't present with goals because, if not achieved, there is no feeling that the result has been taken away from athletes.

Unlike expectations which have a black-or-white, "you achieve it and succeed or you don't and you fail" air to them, another key aspect of goals is that they are about degree of attainment. That is, not every goal can be achieved, but there will almost always be improvement toward a goal and that progress defines success. So, if athletes give their best effort, there is little chance of failure and great opportunity for success.

The emotional experience of goals is also very different from those of expectations. Before a competition in which athletes set goals, they are motivated and excited to compete because they see the goals as challenges to pursue rather than threats to avoid. After an event, if they succeeded in achieving their goal, they feel elated. However, if they fail to meet their goal, unlike an expectation, they certainly feel disappointed, but they also feel pride in knowing that they gave it their all and they remain hopeful that they can achieve the goal at the next opportunity.

From Outcome to Process

According to Lazarus (2000), if athletes can change the meaning of the appraisal, the emotion changes as well. Once athletes understand that they cannot directly control the outcome of a competition due to the complex nature of sports, consultants can pivot the conversation to what is within their control during a performance. For example, they can control their attitude, focus, effort, preparation, self-talk, and routines. This process-oriented approach to performance lifts the weight of outcome expectations from athletes' shoulders. It removes the burden of worrying about the outcome and allows them to fully engage in the present moment of the performance. For the golfer with an expectation of "I should sink this putt," they can shift to a goal of "I can sink this putt." They can then focus on the how of achieving that goal: stick to their pre-shot routine process, approach the ball relaxed and confident, stay in control, trust their swing. This focus on the process in pursuit of their outcome goal ensures that they are prepared to execute the shot well which increases their chances of accomplishing their outcome goal of sinking the putt.

As such, consultants can encourage athletes to set outcome goals, not outcome expectations. Once athletes have established goals for the results they want, they can immediately shift from outcome to process and set goals for what they need to do to achieve their outcome goals. Examples might include setting goals to be totally prepared before an event, focus on specific technique or a particular strategy, or playing as aggressively as possible.

There are several key elements about process goals that distinguish them from outcome goals and, even more, from expectations. First, if athletes achieve the process goals, they are very likely to achieve the outcome goals they set for themselves because they will be better prepared and are more likely to perform well. Second, unlike outcome goals, process goals are entirely within athletes' control, so they have the power to directly accomplish their process goals. Third, because process goals are controllable, athletes will feel confident that they can achieve their process goals and motivated to give their best effort. Finally, athletes are able to exert control over the quality of their efforts and, by extension, the results that they produce.

Change the Relationship with Expectations

Another option is helping athletes and coaches to change the relationship, or appraisal, that they have with expectations and pressure. For example, following their loss in the 2007 World Cup, the New Zealand All Blacks began working with a sport psychologist on (among other skills) how to view "pressure as a privilege" (Hodge & Smith, 2014). Instead of viewing pressure as something that is negative and as a problem to be avoided, they began to talk of pressure as something that is positive and as an opportunity to be embraced and welcomed. Pressure, they began to believe, was a sign of respect and something that was earned. Similarly, in Gould et al.'s (1999) study of Olympic teams, two teams that successfully met or exceeded expectations either embraced the pressure and expectations of winning the games or felt free of expectations and pressure entirely and played "with nothing to lose."

Use Practice to Build Confidence, not Expectations

Practice is another place where athletes can build up expectations that end up hurting their efforts in competitions. It's not uncommon for athletes who perform well in practice to have developed expectations that they will perform well in competitions as well. These athletes turn performing well in practice, which should be a positive, into pressure to be successful in an upcoming competition, which is clearly a negative. They begin to question whether they can continue their good performances in competitions and worry that they won't. As strange as it sounds, after a great practice period, competing actually becomes something to fear rather than embrace. The result is a self-fulfilling prophecy of poor performances in competition.

But it shouldn't be this way. Quite to the contrary, performing well in practice shouldn't weigh athletes down, but rather should lift them up. Doing well in practice should be a good thing; it means athletes "on their game" and are ready to perform well in competition. It should give athletes confidence, not create expectations.

This different relationship between athletes performing well in practice should inspire confidence in them that they are mentally and physically prepared to continue the practice success in competition. From this perspective, athletes can feel motivated, confident, intense, focused, and excited to go out there and compete. The result is a self-fulfilling prophecy of good performance in competition.

Learn Coping Tools

Lastly, consultants can introduce coping techniques to help athletes manage the cognitions and emotions that stem from expectations. Evidence indicates that coping tools can mediate the negative impact of high expectations. For example, Greenleaf, Gould, and Dieffenbach (2001) found that there was a positive relationship between high expectations and performance in Olympic athletes, but only when the athletes had the coping tools required to mitigate the expectations.

Likewise, Durand-Bush and Salmela (2002) noted that as the athletes in their study gained experience, they learned the coping tools necessary to manage and redirect the expectations they felt. Strategies that the research has reported as effective include:

- goal setting;
- positive self-talk;
- mindfulness;
- muscle relaxation;
- deep breathing;
- routines;
- mental imagery; and
- centering.

Summary

- Expectations are defined as "a strong belief that something will happen in the future . . . a belief that someone will or should achieve something."
- Six phrases that create expectations: I must, I have to, I need to, I should, I better, I gotta.
- Expectations take a significant toll on athletes before (e.g., pre-competitive doubt, worry, and anxiety), during (e.g., fearful, tentative, unfocused), and after (e.g., relief, devastation) competitions.
- Research has a consistent relationship between outcome expectations and poor performance.
- Expectations have been found to be associated with choking, negative physical states, difficulty focusing, loss of confidence, and interfering emotions.
- There are a variety of strategies that consultants can use to mitigate or remove expectations including a shift from "I must" to "I would like," from expectations to goals, from a focus on results to a focus on process, helping athletes see expectations as positive, allowing practice success to create confidence, not expectations, and to teach coping tools to athletes so they can better manage the expectations they feel prior to a competition.

References

Durand-Bush, N., & Salmela, J. H. (2002). The development and maintenance of expert athletic performance: Perceptions of world and Olympic champions. *Journal of Applied Sport Psychology, 14,* 154–171.

Gould, D., Guinan, D., Greenleaf, C., Medbery, R., & Peterson, K. (1999). Factors affecting Olympic performance: Perceptions of athletes and coaches from more and less successful teams. *The Sport Psychologist, 13,* 371–394.

Greenleaf, C., Gould, D., & Dieffenbach, K. (2001). Factors influencing Olympic performance: Interviews with Atlanta and Negano US Olympians. *Journal of Applied Sport Psychology, 13,* 154–184.

Gucciardi, D. F., Longbottom, J., Jackson, B., & Dimmock, J. A. (2010). Experienced golfers' perspectives on choking under pressure. *Journal of Sport and Exercise Psychology, 32,* 61–83.

Hodge, K., & Hermansson, G. (2007). Psychological preparation of athletes for the Olympic context: The New Zealand Summer and Winter Olympic Teams. *Athletic Insight, 9,* 1–14.

Hodge, K., & Smith, W. (2014). Public expectation, pressure, and avoiding the choke: A case study from elite sport. *The Sport Psychologist, 28,* 375–389.

Lazarus, R. S. (2000). How emotions influence performance in competitive sports. *The Sport Psychologist, 14,* 229–252.

Mellalieu, S. D., Neil, R., Hanton, S., & Fletcher, D. (2009). Competition stress in sport performers: Stressors experienced in the competition environment. *Journal of Sports Sciences, 27,* 729–744.

Oxford Dictionaries. 2018. Expectation. Retrieved from https://en.oxforddictionaries.com/definition/expectation goal.

Uphill, M. A., & Jones, M. V. (2007). Antecedents of emotions in elite athletes. *Research Quarterly for Exercise and Sport, 78,* 79–89.

Williams, J. M., Nideffer, R. M., Wilson, V. E., Sagal, M., & Peper, E. (2010). Concentration and strategies for controlling it. In J. M. Williams (Ed.), *Applied sport psychology: Personal growth to peak performance,* 6th ed. (pp. 336–358). New York, NY: McGraw-Hill.

EMOTIONS

Sheila Alicea, Melanie Poudevigne, and Jim Taylor

Emotions play an essential, yet often underappreciated, role in athletic performance. The emotions athletes experience during their sports participation underlie their motivation to practice and compete, the enjoyment they gain from their sports involvement, and their ability to perform their best and achieve their sports goals. They also determine how athletes respond to the demands of sports and are a powerful expression of athletes' reactions to success and failure in sports. So-called positive emotions commonly experienced in sports include:

- love;
- happiness;
- passion;
- excitement;
- determination;
- joy;
- surprise;
- elation;
- euphoric;
- exhilaration;
- satisfaction;
- pride;
- inspiration;
- courage;
- contentment;
- amazement.

All of these emotions have a wide-ranging and oftentimes intense impact on athletes in all aspects of their sports lives. They motivate, build confidence, create intensity, and affect how athletes think, perform, and react in the diverse situations in which athletes find themselves.

Conversely, as any athlete will tell you, there are also many so-called negative emotions that are also frequently experienced in sports:

- sadness;
- frustration;
- angry;
- fear;
- unhappy;
- panicked;
- discouraged;
- despair;
- disappointment;
- hopelessness;
- guilt;
- embarrassment;
- humiliation;

- shame;
- grief;
- lonely;
- bored;
- cowardice;
- impatience; and
- jealousy.

Whereas the positive emotions listed above act as propulsion for athletes toward their goals, the negative emotions act as a wall that slows or halts that progress. As a result, emotions are an essential piece of the sports performance puzzle that must be addressed to ensure that athletes have a clear path to their goals. Athletes can help maximize their training and competitive efforts by removing the emotional obstacles. They can also generate positive emotions that facilitate their performances.

Theory and Research

One challenge that athletes face in understanding the impact that emotions have on them is defining emotions (Lox, Martin Ginis, & Petruzzello, 2014; Weinberg & Gould, 2015). Lazarus (2000a) defines emotion as, "an organized psychophysiological reaction to ongoing relationships with the environment, most often, but not always, interpersonal or social" (p. 230). Another definition that has been applied to sport is "a reaction to a stimulus event (either actual or imagined). It involves change in the viscera and musculature of the person, is experienced subjectively in characteristic ways, is expressed through such means as facial expressions and action tendencies, and may mediate and energize subsequent behaviors" (Deci, 1980, p. 85). In sum, emotions are experienced as visceral physiological changes that produce immediate psychological interpretations of the situation causing the emotions, which lead to behavioral reactions that are dependent on the specific emotion that is felt (Jones, 2003; Vallerand & Blanchard, 2000). However, due to the ethereal nature of emotions, none of these definitions (or others considered) do justice to or adequately explain the experience of emotions. Suffice it to say that athletes know what emotions are and usually recognize how emotions affect them.

There are many stimuli in sport that may cause emotional reactions in athletes, from external stimuli, such as a bad call from an umpire, to internal stimuli such as negative self-talk (Jones, 2003). Emotions are often experienced as immediate, short-lived, and, depending on the stimulus, intense (Jones, 2012; Lox et al., 2014). In addition, athletes are not always aware of why they feel an emotion, as the process may occur without conscious thought (Lazarus, 1991). For example, many of the emotions associated with the four previously discussed obstacles, including fear, anger, frustration, and despair, are often derived from athletes' past life experiences and ingrained as unconscious patterns that are counterproductive to their athletic efforts.

The Cognitive–Motivational–Relational Theory (CMRT) (Lazarus, 2000a) proposes that specific emotions in athletes are guided by the interaction between the athlete and the environment. First, athletes bring to any potentially emotional situation genetic predispositions (based in temperament), life experiences that shape longstanding attitudes and beliefs, and immediate perceptions about the current situation. From these "filters," they rapidly assess the risks and rewards involved in a particular sport situation, sometimes consciously, other times unconsciously. From these evaluations, athletes experience a particular emotion which, in turn, leads to an action tendency that they believe will help them best manage the situation (Lazarus, 2000b). For example, an action tendency when an athlete is losing a competition might be to become angry. Anger is described as "a powerful impulse to counterattack in order to gain revenge for an affront or repair a wounded self-esteem" (Lazarus, 2000a, p. 243). The complex relationship between the athlete and the situation will determine how the anger impacts their performance. When losing, anger can cloud thinking, create anxiety and tension, and cause distractions, all of which will hurt performance. However, in sports where aggressiveness can be beneficial, such as boxing, tennis, and soccer, anger can increase motivation, reduce pain and fatigue, and narrow focus, thus producing an improvement in performance (Lazarus, 2000b). Because of this complicated interplay between athletes and their sport, consultants will want to explore what emotions are most productive for a given athlete in a given sport before choosing to intervene on an athlete's emotional experience.

Practical Implications

In approaching how to remove the emotional obstacles that athletes experience, consultants can help them in two ways. First, they can provide short-term strategies to mitigate the obstacles temporarily. Second, they can employ long-term strategies to minimize or remove them permanently. However, doing so requires considerable determination and persistent effort on the part of athletes to diminish the negative impact of emotional obstacles on performance. This challenge can be so daunting because they are often unconscious and deeply ingrained, and produce immediate, intense, persistent, and unproductive habitual patterns of thinking and behavior that hurt performance. Strategies to assist athletes in managing their emotions involve both cognitive and behavioral approaches, most often including personal and situational factors (Weinberg & Gould, 2015).

Short-term Interventions

Reappraisal

The athletes' appraisal of the situation, rather than the situation itself, influences the quality and intensity of the emotional response (Uphill, McCarthy, & Jones, 2009). Reappraisal is a strategy athletes can use to reframe an emotional situation to see it in a less threatening and more positive light (Folkman & Moskowitz, 2000). It is often taught in cognitive-behavioral therapy and assessed using various measures of coping (e.g., Ways of Coping Questionnaire; Folkman & Lazarus, 1988). The use of Socratic dialogue, asking questions with the intent of getting athletes to re-evaluate self-defeating perceptions, thoughts, interpretations, and behaviors, and using storytelling and metaphors can help athletes become more aware of their negative appraisals of emotional situations and increase their use of positive appraisals (Jones, 2003).

Problem-focused Strategies

Problem-focused strategies "involve efforts to alter or manage the problem that is causing the stress for the individual concerned" (Weinberg & Gould, 2015, p. 285). More specifically, these methods are aimed at identifying and solving the problem that is producing the unproductive emotions. For example, if an athlete is experiencing frustration because she can't master a new technical aspect of her sport, having the coach provide a clearer explanation of the technique and offer more effective drills can enhance learning and, in turn, reduce the frustration. This approach can be meaningful because it redirects athletes' attention away from the emotions and onto something within their control, thus fostering feelings of mastery and confidence (Folkman & Moskowitz, 2000). Examples of problem-focused coping strategies include:

- goal setting;
- information gathering;
- analysis;
- decision making;
- time management;
- weighing benefits vs. costs;
- increasing motivation and effort;
- self-talk;
- making training and competition plans; and
- adhering to training and competitive routines.

All of these problem-focused approaches serve several important purposes. If athletes are focused on solving the problem underlying the interfering emotions they are less likely to pay attention to the emotions themselves, thus reducing their impact on them. These strategies inspire and motivate athletes, build their confidence, relax them, and generate countervailing positive emotions that can further mitigate the negative emotions.

Emotion-focused Strategies

Emotion-focused strategies "entail regulating the emotional responses to the problem that causes stress for the individual" (Weinberg & Gould, 2015, p. 285). As will be discussed in Chapter 3, physiological intensity (also referred to as arousal) plays an essential role in sports performance. One powerful way in which it does involves how athletes manage the physical manifestations of the emotions they experience. Sports training and competitive performance require varying levels of intensity (e.g., increased or decreased heart rate, respiration, blood flow) depending on the sport. For sports that involve power or strength, elevated intensity can have a positive effect on performance. In contrast, sports that require endurance or fine motor control, arousal can be detrimental to performance (Landers & Arent, 2001). Moreover, emotions can have the effect of either raising or lowing intensity. For example, fear and frustration boost intensity, whereas disappointment and sadness can lower intensity, both with a commensurate impact on performance.

Consultants can help athletes to minimize the effect of the physiological expression of emotions with a variety of strategies aimed at controlling intensity. Some of these emotion-focused techniques lower the physical symptoms of emotions, others increase it, and still others can be used to either reduce or elevate it. Commonly used methods include (discussed in detail in subsequent chapters; Bood et al., 2013; Gaudreau and Blondin, 2004; Hutchinson & Karageorghis, 2013):

- muscle relaxation;
- breathing;
- meditation;
- self-talk;
- music;
- mental imagery;
- physical movement;
- routines; and
- distractions (internal or external).

Research has shown that facial expressions can influence emotions (Ekman et al., 1987). Smiling is one surprisingly effective emotion-focused strategy. Results from one study showed that participants who smiled when stressed experienced more positive emotions than when they frowned (Philippen, Bakker, Oudejans, & Canal-Bruland, 2012). Consultants can help athletes identify how their facial expressions are influencing their emotions and teach them to smile when they are experiencing unproductive emotions.

Long-term Interventions

Short-term strategies can help athletes to temporarily manage the emotions they experience in their sports participation, but they don't address the root causes of the emotions that lead them to become obstacles in the path toward athletes' goals. This means that athletes will continue to struggle with these emotions whenever the situations that provoke them occur. The ultimate goal for consultants is to assist athletes in removing the sources of the unhelpful emotions. The most common culprits of these emotions are the four previous obstacles discussed in this chapter (i.e., overinvestment, perfectionism, fear of failure, and expectations), as well as the negative side of the building blocks described in Chapter 1 (i.e., lack of ownership, fixed mindset, threat attitude, outcome focus, short-term perspective, and an inability to take risks).

A long-term strategy that is grounded in traditional counseling or psychotherapy can help athletes to let go of this emotional "baggage." There are a variety of methods that might be used in this process including insight-oriented, cognitive-behavioral, and humanistic approaches. The particular strategy that is used depends on the education, training, and theoretical orientation of the consultant working with the athletes. Regardless of which specific technique is chosen, all use some combination of the following process to produce emotional change.

First, they all have a component of self-realization in which athletes identify the precise emotions they are experiencing, what they think, feel, and do when those emotions are present, and how they impact their performances and their lives. For example, an athlete who experiences fear before a competition causes her to have negative self-talk, muscle tension, and difficulty focusing. These changes result in a poor competitive performance.

Second, they examine the exact situations in which the emotions arise. Typically, a consistent pattern will emerge in which similar situations cause the same emotional reactions. Continuing with the previous example, this fear reaction arises in competitions where her parents are present and in which she needs a certain result to qualify for the next level.

Third, athletes explore the source of the emotional obstacles, most likely found in the obstacles earlier in this chapter, and what purpose they serve despite interfering with sports performance. Referring back to the continuing example, the athlete had a fear of failure based in not living up to her parents' expectations and concern with disappointing them.

Fourth, they reflect back on their lives to understand how these obstacles arose. For the athlete that's been described, she realizes her parents have always been very focused on results in their lives and were very critical of themselves when they didn't perform well in school or at work. And they put the same sort of pressure on her in her school and sports.

Fourth, athletes consider alternative perspectives and perceptions that would produce a different emotional reaction. Because the emotional obstacles typically arise from how athletes perceive and interpret situations, if they can alter how they look at them, the associated emotions will change too. For the above athlete, she realized that her parents loved her and thought they were doing the right thing in pushing her to be successful. She also recognized that her parents were human and had their own emotional baggage to contend with. These two realizations caused her to feel a weight lifted off her shoulders.

Finally, with the help of consultants, athletes can identify alternative ways of thinking, feeling, and behaving and, in doing so, can replace the old emotional patterns with new ones. Subsequently, through awareness and practice, athletes can expose themselves to those fear-producing situations and consciously introduce the new ways of thinking, feeling, and responding, thus removing the fear that interfered with their performances. To conclude the above example, the athlete was able to separate her parents' love and good intentions from the pressure she felt from them, thus reducing her fear reaction. In addition, her consultant also helped her to stay confident, relaxed, and focused in competitive situations. The end result was that, over time, her fear diminished and she was able to perform up to her fullest capabilities.

Summary

- The emotions athletes experience during their sports participation underlie their motivation to practice and compete, and their ability to perform their best and achieve their sports goals.
- Commonly experienced positive motions include love, happiness, passion, excitement, joy, elation, exhilaration, satisfaction, pride, and inspiration.
- Commonly experienced negative emotions include sadness, frustration, anger, fear, discouragement, guilt, embarrassment, panic, and disappointment.
- Emotions are an essential piece of the sports performance puzzle that must be addressed to ensure that athletes have a clear path to their goals.
- Emotions are experienced as visceral physiological changes that produce immediate psychological interpretations of the situation causing the emotions, which lead to behavioral reactions that are dependent on the specific emotion that is felt.
- There are many stimuli in sport that may cause emotional reactions in athletes, from external stimuli, such as a bad call from an umpire, to internal stimuli such as negative self-talk.
- Athletes bring to any potentially emotional situation genetic predispositions, life experiences that shape long-standing attitudes and beliefs, and immediate perceptions about the current situation.
- Because of the complicated interplay between athletes and their sport, consultants will want to explore what emotions are most productive for a given athlete in a given sport before choosing to intervene on an athlete's emotional experience.
- Consultants can provide short-term strategies to mitigate emotional obstacles temporarily and long-term strategies to minimize or remove them permanently.

- Short-term interventions include changing how athletes' appraisal of an emotional situation, problem-focused strategies aimed at resolving the problem that is causing the interfering emotions, and emotion-focused strategies that address the physical manifestations of the emotion.
- Common problem-focused strategies include goal setting, time management, self-talk, making training and competition plans, and developing routines.
- Common emotion-focused strategies include muscle relaxation, breathing, meditation, music, mental imagery, and physical movement.
- Long-term interventions are grounded in traditional counseling or psychotherapy that can help athletes to let go of their emotional "baggage."
- Long-term strategies include self-realization that involves identifying the precise emotions, specifying the situations in which they arise, exploring the obstacles that cause the emotions, understanding where the obstacles came from, considering alternative perspectives and perceptions that would produce different emotions, and identifying and implementing new patterns of thinking, feeling, and behaving.

References

Bood, R. J., Nijssen, M., van der Kamp, J., & Roerdink, M. (2013). The power of auditory-motor synchronization in sports: Enhancing running performance by coupling cadence with the right beats. *PLOS One, 8*, e70758. doi: 10.1371/journal. pone.0070758

Deci, E. L. (1980). *The psychology of self-determination.* Lexington, MA: Heath.

Ekman, P., Friesen, W. V., O'Sullivan, M., Diacoyanni-Tarlatzis, I., Krause, R., Pitcairn, T., & Tzavaras, A. (1987). Universals and cultural differences in the judgments of facial expressions of emotion. *Journal of Personality and Social Psychology, 53*(4), 712–717. doi: 10.1037/0022-3514.53.4.712

Folkman, S., & Lazarus, R. S. (1988). *Manual for the Ways of Coping Questionnaire.* Palo Alto, CA: Consulting Psychologists Press.

Folkman, S., & Moskowitz, J. T. (2000). Positive affect and the other side of coping. *American Psychologist, 55*(6), 647–654. doi: 10.1037//0003-066X.55.6.647

Gaudreau, P., & Blondin, J.-P. (2004). Different athletes cope differently during sport competition: A cluster analysis of coping. *Personality and Individual Differences, 36*, 1865–1877. doi: 10.1016/j.paid.2003.08.

Hutchinson, J. C., & Karageorghis, C. I. (2013). Moderating influence of dominant attentional style and exercise intensity on psychological and psychophysical responses to asynchronous music. *Journal of Sport & Exercise Psychology, 35*, 625–643. doi: 10.1123/jsep.35.6.625

Jones, M. V. (2003). Controlling emotions in sport. *The Sport Psychologist, 17*(4), 471–486. doi: 10.1123/tsp.17.4.471

Jones, M. (2012). Emotion regulation in sport. In: S. Murphy (Ed.). *The Oxford handbook of sport and performance psychology* (pp. 154–172). New York, NY: Oxford University Press.

Landers, D. M., & Arent, S. M. (2001). Arousal-performance relationships. In: J. M. Williams (Ed.), *Applied sport psychology: Personal growth to peak performance,* 4th ed. (pp. 206–228). Mountain View, CA: Mayfield.

Lazarus, R. S. (1991). *Emotion and adaptation.* Oxford: Oxford University Press.

Lazarus, R. S. (2000a). How emotions influence performance in competitive sports. *The Sport Psychologist, 14*, 229–252.

Lazarus, R. S. (2000b). Cognitive-motivational-relational theory of emotion. In Y. L. Hanin (Ed.), *Emotions in sport* (pp. 39–63). Champaign, IL: Human Kinetics.

Lox, C. L., Martin Ginis, K. A., & Petruzzello, S. J. (2014). *The psychology of exercise,* 4th ed. Scottsdale, AZ: Holcomb Hathaway Publishers.

Philippen, P. B., Bakker, F. C., Oudejans, R. R. D., & Canal-Bruland, R. (2012). The effects of smiling and frowning on perceived affect and exertion while physically active. *Journal of Sport Behavior, 35*(3), 337–353. Retrieved from http://dare. ubvu.vu.nl/bitstream/handle/1871/50776/2012?sequence=1

Uphill, M. A., McCarthy, P. J., & Jones, M. V. (2009). Getting a grip on emotional regulation in sport. In S. D. Mellalieu & S. Hanton (Eds.), *Advances in applied sport psychology: A review* (pp. 162–194). New York, NY: Routledge.

Vallerand, R. J., & Blanchard, C. M. (2000). The study of emotion in sport and exercise: Historical, definitional, and conceptual perspectives. In Y. L. Hanin (Ed.), *Emotions in sport* (pp. 3–37). Champaign, IL: Human Kinetics.

Weinberg, R. S., & Gould, D. (2015). *Foundations of sport and exercise psychology,* 6th ed. Champaign, IL: Human Kinetics.

3

MENTAL MUSCLES

Introduction

Jim Taylor

In applied sport psychology, there are four mental areas that are considered to be central for athletes to be mentally prepared for athletic success: motivation, confidence, arousal, and concentration. Much of the work done by consultants with athletes involves maximizing these areas, thus maximizing athletes' readiness to perform their best.

Returning to the discussion about a more precise vocabulary begun in the Introduction, the conventional wisdom in our field is that those four mental areas that are commonly addressed in helping athletes to be mentally prepared to perform their best are "skills" that they can improve. Yet, *CASP* would argue that these four areas aren't skills at all. Consider this. A skill is typically defined as "The ability to do something well; expertise." Athletes don't become more skilled or expert at motivation, confidence, arousal, or concentration when they do mental training.

A big part of the work that consultants do with athletes, coaches, and teams is to convince them that mental training should be viewed the same as physical conditioning and the technical aspects of athletic development. A key part of that "sales pitch" is that, like the body, the mind is made up of "muscles" and that physical and mental muscles have much in common. They both can be weak if the muscles aren't exercised regularly. Physical and mental muscles can be injured. In the case of physical muscles, injuries can be sustained by having too much force placed on them, resulting in pulls or tears. Similarly, mental muscles can also be hurt from too much force exerted on them, in the form of struggles, failures, and disappointments. Importantly, both physical and mental muscles can be strengthened with a consistent (physical or mental) conditioning program. Also, like their physical muscles, athletes' only chance to become the best they can be is to commit to making the muscles in your mind as strong as they can be. As such, from this point forward, *CASP* will call what have traditionally been termed mental skills mental muscles.

MOTIVATION

Candace Brown and Jim Taylor

Simply defined, motivation refers to athletes' determination and drive to pursue their sports goals. Motivation is the cornerstone of athletic success. Without motivation, nothing in athletes' development will matter because they won't devote the effort, energy, or time that is necessary, whether in their conditioning, sport training, nutrition, sleep, or mental training, to achieve their goals. For athletes to fully realize their abilities, they must be motivated to initiate the process of athletic development and then sustain their efforts until their goals have been accomplished.

Motivation in sports is so essential for athletic success for several reasons. First, it requires that athletes expend effort consistently in every component of their sports lives including their physical fitness, the technical and tactical aspects of their sport, optimal maintenance of their equipment, and, of course, their mental training. That motivation isn't just restricted to areas with a direct impact on how athletes perform. Additionally, the determination that athletes apply to their sports must also extend to other aspects of their lives that have an indirect, though equally important, influence on their sports performance such as sleeping and eating habits, school or work, use of technology, and relationships.

Second, the pursuit of athletes' own personal greatness is a difficult road rife with fatigue, pain, boredom, failures, frustration, and the desire to do other things that are easier and more fun. As a result, their motivation will determine what place sports assume in their life's priorities and into what activities they spend their time and energy. This conflict is particularly difficult to navigate for young athletes who have to balance many competing priorities including school, other hobbies, and social life, as well as the priorities that their parents have for them.

There is one simple reality that every athlete must come to terms with: Without sufficient motivation that turns talk of big dreams into action toward tangible goals, their sports goals will surely not be realized. In other words, to become the best they can be, athletes must be motivated to do what it takes to maximize their ability.

There are many factors that contribute to how successful athletes will become. First, there are the attributes that they are born with including their genetically endowed athletic ability, body type and composition, and temperament. Because innate qualities are something athletes get from their parents, it is not within their control and, as a result, not worth discussing further.

Second, in terms of preparation, athletes must have the opportunity to fully realize whatever innate ability they have. Opportunity is reflected in having enough money to pay for coaching, equipment, camps, and competitions. Other opportunity factors include geographical location, quality coaching, time to practice, and support from family. Athletes don't always have control over the opportunities that are available to them; for example, their family may not have the financial resources to underwrite their efforts. At the same time, in some cases, motivation can create opportunities where none had existed previously

Third, success in competitions is dependent in part on the difficulty of the event. How difficult a competition is depends on the ability of opponents, the depth of the field of competitors, weather, the conditions at the competitive venue, and fans. Athletes have no control over these factors.

Lastly, motivation plays a central role in sports performance for athletes because it is the one contributor over which they have almost complete control. It influences the time and energy athletes put into their practice. Motivation dictates their willingness to persist in the face of setbacks and failures. To fully illustrate its importance, consider this. If there are two athletes of nearly equal natural ability and opportunity, who will emerge victorious is the one who is the most diligent in their practice efforts, doesn't give up no matter what the competitive circumstances, and who drives themselves to perform at their highest level when it matters most.

Warning Signs of Low Motivation

Motivation isn't just a perception that athletes hold about themselves ("I'm a hard worker") or an aspiration ("I want to be an Olympic champion"). Instead, motivation involves the ability of athletes to turn those beliefs and goals into tangible action. In other words, are athletes willing to do the hard work necessary every day to accomplish their sports goals? To help athletes better understand their motivation and gauge how motivated they really are, consultants can use the following warning signs of low motivation:

- Do athletes often lack the desire to practice as much as they could?
- Do they give less than 100% effort in practice?
- Do athletes skip or shorten their training?
- Do they make choices that don't support their athletic goals (e.g., stay up late, eat unhealthy food)?

If athletes exhibit any of these symptoms of low motivation, they need to reevaluate their commitment to their sport and, if they choose to, find their motivation and learn to work hard enough to achieve their goals.

Theory and Research

Self-determination theory examines what motivates people and determines their behavior (Deci & Ryan, 1995). It is based on the rewards, feedback, praise, and directives that either enhance or diminish outcomes. According to Deci and Ryan, motivation can be extrinsic or intrinsic (Deci & Ryan, 2000, 2008). Extrinsic motivation comes from a desire to receive external rewards such as trophies, attention, praise, acceptance, or money. In contrast, intrinsic motivation provides internally derived rewards including satisfaction, meaning, fun, or sense of mastery. Moreover the absence of motivation, termed "amotivation," involves athletes having neither extrinsic nor intrinsic rewards to engage in the sport. This may be due to a lack of interest, not finding value in the sport, or the sport being an aversive experience (Deci & Ryan, 2000).

Motivation is also either controlled or autonomous. Controlled motivation is typically externally based and used to hold sway over athletes' actions. Controlled rewards can include the expression of love and affection, overt approval, or the use of material incentives. Controlled punishments may involve the use of guilt, shame, disapproval, or the withdrawal of love, affection, or attention. Autonomous motivation comes from within athletes and is, as a result, under their complete control and entirely self-regulated. This healthy form of motivation is derived from athletes' values, interests, and goals. Autonomous motivation is a natural and positive expression of who they are and what they want in their sports lives. Conversely, controlled motivation can be an unhealthy form of motivation because athletes don't have ownership of or influence over it, feel at the mercy of those who exert the control, or the incentives used can do psychological and emotional harm (Deci & Ryan, 2000).

Research has determined that motivation plays a key role in performance in sports. The success of performance is based on various motivational factors including coaching support, motivational climate, and the conditions of the training facility (Gillet & Vallerand, 2016). A coach who is "autonomy supportive" (Deci & Ryan, 1985) will acknowledge athletes' perspectives and feelings, may provide advice or information for guidance, and allow athletes to make decisions without pressure or demands (Black & Deci, 2000). Athletes with coaches who support their autonomy will be more motivated in their practice (Conroy & Coatsworth, 2007) and will want to do what is needed to be the best athlete they can be.

Motivational climate is determined by focusing on achieving mastery (task) or ego (performance) goal. Athletes training under a motivational climate with a mastery focus will give their maximum effort in training and choose challenging tasks, be persistent, and take pride in personal improvement (Ames, 1992), demonstrating more of an intrinsic style of motivation. An ego climate uses comparison among athletes as the basis for defining success. This extrinsic type of climate promotes positive reinforcement to the most competent athletes because winning is deemed more important than personal improvement (McArdle & Duda, 2002).

The environmental conditions of where athletes train can also be motivational. Athletes are more motivated when they benefit from proper training conditions. This is why some athletes will travel to specific locations to train. For a snowboarder, the training environment in Colorado is vastly different than if they trained in Pennsylvania. Additionally, conditions of facilities may increase their pleasure and efficiency of training. Also, a training environment populated by equally motivated and determined athletes will inspire individual athletes to give their best efforts. Motivation can be found through different mechanisms that are psychological, social and environmental. This is why it is important for athletes to be aware of the effect of a training setting on their motivation. Each mechanism can have a positive or negative effect on their motivation and support or hinder their athletic outcomes. Consultants can leverage these forces to create a training environment that maximally fuels their motivation.

Practical Implications

Because motivation plays such an important role in athletic success, it is also the starting point for consultants in their work with athletes. There a number of practical strategies consultants can use to help athletes to gain and maintain their motivation.

Focus on Long-term Goals

For athletes to be their best, they must expend considerable time and effort in the many aspects of their sport. And, as much as they may enjoy their athletic efforts over all, there are going to be many times when those efforts are, as discussed previously, tiring, painful, and monotonous. Yet, it is often those challenging times that can make the difference between success and failure.

When athletes reach that breaking point in their sport efforts, one useful technique to help them through it successfully is for them to focus on their long-term goals. In a nutshell, they must remind themselves why they're working so hard. Athletes can imagine what they want to achieve in their sports lives and tell themselves that the only way they'll be able to find success is to continue to work hard.

Focusing on their long-term goals, particularly when training or competitions get difficult, girds their motivation in several ways. First, when athletes are pushing themselves in practice, their bodies are telling their minds to stop. If their minds capitulate to the messages from their bodies, they will either ease up or give up. Or, if they are losing in a competition and a part of their mind is telling them to quit, it's easy for athletes to give in to those messages. But when athletes focus on their long-term goals during these difficult times, they are recalling why they are suffering. In doing so, they are giving their minds and bodies a reason to keep going despite the protestations to the contrary.

Second, when athletes direct their attention onto their long-term goals, they are distracting themselves from their physical or mental struggles. As a result, the negatives become more tolerable and they are better able to maintain their efforts, whether in practice or competitions.

Third, when athletes remind themselves of why they are so committed to their sport, they experience positive emotions, such as inspiration and pride, that blunt the negative emotions they are experiencing such as frustration, anger, or disappointment. Moreover, those positive emotions reduce their experience of pain.

Have a Training Partner

It's challenging for athletes to stay motivated in their sport efforts on their own day in and day out. When they're tired, stressed, distracted, or just need a break, their motivation will naturally wane. Moreover, with few exceptions, athletes can't push themselves as hard as when they are being pushing by someone else, whether a coach, personal trainer, parent, or teammate. For both reasons then, having a training partner is one of the simplest motivational strategies for athletes to employ.

Training partners may offer several motivational benefits. First, there are going to be days when the motivation isn't there for individual athletes, but it is rare that it will be absent on the same day when athletes train together. On those days, teaming up with a motivated training partner can help harness their power to fuel their individual motivation. Relatedly, on some days, athletes can feel overwhelmed by the immensity of the physical challenge that lies ahead and can feel incapable of overcoming those challenges alone. A training partner can provide social support and encouragement to help athletes to give their best effort (Keegan, Harwood, Spray, & Lavallee, 2009).

Second, a training partner holds athletes accountable. Every athlete has felt like skipping a training session because they are tired or just aren't in the mood. And, in some cases, without any accountability, they would pass on the workout. But, a training partner creates a shared responsibility in which missing a training session would also be letting them down. In other words, training partners create a sense of obligation to be motivated. The bottom line is that training partners will count on each other to stay motivated and do the work necessary.

Third, during workouts that are physically tiring and painful, athletes' bodies will be screaming at their minds to stop. If training alone, they might very well ease up for quit. But, a training partner wouldn't allow that to happen. Instead, they would exhort emotional support to keep their partner going to completion (Keegan, Harwood, Spray, & Lavallee, 2014).

Train Smart

The nature of athletes' pursuing their sports goals is that their training program can be tiring, time consuming, and tedious. Over time, athletes can find themselves exhausted, bored, and unfocused. The result is a loss of motivation and a decline in effort and progress toward their goals. One way to minimize the chances of this happening is to "train smart." Training smart involves a training program that allows for:

- periodization (appropriate phases of training for specific times of the year);
- variety (to keep training fresh and interesting);

- plenty of opportunities for rest and recovery (including low-intensity days and scheduled days off); and
- athletes to listen to their bodies (to respond to the cues of fatigue they are receiving).

When athletes engage in a training regimen that meets the above criteria, they experience two important motivational benefits. First, they are able to maintain optimal motivation for each training session. Second, they put themselves in a position to sustain their motivation and high levels of effort, intensity, and focus throughout a training block. Finally, training smart can assist in athletes achieving their sports goals (Venter, 2014).

Focus on Greatest Competitor

Almost every athlete has opponents whom they see as their primary competition in their sport. Those people may be teammates with whom they share a friendly (though intense) rivalry, or they may be bitter enemies from another team or club. This relationship can be leveraged as another source of motivation. Athletes can identify who those rivals are and use them to bolster motivation. Athletes can use those rivals to keep them motivated and working hard in the face of fatigue, pain, or sheer dislike, whether by placing their name or photo in a noticeable place or just thinking about them during a tough practice session. They can also ask themselves if they are doing the work necessary to beat that adversary when they meet next.

Some athletes do not see others as opponents, but rather focus their attention on beating themselves their own standards. This is often the case with athletes who participate in sports that involve judges' scores (e.g., gymnastics) or objective measures of performance such as time (e.g., swimming) or distance (e.g., javelin). In these cases, athletes' greatest competitors' are those measures of performance. Thus, the motivation is to achieve personal bests (Brown, 2016).

Motivational Cues

Emotions lie at the heart of athletes staying motivated in sports. Feelings, such as excitement, pride, satisfaction, and joy, can enable athletes to stay motivated even when they are struggling. Positive emotions help athletes feel inspired, push them through difficult practices and competitions, help them to stay intense and focused, and allow them to get the most out of their efforts and progress toward their sports goals (Uphill, Groom & Jones, 2014).

One way to actively create those emotions is with motivational cues such as inspirational phrases and photographs. For example, Jonathan Field, a five-time martial arts world champion, has said "Commitment means staying loyal to what you said you were going to do long after the mood you said it in has left you." A quote like this can help athletes stay motivated during challenging times. A photo of an admired Olympic or professional athlete can have the effect of boosting motivation when it's lagging. In both cases, they engender those positive thinking and emotions that increase or maintain athletes' motivation.

Daily Questions

The overall theme of the motivational strategies in this section is for athletes to consistently recall why they are working so hard to stay focused on the tasks that propel them toward their goals. Another way for athletes to keep "their eye on the prize" is to ask themselves two questions every day. First, at the beginning of the day, ask "What can I do today to become the best athlete I can be?" This question immediately connects athletes to their motivation and what they want to accomplish that day. It realigns their thought on how they may improve as an athlete and can inspire them to strive toward their goals. And, at a practical level, it also identifies what precisely they need to do each day to become successful.

To end their day, athletes can ask, "Did I do everything possible today to become the best athlete I can be?" This question holds athletes accountable for what they said they would do and what they actually did. If athletes answer in the affirmative, their motivation will be reinforced with feelings of satisfaction and pride in their efforts. However, if they answer in the negative, they will have to face their failure and possibly experience disappointment or regret. In either case, this question will set the stage for what they choose to do and how they may be more motivated to strive toward their goals the next day.

Motivation is a Moment-to-Moment Choice

Sports are about details. The details involve everything that goes into striving to find success in sports, whether conditioning, technique, tactics, nutrition, equipment, sleep, psychology, or non-sport contributors. Sports are also about frequent choices. Every day, athletes are faced with a myriad of options in their lives. Some of these options support their athletic efforts and other options don't:

- Should I do my warm-up before training?
- Should I go to bed early tonight?
- Should I push through the pain of this workout?
- Should I eat a bag of potato chips?
- Should I turn off my phone, so I can focus on my competitive preparations?

The life of an athlete is rife with those options that impact those details and that ultimately dictate how successful they become. Athletes face these forks in the road many times every day in which they must make a choice between what is best for their sports lives and what might be easier or more fun in other parts of their lives. These choices require athletes' vigilance and deliberate thought because the road away from their goals is often smooth and enticing. Only by athletes keeping their motivation, their drive to accomplish their sports goals, and the priority that they place on those goals in the forefront of their minds, while also being alert to the competing forces for their attention, time, and energy, will they be able to make the best choices that will ultimately lead them to their goals.

Set Goals

There is a robust body of research demonstrating the value of goal setting to motivation. As any athlete knows, setting, putting forth effort toward, and accomplishing a goal is fulfilling and inspiring. The sense of achievement and affirmation that results from the effort encourages athletes to aim even higher. Goal setting will be discussed in depth in Chapter 4.

The Heart of Motivation

The techniques that have been described so far are helpful in increasing athletes' short-term motivation. They can aid athletes in getting through the painful conditioning sessions, frustrating practices, and discouraging competitions. At the same time, motivation involves more than the daily workouts and practices; it also mean finding the motivation in the weeks, months, and years that it takes to work toward and achieve their goals. That kind of enduring and resilient motivation can't be manufactured with motivational techniques. Instead, athletes must identify a compelling reason within themselves to travel down the difficult road of athletic success. There are many motivators that can drive athletes toward their sports goals: fun, satisfaction, mastery, love of competing, high outcome goals. Regardless of the specific motivation athletes have for their sport participation, at its heart must be an unwavering desire and determination to be the best athlete they can be.

Summary

- Motivation refers to athletes' determination and drive to pursue their sports goals.
- Motivation is the cornerstone of athletic success as without it, nothing in athletes' development will matter because they won't have the desire to do what is necessary, whether in their conditioning, sport training, nutrition, sleep, or mental training, to achieve their goals.
- There are many factors that contribute to how successful athletes will become including inborn attributes, opportunities, the difficulty of competitions, and motivation.
- Warning signs for low motivation include a lack of desire to practice, less than 100% effort in practice, shortened or skipped training, and making choices that don't support athletic efforts.
- Motivation can be extrinsic or intrinsic.

- Extrinsic motivation comes from a desire to receive external rewards such as trophies, attention, praise, acceptance, and money.
- Intrinsic motivation provides internally derived rewards including satisfaction, meaning, fun, and sense of mastery.
- Motivation is also either controlled or autonomous.
- Controlled motivation is typically externally based and used to hold sway over athletes' actions.
- Autonomous motivation comes from within the athlete and is, as a result, under their complete control and entirely self-regulated.
- Practical strategies that consultants can use with athletes to bolster their motivation include focusing on long-term goals, having a training partner, training smart, focusing on their greatest competitor, using motivational cues, asking daily motivational questions, making good moment-to-moment choices, and goal setting.
- For enduring and resilient motivation, athletes must identify a compelling reason within themselves to participate in sports and develop an unwavering desire and determination to be the best they can be.

References

Ames, C. (1992). Achievement goals, motivational climate, and motivational processes. In G. C. Roberts (Ed.), *Motivation in sport and exercise* (pp. 161–176). Champaign, IL: Human Kinetics.

Black, A. E., & Deci, E. L. (2000). The effects of instructors' autonomy support and students' autonomous motivation on learning organic chemistry: a self-determination theory perspective. *Science Education, 84,* 740–756.

Brown, C. (2016). The Motives for triathlon participation from an aging Black woman. *Gerontology & Geriatrics: Research, 2*(2): 1009. Retrieved from http://austinpublishinggroup.com/gerontology/fulltext/ggrv2-id1009.php.

Conroy, D. E., & Coatsworth, J. D. (2007). Assessing autonomy-supportive coaching strategies in youth sport. *Psychology of Sport and Exercise, 8,* 671–684.

Deci, E. L., & Ryan, R. M. (1985). *Intrinsic motivation and self-determination in human behavior.* New York, NY: Plenum Press.

Deci, E. L., & Ryan, R. M. (1995). Human autonomy: The basis for true self-esteem. In M.H. Kernis (Ed.). *Efficacy, agency, and self-esteem* (pp.31–49). New York, NY: Springer Science & Business Media.

Deci, E. L., & Ryan, R. M. (2000). The "what" and "why" of goal pursuits: Human needs and the self-determination of behavior. *Psychological Inquiry, 11*(4), 227–268. doi:10.1207/S15327965PLI1104_01

Deci, E. L., & Ryan, R. M. (2008). Facilitating optimal motivation and psychological well-being across life's domains. *Canadian Psychology, 49*(1), 14–23. doi: 10.1037/0708-5591.49.1.14

Gillet, N., & Vallerand, R. (2016). Effects of motivation on sport performance based on self-determination theory: Towards a person-centered approach. *Psychologie Francaise, 61*(4), 257–271. doi: 10.1016/j.psfr.2014.01.001

Keegan, R. J., Harwood, C. G., Spray, C. M., & Lavallee, D. E. (2009). A qualitative investigation exploring the motivational climate in early career sports participants: Coach, parent and peer influences on sport motivation. *Psychology of Sport & Exercise, 10*(3), 361–372. doi: 10.1016/j.psychsport.2008.12.003

Keegan, R. J., Harwood, C. G., Spray, C. M., & Lavallee, D. (2014). A qualitative investigation of the motivational climate in elite sport. *Psychology of Sport & Exercise, 15*(1), 97–107. doi: 10.1016/j.psychsport.2013.10.006

McArdle, S., & Duda, J. K. (2002). Implications of the motivational climate in youth sports. In F. L. Smoll & R. E. Smith (Eds.), *Children and youth in sport: A biopsychosocial perspective,* 2nd ed. (pp. 409–434). Dubuque, IA: Kendall/Hunt.

Uphill, M., Groom, R., & Jones, M. (2014). The influence of in-game emotions on basketball. *European Journal of Sport Science, 14*(1), 76–83. doi: 10.1080/17461391.2012.729088

Venter, R. E. (2014). Perceptions of team athletes on the importance of recovery modalities. *European Journal of Sport Science, 14*(1), S69–S76. doi: 10.1080/17461391.2011.643924

CONFIDENCE

Jennifer Schumacher and Jim Taylor

Confidence is the sense of certainty that athletes possess about their ability to accomplish their sports goals (Vealey, 2001). It can be dispositional, meaning their general degree of belief in their ability to succeed, or situational, meaning their belief in a particular moment (Weinberg & Gould, 2014; Williams, Zinsser, & Bunker, 2015). Several reviews have demonstrated a significant relationship between high levels of confidence and improved performance, as well as lack of confidence undermining performance (Feltz, 1988; Woodman & Hardy, 2003).

Additionally, when athletes experience higher levels of confidence, they also exhibit more positive thoughts, emotions, and effort, leading to better performance outcomes (Hays, Thomas, Maynard, & Bawden, 2009).

Confidence plays such a central role in sports performance because athletes may have other capabilities necessary to be successful (e.g., fitness, technical and technical acumen, the best equipment), but if they lack the fundamental belief in those capabilities, then they aren't likely to perform up to their potential or achieve their competitive goals. As such, as athletes develop themselves physically and technically, they must also devote time and energy to building the commensurate confidence that must accompany those more tangible abilities.

This impact of confidence on sports performance extends well beyond the mind. One way to conceptualize this relationship is by considering how interconnected the mind and body are. Confident thinking on the part of athletes generates positive emotions (e.g., excitement, inspiration) and catalyzes beneficial physiological changes (increased adrenaline and blood flow), leading to improved performance, which reinforces further confident thinking, thus creating a virtuous cycle of confidence and performance (Lazarus, 2000; Williams, Zinsser, & Bunker, 2015). Conversely, this mind–body interaction can also work against athletes. Negative thinking can generate counterproductive emotions (e.g., fear, frustration) and detrimental physiological changes (e.g., muscle tension, insufficient oxygen intake), resulting in weakened performance and the creation of a vicious cycle of negativity and poor performance.

The Challenge of Confidence

Confidence is important not only in driving athletes forward to their goals, but also in how they react when they are struggling in pursuit of those goals. It's easy for athletes to be confident when they are "on their game" because their efforts are being rewarded with success. The challenge for athletes related to confidence is how they react when those efforts aren't being rewarded. Common sport experiences that can hurt confidence include:

- difficulties learning new sport skills;
- poor practice performances;
- subpar competitive performances;
- unexpected losses;
- performance plateaus and declines;
- slumps;
- failing to achieve goals;
- team conflict; and
- non-sport challenges.

These experiences can lead athletes to not only lose their confidence, but also their motivation, intensity, and focus, which can lead to a vicious cycle of diminishing confidence, "injury" to other mental muscles, and progressively worsening performance in practice and competitions.

Warning Signs of Low Confidence

Because of the powerful influence that confidence has on sports performance, it's important for athletes to be aware of their confidence during the inevitable ups and downs of a training session, a competition, or a season. They must be particularly attuned to early warning signs following one or more of the events described above. The goal for athletes is to see these early "red flags" of low confidence so that they can avoid the aforementioned vicious cycle and to take active steps to rebuild confidence. Athletes, and the consultants with whom they might be working, can look for the following warning signs of low confidence:

- Self-doubt: the use of negative self-talk or negative talk to others.
- Anxiety: experiencing intense pre-competitive anxiety as manifested in muscle tension, choppy breathing, and extreme increases in heart rate and respiration.
- Lack of effort: reduced motivation expressed as reluctance to participate, skipping or shortening practice sessions, diminished exertion, and easing up or quitting when faced with challenges.
- Tentative performance: absence of full commitment, cautious performance, and reluctance to take risks.

Theory and Research

Research has demonstrated a significant relationship between high levels of confidence and improved performance, as well as lack of confidence undermining performance (Feltz, 1988; Vealey, 2001; Woodman & Hardy, 2003). When athletes experience higher levels of confidence, they exhibit more positive thoughts, emotions, and effort, leading to better performance outcomes (Hays et al., 2009). Several meta-analyses have demonstrated that high levels of self-reported confidence are moderately correlated with improved performance (Craft, Magyar, Becker, & Feltz, 2003; Moritz, Feltz, Fahrbach, & Mack, 2000). Additionally, one meta-analysis discovered that gender and competitive standard are moderating variables on the relationship between confidence and performance, with effects of confidence having a greater impact on the performance of men and on higher-level competitions (Woodman & Hardy, 2003). It is possible that the gender effect is due to the lack of research on high-competitive standard female athletes at the time of data collection. Further, this analysis revealed that confidence had a greater positive impact on performance than cognitive anxiety's negative impact (Woodman & Hardy, 2003).

Confidence also appears to be one of the strongest indicators of success among athletes participating at the Olympic Games (Gould, Greenleaf, Chung, & Guinan, 2002). Additionally, Hays and colleagues (2009) interviewed 14 world-class athletes and determined that high sport confidence led to facilitated performance by aiding in the ability to maintain appropriate attentional focus for competition. Confidence was described as a "shield" that could protect one from distraction and self-doubt (Hays et al., 2009). Athletes indicated that confidence led to positive emotions, increased enjoyment of the experience, a state of relaxation, and increased automaticity, and that low confidence debilitated performance (Hays et al., 2009).

These findings indicate that confidence is part of successful performance at the highest levels, and that even elite athletes experience shifts in levels of confidence. Thus, athletes at every level of competition can learn from the strategies they use to bolster confidence.

Vealey and colleagues (Vealey, Garner-Holman, Hayashi, & Giacobbi, 1998) proposed the Sport-Confidence Model, identifying nine sources of confidence:

- achievement;
- preparation;
- self-regulation;
- models (vicarious learning);
- feedback and encouragement;
- belief in the coach's leadership;
- environmental comfort;
- physical self-presentation; and
- situational favorableness (such as breaks in momentum or the perception of a competitive advantage).

Practical Implications

For athletes to build and maintain their confidence, they must first take ownership of their thinking by developing awareness and self-control, which can ultimately increase performance (Ravizza & Fifer, 2015). The first step, awareness, involves athletes being cognizant of their thinking as it relates to confidence. Consultants can facilitate this awareness by having athletes check in with them on the quality of their thinking and ensuring that it supports their confidence, particularly following a period of poor performance.

The second step, control, consists of athletes actively strengthening their confidence and minimizing any negative experiences and thoughts that might hurt their confidence. By leveraging a variety of strategies and choosing to focus on their own progress and other positive elements of their efforts, athletes can cultivate confidence in their sports participation (Zinsser, Perkins, Gervais, & Burbelo, 2004).

There are two primary objectives of this second step. First, athletes instill a deep and resilient belief in their athletic capabilities. Second, athletes use that confidence to give their fullest effort and perform their best in the most important competitions of their lives. The following are a set of strategies that consultants can help athletes to use to build and sustain their confidence.

Preparation Breeds Confidence

Preparation is the foundation of athletic performance and, by extension, of confidence. Preparation involves athletes ensuring that every aspect of their sport that impacts performance is maximized: physical, technical, tactical, nutrition, sleep, team, mental, and equipment. It also means that athletes expend the necessary time and effort into all aspect of their training. If athletes can tell themselves that they have prepared these areas as completely as possible, they will likely be confident that they can use that preparation to perform their best. The goal for athletes before a competition is to be able to say, "I'm as prepared as I can be to find success today."

Mental Tools Protect Confidence

As will be discussed in Chapter 4, a key goal for athletes is to create a toolbox filled with mental tools they can use when something "breaks" and needs to be fixed. Consultants can show athletes how they can get the best use out of these tools in two ways. First, athletes can use the tools to make small adjustments that will enable them to perform at their best. For example, mental tools can be deployed to increase motivation, reduce intensity, or improve focus. Second, just like having plumbing tools to fix a leaky kitchen pipe, they can use their mental tools to fix a problem that arises. For instance, if an athlete gets nervous, they can use their breathing tool to fix the nerves.

Mental tools that athletes can place in their toolbox might include:

- motivating quotes or photos to boost their motivation;
- positive thinking to reinforce their confidence;
- deep breathing to settle anxiety; and
- imagery to regain focus.

Tools that help resolve any problems that arise, whether mental, physical, technical, or tactical, by extension, will increase confidence. A variety of the most commonly used mental tools will be described in Chapter 4.

Adversity Ingrains Confidence

One of the most powerful ways to build confidence is through direct experience of being competent. Moreover, these benefits to confidence are amplified when those "hands on" experiences are in the face of adversity. Athletes can expose themselves to various types of adversity:

- physical (e.g., long or tiring practice);
- environmental (e.g., hot weather or poor field conditions);
- opposition (e.g., a more skilled competitor or a frustrating style of play); and
- technical (e.g., complex new skill, difficult combination of skills).

There are several valuable benefits to athletes exposing themselves to adversity. It increases their belief that they have the ability to react productively in similar conditions in competitions because they've already done it in practice. A successful response to adversity teaches athletes how they can adapt to comparable adversity in competitions. Practicing in adverse conditions also enables athletes to see them as familiar and controllable situations for which they are prepared to face successfully. And, overcoming adversity just makes athletes feel tough!

There are several keys to developing a healthy perspective about the inevitable adversity that athletes will experience that will further support and build confidence:

- Develop the attitude that demanding situations are challenges to seek out, not threats to avoid.
- Believe that experiencing challenges is a necessary part of becoming the best athlete they can be.
- Be well-prepared to meet the challenges.

- Stay positive and motivated in the face of difficulties.
- Focus on what athletes need to do to overcome the challenges.
- Accept that they may fail when confronted with new challenges.
- Never give up!

Risk-Taking Deepens Confidence

As discussed in Chapter 1, athletes must be willing to take appropriate risks to be successful. Risk-taking pushes athletes out of their comfort zones and extends the limits of what they believe themselves capable. Risk-taking is a helpful exercise that athletes can use to reach beyond their perceived boundaries of what is possible. Risks might include taking on a better opponent, trying something new technically or tactically in their sport, pushing themselves in their conditioning efforts, or testing new equipment that might make them better.

Successful risk-taking changes the way athletes think, by showing them that they can do things that they previously didn't believe were possible and, as a result, their confidence in those newly expanded capabilities grows. It also has an emotional benefit by creating confidence-building emotions such as satisfaction, excitement, pride, and inspiration.

Support Bolsters Confidence

Success in sports isn't a solo journey, neither one that can be navigated or in which success is possible alone. Rather, for athletes to achieve their sports goals, they need a group of people to support them. These people can provide a variety of support and encouragement. Family, friends, and teammates can offer emotional support, particularly when things aren't going well. Coaches can provide support specifically related to sports performance. A team's administrative staff can facilitate logistical support. Teachers can offer academic support. Other experts can provide tertiary support such as physical conditioning, sports medicine, sport psychology, and nutrition.

Support is important for confidence because athletes will experience many ups and downs throughout a season based on how they are feeling physically and mentally, how well they are practicing, and recent competitive results. Athletes with a strong support team can count on "their people" to have steadfast confidence in them and demonstrate this by giving them a hug, a pat on the back, a reminder of the work put in, or a "You can do this!" when confidence may be wavering.

Because support is so important to building, maintaining, and regaining confidence, consultants should encourage athletes to actively reach out to and create a team of people who can provide the various types of support they will need on their journey toward their sports goals.

Success Affirms Confidence

All of the exercises discussed above aim to develop and maintain confidence yet will fail to do so if athletes don't affirm their efforts with success. Success shows athletes that their confidence in their ability is justified, making it stronger and more resilient. Importantly, success bolsters athletes' motivation by reinforcing their efforts and inspiring them to renew those efforts in further pursuit of their goals, thus creating a virtuous cycle of increased confidence, effort, and performance.

However, athletes and coaches must understand that success and winning are not mutually exclusive. When most people think of success, they think of a victory in competition. It's not uncommon to hear athletes say, "I'll get my confidence back when I win." However, the paradox here is that success isn't likely without confidence. Rather, success is defined more broadly here. The fact is that athletes have many small victories every day, for example, strength gains in the gym, technical improvement in practice, or staying motivated during a demanding workout. Confidence is progressively built from reflecting on those small wins until the time arrives when athletes' confidence, and all of the other contributors to sports performance, come together and result in a big success in competition.

Other Confidence Exercises

In addition to the exercises just described, several others have been found to be effective in strengthening confidence. These exercises include self-talk, mental imagery (Bandura, 1977; Munroe-Chandler, Hall, & Fishburne, 2008; Williams & Cumming, 2012), observational learning (Hall, Munroe-Chandler, Cumming, Law, Ramsey, & Murphy, 2009), modeling (Vargas-Tonsing, Myers, & Feltz, 2004), routines, and goal setting (Beaumont, Maynard, & Butt, 2015). These exercises will be explored in greater depth in subsequent chapters.

Summary

- Confidence is athletes' belief that they can perform their best and accomplish their sports goals.
- Confidence plays such a central role in sports performance because athletes may have the other capabilities necessary to be successful (e.g., fitness, technical and technical acumen, the best equipment), but if they lack the fundamental belief in those capabilities, then they aren't likely to perform up to those capabilities or achieve their competitive goals.
- Confident thinking on the part of athletes generates positive emotions (e.g., excitement, inspiration) and catalyzes beneficial physiological changes (increased adrenaline and blood flow), leading to improved performance, which reinforces further confident thinking, thus creating a virtuous cycle of confidence and performance.
- The challenge for athletes related to confidence is how they react when those efforts aren't being rewarded, for example, when faced with difficulties learning new sport skills, poor practice or competitive performances, unexpected losses, performance plateaus and declines, or slumps.
- Warning signs of low confidence include self-doubt, pre-competitive anxiety, low effort, and tentative performances.
- Research has demonstrated a significant relationship between high levels of confidence and improved performance, as well as lack of confidence undermining performance.
- Athletes can build and maintain their confidence by, first, gaining an awareness of their confidence and, second, taking active steps to build confidence.
- Practical strategies for developing confidence includes preparation, using mental exercises and tools, responding positively to adversity, taking risks, building a support team, experiencing success, imagery, observational learning and modeling, goal setting, and routines.

References

Bandura, A. (1977). Self-efficacy: Toward a unifying theory of behavioral change. *Psychological Review, 84*(2), 191.

Beaumont, C., Maynard, I. W., & Butt, J. (2015). Effective ways to develop and maintain robust sport-confidence: Strategies advocated by sport psychology consultants. *Journal of Applied Sport Psychology, 27*(3), 301–318.

Craft, L. L., Magyar, T. M., Becker, B. J., & Feltz, D. L. (2003). The relationship between the Competitive State Anxiety Inventory-2 and sport performance: A meta-analysis. *Journal of Sport and Exercise Psychology, 25*(1), 44–65.

Feltz, D. L. (1988). Self-confidence and sports performance. *Exercise and Sport Sciences Reviews, 16*, 423–457.

Gould, D., Greenleaf, C., Chung, Y., & Guinan, D. (2002). A survey of US Atlanta and Nagano Olympians: Variables perceived to influence performance. *Research Quarterly for Exercise and Sport, 73*(2), 175–186.

Hall, C. R., Munroe-Chandler, K. J., Cumming, J., Law, B., Ramsey, R., & Murphy, L. (2009). Imagery and observational learning use and their relationship to sport confidence. *Journal of Sports Sciences, 27*(4), 327–337.

Hays, K., Thomas, O., Maynard, I., & Bawden, M. (2009). The role of confidence in world-class sport performance. *Journal of Sports Sciences, 27*(11), 1185–1199.

Lazarus, R. S. (2000). How emotions influence performance in competitive sports. *Sport Psychologist, 14*(3), 229.

Moritz, S. E., Feltz, D. L., Fahrbach, K. R., & Mack, D. E. (2000). The relation of self-efficacy measures to sport performance: A meta-analytic review. *Research Quarterly for Exercise and Sport, 71*(3), 280–294.

Munroe-Chandler, K., Hall, C., & Fishburne, G. (2008). Playing with confidence: The relationship between imagery use and self-confidence and self-efficacy in youth soccer players. *Journal of Sports Sciences, 26*(14), 1539–1546.

Ravizza, K., & Fifer, A. (2015). Increasing awareness for sport performance. In J. M. Williams & V. Krane (Eds.), *Applied sport psychology: Personal growth to peak performance*, 7th ed. (pp. 176–187). New York, NY: McGraw-Hill.

Vargas-Tonsing, T. M., Myers, N. D., & Feltz, D. L. (2004). Coaches' and athletes' perceptions of efficacy-enhancing techniques. *The Sport Psychologist, 18*(4), 397–414.

Vealey, R. S. (2001). Understanding and enhancing self-confidence in athletes. *Handbook of Sport Psychology, 2*, 550–565.

Vealey, R. S., Garner-Holman, M., Hayashi, S. W., & Giacobbi, P. (1998). Sources of sport-confidence: Conceptualization and instrument development. *Journal of Sport and Exercise Psychology, 20*(1), 54–80.

Weinberg, R. S., & Gould, D. (2014). *Foundations of Sport and Exercise Psychology*, 6th ed. Champaign, IL: Human Kinetics.

Williams, J. M., Zinsser, N., & Bunker, L. (2015). Cognitive techniques for building confidence and enhancing performance. In J. M. Williams & V. Krane (Eds.), *Applied sport psychology: Personal growth to peak performance*, 7th ed. (pp. 274–303). New York, NY: McGraw-Hill.

Williams, S. E., & Cumming, J. (2012). Sport imagery ability predicts trait confidence, and challenge and threat appraisal tendencies. *European Journal of Sport Science, 12*(6), 499–508.

Woodman, T., & Hardy, L. (2003). The relative impact of cognitive anxiety and self-confidence upon sport performance: A meta-analysis. *Journal of Sports Sciences, 21*(6), 443–457.

Zinsser, N., Perkins, L. D., Gervais, P. D., & Burbelo, G. A. (2004). Military application of performance-enhancement psychology. *Military Review, 84*(5), 62.

INTENSITY

Dafna Aaronson and Jim Taylor

This section of Chapter 3 explores the physiological changes that athletes experience in their sports participation. Arousal and anxiety are words commonly used to describe these physiological shifts, and are operationally understood as a "general physiological and psychological activation of the organism that varies on a continuum from deep sleep to intense excitement" (Gould & Udry, 1994, p. 33). Current research recognizes arousal and anxiety as interdependent between both physiological and psychological constructs (Craft, Magyar, Becker, & Feltz, 2003; Gould & Udry, 1994). Acknowledging that evidence supports arousal assessment as a multidimensional, this section focuses on the well-understood physiological responses to sport participation separate from its cognitive component.

CASP has chosen the term "intensity," rather than arousal or anxiety to describe this indispensable contributor to athletic performance that involves athletes being aware of, understanding, and regulating their physiological responses to their sports efforts. *CASP* chooses not to use these terms for several reasons. First, arousal has associations with sex which can be a distraction in its use with athletes. Second, anxiety carries with it a negative association; no athlete wants to feel anxious. Yet, every athlete wants to experience some of the physiological changes related to anxiety.

Admittedly, intensity also has different meanings that may sometimes cause confusion with athletes. For example, intensity can be seen as a mental state that is akin to focused effort. At the same time, its advantages outweigh its liabilities including its positive associations with athletic performance and the ability of athletes to assessment themselves along a continuum.

Simply put, intensity is the amount of physiological activation athletes experience as changes in:

- heart rate;
- respiration;
- blood flow and pressure;
- adrenaline;
- muscular activation;
- sensory acuity;
- cortisol; and
- activation of the immune system.

Intensity lies along a continuum from very relaxed (sleep) at one end and very intense (extreme fear). Athletes' ideal intensity, that is, the level at which they are physiologically prepared to perform their best, lies somewhere between those two extremes. Variables impacting how physiological activation is perceived (facilitative or debilitative) includes if the sport is played by a team or individual, if the skill required is open or closed, and the level of athlete (elite or recreational). The sport that athletes participate in also plays a role in the level of intensity that best serves them. Sports have different physiological demands that partially dictate what intensity is most effective to maximize performance. For example, those that engage large muscle groups and require speed, strength, and explosiveness, need higher levels of intensity; for example, sprinting, wrestling, and hammer throw. Conversely, sports that require fine motor skills or endurance necessitate lower intensity; for instance, golf, riflery, and marathon running. Intensity may be the most critical component to athletic performance once the competition begins. Regardless of how mentally prepared athletes are, if their bodies aren't at their ideal intensity, they will not be able to perform at their highest level. The challenge is that "one size doesn't fit all" with intensity. Some athletes perform well relaxed, others moderately intense, and still others extremely intense, based on their genetic make-up and learned experiences.

Intensity affects athletes in two ways. First, they experience intensity physically in a variety of ways including heart rate, respiration, and adrenaline. Second, as previously noted, athletes develop a perception about the intensity, particularly in terms of whether it will help or hurt them in their sports efforts. Specifically, athletes may experience intensity the same way physically, but their perception of it will determine how it influences their performances. For example, does an athlete view their intensity as excitement or anxiety, calm or lethargy? This psychological component is important because that interpretation of intensity has a reciprocal effect on other mental muscles. Athletes' perception of their intensity will affect their motivation, confidence, focus, and emotions, and by extension, how prepared they feel for an upcoming practice or competition. The goal is for athletes to reach and maintain their ideal intensity consistently, thus enabling them to get the most out of their practice efforts and competitive performances.

Warning Signs of Overintensity and Underintensity

Intensity catalyzes many different symptoms that athletes can interpret as either interfering or facilitative to sports performance. Creating an awareness of when athletes aren't at their ideal intensity is the first step in their learning to reach that optimal level.

Overintensity

Also referred to as anxiety and nerves, overintensity has a number of physiological and psychological effects that can hurt sports performance:

- muscle tension;
- short or choppy breathing;
- poor posture;
- stiff gait;
- loss of fine motor coordination;
- decline in motivation and confidence;
- difficulty focusing;
- negative emotions;
- rushed preparations and performances;
- tentative efforts; and
- tense performances.

Underintensity

Though not experienced as much as overintensity, underintensity can also hurt athletes' practice and competitive efforts. A set of red flags that lie at the opposite end of the intensity continuum are indicative of underintensity:

- low energy;
- insufficient muscle activation;
- low strength, stamina, and agility;

- low motivation;
- easily distracted;
- lethargic preparations;
- apathetic efforts; and
- uninspiring performances.

Theory and Research

Four primary theories attempt to explain the relationship between intensity and performance. The original base-line came from the inverted-U theory which suggests that the relationship between intensity and performance is curve-linear, where performance improves with increased intensity up to a point after which greater intensity hurts performance (Yerkes & Dodson, 1908). Yerkes and Dodson's theory dominated the theoretical and empirical investigation of intensity until the latter part of the 20th century at which point three competing theories attempted to more accurately explain the impact of intensity on sports performance.

Catastrophe theory (Hardy, 1990) posited that physiological activation interacts with cognitive anxiety to determine its impact on performance. Hanin's Optimal Zones of Functioning (Hanin, 1980) suggests that athletes react to intensity in different ways with some performing best when arousal is low, others when it is moderate, and still others when it is high. The multidimensional anxiety theory (Burton, 1990) argues that cognitive anxiety and self-confidence mediate the relationship between somatic anxiety (i.e., intensity) and sports performance. Common themes found in these theories include:

- Acknowledging the interplay between physiological intensity and its cognitive interpretation.
- There exists an optimal level of intensity yielding high performance.
- This optimal level is highly individualized and not necessarily at the midpoint along the continuum.
- Because of the cognitive interpretations, excessive levels of intensity are not always associated with lower performance levels.

As such, an athlete's individual recipe for optimal performance depends on their awareness of both their physiological manifestations of their intensity and how they perceive those physical indications.

Studies focusing on the impact of intensity on performance are limited and have not produced conclusive results. For example, compared with cognitive techniques (e.g., attentional focus, imagery) somatic-energizing techniques (e.g., getting pumped up, mad) is linked to improved performance in strength tasks, however ineffective with motor tasks requiring more skill and timing (Gould, Weinberg, & Jackson, 1980; Weinberg, Gould, & Jackson, 1980). Overall, the evidence suggests that performance may benefit from increased intensity in some sports situations, but not in others.

On the other hand, greater focus is given to reducing intensity and regulating somatic experiences with the goal of improving performance. Modalities such as biofeedback, relaxation, cognitive-behavior strategies, and routines are the most commonly used tools for regulating intensity (Zaichkowsky & Fuchs, 1988).

Practical Implications

Given the importance of intensity to sports performance, an essential role consultants can play is to help athletes to identify and reach their ideal intensity, considering both somatic and cognitive effects when matching techniques to athletes' specific cause of over/under intensity (Gould & Udry, 1994). Fortunately, unlike the other mental muscles which are quite ethereal in nature, intensity is tangible, making it easier to recognize and intervene.

Assessing Ideal Intensity

Athletes' intensity is akin to a thermostat whose purpose it is to maintain the temperature of a home. When a home's temperature becomes too hot or too cold, the thermostat is activated and the temperature reaches a more comfortable level. Intensity works the same way. Athletes can become sensitive to their body's "temperature" and adjust their internal "thermostat" to reach their ideal intensity. Athletes can think of their intensity as their internal temperature that needs to be adjusted periodically

Identifying ideal intensity offers athletes several benefits. First, they understand what their ideal intensity is which enables to them to be more sensitive to when it shifts either too high or too low in practice and competitions. Second, athletes can recognize those situations in which their intensity may move away from their ideal level, for example, in important competitions or when they are behind. Finally, they can use a variety of strategies to actively reach and maintain their ideal intensity in practice and competitions.

There are two ways for athletes to identify their ideal intensity. First, they can think back to past competitions in which they performed well and in which they performed poorly, and recall their intensity before each. What were they thinking, how did their bodies feel, and what emotions were they experiencing? Most athletes will see a clear pattern in their intensity when they performed well and a very different pattern when they performed poorly. More real-time assessments can be recorded or journaled shortly prior to and just after a competition to most accurately recall, describe, and reflect on the impact of intensity on their sports performances (Wiggins, 1998).

Athletes can also experiment with different levels of intensity in practice. They can run through drills or simulated competitions at low, medium, and high intensity, and correlate how they feel with how they perform. As with the previous exercise, a distinct pattern will likely emerge in which athletes perform better at one level of intensity. This experiment should be conducted over a period of several days to ensure consistency of results.

Recent advancements in biofeedback provide objective means for observing, gauging, and attaining optimal intensity levels. Biofeedback not only offers athletes the means to directly assess, but also modify their intensity (Fredrikson & Engel, 1985). Once this knowledge has been gained, athletes will have an understanding of their ideal intensity. Consultants can then provide a variety of physical and mental exercises and tools to help athletes reach their ideal intensity. Best results are attained when athletes commit to learning and automating strategies into mental preparation routines (Crews, 1993).

Intensity Exercises

For most athletes, an increase in intensity prior to a competition is natural and inevitable. The associated physical changes are their bodies' way of preparing for the challenge that lies ahead. To some degree, these shifts can help performance. At the same time, if the intensity "temperature" gets turned up too high, it can be perceived as anxiety and can hurt performance. Conversely, though less common, athletes can also experience too low intensity due to a variety of causes including a lack of motivation, overconfidence, or distraction. In either case, not being at ideal intensity means that athletes are physiologically incapable of performing at their highest level. To prevent this turn for the worse in either direction, athletes can employ "psych-down" or "psych-up" exercises and tools ensuring that their intensity reaches and maintains an ideal level.

Breathing

When athletes become overly intense, breathing is an immediate result that impairs performance by limiting the amount of oxygen that gets into their systems. One of the simplest ways, then, to lower intensity, is to have athletes take slow, deep breaths and increase their oxygen intake.

Deep breathing benefits athletes in several physical and mental ways. Foremost, it makes certain that athletes get sufficient oxygen for their bodies to perform optimally. Additionally, they feel more relaxed, comfortable, and in control. Athletes also gain confidence and are able to set aside negative thoughts and emotions that often accompany overintensity. Deep breathing also acts as a focusing tool that brings athletes' attention back to themselves and what they need to do to get prepared. Combining a centering breath with positive self-talk also helps achieve these goals.

Forceful breathing has the opposite effect physically while bringing similar effects mentally. When athletes find themselves under intense, they can use breathing that involves a deep inhale and a forceful exhale. This high-intensity breathing still ensures adequate intake of oxygen and its ancillary benefits. It generates more physical activity and causes athletes to feel more energized. Forceful breathing also triggers increased motivation and confidence, and a more aggressive attitude.

Muscle Relaxation/Activation

Muscle tension is a symptom that overly intense athletes experience before competitions. This warning sign is perhaps the most debilitating because tense muscles don't allow for optimal coordination and mobility. Muscle relaxation offers similar physical and mental benefits as deep breathing, including decreasing oxygen consumption, heart rate, respiration rate as well as a reduction in muscle tension. There are two muscle-relaxation exercises that athletes can use away from, before, and in competitions (during breaks): passive relaxation and progressive relaxation.

Passive relaxation involves athletes imagining that tension is a liquid that permeates their muscles causing physical discomfort. To use passive relaxation, athletes can:

- assume a comfortable position;
- take several deep breaths;
- allow the tension to empty from their bodies; and
- focus on their general state of physical relaxation and the accompanying calm.

Progressive relaxation (Jacobson, 1925) is best used when athletes experience significant muscle tension where passive relaxation isn't effective. It involves relaxing muscle groups (e.g., legs and buttocks, chest and back, shoulders and arms, face and neck).

To use progressive relaxation, athletes can:

- assume a comfortable position;
- beginning with the legs and buttocks, tighten muscles for five seconds, release, take a deep breath, and repeat for each muscle group;
- focus on the differences between tension and relaxation; and
- focus on their general state of physical relaxation and mental calmness.

Intensity is physiological activity in its most basic form. When athletes lack sufficient intensity, they can use muscle activation as a tool to raise intensity. The most immediate means of increasing intensity is for them to simply move their bodies; they can walk, run, jump, and do lunges, push-ups, or squats. Anything that gets their heart pumping, blood flowing, and muscles firing will raise your intensity.

High-energy body language is another tool that athletes can use to raise their intensity. When they, for example, pump their fist or slap your thigh, those physical actions increase intensity and enable athletes to feel more fired up mentally and emotionally.

Self-talk

When athletes experience overintensity, their thinking often goes into overdrive and shifts toward negativity including doubt, pessimism, and worry. This change tends to cause an ever-spiraling vicious cycle of physical overintensity and negative thinking. When this occurs, athletes can use calming self-talk to settle themselves down physically and mentally by saying, for example, "Let's relax," "Calm down," and "Be cool." This self-talk quiets the mind and relaxes the body.

In contrast, a common cause of declines in intensity is letdown self-talk. When athletes think to themselves, "I've got this," "They're done," or "I have no chance," they are sending a signal to their bodies that they can turn off because they no longer need to perform. When this happens, performance declines. To counter letdown self-talk, athletes can use high-energy self-talk such as "Keep going," "Let's finish this," and "Stay fired up." Said with passion and volume, this self-talk activates athletes' physically and increases motivation, confidence, and focus mentally.

Music

Music is a tool that athletes frequently use to control their intensity. Many Olympic and professional athletes use music to help them reach their ideal intensity and even have different playlists depending on how they feel before a competition. Music affects us in a powerful way physically, mentally, and emotional. It can cause us to feel excited, sad, angry, or inspired, and it can also fire us up or calm us down. As such, it is both a powerful and enjoyable way for athletes to adjust their intensity.

Calming music offers athletes several benefits. It slows breathing and relaxes muscles. Quite simply, it makes athletes feel comfortable. Mentally, music causes athletes to feel motivated and confident. It also generates positive emotions such as joy and contentment. Calming music also helps athletes to distract themselves from the pressures of competition and to focus on their preparations. Typical calming music can include classical, jazz, or New Age. The overall sensation of listening to relaxing music is a generalized sense of ease, comfort, and well-being.

Music can also be helpful to athletes who need to increase your intensity and get them psyched up and motivated. High-energy music increases the physical parameters such as hear rate, blood flow, and adrenaline. It generates intense emotions such as excitement and inspiration. High-energy music also instills motivation, confidence, and a "bring it on" attitude. Common types of high-energy music include rock, hip-hop, and heavy metal. The broad experience of listening to high-energy music is a generalized sense of excitement and energy. The impact of music on athletic performance will be explored in greater depth in Chapter 4.

Mental Imagery

Mental imagery is another powerful exercise and tool that athletes can use to achieve their ideal intensity. This technique involves athletes seeing and feeling themselves "in their mind's eye" performing in their sport. Imagery is useful for intensity control because athletes can imagine themselves in either high- or low-intensity situations and then use psych-up or psych-down exercises and tools to reach their ideal intensity see themselves performing well. Mental imagery will be examined further in more detail in Chapter 4.

Mindfulness

The Mindfulness–Acceptance–Commitment (MAC) approach is the most notably studied and formalized approach to the use of mindfulness in sports. MAC emphasizes nonjudgment of one's current internal state and in-the-moment awareness and acceptance of current physiological experiences as opposed to "controlling" them (Gardner & Moore, 2004). MAC is a seven-module protocol that is typically administered by trained consultants or used by athletes on their own. Mindfulness will be explored in detail in Chapter 4.

Smiling

Smiling is one of the most effective exercises and tools that athletes can use to reduce intensity. Considerable research has demonstrated that smiling, even if forced, has a dramatic impact on our psychology and physiology. This relationship occurs for several reasons. First, in our upbringing and culture, we learn through conditioning and association that smiling means we're happy. Second, research has shown that smiling triggers neurochemical and hormonal changes related to the parasympathetic nervous system. These changes include the relief of endorphins and slowed heart rate, respiration, and blood flow. When athletes experience over-intensity, they can mitigate it by smiling. The smiles can be generated externally by engaging in fun activities (e.g., talking to a funny person, watching a funny movie) or internally by thinking pleasing thoughts or telling a joke. They can also be manufactured by simply raising the corners of the mouth and forming a smile. Though genuine smiles appear to have a greater impact physically and psychologically, forced smiles have also been found to produce positive changes.

For all of these intensity exercises and tools to be maximally effective for athletes, athletes should use them regularly and incorporate them into their practice and competitive regimens. The goal is for athletes to build them into their routines and habits so that when they experience overintensity or underintensity, they can use these exercises and tools automatically, their intensity will shift to an ideal level, and they will be better prepared to perform your best.

Summary

- Intensity has been chosen over arousal or anxiety because of its positive associations with performance and its absence of associations related to sex and discomfort, respectively.
- Intensity is the amount of physiological activation athletes experience as changes in heart rate, respiration, blood flow and pressure, adrenaline, muscular activation, sensory acuity, cortisol, and activation of the immune system.
- Intensity is a continuum with very relaxed (sleep) at one end and very intense (extreme fear) at the other.
- Athletes' ideal intensity, that is, the level at which they are physiologically prepared to perform their best, lies somewhere between those two extremes.
- Intensity may be the most critical component to athletic performance once the competition begins because, regardless of how mentally prepared athletes are, if their bodies aren't at its ideal intensity, they will not be able to perform at their highest level.
- The sport that athletes participate in plays a role in the level of intensity that best serves them based on the different physiological demands of each sport.
- Athletes may experience overintensity as muscle tension, choppy breathing, loss of fine motor coordination, difficulty focusing, negative emotions, and tentative efforts.
- They may experience underintensity as low energy, insufficient muscle activation, low strength, stamina, and agility, low motivation, easily distracted, and uninspiring performances.
- Research has demonstrated that intensity is a significant predictor of athletic success.
- Ideal intensity can be assessed by having athletes compare and identifying patterns in how they felt before successful and unsuccessful performances, by experimenting with different levels of intensity in practice, and by using biofeedback.
- Athletes can adjust their intensity to their ideal with breathing, muscle relaxation/activation, self-talk, music, mental imagery, mindfulness, and smiling.

References

Burton, D. (1990). Multimodal stress management in sport: Current status and future directions. In G. Jones & L. Hardy (Eds.), *Stress and performance in sport* (pp. 171–202). Chichester: John Wiley.

Craft, L. L., Magyar, T. M., Becker, B. J., & Feltz, D. L. (2003). The relationship between the Competitive State Anxiety Inventory-2 and sport performance: A meta-analysis. *Journal of Sport and Exercise Psychology, 25,* 44–65.

Crews, D. (1993). Self-regulation strategies in sport and exercise. In R. Singer, M. Murphy, & L. Tennet (Eds.), *Handbook on research in sport psychology* (pp. 557–568). New York, NY: Macmillan.

Fredrikson, M., & Engel, B. (1985). Learned control of heart rate during exercise in patients with borderline hypertension. *European Journal of Applied Physiology, 54,* 315–320.

Gardner, F. L., & Moore, Z. E. (2004). A Mindfulness–Acceptance–Commitment (MAC) based approach to athletic performance enhancement: Theoretical considerations. *Behavior Therapy, 35,* 707–723.

Gould, D., & Udry, E. (1994). Psychological skills for enhancing performance: Arousal regulation strategies. *Medicine and Science in Sports and Exercise, 26,* 478–485.

Gould, D., Weinberg, R., & Jackson, A. (1980). Mental preparation strategies, cognitions, and strength performance. *Journal of Sport Psychology, 2,* 329–339.

Hanin, Y. (1980). A study of anxiety in sports. In W. Straub (Ed.), *Sport psychology: An analysis of athlete behavior.* (pp. 236–249). Ithaca, NY: Movement.

Hardy, L. (1990). A catastrophe model of performance in sport. In G. Jones & L. Hardy (Eds.), *Stress and performance in sport* (pp. 81–106). Chichester: John Wiley.

Jacobson, E. (1925). Progressive relaxation. *The American Journal of Psychology, 36*(1), 73–87.

Weinberg, R., Gould, D., & Jackson, A. (1980) Cognition and motor performance: Effect of psyching-up strategies on three motor tasks. *Cognitive Therapy and Research, 4,* 239–245.

Wiggins, M. S. (1998). Anxiety intensity and direction: Preperformance temporal patterns and expectations in athletes. *Journal of Applied Sport Psychology, 10,* 201–211.

Yerkes, R. M., & Dodson, J. D. (1908). The relation of strength of stimulus to rapidity of habit-formation. *Journal of Comparative Neurology and Psychology, 18,* 459–482.

Zaichkowsky, L., & Fuchs, C. (1988). Biofeedback applications in exercise and athletic performance. *Exercise and Sport Sciences Reviews, 16,* 381–421.

FOCUS

Abby Keenan and Jim Taylor

This section is another example of *CASP* choosing a vocabulary that is different from that used in most of the research and applied writing in applied sport psychology. Concentration and attention are the words that are most frequently used to describe the phenomenon to be discussed in this section. *CASP* opts not to use these words for several reasons. First, concentration has associations with a narrow and singular approach as the "direction of attention on a single object" (Merriam-Webster, 2004a, p. 149), when many sports require broader awareness and focus on more than one cue. Concentration also carries with the sense that athletes have to expend considerable effort in the process of paying attention to relevant cues. Yet, as athletes describe it, when optimized, this experience is effortless. Second, attention typically refers to considering, taking notice of, or applying the mind to something (Merriam-Webster, 2004b). Moreover, "paying attention" carries a negative connotation, especially as an admonition from a parent, coach, or teacher.

CASP has selected the term "focus" because it more accurately represents the experience that athletes have in practice and competition. Focusing involves athletes directing their attention onto something relevant in the sports context and possessing the ability to adjust focus as needed based on the situational demands of a sport along important dimensions as needed. Additionally, focusing goes beyond just the awareness of something in athletes' internal or external sensory fields, but rather includes using that information for analysis and decision making (Furley, Bertrams, Englert, & Delphia, 2013; Hüttermann & Memmert, 2018) as well as communication and action.

Simply put, focus involves athletes directing their awareness, thoughts, and efforts toward a particular goal. It is one of the most critical factors for high-level performance (Janelle & Hatfield, 2008). With appropriately allocated focus, athletes can notice and process the right information at the right time, thus enabling them to perform their best.

Effective focus means athletes attending only to cues that will help them perform up to their fullest ability and avoiding distractions that hurt performance (Furley et al., 2013). Focus can include task-relevant external cues such as teammates, opponents, score, time remaining, and environmental conditions. External cues that benefit focus most often provide information to help athletes make tactical or strategic decisions (Bernier, Codron, Thienot, & Fournier, 2011). At times, effective focus can also involve internal cues such as body mechanics, technique, tactics, confidence, and intensity. An essential aspect of effective focus is the ability of athletes to adjust their focus internally and externally as needed in practice or competition.

Conversely, poor focus involves processing internal and external cues that take athletes' focus away from what they need to do to perform their best (Janelle, Singer, & Williams, 1999). There are two types of harmful cues. *Interfering* cues that hinder performance are those that directly impede it such as negative thoughts, anxiety, or concern over an upcoming opponent. *Extraneous* cues are those that don't directly hurt performance, but rather impair it by diverting focus away from an effective focus such as homework that is due or feeling hungry.

Value of Focus

There are three important benefits to an effective focus for athletes in their practices and competitive performances. First, athletes who are focused are more *effective* in their efforts because they are directing their attention onto what they need to do to perform their best, whether they are working on a new technique in practice or they are attempting to outplay an opponent in competition. Second, when they are focused, athletes are more *efficient* in practice because their focus enables them to get the most out of whatever they are working on, therefore minimizing wasted effort or time. In competition, athletes' performances are more efficient when they are externally focused, as this allows automaticity to take over, therefore taking less time to execute (Weiss, Reber, & Owen, 2008). Finally, the more *consistent* athletes' focus, the more consistent their effort, execution, and performances.

Three Focus Goals

Athletes should have three goals in finding and maintaining their ideal focus. They need to recognize the cues that allow them to focus and perform their best, whether internal (e.g., thoughts, emotions, physical sensations) or external (e.g., targets, conditions). Athletes must also isolate the internal (e.g., negative thoughts, physical anxiety) and external (e.g., spectators, officials) distractions that interfere with ideal focus. Third, they can actively and consistently focus on the helpful cues and ignore or block out the distracting cues (Janelle et al., 1999; Moran, 2009) while shifting focus in order to prepare, execute, and evaluate their performances effectively (Bernier et al., 2011).

Theory and Research

It is important for consultants to understand the properties and functions of focus to best support athletes. These qualities provide clarity on what athletes can and cannot do with their focus as well as how to best leverage it for optimal performance.

Properties of Focus

First and foremost, focus is a resource with limited capacity; we can only consciously focus on one thing at any given time (Schmidt & Lee, 2005; Moran, 2009). According to the dual-task paradigm, when athletes attempt to perform two tasks simultaneously (i.e., multitasking), if the combined demands exceed capacity, the secondary task will interfere with the performance of the primary task (Schmidt & Lee, 2005). Multitasking slows thinking, degrades memory and learning, and elevates stress-related hormones (Kirn, 2007). Of particular relevance to sports, multitasking also slows reaction time and causes athletes to miss relevant situational cues (Strayer & Johnston, 2001). However, if the primary task is automatic, meaning it has been practiced so much that it does not require conscious thought, athletes can perform two or more actions at the same time (Schmidt & Lee, 2005; Moran, 2009). For example, experienced basketball players can dribble the ball and scan the court simultaneously.

Nideffer (1976) described four attentional styles that lie along the dimensions of width (i.e., broad to narrow) and direction (i.e., external or internal):

- broad–internal (e.g., analysis, strategizing);
- broad–external (e.g., environmental awareness);
- narrow–internal (e.g., problem solving); and
- narrow–external (e.g., skill execution).

Within the framework of the aforementioned properties, focus serves three main functions (Petersen & Posner, 2012):

- alerting (reaching and maintaining optimal vigilance or readiness);
- orienting (selecting and attending to particular information); and
- executive control (consciously directing focus by resolving attentional conflict).

Obstacles to Focus

Focus has limits and takes effort on the part of athletes to establish and maintain. As a result, there are several primary obstacles to effective focus. First, distractions can be internal or external, both of which steal focus away from the task at hand (Moran, 2009). Common external distractions are visual or auditory, including spectators, opponents, noise, practice or field conditions, and weather. Frequent internal distractions include physical sensations (e.g., pain or fatigue), negative thoughts (e.g., worry, concern, or doubt), unpleasant emotions (e.g., fear, frustration, disappointment), and a preoccupation with results, the past, and the future (Moran, 2009). Worry can be particularly detrimental as it adds to cognitive load and can athletes to exceed their attentional capacity threshold (Mullen, Hardy, & Tattersall, 2005).

Distractions can also be caused by athletes not having defined goals or a clear process in their practice sessions. Quite simply, if athletes don't know where they are going or what they need to do to get there, they're going to be unable to focus effectively because they won't know where to direct their focus. The result will be unfocused effort, poor quality training, and few gains in practice.

Anxiety also plays a role in athletes' focusing ability. Anxious individuals tend to focus more on potential threats, are less capable of shifting their attention, and are more easily distracted by task-irrelevant cues, all causing decreases in performance (Eysenck, Derakshan, Santos, & Calvo, 2007). Moreover, athletes with anxiety experience cognitive interference, where they become preoccupied with irrelevant thoughts, such as worry about their performance (Sarason, Sarason, & Pierce, 1990). This phenomenon is also seen in young athletes, resulting in negative, irrelevant, or irregular thoughts, resulting poor focus and performance (McCarthy, Allen, & Jones, 2013).

The level of intensity, commonly referred to as arousal or activation in the sport psychology literature, that athletes feel in practice and competition also impacts their ability to focus. If intensity is too low, athletes will lack alertness and their focus will be unfocused or scattered. If intensity is too high, focus will be directed onto the psychological and emotional causes of the overintensity as well as their physical symptoms. With high intensity, athletes tend to pay attention to the wrong cues as their focus becomes narrow (Easterbrook, 1959; Janelle et al., 1999) like "tunnel vision" and gradually becomes more internal (Nideffer, 1976). When this occurs, internal focus on mechanics, or consciously monitoring and controlling movements, can degrade performance in the moment (Weiss et al., 2008) as it causes skilled athletes to break down automatic skills into step-by-step processes (Bernier et al., 2011). Additionally, heightened intensity causes athletes to experience more frequent shifts between relevant and irrelevant cues, thereby decreasing efficiency of focus, particularly resulting in delayed response speed and accuracy (Janelle & Hatfield, 2008).

Another significant obstacle to focus involves athletes focusing on factors outside of their control (Sowa, 1992) such as results and other competitors rather than on the process, particularly during competition. In either case, uncontrollables take athletes' minds off of what they need to do to perform well. Moreover, they cause negative thinking and emotions as well as exacerbate overintensity, which creates additional distractions and further erodes focus.

Practical Implications

With an understanding of what focus is and how it impacts sports performance, consultants can then help athletes to strengthen their focus muscle with various exercises and provide tools for when focus declines.

Assessing Focus

Research indicates that athletes can develop all four attentional styles (narrow–internal, narrow–external, broad–internal, broad–external) and shift focus within practice and competitive situations as needed (Nideffer, 1976). At the same time, athletes tend to have a preferred style with which they are most comfortable and gravitate toward (Nideffer, 1976; Weiss et al., 2008). A key goal in strengthening focus is for athletes to identify their favored style as well as gain flexibility in shifting from style to style based on the practice and competitive demands they experience.

One way to recognize their dominant style is for athletes to remember past competitions when they performed well and poorly (Nideffer, 2001). This analysis can be accomplished by gaining an understanding of all of the styles and reflecting on which they have used previously (Weiss et al., 2008). It's important for athletes to consider what style they tended toward or felt more comfortable with and what style they found difficult to maintain before and during a competition (Nideffer, 2001). Most athletes will demonstrate a pattern in which they perform their best with one style and perform poorly with another style.

Athletes can also experiment with different styles in practice and then in less important competitions. Through direct and immediate experience, they learn which style helps them focus and which they find distracting. As with recalling past competitions, a pattern will likely become apparent in which one style works and the other ones don't.

The ability for athletes to recognize and shift their style when appropriate is important in typical practices as well as competitive preparations and performances. It is especially valuable in pressure situations such as important competitions. There is a tendency for athletes under pressure to revert back to a style that they may be comfortable with, but may interfere with rather than help their performances. For example, if an athlete tends to overthink (narrow-internal), they may find themselves turning their focus inward when the pressure is on in competition, despite needing to extend focus broadly and externally.

Consultants can also have athletes take the Test of Attentional and Interpersonal Style (TAIS; Nideffer, 2001). The TAIS is a self-report questionnaire that was developed for athletes to identify their dominant focus style and their focusing strengths and weaknesses. TAIS results can then be used to develop interventions to strengthen the focus muscle, improve practice and competitive performances, or minimize mistakes (Nideffer, 2001).

Foundation of Focus Control

An essential goal for athletes is to establish and maintain effective focus to ensure that focus helps rather than hurts their practice efforts and competitive performances. The first step in developing focus control is for athletes to understand the broad areas toward which they should direct their focus:

- Focus on what athletes can control: If athletes focus only those areas they can control (e.g., their mind, body, and efforts) and avoid focusing on that which they have no control (e.g., opponents, weather, conditions), they will focus on what they need to do to perform well.
- Process focus: As discussed in detail in Chapter 1, when athletes focus on the process of their performances (e.g., technique, tactics), rather than the possible outcomes (e.g., possible victory or defeat), they are more likely to do what is necessary to get the outcomes they want.
- Thinking vs. focusing: When athletes can focus on their performances (i.e., attend to relevant internal and external cues in an impartial, objective, and unemotional way) instead of thinking about their performances (i.e., analyzing, critiquing, and judging) in the moment, they clear their minds and free their bodies to perform their best.

Focus Exercises and Tools

The above areas lay the foundation for an effective focus. In addition, athletes can employ a variety of exercises and tools to maximize their focus in their practice and competitive efforts.

Have Clear Goals and a Process

A simple fact about focusing is that athletes can't focus on something if they don't know where to direct their focus. The first step in effective focus is to set a goal that specifies athletes' focus and therefore provides direction (Gould, 2010; Weinberg, Butt, & Knight, 2001). In practice, a goal might be technical or tactical. For a tennis player, a practice goal might be "I'm going to work on coming into the net on short balls." In competition, a goal might be to play aggressively or stay on their toes. For a swimmer, a practice goal may be to breathe every five strokes during the main set while a competitive goal might be "I'm going to negative split."

The next step for athletes is to operationalize the goal with a process that provides the appropriate focus. This helps athletes direct focus to task-relevant information that is within their control (Gould, 2010; Moran, 2009). For the above tennis player in practice, the process might be to focus specifically on the early trajectory of the ball, a quick reaction, and aggressive movement toward the net. For the swimmer in practice, the process would involve counting to five strokes throughout the main set.

Once goals are identified, a process involving an internal focus on step-by-step procedures of skill execution is helpful for novices still learning about their sport (Maurer & Munzert, 2013). Conversely, much research suggests that athletes should focus externally while performing in order to maintain automaticity (Wulf & Su, 2007), particularly in closed, self-paced tasks or sports (Lidor, Ziv, & Tenenbaum, 2013) and for experts (Maurer & Munzert, 2013). An external focus involves a movement-induced effect of a skill (e.g., the pendulum-like motion of a club in golf) or focusing on an external cue in the environment (e.g., the black line at the bottom of the pool in swimming or the trajectory of a ball leaving the bat in baseball).

Identify and Limit Distractions

Regardless of how clear athletes' focus goals and processes are, effective focus won't be possible if they are distracted by frequent interfering or irrelevant cues (Janelle et al., 1999). As a result, it's useful for athletes to proactively identify internal and external distractions in their typical practice and competitive environments. In creating a list of distractions, consultants can lead a discussion about how athletes plan to effectively respond to distractions if they occur and when to apply them to practice or competitive situations (Moran, 2009). For example, a basketball player may identify heckling fans during a free throw attempt as a distraction. A consultant could then help her to develop a plan and use focus tools to mitigate the distraction.

Common external distractions include teammates, competitors, coaches, family and friends, media, fans, and the scoreboard. Typical internal distractions include negative thoughts, irrelevant thoughts, unpleasant emotions, and physical anxiety. Once these distractions have been identified, consultants can help athletes to develop internal and external focusing strategies to mitigate or remove them (Lidor et al., 2013). For example, if an athlete is distracted by worry about results before a competition, they can use music (Mesagno, Marchant, & Morris, 2009) or talking to teammates to shift their focus away from the distraction. Consultants and coaches can also help athletes to simulate situations with distractions and practice applying focus tools to prepare for competition.

Keywords

A valuable tool for establishing, maintaining, and regaining focus involves athletes creating and repeating a keyword, or cue, that reminds them of an effective focus for their given sports situation. Keywords should be short (i.e., one word or a short phrase), specific, relevant, vivid, controllable, and positively phrased descriptors that cue athletes to focus appropriately (Moran, 2009). In identifying keywords, it's helpful for athletes to keep their skill level, goals, objectives, preferred focusing style, and performance demands in mind. When saying the keyword, they are keeping it in their mind and are more likely to execute that focus. Cues can direct visual attention (e.g., "see the buoy"), provide instruction about technique (e.g., "pedal circles") or tactics (e.g., "pace"), or direct focus onto physical feelings (e.g., "smooth") or mental states (e.g., "attack") (Hatzigeorgiadis, Zourbanos, Galanis, & Theodorakis, 2011).

Additionally, athletes can use keywords to remind them when to "switch on" and "switch off" their focus in their sport (Moran, 2009). These alerts help athletes to mitigate the limited capacity of focus and therefore allocate it appropriately while taking breaks to reset physically and mentally. This tool is particularly important for sports that involve high intensity and are of an extended duration such as tennis, football, golf, running, and cycling.

Messages on Equipment

When athletes are practicing or competing, they can get so immersed in performing that they lose sight of whatever they should focusing on, particularly during an intense practice session or a high-pressure competitive situation. For example, pre-competitive anxiety can overwhelm athletes to the point that they become focused on the physical symptoms rather than what they can do to relax. It is a challenge to break free of this preoccupation and redirect their focus in a more helpful direction. A tool for helping athletes to regain focus in these situations involves writing focus messages on their equipment. Returning to the anxiety example above, if they have written "breathe" or "calm" on their tennis racquet, baseball bat, or golf bag, it acts as a reminder that can free them from the unhealthy focus and reset their focus on what will help them perform their best.

Visual Focus Training

Particularly relevant for open-skill, team sports (e.g., soccer or volleyball), athletes can engage in computer or field training to expand their attention-window, thereby improving their performances. Consultants can lead computer-based training including the cueing paradigm (i.e., focus on the center of the screen and react to stimuli appearing on the sides), d2 task (i.e., cross out any letter d with two marks above or below as fast as possible), Stroop Task (i.e., look at words that name colors and correctly identify the colors rather than the names), and useful field of view task (i.e., find a specific target briefly presented among similar distractors). Shown to be equally effective, consultants can guide field training alongside coaches, including having athletes engage in exercises to focus on a small area or target object as well as exercises requiring a wider focus, for example, where an increasing the number of teammates involved in a drill (Hüttermann & Memmert, 2018).

Additional Focus Exercises and Tools

There are several other highly effective exercises and tools consultants can teach athletes to use to improve focus. Described briefly below, they will be explored in more detail in Chapter 4:

- Mental imagery: Imagery, by definition, narrows athletes' focus onto their performances and, at the same time, minimizes or removes distractions.
- Breathing: When athletes focus on their breathing, it brings their attention onto themselves and redirects them away from distractions.
- Routines: When athletes focus on their routines, they are directing their attention onto what will enable them to be prepared to perform their best and, in doing so, block out distractions.

Once the appropriate focus exercises and tools have been identified and taught by consultants, it is important for athletes to rehearse them in practice and less-important competitions to gain mastery and comfort with their use. Familiar focus conditions have been shown to improve performance (Maurer & Munzert, 2013). The goal of which is that the strategies will become ingrained and will emerge automatically when athletes perform in their sport.

Summary

- Focus involves athletes directing their awareness, thoughts, and efforts toward a particular goal.
- Effective focus means athletes attending only to cues that will help them perform their best and avoid distractions that hurt performance, for example, external cues such as teammates, opponents, score, time remaining, and field or weather conditions, and internal cues such as technique, tactics, confidence and intensity mindset.
- Poor focus involves processing internal and external cues that take athletes' focus away from what they need to do to perform their best, for instance, negative thoughts, anxiety, concern over who the next opponent will be, as well as homework that is due or feeling hungry.
- Focus is so important to practice efforts and competitive performances because they ensure effectiveness, efficiency, and consistency.
- Three focus goals for athletes include identifying essential cues to perform their best, isolating distractions, and actively focusing on helpful cues and blocking out distracting cues.
- Focus can be conceptualized along two dimensions: broad-narrow and internal-external.
- Focus serves three main functions: alerting, orienting, and executive control.
- Focus can be assessed by recalling past competitions and identifying what focus approach worked and what didn't, and by taking the Test of Attentional and Interpersonal Style.
- Effective focus is grounded in athletes focusing on what they can control, an emphasis on process, and keeping focus impartial, objective, and unemotional.
- Frequently used focus exercises and tools include having clear goals and process, Identifying and limiting distractions, keywords, messages on equipment, mental imagery, breathing, and routines.

References

Bernier, M., Codron, R., Thienot, E., & Fournier, J. F. (2011). The attentional focus of expert golfers in training and competition: A naturalistic investigation. *Journal of Applied Sport Psychology, 23*(3), 326–341.

Easterbrook, J. A. (1959). The effects of emotion on cue utilization and the organization of behavior. *Psychological Review, 66*(3), 183–201.

Eysenck, M. W., Derakshan, N., Santos, R., & Calvo, M. G. (2007). Anxiety and cognitive performance: Attentional control theory. *Emotion, 7*(2), 336–353.

Furley, P., Bertrams, A., Englert, C., & Delphia, A. (2013). Ego depletion, attentional control, and decision making in sport. *Psychology of Sport and Exercise, 14,* 900–904.

Gould, D. (2010). Goal setting for peak performance. In J. M. Williams (Ed.), *Applied sport psychology: Personal growth to peak performance* (pp. 201–220). New York, NY: McGraw-Hill.

Hatzigeorgiadis, A., Zourbanos, N., Galanis, E., & Theodorakis, Y. (2011). Self-talk and sports performance: A meta-analysis. *Perspectives on Psychological Science, 6*(4), 348–356.

Hüttermann, S., & Memmert, D. (2018). Effects of lab- and field-based attentional training on athletes' attention-window. *Psychology of Sport & Exercise, 38,* 17–27.

Janelle, C. M., & Hatfield, B. D. (2008). Visual attention and brain processes that underlie expert performance: Implications for sport and military psychology. *Military Psychology, 20*(Suppl. 1), S39–S69.

Janelle, C. M., Singer, R. N., & Williams, A. M. (1999). External distraction and attentional narrowing: Visual search evidence. *Journal of Sport & Exercise Psychology, 21,* 70–91.

Kirn, W. (2007, November). The autumn of the multitaskers. *The Atlantic,* 150th Anniversary Issue. Retrieved from www.theatlantic.com/magazine/archive/2007/11/the-autumn-of-the-multitaskers/306342

Lidor, R., Ziv, G., & Tenenbaum, G. (2013). The effect of attention allocation instructions on self-paced task performance under quiet and distracted conditions. *Journal of Applied Sport Psychology, 25,* 478–492.

Maurer, H. & Munzert, J. (2013). Influence of attentional focus on skilled motor performance: Performance decrement under unfamiliar focus conditions. *Human Movement Science, 32,* 730–740.

McCarthy, P. J., Allen, M. S., & Jones, M. V. (2013). Emotions, cognitive interference, and concentration disruption in youth sport. *Journal of Sports Sciences, 31*(5), 505–515.

Merriam-Webster. (2004a). Concentration. In *Merriam-Webster's dictionary,* 11th ed. Springfield, MA: Merriam-Webster.

Merriam-Webster. (2004b). Attention. In *Merriam-Webster's dictionary,* 11th ed. Springfield, MA: Merriam-Webster.

Mesagno, C., Marchant, D., & Morris, T. (2009). Alleviating choking: The sounds of distraction. *Journal of Applied Sport Psychology, 21,* 131–147.

Moran, A. (2009). Attention in sport. In S. D. Mellalieu & S. Hanton (Eds.), *Advances in applied sport psychology: A review* (pp. 195–220). New York, NY: Routledge.

Mullen, R., Hardy, L., & Tattersall, A. (2005). The effects of anxiety on motor performance: A test of the conscious processing hypothesis. *Journal of Sport & Exercise Psychology, 27,* 212–225.

Nideffer, R. M. (1976). Test of attentional and interpersonal style. *Journal of Personality and Social Psychology, 34,* 394–404.

Nideffer, R. M. (2001). Theory of attentional and personal style vs. Test of attentional and interpersonal style (TAIS). Retrieved from www.epstais.com/articles/tais.pdf

Petersen, S. E., & Posner, M. I. (2012). The attention system of the human brain: 20 years after. *Annual Review of Neuroscience, 35,* 73–89.

Sarason, I. G., Sarason, B. R., & Pierce, G. R. (1990). Anxiety, cognitive interference, and performance. *Journal of Social Behavior and Personality, 5*(2), 1–18.

Schmidt, R. A. & Lee, T. D. (2005). *Motor control and learning: A behavioral emphasis.* Champaign, IL: Human Kinetics.

Sowa, C. J. (1992). Understanding clients' perceptions of stress. *Journal of Counseling & Development, 71,* 179–183.

Strayer, D. L., & Johnston, W. A. (2001). Driven to distraction: Dual-task studies of simulated driving and conversing on a cellular telephone. *Psychological Science, 12*(6), 462–466.

Weinberg, R., Butt, J., & Knight, B. (2001). High school coaches' perceptions of the process of goal setting. *The Sport Psychologist, 15,* 20–47.

Weiss, S. M., Reber, A. S., & Owen, D. R. (2008). The locus of focus: The effect of switching from a preferred to a non-preferred focus of attention. *Journal of Sports Sciences, 26*(10), 1049–1057.

Wulf, G., & Su, J. (2007). An external focus of attention enhances golf shot accuracy in beginners and experts. *Research Quarterly for Exercise and Sport, 78*(4), 384–389.

4

MENTAL EXERCISES AND TOOLS

Introduction

Jim Taylor

Many athletes believe that the mind is set in stone at an early age and it either can't be changed or change is incredibly difficult. Yet, as discussed in the introduction to Chapter 3, they have no problem believing that the body can be made stronger through a committed conditioning program. That is the challenge that every consultant who wants to help athletes be more mentally prepared faces. Consultants must convince athletes that the mind is no different; if athletes commit the time and effort, they can strengthen their mental "muscles" and change the way they think, feel, and perform.

This is another place in which *CASP* departs from the accepted vocabulary of applied sport psychology. Chapter 4 examines seven strategies that are commonly referred to as mental skills. Yet, it is *CASP's* view that these are not skills; their purpose is not for athletes to get better at or become more skilled at mindfulness, self-talk, routines, etc. Rather, they are exercises used to strengthen the mental muscles discussed in Chapter 3 and tools that are used to "prime" those mental muscles just prior to competition.

Athletes can use these mental exercises to make their minds stronger the same way as they do with their bodies. By exercising those mental muscles in a structured and consistent way, motivation, confidence, intensity, and focus become powerful and resilient, thus allowing them to withstand the forces placed on them and remain strong in practice and competition.

Once the mental muscles have been optimally conditioned, those mental exercises become tools that athletes can place in their mental toolboxes. These tools can be used by athletes in two ways. First, the tools can be used to fix problems that arise in practice and competitions. Here's an analogy to explain this perspective on mental training. Imagine you're driving and get a flat tire. You pull over to the side of the road and see that you have no jack, no spare tire, and no tire iron (and no AAA!). In other words, you're stuck where you are with no means of changing the flat tire. However, if you had the tools and the know-how you needed to replace the flat, you would be back on the road in a short time.

Athletes are going to experience a lot of "flat tires" in their sports lives. For example, athletes will become discouraged, nervous, and distracted. They will get frustrated working on new skills in their sport. And they will perform poorly and fail to accomplish their competitive goals. These difficulties are an inevitable and unavoidable part of sports. What is not a foregone conclusion is whether they surmount those hurdles and continue to progress as athletes. It's up to consultants to provide them with the tools they need to fix the problems and return to the road toward their sports goals.

Additionally, athletes can use these mental tools to fine tune their "engines" to get the most out of their practice efforts and competitive performances. For example, they can adjust their focus, lower their intensity, or boost their confidence with the appropriate mental tools. Using these tools to prime their mental muscles before a practice or competition allows athletes to be maximally prepared to perform their best in any sports performance.

Chapter 4 will explore of the seven mental exercises and tools that consultants can help athletes use to strengthen and prime their mental muscles:

- time-honored mental exercises and tools such as goal-setting and imagery.
- forward-looking mental exercises and tools including as mindfulness and breathing.
- emerging exercises and tools such as music.

GOAL-SETTING

Angel Brutus and Jim Taylor

Goal-setting is a valuable mental exercise and tool that athletes can use to lay the foundation for motivation. The process of setting, working toward, and achieving goals has a powerful emotional resonance that influences how we expend effort and energy in our pursuits. Two emotions play a significant role in how goal-setting influences motivation, *pride* in putting forth effort in striving toward and *inspiration* in having accomplished deeply felt goals.

In addition to the visceral value of goal-setting in fueling motivation, it also has practical benefits. First, goals clarify the destination for where athletes desire to go. This terminus is key because if athletes don't know where they want to go, they cannot direct their effort and energy in any defined direction. Second, goals show athletes how to get to where they want to go. In other words, goals offer athletes a road map for how to get to their destination.

Theory and Research

To understand the influence that goal-setting can have on athletes in their sports development, the theoretical framework that has served as a driver for the efficacy of this mental tool must be acknowledged. The industrial psychologists Edwin Locke and Gary Latham studied human behaviors influenced by conscious purpose, planning, intention, and task-orientation as a motivational aspect that promotes action (Locke & Latham, 1985). Specifically, their research focus for over three decades targeted the relationship between conscious performance goals and relevant task performance behaviors in organizational settings.

There has been an enormous amount of research examining this relationship both outside and within of sport (Locke & Latham, 1985; Kyllo & Landers, 1995). The focus of this line of investigation has been on how goals impact performance and how goal-setting can be used to maximize its value in relation to performance. Most basically, the findings indicate several conclusions. First, people with identified goals outperform those with no goals. Second, people with specific goals perform better than those with "do your best" goals. Third, people who set a series of process goals that lead to an outcome goal do better than those who just set an outcome goal (Latham & Locke, 1991). Moreover, goal-setting results in more concerted and sustained efforts, more determination when faced with roadblocks, and resilience in response to setbacks, especially when personal goals are set by the individual rather than by others.

Practical Implications

Because goal-setting is such a well-documented mental tool and it is tangible in its use, consultants are in a position to leverage it in several ways that will benefit athletes' practice and competitive efforts. They can incorporate goal-setting into a comprehensive mental training program in which goals are established and act as the foundation for developing athletes' overall training plan. Consultants can work with coaches to include it into their practice regimens. They can also use goal-setting for upcoming competitions.

SMARTER Goals

The research has also explicated specific criteria for athletes to get the most out of goal-setting. In particular, the acronym SMARTER signifies seven attributes that enable the value of goal-setting to be maximized (there are variations on what each letter represents and those that are believed to be most effective have been selected):

- **s**pecific;
- **m**easurable;
- **a**ccepted;
- **r**ealistic;
- **t**ime-limited;
- **e**xciting; and
- **r**ecorded.

Specific

Goals must be specific to what athletes want to achieve. For example, a hockey player would want to identify a detailed goal, "I want to increase my assists by three per game" instead of a more imprecise goal, "I want get better with my assists." The more specific athletes can get in their goals, the more they can focus on accomplishing that goal in practice and competitions to develop that area.

Measurable

As noted above, one of the most robust findings from the goal-setting research is that undefined "do your best" goals aren't as effective because they don't provide athletes with a sufficient yardstick to pursue. Instead, athletes want to set goals that are measurable and objective. For example, a swimmer who wants to swim her 50 free faster would be best served by setting a measurable goal of "I want to improve my time by five percent." But this "destination" goal isn't sufficient to leverage goal-setting fully. This type of goal defines the destination that athletes want to arrive at, but it doesn't provide a process for getting there. As a result, they need to create a measurable process goal that shows them how to arrive at their outcome goal: "My goal is to swim ten 50s three times a week at a progressively faster pace across each set."

Accepted

As discussed in Chapter 1, athletes' ownership of their sport is crucial to their athletic success. Ownership is equally vital to effective goal-setting. When goals are set by someone other than athletes themselves, such as parents or coaches, and the athletes feel little ownership of them, the goals lack the power to inspire or motivate completely because athletes don't have a real investment in them. In contrast, when athletes themselves choose goals that come from their most fundamental motivations about their sport, ownership is deeply felt and realization of those goals becomes central to their efforts.

Realistic

If athletes establish goals that are too easily attainable, they know they will achieve the goals without much effort, so the goals will provide little motivational value. Conversely, if they set goals that they perceive as unreachable, athletes will have little incentive to put out any effort. Goals should are realistic and challenging, meaning that the goals are attainable, but only with considerable effort (Locke, Shaw, Saari, & Latham, 1981).

Time-limited

Research has shown that goals that are open ended aren't effective at fostering motivation because they have no sense of urgency behind them; athletes can work toward them when they want (Kyllo & Landers, 1995). The most effective goals have a time limit for their completion. Time limits induce athletes to commit time and energy immediately to meet the deadline. For example, if an Olympic-distance triathlete wants to improve his cycling 40K time by five minutes, a goal might be: "I'm going to do ten hill repeats three times a week for the next six weeks."

Many athletes are familiar with some variation of the five SMART criteria just described. However, relatively few have been introduced to the remaining two factors that augment the goal-setting process.

Exciting

The motivation of athletes to pursue their goals is fueled by the emotions they connect with their goals. As a result, athletes should set goals that inspire and excite them. Emotions are particularly important to goal-setting when athletes are confronted with challenges they are inevitably confronted with as they strive toward their goals including failures, disappointment, fatigue, and injury. As athletes set goals, they can put the goals to the "excitement test;" they can ask themselves whether their goals get them fired up and motivated.

Recorded

According to the goal-setting research, people are more likely to remain motivated when goals are write down (not just typed into a computer; Orlick, 2016). There are several benefits to athletes recording their goals. First, the physical act of writing them down appears to somehow stamp them more deeply in people's minds. Second, goals that are written down feel more concrete and real. Third, people feel more ownership of and accountability toward their goals when they write them down. Fourth, when athletes post their goals where they can be seen frequently the visible goals act as a constant reminder to pursue and achieve them.

Additional Goal-setting Criteria

In addition to the SMARTER criteria, several other guidelines have been shown to maximize the benefits that goal-setting has to offer athletes.

Focus on Degree of Attainment

Goal-setting has been researched for years and there is a solid understanding of how it works. Yet, goal-setting is still an inexact science for athletes. There is no certainly if or when goals will be achieved. Because of this ambiguity, athletes should focus on degree of attainment, rather than absolute attainment.

Absolute attainment involves accomplishing a goal completely and within the time that was established. But following this rigid standard sets athletes up for failure because goal attainment is neither fully predictable nor controllable. In contrast, successful goal-setting is defined by degree of attainment and progress toward a goal (Gardner & Moore, 2007; Orlick, 2016).

Make Goals Public

Still another result that has been found in the goal-setting research is that people are more likely to remain committed to their goals if they are made public. Public airing of goals can involve athletes simply sharing them with coaches, teammates, family, or friends. Or, with the power of the internet, athletes can post their goals on their social media. Making goals public increases accountability and allows for support and encouragement from others.

Review Goals Regularly

Goals are most effective when they are seen as living documents that are dynamic and constantly evolving. They are best used when athletes regularly review, adjust, and recommit to them. Athletes get in the habit of evaluating their goals on a monthly basis, comparing them to actual progress, and modifying them as needed. Athletes can gain additional benefit from goal-setting by discussing them with their coaches who can offer practical feedback to make adjustments that will further motivate them to strive toward their goals.

Types of Goals to Set

Goal-setting involves athletes establishing a series of goals that begin in the future and work backward toward increasingly immediate, specific, and actionable goals.

- Long-term goals: what athletes ultimately want to accomplish in their sport (e.g., compete in college, become an Olympian).
- Yearly goals: what athletes want to achieve in the coming competitive season (e.g., qualifying for a regional championships, earn a certain ranking, or attain a particular won-loss record).
- Competition goals: what results athletes need to attain their yearly goals (e.g., finish in top-ten in a qualifying event, achieve certain game statistics).
- Preparation goals: what they need to accomplish in practice to reach their outcome goals (e.g., physical, technical, mental).
- Lifestyle goals: what they need to do in their general lifestyle to reach the above goals (e.g., sleep, eating habits, study habits).

Athletes can determine what they believe are reasonable goals based on the SMARTER guidelines, as well as the other criteria, above. They are also encouraged to collaborate with their coaches on their goal-setting because coaches often have experience and perspective on athletes' development and progress that can assist them in establishing the most effective goals for motivating them.

Summary

- Goal-setting is a valuable mental exercise and tool that athletes can use to lay the foundation for their motivation.
- The process of setting, working toward, and achieving goals has a powerful emotional resonance that causes us to want to expend effort and energy in their pursuit.
- Goals provide the destination of where athletes want to go and offer athletes a road map for how to get to their destination.
- Research has shown that people with goals outperform those with no goals, specific goals perform better than "do your best" goals, people who set a series of process goals that lead to an outcome goal do better than those who just set an outcome goal, and goal-setting results in more concerted and sustained efforts, more determination when faced with roadblocks, and resilience in response to setbacks.
- The most effective goals are specific, measurable, accepted, realistic, time-limited, exciting, and recorded.
- Additional goal-setting criteria include a focus on degree of attainment, making goals public, and reviewing goals regularly.
- Types of goals to set consist of long-term, yearly, competition, preparation, and lifestyle goals.

References

Gardner, F. L., & Moore, Z. E. (2007). *The psychology of enhancing human performance: The mindfulness-acceptance-commitment (MAC) approach.* New York, NY: Springer Publishing Company.

Kyllo, L., & Landers, D. (1995). Goal setting in sport and exercise: A research synthesis to resolve the controversy. *Journal of Sport & Exercise Psychology, 17*(2), 117.

Latham, G. P., & Locke, E. A. (1991). Self-regulation through goal setting. *Organizational Behavior and Human Decision Processes, 50*(2), 212–247.

Locke, E.A. & Latham, G.P. (1985). The application of goal-setting to sports. *Journal of Sport Psychology, 7,* 205–222.

Locke, E. A., Shaw, K. N., Saari, L. M., & Latham, G. P. (1981). Goal-setting and task performance. *Psychological Bulletin, 90*(1), 125.

Orlick, T. (2016). *In pursuit of excellence,* 5th ed. Champaign, IL: Human Kinetics.

IMAGERY

Philip Post, Duncan Simpson, and Jim Taylor

> I continue to visualize all my races days and weeks before they happen . . . I have never been
> to a competition, including the Olympic Games, where I didn't see myself win in my mental
> images before I got there. It is just part of the whole training package.
>
> *Janet Evans (quoted in Ungerleider, 2005, p. 165)*

Over the past several decades elite athletes in just about every sport have reported using imagery to benefit their
sport performance. These anecdotal accounts have fascinated sport psychologists and have led to numerous
investigations into this mental exercise and tool. This section will highlight some of the important findings and
provide practical suggestions for consultants to help athletes to gain the most benefits from its use.

Imagery has been defined as the creation or re-creation of an experience in the mind (Vealey & Forlenza,
2015). Most athletes' imagery starts off by recalling a prior experience in their mind (Post & Wrisberg, 2012).
For example, a gymnast might rehearse her floor routine before executing it in practice. When she recalls
the routine, she will access her long-term memory and, in doing so, recall specific features associated with
her routine (e.g., kinesthetic sensations, visual cues, emotions associated with performing the routine). As
athletes develop their imagery ability they will begin to create new experiences in their mind (Post, Simpson,
Young, & Parker, 2014; Post & Wrisberg, 2012) that may involve creating new movements, rehearsing skills,
competition scenarios, or desired outcomes. When athletes create an experience in their mind, they do so
by incorporating multiple senses, thoughts, and emotions. For instance, when a golfer sees and feels himself
hitting off the first tee, he might experience being excited (emotion), smell the freshly cut grass (olfaction),
feel his weight transfer during the swing (kinesthetic), hear the ping of the club (auditory), and see the flight
of the ball as it travels through the air (vision). Incorporating multiple senses and emotions during imagery
makes the imagery experience more authentic and influential (Munroe, Giacobbi, Hall, & Weinberg, 2000;
Post & Wrisberg, 2012).

The depth and breadth of imagery leads to an important aspect of imagery that consultants should emphasize
with athletes: it isn't just a mental event. Rather, it is a psychological, emotional, and physiological phenomenon
in which athletes reproduce the actual sports experience in their minds and bodies (Jeannerod, 1994). Because
of this broad impact, imagery can be used to improve every component of sports performance: psychological,
emotional, physical, technical, tactical, and team. A metaphor that athletes can relate to is that imagery is weight
lifting for the mind because it strengthens every mental muscle and so much more.

Theory and Research

Imagery is one of the most studied aspects of applied sport psychology. Research on imagery has produced
a wealth of knowledge about why and how it works, its impact on sports performance, and how to best
use it. Several theories have been proposed to explain the influence that imagery has on athletes' sport performance, cognitions, and affect. Of these theories, Jeannerod's (1994) functional equivalence and Lang's
bio-informational (Lang, 1977, 1979) have attracted the most attention. Imagery interventions based on
these theories have shown to improve sport performance (Callow, Roberts, & Fawkes, 2006; Post, Wrisberg,
& Mullins, 2010; Smith, Wright, Allsopp, & Westhead, 2007). Using emerging neuroimaging technology,
Jeannerod (1994) argued that imagery and physical practice are functionally equivalent in that imagery and
physical practice access common neural mechanisms. Essentially, when an athlete creates a physical movement
in their mind it activates similar neural mechanisms associated with the actual perception, motor control, and
emotions of the overt movement (Holmes & Collins, 2001; Jeannerod, 1994). It is believed that athletes can
strengthen the correct neural mechanisms, connections, and pathways associated with an ideal performance
by engaging in repeated imagery, thus making it more likely that the desired patterns established in imagery
extend to the actual sports performance.

In contrast, Lang (1977, 1979) proposed that individuals store an organized set of stimulus and response propositions in long-term memory. Stimulus propositions elicit the context of a particular event (e.g., the environment)

and response propositions elicit potential responses (e.g., psychological/physiological responses) for that specific event. Through imagery, athletes can become more adept at matching the most effective response propositions to a particular set of stimulus propositions. For example, when a halfpipe snowboarder imagines a specific run, he can recall from long-term memory the contextual elements of what that run is like (e.g., the halfpipe, weather, snow conditions, context). Once this context is created, the snowboarder can imagine how he wants to perform (e.g., the approach to the run, executing elements, being confident). Thus, when the athlete actually encounters the specific situation (i.e., stimulus propositions), he can now respond (i.e., response propositions) optimally to that situation.

Athletes' Use of Imagery

Results from numerous studies have provided detailed information regarding *where, when, why,* and *what* of athletes' imagery (Hall, Mack, Paivio, & Hasusenblas, 1998; Munroe et al., 2000; Post et al., 2014; Post & Wrisberg, 2012). With regard to *where* and *when,* athletes report engaging in imagery during and outside of competition (Munroe et al., 2000; Post & Wrisberg, 2012). In terms of the *what,* athletes report using imagery from two distinct perspectives: internal (i.e., from behind their own eyes) and external (i.e., from a third person perspective; Munroe et al., 2000; Post & Wrisberg, 2012). Athletes use an internal imagery perspective to experience the perceptual and kinesthetic elements of their performance, while an external perspective enables the athlete to observe and evaluate their form (Post & Wrisberg, 2012). In addition to imagery perspectives, athletes report manipulating the speed of their image (Post et al., 2014; Post & Wrisberg, 2012). Real-time imagery is used by athletes to experience the correct timing, tempo, and rhythm of a skill. Slow-motion imagery is used to focus on important parts of a skill or to correct mistakes (Post et al., 2014; Post & Wrisberg, 2012). In addition to speed and perspective, athletes' imagery includes multiple senses and small nuances associated with practice and the competition environment (Munroe et al., 2000).

A primary focus of describing athletes' imagery use has been identifying *why* they use it. To date, researchers have identified five major functions (Hall et al., 1998; Martin, Moritz, & Hall, 1999; Paivio, 1985): *Motivational-Specific* (MS): imagery that represents specific goals and goal-oriented behaviors. *Motivational General-Mastery* (MG-M): imagery that represents effective coping and mastery of challenging situations. *Motivational General-Arousal* (MG-A): imagery that represents feelings of relaxation, stress, and intensity regulation. *Cognitive Specific* (CS): imagery of specific sport skills. *Cognitive General* (CG): imagery of broad strategies associated with a specific sport. These functions are considered to be independent. Thus, an athlete could image game strategies (CG) without imaging being confident (MG-M). At the same time, athletes often report combining various functions to meet desired cognitive, behavioral, or affective outcomes (Martin et al., 1999; Post et al., 2014). Thus, a softball pitcher wanting to practice the proper execution of a rise ball while feeling confident could combine MS and CS imagery to meet her desired behavioral and affective outcome.

Effects of Imagery on Sport Performance

The biggest question among athletes and coaches is usually "does imagery work"? Extensive sport psychology research indicates that it has multiple benefits including enhancing motor performance, skill acquisition, and psychological aspects associated with successful sport performance (for a review see Weinberg, 2008). Imagery interventions have been shown to benefit a variety of motor tasks varying in cognitive and motor demands (Weinberg, 2008). For example, imagery interventions have improved athletes free-throw shooting (Post et al., 2010), field hockey penalty flicks (Smith et al., 2007, study 1), gymnastics routines (Smith et al., 2007, study 2), skiing (Callow et al., 2006), and swimming performance (Post, Muncie, & Simpson, 2012). Imagery has also benefited the skill acquisition of cognitive (Wright & Smith, 2007), gross motor (Post, Williams, Simpson, Berning, 2015), timing (Post et al., 2018), and strength tasks (Wright & Smith, 2009). Finally, imagery has also improved psychological variables associated with successful athletic performance. For example, imagery interventions have enhanced athletes' confidence (Callow, Hardy, & Hall, 2001), self-efficacy (Garza & Feltz, 1998), motivation (Martin & Hall, 1995), selective attention (Calmels, Berthoumieux, & Arripe-Longueville, 2004) and decreased performance anxiety (Mamassis & Doganis, 2004).

While imagery has been shown to enhance various aspects of sport performance to a greater extent than no practice at all, it is not as beneficial as physical practice (Weinberg, 2008). Thus, researchers have recommended that the most significant benefits of imagery are only realized when the skill is combined with athletes' actual physical practice (Post et al., 2012; Post et al., 2018). Like any exercise or tool, imagery has its greatest impact when practitioners integrate it with athletes' overall sport training regimen.

Practical Implications

When athletes and coaches are provided with the overwhelming evidence that imagery works, a common question is, "how can I utilize imagery effectively?" The answer to this question varies depending on what they want to get out of their imagery training.

Maximizing the Value of Imagery

To assist consultants in creating effective imagery interventions for athletes, Holmes and Collins (2001) developed the PETTLEP imagery model, which combines Lang's (1977, 1979) bio-informational and Jeannerod's (1994) functional equivalence theories. The PETTLEP imagery model suggests that effective imagery should include stimulus and response propositions and approximate physical practice along seven factors that comprise the acronym:

- *Physical* refers to imagining the perceived physical sensations experienced by the athlete during the actual performance. Athletes can enhance these sensations by imagining while in their performance stance or by holding a piece of equipment associated with their sport.
- *Environment* involves imagining or supplementing their session with video or photos of the performance setting.
- *Task* refers to making the imagined task similar to the actual task to be executed. Athletes should incorporate focus cues consistent with the cues used during actual performance.
- *Timing* refers to the speed at which imagery is done, which should be similar to the timing of actual performance.
- *Learning* refers to the need for consultants to update imagery scripts so that it matches athletes' current skill level.
- *Perspective* involves imagining from an internal or external perspective. Although proponents of the PETTLEP model suggest that athletes should only adopt a first-person perspective because this perspective is congruent with what athletes actually experience, empirical and consulting evidence supports the use of either first- or second-person perspectives. Moreover, athletes appear to have a preferred perspective that they gravitate to and with which they are most comfortable. It is generally recommended that they use that perspective.

In addition to the seven-function PETTLEP model, consultants also need to incorporate stimulus and response propositions. Specifically, consultants should encourage athletes to select specific situations in which they want to do their imagery (i.e., stimulus responses) and have them think about how they want to perform in those situations (i.e., response propositions). For example, a tennis player who struggles hitting her serve to close out a match needs to practice creating this specific scenario in her imagery (e.g., the match context, the pressure she feels, the thoughts, emotions, and physical sensations she experiences) and then imagine how she would like to respond in that specific situation (i.e., calmly executing her first serve). By considering the seven factors of the PETTLEP model and including stimulus and response propositions, consultants can maximize athletes' imagery training (Smith et al., 2007).

There are also four aspects of imagery that aren't included in the PETTLEP model that are equally important for athletes to get the most out of their imagery training (Taylor, 2017).

Vividness

Vividness involves how clearly athletes see their imagery. Are the visual images blurry or "high-def?" Are their physical sensations elusive or distinct? Are their emotions flat or acute? It's typical for athletes who first use imagery to say that their imagery isn't very good. Consultants can counsel patience and stress that imagery is an exercise and tool time to become skilled at; the more they do it, the better they will get at it. Additionally, due to the extensive use of video in sports, athletes can gain a clear and precise image of what they look like when performing in their sport and can then translate that image into their imagery (Holmes & Collins, 2001).

Control

One of the most frequently reported challenges that athletes experience when they first use imagery is that they make mistakes in their imagined performances. For example, a soccer player will miss an imagined penalty kick or a gymnast will fall off an apparatus. This problem relates to imagery control, which is how well they are able to imagine what they want to imagine (Post & Wrisberg, 2012).

At first blush, this phenomenon seems odd given that athletes should be able to imagine whatever they want. Though there are no articulated theories about why this problem occurs, a few hypotheses can be offered. First, imagery appears to circumvent the conscious mind and taps into unconscious beliefs that athletes hold about themselves. When athletes make an error in their imagery, it may reflect a fundamental lack of confidence in their ability to perform well. A mistake may also signify that athletes haven't fully learned and ingrained a new skill or another aspect of performance into their motor cortex, thus aren't able to access and execute the skill effectively even in their imagery. Lastly, it might suggest that athletes might not have a clear understanding of what they are supposed to imagine.

Feeling

Many athletes, coaches, and consultants call imagery visualization. Though they can and often are used interchangeably, there are differences that justify why *CASP* uses imagery as its preferred term. Visualization places its emphasis on the visual aspects of the experience, that is, athletes seeing themselves perform in their mind's eye. Though the visuals of imagery are important, another key contributor to the power of imagery is in athletes feeling of the imagined performances. This notion of feeling has two elements. There is the kinesthetic reproduction of athletic performances in which whatever athletes feel physically in the actual execution they also experience in their imagery. As research has demonstrated, when athletes imagine themselves performing, they are triggering the same motor programs as when they are physically performing (Jeannerod, 1994). This is strikingly demonstrated by athletes whose bodies move involuntarily while doing imagery. Additionally, athletes want to reproduce the emotional feelings associated with their sports performances. If the emotions are positive and helpful (e.g., excitement, joy), experiencing them through imagery enables athletes to deepen the presence of those emotions in their sports performance. In contrast, if the emotions are negative and interfering (e.g., fear, frustration), athletes can re-create those emotions in their imagery and develop corrective responses that mitigate or replace the emotions.

Total Experience

The most effective imagery involves the complete reproduction of the actual sports experience. Everything that athletes experience in their real performances—sights, sounds, physical sensations, thoughts, and emotions—they should also experience in their imagined performances. As athletes gain more skill and comfort with imagery, they can incorporate more aspects of their sports performance into their imagery. Their goal is to make their imagery as close to the actual athletic experience as possible.

Assessing Imagery Capabilities

To begin the process of athletes using imagery as a mental exercise or tool, it can be helpful for consultants to first assess athletes' imagery capabilities. Formal assessments such as the Movement Imagery Questionnaire (MIQ-3; Williams et al., 2012) or Vividness of Movement Imagery Questionnaire (VMIQ-2; Roberts, Callow, Markland, & Bringer, 2008) offer consultants objective measures of athletes' kinesthetic and visual imagery ability.

Consultants can also informally assess athletes' imagery abilities by having them imagine themselves performing in their sport and have them rate themselves on the PETTLEF dimensions on a one-to-five scale.

Developing an Imagery Program

As discussed earlier, the key for athletes getting the most out of their mental training is to approach it the same way they do their conditioning and sport training. Athletes wouldn't expect to get stronger by lifting weights occasionally. And they wouldn't expect to get better technically by practicing infrequently. The same holds true for mental imagery. The only way for athletes to gain the benefits of imagery is to develop an imagery program that is comprehensive, structured, and consistent (Post & Wrisberg, 2012).

Set Imagery Goals

Consultants can help athletes set specific goals for the areas they want to improve in their imagery. Goals can be technical, tactical, mental, or over-all performance. For example, athletes might focus on a technical improvement, being more confident and positive before competition, or performing with total commitment from start to finish. Before every imagery session, athletes can select a goal they want to accomplish which would then be the focal point of their imagery session.

Climb Imagery Ladder

Practicing sport skills begins in a simple environment and increases in complexity as the skill is ingrained and used automatically in competitions. The same holds true for imagery (Post et al., 2014; Post & Wrisberg, 2012). Consultants can help athletes to create a ladder of practice and competitive scenarios in which they will be performing. The ladder should begin with executing the imagery goals that are established in a simple practice environment. Once that goal is accomplished, athletes can progress up the ladder to more demanding training situations, competitions of less importance, and increase through more important events up to the most important competitions of the season.

Training- and Competition-specific Imagery

Athletes should select practice and competitive situations that are appropriate for their level of sports development. In other words, if an athlete is a high school pole vaulter, they shouldn't imagine themselves performing in the Olympics. Also, for each imagery session, they should choose a specific practice or competition venue under particular conditions. When athletes achieve their imagery goals in a range of practices and competitions, settings, and conditions, they have the opportunity to gain the most benefit from their imagery sessions.

Imagery Content

Each imagery session that athletes do should consist of their pre-performance routine following by either their practice efforts or a competitive performance. For athletes who participate in a sport of relatively short duration (e.g., swimming, ski racing), they can imagine an entire performance. Athletes who compete in a sport of significant length (e.g., golf, tennis, or soccer), they can identify and imagine themselves performing in four or five key parts of the competition.

Imagery Sessions

Given the importance of consistency to gain the most benefit from imagery, consultants can encourage athletes to do three or four imagery sessions each week. Each session should last about 10–15 minutes. Athletes should schedule a time of the day when they know they will be available (just like conditioning and sport practice) and make it a part of their daily routine. It is recommended that they set a reminder and a notification in their phones until the imagery sessions become established parts of their training schedules. Finally, athletes should find a quiet and comfortable place (e.g., bedroom or living room) where they won't be disturbed. They can then sit or lie down and begin their imagery session.

Imagery Journal

One of the challenges of imagery is that, unlike conditioning, the results of imagery aren't concrete. A helpful way to make it more tangible is to keep an imagery journal. In these logs, athletes can note key parts of their imagery sessions including how they performed, thoughts, emotions, and physical sensations they experienced, progress that was made, problems that arose, and what they want to focus on the next session. An imagery journal enables athletes to see improvements in their imagery, thus encouraging them to continue its use.

Incorporating Imagery into Their Sport

Athletes can also benefit from incorporating imagery into their practice sessions and competitive preparations. As a part of the pre-performance routines, they can use imagery for 10–15 seconds to see feel themselves performing the way they want. This use of imagery offers athletes several advantages:

- It blocks out distractions such as other people talking around them or intrusive thoughts.
- It confines their focus to their practice or competitive goal.
- It primes their mind and body for the upcoming effort.
- The positive images, thoughts, and feelings they generate boost motivation and confidence because they are seeing a successful performance before they begin.
- Imagery helps athletes reach their ideal intensity before every performance.

The overall benefit to athletes is that they will be more mentally and physically prepared to perform their best in practice and competitions.

Athletes can also do imagery after a practice or competitive performance to encourage improved performance in your next effort. When they complete a performance, athletes can immediately close their eyes and imagine their just-finished effort. If they had a successful performance, they can "replay" it and ingrain the positive images and feelings they just experienced. If athletes' performances were subpar, they can immediately "replay and edit" the performance, in which they can correct the mistakes they made and substitute the negative images and feelings with the positive images and feelings from a successful imagined performance.

Summary

- Imagery has been defined as the creation or re-creation of an experience in the mind.
- Imagery isn't just a mental event; it is a psychological, emotional, and physiological phenomenon in which athletes reproduce the actual sports experience in their minds and bodies.
- One theory argues that imagery and physical practice are functionally equivalent; when athletes create a physical movement in their minds, it activates similar neural mechanisms associated with the actual perception, motor control, and emotions of the overt movement.
- Another theory suggests that individuals store an organized set of stimulus and response propositions in long-term memory and imagery helps athletes to match the most effective response propositions to a particular set of stimulus propositions.
- Extensive sport psychology research indicates that imagery has multiple benefits including enhancing motor performance, skill acquisition, and psychological aspects associated with successful sport performance.
- Imagery can be maximized by using the PETTLEP model (physical, environmental, task, timing, learning, perspective).
- There are four other aspects of imagery that can increase its value: vividness, control, feeling, and total reproduction of the actual experience.

- Athletes can get the most out of their imagery by developing a structured and consistent program.
- An imagery program would include imagery goals, an imagery ladder, training- and competition-specific imagery, structured imagery sessions, and keeping an imagery journal.
- Imagery can also be used effectively before and after practice and competitions.

References

Callow, N., Hardy, L., & Hall, C. (2001). The effects of a motivational general-mastery imagery intervention on the sport confidence of high-level badminton players. *Research Quarterly for Exercise and Sport*, *72*, 389–400.

Callow, N., Roberts, R., & Fawkes, J. Z. (2006). Effects of dynamic and static imagery on vividness of imagery, skiing performance, and confidence. *Journal of Imagery Research in Sport and Physical Activity*, *1*(1). doi: 10.2202/1932-0191.1001

Calmels, C., Berthoumieux, C., & Arripe-Longueville, F. (2004). Effects of an imagery training program on selective attention of national softball players. *The Sport Psychologist*, *18*, 272–296.

Garza, D. L., & Feltz, D. L. (1998). Effects of selected mental practice on performance, self-efficacy, and competition confidence of figure skaters. *Sport Psychologist*, *12*, 1–15.

Hall, C. R., Mack, D. E., Paivio, A., & Hausenblas, H. A. (1998). Imagery use by athletes: Development of the sport imagery questionnaire. *International Journal of Sport Psychology*, *29*(1), 73–89.

Holmes, P. S., & Collins, D. J. (2001). The PETTLEP approach to motor imagery: A functional equivalence model for sport psychologists. *Journal of Applied Sport Psychology*, *13*, 60–83. doi:10.1080/10413200109339004

Jeannerod, M. (1994). The representing brain: Neural correlates of motor intention and imagery. *Behavioral and Brain Sciences*, *17*, 187–245.

Lang, P. J. (1977). Imagery in therapy: An informational processing analysis of fear. *Behavior Therapy*, *8*, 862–886.

Lang, P. J. (1979). A bio-informational theory of emotional imagery. *Psychophysiology*, *16*, 495–512. doi: 10.1111/j.1469-8986.1979.tb01511.x

Mamassis, G., & Doganis, G. (2004). The effects of a mental training program on juniors pre-competitive anxiety, self-confidence, and tennis performance. *Journal of Applied Sport Psychology*, *16*, 118–137. doi: 10.1080/10413200490437903

Martin, K. A., & Hall, C. R. (1995). Using mental imagery to enhance intrinsic motivation. *Journal of Sport and Exercise Psychology*, *17*, 54–69.

Martin, K. A., Moritz, S. E., & Hall, C. R. (1999). Imagery use in sport: a literature review and applied model. *The Sport Psychologist*, *13*, 245–268.

Munroe, K., Giacobbi, P. R., Hall, C., & Weinberg, R. (2000). The four Ws of imagery use: where, when, why, and what. *The Sport Psychologist*, *14*, 119–137.

Paivio, A. (1985). Cognitive and motivational functions of imagery in human performance. *Canadian Journal of Applied Sport Sciences*, *10*(4), 22S–28S.

Post, P. G., Muncie, S., & Simpson, D. (2012). The effects of imagery training on swimming performance: An applied investigation. *Journal of Applied Sport Psychology*, *24*, 323–337. doi: 10.1080/10413200.2011.643442

Post, P. G., Simpson, D., Young, G., & Parker, J. F. (2014). A phenomenological investigation of divers' lived experience of imagery. Journal of Imagery Research in Sport and Physical Activity, *8*(1). doi: 10.1515/jirspa-2014-0005

Post, P. G., Williams, C., Simpson, D., & Berning, J. (2015). The effects of a PETTLEP imagery intervention on the learning of a complex motor skill. *Journal of Imagery Research in Sport and Physical Activity*, *10*(1). doi: 10.1515/jirspa-2015-0007

Post, P. G., & Wrisberg, C. A. (2012). A phenomenological investigation of gymnasts' lived experience of imagery. *The Sport Psychologist*, *26*, 98–121.

Post, P. G., Wrisberg, C. A., & Mullins, S. (2010). A field test of the influence of pre-game imagery on basketball free throw shooting. *Journal of Imagery Research in Sport and Physical Activity*, *5*(1). doi: 10.2202/1932-0191.1042

Roberts, R, Callow, N., Hardy, L., Markland, D., & Bringer, J. (2008). Movement imagery ability: Development and assessment of a revised version of the vividness of movement imagery questionnaire. *Journal of Sport and Exercise Psychology*, *30*, 200–221.

Smith, D., Wright, C., Allsopp, A., & Westhead, H. (2007). It's all in the mind: PETTLEP-based imagery and sports performance. *Journal of Applied Sport Psychology*, *19*, 80–92. doi: 10.1080/10413200600944132

Taylor, J. (2017). *Train your mind for athletic success: Mental preparation to achieve your sports goals*. Lanham, MD: Rowman & Littlefield.

Ungerleider, S. (2005). *Mental training for peak performance*. Emmaus, PA: Rodale.

Vealey, R. S., & Forlenza, S. T. (2015). Understanding and using imagery in sport. In J. Williams (Ed.), *Applied sport psychology: Personal growth to peak performance*, 7th ed. (pp. 240–273). New York, NY: McGraw-Hill.

Weinberg, R. (2008). Does imagery work? Effects on performance and mental skills. *Journal of Imagery Research in Sport and Physical Activity*, *3*(1). doi:10.2202/1932-0191.1025

Williams, S. E., Cumming, J., Ntoumanis, N., Nordin-Bates, S. M., Ramsey, R., & Hall, C. (2012). Further validation and development of the movement imagery questionnaire. *Journal of Sport and Exercise Psychology*, *34*, 621–646.

Wright, C., & Smith, D. K. (2007). The effect of a short-term PETTLEP imagery intervention on a cognitive task. *Journal of Imagery Research in Sport and Physical Activity*, 2(1). doi: 10.2202/1932-0191.1014

Wright, C., & Smith, D. (2009). The effect of PETTLEP imagery on strength performance. *International Journal of Sport and Exercise Psychology*, 7, 18–31.

ROUTINES

Jim Taylor and Stewart Cotterill

Routines are one of the most commonly used exercises and tools that athletes develop to improve the quality of their conditioning, practice, and competitive efforts. The generic term "routine" can be applied to any behavioral, cognitive or emotional strategy that is used consistently before, during, or after a performance (Bloom, Durand-Bush, & Salmela, 1997). A pre-performance routine can be defined as a "sequence of task relevant thoughts and actions which an athlete engages in systematically prior to his or her performance of a specific sport skill (Moran, 1996, p. 177). The purpose of a routine is to ensure that athletes are comprehensively prepared to perform optimally in a practice or competitive performance. Post-performance routines have been specifically defined as "as a series of behavioral or psychological strategies undertaken after performance execution, yet prior to the PPR of the next performance attempt" (Mesagno, Hill, & Larkin, 2015, p. 88). Most of the attention within applied sport psychology and mental training has been on pre-performance routines, so the term "routines" used in the remainder of this section is intended to refer those that are used to prepare athletes to perform their best in an upcoming practice or competition.

Routines are suggested to provide athletes with many benefits that can help them to maximize their practice and competitive performances including:

- enhance the quality of athletes' practice efforts;
- provide a specific focus for the upcoming performance;
- ingrain skills and habits that allow athletes to more effectively transition from practice to competition;
- reduce controllable problems and errors;
- instill consistently of mind, body, and performance regardless of the practice or competitive situation or conditions;
- direct athletes' focus on the process of the performance, rather than the outcome;
- prime the athletes' mind and body allowing for optimal performance;
- create familiarity, predictability, and control; and
- increase confidence, comfort, and calm.

It's unlikely that there is a professional or Olympic athlete who doesn't have a well-developed routine that they include in their practice and competitive preparations. The development of their routines may have evolved organically during the course of their athletic development or have been created as part of a deliberate process aimed at identifying the approaches, strategies, and tools that help them to perform their best consistently.

Routines are another example of how the use of vocabulary influences how a mental area is understood. Some consultants use the term ritual in place of routine. The distinction between routines and rituals is an important one as rituals don't provide an accurate representation of what routines are actually intended to accomplish. Recall that the point of routines is to ensure that athletes are as prepared as they can be to perform their best in practice and competitions. Everything that a routine comprises serves a specific and practical purpose toward that goal. For example, a physical and technical warm-up and a review of tactics for an upcoming competition are all essential for total preparation.

In contrast, rituals are associated with superstitions and often consist of things that have no real effect on performance. For instance, rituals might include having to eat a specific meal before a competition or tapping the wall when athletes leave the locker room. Routines are also flexible, allowing for adjustments to be made as the competitive situation and conditions warrant. For example, if an athlete arrives late to a venue due to traffic, they can abbreviate their routines and still feel prepared. Rituals, by contrast, can be rigid and ceremonial. Athletes can come to believe that rituals *must* be completed or they will not perform well. At best, rituals act as a placebo in which athletes' belief in them increases confidence and motivation, thereby resulting in improved performance.

At worst, if athletes aren't able to complete their ritual, (e.g., can't eat their lucky meal or find their lucky socks), they may lose confidence and motivation and, as a result, lead to a poor performance. In sum, athletes control routines, but rituals control them.

Theory and Research

The popularity of routines use by athletes across a range of sports and occurring at the highest level of sport stems from the widespread belief that routines help athletes to be maximally prepared physically, technically, tactically, and mentally to perform their best when it matters most. To this end, Boutcher (1992), building on his work with golfers, suggested four main benefits that routines provide by encouraging athletes to:

1. focus their thoughts on the task-relevant cues;
2. help athletes to overcome a natural tendency to dwell on negatives;
3. allow athletes to select the appropriate motor schema; and
4. prevent "warm-up" decrements and the devotion of excessive attention to the mechanics of athletes' automatic skills.

Singer (2002) more generally suggested that the purpose of routines is to "put oneself in an optimal emotional, high self-expectant, confident, and focused state immediately before execution, and to remain that way during the act" (p. 6). Other suggested benefits of routines for sports performances include improving the ability to focus and reducing distractions, acting as triggers for well-learned skills, and enhancing the recall of optimal physical and mental states (Cotterill & Simpson, 2019). Early research suggested that targeting consistent behaviors and crucially consistent timing for those behaviors would be beneficial in routine development (Boutcher & Crews, 1987). However, other research has suggested that inflexibility in the timing of the components of the routine is not desirable and might actually be detrimental to performance. For example, in golf where the accuracy requirements of performance vary from shot to shot (e.g., teeing off vs. putting) which, in turn, impact the time it takes to prepare for a shot (Cotterill, Sanders & Collins, 2010). This finding is relevant for the above discussion that distinguishes routines from rituals.

Still other research (Cotterill, 2011) has also suggested that a cookie-cutter approach, in which one particular routine is used by many athletes, won't be effective. Instead, routines should be individualized based on athletes' physical, technical, tactical, and mental needs, as well as the demands of the sports and the context in which they will be practicing or competing. The specific components must be specific to the needs of the individual athlete. Indeed, the development of routines should be dependent on the personality, coping resources, and situation appraisal of the individual athlete (Cotterill, Sanders, & Collins, 2010).

A number of core mental exercises and tools have been identified as commonly used by athletes in their routines (Cotterill & Simpson, 2019):

- mental imagery;
- keywords;
- positive and motivational self-talk;
- emotional regulation;
- music;
- technical and tactical rehearsal; and
- mindfulness.

Routines also include physical exercises and tools that serve two essential purposes. First, they are aimed at preparing athletes physically for their training and competitive performances. Second, routines help athletes to achieve their ideal physical intensity (see Chapter 3 for more on intensity). Physical exercises and tools that athletes commonly incorporate in their routines include:

- physical movement;
- breathing;

- muscle relaxation;
- meditation; and
- high-energy or calming self-talk.

Developing Routines

A range of approaches to developing routines have been developed over the past 25 years. Singer's (1988) five-step approach consists of (1) readying, (2) imagining, (3) focusing attention, (4) executing, and (5) evaluating. Murphy's four-point model has also been described as a performance management model, which is composed of (1) practice, (2) preparation, (3) performance, and (4) analysis (Murphy, 1994).

Cotterill (2011) adopted a different approach, outlining a five-step process that explicitly focuses on developing a routine for self-paced skills: (1) video-recording performance, (2) clarifying the meaning of pre-existing preparatory behaviors, (3) developing a focus and function for each pre-existing component, (4) routine construction and agreement, and (5) practicing the newly developed routine until it becomes automatic. Hazell, Cotterill, and Hill (2014) built on the work of Cotterill (2011) by adding another step that precedes his four steps: understand the task requirements and the overall aim of the routine.

There has also been a focus in the routine literature on how to teach routines to novice learners. Lidor and Singer (2000) suggested that novices should develop routines as early as possible in the skill-development process. Lidor and Mayan (2005) further recommended that another benefit of developing routines early in the learning process is that it assists athletes in developing a plan of action that activate appropriate physical and mental processes to ensure optimal preparation for practice and competitive performances. This suggests that learners would then know more about how to manage their own mental processes and how to analyze themselves and situational demands. However, there is no research to date that has explored the validity of these assertions. Nor has there been studies examining novices learn routines or how much time is needed to develop and ingrain a new routine sufficiently to improve performance.

Lastly, it is important to remember that the structure and function of routines may evolve as athletes develop. The progression of a routine is influenced by several factors including their level of technical and tactical skill development, physical maturity, psychological and emotional maturity, and knowledge of their ideal physical and psychological states for practice and competitive performances.

Impact of Routines on Performance

There are a number of ways that routines have been found to have a positive impact upon performance. From a theoretical perspective, it has been suggested that routines might reduce the incidence of choking or increase consistency in performance under pressure because an increase in perceived control (Cheng, Hardy, & Markland, 2009). Mesagno et al. (2008) explored this question in a study involving bowlers. Their results demonstrated improved bowling accuracy in high-pressure situations as well as positive psychological outcomes such as decreased self-awareness and less conscious processing. Additionally, Lautenbach et al. (2014) examined the impact of a non-automated routine on performance in a high-pressure tennis environment. The results indicated that a routine can help athletes maintain or improve performance while under pressure.

Practical Implications

Consultants can play an essential role in helping athletes develop routines that best prepare them in three areas within their sport. First, routines are of great value in assisting athletes to get the most out of their practice efforts. Practice routines ensure that athletes are physically and mentally ready to meet the demands of conditioning and technical and tactical development. Second, they are crucial to make certain that athletes are thoroughly prepared to perform their best from the moment a competition begins. Third, for sports composed of a series of short performances (e.g., tennis, golf, football), routines help athletes get ready for each subsequent performance.

Another point worth mentioning is that there is no one ideal routine for every athlete, but all share many of the same elements. Routines are very personal and are based on individual athletes' unique physiology, psychology, needs, and goals. The demands of the sport also must be considered. Consultants can help athletes to decide what they need to include and how best to structure them. Additionally, developing an effective routine is an incremental process, involving experimentation that will take time before an athlete finds one that really works for them.

Practice Routines

For athletes to gain the most benefit from their practice time, they must be optimally prepared before every exercise, drill, and performance. To that end, athletes should develop a brief practice routine that ensures that high level of readiness related to their equipment and physical and mental states. Consultants should start with practice preparations in guiding athletes in the development of routines. The reason to start here is that practice routines identify for athletes what they need to do to perform their best first in practice and later in pre-competitive and between-performance routines. Discussions between consultants and athletes are important to understand what the key areas to include in a routine are, what athletes' optimal levels of relevant physical and psychological parameters are, and what specific exercises and tools to include in the routine.

A practice routine need only take a short time to complete—one-to-three minutes depending on the sport—but will result in athletes being maximally prepared to get the most out of their practice efforts. It will also lay the foundation for using a routine before and during competitions. A practice routine is typically an abbreviated version of a pre-competitive routine. Consultants can help athletes devise a practice routine that meets their needs and goals and those of their sport. A typical practice routine might include:

- adjustment of equipment, gear, or clothing;
- physical warm-up;
- check and adjust intensity;
- focus on the goal or purpose of the practice segment;
- mental imagery rehearsing segment focus; and
- breathing.

Pre-competitive Routines

Pre-competitive routines are more detailed and take longer to complete than practice routines, but include the same basic elements. In fact, these routines should be expanded versions of athletes' practice routines. The first step in designing a pre-competitive routine is to have athletes list everything they feel they need to do before a competition to be physically and mentally prepared to perform their best. A thorough routine is composed of everything that might impact athletes' performances including:

- sleep;
- nutrition;
- physical warm-up;
- technical;
- tactical;
- mental;
- equipment;
- team;
- relationships; and
- social media.

Other more personal areas that might go into a pre-competitive routine include when athletes changing into their competition clothing, when they go to the bathroom, and whom they like to be around before they compete.

Then, athletes can determine in what order they want to complete the routine list as they approach the start of the competition. This decision will be based on both personal needs and external influences including pre-competitive meetings and other activities. For instance, athletes have to take into account arrival time at the competitive venue, the start time of the competition, team meetings to discuss game plans, availability of a warm-up area, and a team warm-up.

Next, athletes must specify where each step of their routine can be completed. For example, some athletes like to do their routines around teammates or friends, while others like to go through their routine alone in a secluded spot. Consultants can help athletes to again knowledge of the competitive venue to determine this aspect of their routine.

Athletes can then establish a time frame and a schedule for accomplishing their routine based on how much time they need to be totally prepared. For instance, some athletes like to arrive at the competition site a short while before they compete. In contrast, others like to arrive hours before. All of these decisions are personal; athletes need to decide what is ideal for them.

Once athletes have established a pre-competitive routine, they can begin to test it in less important competitions. With experience using their routines, they then determine what aspects of their routines that work and which don't. Over time, athletes can fine tune your routines until they arrive at one that feels most comfortable and that is most effective in preparing them to perform their best in a competition.

Finally, athletes must understand that pre-competitive routines only offer them benefit if they are used consistently. When athletes use their routines on a regular basis before competitions, they become ingrained and automatic, requiring little or no thought, yet maximally preparing them for competition.

Between-performance Routines

Many sports consist of a series of many short performances with breaks of various lengths in between, such as baseball, football, tennis, and golf. For these sports, being well-prepared for the first performance is not enough. Rather, athletes in these sports must be prepared for the first and every performance in a competition, regardless of the time, score, conditions, or other variables. Relatedly, one thing that separates the great from the good athletes is their ability not only to be ready at the start of a competition, but also to be consistently prepared for every performance within a competition until it concludes.

The time between performances is essential to consistent competitive performance. What athletes think, feel, and do between performances often determines how they perform and the outcome of the competition. A between-performance routine allows athletes to take control of those breaks to ensure that they are ready every time.

The composition of between-performance routines depends on the sport and the length of the pauses. For example, golf has many minutes between shots, whereas baseball, football, and tennis have less than a minute between pitches, downs, and serves, respectively. A between-performance routine might include:

- physical recovery from the last performance;
- review of the last performance and the development of a strategy for the next one;
- check-in and adjustment of intensity;
- motivational or confidence-building self-talk; and
- refocusing on the ensuing performance.

Taylor (2017) suggests a four-step between-performance routine that he refers to as the Four Rs:

- recover;
- regroup;
- refocus; and
- recharge.

Recover

As soon as a previous performance concludes for sports that require an intensive effort, athletes are likely to be tired and out of breath. As such, the first step of a between-performance routine involves helping the body to recover quickly and fully. This recovery can be accomplished by having them relax their bodies and take several deep breaths. This strategy is particularly useful toward the end of a long competition when athletes are tired and recover between performances is essential yet more difficult. Deep breaths and muscle relaxation also help athletes center themselves and better prepare them for the next R.

Regroup

This step in the between-performance the routine deals with athletes' emotions. Of particular importance when they are not performing well or the competition is at an important point, athletes may experience a range of emotions such as excitement, frustration, anger, or despair. Regrouping allows athletes to be mindful of their emotions and, if the emotions are hurting them, to let go of them so they don't continue to interfere with their subsequent performances. Because of the significant effect that emotions have on sport performance, athletes' ability to "get their act together" emotionally between performances is crucial to how they do in the upcoming performance.

Refocus

For sports of significant duration (e.g., baseball and hockey) or those with many short performances, it is both nearly impossible and unnecessary to have a sustained focus. Instead, athletes in these sports learn to turn their focus on and off as needed. Moreover, a challenge for many athletes is to stay focused on the present and not have their focus drawn to the past—what happened in the previous performance—or to the future—what might happen in the next performance. During the refocus phase of a between-performance routine, athletes can let their focus switch off briefly (depending on the length of the break) and then back on as they prepare the upcoming performance. They can also shift their focus from evaluating the last performance to planning for the next one. The key step is for athletes to begin the ensuing performance with a clear focus on what they need to do to perform your best in the coming moment.

Recharge

The final step in this between-performance routine is for athletes to prepare themselves physically to perform their best. This step is particularly important late in competitions when athletes are tired. Just before the next performance begins, athletes can monitor their physical state and adjust their intensity as needed, either increasing or decreasing it. For athletes who need to calm down, they can consciously slow their pace, take deep breaths, and relax their muscles. In contrast, athletes who need to "rev up" can speed up their pace, take intense breaths, and move their bodies to increase their activation (see Chapter 3 for more intensity tools). The goal in this phase of athletes' between-performance routines is to ensure that they are physically ready to perform at their highest level in every performance within the competition.

Summary

- Routines are one of the most commonly used exercises and tools that athletes develop to improve the quality of their conditioning, practice, and competitive efforts.
- The generic term "routine" can be applied to any behavioral, cognitive or emotional strategy that is used consistently before, during, or after a performance.
- It's unlikely that there is a professional or Olympic athlete who doesn't have a well-developed routine that they include in their practice and competitive preparations.
- The term routine more accurately represents the benefits to athletes as compared to the term ritual.
- Considerable research has demonstrated the value of routines in maximizing athletic performance.
- Consultants can play an essential role in helping athletes develop routines that best prepare them in three areas within their sport: practice, pre-competition, and between-performances.
- There is no one ideal routine for every athlete, but all share many of the same elements; rather routines are very personal and are based on individual athletes' unique physiology, psychology, needs, and goals.

- For athletes to gain the most benefit from their practice time, they must be optimally prepared before every exercise, drill, and performance by developing a brief practice routine that ensures that high level of readiness related to their equipment and physical and mental states.
- Pre-competitive routines are more detailed and take longer to complete than practice routines, but include the same basic elements.
- Many sports consist of a series of many short performances with breaks of various lengths in between, such as baseball, football, tennis, and golf, so they can develop a between-performance routine that consists of recover, regroup, refocus, and recharge.

References

Bloom, G. A., Durand-Bush, N., & Salmela, J. H. (1997). Pre-and postcompetition routines of expert coaches of team sports. *The Sport Psychologist, 11*(2), 127–141.

Boutcher, S. H. (1992). Attentional and athletic performance: An integrated pre-performance routine approach. In T. S. Horn (Ed.), *Advances in sport psychology* (pp. 251–266). Champaign, IL: Human Kinetics.

Boutcher, S. H., & Crews, D. J. (1987). The effect of a preshot attentional routine on a well learned skill. *International Journal of Sport Psychology, 18*, 30–39.

Cheng, W. N. K., Hardy, L., & Markland, D. (2009). Toward a three-dimensional conceptualization of performance anxiety: Rationale and initial measurement development. *Psychology of Sport and Exercise, 10*, 271–278.

Cotterill, S. T. (2011). Experiences of developing pre-performance routines with elite cricket players. *Journal of Sport Psychology in Action, 2*(2), 81–91.

Cotterill, S. T., Sanders, R., & Collins, D. (2010) Developing effective pre-performance routines in golf: Why don't we ask the golfer? *Journal of Applied Sport Psychology, 22*(1), 51–64.

Cotterill, S. T., & Simpson, D. (2019). Routines, Preparation, and Performance. In G Cremades & A. Mugeford & (Eds.), *Sport, exercise and performance psychology: Theories and applications.* Abingdon: Routledge.

Hazell, J., Cotterill, S. T., & Hill, D. (2014). Exploring the impact of taught pre-performance routines on self-efficacy, anxiety and performance in semi-professional soccer players. *European Journal of Sport Science. 14*(6), 603–610.

Lautenbach, F., Laborde, S., Mesagno, C., Lobinger, B. H., Achtzehn, S., & Arimon, F. (2014). Nonautomated pre-performance routine in tennis: An intervention study. *Journal of Applied Sport Psychology, 27*(2), 123–131.

Lidor, R., & Mayan, Z. (2005). Can beginning learners benefit from preperformance routines when serving in volleyball? *The Sport Psychologist, 19*, 343–363.

Lidor, R., & Singer, R. N. (2000). Teaching pre-performance routines to beginners. *Journal of Physical Education, Recreation and Dance, 71*, 34–36.

Mesagno, C., Marchant, D., Morris, T. (2008). A pre-performance routine to alleviate choking in "choking-susceptible athletes." *The Sport Psychologist, 22*, 439–457.

Mesagno, C., Hill, D., & Larkin, P. (2015). Examining the accuracy and in-game performance effects between pre- and post-performance routines: A mixed methods study. *Psychology of Sport and Exercise, 19*, 85–94.

Moran, A. P. (1996). *The psychology of concentration in sports performers: a cognitive analysis.* Hove: Psychology Press.

Murphy, S. (1994). Mental preparation for golf: achieving optimal performance. In A. J. Cochrane & M. R. Farrally (Eds.), *Science and golf II: Proceedings of the World Scientific Congress of golf* (pp. 43–58). London: E. and F. N. Spon.

Singer, R. N. (1988). Strategies and meta-strategies in learning and performing self-paced athletic skills. *The Sport Psychologist, 2*, 49–68.

Singer, R. N. (2002). Pre-performance state, routines, and automaticity: what does it take to realize expertise in self-paced events? *Journal of Sport and Exercise Psychology, 24*, 359–375.

Taylor, J. (2017). *Train your mind for athletic success.* Lanham, MD: Rowman & Littlefield.

SELF-TALK

Megan Pietrucha

Self-talk is one of the most powerful mental exercises and tools that athletes can leverage to help them perform their best. At the same time, it is also one of the most powerful weapons that athletes use against themselves that can hurt their sport efforts. What athletes say to themselves away from their sport, at practice, and before and during competitions can impact their thinking, the emotions they experience, and how they perform. It can also determine the quality of their practices and the outcome of their competitions.

Quite simply, whatever athletes think more of—whether positive or negative—will determine the road they travel down in their sports lives.

The idea that behavior, or athletic performance in the case of sports, can be modified through manipulation of thoughts is not new. In each of their theories related to cognitive behavioral modification, Beck (1975), Meichenbaum (1977) and Ellis (1982) propose that it is the perception of an event, rather than the event itself, that influences subsequent feelings and behavior. Thoughts are also connected to deeper beliefs about the self (i.e., core beliefs) including self-esteem and self-efficacy. Patterns of unhelpful or irrational thoughts can lead to changes in emotions and maladaptive behavior. Thus, when people examine their perceptions of an event and challenge unhelpful thoughts, they can produce more adaptive behavior.

Self-talk is generally defined as a dialogue with the self, which can be either internal or out loud. It is considered a critical mental exercise and tool because of its ability to influence performance. Self-talk has been called the "key to cognitive control" (Williams, Zinsser, & Bunker, 2015) and is one of the most widely used and researched mental exercises and tools in applied sport psychology (Van Raalte, Vincent, & Brewer, 2016). Self-talk is considered to be so useful because it can help athletes build confidence, harness motivation, manage emotions, regulate intensity, control energy and effort expenditure, shift focus, and trigger automatic execution of tasks (Hardy, Hall, & Alexander, 2001; Theodorakis, Hatzigeorgiadis, & Chroni, 2008). Self-talk can also help athletes avoid overthinking during performances or falling victim to "paralysis by analysis" (Beilock, 2010) and improve performance under pressure or "in the clutch" (Swann et al., 2017). Overall, this impact highlights the importance of self-talk on sports performance and explains why should be an integral part of mental training for athletes.

Theory and Research

According to a review of the literature by Latinjak, Zourbanos, López-Ros, and Hatzigeorgiadis (2014), the self-talk research is divided into two paradigms: exploring spontaneous or automatic self-talk and understanding self-talk as an intervention strategy. Spontaneous self-talk was initially defined based on the valence, or the positive or negative direction, of the statement (Hardy, Hall & Hardy, 2004; Latinjak et al., 2014; Van Raalte, Brewer, Rivera, & Petitpas, 1994; Van Raalte et al., 2016). An example of positive self-talk might be, "I can do it!", where as an example of negative self-talk might be, "I'm not good enough to win this game."

Another approach is to categorize self-talk based on the behavioral outcome, or effect, of the self-talk. For example, thoughts that create anxiety or are counterproductive to athletic performance are labeled as negative, whereas self-talk that fosters motivation and confidence is labeled as positive (Latinjak et al., 2014; Van Raalte et al., 2016). Overall, reviews of the literature generally support the hypothesis that positive self-talk is related to positive performance outcomes and vice versa for negative self-talk (Williams & Leffingwell, 2002; Williams et al., 2015). However, since content and outcome are distinct constructs related to self-talk, the labeling of self-talk as positive or negative can be confusing, and more so, oversimplifies the function of self-talk and the impact self-talk can have on the athlete.

From this literature, a two-dimensional model for self-talk was proposed that incorporates valence (positive-negative) and impact (motivational-demotivational) (Hardy et al., 2001). In examining the relationship between valence and motivation, Hardy et al. (2001) found a positive relationship between negative-positive and demotivational-motivational self-talk. Yet, the authors also noticed that negatively valanced self-talk was motivational for some athletes (e.g., "Come on, you idiot, you can't play this bad!"). Likewise, it can be assumed that for some athletes, positively valanced self-talk can potentially be distracting from the demands of the task (Hardy et al., 2001; Van Raalte et al., 2016).

There are three general types of self-talk that are discussed in the literature: cognitive/instructional, motivational, and goal-directed self-talk (Van Raalte et al., 2016). Cognitive/instructional self-talk provides a facilitative function for athletes by giving directions for learning and executing tasks and skills. It is most useful during skill development or to cue athletes into a specific movement (Williams et al., 2015). This type of self-talk is advised to be kept short and simple during early learning, and to be de-emphasized as the skill becomes more automatic.

Motivational self-talk serves athleted by providing encouragement and managing energy and effort. Motivational self-talk can be divided into self-talk aimed at mastery (i.e., focus, confidence; "You can do this!")

or drive (i.e., persistence, staying on track towards goal attainment; "Hang in there!") (Hardy et al., 2004; Hatzigeorgiadis et al., 2009). As discussed in Chapter 3, motivational self-talk also has an intensity function which can be used to "psych up" or "psych down" athletes depending on their own needs as well as the demands of their sport (Hardy et al., 2005). Hatzigeorgiadis et al. (2009) found that the motivational self-talk of tennis players had a positive impact on confidence and reduced cognitive anxiety. The overall results of this study support the connection between motivational self-talk and improved performance on a forehand drive task (Hatzigeorgiadis et al., 2009). Motivational self-talk has also been positively linked to strength performance. In a review exploring the relationship between cognitive strategies and strength performance, self-talk was defined as using a cue word to assist with performance (Tod, Edwards, McGuigan & Lovell, 2015). When compared to instructional self-talk and cognitive restructuring, motivational self-talk was consistently correlated with enhanced muscular strength, whereas instructional self-talk had an indeterminate relationship (Tod et al., 2015). It is hypothesized that motivational self-talk increases energy and effort expenditure and thus increases drive and strength performance (Hardy et al., 2005; Tod et al., 2015).

Goal-directed self-talk focuses athletes on problem solving, decision making, and facilitating progress towards goal attainment (Latinjak et al., 2014). In their exploration of self-talk, these researchers sought to understand the content of goal-directed and undirected self-talk in a group of athletes. The authors suggest that goal-directed self-talk could be classified along two dimensions: activation and time-orientation (Latinjak et al., 2014). Goal directed, activation self-talk aims to control or create positive emotional states (e.g., "Let's stay fired up here!"). The time-orientation dimension classifies self-talk statements on whether they are aimed at dealing with outcomes of the past, present, future, or some combinations of these (e.g., "Let go of that last point").

Athletes use self-talk in practice and competition, but tend to use it more during competition (Hardy et al., 2005). Instructional self-talk was also found to be utilized less from practice to competition situations, and this was hypothesized to be related to a decrease in performance under pressure when using instructional self-talk (Hardy et al., 2005). Lastly, the study also found differences between individual sports and team sports in the use of self-talk; individual-sport athletes tend to use more self-talk compared to team-sport athletes (Hardy et al., 2005).

Social factors, such as coaches, parents, and team culture, can also have an impact on self-talk (Van Raalte et al., 2016). When athletes perceive coaches to be supportive, they tend to have more positive and less negative self-talk (Zourbanos et al., 2011). The authors proposed that the negative relationship between perceived support from coaches and athletes' worry, disengagement, and somatic fatigue self-talk could be important especially during competition and pressured performance situations (Zourbanos et al., 2011). It is recommended that coaches and parents encourage positive self-talk by being mindful of the ways in which they are talking to their athletes.

Practical Implications

In general, self-talk should be present-focused, concise, positive, and focused on the desirable outcome (Williams & Leffingwell, 2002). When used effectively, self-talk can be beneficial to performance. However, self-talk can also hinder performance if it becomes distracting or demotivating (Williams et al., 2015). Keeping self-talk positive and avoiding negative language (e.g., "I can't win") or unwanted outcomes (e.g., "Don't miss the shot!") is generally encouraged for the most effective uses of self-talk. Thus, athletes knowing how and when to use self-talk will help them to maximize the impact that this exercise and tool can have on their practice efforts and competitive performances.

Increasing Awareness with Mindfulness

Though mindfulness has been discussed in depth earlier in this chapter, it is worth focusing briefly on its value in relation to self-talk. Learning how to use self-talk to gain a competitive edge in sports starts with increasing awareness of the thoughts occurring during practice and performance. It is not uncommon for athletes to have limited awareness of how their thoughts are connected to their behavior. In fact, some athletes might strive to minimize thoughts entirely during performance or believe that they can disconnect thought processes from behavior (Williams et al., 2015).

Increasing awareness of thoughts and behaviors can be facilitated with mindfulness. The "in-the-moment" aspect of mindfulness enables athletes to gain awareness of valence and content of their thoughts in practice and during competitions. Research found that athletes were more mindful were more likely to adopt mental exercises and tools including self-talk (Kee & John, 2008; Scott-Hamilton, Schutte & Brown, 2016). Overall, these studies suggest that by using mindfulness, athletes can increase awareness of their self-talk thus leading to more positive performance outcomes.

Thought Log

A thought log is a documented record of athletes' thoughts related to their performances. Keeping a thought log can help athletes identify specific patterns in self-talk with the goal of changing unhelpful thoughts to develop more effective self-talk that promotes optimal performance., In this way, thought logs are similar to the common practice for some athletes of recording conditioning, practice, and competitive experiences that can help them to develop in those areas (Porter, 2003).

The purpose of the thought log is to increase awareness of athlete's thinking before, during, and after practice and competition and provides insights into how self-talk impacts their performances (Williams et al., 2015). A thought log can take many forms, but it should consist of any of the thoughts, emotions, and reactions athletes have related to performance and can include thoughts during practice and competition. This type of monitoring of thoughts can be particularly helpful in identifying negative self-talk patterns as well as bring awareness to the connection between self-talk, emotions, motivation, confidence, intensity, focus, and performance. In some cases, athletes might not even realize how their self-talk impacts their performances until this form of monitoring and analyzing patterns identified by using a thought log illuminates the connection. Once a pattern or problem is identified in the thought log, athletes can begin to intervene by changing their self-talk.

Thought Stopping

Once athletes become aware of the self-talk that are interfering with their performances, they can take active steps to retrain how they talk to themselves. Thought stopping is a strategy that athletes can use to immediately intervene with negative self-talk patterns. First, athletes can use a keyword, such as "stop," or a physical action such as pumping their fist, as soon as they become aware of their negative self-talk (Williams et al., 2015). Then, they can replace the negative self-talk with positive self-talk. With awareness and practice, athletes can retrain their minds in a more positive direction.

Affirmations

Affirmations are positive, confidence-building self-talk that can be used to combat negative thinking. Porter (2003) suggests that affirmations can support what athletes want to believe about themselves in their sports participation that are positive, specific, present tense, process oriented, and personal to have the greatest impact (Porter, 2003). For example, a present-focused affirmation might be, "You can do this." Affirmational self-talk should take the form of second-person "you" statements or third-person, "your name" statements because they have been found to be more effective than first-person, "I" statements (Holohan, 2016). Writing down, rehearsing, and reviewing affirmations regularly also helps to change self-talk to be more effective and positive.

Reframing

Reframing is another effective self-talk strategy to create positive alternatives to negative self-talk. Reframing allows athletes to acknowledge the negative self-talk, but also encourage them to create alternative self-talk by viewing the perceived problem from a solutions-oriented perspective. The resulting self-talk is essentially the "silver lining" or seeing the situation in a positive light and allows for athletes to focus on possibilities and opportunities instead of obstacles (Williams et al., 2015). For example, an athlete might say "Jenny's so much better than I am." To reframe this self-talk more positively, she could say "Jenny gives me a target to aim for as I continue to improve."

Countering

Changing negative self-talk to positive self-talk is no easy feat, even if athletes can recognize that the negative self-talk is hurting their efforts. Change is difficult because negative thoughts can be deeply ingrained and habitual and athletes come to believe in them (Williams et al., 2015). To counter negative thoughts, athletes can search for evidence that disproves the negative thoughts or that offers a more positive perspective that mitigates the impact of the negative thoughts. For instance, returning to the Jenny example above, the athlete might counter her initial negative self-talk with "Jenny may be better than me now, but I'm in this for the long haul, so who knows where we'll be in a few years."

Balance the Scales

An effective tool that consultants can use with athletes is to have them record the amount of positive and negative self-talk they use during practices and competitions. With athletes who have well-entrenched negative self-talk, the ratio of negatives to positives is very high. The goal, ultimately, is to eradicate all negatives and instill only positive. However, such a dramatic shift is unlikely given the habitual nature of self-talk.

To begin this transition from negative to positive, athletes can begin by "balancing the scales." In other words, they can accept that there will continue to be negatives, but to focus on increasing the proportion of positives to negatives. This means athletes being positive when good things happen in practice and competitions.

Once athletes have balanced the scales by boosting their positive self-talk to match their negative self-talk, their next goal is to reach a tipping point in which the positives outweigh the negatives by reducing their negative self-talk. This step of tipping the scales toward positives is so vital because of recent studies have revealed that negative experiences such as negative self-talk, negative body language, and negative emotions carry more weight than positive experiences. In fact, the "positivity ratio" suggests that a three to one ratio of positive to negative emotions serves as the "tipping point" and characterizes people who are "flourishing", resilient, and functioning optimally in their mental health and lives (Fredrickson & Losada, 2005). This research suggests that every time athletes use negative self-talk, they need to have at least three instances of positive self-talk to combat the impact of the one negative thought.

Use Negative Thinking Positively

As described above, there is strong evidence that positive self-talk has a powerful effect on many aspects of sports performance. At the same time, as any athlete knows, it's not always easy to stay positive when things aren't going well. Some negativity is normal and unavoidable when athletes who care deeply about their sport don't perform as well as expected. Negative thinking can also help athletes' efforts, but only if it's the right kind of negative thinking.

There are two types of negative thinking that athletes typically engage in. "Give-up" negative thinking involves their feeling lost, hopeless, and helpless, for example, "I'm so far behind, I've got no chance of winning." Athletes focus on negatives, causing them to lose their motivation, confidence, and intensity, resulting in surrender and defeat. Clearly, give-up negative thinking has no place in sports.

However, "fire-up" negative thinking has a decidedly different effect on athletes. They experience anger and get psyched up. For example, "I'm getting crushed. This is unacceptable!" (said with anger and intensity). Fire-up negative thinking causes an increase in determination, intensity, and feelings of wanting to fight rather than submit, which can improve performance and possibility turn a bad situation around (Taylor, 2017).

REBT and CBT for Sport

Self-talk can also be used to challenge underlying beliefs and thoughts that might be impeding performance (Williams & Leffingwell, 2002). Athletes' self-talk is often the manifestation of their core beliefs about their capabilities. However, just as these beliefs were learned, they can also be unlearned through adapting different ways of thinking and creating new beliefs (Porter, 2003). Rational emotive behavior therapy (REBT; Ellis, 1982, 1994) and cognitive behavior therapy (CBT; Beck, 1975) are structured and empirically supported approaches to identifying irrational and distorted thinking patterns that are negatively impacting cognitive, emotional, and behavioral functioning. Each theory takes a slightly different approach to identifying these thoughts and patterns, but both focus on how the thoughts are also representative of underlying negative beliefs about the self that perpetuate the unhelpful thought patterns and resulting maladaptive emotions and behaviors.

Summary

- Self-talk is generally defined as a dialogue with the self, which can be either internal or out loud.
- Self-talk is a critical mental exercise and tool because of its ability to influence performance through helping athletes focus attention, build confidence, harness motivation, manage emotions, regulate intensity, control energy and effort expenditure, narrow focus, and trigger automatic execution of tasks.
- Self-talk can be categorized based on whether it is positive or negative in its content or on how it impacts performance.
- Three general types of self-talk that occur in the literature are cognitive/instructional, motivational, and goal-directed self-talk.
- Instructional self-talk is most useful during skill development to cue athletes into a specific movement.
- Motivational self-talk serves athletes by providing encouragement and managing energy and emotions.
- Goal-directed self-talk focuses athletes on problem solving, decision making, and facilitating progress towards goal attainment.
- Consultants can help athletes to use self-talk that is present-focused, concise, positive and focused on the desirable outcome.
- Specific strategies for using self-talk include increasing awareness with mindfulness, keeping a thought log, using thought stopping, developing affirmations, reframing or countering negative self-talk, changing the proportion of positives to negatives, using fire-up negative thinking, and employing REBT or CBT.

References

Beck, A. T. (1975). *Cognitive therapy and the emotional disorders.* Madison, CT: International Universities Press.

Beilock, S. (2010). *Choke: What the secrets of the brain reveal about getting it right when you have to.* New York, NY: Atria.

Ellis, A. (1982). Self-direction in sport and life. In T. Orlick, J. Partington, & J. Salmela (Eds.), *Mental training for coaches and athletes* (pp.10–17). Ottawa, ON: Coaching Association of Canada.

Ellis, A. (1994). The sport of avoiding sports and exercise: A rational emotive behavior therapy perspective. *The Sport Psychologist, 8,* 248–261.

Fredrickson, B. L., & Losada, M. F. (2005). Positive affect and the complex dynamics of human flourishing. *The American Psychologist, 60*(7), 678–686. doi: 10.1037/0003-066X.60.7.678

Hardy, J., Hall, C., & Alexander, M. (2001). Exploring self-talk and affective states in sport. *Journal of Sports Sciences, 19* (7), 469–475.

Hardy, J., Hall, C., & Hardy, L. (2005). Quantifying athlete self-talk. *Journal of Sports Sciences, 23*(9), 905–917.

Hardy, J., Hall, C., & Hardy, L. (2004). A Note on Athletes' Use of Self-Talk. *Journal of Applied Sport Psychology, 16*(3), 251–257.

Hatzigeorgiadis, A., Zourbanos, N., Mpoumpaki, S., & Theodorakis, Y. (2009). Mechanisms underlying the self-talk-performance relationship: The effects of motivational self-talk on self-confidence and anxiety. *Psychology of Sport & Exercise, 10* (1), 186–192.

Holohan, M. (2016). Talk to yourself? Here's why experts say that's a good thing. Retrieved from www.today.com/health/talk-yourself-out-loud-here-s-why-experts-say-s-t76531 (accessed January 16, 2019).

Kee, Y. H., & John, W. C. K. (2008). Relationships between mindfulness, flow dispositions and mental skills adoption: A cluster analytic approach. *Psychology of Sport & Exercise, 9* (4), 393–411.

Latinjak, A. T., Zourbanos, N., López-Ros, V., & Hatzigeorgiadis, A. (2014). Goal-directed and undirected self-talk: Exploring a new perspective for the study of athletes' self-talk. *Psychology of Sport & Exercise, 15*(5), 548–558.

Meichenbaum, D. (1977). *Cognitive-behavior modification: An integrative approach.* New York, NY: Plenum.

Porter, K. (2003). *The mental athlete.* Champaign, IL: Human Kinetics.

Scott-Hamilton, J., Schutte, N. S., & Brown, R. F. (2016). Effects of a mindfulness intervention on sports-anxiety, pessimism, and flow in competitive cyclists. *Applied Psychology: Health and Well-Being, 8*(1), 85–103.

Swann, C., Crust, L., Jackman, P., Vella, S. A., Allen, M. S., & Keegan, R. (2017). Performing under pressure: Exploring the psychological state underlying clutch performance in sport. *Journal of Sports Sciences, 35*(23), 2272–2280.

Taylor, J. (2017). *Train your mind for athletic success: Mental preparation to achieve your sports goals*. Lanham, MD: Rowman & Littlefield.

Theodorakis, Y., Hatzigeorgiadis, A., & Chroni, S. (2008). Self-Talk: It Works, but How? Development and Preliminary Validation of the Functions of Self-Talk Questionnaire. *Measurement in Physical Education and Exercise Science, 12*(1), 10–30.

Tod, D., Edwards, C., McGuigan, M., & Lovell, G. (2015). A systematic review of the effect of cognitive strategies on strength performance. *Sports Medicine, 45*(11), 1589–1602.

Van Raalte, J. L., Brewer, B. W., Rivera, P. M., & Petitpas, A. J. (1994). The relationship between observable self-talk and competitive junior tennis players' match performances. *Journal of Sport & Exercise Psychology, 16*(4), 400–415.

Van Raalte, J. L., Vincent, A., & Brewer, B. W. (2016). Self-talk: Review and sport-specific model. *Psychology of Sport & Exercise, 22*, 139–148.

Williams, J. M., & Leffingwell, T. R. (2002). Cognitive strategies in sport and exercise psychology. In J. L. Van Raalte & B. W. Brewer (Eds.), *Exploring sport and exercise psychology* (pp. 75–98). Washington, DC: American Psychological Association.

Williams, J. M., Zinsser, N., & Bunker, L. (2015). Cognitive techniques for building confidence and enhancing performance. In J. M. Williams & V. Krane (Eds.), *Applied sport psychology: Personal growth to peak performance* (pp. 274–303). New York, NY: McGraw Hill.

Zourbanos, N., Hatzigeorgiadis, A., Goudas, M., Papaioannou, A., Chroni, S., & Theodorakis, Y. (2011). The social side of self-talk: Relationships between perceptions of support received from the coach and athletes' self-talk. *Psychology of Sport & Exercise, 12* (4), 407–414.

MINDFULNESS

Sheryl Smith and Heidi Freeman

The New York Knicks (Vorkunov, 2016) and the Los Angeles Lakers (Gordhamer, 2011). Olympic Snowboarder Gretchen Bleiler (Goyanes, n.d.). Gymnast Sam Mikulak (Penny, 2015). Marathon runner Deena Kastor (Carlson, 2015). What do these teams and athletes all have in common? All have incorporated mindfulness into their training regimens. They say it makes them more focused and calm, and helps them to get "in the zone."

What is Mindfulness?

While there exist a variety of approaches to mindfulness leading to a broad array of definitions, the most commonly cited definition of mindfulness is "paying attention, in a particular way, on purpose, in the present moment, and nonjudgmentally" (Kabat-Zinn et al., 1992). Shinzen Young describes three components to mindfulness: concentration power, sensory clarity, and equanimity (the ability to allow experiences to come and go without judgment; Young, 2016). Most definitions of mindfulness emphasize both a heightened awareness of the moment and the uncoupling of sensory experience from its evaluation.

It is important to make the distinction between mindfulness and relaxation. A sense of calm may be a *result* of mindfulness practice, but it is not necessarily its *goal*. Athletes can experience of a range of thoughts and feelings to which to apply nonjudgmental awareness. It is the repeated response of benevolent curiosity toward, and emotional disengagement with, the unfolding awareness of the present moment that results in mindfulness's benefits.

Meditations are the mental practice exercises through which mindfulness is trained. The three most common types are focused attention (FA), open monitoring (OM) meditations, and loving kindness (Lutz et al., 2009). Focused attention meditations involve selecting an object of attentional focus (an anchor), approaching it with an attitude of curiosity, and repeatedly returning one's attention back to it after a distraction. FA meditations can be seen by athletes as drill-based exercises that strengthen the ability to sustain attention. Open monitoring or choiceless awareness meditations have no preselected foci of attention. They consist of practicing nonreactive monitoring of whatever presents itself in the moment. The emphasis here is on noticing whatever arises in one's experience with unattached awareness.

A third type of meditation, loving kindness, is aimed at increasing the experience of compassion (an active stance of wanting to comfort). In loving kindness meditations, instructions are given to direct one's attention toward others and recognize that fears and feelings of inadequacy are universal (common humanity; Neff, 2003).

From a heightened sense of shared vulnerability, meditators practice responding with kindness and compassion by silently repeating expressions wishing all beings well. Loving kindness meditations can also be directed toward the self. Self-compassion meditations practice "turning toward" instead of turning away from painful experiences. Taking an active stance of self-compassion, one practices acknowledging difficult emotions with gentleness and compassionate awareness, making space for them inside one's larger experience of the moment. Nonreactive present moment awareness is required to hold painful thoughts and feelings in balanced awareness for the purpose of self-soothing (Neff, 2003, Germer, 2009).

Theory and Research

Mindfulness has become increasingly popular since the early 2000s, assuming a prominent role in the complementary medicine industry. It has been adopted as a solution to stress and illness and as a promoter of focus and wellness. In 1979, Dr. Jon Kabat-Zinn developed the Mindfulness-Based Stress Reduction (MBSR) program to help chronically ill people reduce their experience of stress. MBSR brings traditional Buddhist principles of nonjudgmental present moment awareness to the secular practice of Western medicine. Studies on the beneficial effects of increased mindfulness have shown that MBSR training reduces anxiety, depression, and the suffering component of pain in clinical populations (Goyal et al., 2014; Hofmann et al., 2010). In addition to self-report measures of cognitive and emotional experiences, recent advances in neuroscience have contributed exciting evidence of the benefits of mindfulness training. Evidence for meditation-induced brain changes comes from fMRI investigations of the brains of meditators. Mindfulness practices have been associated with structural changes in brain areas that promote memory, attention, emotion regulation, self-referential processing, and perspective-taking and compassion (Hözel et al., 2008, 2011a, 2011b; Lazar et al., 2005; Sevinc et al., 2018).

However, as the healthcare, business, and education sectors have embraced mindfulness as a new panacea, concerns have arisen that it has strayed from the foundations of simple meditative practices (Kabat-Zinn, 2015) and that the claims of mindfulness' benefits have outpaced the research that supports it.

With this caution, the usefulness of mindfulness in the context of sports performance factors and athlete well being is examined. There is a growing body of research demonstrating the value of mindfulness training both outside of and within sports. It indicates that mindfulness impacts people psychologically, emotionally, and physiologically in a number of ways. These changes can benefit athletes in their practice efforts and competitive performances. In particular, sports performance can benefit from:

- heightened awareness of the present moment;
- ability to direct and sustain focus;
- ability to accept experiences without judgment; and
- compassionate relationship to the self.

Focus

Focus is one area in which mindfulness training has proven to be effective with athletes.

The ability to focus amid distractions is an essential skill for athletes. They are required to focus on performance-relevant cues and shift attention when appropriate, while also filtering out irrelevant stimuli and distractions (Kaufman, Glass, & Pineau, 2016). As discussed in Chapter 3, athletes must often contend with distractions that are external (e.g., crowd noise, weather, opposing players, officials) and internal (distracting thoughts, emotions, or physical sensations). The core practice of focused attention meditation is essentially focus training, and indeed, within sport contexts, mindfulness training has been shown to improve attention and concentration (Gardner, 2016; Haase, Kentta, Hickman, Baltzell, & Paulus, 2016; Kaufman, Glass, & Pineau, 2016). In addition, open monitoring practices, which emphasize acknowledging thoughts and emotions as they come and then letting them go without judgment or attachment, can help athletes to let go of distracting thoughts, unhelpful emotions, and uncomfortable physical reactions (Gardner & Moore, 2007; Kaufman, Glass, & Pineau, 2016).

Mindfulness meditation training has been shown to improve cognitive control and flexibility (Moore & Malinowski, 2008; Teper & Inzlict, 2013). There is evidence that it strengthens the brain's attention systems and inoculates them from the effects of stress in high-stress situations (Jha et al., 2007, 2017; Zeiden et al., 2010). Mindfulness training is also related to faster and more accurate target detection amid distraction (Jha et al., 2007; Slagter et al., 2007), suggesting that an athlete's ability to attend to important task-relevant cues may improve. Moreover, cognitive effort is reduced (Lutz et al., 2009) and attention resource allocation becomes more efficient after intensive meditation training (Slagter et al., 2007; MacLean et al., 2010; Malinowski, 2013). Mindfulness practice strengthens the brain's systems of attention and executive control and makes them more resilient to pressure, making recognition of distraction and return of focus progressively more effortless and efficient. However, it is unclear how long these beneficial effects persist after a regular program of mindfulness practice is suspended or has ended.

Distress Tolerance and Emotion Regulation

Closely related to attention control is the ability to regulate emotions, especially to tolerate distress. As discussed in Chapter 2, athletes experience a wide range of unpleasant and distressing emotions while practicing and competing including fear, frustration, anger, and disappointment. Along with those emotions, they must also contend with negative thoughts and uncomfortable physical sensations associated with those emotions. The challenge for athletes is to experience those emotions and sensations without being consumed by them to the point that performance suffers. Studies of mindfulness interventions in sport have shown that mindfulness training helps athletes to reduce psychological distress, task-related worries, and task-irrelevant thoughts, and to improve experiential acceptance and non-reactivity, optimism, and goal-directed behavior, as well as body awareness and tolerance of discomfort (Gardner, 2016; Haase et al., 2016; Kaufman, Glass, & Pineau, 2016).

Mindfulness training emphasizes the open and accepting experience of the present moment without judgment and without needing to change it. Another tenet of mindfulness is the understanding that all experiences are transient—they come and go on their own—and therefore do not necessarily need to be acted upon to be resolved, but simply experienced and allowed to pass. Mindfulness training, especially open monitoring meditations, helps athletes to identify thoughts and emotions and experience them without undue reaction or attachment. "Turning toward" meditations deliberately engage awareness with difficult emotions, experiencing them impartially, without escaping or suppressing them. In addition, body awareness may facilitate emotion regulation and reduce cognitive rumination. Brain activity associated with body awareness increases (Farb et al., 2010; Lazar et al., 2005) and amygdala reactivity decreases (Desbordes et al., 2015; Hözel et al., 2013) with mindfulness training. Farb and colleagues (2010, 2012) suggest that mindfulness practice enables the recruitment of brain areas related to body sensation as an *alternative* to ruminative processing of negative emotion. Instead of trying to deny or change their thoughts and emotions, athletes learn to experience and tolerate them, which decreases the amount of attention given to the experience, thus allowing the athlete to focus on their performance.

As athletes improve their ability to tolerate distress and regulate their emotions, there is less need for avoidance behaviors—those that serve the purpose of reducing unpleasant emotions by avoiding the situations in which they arise, but also hurting performances. This self-sabotage can include rushing through movements, shying away from practicing certain skills, giving less effort, or taking oneself out of a play or event. Behaviors that allow an escape from unpleasant experiences are reinforcing and with repetition can become automatic habits; athletes may even have low awareness of when they are engaging in avoidance behaviors. Mindfulness training raises this self-awareness and decouples the link between urge and automatic behavior (Brewer, 2017) and reduces the need for experiential avoidance.

Empathy and Self-compassion

Mindfulness training also has been shown to increase compassion, self-compassion, and empathy (Birnie, Speca, & Carlson, 2010; Evans et al., 2018; Sevinc et al., 2018). Active self-soothing using a benevolent inner voice can be strengthened to counter harsh self-criticism. While self-compassion may seem counter to a sport culture that often emphasizes toughness and grit, Baltzell (2016) argues that the ability to meet unpleasant experiences with compassion and gentleness is what makes distress tolerance *possible* and allows the athlete to let go and refocus on the performance. Meditations that focus on self-comfort such as Hickman's "Finding your compassionate inner coach" (Baltzell, 2016) and those contained in Germer's (2009) "The mindful path to self-compassion" equip athletes to deal with failure, fear, and shame. In addition, team compassion meditations can be used to facilitate a sense of common humanity, create a shared compassionate culture, and build an empathic bridge between teammates in conflict.

Practical Implications

As mindfulness has become more popular in both clinical and sport settings, several mindfulness- and acceptance-based performance enhancement programs have been developed and studied.

Mindfulness–Acceptance–Commitment

The Mindfulness–Acceptance–Commitment (MAC) model was first conceptualized by Frank Gardner and Zella Moore in 2001 as an acceptance-based alternative to traditional mental training programs. The goal of the MAC approach to performance enhancement is to develop athletes' awareness and acceptance of a variety of internal experiences as normal and natural, without judgment or a need to change them. In addition, the MAC approach aims to strengthen athletes' ability to attend to task-relevant cues, regardless of internal states, and to choose values-driven responses (Gardner & Moore, 2007; Gardner, 2016). The MAC protocol consists of seven modules that include psychoeducation, training in mindfulness and cognitive defusion (separating thoughts from events/experiences), values and values-driven behavior, acceptance of experience, commitment, and skill consolidation (Gardner & Moore, 2007, 2017). The protocol also includes in-session and between-session exercises to enhance mindful awareness, acceptance of experience, and commitment to goals, as well as considerations for continuing practice once the intervention concludes. The MAC protocol has been shown to improve attention and awareness, practice intensity, acceptance of internal states, and competitive performance, and to increase flow states and reduce psychological distress (Gardner, 2016; for a full description and manualized protocol, see Gardner and Moore, 2007).

Mindful Performance Enhancement, Awareness, and Knowledge

The Mindful Performance Enhancement, Awareness, and Knowledge (mPEAK) program was developed by Haase and colleagues (2016), and is based, in part, on Jon Kabat Zinn's Mindfulness Based Stress Reduction (MBSR). In addition to increasing mindful awareness and acceptance of experience, the mPEAK program aims to improve athletes' responses to sport stressors (e.g., physical pain or emotional strain) and includes training in self compassion. The mPEAK program is an eight-week intervention built around four "pillars" (Haase et al., 2016):

1. Mindful awareness of the body.
2. Awareness of thoughts and the "wandering mind" and how they can impact performance (with the goal of letting go of unhelpful stories).
3. Acknowledging and accepting difficulty and letting go of the need to avoid or change these experiences.
4. Self-compassion and letting go of perfectionism.

The mPEAK program has been studied with members of the USA BMX Cycling Team and was found to improve awareness of physical and emotional experiences, attentional control, and the ability to cope with distress (Haase et al., 2016). For a more in-depth description of the mPEAK program, see Haase et al. (2016) or visit the UCSD Center for Mindfulness website at http://mbpti.org/programs/mpeak.

Mindful Sport Performance Enhancement

The Mindful Sport Performance Enhancement (MSPE) program was developed by Kaufman and Glass in 2006, and updated in 2017. The MSPE program, also based in part on Jon Kabaat Zinn's MBSR, consists of six sessions, each including didactic and experiential components as well as home practice assignments. The protocol includes education on mindfulness and sport performance, nonjudgment of experience, awareness of the body and of thoughts, non-attachment and acceptance, and the integration of mindfulness into daily training. In addition to traditional practices such as mindfulness of the breath, mindful walking, and the body scan, the MSPE program includes mindful yoga and sport-specific mindfulness practices (e.g., mindful running) (Kaufman, Glass, & Pineau, 2016). Preliminary studies of the MSPE program showed increases in trait and state mindfulness, optimism, flow, and acting with awareness, and decreases in perfectionism, task-irrelevant thoughts and worries, and sport-related anxiety (Kaufman, Glass, & Pineau, 2016). A detailed outline of the MSPE program can be found in Kaufman, Glass, and Pineau (2016) and the full protocol is available in Kaufman and Glass (2017). For an excellent review of the current state of mindfulness and performance, see Baltzell (2016).

Summary

- Most definitions of mindfulness incorporate the elements of heightened awareness of the present moment and uncoupling of sensory experience from the evaluation of it.
- Three most common types of meditations are focused awareness (concentration), open monitoring (choiceless awareness), and loving kindness or compassion.
- Focused attention meditations involve selecting an object of attentional focus (anchor), and repeatedly returning one's attention back to the anchor after a distraction. Open monitoring, or choiceless awareness meditations, have no preselected foci of attention and practice nonreactive noticing of whatever presents itself in the moment.
- Loving kindness meditation is aimed at increasing the experience of compassion (an active stance of wanting to comfort) and can be directed toward the self or others.
- Studies on the beneficial effects of increased mindfulness have shown that MBSR training reduces anxiety, depression, and the suffering component of pain.
- Mindfulness training has proven to be effective in helping athletes with heightened awareness of the present moment, the ability to direct and sustain attention, the ability to accept experiences without judgment, and the opportunity to develop a compassionate relationship to the self.
- Studies of mindfulness interventions in sport have shown that mindfulness training helps athletes to reduce anxiety and apprehension, psychological distress, task-related worries, and task-irrelevant thoughts, and to improve experiential acceptance and non-reactivity, optimism, and goal-directed behavior, as well as body awareness and tolerance of discomfort. Mindfulness training also has been shown to increase compassion, self-compassion, and empathy.
- Empirically based mindfulness interventions include Mindful–Acceptance–Commitment (MAC), Mindful Performance Enhancement, Awareness, and Knowledge (mPEAK), and Mindful Sport Performance Enhancement (MSPE).

References

Baltzell, A. L. (2016). Self-compassion, distress tolerance, and mindfulness in performance. In A. Baltzell (Ed.), *Mindfulness and performance* (pp. 53–77). Cambridge: Cambridge University Press.

Birnie, B. Speca, M., & Carlson, L. E. (2010). Exploring self-compassion and empathy in the context of mindfulness-based stress reduction (MBSR). *Stress and Health*, 26(5), 359–371.

Brewer, J. (2017). *The craving mind: From cigarettes to smart phones to love—why we get hooked and how we can break bad habits*. New Haven, CT: Yale University Press.

Carlson, C. (2015, January 28). How meditation can make you a better athlete. Retrieved from www.shape.com/lifestyle/mind-and-body/how-meditation-can-make-you-better-athlete

Desbordes, G., Gard. T., Hoge, E. A., Hözel, B. K., Kerr, C., Lazar, S. W., Olendzdki, A., & Vago, D. R. (2015). Moving beyond mindfulness: Defining equanimity as an outcome measure in meditation and contemplative research. *Mindfulness*, 6(2): 356–372. doi: 10.1007/s12671-013-0269-8.

Evans, S., Wyka, K., Blaha, K. T., & Allen, E. S. (2018). Self-compassion mediates improvement in well-being in a mindfulness-based stress reduction program in a community-based sample. *Mindfulness*, 9(4), 1280–1287. doi: 10.1007/s12671-017-0872-1

Farb, N. A., Anderson, A. K., Mayberg, H., Bean, J., McKeon, D., & Segal, Z. V. (2010). Minding one's emotions: mindfulness training alters the neural expression of sadness. *Emotion*, 10(1): 25–33.

Farb, N. A., Anderson, A. K., & Segal Z. V. (2012). The mindful brain and emotion regulation in mood disorders. *Canadian Journal of Psychiatry, 57*(2), 70–77.

Gardner, F. L. (2016). Scientific advancements of mindfulness- and acceptance-based models in sport psychology: A decade in time, a seismic shift in philosophy and practice. In A. Baltzell (Ed.), *Mindfulness and performance* (pp. 127–152). Cambridge: Cambridge University Press.

Gardner, F. L., & Moore, Z. E. (2007). *The psychology of enhancing human performance: The mindfulness-acceptance-commitment (MAC) approach.* New York, NY: Springer.

Gardner, F. L., & Moore, Z. E. (2017). Mindfulness-based and acceptance-based interventions in sport and performance contexts. *Current Opinion in Psychology, 16*, 180–184. doi: 10.1016/j.copsych.2017.06.001

Germer, C. K. (2009). *The mindful path to self-compassion: Freeing yourself from destructive thoughts and emotions.* Guilford publications

Gordhamer, S. (2011, April 15). The Lakers meditate? Retrieved from www.mindful.org/the-lakers-meditate/

Goyal, M., Singh, S., Sibinga, E. M., Gould, N. F., Rowland-Seymour, A., Sharma, R., Berger, Z., Sleicher, D., Maron, D. D., Shihab, H. M., Ranasinghe, P. D., Linn, S., Saha, S., & Haythornthwaite, J. A. (2014). Meditation programs for psychological stress and well-being: A systematic review and meta-analysis. *JAMA Internal Medicine, 174*(3): 357–368. doi: 10.1001/jamainternmed.2013.13018.

Goyanes, C. (n.d.). How to meditate with Gretchen Bleiler. Retrieved from www.shape.com/lifestyle/mind-and-body/how-meditate-gretchen-bleiler

Haase, L., Kentta, G., Hickman, S., Baltzell, A., & Paulus, M. (2016). Mindfulness training in elite athletes: mPEAK with BMX cyclists. In A. Baltzell (Ed.), *Mindfulness and performance* (pp. 186–208). Cambridge: Cambridge University Press.

Hofmann, S. G., Sawyer, A. T., Witt, A. A., & Oh, D. (2010). The effect of mindfulness-based therapy on anxiety and depression: A meta-analytic review. *J Consult Clin Psychol, 78*(2): 169–183. doi: 10.1037/a0018555

Hölzel, B. K., Ott, U., Gard, T., Hempel, H., Weygandt, M., Morgen, K., & Vaitl, D. (2008). Investigation of mindfulness meditation practitioners with voxel-based morphometry. *Soc Cogn Affect Neurosci, 3*, 55–61.

Hölzel, B. A., Carmody, J., Vangel, M., Congleton, C, Yerramsetti, A. M., Gard, T., & Lazar, S. (2011a). Mindfulness practice leads to increases in regional brain gray matter density. *Psychiatry Research: Neuroimaging, 191*(1), 36–43. doi: https://doi.org/10.1016/j.pscychresns.2010.08.006

Hölzel, B. K., Lazar, S. W., Gard, T., Schuman-Olivier, Z., Vago, D. R. et al. (2011b). How does mindfulness meditation work? Proposing mechanisms of action from a conceptual and neural perspective. *Perspective Psychol Sci, 6*, 537–559. doi: 10.1177/1745691611419671.

Hölzel, B. K., Hoge, E. A., Greve, D. N., Gard, T., Creswell, J. D., Brown, W. K., Barrett, L. F., Schwartz, C., Vaitl, D., & Lazar, S. W. (2013). Neural mechanisms of symptom improvements in generalized anxiety disorder following mindfulness training. *Neuroimage Clin, 2*, 448–458.

Jha, A. P., Krompinger, J., & Baime, M. J. (2007). Mindfulness training modifies subsystems of attention. *Cogn. Affect. Behav Neurosci, 7*, 109–119.

Jha, A., Witkin, J. E., Morrison, A. B., Rostrup, A., & Stanley, E. (2017). Short-form mindfulness training protects against working memory degradation over high-demand intervals. *J Cogn Enhanc, 1*, 154–171.

Kabat-Zinn, J. (2015). Mindfulness has huge health potential—but McMindfulness is no panacea. Retrieved from www.theguardian.com/commentisfree/2015/oct/20/mindfulness-mental-health-potential-benefits-uk

Kabat-Zinn, J., Massion, A. O., Kristeller, J., Peterson, L. G., Fletcher, K. E., Pbert, L., Lenderking, W. R., & Santorelli, S. F. (1992). Effectiveness of a meditation-based stress reduction program in the treatment of anxiety disorders. *Am J Psychiatry, 149*(7), 936–943.

Kaufman, K. A., & Glass, C. R. (2017). *Mindful sport performance enhancement: Mental training for athletes and coaches.* Washington, DC: American Psychological Association.

Kaufman, K. A., Glass, C. R., & Pineau, T. R. (2016). Mindful sport enhancement (MSPE): Development and applications. In A. Baltzell (Ed.), *Mindfulness and performance* (pp. 153–185). Cambridge: Cambridge University Press.

Lazar, S. W., Kerr, C. E., Wasserman, R. H., Gray, J. R., Greve, D. N., Treadway, M. T., McGarvey, M., Quinn, B. T., Dusek, J. A., Benson, H., Rauch, S. L., Moore, C. I., & Fischl, B. (2005). Meditation experience is associated with increased cortical thickness. *Neuroreport, 16*, 1893–1897.

Lutz, A., Slagter, H. A., Rawlings, N. B. Francis, A. D., Greischar, L. L., & Davidson, R. J. (2009). Mental Training Enhances Attentional Stability: Neural and Behavioral Evidence. Journal of Neuroscience 29(42), 13,418–13,427.

MacLean, K. A., Ferrer, E., Aichele, S. R., Bridwell, D. A., Zanesco, A. P., Jacobs, T. L., King, B. G., Rosenberg, E. L., Sahdra, B. K., Shaver, P. R., Wallace, B. A., Mangun, G. R., & Saron, C. D. (2010). Intensive meditation training improves perceptual discrimination and sustained attention. *Psychol Sci Jun, 21*(6), 829–839.

Malinowski, P. (2013). Neural mechanisms of attentional control in mindfulness meditation. *Front Neurosci, 7*, 8.

Moore, A., & Malinowski, P. (2008). Meditation, mindfulness and cognitive flexibility. *Consciousness and Cognition, 18*, 176–186.

Neff, K. (2003). Self-compassion: An alternative conceptualization of a healthy attitude toward oneself. *Self and Identity, 2*, 85–101.

Penny, B. (2015, August 15). Sam Mikulak chooses mindfulness over playfulness in dominant performance at P&G Championships. Retrieved from www.teamusa.org/News/2015/August/15/Sam-Mikulak-Chooses-Mindfulness-Over-Playfulness-In-Dominant-Performance-At-P-G-Championships

Sevinc, G., Holzel, B. K., Hashimi, J., Greenberg, J., McCallister, A., Treadway, M., Schneider, M.L., Dusek, J. A., Carmody, J., & Lazar, S. W. (2018). Common and dissociable neural activity following mindfulness-based stress reduction and relaxation response programs. *Psychosomatic Medicine, 80*(5), 439–451.

Slagter, H. A., Lutz, A., Greischar, L. L., Francis, A. D., Nieuwenhuis, S., Davis, J. M., & Davidson, R. J. (2007). Mental training affects distribution of limited brain resources. *PLoS Biol, 5*(6), e138.

Teper, R., & Inzlicht, M. (2013). Meditation, mindfulness and executive control: the importance of emotional acceptance and brain-based performance monitoring. *Social Cognitive and Affective Neuroscience, 8*(1), 85–92.

Vorkunov, M. (2016, December 6). Coached by the Zen master, the Knicks try mindfulness. *The New York Times*. Retrieved from www.nytimes.com/2016/12/06/sports/basketball/phil-jackson-zen-master-knicks-mindfulness.html

Young, S. (2016). *The science of enlightenment: How meditation works*. Boulder, CO: Sounds True.

Zeidan, F., Johnson, S. K., Diamond, B. J., & Goolkasian, P. (2010). Mindfulness meditation improves cognition: Evidence of brief mental training. *Consciousness and Cognition, 19*, 597–605.

BREATHING

Kimberlee Bethany Bonura and Jim Taylor

Breathing may be one of the least appreciated and used exercises and tools that athletes have at their disposal. Like all of us, athletes may not even realize the benefits that breathing has to their sports efforts because it is something that humans do without conscious awareness or the need to control every moment of their lives. Moreover, many athletes may view breathing as more of problem—being really out of breath after an intense exertion—than as a powerful means of improving their practice and competitive performances. Clearly, breathing is fundamental for life; it supplies our bodies with the oxygen necessary for life. That very function means that breathing can also have a substantial impact, either beneficial or harmful, on athletes' performances.

It's not uncommon for athletes to either engage in short and choppy breathing or inadvertently hold their breath. This unintentional practice has several effects that prevent athletes from performing at their highest level. Due to a lack of sufficient oxygen in their systems, reduced or impaired breathing may cause athletes to experience the following symptoms:

- more rapid fatigue;
- greater experience of pain;
- muscle tension;
- loss of fine motor control;
- decline in endurance;
- reduction in strength and power;
- decreased mobility;
- loss of motivation and confidence;
- increased stress and anxiety;
- heightened emotional sensitivity; and
- increased distraction.

The cumulative outcome of restricted breathing and reduced oxygen intake is that athletes are no longer physiologically or psychologically capable of performing their best in their sport.

The opposite of this inhibiting effect is that breathing can produce important physical and psychological advantages for athletes. Some of these benefits include:

- greater physiological control;
- increased energy;
- more pain tolerance;
- more efficient muscle activity;
- greater fine motor control;

- enhanced stamina;
- improved strength and power; and
- better mobility.

The overall benefit when athletes use breathing as an exercise or tool is that they gain the ability to ensure that they are physiologically ready to perform at their highest level.

Breathing also brings considerable value to athletes mentally and emotionally. These psychological benefits of deliberate breathing training include:

- greater sense of control;
- reduced stress, anxiety, and fear;
- bolstered motivation and confidence;
- more centered;
- maintain ideal intensity;
- greater emotional resilience;
- improved focus and fewer distractions;
- more process-oriented; and
- greater sense of rhythm and flow in performance.

As a result, athletes should see breathing as more than an autonomic physical experience that occurs outside of their conscious control. Rather, athletes should include breathing as another purposeful exercise and tool they can actively employ to be better prepared physically and mentally to perform their best.

Theory and Research

Breathing is both very simple and very complex. At its simplest, respiration, the process of breathing in oxygen and breathing out carbon dioxide, is part of the autonomic system. The autonomic nervous system is part of the body's control system that maintains unconscious bodily functions such as heart rate, digestion, and the processing and filtration of liquids into blood and urinary waste products. The autonomic nervous system controls breathing as part of daily functioning, outside of awareness, when we are not thinking about breathing. Under normal resting conditions, when breath is managed by the autonomic system and functioning outside of awareness or voluntary control, the average person breathes approximately 14 to 16 times per minute (Seaward, 2002). Under exertion, such as during aerobic exercise, breathing rate can increase to as high as sixty breaths per minute. In situations of high physiological arousal, such as when experiencing acute stress, respiratory rate increases and the breathing pattern becomes shallow, with muscular contraction focused in the chest cavity, rather than allowing for deeper breaths using diaphragmatic contraction (Seaward, 2002). In Selye's (1956) classic General Adaptation Syndrome model of stress, respiratory rate may shift as part of the physiological changes that occur during the three stages of alarm, resistance, and exhaustion. These fluctuations in respiratory rate generally occur outside of our control, as part of the body's natural response to physiological and psychological stressors.

At the same time, we can exert voluntary control over respiration with purposeful awareness and breathing exercises. EEG research indicates that deliberate control of the breath has specific neurological impacts and may actually support organizational hierarchies and strategies in the brain (Herrero, Khuvis, Yeagle, Cerf, & Mehta, 2018). In other words, deliberate breathing training may help to improve how we think, organize and perform. Breath control and training have a variety of functions and breathing exercises may be used in many different ways before, during, and after sports performances to harness its value to athletes.

For instance, one empirical study with runners tested the effects of a four-week breathing intervention. Breathing exercises (thirty breaths, twice per day) were included as part of daily training and before races. The breathing exercises were done as part of the pre-competitive warm-up, just before a race. The results indicated that use of daily breathing training exercises improved race times by 12 percent. Their use in the warm-up before a race improved race times by five to seven percent. When the two strategies were combined (i.e., both daily breath training and specific pre-performance breathing exercises), race times improved by 15 percent (Lomax, Grant, & Corbett, 2011). Research with youth rugby players has found that regular breathing training has broad impact, including improved psychological skills, health, and sport performance (Edwards & Edwards, 2007).

Other research indicates that runners may use a variety of breathing patterns, which in running are reflected as strides per breath, although a 2:1 ratio (i.e., two strides per breath) seems to be favored (Bramble & Carrier, 1983). Ongoing research indicates that breathing patterns in running "minimize antagonistic loading of respiratory muscles, reduce work of breathing and minimize rate of fatigue" (Daley, Bramble, & Carrier, 2013).

Overall, athletes may find that deliberate awareness of and training with breathing strategies may have psychological effects (i.e., improved ability to manage stress and anxiety) and improved sport-related performance outcomes.

Practical Implications

With any mental exercise and tool, regular practices and consistent use is necessary for athletes to experience benefits. Breathing is no different. For breathing to be effective in enhancing athletes' practice efforts and competitive performances, breathing training must be used regularly and become a consistent habit in all areas of athletes' lives. Athletes can use breathing in particular places in practice and competitions to help them be more prepared physically and mentally.

Breathing Basics

Good breathing techniques are relevant in all sports, regardless of their physiological requirements, complexity, or duration. Many people have learned to breathe into their chests, which may reflect cultural preferences for smaller waists and stomachs (Seaward, 2002), but chest-based breathing is more demanding on the body because it requires that the rib cage and shoulders be lifted while breathing, which also limits the capacity of the lungs. In contrast, diaphragmatic breathing, which involves allowing the stomach to relax so that the diaphragm may expand during each inhalation, improves breathing capacity and breathing's relaxation effects.

To practice diaphragmatic breathing, athletes can use this exercise:

- Lie down and assume a comfortable and relaxed position.
- Place one hand on the stomach.
- Inhale and exhale through the nose.
- With each inhalation, focus on allowing the air to come into the body and fill the lungs, so that they expand into the core body—this will cause the stomach to rise and the hand that is on the stomach will lift upward.
- With each exhalation, focus on pushing all of the air out of the body, with the diaphragm moving up into the chest cavity as the lungs contract. This will cause the stomach to contract, and the hand that is on the stomach will fall down toward the body.
- Repeat this for two minutes, while using the hand on the stomach as a physical tool to facilitate breathing "into the belly."

Posture impacts breathing as well and when athletes are slouched (i.e., standing or sitting with poor spinal alignment), it can reduce the quality and integrity of the breath. Good posture with an open chest, spinal alignment, and balanced positioning between the left and right sides can improve the ability of the lungs to expand fully and support complete breathing cycles.

Deliberate breathing is a physical skill and, like any other, it is responsive to practice. Daily practice of deep, diaphragmatic breathing with good posture improves athletes' ability to leverage this type of breathing in practice and competitive situations, and increases the likelihood that they will remember to use deep diaphragmatic breathing deliberately in situations and experiences of stress.

Athletes can then apply these basic strategies for good breathing to the unique demands of their sport. For example, swimmers need to learn to pace strokes with breaths, and patterns may vary by stroke for optimal performance. Competitive shooters find that aim and accuracy are improved if they shoot in the natural pause after the exhalation (Snow, 2014). Competitive shooters (or other athletes who must aim with precision, such as archers) may want to practice breathing which focuses on the pauses between the active inhale and exhale components of the breath. For instance, "square breathing" is a breathing exercise which emphasizes four equal components within the breath. To practice square breathing:

- Identify a time period for each phase—for instance, 2 seconds, 4 seconds, or 8 seconds. For the purposes of this exercise, we'll use 8 seconds, which is a common time goal for square breathing exercises.
- Identify the four phases of the breath (the four sides of the square): the inhalation, the pause between the inhalation and the exhalation, the exhalation, and the pause between the exhalation and the next inhalation.
- Using a stable seated posture, deliberately and slowly inhale through the nose for a count of 8.
- Hold the breath for a count of 8.
- Exhale through the nose for a count of 8.
- Hold the space and emptiness for a count of 8.

Square breathing should be done for at least five minutes to create understanding of the pattern of the breath and can be practiced regularly and for extended periods as a meditation and breath-training strategy. Breath holding may be contraindicated for certain health conditions (for instance, high blood pressure, epilepsy, and pregnancy), so athletes with health conditions should discuss square breathing with their medical practitioner prior to trying this strategy. For competitive shooters, square breathing may be helpful as a way to focus on the calm space between breaths during the moment they pull the trigger to increase focus and accuracy.

In Routines

Breathing can become a consistent part of athletes' daily practices by incorporating them into their practice, pre-competitive, and between-performance routines. Athletes can use breathing in various places in their routines including during physical warm-up, to help in reaching and maintaining their ideal intensity, to redirect their focus inward, during their use of mental imagery, and in the last moments before practice or a competition begins or resumes.

During Performances

As discussed previously, athletes can be known to unintentionally hold their breaths during performances, thus creating physical and mental states that are not conducive to optimal performance. To counter this negative effect, athletes can include breathing in their conditioning, practice, and competitive performance routines. Through awareness and repetition, athletes can, first, learn where breathing may benefit during a performance, for example, for timing a skill, increasing exertion, or to ensure the full range of a movement. Then, they can consciously incorporate the appropriate breathing patterns into their performances until they are deeply ingrained habits that they use automatically in competitions.

In Recovery from Performances

When athletes experience significant physical exertion in their conditioning, practice, or competitive efforts, they are going to be out of breath when finished. For instance, after a series of intervals, a long point in tennis, a 400-meter run, a play in football, or run to the goal in soccer, athletes may feel out-of-breath due to the physical exhaustion. Athletes' ability to recover swiftly and completely is important to sustain consistent performance, particularly in sports that require ongoing engagement through the duration of the event. In these situations, athletes will usually wait until their breathing normalizes on its own. However, this approach may take time that athletes do not have. With the use of purposeful breathing, they can reclaim control of their physiology as quickly as possible. To that end, athletes can gain that control by consciously deepening and slowing their breathing until it moderates. Using breathing as a tool in this way will enable athletes to regain control of their breathing, recoup the oxygen they lost during their effort, accelerate recovery, and return their bodies to an equilibrium that best prepares them for their ensuing performance.

When Athletes Go Negative

Breathing doesn't just offer physical benefits; it can also be a useful exercise and tool to help athletes when their minds turn against them. For example, it's not uncommon for athletes to "go negative" before a competition, where they experience negative self-talk, worry, and anxiety. This reaction usually occurs when they feel out of control, unprepared, uncertain, or uneasy. In these situations, athletes can use breathing to their benefit in several ways. It can help them return a sense of control that comes from actively mitigating the unpleasant physical reactions that are present. For instance, when stressed, athletes may notice its physiological effects including a tight stomach or tense muscles. Deliberate, slow, and focused breathing may help to reduce the physiological effects of stress and regain a sense of physical calm. With this removal of physical symptoms, athletes will feel more comfortable. With both of these responses, they will also feel more confident in facing the challenges presented to them. Breathing also redirects athletes' attention from the causes of the negativity. Breathing brings their focus back onto themselves, to the physical activity of consciously controlling the breath, and allows the athletes to move forward with what they need to do to perform their best.

When Athletes Become Anxious

As discussed in Chapter 3, overintensity, anxiety or stress are common reactions in athletes before a competition. Doubt, worry, expectations, and pressure can all contribute to activation of the sympathetic nervous system including quickened breathing, tense muscles, racing heart, sweating, and excessive adrenaline. In this highly stressed state, optimal athletic performance is a near impossibility.

At the heart of a stress or anxiety reaction is the perception that athletes have lost control of their bodies. The reality is that they can't directly reduce or reverse the physical symptoms of sympathetic nervous system activation. But breathing is the one physiological function that athletes can directly control. By taking control of their breathing, athletes activate the parasympathetic nervous system and indirectly mitigate those interfering physical symptoms. This regained control of their physiology offers athletes mental benefits as well in the form of increased confidence and comfort, more positive emotions, and improved focus.

To Increase Intensity

Breathing is most commonly thought of as an exercise or tool to induce a state of relaxation in athletes. Yet, a calm state isn't always ideal for optimal performance for every athlete and in every sport. In fact, some athletes perform best at a high level of intensity and some sports require more intensity due to their need for powerful and explosive movement (e.g., weight lifting, sprinting, tennis).

To that end, breathing can be a useful exercise and tool for elevating the intensity of athletes. Instead of slow, deep breaths, athletes can take shorter and more forceful breaths. This "aggressive" breathing activates the sympathetic nervous system in a positive and energizing way. Intense breathing also offers mental benefits including more motivation and effort, increased confidence, a sharpened focus, and a more "fired up" attitude.

As a Performance Trigger

For anyone who has ever watched elite athletes in a competition, they may have noticed that these athletes often take a perceptible breath before they perform. Examples include a football player waiting for the snap, a goalie preparing for a penalty kick, or an archer getting ready to release their arrow. Their pre-performance breathing can be brief and forceful or full and gradual. The number of breaths they take is usually from one to three. Their breathing seems to be the last action they take before they perform.

When high-level athletes have been asked why they take breaths, their responses are all unique:

- "It's my signal to bring everything together so I'm totally ready to give it my all."
- "Deep breathing makes me centered and focused."
- "It makes me happy and I play best when I'm happy."
- "Breathing helps me push any nerves or tension I feel out of my body."
- "My breathing turns up the volume on my energy and I'm ready explode forward."
- "I need to be super fired up for me to play well and a few intense breaths get me stoked."
- "My breathing allows me to turn my mind off and let my body do its thing."

These responses sound very different, but they share one common theme: breathing provides them with a trigger that acts as the final point of preparation before the performance (Taylor, 2017).

Athletes can use this same approach to find their own performance triggers. They can first understand what they need to feel before they perform to be completely ready: relaxed or intense, centered on self or outward focused, happy or angry? Second, once identified, athletes can choose a type of breathing that best triggers that feeling. They can also decide how many breathes they want to take and at what point in their final preparations. When athletes know what type of breathing will work best for them as a performance trigger, they can include that breathing into their conditioning, practice, and pre-competition preparations.

Summary

- Breathing may be one of the least appreciated and used exercises and tools that athletes have at their disposal.
- Breathing is so important because without it, athletes will experience more fatigue, greater pain, more muscle tension, loss of motor control, decline in endurance, reduction in strength and power, decreased mobility, loss of motivation and confidence, increased anxiety, heightened emotional sensitivity, and more distractions.
- The benefits of breathing include great physiological control, increased energy, more pain tolerance, more efficient muscle activity, greater motor control, enhanced stamina, improved strength, better mobility, greater sense of control, reduced stress, anxiety, and fear, bolstered motivation and confidence, greater emotional resilience, improved focus, and greater rhythm and flow.
- Diaphragmatic breathing and good posture are essential for effective breathing.
- Considerable research has demonstrated the value of breathing to many aspects of sports performance.
- Breathing can be used by athletes to maximize its benefits in routines, during performances, in recovery from performances, when athletes go negative, when they become stressed or anxious, to increase intensity, and as a performance trigger.

References

Bramble, D., & Carrier, D. (1983). Running and breathing in mammals. *Science, 219*, 251–256.

Daley, M. A., Bramble, D. M., & Carrier D. R. (2013). Impact loading and locomotor-respiratory coordination significantly influence breathing dynamics in running humans. *PLoS ONE, 8*(8): e70752. doi:10.1371/journal.pone.0070752

Edwards, S., & Edwards, D. (2007). Breath-based psychological skills training and rugby players. *African Journal for Physical Health Education, Recreation, and Dance, 13*(4), 380–399.

Herrero, J., Khuvis, S., Yeagle, E., Cerf, M., & Mehta, A. D. (2018). Breathing above the brain stem: Volitional control and attentional modulation in humans. *Journal of Neurophysiology, 119*(1), 145–159.

Lomax, M., Grant, I., & Corbett, J. (2011). Inspiratory muscle warm-up and inspiratory muscle training: Separate and combined effects on intermittent running to exhaustion. *Journal of Sports Science, 29*(6), 563–569.

Seaward, B. (2002). *Managing stress: Principles and strategies for health and wellbeing*, 3rd ed. Boston, MA: Jones and Bartlett Publishing.

Selye, H. (1956). *The stress of life*. New York, NY: McGraw Hill.

Snow, J. (2014). *The ultimate shooting skills manual*. San Francisco, CA: Weldon Owen Publishing.

Sood, A. (2013). *The May Clinic guide to stress-free living*. Philadelphia, PA: Da Capo Life Long.

Taylor, J. (2017). *Train your mind for athletic success: Mental preparation to achieve your sports goals*. Lanham, MD: Rowman & Littlefield.

MUSIC

Leopoldo Ferrer and Jim Taylor

Athletes with headphones have become a ubiquitous sight at competitions in most sports and at every level, from youth to Olympians and professionals. Music is used by athletes to manage both their physiologies and psychologies, and to prepare themselves to perform their best in competitions. Athletes have specific playlists depending on how they feel on a given day. Specifically, athletes use music to:

- increase motivation;
- build confidence;
- generate beneficial emotions;
- shift physical intensity up or down; and
- direct focus inward.

Despite its widespread use, it is only recently emerging as an area receiving scientific attention in applied sport psychology. Music therapy is a growing field of both study and practice that has theoretical approaches, uses passive and active methods, and has demonstrated its benefits outside of sport (Del Olmo, 2009; Wheeler, 2015).

Theory and Research

There is a growing body of research both outside of and within sport demonstrating the value of music as a tool to assist athletes in being better prepared to perform their best. This impact is evident in several primary areas that are relevant to athletes.

Outside of sport, there is considerable research indicating many effects that could be useful to athletes. Music therapy has been shown to reduce nausea, pain, and aggression, modify many physiological parameters, and improve emotion, mood, well-being, life satisfaction, relationships, verbal and gestural communication, fine and gross motor skills, balance, and gait. Other research has found that cognitive functions are also influenced by music including attention, calculation, language, memory, and judgment (Särkämö et al., 2008; Kwon, Gang, & Oh, 2013). It has been theorized that these effects are due to the activation of relevant neural pathways involving both psychological and physiological factors. More specifically, it has been hypothesized that emotion is the central mediator between linked music and performance in its powerful impact on physiology, psychology, cognition, and biomechanics (Baker, 2015; Särkämö et al., 2008).

Emotions

Emotions play a vital role in athletes' experience of and performance in sports. Whether positive emotions, such as excitement, pride, and inspiration, or negative emotions, such as fear, anger, and despair, the causes of these emotions and how athletes react to them often have an significant impact on their sports efforts. Music has been shown to influence both the direction and the intensity of emotions (Tenenbaum et al., 2011; Bishop, Karageorghis, & Loizou, 2007).

Music's evocative impact has both intrinsic and extrinsic sources of emotional responses. Intrinsic sources refer to structural characteristics of the music including tempo and beat. Extrinsic sources of music on athletes are mediated by associations unrelated to the structural aspects of the music including psychological influences such as memories, past emotional experiences, and current thoughts related to the music. Other extrinsic sources of emotional responses consist of friends, videos they have watched, and preferred artists which produce particular emotional reactions to the music (Bharucha, Curtis, & Paroo, 2006). Both kinds of sources lead to a connection between the music and the produced emotions (Bishop et al., 2007). This research revealed that athletes intentionally used music to shift the direction related to the continuum between positive/negative affect, and intensity of their emotions. Music that was used to increase their energy tended to be higher in tempo and volume. Music was also used by athletes to trigger emotion-laden images related to past successes as a means of replicating the emotions and the concomitant high level of performance (Bishop et al., 2007).

Intensity

Music has been used as a tool to manage pre-competitive stress and regulate pre-competitive intensity. For example, Terry, Dinsdale, Karageorghis, and Lane (2006) reported that music was used by athletes to regulate pre-competitive physical states. John et al. (2010) indicated that music improved performance by reducing pre-competitive stress and cortisol release. To counter pre-competitive stress, Kodzhaspirov (1987) found that athletes choose three kinds of music: (1) music that shifts focus away from the causes and symptoms of pre-competitive stress and toward neutral or pleasant thoughts and emotions; (2) music that induces a state of physical calm; and (3) high-energy music that increases intensity and motivation.

Training Effort

Anyone who has ever entered a weight room filled with athletes in which music is blaring out of speakers recognizes the power that music can have in physical conditioning. Whether it is athletes building strength doing sets of squats, improving endurance with intervals on a treadmill, or increasing mobility in a yoga class, music is omnipresent in the conditioning setting. It is an essential tool used by athletes to raise the quality, quantity, and intensity of their efforts to get stronger, faster, and more prepared physically and mentally to perform their best on the field of play.

The role of music in athletes' conditioning efforts has become a topic interest among researchers in sport psychology. For example, music has been used successfully to: (1) increase motivation during physical-endurance tasks (Brooks & Brooks, 2010); (2) associate positive emotions with intense exertion (Hutchinson et al., 2018); (3) reduce perceived exertion, consumed oxygen, and blood lactate during an endurance task due to the synchronization of music rhythm and body movements (Ju-Han & Jing-Horng Lu, 2013; Karageorghis & Priest, 2012); and (4) improve post-exercise recovery by regulating athletes' physiological parameters (Bhavsar, Abhange, & Afroz, 2014). Additionally, high-tempo music was found to increase pace and improve times, as well as heart rate, during a bicycle time trial (Atkinson, Wilson, & Eubank, 2004). In contrast, slow-tempo music accelerated the normalization of heart rate and blood pressure after isotonic exercise (Bhavsar et al., 2014) and reduced blood lactate levels when athletes listened during recovery (Lee & Kimmerly, 2014).

Team Cohesion

Music doesn't just have an impact on individual athletes. In addition, it can be used to influence an entire team. Specifically, music can help a team build cohesion, create a strong bond, and establish a common purpose. Karageorgis et al. (2018) reported that a soccer team used music to create a sense of identity, forge shared meanings, and direct their collective energy.

Practical Implications

Consultants can educate athletes about why and how music can have such a positive impact on their performances. They can also help athletes to understand how to select music that will best serve their personalities and goals. Consultants can start with an assessment of athletes' music interests and relevant performance-related attributes. They can then proceed to the development of a music-training program in which music is incorporated into different aspects of athletes' practice and competitive regimens.

Assessment of Music Needs

Karageorgnis et al. (1999) recommended two ways of understanding athletes' music requirements. First, they can discuss the psychological and physiological needs involved in athletes' performances (Karageorghis, Jones, & Low, 2006; Robazza, Pellizzari & Hanin, 2004), including musical preferences (García, 2004), optimal intensity (Hanin, 2010), and emotional styles. Interviews with and written descriptions of athletes' reactions to specific music, the intrinsic and extrinsic sources that athletes associate with certain music and the specific thoughts and emotions that are evoked to help consultants develop a detailed and nuanced portrait of what music will help athletes the most (Karageorghis et al., 2006; Bishop & Karageorghis, 2012). Second, the Brunel Music Rating Inventory (BMRI) measures extrinsic and intrinsic factors like responses to rhythm, melody, harmony, cultural influence, and extra-musical associations (Karageorghis et al. 1999, 2006).

The information that is gathered from these two sources allows athletes to define the purpose of their music training (e.g., to reduce intensity, increase motivation, build confidence, narrow focus) and, from that, the best music to select for their playlists. The playlists can induce any of the four combinations of direction and intensity: (1) pleasure/high intensity, (2) pleasure/low intensity, (3) displeasure/high intensity, and (4) displeasure/low intensity. Depending on the individual needs and goals of athletes and the demands of the sport, any of these dimensions could help them perform their best (Bishop & Karageorghis, 2012).

Maximizing the Value of Music

Once consultants have an understanding of the genres of music that athletes both prefer and fit with their psychological, emotional, cognitive, and physical needs, they can help athletes to develop playlists for specific practice and competitive situations. For example, in conditioning, athletes might have a high-intensity playlist for strength training and a low- intensity playlist for mobility training. At practice, a playlist might be one without lyrics so as not to distract from the focus of the sessions. For competitions, athletes might have a displeasure/high intensity playlist (e.g., techno or rock) for events in which they may be overconfident, a pleasure/low intensity playlist (e.g., classical or new age) for competitions in which they may feel anxious, a displeasure/high intensity playlist (e.g., hip hop or heavy metal) for events in which aggression may be required, and a pleasure/low intensity playlist (e.g., mood or emo) after a disappointing performance.

Consultants can then help athletes decide where and when to listen to music, particularly before competitions. Some athletes like to listen to music on the way to the venue. Other athletes use it to keep their mind clear during their pre-competitive preparations. And still others prefer it as part of their final preparations before they compete to calm down or get fired up.

Summary

- Music is used by athletes to manage both their physiologies and psychologies, and to prepare themselves to perform their best in competitions.
- Athletes use music to increase motivation, build confidence, generate beneficial emotions, shift physical intensity up or down, and direct focus inward.
- Research has demonstrated that music has a significant impact on emotions, intensity, training effort, and team cohesion.
- Music therapy has been shown to reduce nausea, pain and aggression, modify many physiological parameters, and impact emotion, mood, well-being, life satisfaction, relationships, verbal and gestural communication, fine and gross motor skills, balance, and gait.
- Other research has found that cognitive functions are also influenced by music including attention, calculation, language, memory, and judgment.
- It has been hypothesized that emotion is the central mediator between linked music and performance in its powerful impact on physiology, psychology, cognition, and biomechanics.
- Consultants can educate athletes about why and how music can have such a positive impact on their performances and to understand how to select music that will best serve their personalities and goals.
- Athletes' best music choices can be assessed by identifying their psychological and physiological, optimal intensity, music preferences, and emotional style.
- They can also use the Brunel Music Rating Inventory (BMRI) which measures extrinsic and intrinsic factors like responses to rhythm, melody, harmony, cultural influence, and extra-musical associations.
- The playlists can induce any of the four combinations of direction and intensity: (1) pleasure/high intensity, (2) pleasure/low intensity, (3) displeasure/high intensity, and (4) displeasure/low intensity.
- Once consultants have an understanding of the genres of music that athletes both prefer and fit with their psychological, emotional, cognitive, and physical needs, they can help athletes to develop playlists for specific practice and competitive situations.

References

Atkinson G., Wilson D. & Eubank, M. (2004). Effects of music on work-rate distribution during a cycling time trial. *Int J Sports Med, 8*, 611–615.

Baker, F. (2015) Evidence-based practice in music therapy. In B. Wheeler (Ed.), *Music therapy handbook*. New York, NY: Guilford Press.

Bharucha, J., Curtis, M. & Paroo, K. (2006). Varieties of musical experience. *Cognition, 100* (1), 131–172.

Bhavsar, S. D., Abhange, R. S. & Afroz, S. (2014). Effect of different musical tempo on post-exercise recovery in young adults. *Journal of Dental and Medical Sciences, 13*(5), 60–64.

Bishop, D. & Karageorghis, C. (2012). Managing pre-competitive emotions with music. In A. Bateman & J. Bale (Eds.), *Sporting sounds: Relationships between sport and music* (pp. 59–84). New York, NY: Routledge.

Bishop, D., Karageorghis, C., & Loizou, G. (2007). A grounded theory of young tennis players use of music to manipulate emotional state. *Journal of Sport & Exercise Psychology, 29*, 584–607.

Brooks, K., & Brooks, K. (2010). Enhancing sport performance through the use of music. *J E Ponline, 13* (2), 52–57.

Del Olmo, M. (2009). Musicoterapia con bebés de 0 a 6 meses en cuidados intensivos pediátricos. Doctoral thesis, Universidad Autónoma de Madrid, Spain.

García, F. (2004). *Herramientas psicológicas para entrenadores y deportistas*. La Habana, Cuba: Editorial Deportes.

Hanin, Y. (2010). Coping with anxiety in sport. In A. R. Nicholls (Ed.), *Coping in sport: Theory, methods, and related constructs* (pp. 159–175). Hauppauge, NY: Nova Science.

Hutchinson, J. C., Jones, L., Vitti, S. N., Moore, A., Dalton, P. C., & O'Neil, B. J. (2018). The influence of self-selected music on affect-regulated exercise intensity and remembered pleasure during treadmill running. *Sport, Exercise, and Performance Psychology, 7*(1), 80–92.

John, S., Verma, S., & Khanna, G. (2010). The effect of music therapy on salivary cortisol as a reliable marker of pre competition stress in shooting performance. *Journal of Exercise Science and Physiotherapy, 6*(2), 70–77.

Ju-Han, L., & Jing-Horng Lu, F. (2013). Interactive Effects of Visual and Auditory Intervention on Physical Performance and Perceived Effort. *J Sports Sci Med, 12*(3), 388–393.

Karageorghis, C. I., Bigliassi, M., Tayara, K., Priest, D.-L., & Bird, J. M. (2018). A grounded theory of music use in the psychological preparation of academy soccer players. *Sport, Exercise, and Performance Psychology, 7*(2), 109–127.

Karageorghis, C. I., Jones, L. & Low, D. C. (2006). Relationship between exercise heart rate and music tempo preference. *Research Quarterly for Exercise and Sport, 77*, 240–250.

Karageorghis, C. & Priest, D. (2012). Music in the exercise domain: a review and synthesis (Part I). *International Review of Sport and Exercise Psychology, 5* (1), 44–66.

Karageorghis, C., Terry, P. & Lane, A. (1999). Development and initial validation of an instrument to assess the motivational qualities of music in exercise and sport: The Brunel Music Rating Inventory. *Journal of Sports Sciences, 17* (9), 713–724.

Kodzhaspirov, Y. G. (1987). Optimización del estado precompetitivo de los deportistas mediante la influencia musical. *Teoría y Práctica de la Cultura Física, 4*(1), 19–33.

Kwon, M., Gang, M., & Oh, K. (2013). Effect of the group music therapy on brain wave, behavior, and cognitive function among patients with chronic schizophrenia. *Asian Nursing Research, 7*(4), 168-174.

Lee, S., & Kimmerly, D. (2014). Influence of music on maximal self-paced running performance and passive postexercise recovery rate. *The Journal of Sports Medicine and Physical Fitness, 17*, 34–49.

Robazza, C., Pellizzari, M. & Hanin, Y. (2004). Emotion self-regulation and athletic performance: An application of the IZOF model. *Psychology of Sport and Exercise, 5* (4), 379–404.

Särkämö, T., Tervaniemi, M., Laitinen, S., Forsblom, A., Soinila, S., Mikkonen, M., . . . & Peretz, I. (2008). Music listening enhances cognitive recovery and mood after middle cerebral artery stroke. *Brain, 131*(3), 866–876.

Tenenbaum, G., Reeder, T., Davis, M., Herman, T. & Hutchinson, J. (2011). The influence of music on a supra maximal exercise bout. *International Journal of Sport Psychology, 41*, 135–148.

Terry P. C., Dinsdale S. L., Karageorghis C. I., & Lane A. M. (2006). Use and perceived effectiveness of precompetition mood regulation strategies among athletes. In M. Katsikitis (Ed.), *Psychology bridging the Tasman: Science, culture and practice*, Proceedings of the Joint Conference of the Australian Psychological Society and the New Zealand Psychological Society (pp. 420–424). Melbourne: Australian Psychological Society.

Wheeler, B. (2015). *Music therapy hand book*. New York: Guilford Press.

CREATING EFFECTIVE MENTAL TRAINING PROGRAMS

Graig Chow, Eric Bean, and Jim Taylor

Sport psychology is an interdisciplinary field where practitioners often translate knowledge from sport sciences, psychology, ethics, diversity and culture, and research methods and statistics into applied practice. In contrast to clinical and counseling psychology, there are a lack of evidence-based manualized treatments and intervention protocols in sport psychology that practitioners can use to assist clients with specific presenting concerns (Gardner & Moore, 2007). As a result, consultants must create effective mental training programs guided by theoretical frameworks and empirical findings from both within and outside of sport psychology, while also considering their own personal philosophy (Poczwardowski, Sherman, & Ravizza, 2004), style, and experience, and client needs and goals.

An effective mental training program is characterized by catalyzing meaningful and relevant change in psychological, emotional, behavioral, and performance areas. Congruence among the mental exercises and tools that are used, the targeted mental muscles, and the outcome goals is imperative to establish program effectiveness. For example, a mental training program that incorporates self-talk to enhance confidence in athletes with the goal of improving basketball free-throw shooting percentage must demonstrate that the self-talk produces changes in confidence and that specific performance parameter. Conversely, change in performance (e.g., free-throw shooting percentage) without effective application of appropriate mental exercises and tools and corresponding changes in the targeted mental muscle may be attributed to factors outside of the mental training program such as physical practice or coaching.

Four Principles for Effective Mental Training Programs

In this section, four principles that represent and guide the creation of effective mental training programs are presented. The principles are not necessarily serial but rather should be considered throughout the development and implementation of the program. For each principle, practical ways that consultants can apply the principle are described.

Athlete-centered

The first principle is *athlete-centered*, which involves ensuring that the mental training program aligns with athletes' needs and goals. There are three ways in which consultants can ensure athlete-centered mental training programs: assessment, collaboration, and personalization.

Assessment

A thorough athlete assessment facilitates understanding of both athletes and their presenting issues, case conceptualization, selection of appropriate interventions, and development of a structured intervention plan. Assessment can include interviewing, observation, and inventories as well as feedback from coaches and other stakeholders. The development of effective mental training programs typically begins by conducting an intake interview with athletes. This information gathering often uses structured interviewing protocols that consultants can use to collect sport-specific and general information about clients to identify and understand the presenting issues (Aoyagi, Poczwardowski, Statler, Shapiro, & Cohen, 2017; Taylor & Schneider, 1992; Taylor & Brutus, 2017). Observation allows consultants to witness athlete behaviors in training and competitive settings, and to understand contextual factors unique to athletes' experiences (Holder, Winter, & Orr, 2017). Sport-specific inventories are also available to assess important mental muscles (e.g., motivation, confidence, intensity, focus) and mental exercises and tools (e.g., goal-setting, imagery, self-talk, relaxation) (Chow & Gilson, 2017).

Collaboration

Collaboration involves consultants and athletes (and coaches, when appropriate) working together to identify essential goals and tasks that will form the basis for a mental training program (Bodin, 1979). Consultants and athletes can agree on the identified benefits that will be gained from the program, the intervention strategies that will be used, and a means for evaluating the effectiveness of the program upon its conclusion. Importantly, disagreement or lack of confidence in any part of the working alliance during the creation of a mental training program can result in client disengagement, adherence issues, and premature termination (Swift & Greenberg, 2012).

Personalization

The unique aspects of athletes, including their age, personality, family upbringing, cultural background, experience, time of season, level of competition, and sport-related needs and goals must be considered in creating effective mental training programs. A personalized approach to the design of a mental training program can ensure optimal commitment, maximum effectiveness, and greatest benefits accrued.

Evidence-based Intervention and Delivery

The second principle is *evidence-based intervention and delivery*. The Contextual Model (Wampold, 2015) describes three critical evidence-based factors that lead to successful outcomes. First, consultants must offer athletes interventions that are validated by empirical research or supported through extensive professional experience (American Psychological Association, 2006). Not only will these strategies have a better chance of success, but they will also engender greater confidence and buy-in by athletes.

A strong working alliance between consultants and athletes is also essential. This relationship is vital because researchers in both sport psychology (e.g., Petitpas, Giges, & Danish, 1999) and counseling (Luborsky et al., 2002; Wampold, 2015) have demonstrated that the professional-client relationship is a stronger determinant of intervention outcomes than theoretical orientation and intervention protocol.

Another contributor to the effectiveness of a mental training program is the expectations that athletes hold about it (Wampold, 2015). The success of a mental training program can depend on how well consultants can convince athletes of its efficacy and establish reasonable expectations in terms of the effort that must be expended, the gains that can be made, and the time that it will take to produce meaningful results. These expectations can involve the general notion of what mental training is and is not capable of providing as well as what athletes can reasonably anticipate from their use of mental training.

Empathy from consultants is the third factor that has been shown to be a powerful contributor to intervention outcomes (Wampold, 2015). Related to the consultant-athlete relationship, consultants can provide athletes with a safe place in which to be vulnerable as they enter this new area of sports performance and then respond with empathy which deepens the working relationship and indicates shared experience and understanding by consultants. Over all, when consultants leverage these three factors, they strengthen their ability to positively influence athletes beyond the evidence-based intervention protocols that are used (Wampold, 2015).

The challenge consultants may face with evidence-based interventions is that what works in a laboratory setting may not be effective in real-life sports settings. Given this reality, being an evidence-based consultant means grounding their efforts in science while also adapting them to the individual athletes and the context and dynamics in which they are performing. To achieve a stronger commitment to evidence-based practice while also ensuring effectiveness in the "real world," consultants can examine their experience-based strategies in relation to the best available evidence that supports or contradicts those methods. Consultants should also consider how the intervention protocol will work within the context of the particular athlete and their environment (e.g., athlete needs, values, demographics, relationships).

Progressive Structure

The third principle is *progressive structure*, which involves ensuring that the mental training program is being offered in a structured and systematic manner. Such a systematic approach to mental training involves three stages.

Education

This stage involves consultants educating athletes about general principles of mental training and the specific components of the program. For example, consultants can educate athletes about the impact that self-talk has on performance, the distinction between negative and positive self-talk, how positive self-talk works, and the specific steps for its use.

Self-awareness

Once clients have gained sufficient knowledge of the mental muscles they will be training, consultants can assist athletes in increasing self-awareness through assessment, reflection, and discussion. For example, consultants can solicit situations or events that lead to unproductive psychological, emotional, or performance reactions and guide athletes toward identifying the precise causes of those reactions, the situations in which they arise, and more adaptive responses when they arise.

Initiation

Once athletes are educated about the relevant issues and understand how they relate to them, consultants can initiate the actual mental training program. In this stage, consultants personalize the mental exercises and tools and show athletes how to begin using them in a familiar and comfortable setting. For example, after athletes have been taught how use keywords to improve focus during practice, they can create their own keywords and start to use them in a simple practice situation.

Expansion and Transfer

The final phase of a systematic approach to mental training involves athletes expanding their efforts into more sophisticated training settings and, ultimately, to competitions. As athletes become more experienced in their use of mental exercises and tools, they can apply them to more complex situations that might involve greater physical (e.g., exertion) and task (e.g., difficult skills) demands. In doing so, athletes gain confidence in their use of mental training, thus increasing buy-in as well as confidence and comfort in their use. They figure out ways to adapt the strategies they use to their personal style, needs, and goals. And, with time, the exercises and tools start to become ingrained and automatized. By reflecting on what has worked and what hasn't, athletes can also formulate questions for consultants who can help them modify and refine their use of mental training. For example, when teaching an athlete how to use imagery, the consultant can have them imagine performing in a simple practice drill. After the imagery, the consultant can ask questions to determine the quality of the imagery. With practice, as the quality of the athlete's imagery improves (i.e., greater vividness and controllability), the consultant can increase the internal or external demands by asking the athlete to increase their intensity or perform in a competitive situation, respectively, into their imagery. From there, the consultant can continue to increase the psychological, emotional, and situational demands until the athlete is seeing and feeling themselves perform optimally in a high-level competition.

In addition to taking a structured approach to mental training, consultants can use periodization to determine the order in which they introduce different aspects of mental training based on athletes' needs and goals as well as their training and competitive cycles. Holliday, Burton, Sun, Hammermeister, Naylor, and Freigang (2008) recommended starting with foundational mental training exercises and tools (e.g., goal-setting, imagery, and self-talk) that strengthen foundational mental muscles (e.g., motivation, confidence, and focus).

Evaluation of Effectiveness

The final principle is *evaluation of effectiveness* which should be systematic and ongoing throughout the mental training program. That is, evaluation can occur at the end of a mental training session, after a specific intervention plan has been completed, or at the conclusion of a season. Documenting the effectiveness of the mental training program and its intervention components is essential in determining the extent to which the intervention is accomplishing athletes' previously established mental training goals as well as in making decisions regarding future developments in an ongoing mental training program. In addition, evaluation increases accountability to stakeholders and the profession (Anderson, Miles, Mahoney, & Robinson, 2002). Indicators of effectiveness can be linked to:

- gains in self-awareness;
- better knowledge of mental training;
- greater facility in the use of mental exercises and tools;
- improved strength of mental muscles;
- increases in sport performance;
- objective measures of performance; and
- achievement of previously established performance and outcome goals.

These markers can be assessed using a variety of evaluation procedures including the three forms of assessment previously mentioned (interviewing, observation, and inventories) as well as standardized consultant evaluation forms, reflective practices, and feedback from coaches.

Developing a Mental Training Program

CASP is rife with useful information and many mental exercises and tools that athletes can use to make their mental muscles stronger and to be mentally ready to perform at their highest level in practices and in competitions. However, the final challenge involves athletes being able to take all of that information and turning it into an organized format that can be put into action and adhered to in a committed way. The starting point for this application is for athletes to approach mental training the same way they do physical conditioning and sport training. For both of the latter to be effective, they must be considered in a comprehensive, structured, and consistent way. Consultants can help athletes to embrace this perspective as they collaborate to create such a mental training program. To accomplish that goal, Taylor (2017) has developed a five-step framework that athletes can use to specify the mental muscles they need to strengthen, establish relevant goals for those areas, and then organize a mental training schedule that athletes can commit and adhere to as they train their minds using this regimen.

Step #1: Identify Mental Muscles

As noted above, consultants can begin their collaborative efforts with athletes in designing an effective mental training program by engaging in a thorough assessment. This evaluation will determine the mental muscles that athletes need to strengthen, identify the mental exercise and tools that will be used as interventions, and guide the structure and progression of the program that is developed. As mentioned above, this assessment can include interviewing, inventories, and observation, as well as triangulation with coaches.

Once consultants have completed a thorough assessment of athletes, they can specify the mental muscles they want to focus on in the first phase of the mental training program. Trying to address too many mental muscles will prove to be overwhelming to athletes and prevent them from devoting sufficient time and effort to those that are their priority. It's more effective for athletes to select a few mental muscles to strengthen, and then work on others later. Which mental muscles athletes should choose to focus on initially should be determined based on (1) which mental muscles are most in need of strengthening, (2) athletes' short-term training and competitive needs, and (3) their long-term development.

Step #2: Select Mental Exercises and Tools

Once the mental muscles have been identified, consultants can review the many mental exercises and tools that athletes have at their disposal and help them choose the ones that will most effectively strengthen the specified mental muscles. The mental exercises and tools that are selected should be determined by a combination of those that consultants believe will be most effective and those that athletes are most comfortable with and enjoy using.

Step #3: Create a Mental Training Goal Plan

Establishing a comprehensive plan will offer athletes a clear structure and process to follow in their mental training, just as they have in their physical conditioning and sport training. This mental training plan includes a number of important criteria that consultants can use as they guide athletes in its development.

Setting

Consultants can help athletes to determine where they will engage in their mental training. Athletes can use the mental exercises and tools in three settings:

- Outside of sport, for instance, athletes doing imagery in their bedrooms before they go to school or doing a relaxation procedure before bedtime.
- During sport training to enhance their practice efforts, for example, with positive self-talk to build confidence or using a keyword to maintain focus.
- Before a competition using mental tools such as music, imagery, and routines.

Mental Muscles

Athletes can decide which of the mental muscles they want to focus on in the three settings. For instance, outside of their sport, athletes can train their motivation muscle by setting daily goals and reminding themselves why they're working so hard. During training, they can use their training routine before every drill and exercise and to begin every effort with two deep breaths. At competitions, athletes can use imagery to build their confidence and use psych-up tools to reach their ideal intensity.

Current Status

Prior to the start of a mental training program, consultants can help athletes to evaluate where they are with their mental muscles. This initial evaluation will provide a baseline from which they can determine their progress. For instance, if athletes want to improve their focus during competitions, consultants can ask them to clarify the specific distractions they struggle with and identify the situations in which they get distracted.

Goals

For every mental muscle that is to be exercised, consultants can guide athletes in setting clear goals for how strong they want it to become and what they will do to accomplish the goals in their mental training program. Athletes can use the SMARTER goal-setting criteria described earlier in this chapter to set constructive goals that will provide the purpose and direction to their mental training efforts.

Mental Exercises and Tools

Having set a series of goals that will define and direct their mental training program, consultants can then help athletes to identify the specific mental exercises and tools they will use to achieve their goals. Consultants and athletes can review Chapters 3 and 4 to specify the particular mental exercises and tools that they will use in their mental training program.

Step #4: Create a Mental Training Schedule

Athletes are busy people who are usually trying to juggle many commitments including their sport, school, work, sleep, and social life. The challenge for all athletes is finding the time in their hectic schedules to implement the mental training program that they have designed with their consultants. Fortunately, even a robust program isn't that time consuming. Athletes need only commit about one hour per week outside of their sport and incorporate the mental training into their regular conditioning and sport training.

To ensure full adherence to the mental training program, consultants can collaborate with athletes to create a schedule within their online or paper calendars to assign times each week for the various mental training exercises. For example, if athletes know they are free from 6:30 to 6:45 p.m. every day before dinner, they can schedule 15-minute imagery sessions in that time slot on Mondays, Wednesdays, and Fridays. For including mental training into their conditioning and sport training, athletes can indicate in their training schedules the mental exercises and tools they will be using.

Another challenge for athletes when they first commit to a mental training program is simply remembering to do it. Because mental training hasn't been a part of their overall training regimen before, they are likely to be so busy that they forget. Or, if they do remember, but are feeling rushed, they may deprioritize and skip mental training. Until mental training becomes as ingrained in their schedules as their conditioning and sport training (athletes rarely forget about those commitments), consultants can encourage athletes to set alerts on their phones that will vibrate or sound a tone to notify them of their ensuing mental training session.

Step #5 Commit

When athletes have established their mental training programs using the four principles and four steps described above, the final and most difficult step they need to take is to make a commitment to the program. This commitment means that athletes must approach mental training with the same determination as their conditioning and sport training. It also involves making mental training a priority and following their mental training program exactly as it is scheduled in their calendars. Finally, that commitment requires that athletes give their fullest effort in all aspects of their mental training.

Summary

- An effective mental training program creates meaningful and relevant change in psychological, emotional, behavioral, and performance areas.
- Consultants must create effective mental training programs guided by theoretical frameworks and empirical findings while also considering their own philosophy, style, and experience, and client needs and goals.
- Four principles that represent and guide the creation of effective mental training programs include athlete centered, evidence-based intervention and delivery, progressive structure, and evaluation of effectiveness.
- A challenge in using mental imagery effectively involves athletes being able to take all of that information and turning it into an organized format that can be put into action and adhered to in a committed way.
- Taylor (2017) has developed a five-step framework that athletes can use to specify the mental muscles they need to strengthen, establish relevant goals for those areas, and then organize a mental training schedule that athletes can commit and adhere to as they train their minds using this regimen.
- The five steps are: identify mental muscles to be strengthened, review and select relevant mental muscles, create a mental training plan, create a mental training schedule, and commit.

References

American Psychological Association. (2006). *APA presidential task force on evidence based practice*. Washington, DC: American Psychological Association.

Anderson, A. G., Miles, A., Mahoney, C., & Robinson, P. (2002). Evaluating the effectiveness of applied sport psychology practice: Making the case for a case study approach. *The Sport Psychologist, 16*(4), 432–453.

Aoyagi, M. W., Poczwardowski, A., Statler, T., Shapiro, J. L., & Cohen, A. B. (2017). The Performance Interview Guide: Recommendations for initial consultations in sport and performance psychology. *Professional Psychology: Research and Practice, 48*, 352–360.

Bodin, E. S. (1979). The generalizability of the psychoanalytic concept of the working alliance. *Psychotherapy: Theory, Research, & Practice, 16*(3), 252–260.

Chow, G. M., & Gilson, T. A. (2017). Inventories: Using objective measures. In J. Taylor (Ed.), *Assessment in applied sport psychology* (pp. 83–99). Champaign, IL: Human Kinetics.

Gardner, F. L., & Moore, Z. E. (2007). *The psychology of enhancing human performance: The Mindfulness-Acceptance-Commitment (MAC) approach*. New York, NY: Springer Publishing Company.

Holder, T., Winter, S., & Orr, B. (2017). Observation: Seeing athlete on the field. In J. Taylor (Ed.), *Assessment in applied sport psychology* (pp. 115–126). Champaign, IL: Human Kinetics.

Holliday, B., Burton, D., Sun, G., Hammermeister, J., Naylor, S., & Freigang, D. (2008). Building the better mental training mousetrap: Is periodization a more systematic approach to promoting performance excellence?. *Journal of Applied Sport Psychology, 20*(2), 199–219.

Luborsky, L., Rosenthal, R., Diguer, L., Andrusyna, T. P., Berman, J. S., Levitt, J. T., . . . & Krause, E. D. (2002). The dodo bird verdict is alive and well—mostly. *Clinical Psychology: Science and Practice, 9*(1), 2–12.

Petitpas, A. J., Giges, B., & Danish, S. J. (1999). The sport psychologist-athlete relationship: Implications for training. *The Sport Psychologist, 13*(3), 344–357.

Poczwardowski, A., Sherman, C. P., & Ravizza, K. (2004). Professional philosophy in the sport psychology service delivery: Building on theory and practice. *The Sport Psychologist, 18*, 445–463.

Swift, J. K., & Greenberg, R. P. (2012). Premature discontinuation in adult psychotherapy: A meta-analysis. *Journal of Consulting and Clinical Psychology, 80*(4), 547–559.

Taylor, J. (2017). *Train your mind for athletic success: Mental preparation to achieve your sports goals.* Lanham, MD: Rowman & Littlefield.

Taylor, J., Simpson, D., & Brutus, A. L. (2017). Interviewing: Asking the right questions. In J. Taylor (Ed.), *Assessment in applied sport psychology* (pp. 101–114). Champaign, IL: Human Kinetics.

Taylor, J., & Schneider, B. A. (1992). The Sport-Clinical Intake Protocol: A comprehensive interviewing instrument for applied sport psychology. *Professional Psychology: Research and Practice, 23*, 318–325.

Wampold, B. E. (2015). How important are the common factors in psychotherapy? An update. *World Psychiatry, 14*(3), 270–277.

5

MENTAL STRATEGIES TO MAXIMIZE TRAINING

Introduction

Jim Taylor and Michele Kerulis

This chapter looks at the often-neglected impact of the mind on the quality of sport training in which athletes engage. Using mental strategies as a part of their regular conditioning and sport training regimens enables athletes to put their best effort into and to get the most out of those efforts, thus maximizing improvement, preparation for competitions, and achievement of their long-term sports goals. Consultants can educate athletes on the use of these mental approaches that will lead to gains that are made from sport training. The goal of this chapter is to illuminate the ways in which consultants can assist athletes in optimizing the time they spend training toward their sports goals.

Some sports use the term "training" to describe what they call their athletic development experience, for example, runners, triathletes, ski racers, and weight lifters go to training and train to develop their abilities. Other sports use the term "practice" to describe what they do, for example, basketball, baseball, football, tennis players, golfers, and swimmers all attend practice and practice their sports to improve.

For Chapter 5, "training" and train" will the terminology that is used because, even for sports that involve "practice," other aspects of athletic development are better described as training, for example, conditioning is generally referred to as physical training and mental training is the accepted verbiage for that domain.

Genes undoubtedly have a significant influence on how athletes develop. Most sports typically attract athletes with certain inborn hereditary characteristics, for example, basketball (height) and weight lifting (strength)—as the legendary basketball coach Red Auerbach once said, "You can't teach height." Yet, without the necessary physical and technical development that comes from sport training, those innate capabilities would not be realized or result in substantial athletic success.

Here again is another example of how *CASP* challenges the conventional wisdom and vocabulary of applied sport psychology. "Deliberate practice" (Ericsson et al., 1993) is the phrase most commonly associated with the process for gaining skills in an activity. It is defined as "a special type of practice that is purposeful and systematic." Four criteria are provided to explain deliberate practice:

- Motivation to direct attention and energy toward improvement
- Satisfactory understanding of what needs to be improved to make the necessary changes
- Gather corrective information about what is being practiced
- Sufficient opportunities to learn what is being practiced

These criteria are certainly contributors to gaining the benefits of sport development. At the same time, they are not sufficient to maximize their value to athletes. This understanding doesn't precisely describe how it is accomplished. There is also not adequate clarity on how deliberate practice benefits people.

In its place, the phrase, "quality training" will be used in Chapter 5. Taylor (2017) defines quality training as: "Total readiness and consistent effort that results in maximal physical, technical and mental development resulting in optimal preparation for competitive success" (p. 80). This chapter examines specific attitudes and strategies that enable athletes to achieve four goals related to quality training:

1. Ensure that athletes use their time and efforts in the most effective and efficient way
2. Develop and instill the essential skills in their sport so they can be executed automatically and consistently in their competitive efforts
3. Strengthen the important mental muscles and gain experience in the use of mental exercises and tools that can be transferred to competitive performance
4. Athletes develop all of the trained attributes that will allow them to accomplish their sports goals

This chapter will explore in greater depth what quality training means, how it is achieved, and the benefits that athletes accrue from its consistent application.

Before athletes can begin the practical aspects of engaging in quality training, they must first develop a healthy perspective toward their training efforts. The perspective that athletes have about their training will dictate how they approach it, the effort they expend in it, and how they respond to the challenges that they will inevitably face in their training. It will determine whether their training experiences accelerate their development in their sport or slow their progress toward their sports goals. The perspective that athletes hold affects their ability to engage in quality training in four ways:

- How athletes think about their training: Is their thinking positive or negative? Is their thinking steadfast or indifferent? Are their thoughts inspiring or discouraging?
- Athletes' thoughts cause emotions that are either encourage or dampen their efforts. Are they excited or downhearted? Do they feel calm or agitated?
- Thoughts and emotions impact motivation. Positive and enthusiastic thinking and emotions fuel motivation. By contrast, negative and apathetic thinking and emotions deplete motivation.
- Thoughts, emotions, and motivation are then expressed in the actual efforts that athletes devote in their training. An axiom of training is that the time and energy athletes put into their training is what they will get out of it.

An axiom of sports training is that it is hard; it's physically demanding and mentally draining. Workouts can be exhausting, excruciating and monotonous. Athletes' perspectives on training will dictate how they respond to those challenges. The thoughts and emotions that athletes associate with those difficulties will impact whether they back off or push through them.

Another axiom of sports is that it can be extremely exasperating because progress never comes without substantial time, effort, and energy. Rarely do athletes experience significant or rapid improvements in their development. Instead, the trajectory is slow and uneven.

The protracted and capricious nature of athletic development requires that athletes embrace a positive perspective toward training because, in its absence, pursuing their goals would feel like an insurmountable obstacle. The underpinning of a healthy perspective on training lies in three essential attributes:

- Patience is defined as: "The capacity to accept or tolerate delay, trouble, or suffering without getting angry or upset." Patience helps athletes accept the protracted nature of training and allows them to remain confident and determined at those times when training isn't going their way. The perspective that athletes gain from patience is: "I will do whatever is necessary for as long as is necessary to achieve my goals."
- Persistence involves athletes having a determined and unyielding effort as they strive toward their goals. Their commitment to expend their utmost effort and energy will dictate how much they get out of their training and to what degree their training gains transfer to the competitive field of play.
- Perseverance is what enables athletes to continue their efforts in the face of failures, setbacks, plateaus, and declines along the way. When athletes are confronted by difficulties, perseverance keeps them moving inexorably forward to their goals.

References

Ericsson, K., Krampe, R., Tesch-Römer, C., & Kintsch, W. (1993). The Role of deliberate practice in the acquisition of expert performance. *Psychological Review, 100*(3), 363–406.

Taylor, J. (2017). *Train your mind for athletic success: Mental preparation to achieve your sports goals.* Lanham, MD: Rowman & Littlefield.

QUALITY TRAINING

Megan Buning and Jim Taylor

Before the ways in which the quality of training can be enhanced, the term "quality" must be defined. The traditional dictionary definitions for quality include "the degree of excellence of something" (from *Merriam-Webster*) and "how good or bad something is." Businessdictionary.com defines quality as "It is brought about by strict and consistent commitment to certain standards that achieve uniformity." At a practical level applied to sports, quality is seen as both a variation of process and an outcome. The process involves athletes putting their maximum effort, focus, and intensity into everything they do including conditioning, sport training, nutrition, equipment preparation, and competitive readiness. The outcome comes from the definition of quality training provided in the introduction to this chapter: "resulting in optimal preparation for competitive success."

As can be seen, quality has many meanings and, as a result, has a certain subjective feeling to it. For the purpose of this section, quality will be defined as the degree to which an intentional determination is made to engage in activities that maximize athletes' progress in pursuit of their goals. Before consultants offer practical strategies to athletes about improving the quality of their efforts, they should have a conversation about how athletes can personally define quality. Assisting them with defining quality can help put into context exactly what athletes must do in their training to achieve their sports goals and how consultants can help them improve their efforts in striving toward that subjective definition of quality.

Theory and Research

Coaches often evaluate quality training based on how much effort athletes apply toward their training and competitive performances and then use the perceived effort as a proxy for how committed and motivated they are in their sport. The message that athletes receive is that they must always give their best effort in everything they do. However, athletes may want to give maximum effort, yet physical and mental barriers prevent them from doing so. Physical barriers might include fatigue, illness, or injury. Mental barriers could consist of lack of confidence, inability to focus, stress, or off-field problems

Athletes should give their fullest effort in competitions and should attempt to match that effort during training. Yet, having athletes perform in every training session and complete every training task with the greatest effort is both mentally and physically exhausting. Mental and physical fatigue caused by unnecessary effort can be counterproductive to quality training as athletes may lose focus, motivation, and control, thereby impeding performance and increasing the risk of injury (Hockey, 1997; Marcora, Staiano, & Manning, 2009). Helping athletes and coaches understand the appropriate times to moderate effort may lead to higher quality and more productive training sessions. Additionally, helping athletes understand the difference between mental and physical effort and when to use one or both types of effort may also help them to manage their mental and physical resources in a way that will ensure quality training over a long period (Krausman, Crowell, & Wilson, 2002; Renfree, Martin, Micklewright, & Gibson, 2014). One final suggestion about effort is the beneficial impact it can have in a team setting. Athletes can learn from teammates when and how to best expend effort (Desender, Beurms, & Van den Bussche, 2016; Spink, Crozier, & Robinson, 2013). Encouraging athletes to learn from each other about quality training and appropriate effort can help elevate the quality of training overall in a team.

Mental Effort

Mental effort is the amount of cognitive resources (or energy) individuals have to apply toward a task. The more complex the task, the more mental effort is required (Brisswalter, Collardeau, & René, 2002). Mental effort can dictate how much focus athletes can maintain and for how long (Carver & Scheier, 2000). Additionally, the amount of mental effort a person is willing to give can be related to how motivated the person is to perform the task (Chong et al., 2018; Deci & Ryan, 2000; Pass, Tuovinen, van Merriënboer, & Darabi, 2005), complexity of task, and other external stressors (e.g., fatigue, sleep deficit, poor nutrition, depression) (Boksem, Meijman, & Lorist, 2006; Hockey, 1997; Schraw & Ericsson, 2005; Silvia, Nusbaum, Eddington, Beaty, & Kwapil, 2014).

Consultants can assist athletes in determining how much mental effort they are willing to devote to a training task and for what reasons is crucial in helping them understand why they can give or may not always be able to give their highest levels of mental effort during training (Paas et al., 2005; Renfree et al., 2014). Effort should be dynamic and match the ever-changing flow of training situations for athletes to be able to sustain appropriate cognitive requirements (Hockey, 1997). For example, during a training session, athletes do not need to maximize mental effort when warming up for training. Instead, effort can increase gradually as warm-ups progress. Consultants can map out a training session with athletes by showing them when lower levels (e.g., warm-ups, between drills, station shifts), moderate levels (e.g., receiving instructions/feedback, between repetitions, video review), and higher levels (e.g., during performance of tasks/drills including game simulations) of effort are appropriate. This process can help them become self-aware to better understand and learn how to control their individualized levels of effort (Renfree et al., 2014). Tying mental effort levels into training goals can also benefit athletes in that they will have a better idea of when and how to adjust their mental effort according to the task to ensure optimal quality within training sessions and throughout a season.

Physical Effort

Physical effort is the amount of physical resources (energy) athletes expend toward a task. Physical effort can be, but is not always, related to mental effort in that athletes who are mentally fatigued may perceive greater physical effort and reduce the quality of their efforts sooner (Marcora, Staiano, & Manning, 2009). Consultants can help athletes to understand when to put forth maximum physical effort to improve the quality of their training. In doing so, they can become more aware of and can better apportion their physical energy as needed. For example, athletes may not need to perform a task at full speed (maximum effort) because it may be more valuable to slow the movement down so they can focus on some specific aspect of the task (e.g., sensations, weight shift, balance) (Connors, Galea, Said, & Remedios, 2010; Jain, Janssen, & DeCelle, 2004). In this case, complete mental effort may be necessary, but not complete physical effort. Consultants could use widely accepted methods such as the rating of perceived exertion (RPE) as a tool to help athletes first become aware of how much effort they feel they are expending then how to better allocate that exertion throughout a practice (Eston, 2012).

Consultants can help athletes to understand the specific ebb and flow of their sport and their own personal physical and mental needs to better monitor and adjust their effort as needed during training. Helping athletes understand different models of focus, for example, Nideffer's (1976) theory of attentional and interpersonal style, may be helpful for athletes when attempting to explain ebb and flow during practice. Consultants can also educate athletes on physiological changes and shifts in focus (association and disassociation) as workload and intensity increase (Tenenbaum & Connolly, 2008). This information may help athletes understand practice flow related to focus and why they struggle to focus consistently or differently at times (Seiler, 2010). Additionally, consultants can aid athletes in recognizing that they may not have the same physical or mental resources accessible every day and should adapt their effort accordingly to maximize the resources that are available. Using the mapping exercise described above, athletes can rate the effort they think they should have for training that day based on their training goals and an assessment of their current resources (Birrer & Morgan, 2010; Paas et al., 2005). When athletes can gain this self-awareness and apply their efforts strategically during training, they not only ensure that they engage in quality training that day, but also manage their efforts to also ensure consistent quality training for the duration of a training block.

Observational Learning and Modeling

Considering athletes often rely on self-directed practice (without a coach) or touch-and-go instruction (during team practices), athletes need to understand how to practice effectively and efficiently for maximal gains. They can spend copious amounts of time during practice confused, stalled, or unfocused for various reasons.

Helping athletes understand key strategies to maximize practice time can help them progress more quickly and more effectively. One of those strategies is observational learning that leads to modeling. Many people, including athletes, rely heavily on observational learning to understand how to perform a task (Cumming, Clark, Ste-Marie, McCullagh, & Hall, 2005; Wesch, Law, & Hall, 2007). Observational learning is well-studied and can be traced back to Bandura's (1986) social cognitive theory (SCT; also referred to as social learning theory). SCT posited that people learn most effectively when they observe models demonstrating the desired behavior in context. The more alike a model is to the observer, the more impact the model will have on the observer's behavior. Direct forms of modeling are preferred (i.e., having a person on-site to demonstrate the movement) (Ashford, Bennett, & Davids, 2006; Weiss, McCullagh, Smith, & Berlant, 1998), but indirect forms of modeling (e.g., video analysis) can also be effective and should be used in combination with direct training (Baker, Côté, & Abernethy, 2003). Using video of athletes and a similar model is a useful tool not only for teaching sports technique, but also strengthening tactical decision-making skills (García-González, Moreno, Moreno, Gil, & Del Villar, 2013).

Observational Learning

Observational learning alone may not be as influential on learning as physical action (practice; Sidaway & Hand, 1993) although some argue it can be (Wulf & Shea, 2002); however, used in combination (observe, then do) the two can be most effective (Shea, Wright, Wulf, & Whitacre, 2000; Shea, Wulf, & Whitacre, 1999). Additionally, there is evidence that providing athletes with autonomy to decide how often and when they need to view the models may lead to more learning (Wulf, Raupach, & Pfeiffer, 2005). This can be achieved most easily with video demonstrations accessible to athletes during practice. Another useful strategy is to, first, teach athletes how to ask themselves specific questions about a tactic, skill, or movement following a task and video review that could help their sport-specific expertise (García-González et al., 2013). Then, have them reflect on their efforts with the prompts that come from their answers (Di Stefano, Gino, Pisano, Staats, & Di-Stefano, 2014). Questioning and reflection strategies could be achieved through journaling, dictating, video-journaling, or incorporated with teammates during practice sessions.

Peer Modeling

Peer modeling used for skill development may be more beneficial if athletes are learning new skills or movements (Ashford et al., 2006), but may also be useful for behavior training as previously mentioned (effort; Desender et al., 2016). To help athletes understand how they can incorporate modeling into practice to enhance quality, consultants can start with conversations with athletes about problematic issues. Consultants can observe practices and help athletes identify teammates who exhibit desirable practice behaviors. In addition, encouraging or facilitating video recording of practices followed by discussions with athletes about the above-mentioned strategies could be another way to show athletes how to enhance the quality of their practices (Di Stefano et al., 2014).

Each of these practice characteristics described above are presented using a deliberate practice approach. Consultants can help athletes focus on specific tasks (like the ones above), be available for immediate feedback during sessions (or practices), allow time for athletes to assess their performance on the tasks and work through strategies to overcome issues, obstacles, or barriers, then provide opportunities for athletes to repeat their performance as much as necessary so athletes can improve the performances (Ericsson, 2008). Deliberate practice methods are well-studied and evidence is encouraging that practicing with a deliberate method can lead to automated responses by athletes which may lead to expert performance in the sport (for review see Ericsson, 2008). The key for consultants when working with athletes is establishing a consistent deliberate routine to improve the quality of practice with the understanding that practice alone is not the only factor that can lead to expert performance (Campitelli & Gobet, 2011; Hambrick et al., 2014).

Practical Implications

Quality training does not occur naturally with athletes. Instead, it begins as a deliberate process in which they take steps to ensure that they are physically and mentally committed, engaged, appropriately intense and throughout every training session. With repetition, the psychological, physical, practical, and team aspects of quality training become ingrained (Ericsson, 2008). In time, the thoughts and behaviors that produce quality training become habitual and are expressed without intention or effort in all aspects of athletes' training.

Training Goal and Purpose

Goal-setting was discussed in detail in Chapter 4, but, because it plays a vital role in quality training, it is worth discussing briefly in this context. One of the biggest issues often noticed by consultants is the omission of training goals. Given the rich literature about the utility and effectiveness of goal-setting (Senécal, Loughead, & Bloom, 2008; Stoeber, Uphill, & Hotham, 2009; Wilson & Brookfield, 2009), practice goals are an effective first step in ensuring quality training.

More often than not, coaches create and post training plans, athletes review them in a cursory way, and forget them before they begin training. Without the clear purpose and focus that training goals provide, quality training is already compromised before it begins (Burton, Pickering, Weinberg, Yukelson, & Weigand, 2010; Stoeber, Uphill, & Hotham, 2009).

Training goals should still follow the SMARTER (Locke & Latham, 2002) framework discussed previously, but should be immediate, task-specific, and clear (for a review, see Weinberg, 2013). With a defined goal and purpose, athletes will be more focused on what they need to do to work on in training and, as a result, are more likely to strive for and achieve the goal. For example, if an athlete needs help establishing a routine to ensure readiness, a training goal could be to identify and organize the activities that help them feel optimally prepared before training exercises and drills. Training goals can be targeted to any aspect of training including technical progressions, tactical execution, physiological responses, and cognitive, emotional, behavioral, or performance regulation. For example, a tennis player may have developed a bad habit of dropping her head just before she makes contact with the ball while serving. This causes her point of contact to be lower than desired, resulting in a disproportionate number of serves being hit into the net. A reasonable training goal would be to raise the trajectory of her serves and get more serves over the net. Once the goal is established, athletes can then create a purpose based on that goal. The purpose involves how she is going to accomplish her training goal, in this case, by keeping her head up through the point of contact (Locke & Latham, 2002).

Focus and Intensity

Once athletes begin a training session, two mental muscles play a prominent role in whether it rises to the level of quality training: focus and intensity. Focus refers to athletes being entirely focused on the goal that they have established and the task that will accomplish the goal. Intensity involves their bodies being at a level of physical activation that allows them give the appropriate effort and get the desired results (Centers for Disease Control and Prevention, 2015).

There are two reasons why focus and intensity are so important to quality training. First, they determine whether athletes are fully committed and engaged in their training efforts mentally and physically which would determine the quality of their efforts and the benefits they gain from their training (see Wulf, 2013 for a review). Second, for athletes to transfer their training gains to competition, they should imitate in training what they will need to do in competition. This applies to proper technique and tactics as well as suitable focus and intensity (Cumming & Hall, 2002; Taylor, Gould, & Rolo, 2008). A common problem is that athletes may train at levels of focus and intensity that are different from those at which they need to be in competition. For example, considering the influence of a deliberate practice approach (Ericsson, 2008), if athletes train at 70 percent focus and intensity, that level of commitment could become ingrained leaving them comfortable performing at that level rather than a higher level needed for competition. Moreover, when a competition arrives, that ingrained focus and intensity will emerge rather than a level of focus and intensity that will foster maximum performance in competition. The result is that they may not perform up to their capabilities in the competition.

Focus

One goal of quality training is to establish a specific focus for every task they will be performing. That ideal focus will be based on the goal that athletes set for themselves before their training sessions. Athletes can identify their ideal focus by revisiting their training goal and purpose. Consultants can help athletes distinguish what their specific focus "types" are as presented in Chapter 3 (Wulf, Lauterbach, & Toole, 1999). Returning to the example of the tennis serve, the player's goal was to increase her service percentage. Her purpose was to raise her head through the point of contact of her serve. The focus that this player will have throughout her serving practice then is to keep her eyes and chin up before and after she contacts the ball. This focus might be established by using imagery to see and feel a successful serve while keeping the above focus. It might be maintained during the actual practice serves by repeating a keyword (e.g., "up") throughout her service motion. This highly directed (and deliberate) focus offers two benefits. First, athletes are more likely to execute their training task effectively and, as a result, accomplish their training goal, remove the bad habit, and ingrain a good habit that results in achieving their goal. Second, that consistent focus strengthens their focus muscle enabling athletes to execute the task in competition, be better able to focus in general, and, as a consequence, increase their chances of performing their best (Ericsson, 2008).

Intensity

Another goal of quality training is for athletes to be able to reach and maintain their ideal intensity throughout their training sessions. As noted in Chapter 3, because athletes are physical beings, their intensity will have a significant influence on the quality of their training, the gains they make, and how well those gains translate into competitive performances. The appropriate intensity that athletes experience in training will be dependent on the specific tasks they engage in (Seiler, 2010; Tenenbaum & Connolly, 2008). For instance, mobility exercises would benefit from low intensity. Moderate intensity would be helpful for a technical or tactical focus. And higher intensity would best serve interval training. Athletes can leverage the exercises and tools discussed in Chapters 3 and 4 to achieve their ideal intensity for each training situation.

Athletes gain several benefits when they are consistently vigilant to their intensity in relation to the training task they are doing. First, they are at an ideal level of intensity that will enable them to maximize their training gains (Seiler, 2010). Second, athletes learn to actively reach and maintain their ideal intensity which they can then access before and during competitions to their greatest advantage.

Recovery from Mistakes

One of the most significant obstacles to consistent quality training is the occurrence of mistakes or setbacks during a training session. Quality training can seem easy to accomplish when athletes are performing well. It is an entirely different story when athletes begin to struggle in their training efforts. Those difficulties may include an inability to master a new skill, increasing fatigue as the training session progresses, or getting beat by a teammate in a simulated competition. In all of these cases, quality training is disrupted. Yet, quality training should actually cause these difficulties to occur because athletes are pushing themselves beyond what is comfortable in order to improve and, as a result, are more likely to make mistakes.

There are two powerful lessons that athletes must learn about their experiences of mistakes in training. First, mistakes are not just a result of quality training; they are also a benefit because, as just mentioned, they indicate a process of change and improvement in athletes. Second, the best athletes in the world in every sport struggle with mistakes and setbacks all of the time. So, given that top athletes make mistakes, it is not the mistakes that are the problem. Rather, the essential differentiator that distinguishes superstars from everyone else is not that they do not make mistakes (though they do make fewer of them), but how quickly and fully that they recover from them.

One mistake or setback can trigger an immediate and precipitous decline in the quality of training or it can turn into a series of mistakes and a slow deterioration of training performance for several reasons. First, confidence is hurt which causes athletes to be less willing to commit fully to their effort. Second, setbacks can trigger a constellation of negative emotions including disappointment, frustration, anger, sadness, and possibly even despair (Hanin, 2007, 2010; Lazarus, 2000; Patel et al., 2010). These emotions are discouraging and demotivating, and make quality training a near impossibility (Baumeister, Vohs, Nathan, Zhang, 2007; Grove & Stoll, 1999). Third, mistakes can generate stress and anxiety that if expressed in a unhelpful way can change athletes' physiology that makes quality training difficult. Fourth, mistakes can cause distractions that impair athletes' ability to maintain an effective focus on their training, thus leading to a decline in the quality of their training (Beilock & Gray, 2007; Elbe, Beckman, & Szymanski, 2003; Meeusen et al., 2006). The result can be a cascade of mistakes and physical and mental decline that prevents any chance of quality training. For athletes to ensure quality training in the face of mistakes and setbacks, they can follow these suggestions:

- Recognize that mistakes can be signs that they are engaging in quality training because they are pushing themselves out of their comfort zone.
- Stay positive and motivated in the face of mistakes.
- Let go of the mistake emotionally.
- Actively reestablish ideal intensity.
- Learn from the mistake, so it can be corrected next time.
- Refocus from the mistake to how to correct it.

Start to Finish

When athletes compete in their sport, they must be at their highest level of performance when the kickoff or tip-off happens, when the whistle blows, when the horn goes off, or any number of other ways. So they take very deliberate steps to ensure that they are completely ready to "hit the ground running." Unfortunately, many athletes do not have this sense of urgency in training. Often, athletes work their way into training, gliding through the initial exercises and drills and increasing their effort, intensity, and focus as the training progresses. This approach to training is not conducive to quality training for two reasons. First, athletes simply cannot perform at their highest level consistently if they are not "all in" from the very start of training to its final conclusion. Consultants can help athletes to ensure that they are fully prepared and ready to give their best efforts from the moment that training begins. First, they can show athletes how to reach their ideal intensity for whatever aspect of training they are engaging in. For instance, swimmers working on their shoulder mobility would want to reach a low level of intensity to relax their muscles and increase range of motion. Lacrosse players doing passing drills would strive for moderate intensity to balance the physical demands of running with the fine-motor skills of passing. And football linemen would want to achieve high intensity for a set of blocking drills. Specific exercises and tools to help athletes reach their ideal intensity can be found in Chapters 3 and 4.

Second, athletes must establish an ideal focus before their training drills. Their focus could be technical, tactical, mental, or performance-related. For example, gymnasts could focus on their body position or baseball hitters on keeping their shoulders level throughout their swing. Athletes can find their ideal focus using exercises and tools in Chapters 3 and 4.

For athletes to truly experience quality training, they must not only start every training task and session strong, at their ideal intensity and focused, they must also finish every training task and session the same way. In addition to easing themselves into training, many athletes also ease their way out of training. When they see the end in sight, they let up mentally and physically. The net result is that they lose their focus and intensity, and, in doing so, quality training disappears. Athletes maintaining quality training from start to finish is important because, as noted above, when not doing so, they are ingraining unproductive habits for both training and competitions. Just as a competition begins at a precise point, so does it end at a determined time, so athletes need to be focused and intense all the way to the finish. Yet, it is not uncommon for athletes to be performing well in a competition and, with the end of the event in sight, they ease up, lose focus and intensity, and their performance declines, often costing themselves a victory or a good result.

Never Give Up

There is one behavior that is singularly related to the abrupt end of quality training: giving up. When athletes cease to give their fullest effort, their intensity drops and their focus is lost. In doing so, the quality of their training declines and they lose the ability to gain the benefits of training. Despite this obvious calculus, it is a common sight to see athletes give up in training, usually in reaction to mistakes, difficulty mastering a new skill, the frustration of poor performance, or lack of motivation (Pass et al., 2005). In some cases, athletes will continue to train, but with lackluster effort. In other cases, they will cut their workouts short.

If this behavior occurs frequently in training, it hurts athletes in two ways. First, they do not get the most out of their training. And, second, they get in the habit of giving up and that habit comes out in competitions.

Athletes give up when they develop the belief that their efforts will not produce the results they want. When they give up, they lose all of the psychological and physical forces that are necessary for quality training including the four mental muscles described in Chapter 3: motivation, confidence, intensity, and focus. Consultants can help athletes to understand this relationship and show them ways to keep their effort high. This process begins with the 3 Ps described in the introduction to this chapter and it continues by ensuring that athletes mental muscles are strong (see Chapter 3) and they are adept at the exercises and tools discussed in Chapter 4.

Every Day Can be a Good Day of Training

Athletes love a good training day. They feel rested and energized. The weather and conditions are good. They perform well. Their coaches are happy. And training is just plain fun. Yet, one of the most frequent comments that consultants hear from athletes is, "I'm having a terrible day of training." This declaration is often followed by expressions of frustration, doubt, worry, and disappointment. Most often, the end result is that athletes lose their motivation, confidence, and focus and their training day is ruined (Hanin, 2007, 2010; Lazarus, 2000; Patel et al., 2010).

But, as any athlete knows, every training day is not always a good day of training. In fact, there are plenty of so-called bad training days. They are usually caused by some struggles athletes experience in their efforts:

- feeling physically tired or sick;
- difficulties with technique or tactics;
- making frequent mistakes;
- distracted by non-sport issues;
- not there mentally;
- coaches are not happy with their efforts or performances; and
- conflicts with teammates.

When confronted with these challenges, athletes will often conclude that they are having a bad day of training. However, this disheartening assumption not only fails to help in turning a training day around, but it is also not accurate. These struggles are certainly not pleasant, but they also provide the opportunity to turn tough days of training into a different type of good training day.

This process starts with consultants helping athletes to redefine what bad and good training days mean. The typical definition of a bad training day is when athletes are not performing well and they are not making progress in some aspect of their sport. But a different perspective allows athletes to redefine bad training days in a very different light: *When they turn against and give up on themselves* (McKay, Wulf, Lewthwaite, & Nordin, 2015; Nicholls, Polman, Levy, & Backhouse, 2008).

At the same time, athletes need to expand their definition of a good training day to go beyond feeling good and performing well. This restricted meaning of a good training day misses another aspect of training in which athletes can benefit tremendously, namely, strengthening their mind. More specifically, those training days when athletes are not "on their game" give them the opportunity to become stronger mentally. And this increased mental strength will pay off when they walk onto the field of play on the day of a competition (Birrer & Morgan, 2010). There are a variety of strategies that athletes can use to turn a so-called bad day of training into a good one:

- Before deciding that a training day is bad, try to turn it around using the exercises and tools described in this chapter as well as in Chapters 3 and 4.
- Reframe the training day as a different type of good training day.
- If the training day can't be turned around, accept that it's going to be a tough day and that they will stay committed to getting what they can out of it.
- Choose to respond positively to the adversity that's causing the day to be difficult.
- Use this opportunity get comfortable with the discomfort of the day.

- Decide to keep fighting and not give up, no matter how bad it gets.
- Turn the negative emotions (e.g., frustration, disappointment) into positive ones (e.g., inspiration, pride).
- See the day as an opportunity to become a more resilient and adaptable athlete that will better prepare them for difficult days of competition.

Summary

- Quality training involves athletes putting their maximum effort, focus, and intensity to everything they do including conditioning, sport training, nutrition, equipment preparation, and competitive readiness.
- Athletes can learn to expend mental and physical effort in training that is appropriate to the specific task.
- Athletes can use observational learning and modeling to better understand and master their sport skills.
- Quality training is a deliberate process in which athletes take steps to ensure that they are physically and mentally "totally there" throughout every training session.
- With a defined goal and purpose, athletes will be more focused on what they need to do to work on in training and, as a result, are more likely to strive for and achieve the goal.
- Once athletes begin a training session, two mental muscles play a prominent role in whether it rises to the level of quality training: focus and intensity.
- One of the most significant obstacles to consistent quality training is the occurrence of mistakes or setbacks during a training session and a key goal for athletes is for them to recover quickly from them.
- Maintaining effort, focus, and intensity from the beginning to the end of every training task and session is essential for quality training.
- One of the most important contributors to quality training is athletes' ability to never give up, even when faced with obstacles, struggles, and failures.
- Athletes can see every day as a good day of training if they recognize that the struggles will make them mentally stronger.

References

Ashford, D., Bennett, S. J., & Davids, K. (2006). Observational modeling effects for movement dynamics and movement outcome measures across differing task constraints: a meta-analysis. *Journal of Motor Behavior, 38*(3), 185–205.

Baker, J., Côté, J., & Abernethy, B. (2003). Learning from the experts: Practice activities of expert decision makers in sport. *Research quarterly for exercise and sport, 74*(3), 342–347.

Bandura, A. (1986). *Social foundations of thought and action: A social-cognitive theory*. Englewood Cliffs, NJ: Prentice Hall.

Baumeister, R. F., Vohs, K. D., Nathan DeWall, C., & Zhang, L. (2007). How emotion shapes behavior: Feedback, anticipation, and reflection, rather than direct causation. *Personality and Social Psychology Review, 11*(2), 167–203.

Beilock, S. L., & Gray, R. (2007). Why do athletes choke under pressure? In G. Tenenbaum & R. Eklund (Eds), *Handbook of sport psychology* (pp. 425–444). Hoboken, NJ: Wiley.

Birrer, D., & Morgan, G. (2010). Psychological skills training as a way to enhance an athlete's performance in high-intensity sports. *Scandinavian Journal of Medicine & Science in Sports, 20*, 78–87.

Boksem, M. A. S., Meijman, T. F., & Lorist, M. M. (2006). Mental fatigue, motivation and action monitoring. *Biological Psychology, 72*, 123–132.

Brisswalter, J., Collardeau, M., & René, A. (2002). Effects of acute physical exercise characteristics on cognitive performance. *Sports Medicine, 32*(9), 555–566.

Burton, D., Pickering, M., Weinberg, R., Yukelson, D., & Weigand, D. (2010). The competitive goal effectiveness paradox revisited: Examining the goal practices of prospective Olympic athletes. *Journal of Applied Sport Psychology, 22*(1), 72–86.

Campitelli, G., & Gobet, F. (2011). Deliberate practice: Necessary but not sufficient. *Current Directions in Psychological Science, 20*, 280–285.

Carver, C. S., & Scheier, M. F. (2000). On the structure of behavioral self-regulation. In M. Boekaerts, P. R. Pintrich, & M. Zeidner (Eds.), *Handbook of self-regulation research* (pp. 41–84). San Diego, CA: Academic Press.

Centers for Disease Control and Prevention. (2015, June). Measuring physical activity. Retrieved from www.cdc.gov/physicalactivity/basics/measuring/index.html

Chong, T. T. J., Apps, M. A., Giehl, K., Hall, S., Clifton, C. H., & Husain, M. (2018). Computational modelling reveals distinct patterns of cognitive and physical motivation in elite athletes. *Scientific Reports, 8*(1), 11888.

Connors, K. A., Galea, M. P., Said, C. M., & Remedios, L. J. (2010). Feldenkrais Method balance classes are based on princi-ples of motor learning and postural control retraining: A qualitative research study. *Physiotherapy*, *96*(4), 324–336.

Cumming, J., & Hall, C. (2002). Deliberate imagery practice: the development of imagery skills in competitive athletes. *Journal of Sports Sciences*, *20*(2), 137–145.

Cumming, J., Clark, S., Ste-Marie, D., McCullagh, P., & Hall, C. (2005). The functions of observational learning question-naire (FOLQ). *Psychology of Sport and Exercise*, *6*, 517–537.

Deci, E. L., & Ryan, R. M. (2000). The "what" and "why" of goal pursuits: Human needs and the self-determination of behavior. *Psychological Inquiry*, *11*, 227–268.

Desender, K., Beurms, S., & Van den Bussche, E. (2016). Is mental effort exertion contagious?. *Psychonomic Bulletin & Review*, *23*(2), 624–631.

Di Stefano, G., Gino, F., Pisano, G. P., Staats, B., & Di-Stefano, G. (2014). *Learning by thinking: How reflection aids performance*. Boston, MA: Harvard Business School.

Elbe, A. M., Beckman, J., & Szymanski, B. (2003). The development of the general and sport-specific performance motive of sports school students. *Psychology and Sports*, *10*(4), 134143.

Ericsson, K. A. (2008). Deliberate practice and acquisition of expert performance: a general overview. *Academic Emergency Medicine*, *15*(11), 988–994.

Eston, R. (2012). Use of ratings of perceived exertion in sports. *International Journal of Sports Physiology and Performance*, *7*(2), 175–182.

García-González, L., Moreno, M. P., Moreno, A., Gil, A., & Del Villar, F. (2013). Effectiveness of a video-feedback and questioning programme to develop cognitive expertise in sport. *PloS one*, *8*(12), e82270.

Grove, J. R., & Stoll, O. (1999). Performance slumps in sport: Personal resources and perceived stress. *Journal of Personal & Interpersonal Loss*, *4*(3), 203–214.

Hambrick, D. Z., Oswald, F. L., Altmann, E. M., Meinz, E. J., Gobet, F., & Campitelli, G. (2014). Deliberate practice: Is that all it takes to become an expert?. *Intelligence*, *45*, 34–45.

Hanin, Y. L. (2007). Emotions in sport: Current issues and perspectives. *Handbook of Sport Psychology*, *3*(3158), 22–41.

Hanin, Y. L. (2010). Coping with anxiety in sport. In A.R. Nicholls (Ed.), *Coping in sport: Theory, methods, and related constructs* (pp. 159–175). Hauppauge, NY: Nova Science Publishers.

Hockey, G. R. J. (1997). Compensatory control in the regulation of human performance under stress and high workload: A cognitive-energetical framework. *Biological Psychology*, *45*, 73–93.

Jain, S., Janssen, K., & DeCelle, S. (2004). Alexander technique and Feldenkrais method: a critical overview. *Physical Medicine and Rehabilitation Clinics*, *15*(4), 811–825.

Krausman, A. S., Crowell III, H. P., & Wilson, R. M. (2002). *The effects of physical exertion on cognitive performance*. No. ARL-TR-2844. Aberdeen, MD: Army Research Lab Proving Ground.

Lazarus, R. S. (2000). How emotions influence performance in competitive sports. *The Sport Psychologist*, *14*(3), 229–252.

Locke, E. A. & Latham, G. P. (2002). Building a practically useful theory of goal setting and task motivation. *American Psychologist*, *57*, 705–717.

Marcora, S. M., Staiano, W., & Manning, V. (2009). Mental fatigue impairs physical performance in humans. *Journal of applied physiology*, *106*(3), 857–864.

McKay, B., Wulf, G., Lewthwaite, R., & Nordin, A. (2015). The self: Your own worst enemy? A test of the self-invoking trigger hypothesis. *The Quarterly Journal of Experimental Psychology*, *68*(9), 1910–1919.

Meeusen, R., Duclos, M., Gleeson, M., Rietjens, G., Steinacker, J., & Urhausen, A. (2006). Prevention, diagnosis and treat-ment of the overtraining syndrome. *European Journal of Sport Science*, *6*(1), 1–14.

Nicholls, A. R., Polman, R. C., Levy, A. R., & Backhouse, S. H. (2008). Mental toughness, optimism, pessimism, and coping among athletes. *Personality and individual differences*, *44*(5), 1182–1192.

Nideffer, R. M. (1976). Test of attentional and interpersonal style. *Journal of Personality and Social Psychology*, *34*, 394–404.

Paas, F., Tuovinen, J., van Merriënboer, J. J. G., & Darabi, A. (2005). A motivational perspective on the relation between mental effort and performance: Optimizing learner involvement in instruction. *Educational Technology, Research and Development*, *53*, 25–34.

Patel, D. R., Omar, H., & Terry, M. (2010). Sport-related performance anxiety in young female athletes. *Journal of Pediatric and Adolescent Gynecology*, *23*(6), 325–335.

Renfree, A., Martin, L., Micklewright, D., & Gibson, A. S. C. (2014). Application of decision-making theory to the regulation of muscular work rate during self-paced competitive endurance activity. *Sports Medicine*, *44*(2), 147–158.

Schraw, G., & Ericsson, K.A. (2005). An interview with K. Anders Ericsson. Educational Psychology Review, 17, 389–412.

Seiler, S. (2010). What is best practice for training intensity and duration distribution in endurance athletes?. *International journal of sports physiology and performance*, *5*(3), 276–291.

Senécal, J., Loughead, T. M., & Bloom, G. A. (2008). A season-long team-building intervention: Examining the effect of team goal setting on cohesion. *Journal of Sport and Exercise Psychology*, *30*(2), 186–199.

Shea, C. H., Wright, D. L., Wulf, G., & Whitacre, C. (2000). Physical and observational practice affords unique learning opportunities. *Journal of Motor Behavior*, *32*, 27–36.

Shea, C. H., Wulf, G., & Whitacre, C. A. (1999). Enhancing training efficiency and effectiveness through the use of dyad training. *Journal of Motor Behavior, 31*, 119–125.

Sidaway, B., & Hand, M. J. (1993). Frequency of modeling effects on the acquisition and retention of a motor skill. *Research Quarterly for Exercise and Sport, 64*, 122–126.

Silvia, P. J., Nusbaum, E. C., Eddington, K. M., Beaty, R. E., & Kwapil, T. R. (2014). Effort deficits and depression: The influence of anhedonic depressive symptoms on cardiac autonomic activity during a mental challenge. *Motivation and emotion, 38*(6), 779–789.

Spink, K. S., Crozier, A. J., & Robinson, B. (2013). Examining the relationship between descriptive norms and perceived effort in adolescent athletes: Effects of different reference groups. *Psychology of Sport and Exercise, 14*(6), 813–818.

Stoeber, J., Uphill, M. A., & Hotham, S. (2009). Predicting race performance in triathlon: The role of perfectionism, achievement goals, and personal goal setting. *Journal of Sport and Exercise Psychology, 31*(2), 211–245.

Taylor, M. K., Gould, D., & Rolo, C. (2008). Performance strategies of US Olympians in practice and competition. *High Ability Studies, 19*(1), 19–36.

Tenenbaum, G., & Connolly, C. T. (2008). Attention allocation under varied workload and effort perception in rowers. *Psychology of Sport and Exercise, 9*(5), 704–717.

Weinberg, R. S. (2013). Goal setting in sport and exercise: research and practical applications. *Revista da Educação Física/UEM, 24*(2), 171–179.

Weiss, M. R., McCullagh, P., Smith, A. L., & Berlant, A. R. (1998). Observational learning and the fearful child: Influence of peer models on swimming skill performance and psychological responses. *Research Quarterly for Exercise and Sport, 69*(4), 380–394.

Wesch, N. N., Law, B., & Hall, C. R. (2007). The use of observational learning by athletes. *Journal of Sport Behavior, 30*(2), 219–231.

Wilson, K., & Brookfield, D. (2009). Effect of goal setting on motivation and adherence in a sixweek exercise program. *International Journal of Sport and Exercise Psychology, 7*(1), 89–100.

Wulf, G. (2013). Attentional focus and motor learning: A review of 15 years. *International Review of Sport & Exercise Psychology, 6*(1), 77–104.

Wulf, G., & Shea, C. H. (2002). Principles derived form the study of simple motor skills do not generalize to complex skill learning. *Psychonomic Bulletin and Review, 9*, 185–211.

Wulf, G., Lauterbach, B., & Toole, T. (1999). The learning advantages of an external focus of attention in golf. *Research Quarterly for Exercise and Sport, 70*, 1219–1226.

Wulf, G., Raupach, M., & Pfeiffer, F. (2005). Self-controlled observational practice enhances learning. *Research Quarterly for Exercise and Sport, 76*(1), 107–111.

CONSISTENCY

Alexandra Thompson and Jim Taylor

Will Durant (1926) summarized the Greek philosopher Aristotle's philosophy on the development of excellence when he said, "We are what we repeatedly do" (p. 76). When thinking about the world's best athletes, regardless of the sport in which they compete, a vital component that catapulted them to the top is consistently high-level performance. This old adage also serves as an essential teaching point that the pursuit of excellence requires the consistent development of performance-enhancing habits.

Yet, it is human nature to quickly assume that the successes of these elite athletes are due to their innate qualities rather than their full development of whatever abilities they were born with, something psychologists term the "fundamental attribution error" (Hooper et al., 2015, p. 69). To be sure, star athletes do bring innate genetic gifts (Eynon et al., 2013), but then maximize those biological talents with consistent quality training, preparation, and recovery (Durand-Bush & Salmela, 2002; Issurin, 2017). Returning to Aristotle's sentiments, the world's best athletes became consistently excellent by infusing all of their efforts with consistent excellence.

Consistent Training

We become what we repeatedly do, and we repeatedly like to do what we are good at. Unfortunately, if athletes base their training on what they already do well, it is likely that they will stagnate and not develop the complete skillsets necessary to become elite performers. For example, an athlete who is physically strong but struggles technically might spend more time and energy in the weight room, when a better return on investment might be focusing on technical skills. It is important for consultants to encourage athletes to develop conscientiousness, such that they attend consistently to every aspect of training that impacts their performance (Hardy et al., 2017; Woodman, Zourbanos, Hardy, Beattie, & McQuillan, 2010). A comprehensive program that consistently incorporates physical conditioning, sport skill development, tactical implementation and re-evaluation, and mental training will help athletes to perform at their highest level (Gould & Maynard, 2009).

In addition to regularly encouraging a multifaceted approach to training, there is also value in having athletes frequently reevaluate their greatest needs and goals as they evolve in their sport (Burton, Pickering, Weinberg, Yukelson, & Weigand, 2010). Periodization of training is often recommended to support elite performance in the strength and conditioning world (Lyakh et al., 2016; Turner, 2011), which helps athletes to manage factors such as volume, intensity, and fatigue throughout their preparation and competitive seasons. Similarly, athletes who more frequently reevaluate their needs and goals (e.g., at the beginning and end of competitive seasons, prior to off-season, off-season mid-point) report greater sport confidence and career success (Burton et al., 2010). Regular reevaluation and subsequent goal-setting is vital to creating individualized and specified training programs. For example, conditioning needs are likely to be different at the end of a competitive season relative to pre-season, and those needs are likely to differ from one year to the next as athletes develop.

Consultants can also support their clients' consistent commitment to their sport. As discussed in the previous section, there are many challenges to athletes' consistent effort during the course of training and competitions. Successful athletes demonstrate a consistent level of commitment to a singular goal in a way that less successful athletes do not (Hollings, Mallett, & Hume, 2014). In addition to accumulating a large volume of training (Issurin, 2017), consistent commitment includes training longer and more frequently, investing significant effort, and appreciating the purpose of training (Hardy et al., 2017). As alluded to above, where and how athletes channel these efforts can vary depending on their individual strengths and areas of growth, time of year, and other demands placed on them. However, the commitment must be unwavering to facilitate ongoing athletic development and goal attainment. Consultants can help athletes foster this consistent commitment by encouraging athletes to strengthen their motivation (see more in Chapter 3) and to identify and mitigate obstacles that hinder the expression of athletes' commitment (see more in Chapter 2).

Consistent Mind

The pursuit of high-level performance will be limited if athletes do not consistently adopt an effective psychology. Research attests to such an influence on performance (Hardy et al., 2017; Issurin, 2017; Taylor, Gould, & Rolo, 2008), and Olympic athletes often demonstrate similar attitudes, dispositions, and/or psychological states across sport (Gould & Maynard, 2009). Consultants can educate athletes about attitudes that are effective such as those discussed in Chapter 1 (e.g., ownership, process, challenge). Helping athletes reflect on their attitudes towards training, preparation, and recovery will help them increase their awareness of opportunities for growth and improvement within each domain.

In addition to consistent application of effective attitudes, it is also vital for consultants to help athletes develop consistency in their mental training and preparation (Burton et al., 2010). This will likely include application of some combination of strengthening their mental muscles (e.g., motivation and confidence) and using mental exercises and tools (e.g., self-talk and imagery) discussed in Chapters 3 and 4, respectively. American Olympians have been shown to employ similar mental tools in practice and in competition (e.g., self-talk, imagery, goal-setting; Taylor et al., 2008). However, it is also important to determine the psychological demands of a given sports setting to develop a mental approach using relevant exercises and tools (Birrer & Morgan, 2010). When consultants emphasize the value of having a consistent mind, athletes can create a mental preparation plan that is intentional, specific, appropriate, and consistently applied for each component of their overall mental training program.

As consultants collaborate with athletes to create mental preparation plans, the next crucial step is to consistently apply what they've learned in their training and competitive efforts. Research supports the importance of consistent use of mental training to benefit performance (Altfeld, Langenkamp, Beckman, & Kellmann, 2017; Brown & Fletcher, 2017; Thelwell, Greenlees, & Weston, 2006; Wright et al., 2015), and elite athletes who have been deemed "mentally tough" stress the importance of time, patience, and effort to master all aspects of mental training (Connaughton, Wadey, Hanton, & Jones, 2008). Maintenance is also important, which can be influenced by ongoing use of mental exercises and tools, high motivation, and social support. Thus, mental training should be viewed similar to that of physical conditioning and sport practice: as exercises that create effective habits, which provide a platform for consistent training and competitive performances.

Consistent Wellness

An NCAA Division I head coach said, "Who you are as an athlete is who you are as a person; how you approach anything is how you approach everything" (D. Cutcliffe, personal communication, March 2018). The message from this coach is that, despite athletes' ability to compartmentalize, what they do away from their sport impacts their on-field performances. This perspective encourages athletes to develop habits in their non-sport lives that will support their sports efforts. Consultants can help athletes attend to a broad spectrum of lifestyle habits, but several key domains in which careful attention can significantly impact performance include nutrition and sleep (Close, Hamilton, Philp, Burke, & Morton, 2016; Freeman, Rees, & Hardy, 2009; Rosen, Frohm, Kottorp, Fridén, & Heijne, 2017).

Nutrition

As the level of competition in sport increases, highly driven athletes seek out additional ways to optimize their performances and gain a competitive advantage. Nutrition is one of those areas that many athletes are leveraging. Research has clearly demonstrated that nutrition has a significant impact on training, competitive performance, and recovery (Close et al., 2016; Thomas, Erdman, & Burke, 2016). The nutrition community has established research-based recommendations regarding type, amount, and timing of food and fluid intake for different sports and training scenarios (Thomas et al., 2016; Wardenaar et al., 2017). Taken together, the current research reinforces the fact that consistent and intentionally structured nutrition practices can benefit many aspects of athletes' sport experiences.

Sleep

Maintaining a consistent sleep schedule with good sleep practices is also crucial for athletic performance. Though variance in sleep schedule occurs based on individual circadian rhythm preferences (e.g., morningness–eveningness dimension; Thun et al., 2015), performance can be impaired as a result of sleep deprivation regardless of sleep preferences, particularly in endurance sports (Simpson, Gibbs, & Matheson, 2017). In a review summarizing the effects of sleep loss on athletic performance, Simpson et al. (2017) cited significant decrements in executive functioning, speed, and performance accuracy (e.g., tennis serving, dart throwing, free throw shooting), even with mild sleep loss (e.g., 4–5 hours total of sleep).

Aside from performance impairments, researchers have also found a link between sleep loss and injury (Milewski et al., 2014). Adolescent athletes who slept less than eight hours per night were 1.7 times more likely to incur a significant injury than those who slept more than eight hours per night. Aside from hours of practice, sleep hours were the strongest predictor of injury risk. This research provides evidence for the powerful relationship between sleep and athletic performance, and suggests that consistent, adequate sleep is requisite for elite performances. Moreover, there is also evidence that extending sleep at night or taking naps when sleep debt has accrued may also improve performance (Simpson et al., 2017; Thun et al., 2015). Thus, it is vital for consultants to integrate sleep assessment during the initial intake and provide relevant education about the effects of sleep loss for athletes. They can also help athletes develop a sleep plan to ensure sufficient quality sleep based on their physiological, training, and life needs.

Consistent School

Because athletes don't always grasp the impact that their non-sport life has on their sports efforts, some believe that they can give their fullest effort in their sport, yet can slack off in their school lives without repercussions.

This perception can be especially problematic in youth and collegiate sport because this pattern can be reinforced by a culture of permissiveness and indulgence, particularly of gifted athletes. However, to be eligible for NCAA competition, particularly at the Division I level, athletes are required to complete a certain curriculum and maintain standards of grades and progress (National Collegiate Athletic Association; NCAA, n.d.). Thus, at a practical level, many athletes must, at a minimum, attend to their academics to even be eligible to participate in their sports. Once they reach collegiate sport, academics typically become even more rigorous. On average, student-athletes spend 34 hours each week on academics, just shy of the 38.5 hours per week they spend on athletics-related activities (NCAA, n.d.). Despite the challenges of balancing two almost full-time jobs, research suggested that Division I athletic participation is actually positively associated with academic performance (Bailey & Bhattacharyya, 2017; Hildenbrand, Sanders, Leslie-Toogood, & Benton, 2009). In a study comparing several thousand students and student-athletes over a 4-year period (Hildenbrand et al., 2009), collegiate athletic status at any point resulted in a significant increase in the odds of graduating, such that 68.4% of student-athletes could be expected to graduate relative to only 58.7% of non-athletes. Moreover, researchers suggested that the top athletic teams actually perform significantly better academically when compared to bottom athletic teams (Bailey & Bhattacharyya, 2017). It is unclear if athletic participation naturally draws those who may be academically driven as well, or if athletic participation serves as a protective factor for academic success (due to departmental resource allocation for academic support). Regardless, it is reasonable to interpret that investment of time and effort into academics may be a protective factor for athletic achievement, and a minimal requirement to transition from high school to collegiate athletics.

Despite these findings, it is clear that not every committed athlete is a committed student. Some athletes who have high aspirations in their sport, struggle with or have little interest in academics, or who have not been held accountable for their educations may find that their lack of consistent commitment to their schooling has a negative impact on their athletic pursuits. These athletes may fall behind in classwork, miss assignment deadlines, produce poor quality work, and worry about their eligibility, all which will produce stress and distractions that can impair sports performance. Consultants can support and encourage athletes, regardless of their level of commitment, by providing perspective and guidance about the importance of education, stress management, life balance, and time management.

Consistent Relationships and Support

Relationships and support constitute the final lifestyle domain that can significantly impact the pursuit of elite athletics. Relationships that can influence sports performance can include those within (e.g., coaches, teammates, fans) and outside of sports (e.g., family, friends; Storm, Henriksen, Larsen, & Christensen, 2014). Research has found that perception of social support can contribute to performance improvements (Freeman et al., 2009; Holt & Dunn, 2004; Rees & Freeman, 2010) and self-confidence (Freeman & Rees, 2010), and can be particularly influential both in transition between and across athletic development stages (Storm et al., 2014). In addition, social support, or lack thereof, can have a significant impact on well-being and can contribute to feelings of burnout (DeFreese & Smith, 2014), which has been associated with negative sport experiences and overall well-being (Cresswell & Eklund, 2006; Cresswell & Eklund, 2007). Thus, nurturance of relationships and consistent maintenance of quality support systems is important for athletes' sports performances as well as their overall wellness. Consultants can help athletes to assess and strengthen their relationships and the support they receive in their sports efforts and in their general lives.

Consistent Preparation

Consistent preparation is the final contributor that drives athletes to be their best. Top athletes are scrupulous and resolute in every aspect of their training and competitive performances to ensure that any area that affects those efforts have been maximized (Gould & Maynard, 2009).

Every committed athlete does their best to prepare thoroughly for competitions because they know that without total preparation, optimal performance and competitive success isn't possible. What is noticeable about the best athletes in the world is that they are equally meticulous about their training preparations as well (Issurin, 2017). For example, they take active steps to prepare themselves by utilizing clearly articulated training routines (more on that in Chapter 4) that ensure a high level of readiness in training. This exacting approach to their training makes more certain that they develop the essential physical, technical, and mental capabilities that they can then transfer to their competitive performances.

Consistency in athletes' preparations can have a significant effect on their performances at several levels.

- *Meta preparation* involves the aggregation of athletes' conditioning, sport-specific competencies, and mental training that develops across many years of dedication to their sport.
- *Macro preparation* relates to preparation that athletes do in the short-term, within weeks of a competition, including refining sport skills, tapering their conditioning, increasing rest, and focusing their mental training to emphasize competitive performance.
- *Micro preparation* refers to athletes fine tuning themselves physically and mentally as they ready themselves for competition.

Summary

- When thinking about the world's best athletes, regardless of the sport in which they compete, a vital component that catapulted them to the top is consistently high-level performance.
- It is important for consultants to encourage athletes to develop conscientiousness, such that they attend to every aspect of training that impacts their performance.
- Consultants can help athletes foster consistent commitment by encouraging athletes to strengthen their motivation and to identify and mitigate obstacles that hinder the expression of athletes' commitment.
- The pursuit of high-level performance will be limited if athletes do not consistently adopt an effective mindset.
- Consultants can help athletes develop consistency in their mental training including the application of some combination of strengthening their mental muscles (e.g., motivation and confidence) and using mental tools (e.g., goal-setting and imagery).
- Mental training should be viewed similarly to that of physical training; practice creates effective and consistent habits, which provide a platform for consistent training and competitive performances.
- Consultants can help athletes attend to a broad spectrum of lifestyle habits including nutrition and sleep.
- Consultants can support and encourage athletes regardless of their level of commitment by providing perspective and education about the importance of education, stress management, life balance, and time management.
- Nurturance of relationships and consistent maintenance of quality support systems is important for athletes' sports performances as well as their overall well-being.
- Top athletes are consistently scrupulous and resolute in every aspect of their training and competitive performances to ensure that any area that affects those efforts have been maximized.
- Consistency in athletes' preparations can have a significant effect on their performances in several ways.
- *Meta preparation* involves the aggregation of athletes' conditioning, sport-specific competencies, and mental training that develops across many years of dedication to their sport. It occurs over years of commitment to a sport.
- *Macro preparation* relates to preparation that athletes do in the short-term, within weeks of a competition, including refining sport skills, conditioning taper period, increase rest, and fine mental training emphasizing competitive performance.
- *Micro preparation* refers to athletes fine tuning themselves physically and mentally by adhering to their pre-competitive routines.

References

Altfeld, S., Langenkamp, H., Beckmann, J., & Kellmann, M. (2017). Measuring the effectiveness of psychologically oriented basketball drills in team practice to improve self-regulation. *International Journal of Sports Science & Coaching, 12*, 725–736.

Bailey, S., & Bhattacharyya, M. (2017). A comparison of academic and athletic performance in the NCAA. *College Student Journal, 51*, 173–182.

Birrer, D., & Morgan, C. (2010). Psychological skills training as a way to enhance an athlete's performance in high-intensity sports. *Scandinavian Journal of Medicine in Science and Sports, 20*, 78–87.

Brown, D. J., & Fletcher, D. (2017). Effects of psychological and psychosocial interventions on sport performance: A meta-analysis. *Sports Medicine, 47*, 77–99.

Close, G. L., Hamilton, D. L., Philp, A., Burke, L.M., & Morton, J. P. (2016). Strategies in sport nutrition to increase exercise performance. *Free Radical Biology and Medicine, 98*, 144–158.

Connaughton, D., Wadey, R., Hanton, S., & Jones, G. (2008). The development and maintenance of mental toughness: Perceptions of elite performers. *Journal of Sports Sciences, 26*, 83–95.

Cresswell, S. L., & Eklund, R. C. (2006). The nature of player burnout in rugby: Key characteristics and attributions. *Journal of Applied Sport Psychology, 18*, 219–239.

Cresswell, S. L., & Eklund, R. C. (2007). Athlete burnout: A longitudinal qualitative study. *The Sport Psychologist, 21*, 1–20.

DeFreese, J., & Smith, A. (2014). Athlete social support, negative social interactions, and psychological health across a competitive sport season. *Journal of Sport & Exercise Psychology, 36*, 619–630. doi: 10.1123/jsep.2014-0040.

Durand-Bush, N., & Salmela, J. H. (2002). The development and maintenance of expert athletic performance: Perceptions of World and Olympic champions. *Journal of Applied Sport Psychology, 14*, 154–171.

Drake, D. (1926). What is a mind? Ontological pluralism versus ontological monism. *Mind, 35*(138), 230–236.

Eynon, N., Hanson, E. D., Lucia, A., Houweling, P. J., Garton, F., North, K. N., & Bishop, D. J. (2013). Genes for elite power and sprint performance: ACTN3 leads the way. *Sports Medicine, 43*, 803–817.

Freeman, P., & Rees, T. (2010). Perceived social support from team-mates: Direct and stress-buffering effects on self-confidence. *European Journal of Sport Science, 10*, 59–67.

Freeman, P., Rees, T., & Hardy, L. (2009). An Intervention to Increase Social Support and Improve Performance. *Journal Of Applied Sport Psychology, 21*, 186–200.

Gould, D., & Maynard, I. (2009). Psychological preparation for the Olympic games. *Journal of Sports Sciences, 27*, 1393–1408.

Hardy, L., Barlow, M., Evans, L., Rees, T., Woodman, T., & Warr, C. (2017). Great British medalists: Psychosocial biographies of super-elite and elite athletes from Olympic sports. *Progress in Brain Research, 232*, 1–119.

Hildenbrand, K., Sanders, J., Leslie-Toogood, A., & Benton, S. (2009). Athletic status and academic performance and persistence at a NCAA Division I university. *Journal for the Study of Sports and Athletes in Education, 3*, 41–58.

Hollings, S. C., Mallett, C. J., & Hume, P. A. (2014). The transition from elite junior track-and-field athlete to successful senior athlete: Why some do, why others don't. *International Journal of Sports Science & Coaching, 9*, 457–471.

Holt, N. L., & Dunn, J. G. H. (2004). Toward a grounded theory of the psychosocial competencies and environmental conditions associated with soccer success. *Journal of Applied Sport Psychology, 16*, 199–219.

Hooper, N., Erdogan, A., Keen, G., Lawton, K., & McHugh, L. (2015). Perspective taking reduces the fundamental attribution error. *Journal of Contextual Behavioral Science, 4*, 69–72.

Issurin, V. B. (2017). Evidence-based prerequisites and precursors of athletic talent: A review. *Sports Medicine, 47*, 1993–2010.

Lyakh, V., Mikołajec, K., Bujas, P., Witkowski, Z., Zając, T., Litkowycz, R., & Banyś, D. (2016). Periodization in team sport games: A review of current knowledge and modern trends in competitive sports. *Journal of Human Kinetics, 54*, 173–180.

Milewski, M. D., Skaggs D. L,, Bishop G. A., Pace J. L., Ibrahim D. A., Wren T. A., & Barzdukas A. (2014). Chronic lack of sleep is associated with increased sports injuries in adolescent athletes. *Journal of Pediatric Orthopaedics, 34*, 129–133.

NCAA. (n.d.). *2017–2018 guide for the college bound student-athlete.* Retrieved from www.ncaapublications.com/productdownloads/CBSA18.pdf.

Rees, T., & Freeman, P. (2010). Social support and performance in a golf-putting experiment. *The Sport Psychologist, 189*, 333–348.

Rosen, P., Frohm, A., Kottorp, A., Fridén, C., & Heijne, A. (2017). Too little sleep and an unhealthy diet could increase the risk of sustaining a new injury in adolescent elite athletes. *Scandinavian Journal of Medicine & Science in Sports, 27*, 1364–1371.

Simpson, N. S., Gibbs, E. L., & Matheson, G. O. (2017). Optimizing sleep to maximize performance: implications and recommendations for elite athletes. *Scandinavian Journal of Medicine & Science in Sports, 27*, 266–274.

Storm, L. K., Henriksen, K., Larsen, C. H., & Christensen, M. K. (2014). Influential relationships as contexts of learning and becoming elite: Athletes' retrospective interpretations. *International Journal of Sports Science & Coaching, 9*, 1341–1356.

Taylor, M. K., Gould, D., & Rolo, C. (2008). Performance strategies of US Olympians in practice and competition. *High Ability Studies, 19*, 19–36.

Thelwell, R. C., Greenlees, I. A., & Weston, N. J. V. (2006). Using psychological skills training to develop soccer performance. *Journal of Applied Sport Psychology, 18*, 254–270.

Thomas, D. T., Erdman, K. A., & Burke, L. M. (2016). Position of the Academy of Nutrition and Dietetics, Dietitians of Canada, and the American College of Sports Medicine: Nutrition and Athletic Performance. *Journal of the Academy of Nutrition and Dietetics, 116*, 501–528.

Thun, E., Bjorvatn, B., Flo, E., Harris, A., & Pallesen, S. (2015). Sleep, circadian rhythms, and athletic performance. *Sleep Medicine Reviews, 23*, 1–9.

Turner, A. (2011). The science and practice of periodization: A brief review. *Strength and Conditioning Journal, 33*, 34–46.

Wardenaar, F. C., Ceelen, I. J. M., Dijk, v., J.W, Hangelbroek, R. W. J., Roy, v., L, Pouw, v. d., B., . . . Witkamp, R. F. (2017). Nutritional supplement use by Dutch elite and sub-elite athletes: Does receiving dietary counseling make a difference? *International Journal of Sport Nutrition & Exercise Metabolism, 27*, 32–42.

Woodman, T., Zourbanos, N., Hardy, L., Beattie, S., & McQuillan, A. (2010). Do performance strategies moderate the relationship between personality and training behaviors? An exploratory study. *Journal of Applied Sport Psychology, 22*, 183–197.

Wright, D. J., McCormick, S. A., Birks, S., Loporto, M., & Holmes, P. S. (2015). Action observation and imagery training improve the ease with which athletes can generate imagery. *Journal of Applied Sport Psychology, 27*, 156–170. doi: 10.1080/10413200.2014.968294

EXPERIMENTATION

Michele Kerulis and Jim Taylor

There are widely accepted "best practices" in athletic development that have been shown to facilitate progress in conditioning, sport skills, nutrition, mental training, and other aspects of performance. However, no one has, as yet, identified one clear path to athletic success. Due to individual differences among athletes, applying a "one size fits all" approach is rarely effective in athletes fully realizing their abilities. Moreover, it is often creative and sometimes truly "out of the box" methods of training that have enabled some athletes to achieve remarkable heights.

Because every athlete is different, and sports are constantly changing, athletes must be receptive and, in fact, motivated to attempt new ways of approaching their sport. Only through trying new things will athletes identify the particular "recipe" that allows them to develop most quickly and completely (Bortoli, Bertollo, Hanin, & Robazza, 2012; Hannin, 2008).

When people hear the word *experimentation* they often think about laboratories with bubbling beakers and people in white coats engaging in the scientific method: observation, formulation of a hypothesis, a prediction based on the hypothesis, and performance of an experiment to confirm or nullify the hypothesis. Instead of beakers and Bunsen burners, athletes' "laboratories" are weight rooms, fields of play, and the mind. For the purposes of this section, experimentation is defined as a series of well-planned steps aimed at contributing to athletic development and enhancing sport performance.

The challenge to athletes is that experimentation is uncertain and uncomfortable. There is rarely clarity on what new things they should try. There is no assurance that breaking away from the status quo will work. And athletes' performances may decline in the short run because of the changes that they make. Yet, the willingness to experiment is essential for athletes to have a chance at achieving their sports goals. As an old Texas saying goes, "If all you ever do is all you've ever done, then all you'll ever get is all you've ever got."

Theory and Research

For athletes to gain comfort and confidence with experimentation in their sports lives, they must first understand the barriers that lead to their aversion to experimentation: innate fear and the uncertainty of trying new things. Athletes can develop a healthy perspective on experimentation and can learn to control some of the forces that drive that reluctance. Consultants can then help athletes to eliminate (or mitigate) fear, collaborate with athletes and their coaches to create training settings that are conducive to experimentation, and empower athletes to embrace experimentation as an essential tool for their sports development.

In general, human beings don't like to experiment for several reasons. At an innate level, we are driven through evolution to seek homeostasis which, in primitive times, helped our ancestors to increase the chances of their survival. Back on the Serengeti 250,000 years ago, new things often meant threats to their lives. That same survival instinct that has been wired into us since we climbed out of the primordial muck and began walking upright now hinders people's and, specifically, athletes' willingness to try new things. When many athletes are confronted with that which is unfamiliar and uncertain, their sympathetic nervous system responds with the "fight or flight" reaction that is triggered by the amygdala and attempts are immediately made to return the body to a state of equilibrium by removing the change that caused it in the first place (Carlson, 2013).

There is also a psychological component to this reluctance to experiment. An unavoidable aspect of doing things differently is that athletes will likely fail at first. Drawing on the discussion of obstacles from

Chapter 2, these failures are threatening to athletes' self-identity, self-esteem, and sports goals (Brewer, Van Raalte, & Linder, 1993). Even when athletes know rationally that experimentation is essential to their development, both the primitive and modern parts of their brains attempt to short circuit those efforts.

The innate reactions, emotional responses, and psychological barriers that can prevent athletes from experimenting in the service of progress in their sport is linked to psychological flexibility, a term used in Acceptance and Commitment Therapy (ACT; Blackledge, & Hayes, 2001; Hayes, Luoma, Bond, Masuda, & Lillis, 2006; Kashdan, 2010). Psychological flexibility involves (1) adjusting to changing situational demands, (2) recalibrating psychological resources, (3) altering perspective, and (4) balancing conflicting wishes, needs, and goals (Kashdan, 2010). Psychologically flexible athletes are better able to examine, understand, and override the interfering cognitive, emotional, physiological, and behavioral reactions that hold them back from experimentation. This new approach can lead them to adopt a more open and accepting attitude toward experimentation. Kashdan's (2010) research confirms that "a flexible approach to one's experiences will be associated with health and well-being, even when those experiences are sometimes painful" (p. 873). Consultants can help athletes examine their own psychological flexibility—or inflexibility—as an initial entry into the notion of experimentation. Additionally, mindfulness (see Chapter 4) can be used to help athletes to be conscious of their internal struggles and to use that awareness as a springboard for altering their responses to unhelpful reactions to experimentation.

Encouragement, which is grounded in Adlerian theory (Adler, 1956), is another tool that consultants can use to help athletes change their perspective on, alter their reactions to, and overcome their reluctance to experiment. Adler spoke extensively about encouragement, which "inspires or helps others toward a conviction that they can work on finding solutions and that they can cope with any predicament" (Sweeney & Sweeney, 2009, p. 72). One way consultants can use encouragement with athletes is to collaborate with them and their coaches to create scenarios that allow athletes to gain incremental comfort with experimentation (Adler, 1956; Vygotsky, 1978). The use of encouragement can help athletes understand how to cope effectively with those factors that cause their hesitancy toward experimentation. Encouraging athletes to believe in themselves (confidence) and to understand that "attitudes, expectations, and self-beliefs . . . are within [their] control" (Sweeney & Sweeney, 2009, p. 74) will prime them psychologically and emotionally to take the first steps toward experimentation in their sports lives. Helping athletes understand emotional barriers and their ability to enhance their psychological flexibility through the use of encouragement is essential in laying the foundation for productive and successful experimentation.

Consultants can also use their relationship with athletes to support them as they work to leverage experimentation in their training efforts (Sharp & Hodge, 2014). Many theorists, including Vygotsky (1978), Adler (1956), and Rogers (1951) emphasized the importance of developing trusting relationships to lay the framework for successful outcomes. The trust that athletes have in consultants can be used to help them look for novel solutions to challenges they face in the sports development, which will improve their confidence and comfort in experimenting, as well as strengthen the consulting relationship (Duffy, Haberstroh, & Trepal, 2016; Kaplan, Tarvydas, & Gladding, 2014).

Counseling researchers (Duffy et al., 2016) also advocate for the use of creativity as a therapeutic tool and experimentation can readily be seen as a proxy for creativity in the sports setting. Consultants can adapt this conceptualization of creativity and its connection to the consultation relationship in their work with athletes. Duffy and her colleagues define creativity (experimentation) in counseling as:

> a shared counseling process involving growth-promoting shifts that occur from an intentional focus on the therapeutic relationship and the inherent human creative capacity to affect change. Creativity [experimentation] is as fundamental to practice as the therapeutic relationship. In the best sense, the counseling relationship ignites creative problem solving, understanding, flexibility, and adaptability. In turn, this shared creativity [experimentation] deepens the counseling relationship.
>
> *(Duffy et al., 2016, p. 448)*

Duffy et al.'s ideas, when applied to sport, suggest that engaging in creative problem solving can enhance the consulting relationship which, in turn, will support athletes' shift toward experimentation. Thus, the stronger the consulting relationship, the more athletes will be willing to accept experimentation in their training.

Practical Implications

In preparing athletes to try new things in their sports training, consultants can embolden athletes to adopt an "experimentation mindset" by following steps similar to those of the scientific model described in the beginning of this section. Each step in the process is intended to be a cooperative effort between consultants and athletes and, if involving conditioning or sport-specific training, in concert with coaches. Together, the stakeholders can create appropriate experimentation to advance different aspects of their performances on and off the field. These experiments can be spontaneous and rely intuitively on elements of the scientific method or they can be well planned and highly structured. Obviously, experimentation of any sort should never be initiated shortly before or during a competition. Rather, it should occur during a preparation period in which there is time for the experimentation to run its course and, if successful, for the newly gained benefits to become learned and ingrained. Experimentation can follow a semi-structured process that involves a number of steps:

- Consultants can observe athletes in both training and competition and to have conversations with them (and coaches, if appropriate) that identify the areas in which improvements can be made.
- They can then brainstorm about innovative ways in which to experiment to make the relevant improvements and specify realistic goals that will provide a reasonable measure of success.
- Consultants can elicit buy-in from athletes, instill confidence in their efforts, and ensure full commitment to the experimentation.
- Both consultants and athletes (and coaches, if appropriate) can reflect on how the experimentation went, identify and reward effort and progress, and plan next steps.

As athletes experience success in their experimentation efforts, consultants can continue to encourage experimentation until athletes have gained sufficient comfort and confidence for them to want to continue to experiment in their sports training.

Get Out of the Comfort Zone

As noted earlier in this section, people in general don't like to be uncomfortable and athletes are no different. Yet, one of the realities of sport is that if athletes aren't uncomfortable, they aren't progressing in their sport. In addition to the reasons discussed, many athletes have negative connotations about being out of their comfort zone. It feels bad physically which triggers uncomfortable emotions. In turn, the physical and emotional discomfort hurts their psychology related to being out of their comfort zone including their confidence, motivation, and focus. What begins as a positive experience to pursue, that is, taking steps to improve, becomes a negative experience to avoid. The end result is that athletes eschew experimentation and choose comfort over progress.

Consultants can use concepts from Vygotsky's (1978) zone of proximal development paired with adult learning theory (Knowles, Holton, & Swanson, 2015) to help athletes move out of their comfort zone and close the gap between what they can do on their own (comfort zone) and to realize the potential of what they can learn under the guidance of others (experimentation). Vygotsky identified the zone of optimal functioning as "the distance between actual developmental level as determined by independent problem solving and the level of potential development as determined through problem-solving under . . . guidance, or in collaboration with more capable peers" (Vygotsky, 1978, p. 86). In the case of experimentation, actual developmental level can be considered the athlete's current skill level and consultants serve as the "guidance."

Consultants can help athletes to welcome experimentation by changing the way they think about being out of their comfort zone. They need to shift their thinking about experimentation from "It feels bad" to "It's good to feel bad." This change can occur when athletes understand that so-called feeling bad is positive because it means that they are doing something new and it is making them better athletes (e.g., understanding change in a meaningful context; Adler, 1956; Vygotsky, 1978).

An essential lesson that consultants can help athletes learn is that, as they get out of their comfort zone, they become more comfortable with being uncomfortable (Kashdan, 2010). When viewed through the lens of Vygotsky's (1978) theory, this translates to helping athletes understand that what they are open to learning with assistance (experimenting with a consultant) they will be able to one day do on their own (e.g., being comfortable with ambiguity during experimentation in sport). In this process, their comfort zone expands. As athletes continue to experiment, they become wrapped in an ever-growing comfort zone. And a part of that process is a constant experience of progressing in their sport.

Go to Extremes

One way in which athletes can experiment is to "go to extremes." The human mind and body are wired, again through evolution, to be highly sensitive to sensory changes including temperature, light, feel, and sound. As noted above, this acute awareness helped us survive because recognition of sensory change might portend an imminent threat to life.

This responsiveness to change can also be used as a tool for experimentation in sports. Many parts of sports training, including physical conditioning, sport skills, or mental training, lie along a spectrum in which athletes perform optimally (Hannin, 2008). One strategy that athletes can use in their experimentation is to identify places along that continuum that they can try (Bortoli et al., 2012). In doing so, they specify the location in which they perform their best. This extreme approach can be used in conditioning to see what the limits of their exertions are. With technique, athletes can experiment with different body positions and movement patterns until they find the ones that work best for them. They can also apply this method to their mental training in which they identify their ideal focus, intensity, and emotions by exploring different degrees and types of each (more on this in Chapters 3 and 4).

To demonstrate how athletes can use extremes in their sport training, consider a young tennis player who isn't able to establish a consistent point of contact with her forehand because, her coach has identified, her grip isn't right. Using extremes, the player can start at one end of the range for her grip and incrementally work her way to the other end. In this process, she is able to see clearly which place along her grip continuum enables her to hit her forehand more consistently. Certainly, as soon as she changes her grip, it is going to feel very uncomfortable and will likely result in an initial increase in errors. But, in time, she will identify her ideal grip and learn how to use it consistently with practice.

Bad vs. Good Mistakes

As discussed earlier in this section, mistakes and failure are key reasons why athletes don't want to experiment in their sport training. At the same time, as described in Chapter 2, athletes can't develop in their sport without them. As such, they need to reframe what mistakes and failure mean to them. An important distinction that helps athletes change their attitude toward mistakes is between bad mistakes and good mistakes. Bad mistakes are ones that occur because athletes are uncommitted, unfocused, and tentative in their efforts and execution. Consultants can convey to athletes that bad mistakes should not be a part of their sport training (Allen et al., 2011).

In contrast, good mistakes happen because athletes are experimenting and pushing themselves out of their comfort zones. If athletes are fully committed to and aggressively execute in their training, they should see the mistakes as indicators of progress. With this new attitude toward mistakes, athletes will respond positively both mentally and emotionally, the result of which will be better quality training and consistent improvement.

Experimentation is a Lifestyle Choice

Consultants can help athletes to become comfortable with experimentation. In doing so, they will fully embrace experimentation, seek it out, and make it something they simply do as a part of the sport training. In this light, athletes apply experimentation to all aspects of their training and life as a means of becoming the best athlete they can be.

A practical means by which athletes can achieve this goal is to commit to including experimentation in their daily training and lives. In discussions with consultants and coaches, athletes can examine their weekly schedule and pinpoint places in their training and lives in which they can experiment. For example, one day, athletes could try a new set of mobility exercises in their conditioning or experiment with a new nutritional plan. They can also challenge themselves to experiment in their daily lives by, for instance, answering a question in class or making a new friend.

Summary

- Due to individual differences among athletes, applying a "one size fits all" approach is rarely effective in athletes fully realizing their abilities and it is often creative and sometimes truly "out of the box" methods of training that have enabled some athletes to achieve remarkable heights.
- Experimentation in sports training is defined as a series of well-planned steps aimed at contributing to athletic development and enhancing sport performance.
- For athletes to gain comfort and confidence with experimentation in their sports lives, they must first understand the barriers that lead to their aversion to experimentation: innate fear and the uncertainty of trying new things.
- Psychological flexibility involves (1) adjusting to changing situational demands, (2) recalibrating psychological resources, (3) altering perspective, and (4) balancing conflicting wishes, needs, and goals.
- Adler spoke extensively about encouragement, which "inspires or helps others toward a conviction that they can work on finding solutions and that they can cope with any predicament."
- Counseling researchers advocate for the use of creativity as a therapeutic tool and experimentation can readily be seen as a proxy for creativity in the sports setting.
- The stronger the consulting relationship, the more athletes will be willing to accept experimentation in their training.
- In preparing athletes to try new things in their sports training, consultants can embolden athletes to adopt an "experimentation mindset" by following steps similar to those of the scientific model.
- Consultants can help athletes to welcome experimentation by changing the way they think about being out of their comfort zone and to shift their thinking about experimentation from "It feels bad" to "It's good to feel bad."
- One way in which athletes can experiment is to "go to extremes" which involves identifying a continuum in their physical, technical, or mental training and try performing at different places along that continuum.
- Athletes are better able to accept mistakes in their sports performances when they distinguish between bad mistakes (caused by a lack of commitment and focus) and good mistakes (caused by experimenting and pushing out of their comfort zone).
- Consultants can help athletes to become comfortable with experimentation by having them fully embrace experimentation, seek it out, and make it something they simply do as a part of the sport training.

References

Adler, A. (1956). *The individual psychology of Alfred Adler: A systematic presentation in selections from his writings* (H. L. Ansbacher & R. R. Ansbacher, Eds.). New York, NY: Harper Torchbooks.

Allen, M. S., Jones, M. V., & Sheffield, D. (2011). Are the causes assigned to unsatisfactory performance related to the intensity of emotions experienced after competition? *Sport & Exercise Psychology Review*, 7(1), 3–10.

Blackledge, J. I. & Hayes, S. C. (2001). Emotion regulation in Acceptance and commitment therapy. *Psychotherapy in Practice*, 57, (2), 243–255.

Bortoli, L., Bertollo, M., Hanin, Y. L., & Robazza, C. (2012). Striving for excellence: A multi-action plan intervention model for shooters. *Psychology of Sport and Exercise*, 13, 693–701. doi: 10.1016/j.psychsport.2012.04.006.

Brewer, B. W., Van Raalte, J. L., & Linder, D. E. (1993). Athletic identity: Hercules' muscles or Achilles heel? *International Journal of Sport Psychology*, 24(2), 237–254.

Carlson, N. R. (2013). *Physiology of behavior*, 11th ed. Boston, MA: Pearson.

Duffy, T., Haberstroh, S., & Trepal, H. (2016) Creative approaches in counseling and psychotherapy. In D. Capuzzi and M.D. Stauffer (Eds.) *Counseling and psychotherapy: Theories and interventions* (pp. 445–468). Hoboken, NJ: John Wiley & Sons.

Hanin Y. L. (2008). Emotions in sport: Current issues and perspectives. In G. Tenenbaum & R. Eklund (Eds), *Handbook of sport psychology*, 3rd ed. (pp. 31–58). Hoboken, NJ: Wiley.

Hayes, S. C., Luoma, J. B., Bond, F. W., Masuda, A., & Lillis, J. (2006). Acceptance and commitment therapy: Model, processes and outcomes. *Behaviour Research and Therapy*, 44(1), 1–25. doi: 10.1016/j.brat.2005.06.006

Kaplan, D., M., Tarvydas, V. M., & Gladding, S. T. (2014) 20/20: A vision for the future of counseling: The new consensus definition of counseling. *Journal of Counseling & Development*, 92, 366–372. doi: 10.1002/j.1556-6676.2014.00164.x

Kashdan, T. (2010). Psychological flexibility as a fundamental aspect of health. *Clinical Psychology Review*, 30(7) 865–878. doi 10.1016/j.cpr.2010.03.001

Knowles, M. S., Holton III, E. F., & Swanson, R. (2015). *The adult learner*, 8th ed. New York, NY: Routledge.

Rogers, C. (1951). *Client-centered therapy*. Boston, MA: Houghton Mifflin.

Sharp, L. & Hodge, K. (2014). Sport psychology consulting effectiveness: The athlete's perspective. *International Journal of Sport & Exercise Psychology, 12*(2), 91–105.

Sweeney, T., & Sweeney, T. (2009). *Adlerian counseling and psychotherapy a practitioner's approach* (5th ed.). New York: Routledge.

Vygotsky, L. S. (1978). *Mind in society: The development of higher psychological processes*. Cambridge, MA: Harvard University Press.

TRAIN LIKE YOU COMPETE

Lauren Tashman and Jim Taylor

A question that athletes often ask is: "Should I compete like I train or train like I compete?" An informal survey of thousands of athletes indicates that the majority believe that they should compete like they train. This response makes sense because when athletes train, they are often more confident, calm, focused, and feel less pressure, all conditions that are conducive to optimal performance that they want to replicate when they compete. However, transferring what happens in training to competition isn't always easy because there is a fundamental difference that separates competition from training: Competition matters! Unlike in training, competition often involves expectations (from themselves or others), feelings of pressure, more of a focus on comparison to others, and concerns about results. So, in the real world of competitive sports, few athletes can compete like they train. . .unless they first train like they compete.

This conclusion is based on two essential premises. First, whatever athletes must do in competitions, whether physical, technical, tactical, mental, or what-have-you, they must do it successfully in training first. Training is where the foundation of all sports skills and habits are learned. Moreover, if they are not deeply ingrained in training, athletes will not be able to use them effectively in competitions.

Second, reversing the above premise, whatever athletes learn and ingrain in training is what will come out in competition. The goal of training is for athletes to instill effective skills and habits that will help them to perform their best when they compete. However, the reality of training for many athletes is that they don't engage in quality training and, as a result, practice and ingrain poor skills and habits. As a consequence, those bad skills and habits come out in competition.

Chapter 5 is devoted to ensuring that this scenario doesn't happen; rather, that athletes engage in quality training to develop effective skills and habits that they can use to their advantage when they compete. Consultants can first help athletes to identify what they need to do prior to, during, and after competitions to perform their best. Then, they can assist athletes with optimizing their training so that when they enter the field of play, their bodies and minds will automatically express the positive skills and habits that they ingrained during quality training.

Theory and Research

People often wonder why some athletes perform as well as or better in competition than in training. One of the most plausible explanations is that how they train plays a large role in how they perform in competition, particularly when the competitive stakes are high. This notion of how to maximize the transferability of performance from training to competition isn't just centered around athletes learning the requisite physical, technical, tactical, and mental skills and habits. Rather, another level of quality training involves athletes learning to execute those skills and habits in training in ways that will facilitate their transfer to the high-pressure environment of competition. Research that has explored ways to optimize training suggests that training programs should better represent the specific demands encountered in competition and thus should be designed to enhance motor and perceptual skill acquisition as well as decision making and situational awareness in the context of those demands (Dicks, Davids, Araújo, 2008; Eccles, Ward, & Woodman, 2009; Travassos, Duarte, Vilar, Davids, & Araújo, 2012).

Simulation Training

Simulation training has been advocated for as a means of effectively preparing for competition (Orlick & Partington, 1988). These approaches generally consist of practice competitions and replicating environmental elements as well as the use of performance routines in training that approximate competitive experiences. This allows athletes to gain comfort with and become desensitized to internal and external conditions experienced in competitions. For example, athletes wear their game-day uniforms in training and teams emulate competitive conditions such as recorded crowd noise. Video and imagery rehearsal have also been used as a passive form of competitive simulation. While these approaches can be useful for developing advanced perceptual-motor skills and decision making, environmental comfort, and optimal attention, they are not the only things that will be needed to achieve success on game day. Real-world performance necessitates that other important skills, such as confidence, adaptability, resilience, and emotion regulation also must be optimized in training for athletes to deliver their best in competition (e.g., Jones, Hanton, & Connaughton, 2007; MacNamara, Button, & Collins, 2010; Sarkar & Fletcher, 2014).

Encoding Specificity and Memory

The rationale for aligning training with performance stems from the principle of encoding specificity which states that memories will be more effectively retrieved if the conditions at the time of retrieval are similar to those at the time of encoding and storage (Tulving & Thomson, 1973). Further, memory is assumed to be both context-dependent (e.g., environmental conditions) and state-dependent (e.g., mental and emotional conditions). Thus, research would suggest having athletes practice (real or imagined) in the competition venue would be more effective than practicing in a completely different environment (context-dependent) and that both mental and physical performance could be affected by the emotions, moods, and mental states experienced during training and competition (state-dependent).

Cognition

Humans are built for efficiency with regards to many important processes including perception, cognition, memory, motivation, and behavior. Further, though the world has changed dramatically since the dawn of humankind, people are still driven to self-protect and survive; thus, they are built to adapt and be highly reactive to the situations in which they find themselves (Buss, 2016) and have an innate drive to compete (Bronson & Merryman, 2013). Consultants aiming to help athletes optimize their training efforts to be more aligned with performance should keep in mind several key features of and propositions about human perception.

First, cognitions play a mediating role between athletes' environments and how they respond to them, which in turn feed back into how they perceive and respond to future environments and situations (Wright, 2006). People are meaning-making beings that use appraisals of situations to derive perceptions and emotions about what is and expectations about what may come next (Kelly, 1963; Lazarus, 1982). Second, the perceptions we derive reflect inherent cognitive biases that have implications for not only how we appraise situations, but also the decisions we make. For example, people can be biased towards comfort (e.g., Samuelson & Zeckhauser, 1988) and at times more motivated by what they have to lose rather than what there is to gain (e.g., Kahneman, 2011). Yet, they also seem to increase their sense of comfort through repeated experience (mere exposure effect; Zajonc, 2001) and develop and improve as a result of perceived challenge (Crum & Luddy, 2014; McGonigal, 2015).

Relatedly, our beliefs play a large role in people's in-the-moment perceptions as well as how they react and respond to situations (Crum & Phillips, 2015). When people are in situations that are perceived to be potential threats, whether stressors that are real or imagined, they engage in a cognitive appraisal process in which they evaluate the demand being placed upon them against their capabilities for handling that demand (Lazarus & Folkman, 1984). Their beliefs about their capability (i.e., self-efficacy) can affect both appraisals and behavior (Bandura, 1989). The determination that comes out of that appraisal process often determines whether athletes respond positively or negatively to training or competitive situations. While this process is meant to be facilitative, it can lead to athletes getting caught up in their thinking and appraising which may derail them from attending to what matters most in the moment (Hayes, 2005).

Thus, perceptions will play a large role in how athletes respond to the demands of competition and will, in part, be shaped by how athletes experience training. Well-designed training situations enable athletes to develop facilitative perceptions about their performances that they can then translate to their competitive efforts.

The goal for athletes then, with assistance from consultants and coaches, is to optimize training by: (1) creating realistic environments and tasks in training that are in line with how athletes think and behave in competition; (2) including appropriate stressors in a controlled environment in training that inculcates athletes to the demands of competition; and (3) preparing athletes in authentic ways that will allow them to practice the responses (mental, physical, technical, tactical) that are necessary for optimal performance and competitive success.

Practical Implications

To embark on the process of designing training regimens that will effectively prepare athletes for competition, the first thing consultants need to do is analyze the nature of the sport in general and specific to competition. This is an extension of Brown, Gould, and Foster's (2005) discussion about the importance of developing contextual intelligence in sports. Some of the dimensions associated with contextual aspects of sport include:

- cognitive vs. motor skills, or a combination of both;
- fine vs. gross motor skills;
- conscious vs. intuitive decision making;
- active vs. reactive performance;
- routine vs. adaptive expertise (see Hatano & Inagaki, 1986);
- focus and intensity demands;
- frequency and duration of performances;
- performance level; and
- if a team sport, coactive vs. interactive.

All of these factors must be considered as athletes, coaches, and consultants attempt to create functional equivalencies between training and competitive performances. Once consultants have analyzed the demands of the sport and competitions, they can work with athletes and coaches to design strategies that appropriately simulate the environmental and contextual influences and, as accurately as possible, re-create the competitive experience in training.

Preparing for Everything

Mental contrasting involves athletes imagining a future successful outcome and the obstacles that might stand in their way (Oettingen, Mayer, Sevincer, Stephens, Pak, & Hagenah, 2009). Exploring and rehearsing the best- and worst-case scenarios allows athletes to use imagery and video to see and feel themselves performing optimally in various competitive situations they may encounter. Once obstacles have been identified, consultants can assist athletes with contingency planning in which they develop "if–then" plans for approaching and overcoming events or obstacles that can cause physical, mental, technical, tactical, equipment, or team deviations from ideal scenarios which would interfere with optimal performance. Athletes can then simulate these sub-optimal situations and implement their contingency plans in training. This approach helps athletes get comfortable with the adversity that often arises, provides a clear path for overcoming the obstacles, and builds confidence that they have the capabilities to use these plans effectively should an unexpected occurrence arise at a competition.

As athletes put these "train like you compete" practices into play, consultants can help them improve on and fine tune their plans by guiding them through debriefs and reflections that allow them to process what they experienced, gain its benefits, and encourage them to continue to use the strategies in future training opportunities. For example, Gibbs's (1988) offers the following framework for intentional reflection that can be applied to both training and competitive experiences:

- Have the athlete describe what happened.
- Analyze the thoughts and feelings they had at the time and are having now looking back.
- Evaluate how things went (good and bad), what they did or didn't do, and their reactions.
- Analyze what sense can be made of the situation and what might have helped or hindered what happened.

- Derive lessons learned by considering what else could have been done and what can be changed or done differently for the future.
- Create an action plan so that if this situation or something similar is experienced in the future athletes have a strategy for how to approach it.

Additionally, interpersonal process recall (IPR) can be utilized when video of training or competition is available. IPR is a guided process of self-discovery (Kagan, 1965) that can be used by consultants to help athletes reflect on and make sense of their in-the-moment experiences (e.g., Jambor & Weekes, 1995). Consultants can use the following steps to guide athletes through an IPR:

1. Video record a training session or competition.
2. Briefly describe to athletes the goal and process of doing an IPR.
3. Review all or part(s) of the video by pausing it at various points initiating reflection and exploration using recall leads phrased in the past tense. Recall leads can be aimed at a particular facet of the experience (e.g., emotions, intention, behavior, mutual perceptions) or can be more open-ended to guard against biasing the reflections.
4. Athletes can also pause the video at any point in order to mention something they remember or want to explore.
5. Throughout the process, consultants help guide athletes to explore what was going on at the time, not just what they are thinking/feeling now, and make sure to refrain from providing comments, feedback, opinions, or suggestions, but rather use other recall leads to follow up if needed on what athletes mention.
6. After reviewing the video, consultants can facilitate a collaborative discussion about what came up during the process (can be done directly after or during the next session), helping athletes to apply what was learned back into training and competition.

Mental Fatigue

Research indicates that mental workload and fatigue have implications for environmental awareness and thinking (e.g., Baror & Bar, 2016) and continued motivation (Boksem & Tops, 2008), and can also be a formidable obstacle for physical performance (e.g., McCunn, Thompson, Beavan, & Gibson, 2018; Marcora, Staiano, & Manning, 2009). This research has prompted the advocating for "brain endurance training," in which athletes are cognitively stressed while training as a means of strengthening their resistance to mental fatigue, increasing their mental workload, and decreasing their perceptions of effort (e.g., Marcora, Staiano, & Merlini, 2015). Recommendations for incorporating cognitively taxing drills into training include those focused on:

- Memory (e.g., giving athletes a list of random words to remember prior to a drill and then afterwards asking them to recall as many words as possible verbally or in writing).
- Speed (e.g., at various points during training, asking athletes to identify as many words with a particular starting letter, such as C, as they can in a short period of time).
- Problem solving (e.g., designing a training drill that has a particular process for completion and requiring athletes to figure it out on their own).
- Attention (e.g., having athletes listen to an audiobook segment or podcast during a drill and then asking them to recall as much as they can or asking them targeted questions about what was covered).
- Flexibility (e.g., having athletes switch back and forth from focusing on different aspects of a training drill).

Thus, for example, if a sport is cognitively taxing in terms of requiring attention over a long period of time (e.g., golf, football), persistent motivation and energy over the course of a season (e.g., baseball), or the use of cognitive-perceptual skills (e.g., soccer), or is physically taxing (e.g., wrestling, triathlon), then incorporating brain endurance training may enhance alignment of training with competitive performance by guarding against the negative effects of mental fatigue.

Simulated Pressure

Research has demonstrated the potential negative effects of pressure on performance (e.g., Navarro et al., 2012) and recently an argument has been made for switching the focus away from flow states to better understanding the psychological states underlying clutch performances (e.g., Swann et al., 2017). Given that the greatest difference, in general, between practice and competition is the perceived stress or pressure involved, athletes training like they compete requires finding ways to incorporate those elements into training. Consultants can help athletes and coaches to identify the sources and types of pressure experienced in their sport and during competitions which can then be included in training (e.g., self-induced expectations, pressures from parents or media, situations that require clutch performances).

Consultants and coaches can create adverse conditions that test athletes and require them to perform optimally despite stress and pressure. For example, softball and baseball coaches can induce pressure in hitting practice by, for example, limiting the number of pitches given to each batter, putting a time limit on a hitting drill, incorporating a random variation of pitches, or exposing them to faster pitching speeds. For pitchers, they can have them try to throw ten strikes in a row or throw a sequence of pitches seeing how many they can throw accurately in five minutes. Golfers can place balls with difficult lies, obstacles, or targets, such as in a bunker or out of bounds, requiring them to practice difficult shots that they may face in a tournament. Athletes can also be encouraged to target weaknesses, for example, requiring basketball players to dribble and pass only with their nondominant hand or having two players defend against them while shooting from the perimeter. As the athletes improve their weaknesses, the drills can be made more difficult to continue to practice with increasing amounts of pressure. Lastly, other ways to simulate pressure include incorporating competitions, challenges, and rewards into training to create the feeling that there is something on the line akin to a competition.

The goal is to dial up the difficulty, stress, or pressure that athletes experience in practice, so that the pressure they feel in competitions is not significantly different from the conditions they have in training. By intensifying the pressure athlete experience in training, athletes not only train under more competition-like conditions, but also are provided with regular opportunities to strengthen their mental muscles (see Chapter 3) and practice their mental exercises and tools (see Chapter 4).

Summary

- When athletes are asked: "Should I compete like I train or train like I compete?", most say they should compete like they train.
- Competing like athletes train is difficult because there is a fundamental difference that separates competition from training: Competition matter!
- Few athletes can compete like they train . . . unless they first train like they compete.
- Stress and pressure are often experienced more in competition than in training, providing athletes with limited opportunity to practice being able to perform under these conditions.
- The rationale for aligning training with performance stems from the principle of encoding specificity which states that memories will be more effectively retrieved if the conditions at the time of retrieval are similar to those at the time of encoding and storage.
- Consultants can help athletes to identify what they need to do in competitions to perform their best and then encourage them to do those things consistently in training.
- Another level of quality training involves athletes learning to execute those skills and habits in the high-pressure environment of competition.
- Research suggests that training programs should better represent the specific demands encountered in competition and thus should be designed to enhance motor and perceptual skill acquisition as well as decision making and situational awareness in the context of those demands.
- Simulation training consists of practice competitions and replicating environmental elements as well as the use of performance routines in training that approximate competitive experiences, allowing athletes to gain comfort with and become desensitized to internal and external conditions found in competitions.
- The rationale for aligning training with performance stems from the principle of encoding specificity which states that memories will be more effectively retrieved if the conditions at the time of retrieval are similar to those at the time of encoding and storage.

- Cognitions play a mediating role between athletes' environments and how they respond to them, which in turn feed back into how they will perceive and respond to future environments.
- To embark on the process of designing training regiments that will effectively prepare athletes for competition, the first thing consultants need to do is analyze the nature of the sport in general and specific to competition.
- Consultants can help athletes use mental contrasting (i.e., imagining a future successful outcome and the obstacles that might stand in their way) and contingency planning (i.e., developing "if–then" plans for the various scenarios that are identified in the mental contrasting exercise) to optimize training and prepare for competition.
- Consultants can guide athletes through debriefs and reflections that allow them to intentionally reflect on what they experienced and make action plans for future trainings and competition.
- Mental fatigue can have negative consequences on various aspects of mental (e.g., memory, thinking, focus) and physical performance (e.g., endurance, cognitive-perceptual skills).
- Consultants can help athletes and coaches effectively simulate stress and pressure conditions in training to be better prepared for performing under those conditions in competition.
- Mental training strategies can be used so that athletes practice applying these strategies and can use them in competition when it matters most.

References

Bandura, A. (1989). Human agency in social cognitive theory. *American Psychologist, 44*(9), 1175–1184.

Baror, S., & Bar, M. (2016). Associative activation and its relation to exploration and exploitation in the brain. *Psychological Science, 27*(6), 776–789.

Boksem, M. A., & Tops, M. (2008). Mental fatigue: costs and benefits. *Brain Research Reviews, 59*(1), 125–139.

Bronson, P., & Merryman, A. (2013). *Top dog: The science of winning and losing.* New York, NY: Hachette.

Brown, C. H., Gould, D., & Foster, S. (2005). A framework for developing contextual intelligence (CI). *The Sport Psychologist, 19*(1), 51–62.

Buss, D. A. (2016). *Evolutionary psychology: The new science of the mind,* 5th ed. New York, NY: Routledge.

Crum, A. J., & Luddy, C. (2014). De-stressing stress: The power of mindsets and the art of stressing mindfully. In A. Ie, C. T. Ngnoumen, & E. J. Langer (Eds.), *The Wiley Blackwell handbook of mindfulness.* Hoboken, NJ: Wiley-Blackwell.

Crum, A. J., & Phillips, D. (2015). Self-fulfilling prophecies, placebo effects, and the social-psychological creation of reality. In R. Scott & S. Kosslyn (Eds.), *Emerging trends in the social and behavioral sciences.* Hoboken, NJ: John Wiley and Sons.

Dicks, M., Davids, K., & Araújo, D. (2008). Ecological psychology and task representativeness: Implications for the design of perceptual-motor training programmes in sport. In Y. Hong & R. Bartlett (Eds.), *The Routledge handbook of biomechanics and human movement science* (pp. 129–139). London: Routledge.

Eccles, D. W., Ward, P., & Woodman, T. (2009). Competition-specific preparation and expert performance. *Psychology of Sport and Exercise, 10*(1), 96–107.

Gibbs, G. (1988). *Learning by doing: A guide to teaching and learning methods.* Oxford: Oxford Further Education Unit.

Hatano, G, & Inagaki, K. (1986). Two courses of expertise. In H. A. H. Stevenson & K. Hakuta (Eds.), *Child development and education in Japan* (pp. 262–272).

Hayes, S. C. (2005). *Get out of your mind & into your life: The new acceptance and commitment therapy.* Oakland, CA: New Harbinger Publications.

Jambor, E., & Weekes, E. M. (1995). Videotape feedback: Make it more effective. *Journal of Physical Education, Recreation, & Dance, 66*(2), 48–50.

Jones, G., Hanton, S., & Connaughton, D. (2007). A framework of mental toughness in the world's best performers. *The Sport Psychologist, 21,* 243–264.

Kagan, N. I. (1965). *IPR-interpersonal process recall: Simulated recall by videotape. Exploring studies of counseling and teaching.* East Lansing, MI: Bureau of Educational Research.

Kahneman, D. (2011). *Thinking, fast and slow.* New York, NY: Farnar, Straus and Giroux.

Kelly, G. A. (1963). *A theory of personality: The psychology of personal constructs.* New York, NY: W. W. Norton & Company.

Lazarus, R. S. (1982). Thoughts on the relations between emotions and cognitions. *American Psychologist, 37*(9), 1019–1024.

Lazarus, R. S., & Folkman, S. (1984). *Stress, Appraisal, and Coping.* New York, NY: Springer.

MacNamara, A., Button, A., & Collins, D. (2010). The role of psychological characteristics in facilitating the pathway to elite performance, part 1: Identifying mental skills and behaviors. *The Sport Psychologist, 24*(1), 52–73.

Marcora, S. M., Staiano, W., & Manning, V. (2009). Mental fatigue impairs physical performance in humans. *Journal of Applied Physiology, 106,* 857–864.

Marcora, S. M., Staiano, W., & Merlini, M. (2015). A randomized controlled trial of brain endurance training (bet) to reduce fatigue during endurance exercise. Poster presentation at the 62nd Annual Meeting of the American College of Sports Medicine, San Diego, CA.

McCunn, R., Thompson, C., Beavan, A., & Gibson, N. (2018). Head in the game: Mental fatigue and its potential influence on the perceptual-cognitive element in sport. *The Sport and Exercise Scientist, 57*, 20–21.

McGonigal, K. (2015). *The upside of stress: Why stress is good for you and how to get good at it.* New York, NY: Avery.

Navarro, M., Miyamoto, N., van der Kamp, J., Morya, E., Ranvaud, R., & Savelsbergh, G. J. P. (2012). The effects of high pressure on the point of no return in simulated penalty kicks. *Journal of Sport & Exercise Psychology, 34*(1), 83–101.

Oettingen, G., Mayer, D., Sevincer, A. T., Stephens, E. J., Pak, H-ju, & Hagenah, M. (2009). Mental contrasting and goal commitment: The mediating role of energization. *Personality and Social Psychology Bulletin, 35*(5), 608–622.

Orlick, T., & Partington, J. (1988). Mental links to excellence. *The Sport Psychologist, 2*, 105–130.

Samuelson, W., & Zeckhauser, R. (1988). Status quo bias in decision making. *Journal of Risk and Uncertainty, 1*, 7–59.

Sarkar, M., & Fletcher, D. (2014). Psychological resilience in sport performers: A review of stressors and protective factors. *Journal of Sports Sciences, 32*(15), 1419–1434.

Swann, C., Crust, L., Jackman, P., Vella, S. A., Allen, M. S., & Keegan, R. (2017). Performing under pressure: Exploring the psychological state underlying clutch performance in sport. *Journal of Sports Sciences, 35*(23), 2272–2280.

Travassos, B., Duarte, R., Vilar, L., Davids, K., & Araújo, D. (2012). Practice task design in team sports: Representativeness enhanced by increasing opportunities for action. *Journal of Sport Sciences, 30*(13), 1447–1454.

Tulving, E., & Thomson, D. M. (1973). Encoding specificity and retrieval processes in episodic memory. *Psychological Review, 80*, 352–373.

Wright, J. (2006). Cognitive behavior therapy: Basic principles and recent advances. *Focus, 4*, 173–178.

Zajonc, R. B. (2001). Mere exposure: A gateway to the subliminal. *Current Directions in Psychological Science, 10*(6), 224–228.

PSYCHOLOGICAL RECOVERY FROM TRAINING

Stacy Gnacinski

In the pursuit of excellence in sport, substantial attention is dedicated to the physical, technical, and mental areas of training required for optical conditioning, enhanced skill development and maximum performance. As such, strength and conditioning, sport, and mental coaches, design and deliver periodized and individualized training regimens aimed at systematically increasing performance and athletic capabilities across time. Given the recent and rapid advancements made in both research and practice in the areas of training load prescription and overtraining prevention, it is not surprising that increased attention has been dedicated to the physical and psychological aspects of recovery from sport training (Kellmann et al., 2018). Despite this shift in attention toward recovery, there has been a substantial gap in the literature regarding interventions aimed at enhancing the psychological aspects of recovery for competitive athletes.

Theory and Research

Driven by the competitive pressures of elite sport, performance experts in the many domains of sport are continually challenged to identify the most effective and efficient methods of athlete development and performance enhancement. Across training modalities, researchers have generally supported the notion of a supercompensation principle in which deliberate overloads in training followed by sufficient periods of recovery yield positive training adaptations and enhanced performance (Bosquet, Montpetit, Arvisais, & Mujika, 2007; Fleck, 1999; Gabbett, 2016; Issurin, 2008, 2016). Although the consistent and successful execution of this training principle in practice is challenging due to any number of logistical barriers including length of training blocks, competitive schedules, and the unique needs and goals of individual athletes, the theories underpinning periodization and training load management (e.g., general adaptation syndrome, stimulus-fatigue-recovery-adaptation theory, fitness-fatigue paradigm) suggest beneficial training adaptations and performance gains are all contingent on the effectiveness of recovery periods (Haff & Haff, 2012; Kenttä & Hassmén, 1998; Meeusen et al., 2013). As such, the importance of recovery now appears unanimously embraced by professionals across disciplines (Kellmann et al., 2018). This perspective not only serves as a welcome development from the traditional "no pain, no gain" view of training, but also provides impetus for the development of evidence-based recovery interventions available to athletes and teams such as nutritional supplementation, foam rolling, use of compression garments, and use of cold-water immersion.

Even with the rapid advancement in the literature about recovery intervention efficacy, the majority of scholarly discourse has revolved around physical interventions, with far less attention dedicated to the psychological aspects of recovery. Moreover, recovery as a psychological construct has gained far more traction in the sports medicine literature than in the applied sport psychology literature. In fact, the majority of references made to recovery in applied sport psychology still refers to post-injury recovery (i.e., rehabilitation), as opposed to post-training or post-competition recovery. Given the growing popularity of recovery as a scholarly topic in addition to the persistent adverse consequences of overtraining (Kenttä & Hassmén, 1998; Meeusen et al., 2013), the purposes of this section are to operationalize recovery as a construct, discuss select psychological aspects of the recovery process, and outline individualized and integrated intervention approaches to facilitating athletes' mental recovery from the demands of training, competition, and other areas of their lives.

Per the extensive line of research led by Kellmann on sport overtraining prevention, recovery refers to a passive or active process of restoring psychophysiological balance following a stressful experience (Kallus & Kellmann, 2016). It is theorized that optimum training outcomes are achieved through managing athletes' stress (i.e., training load and strain) and recovery (i.e., restoration of depleted resources) concurrently (Kellmann, 2010). This means that in practice, and in conjunction with the physiological processes of recovery, consultants must be mindful of monitoring the cumulative psychological load and strain imposed on athletes while also providing opportunities for them to psychologically rest, heal, and mentally regenerate within and between training sessions. Since monitoring and assessment techniques fall outside the scope of this chapter, modern discussions around methods for monitoring the psychological load can be found in Saw et al. (2017), Nässi et al. (2017), and Kellmann et al. (2018).

Extending beyond what is known in the sport literature, Sonnentag and colleagues' (2017) work in the occupational domain highlights the importance of distinguishing recovery as a process from recovery as an outcome. More specifically, the process of recovery can be described as the activities and experiences that elicit change in work strain indicators (i.e., what athletes are thinking, feeling, and doing during recovery periods), whereas the outcome of recovery can be described as a psychophysiological state during a period of rest or work break (i.e., if athletes are recovered or not following prescribed periods of time for recovery). Since recovery outcomes are often uncontrollable in sport environments, specific psychological aspects of athletes' recovery process are discussed in detail below.

Practical Implications

Much like the physical recovery from training and competition, psychological recovery should involve an intentional and structured process. Consultant interventions should account for various key areas of psychological recovery that athletes experience, while providing practical means for facilitating this recovery in light of upcoming training and competitive schedules. By accounting for psychological aspects of recovery within designed interventions, athletes' may experience better recovery outcomes during designated breaks from sport.

Relaxation

Consistent with the literature on arousal control in sport (Gould & Udry, 1994; see also Chapter 3, this volume), Thomas et al. (1999) suggested that relaxation represents a process of reducing somatic anxiety. Similarly, Sonnentag et al. (2017) described relaxation as a process of reducing sympathetic activation. At present, it seems the majority of applied sport psychology literature utilizes the term relaxation in terms of "strategies" or "techniques," with an implicit understanding that the purpose of relaxation is to decrease physiological activation (Pelka, Heidari, Ferrauti, Meyer, Pfeiffer, & Kellmann, 2016). Given that various relaxation strategies have long been established in the applied sport psychology literature as foundational, evidence-based interventions for performance enhancement, the strategies offered below reflect specific applications of relaxation techniques in the context of micro- and macro-level recovery opportunities.

Micro-level recovery involves athletes' rejuvenation amidst actual training and competitive situations, for example, during practice breaks, timeouts, and between periods or halves. To facilitate micro-level recovery, athletes may benefit from the implementation of a brief relaxation strategy to conserve energy (Harmison, 2011).

By contrast, macro-level recovery refers to regeneration after training or competitions during non-sport time. To support macro-level recovery during non-sport time, relaxation techniques can be implemented to specifically initiate parasympathetic activity and decrease sympathetic activity (Hunt, Rushton, Shenberger, & Murayama, 2018; Pelka et al., 2016). Common relaxation strategies for performance enhancement include somatic-oriented strategies such as biofeedback, progressive muscle relaxation, as well as cognitive-oriented strategies such as imagery, autogenic training, hypnosis, and meditation (Pelka et al., 2016; Pelka, Kölling, Ferrauti, Meyer, Pfeiffer, & Kellmann, 2017). In recovery-focused relaxation audio scripts designed by consultants, specific language that addresses the physiological aspects of relaxation such as "feel the increased blood flow," "feel the warmth in your muscles," "notice the slowing of your heart rate," or "focus on taking nice slow full breaths," match the goals of parasympathetic nervous system activation and associated restful healing responses in the body. Similarly, particular language can also be included that focus on the psychological aspects of relaxation including "Your mind is clear and calm," "You feel a sense of comfort and ease," and "Embrace positive and relaxing thoughts and emotions." In addition, well-established mind–body strategies such as yoga, sports massage, and sleep hygiene routines may be useful for facilitating mental relaxation during macro-recovery periods (Briegel-Jones, Knowles, Eubank, Giannoulatos, & Elliot, 2013; Nédélec, Halson, Delecroix, Abaidia, Ahmaidi, & Dupont, 2015; Nédélec, McCall, Carling, Legall, Berthoin, & Dupont, 2013). For more relaxation techniques, see Chapters 3 and 4.

Psychological Detachment

Drawing upon the occupational recovery literature, Balk, de Jonge, Oerlemans, & Geurts (2017a) characterized psychological detachment as a physical, cognitive, and emotional break from the resource-costly demands of sport. Likewise, Sonnentag et al. (2017) described psychological detachment as the process of "switching off" from work, or a means of forgetting about and moving on during non-work times. Across studies, psychological detachment is thought to facilitate the recovery process through improvements in well-being, sleep quality, and affective states (Sonnentag et al., 2017).

Although portions of the sport literature to date have involved descriptions of psychological detachment or disengagement from sport as an adverse consequence of the sport experience (Caudroit, Stephan, Brewer, & Le Scanff, 2010), others have characterized psychological detachment as a facilitative element of the recovery experience for athletes. Some of the seminal recovery research conducted by Beckmann and Kellmann (2004) refers to a need for distancing, or the deactivation from a stressful activity, as the first step in the recovery process. They suggest that athletes' inability to cognitively distance themselves from the stresses of sport can prevent them from fully attending to and immersing themselves in recuperative non-sport activities (e.g., social events, food preparation, school, work), disrupt sleep, and hinder the athletes' effective selection and implementation of recovery strategies (Beckmann & Kellmann, 2004). Consistent with these initial thoughts by Beckmann and Kellmann (2004), evidence supporting the influence of psychological detachment on the overall recovery process, sleep, and well-being continues to grow in the sport literature (Balk et al., 2017b).

Findings from the occupational literature suggest that consistent and long-term mindfulness training may facilitate psychological detachment from work (Michel, Bosch, and Rexroth, 2014). Hahn and colleagues (2011) delivered a broad recovery training intervention involving a psychological detachment module focused on intensively engaging in other non-work activities and using transition rituals to separate work from non-work time, and demonstrated significant improvements in participants' psychological detachment from pre- to post-intervention. The concept of a transition ritual from sport to non-sport time parallels recommendations from the post-sport debriefing literature which demonstrates coach or consultant-led debriefing interventions may facilitate psychological recovery following training and competitions (Hogg, 2002; McArdle, Martin, Lennon, & Moore, 2010). In addition, the notion of encouraging athletes to engage in non-sport activities is consistent with the premise of developing a well-rounded identity and merging perspectives on facilitating athletes' simultaneous pursuit of both personal and performance excellence (Miller & Kerr, 2002). And while the majority of recommendations reflect macro-level recovery strategies, micro-level strategies around psychological detachment might include the use of a short "mental reset" routine between drills or plays.

Professional practice knowledge would suggest that psychological detachment from sport may be difficult for athletes who possess a singular focus on achievement outcomes. Thus, it is important for consultants to collaborate with athletes to identify detachment strategies that are personally meaningful to athletes such as spending time with friends or family, watching television or movies, listening to music, reading, cooking, or pursuing hobbies. Concomitantly, it is important for consultants to emphasize the importance of psychological detachment in relation to the achievement of overall health, well-being, and, ultimately, performance enhancement and sports success. In so doing, athletes' may be more willing to see the value of and embrace psychological detachment strategies as an essential tool for pursuing their long-term sports goals as well as for maintenance of their overall health and well-being.

Regardless of the specific recovery interventions that are used by athletes, there are several general recommendations that consultants can make improve their effectiveness. Scholars have emphasized the importance of matching recovery interventions to the stress demands imposed as well as the individual characteristics of athletes (Kellmann, 2010; Kellmann et al., 2018). As with any type of mental training, recovery intervention efficacy is contingent on consultants having a strong and trusting relationship with athletes (Anderson, Miles, Mahoney, & Robinson, 2002; Fifer, Henschen, Gould, & Ravizza, 2008). Reinforcing athletes' perception of control over recovery strategies selection, the ways in which they complete the recovery intervention, and non-sport time in general can also greatly enhance the recovery experience (Sonnentag et al., 2017).

The nature of training, and, by extension, the nature of recovery, should also be an integrative process. To optimize recovery intervention matching as indicated above, consultants' collaboration with coaches, athletic trainers, and other staff involved in training is helpful for adequate understanding of the objective and perceived training loads imposed on athletes. The use of integrative approaches to intervention design and delivery may also be warranted to optimize program effectiveness. For example, athletes may listen to a relaxation audio script recorded by the consultant while doing their ice bath in the athletic training room. Alternatively, athletes, coaches, and the consultant may implement short, structured debriefing sessions after every training session to facilitate athletes' psychological detachment from their sport. The ongoing and consistent reinforcement of athletes' recovery efforts across systems can optimize their long-term effects of recovery across training and competitive cycles.

Summary

- In response to training and competitive demands placed on athletes, there has been considerable progress in recent decades aimed at helping athletes manage and recover from their training and competitive loads.
- The importance of recovery now appears unanimously embraced by professionals across disciplines and this perspective not only serves as a welcome development from the traditional "no pain, no gain" view of training, but also as fuel for the development of recovery interventions available to athletes and teams.
- Psychological recovery should involve an intentional and structured recovery and address various key areas of psychological recovery that athletes experience and provide practical means for facilitating this recovery in light of competitive goals and training schedules.
- Psychological detachment strategies for facilitating recovery include: debriefing, "mental reset" routines, spending time with friends or family, watching television or movies, listening to music, reading, cooking, or participating in other hobbies.
- Both relaxation and psychological detachment strategies can be modified in light of micro- (i.e., rejuvenation during sport) and macro-level (i.e., regeneration after sport) recovery needs.
- Relaxation strategies for facilitating recovery include: biofeedback, progressive muscle relaxation, imagery, autogenic training, and hypnosis.
- Recovery intervention design by consultants should follow an individualized and integrative process, thereby optimizing the possible impact of recovery on athlete performance and well-being.

References

Anderson, A., Miles, A., Mahoney, C., & Robinson, P. (2002). Evaluating the effectiveness of applied sport psychology practice: Making the case for a case study approach. *The Sport Psychologist, 16*, 432–453.

Balk, Y. A., de Jonge, J., Oerlemans, W. G. M., & Geurts, S. A. E. (2017a). Physical recovery, mental detachment and sleep as predictors of injury and mental energy. *Journal of Health Psychology, 27*, 1–11.

Balk, Y. A., de Jonge, J., Oerlemans, W. G. M., & Geurts, S. A. E. (2017b). Testing the triple-match principle among Dutch elite athletes: A day-level study on sport demands, detachment, and recovery. *Psychology of Sport and Exercise, 33*, 7–17.

Beckmann, J., & Kellmann, M. (2004). Self-regulation and recovery: Approaching an understanding of the process of recovery from stress. *Psychological Reports, 95*, 1135–1153.

Bosquet, L., Montpetit, J., Arvisais, D., & Mujika, I. (2007). Effects of tapering on performance: A meta-analysis. *Medicine & Science in Sports & Exercise, 39*, 1358–1365.

Briegel-Jones, R. M. H., Knowles, Z., Eubank, M. R., Giannoulatos, K., & Elliot, D. (2013). A preliminary investigation into the effect of yoga practice on mindfulness and flow in elite youth swimmers. *The Sport Psychologist, 27*, 349–359.

Fifer, A., Henschen, K., Gould, D., & Ravizza, K. (2008). What works when working with athletes. *The Sport Psychologist, 22*, 356–377.

Fleck, S. J. (1999). Periodized strength training: A critical review. *Journal of Strength and Conditioning Research, 13*, 82–89.

Gabbett, T. J. (2016). The training-injury prevention paradox: Should athletes be training smarter and harder? *British Journal of Sports Medicine, 50*, 273–280. doi: 10.1136/bjsports-2015-095788

Gould, D., & Udry, E. (1994). Psychological skills for enhancing performance: Arousal regulation strategies. *Medicine & Science in Sports & Exercise, 26*, 478–485.

Haff, G. G., & Haff, E. E. (2012). Training integration and periodization. In J. Hoffman (Ed.), *Strength and conditioning program design* (pp. 209–254). Champaign, IL: Human Kinetics.

Hahn, V. C., Binnewies, C., Sonnentag, S., & Mojza, E. J. (2011). Learning how to recover from job stress: Effects of a recovery training program on recovery, recovery-related self-efficacy, and well-being. *Journal of Occupational Health Psychology, 16*, 202–216.

Harmison, R. J. (2011). Peak performance in sport: Identifying ideal performance states and developing athletes' psychological skills. *Sport, Exercise, and Performance Psychology, 1*, 3–18.

Hogg, J. M. (2002). Debriefing: A means to increasing recovery and subsequent performance. In M. Kellmann (Ed.), *Enhancing recovery: Preventing underperformance in athletes* (pp. 181–198). Champaign, IL: Human Kinetics.

Hunt, M. G., Rushton, J., Shenberger, E., & Murayama, S. (2018). Positive effects of diaphragmatic breathing on physiological stress reactivity in varsity athletes. *Journal of Clinical Sport Psychology, 12*, 27–38.

Issurin, V. (2008). Block periodization versus traditional training theory: A review. *Journal of Sports Medicine and Physical Fitness, 48*, 65–75.

Issurin, V. B. (2016). Benefits and limitations of block periodized training approaches to athletes' preparation: A review. *Sports Medicine, 46*, 329–338. doi: 10.1007/s40279-015-0425-5

Kallus, K. W., & Kellmann, M. (2016). *The Recovery-Stress Questionnaires: User manual.* Frankfurt, Germany: Pearson.

Kellmann, M. (2010). Preventing overtraining in athletes in high-intensity sports and stress/recovery monitoring. *Scandinavian Journal of Medicine & Science in Sports, 20*(S2), 95–102. doi: 10.1111/j.1600-0838.2010.01192.x

Kellmann, M., Bertollo, M., Bosquet, L., Brink, M., Coutts, A., Erlacher, D., . . . Beckmann, J. (2018). Recovery and performance in sport: Consensus statement. *International Journal of Sports Physiology and Performance, 13*, 240–245.

Kenttä, G. & Hassmén, P. (1998). Overtraining and recovery. A conceptual model. *Sports Medicine, 26*, 1–16. doi: 10.2165/00007256-199826010-00001

McArdle, S., Martin, D., Lennon, A., & Moore, P. (2010). Exploring debriefing in sports: A qualitative perspective. *Journal of Applied Sport Psychology, 22*, 320–332.

Meeusen, R., Duclos, M., Foster, C., Fry, A., Gleeson, M., Nieman, D., . . .Urhausen, A. (2013). Prevention, diagnosis, and treatment of the overtraining syndrome: Joint consensus statement of the European College of Sport Science and the American College of Sports Medicine. *Medicine & Science in Sports & Exercise, 45*, 186–205. doi: 10.1249/MSS.0b013e318279a10a

Michel, A., Bosch, C., & Rexroth, M. (2014). Mindfulness as a cognitive-emotional segmentation strategy: An intervention promoting work-life balance. *Journal of Occupational and Organizational Psychology, 87*, 733–754.

Miller, P. S., & Kerr, G. A. (2002). Conceptualizing excellence: Past, present, and future. *Journal of Applied Sport Psychology, 14*, 140–153.

Nässi, A., Ferrauti, A., Meyer, T., Pfeiffer, M., & Kellmann, M. (2017). Psychological tools used for monitoring training responses of athletes. *Performance Enhancement & Health, 5*, 125–133.

Nédélec, M., Halson, S., Delecroix, B., Abaidia, A-E., Ahmaidi, S., & Dupont, G. (2015). Sleep hygiene and recovery strategies in elite soccer players. *Sports Medicine, 45*, 1547–1559.

Nédélec, M., McCall, A., Carling, C., Legall, F., Berthoin, S., & Dupont, G. (2013). Recovery in soccer: Part II-recovery strategies. *Sports Medicine, 43*, 9–22.

Pelka, M., Heidari, J., Ferrauti, A., Meyer, T., Pfeiffer, M., & Kellmann, M. (2016). Relaxation techniques in sports: A systematic review on acute effects on performance. *Performance Enhancement & Health, 5*, 47–59.

Pelka, M., Kölling, S., Ferrauti, A., Meyer, T., Pfeiffer, M., & Kellmann, M. (2017). Acute effects of psychological techniques between two physical tasks. *Journal of Sports Sciences, 35,* 216–223.

Saw, A. E., Kellmann, M., Main, L. C., & Gastin, P. B. (2017). Athlete self-report measures in research and practice: Considerations for the discerning reader and fastidious practitioner. *International Journal of Sports Physiology and Performance, 12,* S2127–S2135. doi: 10.1123/ijspp.2016-0395

Sonnentag, S., Venz, L., & Casper, A. (2017). Advances in recovery research: What have we learned? What should be done next? *Journal of Occupational Health Psychology, 22,* 365–380.

Thomas, P. R., Murphy, S. M., & Hardy, L. (1999). Test of performance strategies: Development and preliminary validation of a comprehensive measure of athletes' psychological skills. *Journal Sports Sciences, 17,* 697–711.

6

SPECIAL TOPICS

Introduction

Jim Taylor

The first five chapters of *CASP* have been devoted to introducing and describing the key mental areas that most impact athletic performance. It has also focused on practical and evidence-based means by which consultants can help athletes to maximize those areas. In a way, the content of *CASP* thus far has been laying the foundation for athletes to be mentally prepared to perform their best, at least under normal circumstances. At the same time, as every athlete, coach, and consultant knows, getting to that point is really just the beginning to finding true sports success. Once the basics of conditioning, technique, tactics, and psychology have been established, the next level in the pursuit of athletes' goals is to prepare them for the many challenges that they will inevitably face as they climb the competitive ladder. It is this next level of performance that separates the very best from the very good.

Chapter 6 will explore four of the most frequently experienced challenges that athletes face in their sports lives. In a sense, these additional demands take the normal challenges of being an athlete and turn the volume way up on them. One key differentiator of the world's best athletes is their ability to perform their best on the biggest stage (e.g., Super Bowl, Olympics, World Series) under the spotlight with all of the accompanying attention, distractions, and pressure. Thus, the first challenge involves preparing for big competitions.

It's not just what athletes do before a competition of great consequence that can affect the trajectory of their sports lives; rather, what happens after matters too. The second challenge involves the aftermath of a big competition, whether a ringing success or a crushing disappointment. How athletes respond to it has a big impact on their future efforts and successes in equally important events.

One of the most discouraging challenges that athletes experience are performance slumps that often arise suddenly, inexplicably, and seemingly intractably. When slumps occur, athletes quickly plummet from the highest of highs in their performances to the lowest of lows. The third challenge then focuses on what causes slumps and how athletes can get out of them as soon as possible.

Finally, perhaps the most distressing aspects of sports are injuries. Almost every committed athlete will experience an injury of some sort that keeps them away from their sport and many suffer serious injuries that prevent them from playing for extended periods and may be career threatening. Yet, the injury itself may be the least of athletes' worries as the long and arduous rehabilitation and return to sport present immense physical and psychological obstacles that they must overcome. In addition to the obvious physical difficulties of injury rehabilitation, the mind also becomes "injured" and must also be rehabilitated. Thus, the fourth challenge involves athletes ensuring that their minds heal and regain their strength as they progress from injured athlete to rehabilitating athlete to, ultimately and hopefully, an athlete who is physically and psychologically capable of returning to and surpassing their pre-injury level of performance.

PREPARING FOR A BIG COMPETITION

Brandon Orr and Jim Taylor

Perhaps the greatest challenge that athletes face, at every level of sports, is being able to perform their best in the biggest competitions of their lives. Certainly, the best athletes in the world distinguish themselves from everyone else not just by their ability to perform well in practice and routine competitions, but rather in their ability to excel when it matters the most. Achieving success in important events, such as the Olympics, soccer's World Cup, or baseball's World Series, tests the ability of athletes to overcome the psychological and emotional challenges that they present to athletes. A survey of Olympic teams that compared those who medaled from those who did not found that the factors affecting performance in big competitions were: travel, team cohesion, lack of experience in big competitions, coaching decisions, and focus (Gould, Guinan, Greenleaf, Medbery, & Peterson, 1999). Because of these and other factors that in evidence, athletes must understand the challenges they face and develop an array of attitudes, approaches, and tools they can use to mitigate the impact of these challenges and ensure total preparation so they can perform at their highest level under the spotlight of big events.

Theory and Research

Because of the powerful impact that preparation has on performances in important competitions, there is a growing body of research that attempts to explain this relationship that is so fundamental to athletes. Several areas have been identified that have significant implications for athletes who are determined to perform their best on the biggest stages of their sports careers.

Context

Athletes don't perform in a vacuum; rather, the context in which they engage in their sport has a substantial influence on how they think about, respond emotionally, behave, and perform. Context explains why some athletes perform well in practice, others are considered "game players," and still others show themselves to be "big game players." Consultants would be well-served to recognize the impact of context as they help athletes to prepare for big events.

In contrast to previous thinking that athletes' motivations and goals are dispositional, recent arguments have suggested a more contextualized lens of motivation that is situational (Harwood, 2002; Van de Pol, Kavussanu, & Ring, 2012); how athletes' definitions of success orient their motivations and goals can shift from one setting to another. This contextualized framework is more reflective of the influence that competition holds over the physical and psychological systems of athletes. This perspective also encourages consultants to better explore and understand athletes' attitudes toward big competitions. As much as there are physical aspects of sport that are the foundation of success, the psychological side of sports may be the ultimate determinant of how athletes perform and whether they find success in their efforts (Gardner & Moore, 2007). Moreover, that psychological impact is significantly shaped by the specific contexts that athletes find themselves in, particularly in big competitions. Consultants can help athletes to tease out the context-relevant forces that impact how they approach important events, either positively or negatively, and guide them in ensuring that they maintain healthy perspectives, attitudes, and practices when confronted by those contexts in the big competitions.

Emotions

Consequential competitions represent a context that is both quantitatively (e.g., better opponents, bigger venues, more fans and media attention) and qualitatively (e.g., more pressure and distractions) different from training and normal competitions (Harwood, 2002). These differences often lead to a shift in athletes' emotions and their accompanying physiology (Lazarus, 2000). Emotions such as worry, fear, and frustration that often arise in big events are clearly not conducive to optimal performance. In turn, the physiological changes that are typically associated with these interfering emotions, including choppy breathing, racing heart, muscle tension, and excessive adrenaline, can further inhibit performance (see more in Chapter 3).

Emotions in sport represent a telling comparison to the Greek construct of the pharmakon wherein a given substance can be both a poison and a remedy (Derrida, 1981). Emotions have been shown to lead to both positive and negative changes in focus, thinking, and decision-making, all of which play a critical role in performance in big competitions (Hanin, 2000; Lazarus, 2000; Uphill et al., 2009). As such, sports performance can be negatively impacted if athletes have not developed of emotional control for when their emotions turn problematic (Lazarus, 2000; Uphill et al., 2009). Consultants can work with athletes to help them understand the emotions they are likely to experience in important competitions and provide them with tools to best manage those emotions to their advantage (more on emotions in Chapter 2).

Focus

A change in focus is a commonly reported reaction among athletes before a big competition. This shift typically occurs when athletes move from a beneficial focus on the process of performance (i.e., what they need to do to perform their best) to a impeding focus on the potential outcome of the event (i.e., winning or losing) because of the personal, team, and cultural weight placed on important events and the potential consequences that might accrue.

This move from process to outcome happens despite its paradoxical impact on performance. Specifically, as noted in Chapter 1, contrary to what many athletes believe, when they focus on the outcome of a competition they actually make it less likely that they will achieve the results they strive for. The outcome of a competition happens at the end of the contest. If athletes are focused on the outcome, they aren't focusing on what they need to do from the beginning to the end to achieve their desired outcome. Also, many athletes experience unhelpful thoughts and emotions, as well as, anxiety before competitions, especially important ones, in reaction to concerns that they will lose. This psychological, emotional, and physiological reaction further interferes with athletes performing their best. As a result, this shift in focus away from the process and onto the outcome that often arises before a big event is, in fact, self-sabotaging.

In contrast, when athletes can maintain a process focus, they improve their odds of achieving the outcome they want. If they are focused on what they need to do to perform well, they are more likely to execute effectively and perform well, the end result being that they get the outcome that they wanted. A significant emphasis for consultants helping athletes prepare for an important competition is to constantly direct their focus away from results and onto the process.

Performance Goals

A significant problem that can occur in important competitions is that, along with the shift in focus from process to outcome, athletes may also shift from striving toward their performance goals to goals that are context-specific. This change often occurs in reaction to key incidences during a competition and the greater meaning they take on in big contests. These occurrences that are perceived to be significant lead to an increase in cognitive activity (i.e., overthinking) in athletes (Swann, Crust, Jackman, Vella, Allen, & Keegan, 2017), as well as anxiety, and a shift toward an outcome focus. A significant problem that can occur in important competitions is that, along with this shift, athletes may also shift from striving toward their performance goals (e.g., running sub 18-minute 5K, reaching a quarterback rating 85 or higher, achieving a batting average of .400 or higher, or scoring higher than 9.8 on the beam in gymnastics) to goals that are context-specific (e.g., "I just want to beat Garret in the 5K" or "I just want to player better than the other team's quarterback" or "I just want to get more hits than Marco" or "I just want to score higher on beam than Brynna").

The more athletes focus on these seemingly consequential context-specific events, the less they focus on their performance goals and the more their performances decline. Performance goals can be powerful tools for athletes to use to combat the debilitating effects of contextual occurrences that that can arise related to the competition, competitive environment, and outcome-related threat concerns (Eys, Carron, Bray, & Beauchamp, 2005; Newin, Bloom, & Loughead, 2008). Consultants can help athletes to keep their performance goals at the forefront of their minds, so when these consequential occurrences happen, athletes can use their previously determined performance goals to resist the distraction of contextual events to stay focused on their competitive tasks and maintain the quality of their performances (Smith, 1996; Stoebel et al., 2008).

Teams

In team sports, teams can struggle with some of the same challenges as individual athletes as an important competition approaches. As such, the need to prepare a team is equally valuable. Just as consultants can help athletes get ready for a big event, so too can they understand and facilitate key areas that impact team performance. In particular, there are two areas that most influence how a team responds to a consequential competition.

Task Cohesion

When it comes to preparing for big competitions, a key distinction that is helpful to make is between social cohesion and task cohesion (Bernthal & Insko, 1993; Loughead & Bloom, 2013). Social cohesion refers to how closely connected members of a group feel to one another. The emphasis with social cohesion is on relationships, collective experience, and emotions. While social cohesion is the more frequent focus of research in applied sport psychology and of importance in the overall functioning of a team, there is little evidence that it is predictive of team success (Loughead & Bloom, 2013). Task cohesion involves a team's ability to work together to accomplish shared goals (Bernthal & Insko, 1993). In contrast to social cohesion, task cohesion has been found to have an impact on team performance (Dunlop, Falk, & Beauchamp, 2012; McEwan & Beauchamp, 2014; Newin et al., 2008). More significantly, there is evidence that low task cohesion is a contributor to poor performance in big competitions (Gould et al., 1999). Task cohesion includes performance goals combined with team-member roles and individual responsibilities related to the team goal (Dunlop et al., 2012; Eys et al., 2005).

Consultants can facilitate task cohesion leading up to big competitions by working with athletes and teams to establish (or re-emphasize if already established) team values, goals, and responsibilities. This renewed clarity has a direct impact on how each individual team member approaches their given responsibilities related to individual and team performance goals. It can also act as armor against the intrusions that are common to big competitions including a focus on results, pressure, distractions, and practical and contextual differences that are present.

Team Roles

The identification of task-specific behaviors related to team roles and performance goals for athletes has been identified in the literature as a positive coping mechanism for performance anxiety (Beauchamp, Bray, Eys, & Carron, 2003; Papaioannou & Kouli, 1999; Smith, Smoll, & Cumming, 2007). As such, consultants can work with athletes and, where appropriate, the coaching staff, to identify tasks and behaviors relevant to the athletes' team roles, particularly in preparation for big competitions (McArdle & Duda, 2002; Taylor, 1995; Vazou, Ntoumanis, & Duda, 2006). Athletes can benefit from these explorations both well before and immediately prior to important competitions so that they have these process-oriented tools at their disposal when contextual outcome cues begin to impose themselves (Smith et al., 2007).

Practical Implications

In addition to the evidence-based strategies just discussed, there are a variety of approaches, attitudes, and practical tools that have stood the test of time among consultants that they can use to help athletes and teams prepare effectively for an important competition. Well before big events approach, consultants can set the stage for athletes' readiness to perform their best by ensuring that they approach them in the most positive, relaxed, and focused way.

KISS Principle

Sports have a lot of moving parts, meaning they are complicated. Athletes have a lot to figure out, focus on, and learn as they develop. As athletes strive toward their goals, they must contend with many factors that impact their performances including physical, technical, tactical, equipment, mental, weather, conditions, team, and opponents, just to name a few. That complexity increases with important competitions as athletes have more to do, there are more people involved, more to think about, stronger emotions, more distractions, and more at stake.

These complications can overwhelm athletes, causing their minds to be filled with clutter including doubt, worry, expectations, stress, and fear.

As athletes head toward the increased demands of big events, consultants can do athletes a great service by introducing them to the KISS principle. KISS principle is commonly known as "Keep it Simple, Stupid", but a more accurate representation is "Keep it Simple, Smart" because, if athletes are smart, they'll simplify their lives as much as possible as they approach important competitions.

Athletes can use the KISS principle to their advantage in several ways. They can start by reminding themselves why they are going to the big event. Even most the most experienced athletes can lose perspective and get caught up in the excitement, tangential activities, and other distractions including people, events, and attention associated with the competition, as well as talk about winning. Returning to the basics of their goals, having fun, and showing themselves what they're capable of can be powerful reminders that keep them grounded and focused before a consequential competition.

Athletes can then identify aspects of the upcoming big events that might clutter their minds and be aware when they begin to become obstacles to their preparations. Finally, they can pinpoint the most essential facets of their preparations, so they have a clear idea of what they want to focus on, while blocking out everything that might crowd their minds and distract them.

"Dance with the One Who Brung Ya"

Though this expression is clearly bad English, it also communicates another important lesson that consultants can teach athletes. Particularly for athletes who haven't experienced a specific big competition before, they can feel the need to "step it up" or "raise their game" to achieve their goals. Paradoxically, this approach is most often self-defeating. To the contrary, as the expression suggests, consultants want to encourage athletes to continue to do everything that has gotten them to brink of the important event.

"Dancing with the one who brung ya" means athletes should return to the basics of what has worked for them in the recent past. Whether physical, technical, mental, social, or some other contributor to performance, if it's working, athletes should keep doing it.

Four Approaches to Big-Event Success

If the top athletes in any given sport were asked what the keys to their success were, they would likely give 20 different answers. At the same time, they probably all would find several fundamental themes in their responses:

- **Control or not to control**. Elite athletes ignore what is outside of their control (e.g., the conditions, competitors, and conditions) and focus on what they can control (their attitude, efforts, thoughts, emotions, behavior, preparation). This approach results in fewer distractions, less stress, anxiety, and frustration, and more motivation, confidence, intensity, and focus.
- **Have a game plan**. Successful athletes prepare for big competitions by developing and following a defined and practical plan for what they will need to do to perform at a high level and accomplish their goals. They also have a plan B for what they will do if plan A doesn't work.
- **Be flexible and adapt**. Because of the uncontrollable nature of sports, competitions don't always play out the way athletes want. If they want to have a chance of "snatching victory from the jaws of defeat," they must be flexible and make adjustments as soon as problems appear. This approach requires that athletes be vigilant to what is working and what isn't, and then be adaptable enough to make the necessary changes that will enable them to stay or return to competitiveness when it matters most.
- **Expect the unexpected**. One of the biggest challenges to athletes in big competitions is when something unexpected happens that causes stress, disrupts their focus, and threatens their confidence. Athletes can first do what they can to prevent unexpected events by expecting the unexpected. Before a big event, they can list everything they can think of that could go wrong and create a solution to the problem. Then, when an unexpected event, they have a prepared response that will keep them on track. Also, because not all situations can be anticipated, athletes can quickly accept the unexpected and focus on staying positive, calm, and determined.

Mental Tools for Big-game Preparation

Once athletes have established healthy attitudes and approaches to the upcoming big event, they are now in a position to leverage some useful mental tools to more directly prepare them to perform their best. Consultants can play a vital role in providing these tools to athletes and showing them how to use them to their fullest advantage.

Imagery

Mental imagery has long been identified as tool that athletes can use to enhance their sports performances. Moreover, there is a robust body of research that it can benefit athletes physically, technically, tactically, and mentally. The power of imagery has been explored in depth in Chapter 4, so further discussions here will focus solely on how athletes can best leverage it as they prepare for big competitions. One particular benefit of imagery in this context involves allowing athletes to see and feel themselves performing their best in the upcoming big event prior to its occurrence, so that when they compete, they feel as if they have a already been there many times before.

Consultants can collaborate with athletes to create imagery scenarios that meet their needs and goals for the big event. Ways in which athletes can use imagery in their preparations include imagining:

- all of the activities, people, uncontrollables, and distractions around the big competition while remaining relaxed and focused, and performing their best;
- a realistic competitive environment that includes the venue, crowds, officials, opponents, and opposing coaches;
- adapting to different environmental and competitive conditions;
- key technical or tactical aspects of their competitive performances;
- consistency of performance from start to finish of the competition;
- optimal overall performance;
- overcoming unexpected occurrences before and during the competition;
- the range of emotions that athletes may experience at the event;
- when ahead in the competition;
- when behind in the competition;
- execution of plan a;
- adoption of plan b when plan a isn't working; and
- emotions athletes will feel after a successful competitive performance.

Pre-competitive Routines

While there has been considerable research demonstrating the value of pre-competitive routines (Cotterill, Sanders, & Collins, 2010), one particular study (Gould, Ecklund, & Jackson, 1992) examining Olympic medalists and non-medalists highlights the importance of routines in big competitions. The results of this study found that the key differentiator between seeded wrestlers who earned Olympic medals and those who did not was whether they adhered to a pre-competitive routine. Moreover, seeded competitors who did not medal only used a pre-competitive routine when competing against another ranked opponent or when competing against an opponent they perceived to have greater ability.

Because routines have been discussed at length in Chapter 4, the implications of pre–competitive routines for big competitions will be the focus here. Pre-competitive routines serve several essential roles in helping athletes perform their best in important events:

- ensure complete preparation in environments that can disrupt their typical regimens;
- help athletes to focus on what they can control and disregard that which they can't;
- create an atmosphere that is familiar, predictable, and comfortable; and
- optimize every contributor to athletic performance.

Consultants can assist athletes in developing pre-competitive routines that best meet their needs and goals for big competitions. These routines should not only be used immediately before the competition, but also upon athletes' arrival at and entire stay leading up to the event. Consultants can also help identify when and where athletes will do their routines. Athletes can enhance the value of their routines by recognizing pre-competitive situations and interactions that can upset their preparations. Finally, consultants can help athletes to be flexible and adjust their pre-competitive routines as scheduling, location, other responsibilities, real-time events, and disruptions warrant.

Mindfulness-based Practices

Big competitions take the normal practices and mental processes that go into competitive preparation and do everything they can to throw them for a loop. At every important event, there are practical, perceived, and social factors that challenge athletes from well before the competition begins to its conclusion. The three most impacted mental areas as the event approaches are intensity, emotions, and focus (more on these mental muscles in Chapter 3). Expectations, pressure, and stress conspire to pull athletes away from their ideal intensity. Consequential competitions can also wreak havoc with athletes' emotions, causing them to experience feelings that can interfere with their competitive efforts including anxiety, fear, worry, and frustration (see Chapter 2 for more on emotions). The emphasis on winning and increased numbers of people and activities, as well as the negative influences just mentioned, also provide a plethora of distractions at a time when athletes need to have a laser focus. In sum, athletes' ability to manage these psychological and physiological challenges may determine how they perform and whether they achieve their goals in the big competition.

Mindfulness is a practice that is receiving more scientific and practical attention in applied sport psychology, as well as in the broader population (see Chapter 4 for more). Its benefits align well with the big-event challenges that were just discussed and can offer itself as an ameliorative to athletes who must overcome them. Mindfulness provides a framework for consultants to help athletes manage the flood of thoughts, feelings, and emotions that can arise in the run-up to big competitions as well as in the competition itself.

Mindfulness first heightens athletes' awareness of their psychological and physiological states, enabling them to decide whether and how they must make adjustments to maintain their ideal performance state. With this information, they can use mindfulness strategies, including breathing, meditation, relaxation, and centering (Gardner & Moore, 2004, 2012), to their benefit as they prepare for an important competition in several ways. First, athletes can moderate their intensity in response to stress or anxiety. Second, they can experience, acknowledge, and let go of unhelpful emotions that arise due to the magnitude of the event. Lastly, athletes can use mindfulness to draw their attention away from the many distractions that exist before and during big events and redirect their focus onto factors that are central to their preparations and upcoming performances.

Preparation is a Collaborative Effort

Finally, consultants can't successfully prepare athletes on their own. Instead, they must enlist and collaborate with coaches and support staff involved in training athletes and to create an integrated program that prepares athletes comprehensively to perform their best in the biggest competitions of their lives (see Chapter 12 for more on staff collaboration). Ultimately, sport performance involves a nexus of physical, psychological, contextual, and social factors that impacts performance. The athletes who can consistently deliver their best in every performance-related domain are those who enjoy the highest levels of success, particularly in the big competitions (Crust, 2008; Crust & Azadi, 2010; Durand-Bush & Salmela, 2002; Gould et al., 1999). Of particular value is for consultants to work closely with athletes' support team to ensure that every base is covered as they prepare for the competitions that matter the most (Crust & Azadi, 2010; Durand-Bush & Salmela, 2002).

Summary

- Achieving success in big competitions such as the Olympics, soccer World Cup, or baseball World Series tests the ability of athletes to overcome the psychological and emotional obstacles that these events place in the path toward their goals.

- Research has reported that context, emotions, focus, and performance goals play a central role in how athletes perform in important events.
- In response to the complicated nature of big competitions, athletes are encouraged to embrace the KISS principle (Keep it Simple, Smart) and identify and focus on just a few key areas as they prepare to compete.
- Consultants can ensure that athletes trust and do what they've been trained to do rather than feeling the need to do something different in an important event.
- To mitigate the stresses of an important event, athletes can focus on what they can control, have a game plan, be flexible and adapt, and expect the unexpected.
- Practical tools that athletes can use to prepare for a big competition include mental imagery, routines, and mindfulness.

References

Beauchamp, M. R., Bray, S. R., Eys, M. A., & Carron, A. V. (2003). The effect of role ambiguity on competitive state anxiety. *Journal of Sport and Exercise Psychology, 25*(1), 77–92.

Bernthal, P. R., & Insko, C. A. (1993). Cohesiveness without groupthink: The interactive effects of social and task cohesion. *Group and Organization Management, 18*(1), 66–87.

Cotterill, S. T., Sanders, R., & Collins, D. (2010). Developing effective pre-performance routines in golf: Why don't we ask the golfer? *Journal of Applied Sport Psychology, 22*(1), 51–64.

Crust, L. (2008). A review and conceptual re-examination of mental toughness: Implications for future researchers. *Personality and Individual Differences, 45*(7), 576–583.

Crust, L., & Azadi, K. (2010). Mental toughness and athletes' use of psychological strategies. *European Journal of Sport Science, 10*(1), 43–51.

Derrida, J. (1981). "Plato's Pharmacy." In his *Dissemination* (trans. B. Johnson; pp. 61–172). London: Athlone Press.

Dunlop, W. L., Falk, C. F., & Beauchamp, M. R. (2012). How dynamic are exercise group dynamics? Examining changes in cohesion within class-based exercise programs. *Health Psychology, 32*, 1240–1243.

Durand-Bush, N., & Salmela, J. H. (2002). The development and maintenance of expert athletic performance: Perceptions of World and Olympic champions. *Journal of Applied Sport Psychology, 14*(3), 154–171.

Eys, M., Carron, A., Bray, S., & Beauchamp, M. (2005). The relationship between role ambiguity and intention to return the following season. *Journal of Applied Sport Psychology, 17*(3), 255–261

Gardner, F., & Moore, Z. E. (2004). A mindfulness-acceptance-commitment based approach to athletic performance enhancement: Theoretical considerations. *Behavior Therapy, 35*(4), 707–723.

Gardner, F., & Moore, Z. E. (2007). *The psychology of enhancing human performance: The mindfulness–acceptance–commitment approach.* New York, NY: Springer Publishing.

Gardner, F., & Moore, Z. E. (2012). Mindfulness and acceptance models in sport psychology: A decade of basic and applied scientific advancements. *Canadian Psychology/Psychologie Canadienne, 53*(4), 309–318.

Gould, D., Ecklund, R., Jackson, S. (1992). 1988 US Olympic Wrestling excellence: I. Mental preparation, precompetitive cognition, and affect. *The Sport Psychologist, 6*(4), 358–382.

Gould, D., Guinan, D., Greenleaf, C., Medberry, R., & Peterson, K. (1999). Factors affecting Olympic performance: Perceptions of athletes and coaches from more and less successful teams. *The Sport Psychologist, 13*(4), 371–394.

Hanin, Y. L. (2000). *Emotions in sport.* Champaigne, IL: Human Kinetics.

Harwood, C. (2002). Assessing achievement goals in sport: Caveats for consultants and case for contextualization. *Journal of Applied Sport Psychology, 14*(2), 106–119

Lazarus, R. S. (2000). How emotions influence performance in competitive sports. *The Sport Psychologist, 14*(3), 229–252. doi: 10.1123/tsp.14.3.229

Loughead, T. M., & Bloom, G. A. (2013). Team cohesion in sport: Critical overview and implications for team building. In P. Potrac, W. Gilbert, & J. Denison (Eds.), *Routledge handbook of sports coaching* (pp. 345–356). New York, NY: Routledge.

McArdle, S., & Duda, J. K. (2002). Implications of the motivational climate in youth sports. In F. L. Smoll & R. E. Smith (Eds.), *Children and youth in sport: A biopsychosocial perspective* (2nd ed., pp. 409–434). Dubuque, IA: Kendall/Hunt.

McEwan, D., & Beauchamp, M. R. (2014). Teamwork in sport: A theoretical and integrative review. *International Review of Sport and Exercise Psychology, 7*, 229–250.

Newin, J., Bloom, G. A., & Loughead, T. M. (2008). Youth ice hockey coaches' perceptions of a team-building intervention program. *The Sport Psychologist, 22*, 54–72.

Papaioannou, A., & Kouli, O. (1999). The effect of task structure, perceived motivational climate and goal orientations on students' task involvement and anxiety. *Journal of Applied Sport Psychology, 11*(1), 51–71.

Smith, R. E. (1996). Performance anxiety, cognitive interference, and concentration enhancement strategies in sports. In I. G. Sarason, G. R. Pierce, & B. R. Sarason (Eds.), *Cognitive interference: Theories, methods, and findings* (pp. 261–283). Mahwah, NJ: Lawrence Erlbaum Associates.

Smith, R. E., Smoll, F. L., & Cumming, S. P. (2007). Effects of motivational climate intervention for coaches on young athletes' sport performance anxiety. *Journal of Sport and Exercise Psychology, 29*(1), 39–59.

Stoeber, J., Stoll, O., Pescheck, E., & Otto, K. (2008). Perfectionism and achievement goals in athletes: Relations with approach and avoidance orientations in mastery and performance goals. *Psychology of Sport and Exercise, 9*(2), 102–121.

Swann, C., Crust, L., Jackman, P., Vella, S.A., Allen, M.S., & Keegan, R. (2017). Performing under pressure: Exploring the psychological state underlying clutch performance in sport. *Journal of Sport Sciences, 35*(23), 2272–2280.

Taylor, J. (1995). A conceptual model for integrating athletes' needs and sport demands in the development of competitive mental preparation strategies. *The Sport Psychologist, 9*, 339–357.

Uphill, M. A., McCarthy, P. J., & Jones, M. V. (2009). Getting a grip on emotion regulation in sport: Conceptual foundations and practical application. In S. D. Mellalieu & S. Hanton (Eds.), *Advances in applied sport psychology: A review* (pp. 162–194). New York, NY: Routledge.

Van de pol, P. K. C., Kavussanu, M., & Ring, C. (2012). The effects of training and competition on achievement goals, motivational responses, and performance in a golf-putting task. *Journal of Sport and Exercise Psychology, 34*(6), 787–807.

Vazou, S., Ntoumanis, N., & Duda, J.L. (2006). Predicting young athletes' motivational indices as a function of their perceptions of the coach- and peer-created climate. *Psychology of Sport and Exercise, 7*, 215–233.

REFLECTIONS AFTER A BIG COMPETITION

Abby Keenan and Jim Taylor

Picture this: athletes who just finished a Saturday in-season competition grab dinner with teammates. They have a day off from their sport on Sunday, during which they do homework and have some downtime. On Monday, they return to school and practices for the upcoming week's competition. The athletes follow this routine for months on end.

The problem with this scenario is that, though athletes devote enormous amounts of time to their sports lives, they aren't necessarily maximizing the benefits of that time commitment. As a general rule, athletes love to participate in their sport, in both training and competition. At the same time, they are less prone to want to think or talk about their sport, particularly in a reflective and analytical way. Yet, it is this lack of reflection that may prevent athletes from becoming the best they can be.

Outside of sport, Dewey (1933) originally defined reflection as the "reconstruction or reorganization of experience which adds to the meaning of experience and which increases ability to direct the course of subsequent experience" (p. 76). Or, to quote the philosopher George Santayana (1905), "Those who cannot remember the past are condemned to repeat it" (p. 284). By following action with reflection, athletes can more effectively learn and grow from their experiences and develop more fully and more quickly over time. Athletes should engage in their sports experiences committedly, observe and reflect on their experiences from a variety of perspectives, integrate their introspections into concrete actions, and apply those actions to their future sports efforts. This four-stage process is known as the Experiential Learning Cycle (Kolb & Kolb, 2009):

1. Stage one, *concrete learning*, involves athletes having a new experience such as a training session or competition.
2. Stage two, *reflective observation*, occurs when athletes reflect on the experience, identifying what worked and what didn't.
3. Stage three, *abstract conceptualization*, refers to athletes generating new ideas that are based on the reflections of the experience.
4. Stage four, *active experimentation*, involves athletes using their new knowledge gained from the first three stages to make changes to improve future sports experiences.

After a practice or competition, athletes can intentionally engage in the process of reflection by sharing the tangible aspects of the sports experience including what they did and how it turned out, their reactions, and observations. This process involves their reflecting on what happened and why, connecting reflections to other sports experiences, and determining how to apply what they learned to future sport situations (Cleary & Zimmerman, 2001; Cummings, 2008). Athletes can reflect on their own, reflect with their teammates and coaches, or participate in reflection facilitated by a consultant. In any case, reflection can also be known by other terms such as debriefing, processing, or reviewing (Cummings, 2008). Regardless, "the initial reaction of most people after a powerful experience is to want to talk about it. People naturally want to describe what happened to them and how it felt" (Jacobson & Ruddy, 2015, p. 50). This propensity to want to share experiences can be used by consultants to encourage the process of reflection and learning, particularly after big competitions.

At the same time, despite this immediate desire to share experiences, getting athletes to open up about their competitive experiences in a deep and substantive way, particularly following failed efforts that evoke unpleasant emotions, can be challenging. Additionally, it requires introspection, critical thinking, and a willingness to be vulnerable, all qualities not necessarily valued in the sports community. Furthermore, reflection involves athletes taking ownership and being accountable for their actions; again, something that they might be reluctant to do following a defeat. In spite of these potential hurdles, it is valuable for consultants to integrate self-directed or guided reflection into their work with athletes and teams. This process helps athletes to develop self-awareness (Ravizza, 2010), gain insight into training and competitive experiences (Lederman, 1992), create connections between past and future experiences (Kolb, 1984), provide useful information for subsequent efforts (Cleary & Zimmerman, 2001), and bring closure to their past performances (Lederman, 1992; Ravizza, 2010).

The reflective process can be particularly beneficial to athletes following an important competition. As such events are, by definition, rare, athletes don't have many opportunities to experience and learn from them. Yet, experience is vital to improved performance, especially in competitions of consequence. To ensure that athletes are well-prepared for their next big event, they must garner as much information about their recent experience, positive or negative, to apply it to subsequent competitions (McArdle, Martin, Lennon, & Moore, 2010). Moreover, due to the complexity of these events, without an intentional process of reflection, analysis, and planning, key contributors or obstacles to performance may be missed and, in those squandered opportunities, athletes also lose out on valuable information that could benefit them the next time they compete in an important event. The goal of consultants is to convince athletes of the value that reflection has to their sports development and provide them with tools to formalize its use and maximize its impact.

Overview

Though reflection occurs after an important competition, it actually begins beforehand as part of consultants' efforts to prepare athletes for the big event. It starts with introducing athletes to a framework for how reflection will be used before and after the competition of consequence. This process begins with consultant-led experiences prior to the important event (e.g., mental training and team-building sessions) and concludes with structured and unstructured reflections.

Plan

The process of reflection begins with consultants explaining to athletes what reflection is, why it's important, and how it works. By educating athletes to its purpose and value, they can take a process that can be cerebral and ethereal and turn it into a tangible exercise that they can more easily embrace. In doing so, athletes can more readily take ownership of reflection as a means of maximizing their sports development and competitive performances.

Based on the personalities of athletes and, in the case of a team, its culture, as well as the upcoming competition, consultants can first determine if they want athletes to reflect on their own or if they will be leading athletes through reflection individually and/or collectively. Most often, consultants lead the reflection if they are working with a team or they incorporate the reflection into their mental training sessions. Next, consultants can select a reflection method and materials (Lederman, 1992), keeping the needs and goals of the athletes and the objectives of the competition in mind (Jacobson & Ruddy, 2015). Consultants can then determine when (e.g., shortly after or at a distance from the competition) and where reflection will occur, and how much time is needed (McArdle et al., 2010). Ideally the reflection will occur immediately after an experience before it is forgotten (Cain, Cummings, & Stanchfield, 2004), though this proximity may not be logistically possible (e.g., the need to travel or return immediately to school responsibilities). In this latter case, consultants can ask athletes to take some time on their own to write down their reflections while they are fresh in their minds. The amount of time devoted to post-competitive reflection will depend on the purpose, method, complexity, and intensity of the reflection as well as the responsiveness of the individual or team (Dennehy, Sims, & Collins, 1998). It can be accomplished with minimal resources in a few minutes or can take up to two days with evidence from video analysis or performance statistics (McArdle et al., 2010). Finally, in preparation for the important competition, consultants can provide clarity of purpose for the reflection exercise, identify the parameters for the reflection (i.e., what athletes should be expected to reflect on), and establish specific goals for what they want to get out of it.

Observe

When possible, consultants can observe athletes' competitive experiences. This observational data provides consultants with valuable information they can use in leading athletes through a post-competition reflection. Jacobson and Ruddy (2015) recommend using a scientific, anthropological, or psychological approach to observation. In looking for scientific data, consultants can collect quantifiable aspects of the competitive performance, such as individual and team performance statistics, who contributed and how much to the team performance, what tactics were employed and with what success, and whether competitive goals were achieved. From an anthropological perspective involving team reflections, consultants can look at the relationships among team members, who had influence and how it was acquired, rules that the team operated by, the quality of the communications, how conflicts were resolved, and which rules were followed and broken. Finally, consultants can focus on observing the psychological aspects of athletes' performances as a means of identifying what mental factors influenced their competitive efforts and outcomes. For example, consultants can assess athletes' motivation, confidence, intensity, focus, and emotions during the big event. They can also observe how much athletes used mental tools such as self-talk, breathing, and imagery during the competition. Detailed observation can help consultants to lead reflection in an informed way that also enables them to customize the process to meet the identified needs and goals of athletes and teams.

Facilitate

As reflection isn't an exercise that athletes are accustomed to or trained to do, consultants can facilitate its use by providing a structure and process for how to do it, whether athletes do it on their own or are led by consultants. When athletes reflect on their own, consultants can define their expectations about what they want athletes to do and what they want athletes to gain from the experience. This clarity includes providing athletes with information about the purpose, materials needed, timing, and step-by-step instructions for its use. Once athletes complete their reflection, they can share it with their coaches, parents, consultant, or whomever has a stake in their development. The triangulation that comes from these discussions and resulting feedback can add further nuance and value to the conclusions the athletes themselves garner from the exercise.

When consultants lead reflections, they can provide structure, direction, comfort, and feedback that can increase its value to athletes. Cain et al. (2004) recommend creating a safe and positive environment so individuals are willing to share ideas, reactions, and opinions. In a team setting, often this is physically demonstrated by gathering everyone into a circle. Then, consultants can offer encouragement, actively listen, ask intentional questions, share their own observations, provide feedback and insights, respond to concerns, and empower athletes to learn important lessons from their competitive experience.

Follow Up

Regardless of the method, the goals of reflection are for athletes to learn valuable new information about their big-event experience and then turn that information into actionable strategies that will better prepare them for their next important competition. Consultants and coaches can help athletes make this transition by encouraging them to focus on what's controllable, holding them accountable for what they learn, and giving them opportunities to put their reflections into action (Collins & Durand-Bush, 2014). Regular follow up and check-ins with athletes about how well they are accomplishing these reflection goals can provide them with the encouragement, support, and feedback they need to get the most out of their reflections.

Reflection Methods

There is no single method of reflection that works for everyone. The one that is chosen depends on the personality and style of both the consultant and the athletes. Reflection methods can be structured, semi-structured, or free flow. They can also proceed around the temporal framework of a competition (e.g., the quarters in a football game), the occurrence of consequential events in a competition, the spontaneous musings of the athlete, or any other means by which athletes' reflections are catalyzed.

Discussion Question Models

After athletes compete in a big competition, consultants can facilitate a reflection discussion with individual athletes and teams (Ravizza, 2010) using one of the following question models. The questions in each model are meant to be a starting point; consultants can tailor the follow-up questions to meet athletes' specific needs and goals. Each of these models can take 10–30 minutes, depending on the competitive experience that precedes it, the purpose and goals of the reflection, and the engagement of the athletes or team.

Three-question Model

1. What? (What happened?)
2. So What? (Why is that important?)
3. Now What? (How can we use this information?)

(Schoel, Prouty, & Radcliffe, 1988; Cummings, 2008)

Five-question Model

1. Did you notice . . .?
2. Why did that happen?
3. Does that happen in life?
4. Who? What? Where? When? Why?
5. What will you do now?

(Jacobson & Ruddy, 2015)

Six-phase Model

1. How do you feel?
2. What happened?
3. What did you learn?
4. How does this relate to the real world?
5. What if?
6. What next?

(Thiagarajan, 2004)

Sport-Performance Reflection Forms

In general, athletes and coaches have commonly used post-performance reflections after important competitions to learn from them as a means of preparing for and improving on future performance (Hogg, 2002). In addition to the more conversational approach described above, a post-competitive reflection can be accomplished by athletes' use of structured questionnaires that prompt them to respond to a variety of relevant data points that have been determined by consultants and coaches. This type of reflection can be completed by athletes themselves or in conjunction with consultants or coaches. As noted above, ideally athletes can process their performance immediately following its conclusion while the experience is fresh in their minds. This timeliness can be facilitated by consultants preparing sport-performance reflection forms in advance that prompt athletes to key reflections about a particular event. Additionally, though not offering the opportunity to use as an interactive tool immediately with consultants, coaches, or teammates because they are completed by athletes on their own, these forms can be used as a starting point for more guided reflections by consultants for when time allows. Moreover, they are efficient to administer to groups of athletes.

Reflection forms can be created by consultants on their own or with input from athletes and coaches to align questions with goals and performance indicators. Questions can be open-ended or include a rating scale, and can be focused on different components of the competition including preparation, overall individual and team performance, technical, tactical, or mental factors, and lessons learned. Questions that might be included are:

1. Rate each of the following areas on a 1–10 scale where 1 is poor and 10 is excellent:

   a. Preparation
   b. Technical execution
   c. Tactical execution
   d. Team execution (if a team sport)
   e. Determination
   f. Resilience
   g. Confidence
   h. Intensity
   i. Focus
   j. Emotions

2. What did you do well? What did you not do well?
3. What did you learn from this competition?
4. What do you want to continue doing in your next competition?
5. What do you want to do differently in your next competition?
6. What will be important for you to work on in upcoming practices?
7. What else do you want your coach or consultant to know?

Other examples of reflection forms include the performance feedback sheet (Ravizza, 2010), the Mental States of Readiness and Satisfaction (Hogg, 2002), and journaling (Dennehy et al., 1998; Ravizza, 2010).

In addition to a documented reflection form, Hogg (2002) outlines recommendations for the post-competition debriefing process:

1. Jointly determine the time, place, and purpose of the discussion.
2. Athletes engage in self-reflection while consultants and/or coaches also reflect.
3. Athletes share their reflections first, then everyone collectively determines what they should work on physically, technically, tactically, and mentally.
4. New strategies, plans, and goals are determined.

Summary

- By following big competitions with reflection, athletes can more effectively learn and grow from their experiences and develop more fully and more quickly over time.
- This process involves their reflecting on what happened and why, connecting reflections to other sports experiences, and determining how to apply what they learned to future sport situations.
- The goal of consultants is to convince athletes of the value that reflection has to their sports development and provide them with tools to formalize its use and maximize its impact.
- Based on the personalities and, in the case of a team, its culture, as well as the upcoming competition, consultants can first determine if they want athletes to reflect on their own or if they will be leading athletes through reflection.
- Athletes can engage in reflection on their own or participate in reflection facilitated by a consultant; either way, this requires that they plan, observe, facilitate, and follow up.
- Ideally, athletes process their performance immediately following its conclusion while the experience is fresh in their minds.

- The amount of time devoted to post-competitive reflection will depend on the purpose, method, complexity, and intensity of the reflection as well as the responsiveness of the individual or team.
- Post-performance reflections can incorporate open-ended questions and rating scales about sport performance indicators and/or mental skills.
- When consultants lead post-competition reflection, it is important to allow the athlete time to reflect and share first, then provide input and feedback, working together to align on next steps.

References

Cain, J., Cummings, M., & Stanchfield, J. (2004). *A teachable moment: A facilitator's guide to activities for processing, debriefing, reviewing, and reflecting*. Dubuque, IA: Kendall Hunt.

Cleary, T. J. & Zimmerman, B. J. (2001). Self-regulation differences during athletic practice by experts, non-experts, and novices. *Journal of Applied Sport Psychology, 13*, 185–206.

Collins, J. & Durand-Bush, N. (2014). Strategies used by an elite curling coach to nurture athletes' self-regulation: A single case study. *Journal of Applied Sport Psychology, 26*(2), 211–224.

Cummings, M. (2008). *A teachable moment: Processing the experience* [PDF].

Dennehy, R., Sims, R., & Collins, H. (1998). Debriefing experiential learning exercises: A theoretical and practical guide for success. *Journal of Management Education, 22*(1), 9–25.

Dewey, J. (1933). *How we think: A restatement of the relation of reflective thinking to the educative process*. Boston, MA: Heath.

Hogg, J. M. (2002). Debriefing: A means to increasing recovery and subsequent performance. In M. Kellmann (Ed.), *Enhancing recovery: Preventing underperformance in athletes* (pp. 181–198). Champaign, IL: Human Kinetics.

Jacobson, M. & Ruddy, M. (2015). *Open to Outcome*, 2nd ed. Bethany, OK: Wood N. Barnes.

Kolb, D. (1984). *Experiential learning: Experience as the source of learning and development*. Englewood Cliffs, NJ: Prentice Hall.

Kolb, A. Y. & Kolb, D. A. (2009). The learning way: Meta-cognitive aspects of experiential learning. *Simulation & Gaming, 40*(3), 297–327.

Lederman, L. (1992). Debriefing: Toward a systematic assessment of theory and practice. *Simulation & Gaming, 23*(2), 145–159.

McArdle, S., Martin, D., Lennon, A., & Moore, P. (2010). Exploring debriefing in sports: A qualitative perspective. *Journal of Applied Sport Psychology, 22*(3), 320–332.

Ravizza, K. (2010). Increasing awareness for sport performance. In J. M. Williams (Ed.), *Applied sport psychology: Personal growth to peak performance* (pp. 189–200). New York, NY: McGraw-Hill.

Santayana, G. (1905). *The life of reason: Reason in common sense*. New York, NY: Scribner's.

Schoel, J., Prouty, D., & Radcliffe, P. (1988). *Islands of healing*. Hamilton, MA: Project Adventure.

Thiagarajan, S. (2004, February). Six phases of debriefing. Retrieved from http://thiagi.net/archive/www/pfp/IE4H/february2004.html

PERFORMANCE SLUMPS

Kimberly Cologgi and Jim Taylor

Performance slumps are one of the great enigmas of sport. They are virtually inevitable, usually inexplicable, exceedingly frustrating, incredibly exhausting mentally and physically, difficult to get out of, and despite their persistent presence in athletes' lives, little is known about why they occur. Typically viewed as unexplained drops in performance, slumps are a source of concern for athletes and coaches. While their presence is confounding, there are ways to define, identify, and overcome slumps.

Defining and Identifying Slumps

Performance declines, regression to the mean, or even the infamous Madden Curse are all synonyms for the same thing, a slump. Slumps are used to describe a plethora of experiences, however, all center around one simple fact: a sudden and inexplicable decline in performance. Some believe slumps are solely mental, created in the minds of athletes. While others think slumps are due to unseen technical changes. Still others assert they are caused by an assortment of subtle physical changes (Grove & Stoll, 1999). Due to the use of the term to describe many experiences there has been no clear definition of what a slump in sports entails.

The *Oxford English Dictionary* defines a slump as "Undergoing a sudden, severe or prolonged fall in price, value, or amount" (Oxford Dictionaries, 2018). Though a starting point for understanding slumps in sports, this definition lacks appropriate specificity and context to sports.

In sport, numerous variables contribute to properly defining slumps. The first question is what degree of decline in performance is sufficient to warrant being labeled a slump. The answer to this is that it is subjective. For example, baseball player "X" may generally bat .310 in the regular season. If he proceeds to go 15 games without getting a hit, it is reasonable to say he is in a slump. However, if player "Y" also bats .310 in the regular season and over the next 15 games also does not record a hit but has competitive at bats and a high on base percentage, one might not qualify it as a slump. As a consequence, at least in some sports, a universal criterion of performance cannot be applied to the identification of slumps (Taylor, 1988).

The next question involves how long the decline in performance must last to be deemed a slump. Again, this determination is subjective. A basketball player missing two for eight from the foul line may not be in a slump, but going four for 24 likely would be. Instead of attempting to quantify a slump, a better measure may be to look to the athlete to determine when they feel their performance has dropped significantly enough to be called a slump.

Lastly, slumps are categorized by not having a readily apparent cause. If the reason for the decline in performance was clear, such as a technical flaw, injury, or life stressor, then it could be addressed, and performance could be restored to its baseline level. However, an inherent aspect of slumps is that their cause is not easily identified (Taylor, 1988).

Taylor (1988) offers a comprehensive definition of performance slumps that addresses the above issues. Thus, the following definition of slump is offered: "An unexplained decline in performance from a previously determined baseline level of a particular athlete that extends longer than would be expected from normal cyclic variations in performance in a given sport" (Taylor, 1988, p. 40). This definition provides three criteria for identifying a slump: unclear cause of decline, average performance comparison, and cyclic variation of performance.

Consultants can take several steps to determine if athletes are experiencing a slump. The first step is to evaluate the average standard of performance, a process that is easy to accomplish due to the statistical nature of most sports (e.g., race times, points scored). Since slumps are highly subjective, consultants can help athletes to decide which factors are important and then compare their average level of performance with their current level and decide whether there is evidence of a slump. Plotting data on a graph allows consultants, athletes, and coaches to identify patterns and trends in performance.

Next, consultants can compare recent performance to both baseline levels of performance and normal cyclic variations in performance. If current performance data are well below baseline and outside normal variation, these findings provides more evidence that the decline in performance may be a slump.

Finally, stakeholders can explore possible causes for the drop in performance. If a cause is found, whether physical, technical, or mental, the performance decrease would not fit the strict definition of a slump, a solution can be found, and the decline can be reversed. However, if no clear cause emerges, then the performance drop may be declared a slump.

Theory and Research

Taylor (1988) identified four broad categories of slumps: physical, technical, equipment, and psychological. Physical causes include a wide variety of sport-specific ailments that are too subtle to notice upon an initial examination including muscle fatigue, minor injuries, and competitive stress. General physical health and wellness causes may also be evident such as lack of sleep, poor nutrition, and life stress. Technical causes involve unnoticed changes in athletes' form and execution in their sport, for example, body position, range of motion, and timing in a sport. Particularly in sports that require fine motor skills (e.g., golf, tennis, baseball), subtle changes in technique can have dramatic effects on performance. Slumps may also be caused by unseen changes in equipment. For example, the tension of tennis racquet strings, a loose running shoe, the weight of a baseball bat, or the hockey skate that isn't sufficiently sharp can all have significant effects on how athletes perform.

Lastly, slumps can be caused by psychological factors. Mental contributors to performance declines can be within and outside of sports. On the field of play, changes in motivation, confidence, intensity, focus, and emotions can lead to performance decreases. Additionally, research has found that causal attributions (athletes blaming themselves for poor performance), and a sense of loss of control can lead to slumps (Ball, 2013; Grove & Stoll, 1999). Away from sport, psychological issues including relationship difficulties, financial pressure, academic struggles, and mental health challenges can all lead to declines in performance and slumps.

Practical Implications

With the theoretical and empirical understanding of slumps, the fundamental concern for any consultant is to help athletes get out of them as soon as possible. This process requires collaborative detective work between consultants, athletes, coaches, and other staff involved in athletes' training and competitive efforts (e.g., conditioning, sports medicine). The goal is to explore all of the possible causes for the slump and uncover its root cause. Once identified, steps can be taken to resolve the slump and get athletes back to their pre-slump levels of performance.

Prevention

The best approach to addressing slumps is for consultants to help athletes prevent them from occurring in the first place. Slumps can be averted by understanding their primary causes and taking proactive steps to reduce the chances of those causes happening. When slumps do arise, athletes can respond quickly and effectively to keep the slump to a minimum in terms of impact and duration.

Physical

Slumps can be caused not by a single event, but rather by the typical physical grind of the competitive season. Athletes can get progressively worn down as the season progresses until it finally takes a toll on their performances and leads to a slump (Ball, 2013).

One common physical cause of slumps is the deterioration of athletes' fitness as the season unfolds. If athletes can remain well-conditioned, they will be less vulnerable to fatigue, injury, and illness. As such, one way to prevent the physical causes of slumps is to ensure that athletes engage in an intensive physical conditioning program in the off-season and physical-maintenance program during the competitive season that will mitigate the chances of a slump occurring due to physical deterioration (Greenspan & Feltz, 1989).

Rest is another influential way to prevent slumps. Physical erosion can be reduced by ensuring that athletes incorporate periods of rest into their pre-season and competitive season programs. Sufficient rest can be gained in several ways. Mandatory days off, usually following a competition day, can be included in athletes' weekly training regimens allowing them opportunities for recovery and rejuvenation.

The concept of periodization (Lyakh, Mikołajec, Bujas, & Litkowycz, 2014) involves adjusting the intensity and volume of training that athletes engage in during the course of the year. By reducing the quantity and increase the quality of training as the season progresses, athletes are able to stay healthy and energized and, as a result, are less susceptible to slumps due to physical fatigue.

Consultants can also help athletes and coaches develop a responsible competition schedule that will reduce the chances of slumps occurring. Because competitions themselves can be physically taxing, athletes who compete too frequently are putting themselves at risk of a slump. Athletes and coaches must be highly selective of the chosen competition schedule, only choosing those events that have a clear value and avoiding those that do not have a pre-determined purpose in athletes' competitive goal plan.

With a big competition approaching (e.g., playoffs, championships), consultants can encourage athletes to plan a break two to three weeks prior to the event. This tactic enables athletes to get rested, get over lingering illnesses and injuries, and become reinvigorated physically and mentally, ensuring that they are ready to perform their best in the important competitions that often occur late in the competitive season.

One of the most important lessons that consultants can teach athletes to prevent slumps caused by physical breakdowns is to listen to their bodies. Increasing athlete's self-awareness will give them the ability to recognize and respond to tiredness, illness, and injury, particularly their early subtle symptoms, can enable athletes to prevent slumps before they become a problem (Martin, Wrisberg, Beitel, & Lounsbury, 1997).

Technical

One thing that often occurs when athletes struggle physically is that their technique deteriorates. Their bodies are simply not able to execute properly. Technique is ideally learned and ingrained in the off-season when athletes can concentrate on technical progress without concern for preparing for competitions. Technique-related slumps can also be averted by athletes not attempting to make significant technical changes during the competitive season.

Focusing on technique between competitions can interfere with technique that is working. It can hurt athletes mentally by reducing confidence, causing overthinking and stress, and distracting athletes from just performing their best (Ball, 2013). Also, consultants can help athletes create a library of video "highlights" that can remind them of solid technique and to compare current with previous technique (Greenspan & Feltz, 1989).

Equipment

For sports that are equipment intensive (e.g., tennis, golf, ski racing, archery, sailing), slumps caused by equipment issues usually occur for two reasons. First, equipment breaks down over the course of a season, so it simply cannot do what athletes expect of them. Athletes should inspect and test their equipment on a regular basis to ensure that it is not showing signs of wear. Second, athletes do not take adequate care of their equipment. This issue can be resolved readily by athletes ensuring that they keep their equipment in top condition consistently.

Mental

As discussed above, slumps can be caused by psychological changes at two levels: within and outside of sport. The best way to prevent slumps is for athletes to engage in a comprehensive and consistent mental training program that keeps them mentally sharp through the season (Martin et al., 1997). This preventive approach keeps mental muscles, including motivation, confidence, intensity, and focus, strong. Just like physical muscles, strong mental muscles will be less vulnerable to "injuries" that might be caused by declines in performance or competitive defeats. A thorough mental training program also helps athletes create a mental toolbox that has the tools they need to repair problems quickly and completely when they arise. In addition, this approach to the mental side of slumps gives athletes the means to actively resist the psychological and emotional harm that can occur from disappointing performances. It safeguards athletes from getting trapped in a vicious cycle of negativity and poor performance that can result in a slump.

Second, slumps that occur in sports can be caused by challenges that athletes face outside of their sport including conflicts among family and friends, financial difficulties, and struggles in school or at work. Athletes can prevent these problems from occurring by doing their best to maintain a life in which they manage their stress effectively (Hobfoll, 1988). When difficulties occur off the field, consultants can help athletes to find the support they need and offer guidance for resolving the problems so that the impact on their sports lives will be minimized and slumps caused by these challenges can be avoided.

Slump Intervention Plan

Even the best efforts by athletes to prevent slumps from occurring don't guarantee that they won't. As noted above, slumps are an almost unavoidable aspect of the high-level sports experience. An essential role that consultants can play with athletes involves helping them, when a slump does strike, to get out of it as quickly as possible. For athletes to get out of a slump in the most timely manner, it must be confronted in a structured and committed way. When athletes recognize that they are experiencing a slump, consultants can help them to identify each possible cause and decide how best to resolve it. Athletes' attitude toward the slump also has an impact on their ability to climb out of it and consultants can also help to ensure that athletes establish and maintain a constructive attitude. Some athletes believe that if they are patient, they can ride out the slump. However, in most cases, inaction simply prolongs the slump. Additionally, many athletes have the perception that they can get out of a slump as quickly as they got into it. Yet, slumps require patience combined with taking active steps to get out of them. Athletes must be committed to doing the work and putting in the time necessary to return to their pre-slump level of performance.

Time-out

Before athletes do anything to get out of their slump, consultants can encourage them to take a break from their sport if at all possible. The reason for this change is that as long as athletes stay in the environment in which they are experiencing the slump, the thoughts, emotions, and physiology of the slump will usually maintain its grip on them.

This time-out provides athletes with several benefits. First, the break enables athletes to create physical distance which also creates psychological and emotional distance which, in turn, helps athletes to free themselves from the negative thoughts and emotions that accompany a slump and which makes it easier for them to reorient themselves in a more positive direction. In a sense, the break gives athletes a psychological vacation and, with that distance, offers them the chance to shift to a more constructive perspective with which they can look forward to returning to their sport and relieve themselves of their slump.

Second, slumps take a physical toll on athletes. A time-out enables athletes to rest and rejuvenate, giving them the energy they will need to turn their slump around and return to competitive form.

Third, because slumps rarely disappear on their own, the break offers athletes the chance to study the slump, identify its causes, and develop a plan to surmount it. The time-out also helps athletes to examine the slump dispassionately and objectively and gather the necessary information to respond positively to it.

Analysis

From the unemotional perspective just mentioned, consultants can then collaborate with athletes and their coaches to identify the cause of the slump. They should explore every possible contributor to the decline in performance. Slumps don't just appear for no reason, so even when no cause is evident, sufficient exploration will usually result in finding the cause. Once the cause has been specified, consultants can continue their partnership with athletes and coaches to directly address and resolve the causes.

Goal-setting

A key aspect of the slump intervention plan involves creating a structured program that will alleviate the slump in a progressive manner. This program should consist of a set of goals and use the criteria related to the SMARTER goals described in Chapter 4. The goals should begin with the ultimate goal of relieving the slump and returning to competitive form.

1. **Return-to-form goal.** This goal specifies the level of performance to which athletes want to return.
2. **Causal goals.** These goals address resolving the specific causes of the slump. focus on the level of performance associated with the particular causes of the slump. In cases where there are multiple causes, a goal should be established for each one.
3. **Daily training goals.** These goals involve identifying the specific means by which athletes will relieve the causal goals. In other words, athletes should clarify what exactly they must do in training every day that will progressively address the causes.
4. **Daily performance goals**. Often, athletes don't have the luxury of taking a break from their sport, particularly if the slump arises in the middle of the competitive season or before big events. Consequently, they must continue to perform and compete as they also work to get themselves out of their slump. Daily performance goals offer athletes improved levels of performance that incrementally guide their efforts back toward their pre-slump form.

When athletes commit to and strive toward these goals, they will usually move upward steadily out of their slump. Slump intervention plan offers athletes several important benefits. It gives them hope when the slump has taken it away. The plan offers athletes a greater sense of control when the uncontrollability of slumps can cause them to feel helpless. It also provides them with a clear focus on what they need to do in the present when the distractions of how low they have sunk and worry about whether they can get back can creep into their minds. Lastly, slump intervention plan offers athletes a clear objective they can strive for, which can fuel their motivation to get out of the slump as quickly as possible.

Summary

- Performance slumps are one of the great enigmas of sport because they are virtually inevitable, usually inexplicable, exceedingly frustrating, incredibly exhausting, can be difficult to get out of.
- A slump is defined as "an unexplained decline in performance from a previously determined baseline level of a particular athlete that extends longer than would be expected from normal cyclic variations in performance in a given sport."
- There are four broad categories of slumps: physical, technical, equipment, and psychological.
- The goal for overcoming a slump is to explore all of the possible causes for the slump, uncover its root causes, take steps to resolve the slump, and get athletes back to their pre-slump levels of performance.
- The best approach to addressing slumps is for athletes to prevent them from occurring by staying healthy, rested, and fit, maintaining proper technique, keeping their equipment well maintained, and staying mentally sharp.
- The most effective way to overcome slumps is for athletes to develop a slumpbusting plan that includes having them take a short break from their sport, conducting any analysis to identify the causes, setting specific training and performance goals toward which athletes can aim, and making a committed effort to achieve the goals, and, in doing so, resolve the slump.

References

Ball, C. T. (2013). Unexplained sporting slumps and causal attributions. *Journal of Sport Behavior, 36*(3), 233–242.

Greenspan, M. J., & Feltz, D. F. (1989). Psychological interventions with athletes in competitive situations: A review. *The Sport Psychologist, 3*, 219–236.

Grove, R., & Stoll, O. (1999) Performance slumps in sport: Personal resources and perceived stress. *Journal of Personal & Interpersonal Loss, 4*(3), 203–214.

Hobfoll, S. E. (1988). *The ecology of stress.* New York, NY: Hemisphere.

Lyakh, V., Mikołajec, K., Bujas, P., & Litkowycz, R. (2014). Review of Platonov's "Sports Training Periodization: General Theory and its Practical Application"—Kiev: Olympic literature, 2013. *Journal of Human Kinetics, 44*, 259–263. doi: 10.2478/hukin-2014-0131

Martin, S. B., Wrisberg, C. A., Beitel, P. A., & Lounsbury, J. (1997). NCAA Division I athletes' attitudes toward seeking sport psychology consultation: The development of an objective instrument. *The Sport Psychologist, 11*, 201–218.

Oxford Dictionaries. (2018). Slump. Retrieved from https://en.oxforddictionaries.com/definition/slump

Taylor, J. (1988). Slumpbusting: A systematic analysis of slumps in sports. *The Sport Psychologist, 2*, 39–48.

PSYCHOLOGICAL REHABILITATION OF PHYSICAL INJURY

Karla Kubitz and Jim Taylor

An unfortunate fact of the life of athletes is that most will sustain a serious injury at some point that will put an end to their competitive seasons and, in some cases, threaten their careers. Whether a baseball or softball player's torn rotator cuff, a soccer player's broken ankle, a ski racer's ACL tear, a cyclist's broken collarbone, or a runner's torn Achilles tendon, injuries present athletes with an incredibly difficult physical challenge in healing, rehabilitating, and returning to their sport.

Thankfully, surgical procedures and physical therapy protocols have become so effective at repairing and rehabilitating injuries that a complete physical recovery and return to sport from an injury that two decades ago might have put an end to athletic careers is more the rule than the exception these days. Yet, a thorough physical recovery from injury doesn't guarantee that athletes will return to their pre-injury level of performance.

Another realization that athletes who experience a serious injury have is that it's not just their bodies that are damaged and that need to heal. Rather, they quickly see that their minds also suffer from the physical injury. Athletes experience an array of unpleasant emotions including sadness, frustration, and anger. Their thinking turns negative as they doubt whether they can recover fully. They experience stress, anxiety, and fear as they wonder if they will ever play the sport they love again. These psychological and emotional burdens take a toll on the athletes' abilities to focus on healing, causing a preoccupation with their injuries. These psychological challenges hurt motivation and confidence, both of which are essential for a successful recovery and return to sport.

Despite the recognized mental difficulties of rehabilitating from a serious injury, athletes hear little from surgeons, physical therapists, and athletic trainers about how to recover psychologically and emotionally from their injuries. This section will explore what injured athletes can do to rehabilitate their bodies *and* their minds, so they are fully capable of returning to their sport truly prepared to return to or surpass their pre-injury level of performance.

Theory and Research

A growing body of research is showing that injuries take an immense toll on athletes. Words they use to describe their feelings about their injuries include disappointed, depressed, devastated, annoying, irritable, fearful, worried, isolated, and highly stressed (Mankad, Gordon, & Wallman, 2009). Athletes also report threats to their athletic identity during their rehabilitations, especially when their recovery progress is slow (Brewer, Cornelius, Stephan, & Van Raalte, 2010). Negative psychological reactions can be problematic physically as well; they are positively correlated with self-reported pain during recovery (Brewer et al., 2007).

In the aftermath of a serious injury, athletes do their best to focus on appraising the injury, adopting a positive mindset, and disengaging from the team sport environment, despite the challenges they are confronted with (Ruddock-Hudson, O'Halloran, & Murphy, 2014). As their rehabilitations progress, they are acutely sensitive to the rehabilitation "roller coaster," the challenges of isolation, and finding a sense of renewed optimism (Ruddock-Hudson et al., 2014). Athletes also worry about the consequences of injury on their sport lives, their emotions and their social support, and their relationships with rehabilitation staff (Roy, Mokhtar, Karim, & Mohanan, 2015).

During their return to sport, athletes struggle with the mixed emotions they experience, dealing with the uncertainty and pressure to perform at a high level again, creating psychological readiness to return-to-play, and reaching a positive outcome from the injury experience (Ruddock-Hudson et al., 2014). They also worry about (Podlog, Dimmock, & Miller, 2011; Podlog & Eklund, 2009):

- returning to their pre-injury performance;
- achieving their pre-injury goals;
- establishing realistic expectations for their post-injury performance;
- knowing they've played well in the past, but feeling uncertain about the future;
- staying uninjured;
- feeling isolated from their teammates and coaches and lacking social support;
- feeling pressured by coaches and parents to return to sport;
- letting their coaches and teammates down; and
- overcoming the many challenges of rehabilitation and return to sport.

How athletes react to their injuries, recoveries, and return to sport depends on a number of factors. They are shaped by the team sport emotional climate (i.e., the norms related to risk-taking and pain tolerance; Mankad et al., 2009) and by the athletes' gender (Kontos, Elbin, Newcomer Appaneal, Covassin, & Collins, 2013). Kontos et al. found that females use planning, humor, instrumental support, and venting more than males. In addition, the coping strategies that athletes use change across the phases of rehabilitation and return to sport (Carson & Polman, 2008; Carson & Polman, 2010). Early in their recoveries, injured athletes cope by gathering information on their injury and treatment, using positive self-talk, imagining being fit, finding ways to tolerate pain, and seeking social support. Later, athletes cope by:

- setting short-term rehabilitation goals;
- taking up new hobbies;

- spending time with family and friends;
- seeking support from their rehabilitation team; and
- deepening their understanding of their sport by observing practices, watching video, and listening to coaches.

As athletes return to their sport, they focus on reaching rehabilitation targets; setting specific and realistic return-to-sport goals; seeking support from their teammates and coaches; and continuing to explore their hobbies and other non-sport interests.

A key contributor to a positive rehabilitation experience involves athletes' abilities to develop and maintain a positive attitude during their recoveries. Research has found four important factors that influence whether athletes can maintain a positive mindset throughout their recoveries. First, athletes benefit from developing mental toughness which is defined as a "natural or developed psychological edge that enables mentally tough performers to generally cope better than their opponents with the demands and related pressures that occur at the highest level in sport" (Connaughton, Hanton, & Jones, 2010, p. 168). Mentally tough athletes adhered better during rehabilitation, had more positive attitudes, and used more desirable coping strategies (Levy, Polman, Clough, & McNaughton, 2006; Madrigal, Wurst, & Gill, 2016).

Second, they benefit from developing hardiness which involves: "(a) the belief that they can control . . . the events of their experience, (b) an ability to feel deeply involved in or committed to the activities of their lives, and (c) the anticipation of change as an exciting challenge" (Kobasa, 1979, p. 3). Hardiness predicts the use of more desirable coping strategies during rehabilitation (Wadey, Evans, Hanton, & Neil, 2012).

Third, athletes benefit from making internal, stable, and controllable attributions during recovery. In other words, they benefit from attributing their progress in rehabilitation to their hard work, fitness level, dedication to rehabilitation, and their general good health. Athletes seem to recover more quickly when their attributions align with the self-serving bias (Laubach, Brewer, Van Raalte, & Pepitas, 1996).

Fourth, athletes benefit from showing self-compassion through their struggles which means they experience "understanding, kindness, and openness to one's own suffering" (Huysmans & Clement, 2017, p. 56). Research has found that self-compassion is inversely related to cognitive and somatic anxiety as well as to the use of less desirable coping strategies (Huysmans & Clement, 2017).

Interestingly, athletes also report that their injuries and recoveries can be seen as positive experiences that benefit them in their lives both within and outside of their sports. For example, injured athletes indicate (Brewer, Cornelius, Van Raalte, & Tennen, 2017; Wadey, Evans, Evans, & Mitchell, 2011):

- increased knowledge of anatomy;
- enhanced ability to regulate their emotions;
- stronger social networks;
- improved academic performance;
- improved relationships with their coaches;
- greater tactical awareness;
- healthier nutritional intake and improved fitness;
- elevated confidence;
- greater resilience; and
- more empathy toward other injured athletes.

To get to where they can see their injuries and ensuing rehabilitations as positive, athletes benefit from meta-cognition (i.e., reflecting on their thinking), positive cognitive reappraisal (i.e., changing their negative thinking), positive emotions (e.g., finding hope and optimism), and facilitative responses (e.g., seeking knowledge and committing to rehabilitation; Roy-Davis, Wadey, & Evans, 2017).

Practical Implications

The above review of the extant research provides strong evidence that, when athletes sustain a physical injury, their mind can also become injured. The research also indicates that the mind can play a significant role in helping athletes recover from their injuries and return to their sport. This section will explore practical approaches and strategies that athletes can use in this process.

Keep Perspective

A key first step for consultants who are helping athletes rehabilitate and return to their sport as quickly and safely as possible is to offer them healthy perspectives that will set a positive tone for their recoveries.

Acceptance

This perspective begins with athletes simply accepting that getting injured is unfortunate and that they will feel awful for a while, both physically and mentally, particularly in early in their recoveries. They will experience considerable pain. Athletes will feel unpleasant emotions including despair and frustration. They may also want to give up even before the rehabilitation process has begun. It's important for consultants to convey to athletes that these reactions are a natural, expected, and mostly healthy part of their injury experience because athletes have experienced a loss and they must be allowed to grieve.

Yet, when athletes maintain that negative and emotional orientation, their recoveries will be inhibited both physically and psychologically. Consultants can also play an important role in this transition by helping athletes to shift from negative to positive, from past or future to present, from outcome to process, and from hopelessness to hopefulness.

Long Term

When athletes experience a serious injury, it can, in the moment, feel like a monumental disruption of their journey toward their sports goals. However, with the benefit of hindsight, it can often be seen as a blip on the radar screen of their careers, a temporary hurdle in a sports life full of challenges. Consultants can also help athletes to recognize this long-term perspective which will make the injury less momentous and more manageable.

Rehabilitation is Athletic Performance

Another valuable perspective that athletes can embrace is that rehabilitation is athletic performance. When athletes get hurt, they can feel as if they are no longer athletes and that they are no longer making progress toward their sports goals. Yet, every aspect of a rehabilitation program involves athletic performance. Just like a set of strengthening exercises in the weight room or a set of drills in practice, rehabilitation exercises require many of the same attributes: physical preparation, high motivation and confidence, appropriate intensity, and effective focus. Injured athletes who are able to adopt the perspective that rehabilitation is athletic performance can strengthen their mental muscles and become adept at the mental exercises and tools that are described in Chapters 3 and 4. By strengthening the mental muscles and ingraining the mental exercises and tools during rehabilitation, athletes will be able to transfer them to their sport when they return to the field of play and use them in training and competition more readily and effectively.

Stick with the Rehab Program

One of the most fundamental axioms expressed by sports medicine professionals is that if athletes stick with their rehabilitation program, they will get better and return to their sport as quickly and completely as possible. Unfortunately, athletes can veer away from their rehabilitation regimens in two different directions. First, because physical therapy can be exhausting, painful, and tedious, athletes may lose their motivation and commitment to their programs by either not giving their best effort, cutting short, or failing to show up for rehabilitation sessions. These athletes slow their returns to sport because they are simply not putting in the time and effort necessary to heal and recover fully in the timeliest manner.

At the other end of the continuum of commitment lie athletes who are excessively motivated. This hyper-determination causes these athletes to believe that more is better. As a result, they put in extra physical therapy sessions and do more sets and reps than prescribed by their sports medicine team. Contrary to their intentions, these athletes often slow their rehabilitations by stressing excessively the injured area prematurely and often incur overuse or compensatory injuries. In both cases, whether under- or over-adhering, these athletes' efforts are counterproductive and self-defeating. To reiterate the axiom stated at the beginning of this section: Athletes should adhere precisely, no more and no less, to what their sports medicine team prescribes.

Become a Better Athlete

Serious injuries aren't always the curse that athletes perceive them to be. Instead, they can actually help athletes become more successful in the long run. Injuries do prevent athletes from participating in their sport, thus slowing their technical and tactical progress. They also keep athletes from continuing to improve their physical conditioning. At the same time, injuries also provide valuable opportunities that can help them to become better athletes physically or mentally. The experience of rehabilitating from an injury can help athletes to (Brewer et al., 2017; Roy-Davis et al., 2017; Wadey et al., 2011):

- find their deepest passion and motivation for their sport;
- commit their fullest effort in physical therapy;
- teach them resilience in the face of its many challenges;
- improve their fitness and athleticism around their injury;
- gain confidence in their physical and mental capabilities;
- manage their emotions more effectively; and
- direct their focus to get the most out of their rehabilitation sessions.

As a result, an injury can enable athletes to return to their sport more physically and mentally prepared for success.

There are two challenges that all athletes face when a serious injury keeps them away from their sport. First, they can feel that they are falling behind their teammates and competitors. So, another way in which injured athletes can continue to make progress is to stay involved in their sport and improve some aspect of it. For example, standing on the sidelines and observing practices and competitions can offer athletes an entirely new perspective on and understanding of their sport that can benefit them when they return to their sport after rehabilitation. Injured athletes can identify areas in which they can learn more, such as technique and tactics, and become students of their sport. They can become volunteer or apprentice coaches during their rehabilitations, allowing them to listen in on and learn from their coaches.

Second, the lives of serious athletes usually revolve around their sport. An injury, and the separation from their team that occurs during rehabilitation, can cause them to feel isolated from and unsupported by their teammates. This feeling of not being a regular part of their team can hurt injured athletes psychologically and emotionally, draining their motivation and confidence, and causing feelings of sadness and frustration. Many of the positive things they used to gain from their sport are no longer available. Injured athletes should actively maintain their relationships with their teammates and seek out opportunities to interact with them on a regular basis.

Redirect Their Energy

Perhaps the most challenging aspect of sustaining a serious injury is that athletes aren't able to express their athletic identities and do what they love to do. This obstacle can cause athletes to feel adrift in their lives and unclear on where to direct the energy that would ordinarily be put into their sport. An additional drawback is that athletes no longer have the source from which they have received significant affirmation, value, fulfillment, and enjoyment in their lives.

The best antidote to this psychological and practical loss is for athletes to seek out other avenues toward which they can direct their time and energy. Examples can include school, family and friends, reading, music, and cooking. The specific activity is less important than the fact that it provides athletes with a way to spend their time and a source of satisfaction that they had previously gotten from their sport. This strategy has several benefits. It makes athletes feel better about themselves at a time when they are in need of affirmation. The activity generates positive emotions when athletes struggle against a torrent of negative emotions. It also distracts them from the disappointment caused by injury and the many challenges they face in their recoveries.

Set Goals

Just like in other aspects of their sports lives, goal-setting can be an effective tool for instilling motivation and providing direction to injured athletes as they progress through their rehabilitations and returns to sport. Research has shown the value of goal-setting in the recovery from injury. It benefits rehabilitation self-efficacy and rehabilitation adherence (Evans & Hardy, 2002a, 2002b). Levack et al. (2016) also reported that structured goal-setting had a significant effect on self-reported emotional status and patient self-efficacy.

There should be three foci as athletes set goals around their recoveries. One set of goals should be established related to their physical rehabilitation including long-term and daily goals. Another set of goals should be directed toward improving themselves mentally. A third set of goals should be aimed at developing different aspects of their sports performances. Consultants can refer to Chapter 4 as they guide injured athletes in developing a goal-setting program that encompasses these three areas of surrounding their rehabilitation and return to sport.

Develop a Rehab Imagery Program

Mental imagery may be the single most powerful mental exercise that injured athletes can use to facilitate their rehabilitations and return to their sport. As discussed in detail in Chapter 4, imagery is a psychological and physical experience that can help athletes in many ways.

Imagery produces a plethora of physiological benefits including improvements in muscle activation (Lebon, Guillot, & Collet, 2012), ability to walk (Cho, Kim, & Lee, 2013; Li, Li, Tan, Chen, & Lin, 2017), shoulder function (Hoyek, Di Rienzo, Collet, Hoyek, & Guillot, 2014), knee function (Maddison et al., 2012; Wilczyńska, Łysak, & Podczarska-Głowacka, 2015), and pain (Hoyek et al., 2014; Wilczyñska et al., 2015). It also results in decreases in the neurotransmitters associated with stress (Maddison et al., 2012). Imagery produces psychological and behavioral benefits, including increased satisfaction with rehabilitation (Cressman & Dawson, 2011) and increased rehabilitation adherence (Wesch et al., 2012). In addition, Driediger, Hall, and Callow (2006) found that athletes used imagery to:

- relearn previously automated skills;
- motivate themselves during rehabilitation;
- control stress and facilitate relaxation;
- maintain focus during rehabilitation exercises;
- speed healing;
- manage pain; and
- prevent reinjury.

Considerable research has demonstrated that athletes can improve their sports skills with the consistent use of imagery (Catenacci, Harris, Langdon, Scott, & Czech, 2015; Davies, Boxall, Szekeres, & Greenlees, 2014; Marshall & Gibson, 2017; Ploszay, Gentner, Skinner, & Wrisberg, 2006; Slimani et al., 2016). The use of imagery benefits injured athletes by helping them to feel that they are continuing to improve rather than falling behind in their sport. When injured athletes do imagery, seeing and feeling themselves perform in their sport increases motivation, builds confidence, and maintains and strengthens focus (Driediger et al., 2006; Evans, Hare, & Mullen, 2006; Hare, Evans, & Caddick, 2008).

The value of imagery can be strengthened further by combining it with action observation, which refers to "observing oneself (via video) or a model (via video or live) executing the desired action successfully" (Neuman & Gray, 2013, p. 11). Scott, Taylor, Chesterton, Vogt, and Eaves (2018) compared imagery and imagery combined with action observation and found that the latter condition increased physical strength more than the former condition. They contend that imagery combined with action observation "offers a well-suited addendum to current practice in sports training and injury rehabilitation" (Scott et al., 2018, p. 1449).

Rehabilitating athletes will gain the full benefits of imagery by developing and implementing a structured and consistent imagery program that focuses on both the rehabilitation process and their sports performance. Consultants can help them to create an imagery program that will meet their needs and goals during their recoveries and returns to sport using the information provided in Chapter 4 and applied to injury rehabilitation.

Journaling

Journaling is a strategy that hasn't received very much attention as a practical tool for facilitating injury rehabilitation and return to sport. At the same time, there is an emerging body of evidence demonstrating its value to athletes psychologically and physically. Research suggests that journaling is an effective tool for managing emotions during recovery. For example, Mankad and Gordon (2010) examined the effects of therapeutic writing sessions on athletes' post-injury grief responses. They found writing resulted in lower levels of grief responses (i.e., feeling devastated, dispirited, and cheated). Along the same lines, Duncan et al. (2013) examined the effects of writing sessions on psychological distress (i.e., mood, reinjury anxiety, and depression) and injury mobility. Over a three-day period, athletes wrote about: (1) "the occurrence of the injury"; (2) "the emotions and feelings at the time of injury"; and (3) "their current perspective on the injury, possible psychological growth, and future coping" (Duncan et al., 2013, p. 3). Duncan and colleagues found that participants in the injury-writing group had higher levels of mobility at the posttest as compared to the pretest. It's likely that this physical effect is mediated by a decrease in anxiety and related muscle tension.

Because journaling is outside the normal approaches to injury rehabilitation, consultants are encouraged to take several steps to get the injured athletes' buy-in for its use. They can explain its rationale and provide a structure for journaling to the athlete. Consultants can enlist the sports medicine team to support its use. They can also hold athletes accountable by asking them to share their reflections when they meet.

Bottom Line

There is no doubt that a serious injury is a major setback for athletes and can take an immense toll on them physically and psychologically. At the same time, the more difficult challenge, particularly in the long run, is when athletes are not returning completely or as quickly to their sport as they could have. For athletes to have a successful rehabilitation and return to sport, they must take advantage of every opportunity and leverage every tool at their disposal. That includes fully committing to their physical therapy regimen. It also involves devoting time and energy to rehabilitating their minds alongside of their bodies. The goal is that when athletes return to their sport, they are physically and mentally prepared to return to and surpass their pre-injury level of performance.

Summary

- An unfortunate fact of the life of an athlete is that most will sustain a serious injury at some point that will put an end to their competitive seasons and, in some cases, threaten their careers.
- Surgical procedures and physical therapy protocols have become so effective at repairing and rehabilitating injuries that a complete physical recovery and return to sport from an injury that 20 years ago might have put an end to athletic careers is more the rule than the exception these days.
- A realization that athletes who experience a serious injury have is that it's not just their bodies that are damaged and that need to heal; rather, they quickly see that their minds also suffer from the physical injury.
- A growing body of research is showing that injuries take an immense toll on athletes. They describe their feelings about their injuries using words like disappointed, depressed, devastated, annoying, irritable, fearful, worried, isolated, and highly stressed.
- Research has found four important elements that influence whether athletes can maintain a positive mindset throughout their recoveries: mental toughness, a sense of control, making internal, stable, controllable attributions during recovery, and showing self-compassion.
- Athletes lay the foundation for a successful recovery and return to sport by adopting a perspective that includes accepting their injury, looking long term, and looking at rehabilitation as a form of athletic performance.

- One of the most fundamental axioms expressed by sports medicine professionals is that if athletes stick with their rehabilitation program, they will get better and return to their sport as quickly and completely as possible.
- Athletes can use their injuries as an opportunity to become better athletes.
- Athletes can redirect their energies towards other aspects of their lives.
- Practical strategies that athletes can use during their recoveries include goal-setting, imagery, and journaling.

References

Brewer, B. W., Cornelius, A. E., Sklar, J. H., Van Raalte, J. L., Tennen, H., Armeli, S., . . . Brickner, J. C. (2007). Pain and negative mood during rehabilitation after anterior cruciate ligament reconstruction: A daily process analysis. *Scandinavian Journal of Medicine and Science in Sports*, 17(5), 520–529. doi: 10.1111/j.1600-0838.2006.00601.x

Brewer, B. W., Cornelius, A. E., Stephan, Y., & Van Raalte, J. (2010). Self-protective changes in athletic identity following anterior cruciate ligament reconstruction. *Psychology of Sport and Exercise*, 11(1), 1–5. doi: 10.1016/j.psychsport.2009.09.005

Brewer, B. W., Cornelius, A. E., Van Raalte, J. L., & Tennen, H. (2017). Adversarial growth after anterior cruciate ligament reconstruction. *Journal of Sport and Exercise Psychology*, 39(2), 134–144. doi: 10.1123/jsep.2016-0210

Carson, F., & Polman, R. C. J. (2008). ACL injury rehabilitation: A psychological case study of a professional rugby union player. *Journal of Clinical Sport Psychology*, 2, 71–90.

Carson, F., & Polman, R. C. J. (2010). The facilitative nature of avoidance coping within sports injury rehabilitation. *Scandinavian Journal of Medicine and Science in Sports*, 20(2), 235–240. doi: 10.1111/j.1600-0838.2009.00890.x

Catenacci, K. L., Harris, B. S., Langdon, J. L., Scott, M. K., & Czech, D. R. (2015). Using a MG-M imagery intervention to enhance the sport competence of young special Olympics athletes. *Journal of Imagery Research in Sport and Physical Activity*, 2015(1), 1–12. doi: 10.1515/jirspa-2015-0002

Cho, H., Kim, J., & Lee, G.-C. (2013). Effects of motor imagery training on balance and gait abilities in post-stroke patients: a randomized controlled trial. *Clinical Rehabilitation*, 27(8), 675–680. doi: 10.1177/0269215512464702

Connaughton, D., Hanton, S., & Jones, G. (2010). The development and maintenance of mental toughness in the world's best performers. *Framework*, 24(2002), 168–193. doi: 10.1080/02640410701310958

Cressman, J. M., & Dawson, K. A. (2011). Evaluation of the use of healing imagery in athletic injury rehabilitation. *Journal of Imagery Research in Sport and Physical Activity*, 6(1), 1–25.

Davies, J., Boxall, S., Szekeres, Z., & Greenlees, I. (2014). Developing equestrian training quality and self-efficacy using cognitive-specific imagery. *Sport & Exercise Psychological Society*, 10(1).

Driediger, M., Hall, C., & Callow, N. (2006). Imagery use by injured athletes: A qualitative analysis. *Journal of Sports Sciences*, 24(3), 261–271. doi: 10.1080/02640410500128221

Duncan, E., Gidron, Y., Lavallee, D., Lin, K.-H., Schmitter-Edgecombe, M., & Wu, Y. (2013). Can written disclosure reduce psychological distress and increase objectively measured injury mobility of student-athletes? A randomized controlled trial. *ISRN Rehabilitation*, article 784249. doi: 10.1155/2013/784249

Evans, L., & Hardy, L. (2002a). Injury rehabilitation: A goal-setting intervention study. *Research Quarterly for Exercise & Sport*, 73(3), 310–319.

Evans, L., & Hardy, L. (2002b). Injury rehabilitation: A qualitative follow-up study, 73(3), 320–329.

Evans, L., Hare, R., & Mullen, R. (2006). Imagery use during rehabilitation from injury. *Journal of Imagery Research in Sport and Physical Activity*, 1(1). doi: 10.2202/1932-0191.1000

Hare, R., Evans, L., & Caddick, N. (2008). Imagery use during rehabilitation from injury: A case study of an elite athlete. *The Sport Psychologist*, 22, 405–422. doi: 10.1123/tsp.22.4.405

Hoyek, N., Di Rienzo, F., Collet, C., Hoyek, F., & Guillot, A. (2014). The therapeutic role of motor imagery on the functional rehabilitation of a stage II shoulder impingement syndrome. *Disability and Rehabilitation*, 36(13), 1113–1119. doi: 10.3109/09638288.2013.833309

Huysmans, Z., & Clement, D. (2017). A preliminary exploration of the application of self-compassion within the context of sport injury. *Journal of Sport and Exercise Psychology*, 39(1), 56–66. doi: 10.1123/jsep.2016-0144

Kobasa, S. C. (1979). Stressful life events, personality, and health: An inquiry into hardiness. *Journal of Personality and Social Psychology*, 37(1), 1–11. doi: 10.1037//0022-3514.37.1.1

Kontos, A. P., Elbin, R. J., Newcomer Appaneal, R., Covassin, T., & Collins, M. W. (2013). A comparison of coping responses among high school and college athletes with concussion, orthopedic injuries, and healthy controls. *Research in Sports Medicine*, 21(4), 367–379. doi: 10.1080/15438627.2013.825801

Laubach, W. J., Brewer, B. W., Van Raalte, J. L., & Pepitas, A. (1996). Attributions for recovery and adherence to sport injury rehabilitation. *The Australian Journal of Science and Medicine in Sport*, 28(1), 30–34.

Lebon, F., Guillot, A., & Collet, C. (2012). Increased muscle activation following motor imagery during the rehabilitation of the anterior cruciate ligament. *Applied Psychophysiology Biofeedback*, 37(1), 45–51. doi: 10.1007/s10484-011-9175-9

Levack, W. M. M., Weatherall, M., Hay-Smith, E. J. C., Dean, S. G., Mcpherson, K., & Siegert, R. J. (2016). Goal setting and strategies to enhance goal pursuit in adult rehabilitation: summary of a Cochrane systematic review and meta-analysis. *European Journal of Physical and Rehabilitation Medicine, 52*(3), 400–416.

Levy, A. R., Polman, R. C. J., Clough, P. J., & McNaughton, L. R. (2006). Adherence to sport injury rehabilitation programmes: A conceptual review. *Research in Sports Medicine, 14*(2), 149–162. doi: 10.1080/15438620600651132

Li, R. Q., Li, Z. M., Tan, J. Y., Chen, G. L., & Lin, W. Y. (2017). Effects of motor imagery on walking function and balance in patients after stroke: A quantitative synthesis of randomized controlled trials. *Complementary Therapies in Clinical Practice, 28*(1), 75–84. doi: 10.1016/j.ctcp.2017.05.009

Maddison, R., Prapavessis, H., Clatworthy, M., Hall, C., Foley, L., Harper, T., . . . Brewer, B. (2012). Guided imagery to improve functional outcomes post-anterior cruciate ligament repair: Randomized-controlled pilot trial. *Scandinavian Journal of Medicine and Science in Sports, 22*(6), 816–821. doi: 10.1111/j.1600-0838.2011.01325.x

Madrigal, L., Wurst, K., & Gill, D. L. (2016). The role of mental toughness in coping and injury response in female roller derby and rugby athletes. *Journal of Clinical Sport Psychology, 10*(2), 137–154. doi: 10.1123/JCSP.2015-0021

Mankad, A., & Gordon, S. (2010). Psycholinguistic changes in athletes' grief response to injury after written emotional disclosure. *Journal of Sport Rehabilitation, 19*, 328–342. doi: 10.1123/jsr.19.3.328

Mankad, A., Gordon, S., & Wallman, K. (2009). Perceptions of emotional climate among injured athletes. *Journal of Clinical Sport Psychology, 3*(1), 1–14. Retrieved from http://ezaccess.libraries.psu.edu/login?url=http://search.ebscohost.com/login.aspx?direct=true&db=sph&AN=36829440&site=ehost-live&scope=site

Marshall, E. A., & Gibson, A. M. (2017). The effect of an imagery training intervention on self-confidence, anxiety and performance in acrobatic gymnastics: A pilot study. *Journal of Imagery Research in Sport and Physical Activity, 12*(1). doi: 10.1515/jirspa-2016-0009

Neuman, B., & Gray, R. (2013). A direct comparison of the effects of imagery and action observation on hitting performance. *Movement & Sport Sciences—Science & Motricité, 21*(79), 11–21. doi: 10.1051/sm/2012034

Ploszay, A. J., Gentner, N. B., Skinner, C. H., & Wrisberg, C. A. (2006). The effects of multisensory imagery in conjunction with physical movement rehearsal on golf putting performance. *Journal of Behavioral Education, 15*(4), 247–255. doi: 10.1007/s10864-006-9034-6

Podlog, L., Dimmock, J., & Miller, J. (2011). A review of return to sport concerns following injury rehabilitation: Practitioner strategies for enhancing recovery outcomes. *Physical Therapy in Sport, 12*(1), 36–42. doi: 10.1016/j.ptsp.2010.07.005

Podlog, L., & Eklund, R. C. (2009). High-level athletes' perceptions of success in returning to sport following injury. *Psychology of Sport and Exercise, 10*(5), 535–544. doi: 10.1016/j.psychsport.2009.02.003

Roy, J., Mokhtar, A. H., Karim, S. A., & Mohanan, S. A. (2015). Cognitive appraisals and lived experiences during injury rehabilitation: A narrative account within personal and situational backdrop. *Asian Journal of Sports Medicine, 6*(3). doi: 10.5812/asjsm.24039

Roy-Davis, K., Wadey, R., & Evans, L. (2017). A grounded theory of sport injury-related growth. *Sport Exercise and Performance Psychology, 6*(1), 35–51. doi: 10.1037/spy0000080

Ruddock-Hudson, M., O'Halloran, P., & Murphy, G. (2014). The psychological impact of long-term injury on Australian Football League players. *Journal of Applied Sport Psychology, 26*(4), 377–394. doi: 10.1080/10413200.2014.897269

Scott, M., Taylor, S., Chesterton, P., Vogt, S., & Eaves, D. L. (2018). Motor imagery during action observation increases eccentric hamstring force: an acute non-physical intervention. *Disability and Rehabilitation, 40*(12), 1443–1451. doi: 10.1080/09638288.2017.1300333

Slimani, M., Bragazzi, N. L., Tod, D., Dellal, A., Hue, O., Cheour, F., . . . Chamari, K. (2016). Do cognitive training strategies improve motor and positive psychological skills development in soccer players? Insights from a systematic review. *Journal of Sports Sciences, 34*(24), 2338–2349. doi: 10.1080/02640414.2016.1254809

Wadey, R., Evans, L., Evans, K., & Mitchell, I. (2011). Perceived benefits following sport injury: A qualitative examination of their antecedents and underlying mechanisms. *Journal of Applied Sport Psychology, 23*(2), 142–158. doi: 10.1080/10413200.2010.543119

Wadey, R., Evans, L., Hanton, S., & Neil, R. (2012). An examination of hardiness throughout the sport injury process. *British Journal of Health Psychology, 17*(1), 103–128. doi: 10.1111/j.2044-8287.2011.02025.x

Wesch, N., Hall, C., Prapavessis, H., Maddison, R., Bassett, S., Foley, L., . . . Forwell, L. (2012). Self-efficacy, imagery use, and adherence during injury rehabilitation. *Scandinavian Journal of Medicine and Science in Sports, 22*(5), 695–703. doi: 10.1111/j.1600-0838.2011.01304.x

Wilczyńska, D., Łysak, A., & Podczarska-Głowacka, M. (2015). Imagery use in rehabilitation after the knee joint arthroscopy. *Baltic Journal of Health & Physical Activity, 7*(4), 93–101.

PART II

Athlete Physical and Mental Health

7

ATHLETE HEALTH AND WELL-BEING

Introduction

Faye F. Didymus and Jim Taylor

Success on the field of play doesn't just mean that athletes must focus on developing specific aspects of their sport such as conditioning, technique, tactics, and equipment. What happens away from their sport matters as well. They must consistently balance their athletic efforts, including conditioning, sport training, recovery, competition, with other aspects of their lives such as school, work, and relationships. As noted previously, when athletes enter the competitive arena, they don't leave their "personness" on the sidelines. What is going on in their broader lives has a direct impact on athletes physically and psychologically, and, by extension, their practice and competitive efforts. Second, most athletes are only serious athletes for a part of their daily lives; they also attend school, work, engage in a variety of other activities, and are family members and friends. Additionally, if they are fortunate, athletes' careers will last into their thirties and, for most, their careers will last a much shorter time. So, they will have many decades ahead of them in which their primary identity will be as people, not athletes. As a result, it is incumbent on athletes, and the consultants with whom they work, to broaden their view of themselves beyond the role of athlete and consider themselves in the broader context of their overall health and well-being.

Simply put, for athletes to perform at their highest levels, they must also maintain optimal health and well-being in their lives. This chapter focuses on five essential areas that influence this relationship between sports and life. The first section explores the impact of athletes' *physical health* on sports performances and general health and well-being. It also examines the importance of sleep and the roles that nutrition and hydration play in performance and health. The second section focuses on athletes addressing *stress* both within and outside of their sports lives. The third section discusses the roles of *well-being* in performance and health. In the fourth section, the challenges of *at-risk athletes* are explored. Finally, the fifth section considers the impact of *athletic career transition* on athletes' sports participation and life after sport. Collectively, these sections provide insight into contemporary thinking that will help consultants to better understand the interaction between sports performance and the health and well-being of athletes. This chapter also provides consultants with valuable information and useful tools they can use to ensure that athletes' health and well-being is their foremost priority.

PHYSICAL HEALTH

Sharon A. Chirban, Robin Amylon, and Christina Figueroa

Athlete health is a complicated subject. Athletes are tasked by parents, coaches, and themselves with performing at their highest level consistently in pursuit of their sports goals. Unfortunately, the singular quest for athletic success often has its costs in which many aspects of their broader lives are relegated to lower priority than sport.

Student-athletes have particular challenges because they must make a significant commitment to their sport, but also make a similar commitment to their academics.

Consultants can have a meaningful impact on athletes not only in their athletic lives, but also in their general health. In fact, it could be argued that consultants' first and foremost responsibility is to the athletes' health for several reasons. First, athletes will be committed athletes for only so many years, but they will be people their entire lives. Second, consultants should prioritize athletes' long-term health over results. Third, when athletes pay attention to their health, their competitive performances frequently improve.

Theory and Research

The life of dedicated athletes who also strives for health is an ever-challenging dance of meeting sometimes-conflicting needs and goals. It requires that athletes find a balance between what happens on and off the field. This balance is difficult to find and maintain because an certain ethos about sports has been cultivated in the contemporary sports culture that highlights prioritizing sports over everything else, sacrificing all else for the sport, striving to be the best, taking risks, and challenging limits as a model for behavior (Hughes & Coakley, 1991). Hence, committed participation in sport becomes especially vulnerable to corruption (Hughes & Coakley, 1991) and it can prove to be a destructive rather than life-affirming experience for athletes. This ethos, though ostensibly beneficial for athletic success, can also unintentionally put athletes at risk. Athletes often fall out of balance in their lives in ways that have significant physical and psychological implications. This conflict is especially impactful when they develop an over-commitment and over-conformity to the demands of their sport. This mindset is adopted when athletes prioritize their sports participation over other aspects of their lives without fully understanding the effects it will have on their broader lives. Indeed, highly committed athletes often have a belief that they must do anything to achieve a high level of performance and accomplish their sport goals (Hughes & Coakley, 1991).

Overcommitment and Overconformity

A decline in health have been observed when athletes care too much for, accept too completely, and over-conform to what has become the value system of sport itself (Hughes & Coakley, 1991). The notions of overcommitment and overconformity are behavioral manifestations of the concept of overinvestment described in Chapter 2. One example of an over-committed athlete is a collegiate thrower who used the "110% rule" every time he trained. After disk fusion surgery and eleven months of physical therapy, his surgeon instructed him that back squatting was no longer a safe activity if he wanted to stay injury free and continue competing. During that season's max lift session, he could not say no when the strength coach put him under the rack to back squat (*do what he is told*). As his numbers increased and his teammates were cheering with excitement, he hit a 500-pound one-rep max, the highest weight of his cohort that day (*be the best*). He felt a twinge in his back with some numbness which he kept to himself and continuing to smile, despite the discomfort (*do not show weakness*), as he relished his teammates' admiration. In his next sport psychology consultation, he berated himself for his "stupidity" because he had become quite anxious that his inability to resist the coach and the ego-stroking of his strength numbers may have put his back's health and his last eligible season in jeopardy.

This kind of excessive and detrimental commitment to the sport ethos creates a counterintuitive shift in behavior for athletes. What often is perceived as being in the service of sport may lead to overuse or acute injury, burnout, eating disorders, substance abuse, loss of motivation, and early retirement. Overconformity is often prevalent among athletes whose self-identities are excessively dependent on their sports efforts for validation, have low self-esteem, and are unable to resist the messages of the sport ethos from their coaches, parents, and others. Additionally, overconformity is found in athletes who perceive few options for success in their lives, so come to believe that their only path to success is through sport. With this belief, they feel compelled to accept the extreme demands and commitment that the prevailing sports culture imposes on them. The result is that these overinvested athletes who overcommit and overconform often engage in behaviors that are ultimately self-defeating to their sports aspirations and their general physical health.

Sleep

The days when athletes bragging about sleep deprivation as an indication of toughness are over. The importance of sleep to athletic performance is well documented. For example, one hour less sleep from an athlete's sleep routine causes naturally occurring human growth hormone to be compromised. Sleep is essential to athlete reaction time, focus, and physical recovery. Athletes in youth, high-school, and collegiate sports are often trying to balance the demands of sport with many other life demands and sleep is often sacrificed. Inadequate sleep is also associated with increased injury risk (Luke et al., 2011). Thun et al. (2015) indicate that sports requiring longer sustained effort, such as running and cycling, do not improve after athletes experience insufficient sleep. These sleep studies also showed that participants who were sleep deprived were less motivated to endure discomfort from physical activity after experiencing sleep deprivation. They also found that extending sleep over a period of time and incorporating naps into a daily schedule can improve performance (Thun et al., 2015). A newly held belief is that athletes not only need adequate sleep at night, but also that strategically placed naps can serve the overall performance and recovery of athletes.

Sleep for committed athletes functions as a restorative effect for the endocrine system, helps recovery from the nervous and metabolic cost of being awake, and helps cognitive development because sleep plays a critical role in learning and memory (Fullagar et al., 2015). Studies comparing athletes who get enough sleep to those who do not demonstrate significant differences in motor tasks. Particularly before and after competitions, it is essential for athletes to get enough sleep so that they are properly rested both physically and mentally for competition and so they can recover effectively after competition, respectively.

Serious athletes follow long and intensive practice and competitive schedules that can lead to fatigue, illness and injury. Demanding sports regimen, including early morning practices, double workouts, and night-time competitions, can create an imbalance in athletes' lives and prevent them from finding time in their schedule to get the seven or more hours of sleep they need to perform at their optimal performance level. According to several reports, athletes can experience poorer mood states after sleep restriction, decreases in vigor, and increases in depression, sleepiness, and confusion (Fullagar et al., 2015). These negative mood states have been linked to athletes who are over-training and participating too much in their sport (Fullagar et al., 2015).

Insufficient sleep in athletes also affects their cognitive capabilities. An increase in physiological fatigue due to decrease in sleep can create a "neurocognitive state not conducive for either engaging in physical activity requiring a high motivational component or employing optimal decision making" (Fullagar et al., 2015, p. 180). When athletes are not getting enough sleep, deficits of motivation, confidence, and intensity, and focus can lead to a decline in performance, increased risk of injury, poor decision making, and a loss of enjoyment and desire to continue to their participation in their sport.

Nutrition

Nutrition is another important contributor to athletes' health. Simply put, nutrition is the fuel that propels sports performance. It plays an essential role in:

- overall physical health (both immediate and long-term);
- mental health;
- motivation;
- energy level;
- focus;
- training quality;
- competitive effort;
- injury prevention; and
- recovery from training.

Proper nutrition before, during, and after intense training and competitive efforts is critical for optimizing athletic performance. A successful nutrition plan should be individualized for athletes taking into account:

- demands of the sport;
- position played;
- training load;
- lifestyle;
- personal physiology;
- time in the season;
- individual nutrition needs;
- level of stress; and
- co-occurring medical complications (e.g., eating disorders, osteopenia/osteoporosis, diabetes).

Adequate caloric intake is also important to maintain lean muscle mass, reduce unnecessary weight gain or loss, normal functioning of the reproductive and immune systems, and enhance athletic performance (Thomas, Erdman, & Burke, 2016).

To help demonstrate the effects that nutrition has on athletic performance, it will be useful to describe the negative consequences of inadequate nutrition. Athletes who do not consume adequate energy are at increased risk of fatigue, nutrient deficiencies, infection, illness, injury, anemia, and decreased strength, endurance, mobility and muscle mass. When severe caloric restriction continues, even more severe consequences arise including excessive weight loss, decreased basal metabolic rate, decreased bone mineral density, cardiovascular and gastrointestinal issues, loss of menstrual periods in female athletes, decreased testosterone levels in male athletes can occur, and a decline in athletic performance (Rosenbloom & Coleman, 2012; Thomas et al., 2016). The effects of insufficient nutrition on athletic performance can include decreases in:

- energy;
- response to training;
- endurance;
- concentration;
- muscle strength;
- glycogen stores; and
- coordination.

Other effects include increased risk of injury, depression, and irritability, and impaired judgement. Athletes must consume adequate kilocalories to avoid fatigue, preserve lean body mass, and avoid negative side effects associated with chronic low energy intake (Rosenbloom & Coleman, 2012; Thomas et al., 2016).

The majority of an athlete's diet should consist of carbohydrates (Rosenbloom & Coleman, 2012; Thomas et al., 2016). Adequate carbohydrate stores are crucial for optimal performance during endurance and high-intensity training. Hansen et al. (2014) found that marathon runners who consumed a higher carbohydrate diet were significantly faster than those who consumed a lower carbohydrate diet. Wilson et al. (2013) reported that marathon runners who ingested carbohydrates the day before and morning of a marathon had significantly faster times than those who did not. Protein is also necessary to repair and maintain muscle tissue (Rodriguez, 2013). Protein needs are increased for athletes to maintain lean body mass, promote muscle synthesis, and recover and repair muscle damage after intense exercise. Athletes who do not consume adequate amounts of protein or kilocalories have an increase in protein degradation. Athletes should consume adequate protein and kilocalories to support lean body mass and overall health (Rodriguez, 2013).

Adequate fluid and micronutrient intake are also important. Indeed, dehydration of as little as 2% body weight can impair athletic performance. It is important that athletes consume adequate fluids before, during, and after their training and competitive efforts to maintain and replenish their hydration levels. Stresses from exercise may also increase the need of certain micronutrients such as vitamin D, calcium, iron, and antioxidants. Athletes who consume an inadequate diet due to energy restriction, elimination of certain food groups, or extreme weight-loss practices are at increased risk of micronutrient deficiency (Thomas et al., 2016).

Practical Implications

As discussed in great length in Chapter 2, consultants can play an essential role in helping athletes to address the challenges of overcommitment and overconformity (referred to as overinvestment in Chapter 2).

Consultants can work with athletes to reduce their investment of their self-identities, self-esteem, and goals to a healthy level, provide balance in their lives, to develop or shift attitudes related to overinvestment that will lay the foundation for practices and habits that will foster their physical health and, by extension, their sports performances.

Additionally, few consultants in applied sport psychology or mental training also have expertise in the physical health aspects of athlete performance such as nutrition and sleep. As a consequence, consultants would be well served to collaborate with experts in these two areas of physical health to ensure that the athletes with whom they work are engaging in sleep and nutritional practices that support their sports efforts.

At the same time, consultants can, with the support of the domain experts, help athletes to integrate these physical health areas into their overall sports development and performance regimens. Consultants can help athletes develop a sleep plan that will ensure that they get a sufficient amount of rest each night to allow their bodies to recover and regain the energy they lost from the previous day's sport-related efforts. In addition, Individualized self-awareness programs integrating metrics (e.g., hours of sleep each night, meal and nutrition tracking) around physical health will help athletes attend to the ever-shifting balance between exertion and recovery. Consultants can help athletes reality test their perceptions of their overall physical health and daily health-relate habits to ensure that they are maximally every physical area that may impact their sports performances.

Summary

- The singular quest for athletic success often has its costs in which many aspects of their broader lives, including their physical health, are relegated to lower priority than sport.
- This balance is difficult to find and maintain because a certain ethic about sports has been cultivated in the contemporary sports culture that prioritizes sports over everything else, sacrifice for the sport, striving to be the best, taking risks, and challenging limits as a model for behavior.
- Physical health can suffer when athletes care too much for, accept too completely, and overconform to what has become the value system of the sport in which they participate.
- This kind of commitment to the sport ethos creates a counterintuitive shift in behavior for athletes in which what may be perceived as in service of sport may lead to overuse or acute injury, burnout, eating disorders, substance abuse, or early retirement.
- Consultants can have a meaningful impact on athletes not only in their athletic lives, but also in their general physical health.
- Consultants' first and foremost responsibility is to the athletes' health because athletes will be committed athletes for only so many years, but they will be people their entire lives, consultants should prioritize athletes' long-term health over results, and when athletes pay attention to their health, their competitive performances frequently improve.
- Sleep research has found that athletes who experience insufficient sleep suffer many physical and psychological consequences.
- A newly held belief is that athletes not only need adequate sleep at night, but also that strategically placed naps can serve the overall performance and recovery of athletes.
- Consultants can help athletes develop a sleep plan that will ensure that they get a sufficient amount of sleep each night to allow the body to recover, reset, and regain the energy it lost from the previous day's sport-related efforts.
- Nutrition is another important contributor to athletes' health acting as the fuel that propels sports performance.
- Athletes who do not consume adequate energy are at increased risk of fatigue, nutrient deficiencies, infection, illness, injury, anemia, and decreased strength, endurance, mobility, and muscle mass.
- The majority of an athlete's diet should consist of carbohydrates. It is important that athletes consume adequate fluids before, during, and after their training and competitive efforts to maintain replenish their hydration levels.
- A successful nutrition plan should be individualized for athletes taking into account the demands of the sport, the position played, training load, lifestyle, personal physiology, time in the season, individual nutrition needs, level of stress, and co-occurring medical complications (e.g., eating disorders, osteopenia/osteoporosis, diabetes).
- Few consultants also have expertise in the physical health aspects of athlete performance such as nutrition and sleep, so they would be well served to collaborate with experts in these two areas of physical health to ensure that the athletes with whom they work are engaging in sleep and nutritional practices that support their sports efforts.

References

Fullagar, H. K., Skorski, S., Duffield, R., Hammes, D., Coutts, A. J., & Meyer, T. (2015). Sleep and athletic performance: The effects of sleep loss on exercise performance, and physiological and cognitive responses to exercise. *Sports Medicine, 45,* 161–186.

Hansen, E. A., Emanuelsen, A., Gertsen, R. M., & Sorensen, S. R. (2014). Improved marathon performance by in-race nutritional strategy intervention. *International Journal of Sport Nutrition and Exercise Metabolism, 24,* 645–655.

Hughes, R., & Coakley, J. (1991). Positive deviance among athletes: The implications of overconformity to the sport ethic. In A. Yiannakis, M. J. Melnick, A. Yiannakis, M. J. Melnick (Eds.), *Contemporary issues in sociology of sport* (pp. 361–374). Champaign, IL: Human Kinetics.

Luke, A., Lazaro, R. M., Bergeron, M. F., Keyser, L., Benjamin, H., Brenner, J., d'Hemecourt, P., Grady, M., Philpott, J., & Smith, A. (2011). Sports-related injuries in youth athletes: Is overscheduling a risk factor? *Clinical Journal of Sport Medicine, 21,* 307–314.

Rodriguez, N. R. (2013). Training table to the battlefield: Protein recommendations for warfighters. *The Journal of Nutrition, 143,* 1834S–1837S.

Rosenbloom, C. A., & Coleman, E. J. (2012). *Sports nutrition a practice manual for professionals.* Chicago, IL: American Dietetic Association.

Thomas, D. T., Erdman, K. A., & Burke, L. M. (2016). Position of the Academy of Nutrition and Dietetics, Dietitians of Canada, and the American College of Sports Medicine: Nutrition and athletic performance. *Journal of the Academy of Nutrition and Dietetics, 116,* 501–528.

Thun, E., Bjorvatn, B., Flo, E., Harris, A., & Pallesen, S. (2015). Sleep, circadian rhythms, and athletic performance. *Sleep Medicine Reviews, 23,* 1–9.

Wilson, P. B., Ingraham, S. J., Lundstrom, C., & Rhodes, G. (2013). Dietary tendencies as predictors of marathon time in novice marathoners. *International Journal of Sport Nutrition and Exercise Metabolism, 23,* 170–177.

STRESS

Faye F. Didymus and Jim Taylor

Competitive sports are, by their very nature, stressful. Whether stressors relate to training, competitions, conditions, or expectations, or stress is physical, psychological, emotional, or social, all athletes experience stress on a daily basis. Stress is thought to be prevalent among athletes who compete at all levels but those in high-performance or dual-career (e.g., student-athlete) environments may be particularly susceptible to the experience and potentially detrimental effects of stress. The extent to which stress is harmful depends on the genetic, physiological, and psychological make-up of individual athletes which, in turn, impacts the ways that they perceive, experience, and respond to stressors (Lazarus, 1999). Indeed, athletes are likely to experience different cognitions, emotions, and behaviors, each of which will subsequently influence their health, well-being, and performance. As a result, stress has wide-reaching implications for athletes. Thus, consultants should be adept at helping athletes develop the ability to optimally manage stress in ways that will promote their health, well-being, and sports performances (Didymus & Fletcher, 2017a, 2017b).

Theory and Research

To understand the impact of stress for athletes and different approaches to stress management interventions, it is necessary to first understand the theoretical and empirical underpinnings of stress.

Stress in Perspective

Stress in an umbrella term that refers to stressors, appraising, emotions, coping, and outcomes of stress transactions. It involves physiological and psychological reactions to a perceived threat to athletes' health, well-being, and performances. Stress originated in the primitive survival instinct and its associated flight-or-flight reaction intended to ensure our survival. The activation of the sympathetic nervous system triggers changes in the brain and body that mobilize action in response to a perceived threat to survival.

Stress involves individuals experiencing one or more stressors, making appraisals of those stressors, experiencing emotions, and attempting to cope. Stress is a normal part of any environment that is driven by high goals and expectations, and sports are no exception. Despite what some may think, stress is an important and adaptive experience (to a point) that athletes engage with every day. Stress can help them to respond physically by encouraging more effort, building strength, and enhancing stamina when athletes are confronted with the often intense and exhausting schedules that they must keep. Stress can also generate emotions that can be perceived as facilitative such as excitement, pride, and happiness. Stress can also sharpen athletes' thinking and focus, which can help them to make better sports-related decisions and perform better in training and competitions.

At the same time, stress can be detrimental to health, well-being, and performance when athletes perceive stressors as a threat, feel helpless to respond to it or with a sense of harm or loss. These perceptions usually arise when athletes perceive that they no longer have the ability to cope with stressors effectively or have a lack of control over the situations they find themselves in. When stress becomes detrimental, several red flags may appear:

- athletes may feel psychologically overwhelmed and emotionally vulnerable;
- the quality of their efforts in training and competitions may decline;
- their health deteriorates;
- they may lose enjoyment and lack motivation in their athletic lives; and
- their general quality of life may decrease.

Stressors

To date, sport psychology researchers have highlighted that stressors are prominent in sport environments and that a variety of organizational stressors (e.g., those relating to funding, selection, travel to and accommodation during competitions, role conflict, leadership, and referees' decisions) are experienced and recalled more frequently than those related to competitive performance or athletes' personal lives (Hanton, Fletcher, & Coughlan, 2005). In addition, researchers have noted that group differences (i.e., between males and females; individual and team sports athletes; and international, national, or regional level performers) exist in the type and frequency of stressors that athletes experience and that stressors are encountered more often among athletes competing at an elite level than by those performing at a non-elite level. Additionally, student-athletes may experience a unique blend of stressors when trying to balance the demands of high-level sport and education. Indeed, student-athletes are thought to encounter stressors such as schedule clashes, fatigue, and financial pressure, and have reported a perceived need to prioritize sport to the detriment of education to overcome the stressors that they encounter (Cosh & Tully, 2014). Stressors can relate to both external and internal factors:

- External stressors include time pressure; workload; practice duration and intensity; weather; social conflicts; pressure from family; friends; and media; and financial problems.
- Internal stressors involve lack of perceived control; insufficient resources or skills; negativity; personal standards and expectations; doubt, worry, and fear; lack of support; poor physical health (e.g., illness, injury); and mental health difficulties.

Appraising

Though stressors are real and have a potentially impact on athletes, they do impact every athlete in the same way. The fundamental experience of whether stressors are harmful depends on how athletes appraise them and whether they believe they have the capabilities to manage them effectively. Stress is most acute and debilitating when athletes sense that the demands placed on them are greater than the resources they believe they can marshal in response.

Contemporary conceptualizations of stress place emphasis on the transactional nature of person-environment relationships and on the relational meaning that individuals construct from them (Lazarus, 2000a). These contemporary perspectives suggest that athletes will engage in cognitive-evaluative processes to ascribe meaning to the stressors that they encounter and attempt to cope with them (Lazarus, 1999). At the theoretical heart of stress transactions is appraising, which refers to evaluations of situations that can affect athletes' beliefs, values, and or goals (Lazarus, 1999). Put simply, appraising is the act of making an evaluation and paves the way for psychological, physiological, emotional, and behavioral outcomes (see e.g., O'Donovan et al., 2012; Schneider, 2004). Researchers who have examined the ways in which athletes appraise stressors have found that athletes often respond negatively to stressors although they do have the potential to appraise stressors in positive ways (Didymus & Fletcher, 2012).

Symptoms

How athletes react to stress can be expressed by athletes in five main ways:

1. **Physical:** Increased heart rate, respiration, and adrenaline; frequent illness due to immune system deficiency; physical complaints (e.g., headache, stomach aches, GI distress, muscle pain); sleeping problems (e.g., exhaustion, insomnia, nightmares); fatigue; and changes in appetite (e.g., either overeating or calorie restriction).
2. **Cognitive:** Racing thoughts, excessive negativity and criticalness, low confidence, increased doubt and worry, poor focus, unrealistic expectations, memory lapses, learning struggles, decision-making difficulties, and obsessive thinking.
3. **Emotional:** Frustration, anger, moodiness, panic, worry, and excessive or inappropriate emotional expression.
4. **Social:** Social withdrawal, difficulty communicating, and increased conflict (e.g., between teammates).
5. **Performance:** Tentative performances, unusually high numbers of mistakes, inconsistency, reduced or excessive effort, lack of enjoyment, "give-up" syndrome, poor adaptability to changing conditions, and low resilience.

Coping

Coping is defined as "constantly changing cognitive and behavioral efforts a person makes to manage specific external and/or internal demands that are appraised as taxing or exceeding the resources of the person" (Lazarus, 1999, p. 110). An inability to cope with stress is thought to be an important factor in athletes underperforming during competition (Lazarus, 2000b) and in reduced health and well-being. Researchers who have focused on the coping strategies used by athletes (e.g., Didymus & Fletcher, 2014; Kristiansen, Murphy, & Roberts, 2012) have suggested that social support, self-reliance, pre-performance routines, thought stopping, and avoidance of stressful situations are important coping options.

Stress reduction

Various approaches to stress reduction have been explored in sport, which can be broadly categorized into three levels of intervention: primary, secondary, and tertiary. Primary-level interventions are preventive in that they aim to alter the environment to reduce or eliminate stressors (e.g., reducing the emphasis on winning, fewer practices; Dewe, O'Driscoll, & Cooper, 2010). This type of intervention is often more resource intensive than secondary- and tertiary-level interventions and require substantial buy-in from sport organizations because they may involve organizational restructuring or the development and application of new philosophies, policies, and procedures (e.g., improved communication channels and talent development; see Rumbold, Fletcher, & Daniels, 2018). The potential for primary-level interventions to create environments that minimize stress among athletes and coaches is significant but further research is required to better understand how to implement and evaluate them in sport. The effectiveness of this level of intervention in sport has not been evaluated more widely because of the challenges of instigating organizational change and the difficulties in trying to remove stressors from an activity that is inherently stressful.

The majority of sport psychology literature that has explored the efficacy and effectiveness of stress reduction interventions has focused on secondary-level techniques (see, for a review, Rumbold, Fletcher, & Daniels, 2012).

These interventions have been described as the reduction "of experienced stress by increasing awareness and improving the stress management skills of the individual through training and educational activities" (Cooper & Cartwright, 1997, p. 8). These types of interventions do not attempt to eliminate stressors but, rather, focus on how athletes can mitigate or relieve negative outcomes of stressors (Rogissart & Martinent, 2017). Secondary-level interventions include psychoeducation, relaxation, psychological skills training, synchronous music, motivational general imagery, hypnosis, and cognitive restructuring (Rumbold et al., 2012), as well as meditation, yoga, and biofeedback. Little research exists that compares the effectiveness of different secondary-level interventions but the work that has been published suggests that multimodal interventions may be more effective than unimodal interventions (Rumbold et al., 2012).

The third group of interventions (tertiary level) involves techniques (e.g., counseling) that aim to address the outcomes of stressful experiences, rather than addressing the precipitating stressors (primary level) or individuals' experiences of them (secondary level). These types of interventions are considered to be reactive or rehabilitative and are typically introduced once athletes are already suffering from negative outcomes of stress (e.g., diminished psychological well-being, emotional exhaustion, burnout). Tertiary-level interventions in sport that involve counseling, for example, have been conducted in the contexts of injury support (Gutkind, 2004) and career change-events (Samuel, 2013). Outside of sport psychology, counseling has been widely discussed as an effective technique for helping individuals to cope with psychological (e.g., depression) and physical (e.g., infertility) conditions, difficult life events (e.g., bereavement), and various affective situations (e.g., low self-esteem; Van den Broeck, Emery, Wischmann, & Thorn, 2010). Despite this promising body of evidence, rehabilitative approaches to stress reduction shift focus away from prevention and towards reactive interventions that only help athletes after stress has had a debilitating impact on them.

Practical Implications

An essential role that consultants play when helping athletes to achieve their goals is to help them learn to cope with the inevitable stressors that they will experience both within and outside of sport. As such, consultants must have at their disposal a well-stocked "toolbox" of techniques that address stress directly while leveraging the consultant-client relationship that is built on credibility and trust. This combination can then be used to optimize stress transactions that will both enhance athletes' performances and safeguard their overall health and well-being (Didymus & Fletcher, 2017a).

Approaches to Overcoming Stress

Consultants' work with athletes in helping them to cope effectively with stress begins with establishing a way they can approach stressors in a helpful manner. Athletes can think about stress much as they would the thermometer and thermostat in their homes. When their home gets too hot, they adjust the thermostat to a more comfortable level. The same applies to athletes' experiences of stress. They know when stress is at a manageable level and need to recognize when it is becoming problematic. When that happens, athletes can to adjust their stress thermostat (Mohr, 2010), that is, reduce the stressors they experience, adjust their appraisal of them, or increase their coping resources. By adjusting their stress thermostat in one of these ways, athletes not only lessen the potential for negative outcomes of stress but also take control of their experiences and feel empowered to cope more effectively.

Another part of consultants' work with athletes involves explorations of how they perceive their ability to respond to stressors in training, competition, and outside of sport. As noted in the Introduction, *CASP* is deliberate about the vocabulary it uses to describe the wide range of phenomena that are discussed and stress is no different. The conventional terminology for addressing harmful stress is "stress management." Yet, the term management has the connotations of just getting by or barely dealing with a situation. Such an understanding of management doesn't do justice to what athletes need to do overcome harmful stress in their lives, whether within or outside of their sport. Nor does it suggest true empowerment in taking control of the stress in their lives. Consequently, the term "stress mastery" is used to describe a proactive, assertive, and vigorous approach to addressing stress among athletes. Moreover, this perception can be of a victim, manager, or master:

- Stress victim: suffer from and controlled by stress, loss of motivation to succumb to stress quality of effort deteriorates, depression and or anxiety may be evident.
- Stress manager: respond to stress but most often reactively so there is little sense of control, get by, hang on, short-term relief but long-term negative impact.
- Stress master: accept stress, positive attitude toward stress, prepare for stress proactively, feel in control of stress, thrive in stressful situations.

A key goal for consultants is to help athletes see themselves as stress masters. The notion of mastery (see, e.g., Ntoumanis & Biddle, 1999) is already woven into the fabric of sports in terms of mastering skills, conditions, and their opponents. That same feeling associated with mastery—more control and empowerment—can be helpful in when coping with stressors that they will inevitably face during their sports careers.

Steps to Stress Mastery

Consultants can help athletes to achieve mastery of their stress experiences by, first, having them take active steps to understand stress and gain control of it. This first step involves athletes accepting stress as a normal part of their athletic career (Weston, Thelwell, Bond, & Hutchings, 2009). So, when stressors present, they are not fully unexpected but are seen as an inevitable part of their journey toward their goals. The second step is for athletes to recognize when, where, and with whom stress often occurs. Consultants can point out patterns in the situations, people, and experiences in which athletes experience stress. When athletes know in what situations stress is likely to arise, it is partially mitigated because they see it as more predictable (Didymus & Fletcher, 2012) and controllable, and they are in a better position to prepare and respond positively. The third step involves identifying athletes' recurring stressors. In doing so, consultants can explore the most common stressors and their root causes. The fourth step is for consultants to assist athletes in shifting their focus away from being overwhelmed by or wallowing in stressors and onto optimization of their coping resources. With this emphasis, athletes tend to feel more in control, confident, and emboldened to cope with stress effectively.

When athletes experience stressors, consultants can show athletes that they have three possible solutions to pursue. First, they can try to change the stressors themselves. For example, if an athlete is part of a team that is led by a coach who is overly focused on winning and can act abusively toward his players, the athlete can join a different team with a coach who focuses on fun and process. Second, athletes can alter their appraisals of stressors (Didymus & Fletcher, 2017a). For instance, imagine that two swimmers of equal ability have a big meet approaching and are experiencing pressure from their parents to win their events. In this case, each athlete is experiencing the same stressors but can appraise them in very different ways. Swimmer A appraises the stressors as threats to her goals and well-being and is overwhelmed and paralyzed by them. In contrast, Swimmer B appraises the stressors as a challenge and is excited and energized by the stressful experience. In all likelihood, Swimmer B will outperform Swimmer A because challenge appraisals lead to more beneficial coping and performance outcomes. Third, when confronted with stressors, athletes can attend to the outcomes of stress. For example, consultants may teach athletes how to use a variety of stress-mastery tools. Physical tools include meditation, massage, biofeedback, and exercise. Mental tools include perspective taking, positive thinking, refocusing, and emotional redirection.

The final step is for consultants to fill a "toolbox" with stress-mastery tools that athletes can access when they experience stressors both within and outside of their sports lives. Though stress is inevitable in sports, the potential for negative outcomes can be exacerbated when athletes do not believe that they have the means to cope effectively with stressors. Conversely, stress can be mitigated substantially when athletes feel more in control of and capable of mastering it. This position of strength can occur when athletes have access to a variety of coping techniques with which they can proactively and reactively address stressors.

Given the breadth of issues that stress encompasses (e.g., stressors, appraisals, emotions, and coping) and the individual differences (e.g., personality, resilience, trait anxiety; e.g., Kaiseler, Polman, & Nicholls, 2009) that influence athletes' responses, consultants are not likely to find success by using a "one size fits all" approach to stress mastery. Instead, consultants can approach their stress-related work with athletes with a well-stocked toolbox from which they and athletes can choose tools that will be most effective for their particular needs and goals. As noted earlier in this section, stress can be addressed at many levels of the experience and specific tools can be offered at each of those levels.

General Tools

Consultants can show athletes some general tools that can be used to relieve stress:

- **Manage time and energy:** Athletes should do what they need to do in their sports and overall lives but should not over strive or over commit.
- **Have healthy outlets:** Athletes should have activities (e.g., cultural and spiritual pursuits, cooking, reading, and watching movies) that provide them with joy, excitement, meaning, satisfaction, inspiration, and pride that can "refill their tanks" when they experience stress.
- **Build a social support network:** One robust finding in published research on stress is that social support acts as a buffer against stress and that family, friends, and significant others (e.g., coaches, teammates) can provide emotional support, sympathy, problem solving, encouragement, perspective, and distraction from stressors.
- **Increase coping resources:** Negative outcomes of stress often arise when the real or perceived demands of a situation exceed athletes' real or perceived resources to cope. By increasing their coping resources (e.g., by getting help from others, gaining relevant information and skills, or giving themselves more time), athletes are able to tip the scales of resources and stressors into a healthy balance.
- **Rest:** Where stress can negatively impact athletes' bodies and minds, rest heals and restores them.
- **Eat well:** A healthy and balanced diet bolsters athletes' immune systems and gives them the energy they need to meet the stressors they experience.
- **Exercise:** Exercise provides athletes with opportunities to boost strength and stamina that can protect them from negative outcomes of stress, and also acts as a temporary escape and distraction from stressors.
- **Take a break:** By taking a break from the situations in which stressors occur, athletes distance themselves physically and psychologically and, thus, its effects on them.

Physical Tools

Consultants can also teach athletes a variety of physical tools that can help their bodies and minds to counteract negative outcomes of stressors. When experiencing stressors, physical strategies can lessen the immediate symptoms and make athletes feel more relaxed and comfortable:

- **Breathing:** Slow and deep breathing has a direct impact when stress has caused changes to heart rate, neurochemicals, and muscle tension. Breathing exercises provide additional oxygen that slows heart rate, reduces stress-inducing neurochemicals, relaxes muscles, and increases athletes' sense of comfort and well-being, while also taking their minds off of the stress experience.
- **Muscle relaxation:** During stressful encounters, muscle tension increases to protect the body and prepare for fight or flight. When athletes engage in relaxation exercises (e.g., meditation, yoga, or targeted relaxation), muscle tension is relieved, and athletes' bodies are better able to withstand stress.
- **Music:** Music has a profound influence on athletes psychologically, emotionally, and physically by transporting them from their stressful lives into worlds of tranquility or excitement, either of which, depending on their musical tastes, can relieve outcomes of stress and re-instill a sense of relaxation and comfort.
- **Biofeedback:** Using technology that provides objective information about their physical responses to stress (e.g., heart and respiration rates), athletes are able to gain awareness of and control over the physical outcomes of stress.

Mental Tools

How athletes think about the stressors they experience impacts their physical and psychological reactions to them. As a result, by changing the way athletes perceive, interpret, and feel about stress, they also alter the degree to which stress affects them:

- **Positive thinking:** When athletes view stress in a positive light and talk to themselves positively, the potential for negative outcomes of stress is lessened.

- **Mindfulness:** The practice of mindfulness increases athletes' awareness of stress, centers them, and has relaxing effects on their minds and bodies.
- **Imagery:** When athletes see and feel themselves performing well and transacting positively and calmly with stressors, their minds and bodies respond accordingly.
- **Journaling:** Writing down their thoughts and feelings related to stress transactions can act as a cathartic coping technique for athletes.
- **Problem solving:** If stressors relate to controllable situations, athletes can find solutions that directly alter or manage the stressor(s).
- **Distraction:** Athletes can ease the immediate experience of stress by thinking about other things, interacting with people, or engaging in a diverting activity.
- **Have fun:** Doing enjoyable activities, smiling, and laughing distracts athletes from stress, produces pleasant emotions, generates positive thinking, and activates the parasympathetic nervous system, all of which counteract negative outcomes of stress.

All of the above mental tools have been discussed in greater detail earlier in *CASP*. Consultants can use the general information and approaches from the previous chapters and apply them to stress mastery with athletes.

Summary

- Whether stressors relate to training, competitions, conditions, or expectations, or stress is physical, psychological, emotional, or social, all athletes experience stress on a daily basis.
- Stress has wide-reaching implications for athletes and, thus, consultants should be adept at helping athletes develop attitudes and tools to optimally manage their experiences in ways that will promote health, well-being, and sports performances.
- Despite what some may think, stress is an important and adaptive (to a point) experience that athletes engage with every day.
- Stress can help athletes to respond physically by encouraging more effort, building strength, and enhancing stamina when athletes are confronted with the often intense and exhausting schedules that they must keep.
- Stress can be detrimental when athletes perceive stressors as a threat or with a sense of harm/loss. These perceptions usually arise when athletes perceive that they no longer have the ability to cope with stressors effectively or have a lack of control over the situations they find themselves in.
- External stressors include time pressure, workload, practice duration and intensity, weather, social conflicts, pressure from family, friends, and media, and financial problems.
- Internal stressors involve lack of perceived control, insufficient resources or skills, negativity, personal standards and expectations, doubt, worry, and fear, lack of support, poor physical health (e.g., illness, injury), and mental-health difficulties.
- How athletes appraise stressors determines the physical, psychological, and behavioral outcomes of stress.
- Negative outcomes of stress relate to physical, cognitive, emotional, social, and performance changes.
- Red flags of stress include athletes feeling psychologically overwhelmed and emotionally vulnerable, reductions in the quality of athletes' efforts in training and competitions, health deterioration, loss of enjoyment and motivation, and general decreases in quality of life.
- Three ways in which athletes can address stress is to prevent the stressors before they arise, relieve the outcomes as they occur, or address the effects of stress after it happens.
- Athletes can respond to stress as victims, managers, or masters.
- Athletes can master stress in several steps including accepting it as normal, identifying their most common stressors, recognizing when and where stressors occur, shifting focus away from the experience of stress and on to resolving it, and developing a toolbox of strategies to cope.
- General tools for mastering stress include managing time and energy, having healthy outlets, building a social support network, increasing resources, getting rest, eating well, exercising, and taking a break.
- Physical tools for mastering stress involve breathing, muscle relaxation, music, and biofeedback.
- Mental tools for mastering stress include positive thinking, mindfulness, imagery, having fun, problem solving, journaling, and distraction.

References

Cooper, C. L., & Cartwright, S. (1997). An intervention strategy for workplace stress. *Journal of Psychosomatic Research, 43*, 7–16.

Cosh, S., & Tully, P. J. (2014). "All I have to do is pass": A discursive analysis of student athletes' talk about prioritizing sport to the detriment of education to overcome stressors encountered in combining elite sport and tertiary education. *Psychology of Sport and Exercise, 15*, 180–189.

Dewe, P. J., O'Driscoll, M. P., & Cooper, C. L. (2010). *Coping with work stress: A review and critique.* Chichester: Wiley-Blackwell.

Didymus, F. F., & Fletcher, D. (2012). Getting to the heart of the matter: A diary study of swimmers' appraisals of organizational stressors. *Journal of Sports Sciences, 30*, 1375–1385.

Didymus, F. F., & Fletcher, D. (2014). Swimmers' experiences of organizational stress: Exploring the role of cognitive appraisal and coping strategies. *Journal of Clinical Sport Psychology, 8*, 159–183.

Didymus, F. F., & Fletcher, D. (2017a). Effects of a cognitive-behavioral intervention on field hockey players' appraisals of organizational stressors. *Psychology of Sport and Exercise, 30*, 173–185.

Didymus, F. F., & Fletcher, D. (2017b). Organizational stress in high-level field hockey: Examining transactional pathways between stressors, appraisals, coping and performance satisfaction. *International Journal of Sports Science and Coaching, 12*, 252–263.

Gutkind, S. M. (2004). Using solution-focused brief counseling to provide injury support. *The Sport Psychologist, 18*, 75–88.

Hanton, S., Fletcher, D., & Coughlan, G. (2005). Stress in elite sport performers: A comparative study of competitive and organizational stressors. *Journal of Sports Sciences, 23*, 1129–1141.

Kaiseler, M., Polman, R., & Nicholls, A. (2009). Mental toughness, stress, stress appraisal, coping and coping effectiveness in sport. *Personality and Individual Differences, 47*, 728–733.

Kristiansen, E., Murphy, D., & Roberts, G. C. (2012). Organizational stress and coping in US professional soccer. *Journal of Applied Sport Psychology, 24*, 207–223.

Lazarus, R. S. (1999). *Stress and emotion: A new synthesis.* New York, NY: Springer.

Lazarus, R. S. (2000a). How emotions influence performance in competitive sports. *The Sport Psychologist, 14*, 229–252.

Lazarus, R. S. (2000b). Cognitive-motivational-relational theory of emotion. In Y. L. Hanin (Ed.), *Emotions in sport* (pp. 39–63). Champaign, IL: Human Kinetics.

Mohr, D. C. (2010). *The stress and mood management program for individuals with multiple sclerosis.* Oxford: Oxford University Press.

Ntoumanis, N., & Biddle, S. J. (1999). A review of motivational climate in physical activity. *Journal of Sports Sciences, 17*, 643–655.

O'Donovan, A., Tomiyama, A. J., Lin, J., Puterman, E., Adler, N. E., Kemeny, M., Wolkowitz, O. M., Blackburn, E. H., & Epel, E. S. (2012). Stress appraisals and cellular aging: A key role for anticipatory threat in the relationship between psychological stress and telomere length. *Brain, Behavior, and Immunity, 26*, 573–579.

Rogissart, A., & Martinent, G. (2017). The effects of a multimodal intervention program on national competitive swimmers' state anxiety and coping. In J. F. A. Cruz & R. M. C. Sofia (Eds.), *Anger and anxiety: Predictors, coping strategies, and health effects* (pp. 269–294). Hauppauge, NY: Nova Science.

Rumbold, J. L., Fletcher, D., & Daniels, K. (2012). A systematic review of stress management interventions with sport performers. *Sport, Exercise, and Performance Psychology, 1*, 173–193.

Rumbold, J. L., Fletcher, D., & Daniels, K. (2018). Using a mixed method audit to inform organizational stress management interventions in sport. *Psychology of Sport and Exercise, 35*, 27–38.

Samuel, R. D. (2013). Counseling athletes in career change-events: Applying the scheme of change for sport psychology practice. *Journal of Sport Psychology in Action, 4*, 152–168.

Schneider, T. R. (2004). The role of neuroticism on psychological and physiological stress responses. *Journal of Experimental Social Psychology, 40*, 795–804.

Van den Broeck, U., Emery, M., Wischmann, T., & Thorn, P. (2010). Counselling in infertility: Individual, couple and group interventions. *Patient Education and Counselling, 81*, 422–428.

Weston, N. J. V., Thelwell, R. C., Bond, S., & Hutchings, N. V. (2009). Stress and coping in single-handed round-the-world ocean sailing. *Journal of Applied Sport Psychology, 21*, 460–474.

WELL-BEING

Gloria Park

Why is it important to support the mental health and well-being of athletes? Athletes are more than the sum total of their best performances, and sense of self-worth, happiness, and fulfillment should be tied to more than just their athletic accomplishments. This is particularly true since even the most successful athletes will remain competitive into their thirties as Olympians and professionals, but for the vast majority of athletes, their serious sports careers end in high school. The field of applied sport psychology focuses on supporting processes that contribute to optimal performance. While the quality and consistency of athletic performance itself are of chief interest, consultants should understand that other outcomes, for example, the development of character, psychological flourishing, and enduring social connections, should be outcomes that matter just as much as discrete moments of athletic performance.

Athletes' lives outside of the domain of practice and competitions are impacted by their sports experience. Conversely, when athletes perform in their sport, they don't leave their "personness" on the sideline. Thus, athletes' well-being influences their capacity to perform, and in turn, their sports experiences can powerfully impact their well-being. For example, competitive failures may hurt self-worth, produce negative emotions, and interfere with relationships. However, armed with the right attitudes and tools, those competitive failures can become fruitful opportunities to cultivate motivation, confidence, and resilience. Happiness and well-being can support and precede performance and success across a broad range of domains (Lyubomirsky, King, & Diener, 2005). It is well accepted that the primary focus of the field of applied sport psychology is on helping athletes to perform their best and achieve their goals in their sport. At the same time, given the importance of well-being in both the immediate and long-term lives of athletes, it is also incumbent on consultants to understand that other aspects of the sports experience matter apart from simply competitive outcomes. On the way to supporting athletes' goal attainment, consultants can integrate opportunities to teach strategies that can help them cultivate and sustain their well-being. In fact, the mental muscles (e.g., motivation, confidence, focus) and the mental exercises and tools (e.g., goal setting, mindfulness, self-talk, breathing) that were described in Chapters 3 and 4 are equally beneficial for the development of well-being in athletes and can be used to facilitate lifelong mental health and success in other domains of life (Moore & Bonagura, 2017).

Theory and Research

Because Chapter 8 examines clinical issues among athletes, this section will not focus on "mental health," but rather on "mental wealth" (Uphill, Sly, & Swain, 2016). Mental health traditionally refers to the absence of pathology. In contrast, mental wealth relates to key psychological functions that enable enriching and engaging lives, the capacity to overcome challenges and adversity, and flourishing in meaningful areas of athletes' lives. This notion of mental wealth can be useful to consultants in their work with athletes as they make progress toward their goals in sports and other areas of their lives.

Approaches to supporting "mental health" are not the same as cultivating "mental wealth" (Uphill, Sly, & Swain, 2016): Simply attaining "mental health"—defined as the absence of pathology—does not necessarily contribute to athletes' "mental wealth"—or the presence of positive psychological strengths such as purpose and grit, since resolutions in pathology can be orthogonal to the development of positive mental states. Clarifying this distinction is beneficial to consultants as they navigate the sometimes murky waters of intervention with athletes. As will be noted in Chapter 8, only licensed professionals are qualified to address mental-health challenges that rise to the level of a clinical diagnosis. With their training, clinicians can effectively diagnose, target, and intervene with athletes to resolve the presence of mental illness.

Well-being, however, does not exist simply in the absence of mental illness. Well-being is defined independently as the presence of positive mental health, which includes dimensions of positive emotional states, self-actualization, as well as meaning, purpose, and functioning within a societal or community structure (Westerhof & Keyes, 2010). Although there are various theories underlying well-being (see Grenville-Cleave & Brady, 2018), the two-continuum model of mental health by Keyes (2002) might be the most relevant for thinking about how to move beyond a pathology-focused approach and broaden consultants' understanding of how to support both performance outcomes and well-being. The two-continuum model views mental health and mental illness as distinct (but related) phenomena rather than opposite ends of a single continuum (see Uphill, Sly, & Swain, 2016 for a complete description). This model helps explain how athletes struggling with mental health issues may still be able to experience success in their sport.

Understanding the two-continuum model can aid consultants in better identifying when to refer clients to licensed clinicians, and to broaden their thinking around available intervention strategies since (unlike with clinical issues) consultants with a broad range of education, training, and experience can intervene to support the development of mental wealth, enhanced performance, and well-being. A focus on building mental wealth, strengths of character, and means of resilience can also serve to circumnavigate the stigma around mental illness and weakness that can impede athletes' willingness to seek help.

PERMA

The PERMA model of well-being (Positive Emotion, Engagement, Relationships, Meaning, and Achievement; Seligman, 2018) suggests that well-being is composed of some combination of its elements and the makeup of what flourishing looks like can vary from individual to individual. The PERMA framework provides opportunities for consultants to actively explore and develop new pathways to athletes' well-being just as mental training allows them to impact their mental preparation in their sport positively. Consultants can work with athletes on a broad range of strategies considering all elements of PERMA in their quest toward athletic success and life beyond sport. This subsection will present a conceptual understanding of how consultants can support "mental wealth" of athletes through positive interventions and introduce a sampling of strategies based on the PERMA model that can help athletes build the essential psychological building blocks for flourishing (see Park-Perin, 2010 for additional approaches).

Positive Emotions

Positive emotions, such as joy, excitement, pride, awe, and inspiration, serve distinct functions from negative emotions, contribute to the experience of fulfilling lives, and serve to build critical social and psychological resources across the lifespan (Fredrickson, 2009). Many consultants are adept at helping athletes understand how negative emotions impact their sports participation and performance and sharing ways to productively leverage negative emotions in the service of performance. By understanding the functional role of positive emotions, consultants can help athletes to better embrace the full range of human emotions and be more purposeful and intentional about cultivating more of these emotions as a means of achieving optimal performance and well-being. They can help athletes to identify the situations in which positive emotions are most commonly experienced and become more mindful when they arise so that these emotions can be savored and sustained. Consultants can also help athletes understand how the induction of positive emotion can shift cognitive perceptions, fuel motivation, and support recovery from challenges and setbacks.

Engagement

Deep engagement and absorption in sports can lead to optimized performance in a discrete moment, as well as optimized experiences across a broad range of performance domains (Nakamura & Csikszentmihalyi, 2014). Consultants often work with athletes to better clarify the antecedents of flow (namely challenge–skills balance, clear goals, and unambiguous feedback). Consultants can target changes in flow by leveraging existing mental training approaches including imagery, mindfulness, and pre-performance routines (Norsworthy, Gorczynski, & Jackson, 2017). With this knowledge, athletes can become better architects of flow experiences and understand how moments of deep and powerful engagement contribute to sport success and well-being. While deep engagement and flow experiences can foster optimal performance, consultants can also explore ways to help athletes disengage to enable full rest and recovery, and more balance off the field. Finally, as athletes transition out of their often-brief careers, consultants can help athletes learn how to bring the strengths they developed in sports to bear to pursue goals outside of the athletic domain.

Relationships

Much of the research on how to cultivate well-being can be boiled down to a single phrase: "Other people matter" (Peterson, 2006). In a variety of ways, an individual's sense of well-being hinges greatly on the quality of the connections they share with others. For athletes, these connections can be an important source of support, belongingness, and encouragement or they can be a significant source of stress, conflict, and ill feelings. Interpersonal skill development is also an area ripe for exploration and intervention with athletes as it relates to well-being. Consultants can work with athletes and their broader network of social support to enhance the quality of relationships with family, partners, friends, teammates, and coaches. When presented with opportunities to work with key figures who influence the success and well-being of athletes, consultants can consider concepts like Active Constructive Responding (ACR; Gable & Reis, 2010). ACR provides guidance on how to provide meaningful, positive feedback in a way that also builds relationships and supports future performance efforts.

Meaning

In the daily grind of athletes' lives, it can be easy for them to keep their eyes on the prize of outcomes and goals but lose sight of the sense of meaning and purpose underlying their sports pursuits. Meaning and purpose contribute greatly to well-being in a distinctly different way than happiness and positive emotions, and their presence is a hallmark of those living enriching and fulfilling lives. Consultants can encourage athletes to regularly identify, clarify, and connect with their values. Because consultants are often with athletes during the peaks and valleys of their competitive careers, they can help them to make sense of their how deepest failures, most challenging setbacks, as well as their greatest successes, fit into the larger narrative of their lives. Additional approaches to cultivate meaning come from strengthening connections to others, intentionally working toward purpose, storytelling, and seeking out transcendent experiences (Esfahani Smith, 2017). As athletes transition out of the competitive sphere, consultants can help them explore ways to give back to others through sports, through coaching, mentoring, or passing along their skills and experience in other significant ways.

Accomplishment

Because high-achieving, goal-oriented athletes are so focused on their sports performances, it can be difficult for them to consider what well-being means to them apart from the results they produce. Well-being for this population is often equated to wins, personal bests, awards, and status. This relationship to well-being is best understood by athletes because their accomplishments, as expressed through objective measures of success, reward their engagement, generate affirming emotions, foment relationships, and are powerful incentives for their ongoing commitment in pursuit of their goals. Consultants can help athletes redefine and broaden their understanding of accomplishment as something more than attaining objective goals. Well-being often also comes from the pursuit of mastery-oriented activities (Bradford & Keller, 2016), and consultants can help athletes shift focus to process-related and more subjective metrics of success. They can also work with athletes to develop the mental tools and healthy character attributes necessary to sustain their efforts along the way, including confidence, grit, resilience, and focus.

Practical Implications

The distinction between mental health and mental wealth, and the discussion of PERMA, provides a theoretical foundation for empirically validated approaches to fostering well-being. The three perspectives outlined below are examples of approaches that span across multiple dimensions of PERMA, and contributors to well-being that consultants can bring to light and leverage for athletes.

Pursuing Purpose and Passion

Consultants can encourage athletes to simultaneously pursue success and well-being through understanding and cultivating harmonious passion (Vallerand et al., 2008). Athletes are willing to put forth energy and effort toward their sport often year after year because they enjoy the pursuit and the activity. The way that their chosen activity becomes integrated into an athletes' identity can be categorized as either *harmonious* or *obsessive*, according to the Dualistic Model of Passion (Vallerand, 2010). Harmonious passion is characterized by autonomous internalization, where a person feels free to choose whether or not they engage in an activity and where the activity exists in harmony with other salient dimensions of a person's life. Conversely, obsessive passion results from controlled internalization and characterized by a compulsive drive to engage in an activity, and therefore the activity exists in conflict with other dimensions of life (Vallerand et al., 2008).

Passion is the fuel that enables individuals to sustain engagement in highly demanding activities, and although it is commonly assumed that high levels of performance come only from passion that is more closely character-ized as obsessive, Vallerand and colleagues (2008) have found that both harmonious and obsessive passion are predictors of behaviors that contribute to performance. Achievement does not have to come at the cost of other valued and meaningful aspects of life. While sport psychology continues to focus on goal-setting as a primary pathway to performance optimization, more needs to be understood about the unhealthy ways that overem-phasis on goals and perseverance can unintentionally hinder long-term success and performance sustainability. Performance excellence at the elite level can often come at a cost to other life domains, such as academic and social relationships. Harmonious passion, characterized by less goal conflict and higher levels of positive affect and enjoyment, can help individuals find balance in their lives is central to performance coaching in other domains. Consultants can focus on aiding athletes in finding more balance between work and their social and familial lives, leisure activities, in addition to helping them develop tools to better manage their time and energy. Sport psychology consultants can help their clients define, prioritize, and devise effective ways to find balance in their own lives through cultivating other pathways to well-being.

An emphasis on "peak performance" sometimes undermines greater opportunities to hone in on meaning and purpose. When deeply committed to a specific sport, it can be difficult to see how that activity connects athletes to more long-term objectives. While consultants offer excellent guidance on how to set and obtain goals, they can also help athletes find ways to use their physical skills and talents outside the competitive arena and in service of others and their community. They can encourage athletes to find time to teach and mentor others through coaching, get involved in social justice initiatives or volunteer service, or pursue career fields that continue to allow them to be part of a sport culture in a different capacity. During periods of major transitions or retirement out of competitive sports, consultants can also provide opportunities for athletes to help understand how sport participation has helped them become who they are, regardless of the outcomes they have or have not achieved.

Supporting Strengths

Athletes likely spend a lot of mental energy thinking about what they need to do to improve themselves and their performance. Reflecting on deficiency is healthy and productive when it leads athletes to engage in strate-gies to support growth and development. However, fixing weakness is just one pathway to fully optimizing performance. Many people have difficulty thinking about their strengths beyond the scope of something they *do* well, like sink free throws or slay backhands. Strengths are more than skilled execution: they are who they are at their best, a reflection of how their deeply held values and beliefs show up in their daily actions and attitudes. Operating from strengths can support feelings of authenticity, support intrinsic motivation, and reduce burnout (Peterson & Seligman, 2004).

Identifying, naming, and learning how to use strengths can help reduce stress, increase well-being and decrease depression (Duan & Bu, 2019), and overcome illness and injury (Peterson & Seligman, 2006). Consultants can help athletes understand what their strengths are by providing them with language and dedicated time to reflect on what their strengths might be. Consultants can also help athletes redefine strengths as more than competency with a particular skill: Strengths redefined as reflections of deeply held beliefs and values, as well as behaviors that feel energizing, authentic, and intrinsically motivating can help them figure out how to bring more of those strengths to bear across all aspects of life. Through assessments like the Values in Action Inventory of Strengths (VIA-IS; Peterson & Seligman, 2004) it is possible to gain more perspective on how strengths influence goal pursuit, how athletes may engage with the world and others, and learn how to bring them more fully on and off the field. Using strengths every day can help transform tasks that you might not enjoy doing and fuel perse-verance. From an interpersonal and team perspective, team strengths use predicted flourishing, and feelings of interconnectedness and embeddedness within a team (Stander, Rothman, & Botha, 2017). The goal is intelligent use of strengths, which also involves understanding how strengths aren't working in certain situations or with no regard for others, and how these conflicts might undermine performance or work to the detriment of the team.

Cultivating Gratitude

Reaching and sustaining the highest levels of performance and success requires athletes to be stereotypically self-oriented, possess a singular focus on achieving their goals, and be self-critical of their flaws, mistakes, setbacks, and failures. The human brain has a hardwired tendency called the negativity bias, which is an evolutionary artifact that aids with helping to quickly identify threats in the environment and respond to them with speed and accuracy (Baumeister, Finkenauer, & Vohs, 2001). For athletes, the negativity bias may be supercharged by the motivation to identify and overcome any weaknesses in their sport to facilitate goal attainment. Indeed, focus on growth, mastery, and constant improvement, which is necessary and adaptive in many ways, can further exacerbate athletes' tendencies to focus on, give more weight to, and remember the negative. Positive experiences and beneficial feedback by comparison are much less sticky and more fleeting than the negative. Negativity can catalyze motivation and performance in certain situations but, when it dominates cognitions and emotions, can lead to more serious outcomes including a decline in well-being and mental health.

Consultants can help athletes to minimize the impact of this sometimes destructive self-focus by encouraging them to cultivate gratitude. This practice can support well-being by providing a counterbalance or a positivity offset to the negativity bias. Interventions that focus on cultivating gratitude "can have positive benefits for people in terms of their well-being, happiness, life-satisfaction, grateful mood, grateful disposition, and positive affect, and they can result in decreases in depressive symptoms" (Dickens, 2017, p. 204). Although gratitude has not been shown to be directly related to sport performance outcomes (Chen, 2018), gratitude interventions can generate positions emotions, foster a more relaxed physical state, encourage athletes to reflect on strategies that lead to good performances as well as lift the weight of expectations that they may feel from themselves or others. By intentionally seeking out opportunities to notice good things each day, athletes can train their attention to more habitually notice and remember positive dimensions of their lives. Consultants can teach athletes gratitude exercises including journaling, writing about three good things and reflections on why those good things happened, and regularly thanking others who have supported their sports efforts (most notably, parents, family, and coaches).

Expressions of interpersonal gratitude are mutually beneficial for both the sender and the recipient. Expressions of gratitude from coaches and teammates can reinforce positive behaviors that contribute to individual or team success. When athletes are on the receiving end of appreciation from teammates and coaches, it can create social benefits by inspiring them to pay the goodness forward to others and create positive social contagion. Gratitude can also encourage athletes to focus on personal growth, meaning, and mastery as indicators of success rather than the tangible measures of success (Polak & McCullough, 2006).

Summary

- Athletes are more than the sum of their successes on the field of play and their sense of self-worth, happiness, and fulfillment should be tied to more than just athletic efforts.
- Well-being can be characterized as people's sense of being healthy, happy, and comfortable in their lives and typically encompasses physical and mental health, nurturing relationships, a stable environment, an enjoyable and satisfying school or work setting, and economic sustainability.
- Given the importance of well-being in both immediate and long-term lives of athletes, it is also incumbent on consultants to understand that other aspects of the sports experience (e.g., character development, mental health, emotional stability, and healthy relationships) should also be outcomes that matter to both the athlete and consultants.
- Mental wealth involves helping mentally healthy athletes to more fully develop themselves psychologically and emotionally with the goal of maximizing sports performance in pursuit of their goals.
- Consultants with a broad range of education, training, and experience can intervene on issues related to mental wealth, performance enhancement, and well-being.
- The PERMA model (Positive Emotion, Engagement, Relationships, Meaning, and Achievement of well-being provides a structured framework that consultants can use with athletes to foster their well-being both away from and in their sport.
- In addition to pursuing healthy passions, supporting strengths, and cultivating gratitude, consultants can bring to light and leverage approaches to support the broad range of elements described in the PERMA model.

References

Baumeister, R. F., Finkenauer, C., & Vohs, K. D. (2001). Bad is stronger than good. *Review of General Psychology*, *5*, 323–370.

Bradford, G., & Keller, S. (2016). Well-being and achievement. In G. Fletcher (Ed.), *The Routledge handbook of philosophy of well-being* (pp. 271–280). New York, NY: Routledge.

Chen, L. H. (2018). Gratitude and athletes' well-being. In A. Brady & B. Grenvill-Cleave (Eds.), *Positive psychology in sport and physical activity* (pp. 129–139). New York, NY: Routledge.

Dickens, L. R. (2017) Using gratitude to promote positive change: A aeries of meta-analyses investigating the effectiveness of gratitude interventions. *Basic and Applied Social Psychology*, *39*, 193–208.

Duan, W., & Bu, H. (2019). Randomized trial investigating of a single-session character-strength-based cognitive intervention on freshman's adaptability. *Research on Social Work Practice*, *29*(1), 82–92.

Esfahani Smith, E. (2017). *The power of meaning: Creating a life that matters*. New York, NY: Crown.

Fredrickson, B.L. (2009). *Positivity*. New York, NY: Crown.

Gable, S. L., & Reis, H. T. (2010). Good news! Capitalizing on positive events in an interpersonal context. *Advances in Experimental Social Psychology*, *42*, 195–257.

Grenville-Cleave, B., & Brady, A. (2018). The components of well-being. In A. Brady & B. Grenville-Cleave (Eds.), *Positive psychology in sport and physical activity* (pp. 20–34). New York, NY: Routledge.

Keyes, C. L. M. (2002). The mental health continuum: From languishing to flourishing in life. *Journal of Health and Social Behavior*, *43*, 207–222.

Lyubomirsky, S., King, L. A., & Diener, E. (2005). The benefits of frequent positive affect: Does happiness lead to success? *Psychological Bulletin*, *131*, 803–855.

Moore, Z. E., & Bonagura, K. (2017). Current opinion in clinical sport psychology: From athletic performance to psychological well-being. *Current Opinion in Psychology*, *16*, 176–179.

Nakamura, J. & Csikszentmihalyi, M. (2014) The concept of flow. In *Flow and the foundations of positive psychology* (pp. 239–263). Dordrecht: Springer.

Norsworthy, C., Gorczynski, P., & Jackson, S. A. (2017). A systematic review of flow training on flow states and performance in elite athletes. *Graduate Journal of Sport, Exercise, and Physical Education Research*, *6*, 16–28.

Park-Perin, G. (2010). Positive psychology. In S. J. Hanrahan & M. B. Andersen (Eds.), *Routledge handbook of applied sport psychology* (pp. 141–149). New York City, NY: Routledge.

Peterson, C. (2006). *A primer in positive psychology*. New York, NY: Oxford University Press.

Peterson, C., & Seligman, M. E. P. (2004). *Character strengths and virtues: A handbook and classification*. New York, NY: Oxford University Press.

Polak, E. L., & McCullough, M. E. (2006). Is gratitude an alternative to materialism? *Journal of Happiness Studies*, *7*, 343–360.

Seligman, M. E. P. (2018). PERMA and the building blocks of well-being. *The Journal of Positive Psychology*, *13*, 333–335.

Stander, F., Rothmann, S., & Botha, E. (2017). Pathways to flourishing of athletes: the role of team and individual strength use. *South African Journal of Psychology*, *47*(1), 23–34.

Uphill, M., Sly, D., & Swain, J. (2016). From mental health to mental wealth in athletes: Looking back and moving forward. *Frontiers in Psychology*, *7*, 6.

Vallerand, R. J. (2010). On passion for life activities: The dualistic model of passion. In M. P. Zanna (Ed.), *Advances in experimental social psychology* (pp. 97–193). San Diego, CA: Academic Press.

Vallerand, R. J., Mageau, G. A., Elliot, A. J., Dumais, A., Demers, M., & Rousseau, F. (2008). Passion and performance attainment in sport. *Psychology of Sport and Exercise*, *9*, 373–392.

Westerhof, G.J. & Keyes, C.L.M. Mental illness and mental health: The two-continua model across the lifespan. *Journal of Adult Development*, *17*(2), 110–119.

AT-RISK ATHLETES

Latisha Forster-Scott

The purpose of this section is to discuss factors that place athletes, particularly student-athletes, at risk for dropping out of sport. When "at-risk" athletes are addressed in the literature, it is typically along the lines of injury, drug, alcohol, and steroid use (Buckman et al., 2011; Cimini et al., 2015; Hoff, 2012; Rattner et al., 2011). For the purpose of this discussion, however, "at-risk" will be defined more broadly as athletes who have a greater probability of dropping out of sport due to daily stressors outside of sport that include academic performance, learning disabilities, legal issues, poverty, homelessness, food insecurity, transportation, familial issues, and problems within the community. Athletes often live insulated lives while they are dedicated to meeting the demands of their sport. At the same time, they are not immune to challenges that arise in their wider lives and these matters can negatively impact their mental and physical health, well-being, and sport engagement.

Consultants can be valuable resources for at-risk athletes due to their professional credibility and the trusting relationships they establish. Moreover, consultants may have greater access to the particular details of athletes' lives because athletes may feel more comfortable sharing specific information with them as compared to parents, family, coaches, or teammates. Consultants can be better trusted to maintain confidentiality with athletes and there is less of a concern by athletes about consultants influencing decisions related to their place on the team or in their sport. As a result, athletes may be more forthcoming about their lives without fear of judgment. Whether a consultant works with high school athletes, collegians, Olympians, or professionals, there is a likelihood that they will come across athletes who are struggling with issues unrelated to their sport, yet those issues are putting them at risk in their sport as well as having a potentially negative impact on their future life trajectories.

Theory and Research

Athletes can become at risk in their sports lives for a variety of reasons. Moreover, these struggles are often outside of their control, so they are unable to directly and constructively respond to the challenges. An understanding of these difficulties will help consultants to empathize with, support, and respond in helpful ways to at-risk athletes.

Lack of Basic Needs

The prevalence of poverty, homelessness, and food insecurity in the United States is significant. Research indicates that in K–12 education, 1.3 million children are homeless and 8 million live in households where there are low levels of food security (Broton & Goldrick-Rab, 2017). Indeed, 22%-36% of college students reported being hungry and not having enough money for food, 7–11% of college students reported not eating for a whole day due to a lack of money, up to 14% of community college students and 2% of four year college students report homelessness, and 1 in 10 report housing insecurity. To believe that student-athletes are not impacted by these issues is a false sense of reality. Even when student-athletes receive scholarships and financial aid, a percentage of them will still experience insecure housing and food resources. Additionally, most student-athletes do not receive scholarships and, if they do, they only cover a portion of their college expenses. The portion that scholarships typically cover goes toward tuition and, as a result, they must decide how to pay for necessities such as housing, food, books, transportation, and daily expenses. If the family of the student-athlete is unable to provide financial support to supplement scholarships, this leaves the student-athlete vulnerable. Unlike non-athletes who may be able to secure jobs based on their marketable talents, many athletes are unable to do so due to the high demands of sport participation, as well as the restrictions placed on them by sport governing bodies such as the NCAA when it comes to ways in which they can earn money (NCAA, 2018). For some athletes, the costs of sport participation begin to outweigh the benefits, thus they make the choice to drop out or allow themselves to fail out.

Athletic-academic Balance

Student-athletes who are near completion of their athletic eligibility, but are not academically close to graduating, may also drop out of sport prior to completion of their eligibility for athletic competition. For athletes who have desires of competing at a professional level and realize that those aspirations are not a realistic possibility, this could trigger a significant loss of motivation in school and sports. This is particularly relevant where school was a means to an end to compete in professional sports because, once collegiate sports appear to no longer be an avenue that will lead to professional career, athletes may lose motivation to work hard in school simply because there is less of a commitment to academics to begin with. Being a collegiate athlete is a substantial obligation in which most athletes will spend over 40 hours per week dedicated to their sport and less time on academic work (Rankin et al., 2016). Additionally, many athletes must regularly miss class to travel and compete. It is understandable then why some student-athletes choose to drop out as some will determine that the psychological, emotional, and physical costs of remaining committed academically are too high.

It is also possible athletes are dealing with some level of identity foreclosure due to investing little time in other long-term career options (Beamon, 2012; Murphy et al., 1996). Thus, school has less meaning and, once student-athletes lose academic eligibility, they also lose the privilege to engage in collegiate sports. If athletes have a pessimistic outlook on their current opportunities in their sport and in their long-term prospects, there is a greater likelihood that they will not graduate.

Research from a large sample of athletes indicates that student-athletes tend to have better outcomes academically and athletically when they have better relationships with faculty and athletic personnel. However, research also indicates that many faculty have negative perceptions of athletes and significantly underestimate the amount of time student-athletes commit to sport (Rankin et al., 2016; Forster-Scott & Rosendahl, 2011). Furthermore, many athletes deal with stereotype threat when it comes to identifying as an athlete, meaning the stereotype of "dumb jocks" or "over-privileged" athletes makes it more difficult for some athletes to approach and forge relationships with faculty and non-athlete students (Yopyk & Prentice, 2005). Consultants can be instrumental in helping the student-athlete to identify alternative educational and career options, explore how personal strengths are transferable to other areas beside sport, and how to navigate relationships outside of the sport setting.

Learning Disabilities

Another area of concern is the transition from high school to college particularly for athletes with learning disabilities. It is estimated that 11% of undergraduate students have a learning disability and that, if student-athletes have a learning disability, they may struggle upon entry into college. This transition can be especially difficult for talented athletes who are often "passed through" their high school academic experience by being allowed to take easy classes, given certain "accommodations" in their grades, and receiving extra support (both ethical and unethical) from parents, coaches, teachers, and administrators.

Additionally, as part of the transition from high school to college, many athletes, parents, coaches, and high school academic counselors are unfamiliar with the recruiting and acceptance practices for student-athletes with special needs. It is estimated that every year approximately 1500 student-athletes with learning disabilities seek NCAA eligibility certification and about one third of them are denied (Denbo, 2003). This number does not account for students who have special classification status in high school and do not attempt to seek classification status in college yet enter college anyway. Many of these athletes will forego the process of getting approval for college-level special-needs accommodations because they do not know the process exists, are not aware that it is an option, don't know how to do it themselves, or receive no support in navigating the system. These student-athletes are at particular risk because once they get into college through the regular admissions process, it typically means they barely met the requirements but now will not have the accommodations they need to effectively pursue and experience academic success. These student-athletes end up struggling and eventually fail or drop out. Adding to the problem is that, unlike in high school where the majority of the resources are located in one building, at many colleges and universities, the necessary resources are typically dispersed throughout the campus (e.g., the writing center, academic and career advisement, specific departments to meet with faculty for additional help; Weiss & Robinson, 2013) and these student-athletes aren't given a road map for seeking out these resources.

Practical Implications

Consultants have either experience in treating serious mental-health issues or the relationships and resources to refer out to an appropriately trained professional when they lack the specialized training. In a similar manner, consultants need to be capable of providing expertise, resources, or referrals for at-risk athletes who are dealing with the challenges discussed above. This is especially important for those consultants who are working in high school or collegiate settings. Additionally, because of the culturally diverse nature of colleges and universities and the diversity found in many collegiate sports, it is also important that consultants are culturally aware and competent in understanding how these issues may impact at-risk athletes more than others. Issues related to poverty and disability status disproportionately impact racial and ethnic minorities and students attending community colleges versus four-year colleges.

In practical terms, this means getting to know more intimate details about the athlete population that consultants are working with, the school climate and culture in which they are operating, and gaining a clear understanding of what resources are available on campus settings versus those that may be provided off-campus. Consultants can develop appreciation for the challenges that at-risk athletes face by getting out of their offices and becoming familiar with the various environments in which they inhabit. Consultants can visit the neighborhoods in which they live, walk the streets they walk, attend practices and competitions, spend time in the athletic training room and conditioning facility, and attend team meetings. In other words, consultants are encouraged to "walk in their shoes" as much as possible to gain an in-depth understanding of who at-risk athletes are, how they live, and the challenges they face.

Cultural competency on the part of consultants also means that they will be conscientious not to pass judgement from a "socionormative" perspective that stems from their own life experiences and attitudes. This means deeply examining personal assumptions based on what they perceive as social norms and going out of their comfort zone to provide services which meet the needs of the population they are serving. How athletes respond to the challenges discussed in this section will depend on a combination of personal, cultural, and contextual issues. Effective consultants will have a professional toolbox to help these athletes navigate the wide range of psychological, emotional, social, academic, financial, and physical challenges they face in their lives.

Resources for consultants should include names, phone numbers, and website addresses where athletes can go if public assistance is needed. To support their efforts where social discomfort or communication difficulties may be evident, consultants should be ready and willing to provide introductions and be available for transitions to the support organizations and professionals. There may also be campus resources that student-athletes can take advantage of that the consultants should be aware of. Consultants should have a readily accessible list of places where at-risk athletes can go for food, shelter, acute medical care, legal counseling (e.g., immigration, disability, child-support issues). In some instances, particularly if athletes are well known, having off-campus resources may be preferable to protect their privacy.

Here is a suggested list of contact information all consultants should have as part of their toolbox for sharing referrals and resources with athletes:

1. **Practical support:** Food banks, housing assistance, emergency fund assistance, language and immigration support, legal counsel and religious institutions. Identify campus and off-campus resources. Religious institutions can often be very helpful in providing financial resources, shelter, food and clothing.
2. **Licensed clinician contacts:** Particularly those who specialize in anxiety and depression, psychiatric disorders, eating disorders, drugs and alcohol, family and relationship counseling. Providing resources not directly associated with campus communities may be more suitable for athletes concerned about their privacy.
3. **Academic support:** Do not assume that families and educational institutions have adequate support for these areas in place. It is also possible that certain campus communities have programs that are largely overwhelming and difficult to identify and access, particularly if there is not an academic support program geared specifically to athletes.
4. **Learning disabilities and special needs:** This is an area where a consultant may need to spend time working with athletes to advocate for themselves. Do not assume that parents, coaches, and educational counselors know the rules and guidelines associated with sport when it comes to the special needs population. It is important for athletes with special needs to know and understand their legal rights and services that are available. These resources can often make the difference in an athlete's tenure and success.

Helping athletes to prepare mentally for their training and competitive efforts is a given part of the consultant's role. However, it is the whole person that they must prioritize and care most for. If athletes are experiencing issues like those discussed above, it is incumbent on consultants to assist and support them to the best of their abilities in overcoming these challenges.

Summary

- "At-risk" will be defined as athletes who have a greater probability of dropping out of sport due to daily stressors outside of sport that include academic performance, learning disability, legal issues, poverty, homelessness, food insecurity, transportation, familial issues, and problems within the community.

- Athletes often live insulated lives while they are dedicated to meeting the demands of their sport, yet they are not immune to challenges that arise in their broader lives and these matters can negatively impact their daily lives and sport engagement.
- Consultants may have greater access to the particular details of athletes' lives simply because athletes may feel more comfortable sharing specific information with them when compared to parents, family, coaches, or teammates.
- Athletes can become at risk in their sports lives for a variety of reasons which are often outside of their control, so they are unable to directly and constructively respond to the challenges.
- 22–36% of college students reported being hungry and not having enough money for food, 7–11% of college students reported not eating for a whole day due to a lack of money, up to 14% of community college students and 2% of four-year college students report homelessness, and 1 in 10 report housing insecurity.
- Student-athletes who are near completion of their athletic eligibility but are not academically close to graduating may also drop out of sport prior to completion of their eligibility for athletic competition.
- This is particularly relevant where school was a means to an end to compete in professional sports because, once the sport appears to no longer be an avenue that may lead to bigger things, the athlete is de-motivated to perform well in school simply because there was less of a commitment to academics to begin with.
- It is estimated that 11% of undergraduate students have a learning disability and that, if student-athletes have a learning disability, they may struggle upon entry into college.
- These student-athletes are at particular risk because once they get into college through the regular admissions process, it typically means they barely met the requirements but now they will not have the accommodations that could make it more manageable to succeed academically.
- Consultants need to be capable of providing expertise, resources, or referrals for athletes who are dealing with the challenges discussed above, particularly for those working in an education setting.
- Because of the culturally diverse nature of colleges and universities and the diversity found in many collegiate sports, it is also important that consultants are culturally aware and competent in understanding how these issues may impact at-risk athletes more than others.
- Resources for consultants should include names, phone numbers, and website addresses where athletes can go if public assistance is needed and, to support their efforts where social discomfort or communication difficulties may be present, consultants should be willing to provide introductions and be available for transitions to the appropriate support professional.
- Because consultants are most concerned with the holistic health and well-being of athletes, if athletes are experiencing issues discussed above, it is incumbent on consultants to assist and support them to the best of their abilities in overcoming these challenges.

References

Beamon, K. (2012). "I'm a baller": Athletic identity foreclosure among African American former student athletes. *Journal of African American Studies*, 16(2), 195–208.

Broton, K., & Goldrick-Rab, S. (2017). Going without: An exploration of food and housing insecurity among undergraduates. *Educational Researcher*, 47, 121–133.

Buckman, J. F., Yusko, D. A., Farris, S. G., White, H. R., & Pandina, R. J. (2011). Risk of marijuana use in male and female college student-athletes and non-athletes. *Journal of Studies on Alcohol & Drugs*, 72, 586–591.

Cimini, M. D., Monserrat, J. M., Sokolowski, K. L., Dewitt-Parker, J. Y., Rivero, E. M., & McElroy, L. A. (2015). Reducing high-risk drinking among student-athletes: The effects of a targeted athlete-specific brief intervention. *Journal of American College Health*, 63, 343–352.

Denbo, S. (2003). Disability lessons in higher education: Accommodating learning-disabled students and student-athletes under the Rehabilitation Act and the Americans with Disabilities Act. *American Business Law Journal*, 41, 145–203.

Forster-Scott, L., & Rosendahl, B. V. (2011). "The teacher doesn't like me": Exploring the relationship between teacher attitudes toward student-athletes and academic performance. *Academic Leadership: The Online Journal*, 9, Spring.

Hoff, D. (2012). Doping, risk and abuse: An interview study of elite athletes with a history of steroid use. *Performance Enhancement and Health*, 1, 61–65.

Murphy, M. M., Petitpas, A. J., Brewer, B.W. (1996). Identity foreclosure, athletic identity, and career maturity in intercollegiate athletes. *The Sport Psychologist*, 10(3), 239–246.

NCAA (2018, June 8). Academic year 2018–2019 summary of NCAA Regulations—NCAA Div I. Retrieved from www.ncaa.org/sites/default/files/2018-19_Summary_of_NCAA_Regulations_20180608.pdf.

Rankin, S., Merson, D., Garvey, J. C., Sorgen, C. H., Menon, I., Loya, K., & Oseguera, L. (2016). The influence of climate on the academic and athletic success of student-athletes: Results from a multi-institutional national study. (2016). *The Journal of Higher Education*, *87*, 701–730.

Rattner, J., Matyas, J., Barclay, L., Holowaychuk, S., Sciore, P., Lo, I., Shrive, N., Frank, C. B., Achari, Y., & Hart, D. A. (2011). New understanding of the complex structure of knee menisci: Implications for injury risk and repair potential for athletes. *Scandinavian Journal of Medicine and Science in Sports*, *21*, 543–553.

Weiss, S., & Robinson, T. (2013). An investigation of factors relating to retention of student-athletes participating in NCAA Division II athletics. *Interchange: A Quarterly Review of Education*, *44*, 83–104.

Yopyk, D., & Prentice, D. (2005). Am I an athlete or a student? Identity salience and stereotype threat in student-athletes. *Basic and Applied Social Psychology*, *27*, 329–336.

ATHLETIC CAREER TRANSITION

Claire-Marie Roberts, James Tabano, and Jim Taylor

Typically, the careers of athletes feature progression, plateaus, and declines (Hendry & Kloep, 2002), are characterized by a high degree of uncertainty (Coupland, 2015) and comprise many transitions. These transitions may be related to athletic, personal and social development, educational level, setbacks such as injuries, new teams, the loss of a coach, deselection, and ultimately, the conclusion of sport careers (Roberts & Davis, 2017). The depth and breadth of the athletic experience are many and often-times extreme compared to the non-sport population. Of all the impactful experiences athletes have, perhaps the most difficult is that of the end of their sport career. Moreover, retirement from sports consists of a range of experiences that are unique in comparison to those encountered in traditional retirement from careers later in life (Stambulova & Ryba, 2014; Wylleman, Alfermann, & Lavallee, 2004).

In reaction to the recognition that this phase of an athletes' life can be difficult, over the past three decades, there has been a growing body of theoretical, empirical, and applied work focusing on identifying and understanding the challenges of athletic career transition and providing services for individuals as they progress through their sports careers to their end. This section will offer a broad and deep perspective on career transition among athletes. The issues that will be explored will emphasize the career transition of athletes whose involvement in sports are a significant part of their self-identities and comprise a substantial portion of their time and energy in their lives. Athletes that fit into this category can include high-level collegiate athletes, Olympians, and professionals.

Theory and Research

Transitions are defined as "a turning phase in athletes' development that brings about a set of demands (usually appraised as stressors) and requires adequate coping processes in order to continue athletic and parallel careers such as education or work" (Stambulova & Wylleman, 2014, p. 601). As suggested, the most significant transition of all is athletic career transition, requiring the individual to re-craft a new career and re-construct a version of themselves. Such is the magnitude of this transition that around 20% of athletes experience helplessness at this juncture and require professional assistance to cope (Alfermann & Stambulova, 2007; Stambulova & Wylleman, 2014). The outcome of the individual's inability to cope at this time is termed a crisis transition (Stambulova, 2017) which can ultimately result in psychopathological behavior and social difficulties (Taylor & Ogilvie, 1994), acute depression (Reardon & Factor, 2010), identity crises (Brewer, Van Raalte, & Linder, 1993), difficulties with body image (Kerr & Dacyshyn, 2000), and occupational problems such as zeteophobia (Lavallee, Grove, & Gordon, 1997).

To help define and further understand athletic career transition specifically, Taylor and Ogilvie (1994) presented a comprehensive conceptual model that consists of a multi-stage framework that explores the relevant issues for all aspects of the transition from athlete to retired athlete.

1. **Causes:** Age, deselection, injury, free choice.
2. **Factors related to adaptation:** Personal investment in sports, self-identity, social identity, perceptions of control, life stress, physical health, socioeconomic status, minority status.
3. **Available resources:** Coping skills, social support, pre-retirement planning, medical assessment and guidance.

4. **Intervention:** Stress management, emotional counseling, social networking beyond sports, skills assessment, continuing education, and job training.
5. **Quality of career transition:** High, moderate, poor.

In essence, the model illustrates that successfully negotiating athletic career transition is centered around the process of coping with a set of demands by accessing resources and employing interventions. This coping process involves leveraging internal and external resources against barriers that athletes are confronted with (Stambulova, 2017). The effectiveness of this coping process leads to how successful the transition out of sport turns out to be for athletes.

Theoretical positions such as Taylor and Ogilvie's (1994) model of adaptation to retirement among athletes and Stambulova's athletic career transition model (Stambulova, 2003, 2009, 2017) present two possible transition outcomes: a successful transition or a crisis transition. According to former model, a successful transition results when athletes have deployed effective coping to overcome the demands of the transition, using their internal and external resources to avoid potential barriers. At the other end of the spectrum is a crisis transition which is a product of ineffective coping, as a result of a paucity of internal and external resources, many and significant barriers, and in some cases, the personality attributes of athletes (Stambulova, 2017). At the point of a crisis transition, Stambulova's athletic career transition model (Stambulova, 2003, 2009, 2017) identifies secondary outcomes of (a) a delayed successful transition when interventions are deployed to reverse the outcome, (b) an unsuccessful transition resulting in premature departure from sport, and (c) other negative reactions to the failure of the transition.

Those negative reactions often manifest sub-clinically or clinically. For example, failing to negotiate an effective transition out of sport may lead to athletes to experience a decrease in self-esteem, lasting emotional discomfort, increased sensitivity to mistakes and failures, an increase in the number of internal barriers (e.g., low motivation and self-efficacy), and disorientation in decision-making and behavior (Stambulova, 2000, 2003). When these sub-clinical reactions (Wolanin, Gross, & Hong, 2015) are evident, an expedient reactive counseling intervention may help athletes cope more effectively and hence reverse the transition outcome (to be discussed in greater depth below; Schinke, Stambulova, Si, & Moore, 2017).

In some cases, clinical reactions to crisis transitions may result if athletes do not receive support and assistance from family and professionals and lack the capabilities to navigate the transition on their own. These reactions often include mental-health problems such as depression (Reardon & Factor, 2010) and maladaptive behaviors such eating disorders, alcohol abuse, drug abuse, and suicidality (Stambulova, 2003, 2009). Theoretically, the conceptualization of athletic transition outcomes is intuitive, yet empirical research on athletic career transition does not always support a dichotomous conceptualization of the outcome (i.e., either healthy or unhealthy; Roberts, Mullen, Evans & Hall, 2015). Instead, it is recommended that consultants keep in mind that athletes may, in fact, fall somewhere on a continuum between these two extremes (Roberts et al., 2015). Whatever the outcome, it is crucial that athletes are supported in their adaptation to life after their sports career, as the vast majority are required to move into a second career path as the money earned during a sport career may not allow for the accumulation of sufficient wealth to sustain them past retirement (Padrão dos Santos, Rosa Nogueira, & Böhme 2016).

Practical Implications

There are two approaches to supporting athletes through to the end of, and beyond, their athletic careers as a means of fostering their long-term health and well-being. These can be succinctly summarized as proactive and reactive.

Proactive Support

Proactive approaches to support mean that sports organizations (e.g., colleges, Olympic and professional teams) take time to assess any potential barriers to a healthy transition and identify and suggest resources to help them overcome these (Morris, Tod, & Oliver, 2015). Resources may involve needs and goals analyses, the identification of available and relevant life skills, the exploration and implementation of educational and career programs as well as assistance with planning their transitions. This support is delivered through psychoeducational workshops, one-to-one personal development sessions, the provision of educational or vocational experiences, and networking opportunities. Additionally, such programs aim to engage athletes throughout their careers by enhancing both sports performance and personal development (Park, Lavallee, & Tod, 2013).

There are more than 60 different programs available internationally (Stambulova & Ryba, 2014) that leverage a wide variety of proactive support strategies to help athletes prepare for life after sport. However, these interventions can also be delivered outside of a programmatic structure, by different types of practitioners who intervene at different stages of an athletic career. To illustrate, in the United States, there is an athlete career education (ACE) program provided by the United States Olympic Committee (USOC). This program supports Olympic and Paralympic athletes with teaching educational and life skills development in parallel to their sport careers. In addition, they offer individualized career coaching services for athletes looking for a part-time job while training and competing, thus enabling them to prepare for their career transition or determine their next steps on a long-term career journey.

In professional sports, proactive support may be outsourced to a specialist organization or discrete interventions may be delivered by an athlete development specialist or consultant. The emergence of the role of the athlete development specialist is a relatively new phenomenon promoted (in the US) by the Professional Association of Athlete Development Specialists (PAADS) which is dedicated to helping organizations and individuals develop the whole person in an athletic context. Naturally, the majority of consultants that work in the sport psychology field possess the requisite skills to support athlete development, and due to their existing role with individual athletes or teams, they are likely to be the natural choice to provide this proactive support. Having said that, there is often a lack of role clarity for both athlete development specialists and those working in the sport psychology field. This may contribute to the portrayal of proactive lifestyle support within the literature as focusing solely on practical skill development rather than the personal, psychological, and emotional support required.

Providing preventive holistic athlete development interventions and pre-retirement planning throughout the individual's sport career is considered fundamental to the resulting transition experience. For example, providing such support during adolescence, and, therefore, in the early stages of an athletic career, may seem premature, but this is the stage at which identity, cognitive motivational strategies, and the social and organizational skills that may impact the educational choices and career aspirations of individuals are being formed (Nurmi, 2004). Additionally, a concerted effort on proactive support during the early stages of retirement (or put differently, the latter stages of an athletic career) is likely to be beneficial (Park, Tod, & Lavallee, 2012) as it is likely to be targeted and timely. While the proactive support in the early stages of a sport career can be more broad-based in its focus, it is crucial that the support in the latter stages of the career is fully individualized.

There are a number of different approaches that consultants can take to an athlete development or a proactive transition intervention. For example, Danish, Petitpas and Hale's (1995) Life Development Intervention and Stambulova's (2010) Five Step Career Planning Strategy both feature the development of goal-setting skills and the identification and utilization of skills developed during the course of an athletic career for the benefit of a second career. In addition, consultants can intervene proactively by helping athletes to balance their investment in their sport and the degree that their self-identity is consumed by sport. They can guide athletes in expanding their social networks beyond sports. Consultants can show athletes ways to increase their sense of personal control in their lives outside of sports and identify a variety of resources that athletes can leverage during and after their playing days that will benefit them after career transition.

Essential resources can include academic counselors to encourage continuing their educations, financial advisers to bolster economic responsibility, and community business leaders to act as mentors for pre-retirement planning and future career direction. The benefits of proactive, holistic athlete development and pre-retirement planning is considered to be one of the most significant predictors of a healthy career transition. Yet, there is often general resistance to engaging in these types of activities, centered on the myth that they distract from sport performance (Park et al., 2013). In a convincing challenge to this way of thinking, Lavallee (2018) recently concluded that engaging in proactive support throughout an athletic career actually predicted team selection and career tenure.

Reactive Support

Athletes who fail in their efforts to cope with athletic career transition and are facing a crisis transition, can benefit in the immediate term from reactive support. Such support can be provided by consultants and is aimed at helping athletes enhance their awareness and understanding of their transition, to facilitate sound decision-making, and develop resources to enhance the effectiveness of their coping (Stambulova, 2017). The mobilization model of counseling in crisis transitions proposed by Stambulova (2011) is six-step educational intervention designed to help support athletes to develop a problem-solving orientation in reaction to their transition. Typically, this involves:

- collecting out information relevant to athletes' transitions;
- identifying, prioritizing, and articulating the problem issues;
- analyzing athletes' current coping resources and barriers;
- discussing options resulting in athletes' making a decision about how best to move forward;
- goal setting and program planning to put the decision into action; and
- follow-up assessment, evaluation, and program adjustment.

As a result of, or in addition to the educational intervention described above, athletes may benefit from stress reduction interventions, emotional counseling, education and career planning, networking, and account-making and narrative therapy (Carless & Douglas, 2008; Lavallee, Nesti, Borkoles, Cockerill, & Edge, 2011). Where consultants encounter athletes exhibiting clinical symptoms as a result of a crisis transition, a referral to a appropriately trained mental health professional should be considered (e.g., Roberts, Faull, & Tod, 2016). These reactive interventions are designed to help athletes convert their ineffective coping efforts into effective ones. If the crisis transition is unresolved, negative symptoms often persist, and there is little capacity to face new challenges (Stambulova, 2017).

Despite the suggested content of proactive and reactive support available to athletes there is a lack of research examining the effectiveness of specific content of athlete development and transition interventions (Stambulova & Ryba, 2014). Because little of the content is known, their use, effectiveness, and athlete perceptions of their benefits have not been systematically examined (Park et al., 2013). As such, it is currently unclear as to whether the support described is beneficial to athletes in transition. For this reason, it is suggested that this is an area ripe for further exploration.

Summary

- High-level sports participation is punctuated by transitions based on athletic development, educational level, setbacks such as injuries, new teams, and, ultimately, the conclusion of sports careers.
- Of all the impactful experiences athletes have, perhaps the most difficult is that of the end of their sports careers.
- Over the past three decades, there has been a growing body of theoretical, empirical, and applied work focusing on identifying, understanding, and providing services for athletes as they progress through their sports careers to its end.
- Transitions are defined as "a turning phase in athletes' development that brings about a set of demands (usually appraised as stressors) and requires adequate coping processes in order to continue athletic and parallel careers such as education or work."
- Taylor and Ogilvie offer a multi-stage model of athletic career transition that includes causes, factors related to adaptation, available resources, intervention and quality of career transition.
- A successful transition results when athletes have deployed effective coping to overcome the demands of the transition, using their internal and external resources to avoid potential barriers, while a crisis transition is a product of ineffective coping as a result of a paucity of internal and external resources, many and significant barriers, and the personality attributes of athletes.
- Negative reactions to career transition can manifest themselves sub-clinically (e.g., low self-esteem, emotional discomfort, and indecision) and clinically (e.g., depression, anxiety, substance abuse, and suicide).

- Career transition programs and services are on offer in most Olympic federations and professional leagues, providing educational guidance, career planning, and transition support.
- Consultants can support athletes in transition individually by proactively helping them to balance their investment in their sport and the degree that self-identity is consumed by sport, expand their social networks beyond sports, and show athletes ways to increase their sense of personal control in their lives outside of sports.
- Effective interventions that consultants can use with athletes include skills, needs, and goals assessments, stress management, emotional counseling, and networking.
- Consultants can identify a variety of resources that athletes can leverage during their playing days that will benefit them during and after career transition including academic counselors to encourage continuing their educations, financial advisers to bolster financial responsibility, and community business leaders to act as mentors for pre-retirement planning and future career direction.

References

Alfermann, D., & Stambulova, N. B. (2007). Career transitions and career termination. In G. & R. C. Eklund (Eds.), *Handbook of sport psychology* (3rd ed., pp. 712–736). New York: Wiley.

Brewer, B. W., Van Raalte, J. L., & Linder, D. E. (1993). Athletic identity: Hercules' muscles or Achilles Heel? *International Journal of Sport Psychology, 24,* 237–254.

Carless, D., & Douglas, K. (2008). Narrative, identity and metal health: How men with serious mental illness re-story their lives through sport and exercise. *Psychology of Sport & Exercise, 9,* 576–594.

Coupland, C. (2015). The game of (your) life: Professional sports careers. In M. Barry & J. Skinner (Eds.), *The research handbook of employment relations in sport.* Cheltenham: Edward Elgar.

Danish, S. J., Petitpas, A., & Hale, B. D. (1995). Psychological interventions: A life development model. In S. M. Murphy (Ed.), *Sport psychology interventions* (pp. 19–38). Champaign, IL: Human Kinetics.

Hendry, L., & Kloep, M. (2002). *Adolescence and adulthood. Transitions and transformations.* London: Macmillan.

Kerr, G., & Dacyshyn, A. (2000). The retirement experiences of elite female gymnasts. *Journal of Applied Sport Psychology, 12,* 115–133.

Lavallee, D. (2018). Engagement in sport career transition planning enhances performance. *Journal of Loss and Trauma, 24.*

Lavallee, D., Grove, J. R., & Gordon, S. (1997). The causes of career transition from sport and their relationship to post-retirement adjustment among elite-amateur athletes in Australia. *Australian Psychologist, 32,* 131–135.

Lavallee, D., Nesti, M., Borkoles, E., Cockerill, I., & Edge, A. (2011). Intervention strategies for athletes in transition. In D. Lavallee & P. Wylleman (Eds.), *Career transitions in sport: International perspectives* (pp. 111–130). Morgantown, WV: Fitness Information Technology.

Morris, R., Tod, D., & Oliver, E. J. (2015). An analysis of organizational structure and transition outcomes in the youth-to-senior professional soccer transition. *Journal of Applied Sport Psychology, 27,* 216–234.

Nurmi, J. E. (2004). Socialization and self-development. *Handbook of Adolescent Psychology, 2,* 85–124.

Padrão dos Santos, A., Rosa Nogueira, M. P., & Böhme, M. T. S. (2016). Elite athletes' perception of retirement support systems. *International Journal of Physical Education, Sport and Health, 3,* 138–139.

Park, S., Lavallee, D., & Tod, D. (2013). Athletes' career transition out of sport: A systematic review. *International Review of Sport & Exercise Psychology, 6,* 22–53.

Park, S., Tod, D., & Lavallee, D. (2012). Exploring the retirement from sport decision- making process based on the transtheoretical model. *Psychology of Sport and Exercise, 13,* 444–453.

Reardon, C. L., & Factor, R. M. (2010). Sports psychiatry: A systematic review of diagnosis and medical treatment of mental illness in athletes. *Sports Medicine, 40,* 961–980.

Roberts, C.-M., & Davis, M. O. (2017). Career transitions. In J. Taylor (Ed.), *Assessment in sport psychology.* Champaign, IL: Human Kinetics.

Roberts, C.-M., Faull, A. L., & Tod, D. (2016). Blurred lines: Performance enhancement, common mental disorders and referral in the U.K. athletic population. *Frontiers in Psychology, 7,* 1067.

Roberts, C.-M., Mullen, R., Evans, L., & Hall, R. J. (2015). An in-depth appraisal of career termination experiences in professional cricket. *Journal of Sport Sciences, 33,* 935–944.

Schinke, R. J., Stambulova, N. B., Si, G., & Moore, Z. (2017). International society of sport psychology position stand: Athletes' mental health, performance, and development. *International Journal of Sport and Exercise Psychology, 16,* 35–52.

Stambulova, N. B. (2000). Athlete's crises: A developmental perspective. *International Journal of Sport Psychology, 31,* 584–601.

Stambulova, N. B. (2003). Symptoms of a crisis transition: A grounded theory study. In M. Hassmén (Ed.), *Sipf Yearbook 2003* (pp. 97–109). Örebro, Sweden: Örebro University Press.

Stambulova, N. B. (2009). Talent development in sport: A career transition perspective. In E. Tsung-Min Hung, R. Lidor, & D. Hackfort (Eds.), *Psychology of sport excellence* (pp. 63–74). Morgantown, WV: Fitness Information Technology.

Stambulova, N. (2010). Counselling athletes in career transitions: The five-step career planning strategy. *Journal of Sport Psychology in Action, 1*, 95–105.

Stambulova, N. B. (2011). The mobilization model of counseling athletes in crisis-transitions: an educational intervention tool. *Journal of Sport Psychology in Action, 2*, 156–170.

Stambulova, N. B. (2017). Crisis-transitions in athletes: current emphases on cognitive and contextual factors. *Current Opinion in Psychology, 16*, 62–66.

Stambulova, N. B., & Ryba, T. V. (2014). A critical review of career research and assistance through the cultural lens: Towards cultural praxis of athletes' careers. *International Review of Sport and Exercise Psychology, 7*, 1–17.

Stambulova, N. B., & Wylleman, P. (2014). Athletes' career development and transitions. In A. Papaioannou & D. Hackfort (Eds.), *Routledge companion to sport and exercise psychology* (pp. 605–621). Abingdon: Routledge.

Taylor, J., & Ogilvie, B.C. (1994). A conceptual model of adaptation to retirement among athletes. *Journal of Applied Sport Psychology, 6*, 1–20.

Wolanin, A., Gross, M., & Hong, E. (2015). Depression in athletes: Prevalence and risk factors. *Current Sports Medicine Reports, 14*, 56–60.

Wylleman, P., Alfermann, D., & Lavallee, D. (2004). Career transitions in sport: European perspectives. *Psychology of Sport & Exercise, 5*, 7–20.

8

MENTAL HEALTH

Introduction

Kathy Pruzan and Jim Taylor

Recently, several well-known athletes have publicly discussed the mental health struggles they have had, in particular, anxiety, depression, and sexual abuse. This openness on the part of professional athletes to share their difficulties may signal a shift in how athletes view mental health concerns where they have historically been reluctant to express their vulnerabilities and held negative beliefs about seeking mental health support. In fact, athletes identify a range of barriers to seeking mental health treatment including the stigma associated with mental illness, lack of awareness of mental health issues, and not knowing where to seek treatment, as well as concerns about privacy and how it might affect their sports careers.

Additionally, the prevailing sports culture has traditionally not encouraged or supported discussions about the mental health of athletes. From this perspective, athletes are supposed to be "mentally tough" and, as a result, superhuman and immune to human frailty. As such, many athletes have avoided coming forward when they are struggling with psychiatric issues for fear of being stigmatized by coaches, teammates, administrators, fans, and the media.

In addition to the focus of enhancing sports performance through the mental training of athletes, consultants also have an even more important responsibility and obligation to serve as a starting point for screening, referrals, and treatment for the overall mental health of athletes regardless of their education, training, or experience. Consultants who have clinical training can often treat the mental illness that athletes present with in concert with mental training. Those consultants without specialized mental health training can still play a vital role in screening for and, if necessary, referring out to appropriately trained professionals for treatment.

Because consultants are grounded in the sports world, they can be an initial source of trust toward whom athletes can express their concerns and, in turn, get the help they need. As a result, it's critical that consultants have, at a minimum, a working knowledge of the range of mental health difficulties that athletes may face, as well as an understanding of screening, assessment, and treatment options. It's also important for consultants to know the limits of their professional capabilities when referral to a specific provider or team would be the better choice for helping athletes with a particular clinical issue. This notion holds true for both sport-science and psychology-training professionals because just because a consultant has clinical training doesn't mean they are qualified to treat every form of mental illness that athletes may present with.

ANXIETY

Penny Levin

By its very nature, sports are inherently anxiety-provoking. "Competitive" or "Performance" anxiety refers to an athlete's tendency to approach and respond to competitive sports experiences with some level of fear and tension (Behzadi et al., 2011), and is accepted as a normal part of the competitive process. Typical symptoms of competitive anxiety include a racing heart, quick and shallow breathing, rushing adrenaline, muscle tension, a narrowing of focus (see Chapter 3 for more). Research indicates that female athletes report higher levels of competitive anxiety than males (Thanopoulos & Platanou, 2017) and athletes competing in individual sports generally experience higher levels of competitive anxiety than those competing in team events (Kumar, 2016). Though often viewed negatively, competitive anxiety can be a healthy and adaptive response to sports competition whereby athletes' bodies are preparing for the challenges that lie ahead.

However, it is important to differentiate typical competitive anxiety from clinical anxiety. Competitive anxiety is sport- and often situation-specific, and short lived. By contrast, diagnosed anxiety disorders are debilitating, persistent, and impact all aspects of athletes' lives long after the competitive event has ended.

Theory and Research

Anxiety disorders are characterized by uneasiness, excessive worry that is difficult to control, hypervigilance, emotional reactivity, and fear of the future. In addition to these psychological red flags, anxiety disorders are often accompanied by a range of physiological symptoms, including restlessness, agitation, fatigue, accelerated cardiac and respiratory activity, muscle tension, and sleep disturbances, and eating disruptions (American Psychiatric Association, 2013), as well as behavioral and social changes and cognitive impairment (Khdour et al., 2016). Despite improved access to mental health treatment, anxiety disorders remain among the most commonly diagnosed mental disorders (National Institute of Mental Health, 2017), with a third of all Americans experiencing an anxiety disorder at some point in their lives (Kessler et al., 2005). Unlike performance anxiety, these conditions extend far beyond athletes' sports lives and negatively impact many aspects of their daily functioning.

The *Diagnostic and Statistical Manual of Mental Disorders*—Fifth Edition (DSM-V) (American Psychiatric Association, 2013) identifies a range of anxiety disorders. Because of their particular importance and prevalence among athletes, this section will consider generalized anxiety disorder (GAD), social anxiety disorder (SAD), and panic disorder (PD). Individuals with GAD experience persistent worry that is difficult to control and causes significant distress. It is often accompanied by muscle tension, restlessness, fatigue, gastrointestinal discomfort, and difficulty sleeping, and impacts people across a range of settings. Because symptoms may appear to be physical rather than psychological and overlap with those commonly associated with depression, misdiagnosis may occur and treatment may be delayed (Bandelow et al., 2013).

Social anxiety is distinguished by a persistent fear of one or more social or performance situations in which athletes expect to be exposed to unfamiliar people or possible scrutiny, judgment, or criticism by others (e.g., tryouts). These fears are often accompanied by concerns about embarrassment or humiliation. Typical indications of social anxiety include:

- fear in anticipation of a social activity;
- extreme feelings of shyness or discomfort in social situation;
- self-defeating expectations;
- avoidance of social situations;
- social withdrawal;
- reluctance to speak up in groups; and
- self-criticism of social experiences.

People with social anxiety disorder manage their anxiety by avoiding social events, not attending school or work, not initiating conversations, avoiding eye contact, and not entering a room alone, asserting themselves with others, and dating (American Psychiatric Association, 2013).

Panic disorder involves recurrent and unexpected episodes of intense fear, accompanied by severe physiological symptoms such as palpitations, chest pain, nausea, numbness, dizziness or sweating, followed by fear of either another panic attack or a physical condition such as a heart attack (American Psychiatric Association, 2013). Behavioral signs include (Jacofsky, Santos, Khemlani-Patel, & Neziroglu, n.d.):

- avoidance of the panic-provoking situation;
- attempts to escape the threatening situation;
- self-medication with alcohol or drugs;
- engaging in self-sabotage as a means of removing the perceived threat;
- narrowing the scope of one's life to minimize anxiety; and
- developing an excessive attachment to an object or person that provides comfort.

While little information about the prevalence of anxiety disorders among American athletes is available, a study examining anxiety in elite Australian athletes reported that 14.7% experienced social anxiety, 7.1% experienced generalized anxiety disorder, and that 4.5% experienced panic disorder (Gulliver et al., 2015). A survey of French athletes found that GAD was the most prevalent disorder and was more common in women than in men (Schaal et al., 2011). Interestingly, the anxiety level of coaches has also been shown to impact their players' anxiety and negatively impacts their athletic performance (Mottaghi et al., 2013).

Until recently, the broader category of anxiety disorders also included both obsessive-compulsive disorder (OCD) and post-traumatic stress disorder (PTSD) (American Psychiatric Association, 2000), both relevant to athletes. Now, OCD is among the "Obsessive-Compulsive and Related Disorders" and PTSD is subsumed by "Trauma- and Stressor-Related Disorders" (American Psychiatric Association, 2013). These changes were made to allow for greater precision in identifying specific disorders (Kupfer, 2015).

Some studies suggest that rates of OCD among athletes are higher than the general population and that common traits in athletes, such as perfectionism, superstitions, rituals, and body hyper-focus, might mask OCD identification (Reardon & Factor, 2010). A recent survey of 270 NCAA Division I collegiate athletes across 13 sports who had not received a diagnosis of OCD found that more than a third reported OCD symptoms, 16% screened positive for OCD, and 5% met full criteria for the disorder (Cromer et al., 2017).

PTSD is now subsumed under "Trauma- and Stressor-Related Disorders." Symptoms of PTSD include re-experiencing the trauma through memories, flashbacks, and nightmares, lack of emotional detachment, avoidance of reminders of the trauma, panic attacks, and other expressions of intense anxiety and fear (American Psychiatric Association, 2013). PTSD has been found to be present among injured athletes, so consultants should be aware that athletes typically experience greater anxiety and lower self-esteem in the aftermath of an athletic injury (O'Connell & Manschreck, 2012). Symptoms of PTSD may be present after an injury (Bateman & Morgan, 2017) and approximately 10% of athletes suffer long-term psychological consequences from sport-related injuries (O'Connell & Manschreck, 2012).

Another area in which PTSD may be evident among athletes is in sexual abuse by trusted people such as coaches and medical professionals. The recent sex abuse scandal in USA gymnastics, in which more than 150 female gymnasts were sexually molested by a team physician over several decades, highlights the harm that can occur (Kirby, 2018). With these and other cases of sexual abuse in the news so frequently, it is incumbent on consultants to be sensitive to and aware of indications of such treatment of athletes by people in power in sports (to be discussed in detail later in this chapter).

Practical Implications

Anxiety disorders can have a serious impact on athletes both within and outside of their sports lives. Consultants would best serve athletes with whom they work by having an appropriate level of understanding of anxiety disorders, depending on their education, training, and experience, that would enable them to assist athletes who present with indications of an anxiety disorder in getting the help they need to facilitate their mental health, well-being, and sports performance. Consultants with a thorough understanding of the difference between performance and clinical anxiety will feel more comfortable knowing when to provide appropriate mental training and when to refer athletes for mental health evaluation and treatment.

Assessment

Regardless of whether consultants have clinical training, an essential part of their intake with athletes should be some type of mental-status assessment. Important questions that should be a part of an intake include (Reynolds & Kamphaus, n.d.):

- Does your family have a history of anxiety?
- Have you ever been diagnosed with anxiety?
- Do you experience any of the following symptoms:

  - A. Excessive anxiety and worry (apprehensive expectation), occurring more days than not for at least 6 months, about a number of events or activities (such as work or school performance).
  - B. Difficulty controlling the worry.
  - C. Anxiety and worry associated with three (or more) of the following six symptoms (with at least some symptoms having been present for more days than not for the past 6 months). In consulting with children, only one of these symptoms needs to be present.
    - Restlessness, feeling keyed up or on edge.
    - Being easily fatigued.
    - Difficulty concentrating or mind going blank.
    - Irritability.
    - Muscle tension.
    - Sleep disturbance (difficulty falling or staying asleep, or restless, unsatisfying sleep).
  - D. Anxiety, worry, or physical symptoms that causes clinically significant distress or impairment in social, occupational, or other important areas of functioning.
  - E. The disturbance is not attributable to the physiological effects of a substance (e.g., a drug of abuse, a medication) or another medical condition (e.g., hyperthyroidism).

In addition, there are several objective measures for assessing clinical anxiety, including the Structured Clinical Interview for DSM-5 (First, Williams, Karg, & Spitzer, 2015) and The Beck Anxiety Inventory (Steer & Beck, 1997). In terms of performance anxiety, the Competitive State Anxiety Inventory-2 (Cox et al., 2003) and the Sport Competition Anxiety Test (Martens, 1977) have been developed to specifically measure sports anxiety. These measures are short, easily administered, and free to use. Particularly for those without clinical training, the objective results can provide a clear basis for the need for a referral to an appropriately trained mental health professional.

Treatment

Historically, standard treatments for anxiety disorders have included cognitive-behavioral therapy (CBT) and medication. Both of these treatments have been found to be effective in the management of clinical anxiety, and both are widely used both separately and in combination (Roshanaei-Moghaddam et al., 2011; McArdle & Moore, 2012).

Cognitive-behavioral therapy (Burns, 2006) is founded on the fundamental assumption that how people think directly impacts how they feel and behave. External events or internal beliefs are assumed to trigger dysfunctional thoughts in anxious clients, and it is these negative patterns and distorted thinking that result in symptoms of anxiety. Examples of dysfunctional ideas include those that are overgeneralized, catastrophic, or focus only on the negative aspects of a situation. Treatment is focused on recognizing and systematically reformulating and refuting the inaccurate ideas and developing more accurate and nuanced patterns of thought. Because CBT utilizes techniques similar to those taught in evaluating "self-talk," this modality may be better accepted by athletes than other psycho-therapeutic modalities.

FDA-approved medications that have typically been considered to be the first line of therapy for anxiety disorders include:

- **SSRI medications:** Citalopram (Celexa), Escitalopram (Lexapro), Fluoxetine (Prozac), Paroxetine (Paxil), Sertraline (Zoloft). Vilazodone (Viibryd).
- **SNRI medications:** Desvenlafaxine (Pristiq, Khedezla), Duloxetine (Cymbalta), Levomilnacipran (Fetzima) and Venlafaxine (EffexorDuloxetine (Cymbalta).

In the past, benzodiazepines, including Valium and Xanex, were widely used to treat anxiety conditions, but pose risks, including addiction, with chronic use. SSRIs and SNRIs, while effective, have been shown to increase the risk of suicidality, and these drugs can cause weight gain and sexual dysfunction, which may be of particular concern to athletes (Bystritsky et al., 2013).

More recently, modalities such as mindfulness-based interventions have proven successful with a range of anxiety disorders, even when offered remotely through internet applications. These techniques do not attack symptoms directly, but seek to improve the conscious regulation of attention and foster an attitude of openness and self-acceptance through the use of a range of meditation exercises (Boettcher et al., 2014). Exercise has also become a focus in recent years as a treatment for anxiety disorders. A recent meta-analysis suggests that exercise may be equivalent to more established treatment modalities in the treatment of anxiety. However, issues such as the range of definitions of "exercise" and other significant methodological limitations suggest that additional research is needed to establish physical activity as a viable treatment modality (Stonerock et al., 2015). In addition, for consultants, the fact that clients generally are already exercising regularly suggests the need to consider other treatment options.

Summary

- By its nature, sports competition is inherently anxiety provoking. "Competitive" or "performance" anxiety refers to an athlete's tendency to respond to competitive situations with some level of fear and tension and is accepted as a normal part of the competitive process.
- However, it is important to differentiate competitive anxiety from clinical anxiety, whereas competitive anxiety is sport- and often-situation-specific, and short lived, diagnosed anxiety disorders are debilitating, persistent, pervasive, global, and impact all aspects of athletes' lives long after the competitive event has ended.
- Anxiety disorders are characterized by uneasiness, excessive worry that is difficult to control, hypervigilance, emotional reactivity, and fear of the future and are accompanied by a range of physiological symptoms, including restlessness, agitation, fatigue, accelerated cardiac and respiratory activity, tension, and sleep disturbances, and eating disruptions as well as behavioral and social changes and even cognitive impairment.
- Because of their particular importance in consultation with athletes, this chapter will consider generalized anxiety disorder (GAD), social anxiety disorder (SAD), and panic disorder (PD).
- Individuals with GAD experience persistent worry that is difficult to control and causes significant distress.
- Social anxiety is distinguished by a persistent fear of one or more social or performance situations in which athletes expect to be exposed to unfamiliar people or possible scrutiny, judgment, and criticism by others.
- Panic disorder involves recurrent and unexpected episodes of intense fear, accompanied by severe physiological symptoms such as palpitations, chest pain, nausea, numbness, dizziness or sweating, followed by fear of either another panic attack or a physical condition such as a heart attack.
- Anxiety disorders can have a serious impact on athletes both within and outside of their sports lives.
- Depending on their education, training, and experience, consultants would best serve athletes with whom they work by having a level of understanding of anxiety disorders that would enable them to assist athletes in getting the help they need to facilitate their mental health, well-being, and sports performance.
- Regardless of whether consultants have clinical training, an essential part of their intake with athletes should be some type of mental-status assessment.
- There are several measures for assessing clinical anxiety, including the Structured Clinical Interview for DSM-5 and The Beck Anxiety Inventory.
- Standard treatment for anxiety disorders includes cognitive-behavioral therapy (CBT), medication, mindfulness and exercise.

References

American Psychiatric Association (2000). *Diagnostic and statistical manual of mental disorders*, 4th ed. (DSM-4). Arlington, VA: American Psychiatric Association.

American Psychiatric Association. (2013). *Diagnostic and statistical manual of mental disorders*, 5th ed. (DSM-5). Arlington, VA: American Psychiatric Publishing.

Bandelow, B., Boerner R., Kasper, S., Linden, M., Wittchen H. U., & Moller, H. J. (2013). The diagnosis and treatment of generalized anxiety disorder. *Deutsches Arzteblatt, 1110*, 300–310. doi: 10.3238/arztebl.2013.0300

Bateman, A., & Morgan, K. A. (2017). The Post-Injury Psychological Sequelae of High-level Jamaican Athletes: Exploration of a Post-Traumatic Stress Disorder–Self-Efficacy Conceptualisation. *Journal of Sport Rehabilitation, 18*, 1–33.

Behzadi, F., Hamzei, M., Nori, S., & Salehian, M. H. (2011). The relationship between goal orientation and competitive anxiety in individual and team athletes fields. *Annals of Biological Research, 2*(6), 261–268.

Boettcher, J., Åström, V., Påhlsson, D., Schenström, O., Andersson, G., & Carlbring, P. (2014). Internet-based mindfulness treatment for anxiety disorders: A randomized controlled trial, 2014, *Behavior Therapy, 45*(2), 241–253.

Burns, D. (2006). *When panic attacks.* New York, NY: Broadway Books.

Bystritsky, A., Khalsa, S., Cameron, M., & Schiffman, J. (2013). A current diagnosis and treatment of anxiety disorders. *P&T, 38*(1): 30–57.

Cox, R. H., Martens, M. P., & Russell, W. D. (2003). Measuring anxiety in athletics: The Revised Competitive State Anxiety Inventory-2. *Journal of Sport and Exercise Psychology, 25,* 519–533.

Cromer, L., Kaier, E., Davis, J., Stunk, K., & Stewart, S. (2017). OCD in College Athletes. *American Journal of Psychiatry, 174*(6), 595–597.

First, M. B., Williams, J. B. W., Karg, R. S., & Spitzer, R. L. (2015). *Structured Clinical Interview for DSM-5, Clinician Version* (SCID-5-CV). Arlington, VA: American Psychiatric Association.

Gulliver, A., Griffiths, K. M., Mackinnon, A., Batterham, P. J., & Stanimirovic, R. (2015). The mental health of Australian elite athletes. *Journal of Science and Medicine in Sport, 18*(3), 255–261.

Jacofsky, M. D., Santos, M. T., Khemlani-Patel, S., & Neziroglu, F. (n.d.). The symptoms of anxiety. Gracepoint. www.gracepointwellness.org/1-anxiety-disorders/article/38467-the-symptoms-of-anxiety

Kessler, R. C., Chiu, W. T., Demler, O., Merikangas, K. R., & Walters, E. E. (2005). Prevalence, severity, and comorbidity of twelve-month DSM-IV disorders in the National Comorbidity Survey Replication (NCS-R). *Archives of General Psychiatry, 62*(6), 617–627.

Khdour, H. Y., Abushalbaq, O. M., Mughrabi, I. T., Imam, A. F., Gluck, M. A., Herzallah, M. M., & Moustafa, A. A. (2016). Generalized anxiety disorder and social anxiety disorder, but not panic anxiety disorder, are associated with higher sensitivity to learning from negative feedback: Behavioral and computational investigation. *Frontiers in Integrative Neuroscience, 10,* 20.

Kirby, J. (2018). The sex abuse scandal surrounding USA Gymnastics team doctor Larry Nassar, explained. Retrieved from www.vox.com/identities/2018/1/19/16897722/sexual-abuse-usa-gymnastics-larry-nassar-explained

Kumar, A. (2016). Pre-competitive anxiety levels in female players competing in individual versus team games. *International Journal of Physical Education, Sports and Health, 3,* 303–304.

Kupfer, D. J. (2015). Anxiety and DSM-5. *Dialogues in Clinical Neuroscience, 17*(3), 245.

Martens, R. (1977). *Sport Competition Anxiety Test.* Champaign, IL: Human Kinetics Publishers.

McArdle, S., & Moore, P. (2012). Applying Evidence-Based Principles from CBT to Sport Psychology. *The Sport Psychologist, 26*(2), 299–310.

Mottaghi, M., Atarodi, A., & Rohani, Z. (2013). The relationship between coaches' and athletes' competitive anxiety, and their performance. *Iranian Journal of Psychiatry and Behavioral Sciences, 7*(2), 68.

National Institute of Mental Health. (2017). Any Anxiety Disorder. Retrieved May 30, 2018, from www.nimh.nih.gov/health/statistics/any-anxiety-disorder.shtml.

O'Connell, S., & Manschreck, T. C. (2012). Playing through the pain: Psychiatric risks among athletes. *Current Psychiatry, 11*(7), 16–20.

Reardon, C. L., & Factor, R. M. (2010). Sport psychiatry. *Sports Medicine, 40*(11), 961–980.

Reynolds, C. R., & Kamphaus, R. W. (n.d.) Generalized anxiety disorder. Retrieved from https://images.pearsonclinical.com/images/assets/basc-3/basc3resources/DSM5_DiagnosticCriteria_GeneralizedAnxietyDisorder.pdf

Roshanaei-Moghaddam, B., Pauly, M., Atlins, D., Baldwin, S., & Stein, M. (2011). Relative effects of CBT and pharmacotherapy in depression versus anxiety: Is medication somewhat better for depression, and CBT somewhat better for anxiety? *Depression and Anxiety, 28,* 560–567.

Schaal, K., Tafflet, M., Nassif, H., Thibault, V., Pichard, C., Alcotte, M., & Toussaint, J. F. (2011). Psychological balance in high level athletes: gender-based differences and sport-specific patterns. *Plos ONE, 6*(5), e19007.

Steer, R. A., & Beck, A. T. (1997). Beck Anxiety Inventory.

Stonerock, G. L., Hoffman, B. M., Smith, P. J. et al. (2015). Exercise as treatment for anxiety. *Ann Behav Med, 49,* 542.

Thanopoulos, V., & Platanou, T. (2017). Pre-competitive anxiety in swimmers and water polo players in relation to gender and age. *Facta Universitatis, Series: Physical Education and Sport,* 347–354.

DEPRESSION

Erin Haugen

Major depressive disorder, most commonly referred to as depression, is one of the most commonly diagnosed psychiatric disorders among the general and athletic populations. As noted in the Introduction of Chapter 8, more and more professional and Olympic athletes have shared their struggles with depression (Weitz, n.d.).

This vulnerability has helped to make discussing depression less taboo. In doing so, other athletes afflicted with depression are more comfortable seeking help rather than hiding it and suffering in silence.

Theory and Research

Depression is characterized by a period of at least two weeks of depressed mood and/or loss of interest/pleasure in activities in nearly all activities plus at least five of the following symptoms in the same two-week period:

- change in weight/appetite;
- change in sleeping;
- psychomotor agitation or retardation;
- fatigue or loss of energy;
- feeling worthless or inappropriate guilt;
- difficulty concentrating or indecisiveness; and
- recurrent thoughts of death, suicidal ideation, a suicide attempt, or a plan to die by suicide (American Psychiatric Association, 2013).

It is considered a depressive episode once these symptoms are present for most days for at least a two-week period.

Among the various forms of mental illness that afflict athletes, depression has been the most vigorously and comprehensively studied by researchers. This body of evidence includes a wide range of athlete populations from several countries. Similar to the general population, the findings demonstrate clearly that depression is a significant problem among athletes at many levels of sport.

Depression in Athlete Populations

Studies of the global population suggest the prevalence rate of depression is 4.4% (World Health Organization, 2017), although this varies based upon demographics (e.g., age, gender, national origin). In athlete samples across cultures, the rate of depression ranges from 3.6% (Schaal et al., 2011) to 27% (Gulliver, Griffiths, Mackinnon, Batterham, & Stanimirovic, 2015). Although Gouttebarge and colleagues found rates of up to 45% (Gouttebarge et al., 2017), the measure utilized evaluated both anxiety and depressive symptoms. As a result, the findings suggest that the two disorders may have been conflated, thus producing the astonishingly high rate. One study found rates of depression to vary based upon competitive level with 10% of professional athletes and 28% of elite junior athletes reporting depression (Jensen, Ivarsson, Fallby, Dankers, & Elbe, 2018). In one of the only studies to use a diagnostic interview, Hammond, Gialloreto, Kubas, and Davis (2013) found that 68% of their sample of elite swimmers met diagnostic criteria for depression in the previous 36 months.

Several athlete samples have found that depression is often co-occurring with other disorders. Yang et al. (2014) found 86% of athletes experiencing depression also experienced anxiety. Depressive symptoms were also found to correlate with chronic stress (Frank, Nixdorf, & Beckman, 2017; Nixdorf, Frank, Hautzinger, & Beckman, 2013). Miller and colleagues (2002) found 14% of athletes consuming high rates of alcohol exceeded depressive cutoff scores. Therefore, it is important to consider a wide range of mental health diagnoses when depression may be in evidence.

Suicide is another crucial factor to consider within the context of depression. In a retrospective analysis of college student-athlete deaths, 7% were deaths by suicide with 82.9% of these deaths being male. At the same time, student-athletes were less likely to die by suicide than the general population (Rao, Asif, Drezner, Toresdahl, & Harmon, 2015) and may report suicidal ideation less often than non-athletes (Schaal et al., 2011). Moreover, there is some evidence suggesting that adolescent athletes may experience less hopelessness, suicidal ideation, and suicidal behavior than their peers in the general population, but athlete suicide attempts may result in more serious injury (Sabo, Miller, Melnick, Farrell, & Barnes, 2005). It is also important to note that suicide does not exist exclusively within the context of depression; athletes experiencing other mental health conditions, such as anxiety or substance misuse, may also experience difficulties with suicide.

Unfortunately, due to a variety of methodological limitations, such as use of screening questionnaires to estimate rates rather than diagnostic interviews (Rice, Purcell, De Silva, Mawren, McGorry, & Parker, 2016) and sampling athletes at various times of the competitive season, it is difficult to determine true prevalence rates for depression in athletes. Moreover, researchers often use different questionnaires or cutoff scores to identify cases of depression making it difficult to compare results across studies. At the same time, based on the extant literature and reports from consultants who work with athletes, there is sufficient evidence to suggest that depression should be a significant concern for all stakeholders in the sports community.

Risk Factors in Athlete Populations

Many athletes use physical activity to manage emotional difficulties, although there may be a critical point where athletes feel trapped, sport becomes a stressor, and depressive symptoms are exacerbated rather than mitigated. A variety of demographic factors are associated with depressive symptoms in athletes. Beable, Fulcher, Lee, and Hamilton (2017) found that athletes under age 25 were more likely to report depressive symptoms than older athletes, whereas Belz, Kleinert, Ohlert, Rau, and Allroggen (2018) found elite athletes younger than 18 were more vulnerable to depression than elite adult athletes. Most studies find that female athletes report higher levels of depression than male athletes. One study found college female student-athletes tended to report higher levels of depression as the season progressed (McGuire, Ingram, Sachs, & Tierney, 2017). Gender-based differences in depression may also vary based upon sport type. For example, in a sample of collegiate student-athletes, Wolanin, Hong, Marks, Panchoo, and Gross (2016) found female student-athletes tended to report higher rates of depression than male student-athletes. Track and field athletes reported the highest rates of depression for women (37.7%) and men (25.0%), whereas lacrosse had the lowest rates of depression for women (16.7%) and men (11.6%). However, other studies found no gender difference regarding depressive symptoms (Beable et al., 2017).

Similar to non-athlete populations, several studies found a variety of factors associated with increased depression levels. Factors such as experiencing recent major life events (Gouttebarge et al., 2017; Kilic et al., 2017) or daily hassles (Beable et al., 2017) were associated with higher levels of depressive symptoms in athletes. One study of elite rugby players found players with a history of depression were up to 22 times more likely to experience clinical levels of depression in-season compared to those without a depression history (Du Preez et al., 2017). Moreover, in samples of elite junior athletes, researchers found perfectionism indirectly related to depression through competitive anxiety (Jensen et al., 2018) and negative attributional style (Nixdorf, Frank, & Beckmann, 2016).

The sport environment poses several unique challenges that have been associated with depressive symptoms. Several studies found injured athletes reported higher rates of depression than non-injured athletes (Gulliver et al., 2015; Vargas, Rabinowitz, Meyer, & Arnett, 2015) and were rated by clinicians as more depressed than non-injured athletes at one week and one month post-injury (Appaneal, Levine, Perna, & Roh, 2009). Higher depression scores were also associated with greater time lost due to injury (Galambos, Terry, Moyle, & Locke, 2005), ongoing injury pain, and pain intensity (Sanders & Stevinson, 2017). Moreover, athletes who experienced depression at baseline were more than four times more likely to experience depression and more than three times more likely to experience anxiety after a concussion than athletes without depression at baseline (Yang, Peek-Asa, Covassin, & Torner, 2015).

The relationship between depression and injury may differ based upon the type of injury. In a longitudinal study, injured college student-athletes had elevated depression scores at one-week post-injury. At one month, this trend continued for athletes with orthopedic injuries, but depression symptoms decreased for athletes experiencing a concussion (Roiger, Weidauer, & Kern, 2015). At the same time, some studies found a greater number of concussions to be associated with greater likelihood of being diagnosed with depression (Du Preez et al., 2017; Guskiewicz et al., 2007; Kerr, Marshall, Harding, & Guskiewicz, 2012), although these studies were methodologically limited (i.e., the data collection was either retrospective or players self-identified as having concussions).

There is little research examining the relationship between injury and suicidal ideation or behavior. One study found that adolescent athletes experiencing severe injury or a long injury rehabilitation period were at-risk for suicide (Smith & Milliner, 1994). In an examination of publicly available information, Webner and Iverson (2016) found 80.8% of American football players that died by suicide since 1920 had documented stressors or medical conditions (e.g., injury). Although there is no compelling information to establish a causal relationship between sport injury and suicide, it is recommended that injured athletes be monitored for suicidal ideation (Kontos & Collins, 2018).

Athletic retirement has also been associated with depression symptoms. Beable et al. (2017) found athletes who were uncertain about retirement or had impending retirement were more likely to report depressive symptoms than athletes not retiring. Giannone, Haney, Kealy, and Ogrodniczuk (2017) found that college athletes with strong athletic identities were more likely to experience depressive symptoms three months into retirement than athletes without a strong athletic identity. There is also evidence to suggest athletes who were forced to retire due to injury were more likely to exhibit depressive symptoms. One study found 38.9% of athletes retiring due to injury reported depressive symptoms and the odds of experiencing depression increased more than threefold when an athlete retired due to injury (Sanders & Stevinson, 2017).

Several other unique sport factors have been reported to be associated with higher depressive symptoms: competitive failures (Hammond et al., 2013), participating in an individual sport (Beable et al., 2017; Nixdorf et al., 2013, 2016; Wolanin et al., 2016); being a high-performing (Hammond et al., 2013) or current student-athlete (Weigand, Cohen, & Merenstein, 2013); and participating in aesthetic sports (Schaal et al., 2011). Therefore, it is important to consider a wide range of variables when evaluating athletes for depression.

Practical Implications

The prevalence and impact of depression on athletes has demonstrated clearly that it is a condition worthy of significant concern within the sports community. Moreover, depression, like other forms of mental illness, is unfortunately still stigmatized by many athletes. Athletes seeking help is still the exception and not the rule. Fortunately, consultants can establish an unusually high level of trust with athletes because of their place in the sports world and depth and breadth of their relationships with athletes. As a result, they are uniquely positioned to identify and create dialogues about depression concerns that others in athletes' lives may not be capable of or comfortable with broaching. A fundamental responsibility for consultants, then, should be to recognize and either treat, if they have mental health licensure, or refer athletes with any indications of depression during the course of their work with them.

Assessing Depression in Athletes

As part of their intake protocol, consultants should include questions about any family history of depression; past experience of, diagnosis, or treatment of depression; and athletes' current status relative to depression. For a more formal and thorough assessment of depression, consultants can evaluate symptoms of depression in athletes using either structured clinical interviews or self-report inventories. The Structured Clinical Interview for DSM-5, Clinician Version (SCID-5-CV; First, Williams, Karg, & Spitzer, 2015) is a structured diagnostic interview that contains modules to evaluate a variety of mood disorders, including major depressive disorder. A wide variety of self-report or screening inventories exist for depression. Haugen, Thome, Pietrucha, and Levin (2017) recommended using the Center for Epidemiological Studies Depression Scale—Revised (CESD-R; Eaton, Muntaner, Smith, Tien, & Ybarra, 2004) for its ease of use and availability in the public domain. The CESD-R is also utilized frequently in research with athletes. Another widely used self-report inventory for depression is the Beck Depression Inventory–Second Edition (BDI-II; Beck, Steer, & Brown, 1996). It is similarly easy to use, although it requires certain credentials to purchase the inventory. Both inventories contain items inquiring about suicide. However, Haugen et al. (2017) suggest this may not be sufficient and recommend administering an inventory such as the Suicidal Behaviors Questionnaire-Revised (SBQ-R; Osman et al., 2001). It is important to address any endorsement of items evaluating suicide with the athlete and make referrals for mental health treatment promptly.

Treating Depression in Athletes

The most common treatments for depression are psychotropic medication and psychotherapy. Selective-serotonin reuptake inhibitors (SSRIs) are considered the first choice of antidepressant medications, although other classes (e.g., mixed reuptake inhibitors) may be used (see Reardon & Factor, 2010, for additional discussion).

Regarding psychotherapy, two approaches have the most evidence supporting their efficacy in non-athlete populations: cognitive-behavioral therapy (CBT) and interpersonal psychotherapy (IPT; Barlow & Durand, 2015).

CBT involves identifying and modifying maladaptive thinking processes, whereas IPT focuses on resolving inter-personal problems and forming adaptive relationships with others. Researchers generally find a combination of medication and psychotherapy to be effective short- and long-term, although either type of treatment produces some improvement (Karyotaki et al., 2016).

There is little research examining the efficacy of various treatment approaches for athletes experiencing depression. Studies that have been conducted with athlete populations generally tailor existing therapy models to include strength-based approaches. With this therapeutic modality, consultants focus on identifying and increasing awareness of athletes' strengths, positive attributes, and resources, particularly those that are not evident to athletes, and then using those assets to problem solve and develop a plan moving forward that builds resilience and alleviates the depressive symptoms (Padesky & Mooney, 2012). In a case study with a 21-year-old female rower, Gabana (2016) discussed concurrent antidepressant treatment with strengths-based CBT. The athlete was noted to have improvement of symptoms that continued one year after termination of CBT. However, this improvement was based upon subjective report and not quantified through assessment measures.

Donohue and colleagues adapted family behavior therapy (FBT) for use in athletic populations such that performance and mental health goals can be addressed simultaneously. Although studies examining FBT have not targeted depressive symptoms, per se, (the entry criteria for inclusion was substance use or dependence; Donohue et al., 2015) a variety of case studies demonstrated reduction in depressive symptoms throughout the course of the intervention (Chow et al., 2015; Donohue et al., 2015). In two studies examining FBT, the mean BDI-II levels elevated to nearly pre-intervention levels at 3-month follow-up (Donohue et al., 2015; Pitts et al., 2015). However, a more comprehensive study comparing FBT to services as usual (SAU; Donohue et al., 2018) indicated student-athletes in FBT consistently demonstrated better outcomes, including reduced depression, than those in SAU, and these gains were generally maintained eight months post-treatment. These effects were particularly likely for student-athletes with greater diagnostic severity (i.e., more than one mental health diagnosis).

There is also an emerging body of research examining mindfulness-based approaches in athlete populations. In non-athlete populations, mindfulness-based approaches, particularly mindfulness-based cognitive therapy (MBCT; Segal, Williams, & Teasdale, 2012) are focused on reducing relapse rates for depression by decreasing mood related negative cognitions (i.e., cognitive reactivity). Mindfulness-based approaches are typically centered on tolerating and accepting uncomfortable thoughts, emotions, and experiences with the goal of helping athletes intentionally choose their response rather than react to them. Preliminary evidence suggests no change in psychological distress (i.e., depression and anxiety) after a mindfulness-based intervention. However, student-athletes involved in this study also exhibited relatively low levels of distress at baseline (Goodman, Kashdan, Mallard, & Schumann, 2014). Therefore, additional research on mindfulness-based interventions for depression in athletes is warranted.

Summary

- Major depressive disorder, most commonly identified as depression, is one of the most commonly diagnosed psychiatric disorders among the general population and the athletic population.
- Depression is characterized by a period of at least two weeks of depressed mood and/or loss of interest/pleasure in activities in nearly all activities plus at least five symptoms in the same two-week period.
- Among the various forms of mental illness that afflicts athletes, depression has been the most vigorously and comprehensively studied by researchers, and, much as with the general population, the findings demonstrate that depression is a significant problem among athletes at many levels of sport.
- In athlete samples across cultures, the rate of depression ranges from 3.6% to 27%.
- Suicide is another crucial factor to consider within the context of depression and other mental health conditions.
- A variety of demographic factors are associated with depressive symptoms in athletes: being under age 25, female, injured, and perfectionistic, having a strong athletic identify, and experiencing recent major life events, stressful daily hassles, and retirement from sport.
- Because consultants can establish aa high level of trust with athletes due to their place in the sports world and depth and breadth of their relationships with athletes, they have the ability to identify and create in athletes an openness to discuss concerns about depression that others in athletes' lives may not be capable of or comfortable with.

- As part of their intake protocol, consultants should include questions about any family history of depression; past experience of, diagnosis, or treatment of depression; and athletes' current status relative to depression.
- For more formal and thorough assessment of depression, consultants can evaluate symptoms of depression in athletes using either structured clinical interviews or self-report inventories.
- The most common treatments for depression are psychotropic medication and psychotherapy.
- Selective-serotonin reuptake inhibitors (SSRIs) are considered the first choice of antidepressant medications, although other classes (e.g., mixed reuptake inhibitors) may be used.
- Regarding psychotherapy, two approaches have the most evidence supporting their efficacy in non-athlete populations: cognitive-behavioral therapy (CBT) and interpersonal psychotherapy.

References

Appaneal, R. N., Levine, B. R., Perna, F. M., & Roh, J. L. (2009). Measuring postinjury depression among male and female competitive athletes. *Journal of Sport & Exercise Psychology, 31*, 60–76.

Barlow, D. H., & Durand, V. M. (2015). *Abnormal psychology: An integrative approach*, 7th ed. Stamford, CT: Cengage Learning.

Beable, S., Fulcher, M., Lee, A. C., & Hamilton, B. (2017). SHARPSports mental health awareness research project: Prevalence and risk factors of depressive symptoms and life stress in elite athletes. *Journal of Science and Medicine in Sport, 20*, 1047–1052. doi: 10.1016/j.jsams.2017.04.018

Beck, A. T., Steer, R. A., & Brown, G. K. (1996). *Manual for the Beck Depression Inventory—II*. San Antonio, TX: Psychological Corporation.

Belz, J., Kleinert, J., Ohlert, J., Rau, T., & Allroggen, M. (2018). Risk for depression and psychological well-being in German national and state team athletes—Associations with age, gender, and performance level. *Journal of Clinical Sport Psychology, 12*, 160–178. doi: 10.1123/jcsp.2016-0024

Chow, G. M., Donohue, B., Pitts, M., Loughran, T., Schubert, K. N., Gavrilova, Y., & Diaz, E. (2015). Results of a single case controlled study of the Optimum Performance Program in Sports in a collegiate athlete. *Clinical Case Studies, 14*, 191–209. doi:10.1177/1534650114548313

Donohue, B., Chow, G. M., Pitts, M., Loughran, T., Schubert, K. N., Gavrilova, Y., & Allen, D. N. (2015). Piloting a family-supported approach to concurrently optimize mental health and sport performance in athletes. *Clinical Case Studies, 14*, 159–177. doi:10.1177/1534650114548311

Donohue, B., Gavrilova, Y., Galante, M., Gavrilova, E., Loughran, T., . . . Allen, D. N. (2018). Controlled evaluation of an optimization approach to mental health and sport performance. *Journal of Clinical Sport Psychology, 12*, 234–267. doi: 10.1123/jcsp.2017-0054

Du Preez, E. J., Graham, K., Gan, T. Y., Moses, B., Ball, C., & Kuah, D. E. (2017). Depression, anxiety, and alcohol use in elite rugby league players over a competitive season. *Clinical Journal of Sports Medicine, 27*, 530–535.

Eaton, W. W., Muntaner, C., Smith, C., Tien, A., & Ybarra, M. (2004). Center for Epidemiologic Studies Depression Scale: Review and revision (CESD and CESD-R). In M. E. Maruish (Ed.), *The use of psychological testing for treatment planning and outcomes assessment*, 3rd ed. (pp. 363–377). Mahwah, NJ: Lawrence Erlbaum.

First, M. B., Williams, J. B. W., Karg, R. S., & Spitzer, R. L. (2015). *Structured Clinical Interview for DSM-5, Clinician Version* (SCID-5-CV). Arlington, VA: American Psychiatric Association.

Frank, R., Nixdorf, I., & Beckman, J. (2017). Analyzing the relationship between burnout and depression in elite junior athletes. *Journal of Clinical Sport Psychology, 11*, 287–303. doi: 10.1123/JCSP.2017-0008

Gabana, N. (2016). A strengths-based cognitive behavioral approach to treating depression and building resilience in collegiate athletics: The individuation of the identical twin. *Case Studies in Sport and Exercise Psychology, 1*, 4–15. doi: 10.1123/cssep.2016-005

Galambos, S. A., Terry, P. C., Moyle, G. M., & Locke, S. A. (2005). Psychological predictors of injury among elite athletes. *British Journal of Sports Medicine, 39*, 351–354.

Giannone, Z. A., Haney, C. J., Kealy, D., & Ogrodniczuk, J. S. (2017). Athletic identity and psychiatric symptoms following retirement from varsity sports. *International Journal of Social Psychiatry, 63*, 598–601. doi: 10.1177/0020764017724184

Goodman, F. R., Kashdan, T. B., Mallard, T. T., & Schumann, M. (2014). A brief mindfulness and yoga intervention with an entire NCAA Division I athletic team: An initial investigation. *Psychology of Consciousness: Theory, Research, and Practice, 1*, 339–356. doi: 10.1037/cns0000022

Gouttebarge, V., Jonkers, R., Moen, M., Verhagen, E., Wylleman, P., & Kerkoffs, G. (2017). The prevalence and risk indicators of symptoms of common mental disorders among current and former Dutch elite athletes. *Journal of Sports Sciences, 35*, 2148–2156. doi: 10.1080/02640414.2016.1258485

Gulliver, A., Griffiths, K. M., Mackinnon, A., Batterham, P. J., & Stanimirovic, R. (2015). The mental health of Australian elite athletes. *Journal of Science and Medicine in Sport, 18*, 255–261.

Guskiewicz, K. M., Marshall, S. W., Bailes, J., McCrea, M., Harding, H. P., Matthews, A., Mihalik, J. R., & Cantu, R. C. (2007). Recurrent concussion and risk of depression in retired professional football players. *Medicine & Science in Sports & Exercise*, *39*, 903–909.

Hammond, T., Gialloreto, C., Kubas, H., & Davis, H. H. (2013). The prevalence of failure-based depression among elite athletes. *Clinical Journal of Sports Medicine*, *23*, 273–277. doi: 10.1097/JSM.0b013e318287b870

Haugen, E. N. J., Thome, J., Pietrucha, M. E., & Levin, M. P. (2017). Mental health screening: Identifying clinical issues. In J. Taylor (Ed.). *Assessment in applied sport psychology* (pp. 88–107). Champaign, IL: Human Kinetics.

Jensen, S. N., Ivarsson, A., Fallby, J., Dankers, S., & Elbe, A.-M. (2018). Depression in Danish and Swedish elite football players and its relation to perfectionism and anxiety. *Psychology of Sport and Exercise*, *36*, 147–155. doi: 10.1016/j.psychsport.2018.02.008

Karyotaki, E., Smit, Y., Holdt Henningsen, K., Huibers, M. J. H., Robays, J., de Beurs, D., & Cuijpers, P. (2016). Combining pharmacotherapy and psychotherapy or monotherapy for major depression? A meta-analysis on the long-term effects. *Journal of Affective Disorders*, *194*, 144–152. doi: 10.1016/j.jad.2016.01.036

Kerr, Z., Marshall, S. W., Harding, H. P., & Guskiewicz, K. M. (2012). Nine-year risk of depression diagnosis increases with increasing self-reported concussions in retired professional football players. *The American Journal of Sports Medicine*, *40*, 2206–2212.

Kilic, Ö., Aoki, H., Haagensen, R., Jensen, C., Johnson, U., Kerkoffs, G. M. M. J., & Gouttebarge, V. (2017). Symptoms of common mental disorders and related stressors in Danish professional football and handball. *European Journal of Sport Science*, *17*, 1328–1334. doi: 10.1080/17461391.2017.1381768

Kontos, A. P., & Collins, M. W. (2018). *Concussion: A clinical profile approach to assessment and treatment*. Washington, DC: American Psychological Association. doi:10.1037/0000087-002

McGuire, L., Ingram, Y. M., Sachs, M. L., & Tierney, R. T. (2017). Temporal changes in depression symptoms in male and female college student athletes. *Journal of Clinical Sport Psychology*, *11*, 337–351. doi: 10.1123/JCSP.2016-0035

Miller, B. E., Miller, M. N., Verhegge, R., Linville, H. H., & Pumariega, A. J. (2002). Alcohol misuse among college athletes: Self-medication for psychiatric symptoms? *Journal of Drug Education*, *32*, 41–52.

Nixdorf, I., Frank, R., & Beckmann, J. (2016). Comparison of athletes' proneness to depressive symptoms in individual and team sports: Research on psychological mediators in junior elite athletes. *Frontiers in Psychology*, *7*, 893. doi: 10.3389/fpsyg.2016.00893

Nixdorf, I., Frank, R., Hautzinger, M., & Beckmann, J. (2013). Prevalence of depressive symptoms and correlating variables among German elite athletes. *Journal of Clinical Sport Psychology*, *7*, 313–326. doi: 10.1123/jcsp.7.4.313

Osman, A., Bagge, C. L., Gutierrez, P. M., Konick, L. C., Kooper, B. A., & Barrios, F. X. (2001). The Suicidal Behaviors Questionnaire-Revised (SBQ-R): Validation with clinical and nonclinical samples. *Assessment*, *5*, 443–454.

Padesky, C. A., & Mooney, K. A. (2012). Strengths-based cognitive-behavioural therapy: a four-step model to build resilience. *Clinical Psychology and Psychotherapy*, *19*(4), 283–290.

Pitts, M., Donohue, B., Schubert, K. N., Chow, G. M., Loughran, T., & Gavrilova, Y. (2015). A systematic case examination of The Optimum Performance Program in Sports in a combat sport athlete. *Clinical Case Studies*, *14*, 178–190. doi: 10.1177/1534650114548312

Rao, A. L., Asif, I. M., Drezner, J. A., Toresdahl, B. G., & Harmon, K. G. (2015). Suicide in National Collegiate Athletic Association (NCAA) athletes: A 9-year analysis of the NCAA resolutions database. *Sports Health*, *7*, 452–457. doi: 10.1177/1941738115587675.

Reardon, C. L., & Factor, R. M. (2010). Sport psychiatry: A systematic review of diagnosis and medical treatment of mental illness in athletes. *Sports Medicine*, *40*, 961–980.

Rice, S. M., Purcell, R., De Silva, S., Mawren, D., McGorry, P. D., & Parker, A. G. (2016). The mental health of elite athletes: A narrative systematic review. *Sports Medicine*, *46*, 1333–1353. doi:10.1007/s40279-016-0492-2

Roiger, T., Weidauer, L., & Kern, B. (2015). A longitudinal pilot study of depressive symptoms in concussed and injured/nonconcussed National Collegiate Athletic Association Division I student athletes. *Journal of Athletic Training*, *50*, 256–261.

Sabo, D., Miller, K. E., Melnick, M. J., Farrell, M. P., & Barnes, G. M. (2005). High school athletic participation and adolescent suicide: A nationwide US study. *International Review for the Sociology of Sport*, *40*, 5–23.

Sanders, G., & Stevinson, C. (2017). Associations between retirement reasons, chronic pain, athletic identity, and depressive symptoms among former professional footballers. *European Journal of Sport Science*, *10*, 1311–1318. doi: 10.1080/17461391.2017.1371795

Schaal, K., Tafflet, M., Nassif, H., Thibault, V., Pichard, C., Alcotte, M., & . . . Uddin, M. (2011). Psychological balance in high level athletes: Gender-based differences and sport-specific patterns. *Plos ONE*, *6*(5), doi:10.1371/journal.pone.0019007

Segal, Z. V., Williams, J. M. G., & Teasdale, J. D. (2012). *Mindfulness-based cognitive therapy for depression*, 2nd ed. New York, NY: The Guilford Press.

Smith, A. M., & Milliner, E. K. (1994). Injured athletes and the risk of suicide. *Journal of Athletic Training*, *29*, 337–341.

Vargas, G., Rabinowitz, A., Meyer, J., & Arnett, P. A. (2015). Predictors and prevalence of postconcussion depression symptoms in collegiate athletes. *Journal of Athletic Training*, *50*, 250–255.

Webner, D., & Iverson, G. L. (2016). Suicide in professional American football players in the last 95 years. *Brain Injury, 30,* 1718–1721.

Weigand, S., Cohen, J., & Merenstein, D. (2013). Susceptibility for depression in current and retired student athletes. *Sports Health, 5,* 263–266.

Weitz, A. (n.d.) 16 pro athletes who have depression. Retrieved from www.sadrunner.com/2015/athletes-who-have-depression

Wolanin, A., Hong, E., Marks, D., Panchoo, K., & Gross, M. (2016). Prevalence of clinically elevated depressive symptoms in college athletes and differences by gender and sport. *British Journal of Sports Medicine, 50,* 167–171. doi: 10.1136/bjsports-2015-095756

World Health Organization. (2017). Depression and other common mental disorders: Global health estimates. Retrieved from http://apps.who.int/iris/bitstream/handle/10665/254610/WHO-MSD-MER-2017.2-eng.pdf;jsessionid=44D708803C1E85770B6BC31628D73EC5?sequence=1

Yang, J., Cheng, G., Zhang, Y., Covassin, T., Heiden, E. O., & Peek-Asa, C. (2014). Influence of symptoms of depression and anxiety on injury hazard among collegiate American football players. *Research in Sports Medicine, 22,* 147–160.

Yang, J., Peek-Asa, C., Covassin, T., & Torner, J. C. (2015). Post-concussion symptoms of depression and anxiety in Division I collegiate athletes. *Developmental Neuropsychology, 40*(1), 18–23. doi: 10.1080/87565641.2014.973499

EATING DISORDERS

Megan Pietrucha and Jenni Thome

Disordered eating and eating disorders is an area of significant concern among mental health practitioners who work with athletes in sports in which physical aesthetics and body weight impact performance and results. Most often considered a "female issue," disordered eating and eating disorders are prevalent in gymnastics, figure skating, synchronized swimming, among other women's sports. At the same time, both can also be found in male-oriented sports such as wrestling, weightlifting, boxing, and bodybuilding, to name a few, in which either leanness or weight classes play a role. In all cases, pressures to appear attractive, perform at a so-called ideal weight, or "make weight" aimed at maximizing performance can have harmful physical and psychological effects for athletes of both genders.

Disordered eating and eating disorders include abnormal eating and weight-control behaviors such as restricted food intake, binge eating and purging, and other compensatory behaviors such as excessive or compulsive exercise, and laxative and diuretic abuse. These symptoms are typically, though not always, accompanied by body dissatisfaction, and are frequently comorbid with other mental health issues such as depression, anxiety, and low self-esteem (Johnson & Wardle, 2005; Thome & Espelage, 2004).

The DSM-5 (American Psychiatric Association, 2013) includes diagnostic criteria for four eating disorders and related concerns:

- **Anorexia nervosa** (AN): Characterized by distorted body image and excessive dieting behavior leading to significantly low body weight, with an accompanying fear of becoming fat or gaining weight.
- **Bulimia nervosa** (BN): A repetitive cycle of dysregulated eating, including recurrent episodes of binge eating followed by compensatory behaviors such as vomiting, laxative abuse, or excessive exercise.
- **Binge eating disorder** (BED): Recurrent episodes of binge-eating behaviors without compensatory purging or non-purging behaviors following the binge and is more common than AN and BN combined.
- **Avoidant/restrictive food intake disorder** (ARFID): Typically diagnosed in childhood, this eating or feeding disturbance may include a lack of interest in food, avoidance of food based on sensory characteristics, and concern about aversive consequences of eating. This leads to significant weight loss, nutritional deficiency, dependence on nutritional supplements, and marked interference with psychosocial functioning.

Theory and Research

Methodological limitations within research studies make the prevalence of eating disorders among athletes difficult to estimate (Nattiv et al., 2007). However, some well-designed studies suggest that eating disorders such as AN and BN may be more prevalent among athletes than nonathletes, and in female as compared to male athletes, particularly in aesthetic and lean sports such as gymnastics, cross country running, and figure skating (46.7%)

versus controls (21.4%) (Torstveit, Rosenvinge, & Sundgot-Borgen, 2008). Additionally, higher rates of eating disorders may be found in elite versus recreational athletes (Knapp, Aerni, & Anderson, 2014; Sundgot-Borgen & Torstveit, 2004). Some studies suggest eating disorder prevalence rates of 25–31 percent among elite athletes, compared with 5–9% in control groups.

The nature of sport may make it challenging to identify athletes struggling with eating concerns. For example, athletes who engage in high levels of sport-specific training, conditioning, and nutrition may have leaner body compositions than non-athlete peers through genetic self-selection or commitment to their sport, Additionally, athletes may have unusual exercise and eating habits that may or may not necessarily be unhealthy. Even in medical settings, symptoms of concern in nonathlete populations, such as amenorrhea, low blood pressure, and low resting heart rate, may be attributed to an athlete's activity status rather than identified as indicators of eating concerns (Maron & Pelliccia, 2006), and thus left unaddressed.

At the same time, the veneer of athletes' commitment to conditioning and sport training, nutrition, fueling for competition, and healthy eating may, in fact, mask an eating disorder. Several "good athlete" traits, such as perfectionism and overcompliance, are similar to traits found among people with AN and may be valued and reinforced by coaches, trainers, and teammates (Thompson & Sherman, 1999).

Practical Implications

Consultants must be sensitive to disordered eating and potential eating disorders, particularly in sports that encourage them and in athletes whose unhealthy practices may be covered by a façade of being "model" athletes. Being vigilant to and exploring below the surface of athletes' training, exercise, and eating habits can reveal eating challenges that may not be readily evident otherwise. Consultants' ability to make these distinctions and notice unhealthy habits that either may lead to or have already led to eating disorders is one of their fundamental responsibilities in their concern for athletes' mental health and well-being.

Screening and Assessment

Indications that an athlete is struggling with an eating disorder are diverse, as these individuals may be underweight, average weight, or overweight/obese. Physical signs that may be noticeable or reported include marked weight fluctuations, swollen cheeks/face, blood-shot eyes, sore throat, blood in vomit, thinning hair, stress fractures, knuckle abrasions, dental enamel erosion, easily bruising, yellow skin, constipation, fatigue, amenorrhea, dehydration, and osteoporosis, among others (Academy for Eating Disorders, 2016). The reality is that there is no single appearance to eating disorders, but the physical complications associated with these disorders can be severe and require professional medical oversight.

Given the complex presentation of eating disorders, screening tools can be very useful. The International Olympic Committee (IOC, 2009), American College of Sports Medicine (ACSM; Nattiv et al., 2007), and National Athletic Trainers' Association (NATA; Bonci et al., 2008) advocate for screening of eating disorders during the preparticipation evaluation and periodically thereafter, though there is no consensus about how this should be done or which screening tools should be used. Any screening and assessment tools that are used should be sensitive to athlete's age and competitive level, and include multiple sources of information (Mitchell & Robert-McComb, 2014). Several measures have been developed and validated for the general assessment of eating disorders, and many have been used in studies with athletes (see Pope, Gao, Bolter, & Pritchard, 2014). Though not an exhaustive list, the below measures have been found to be effective assessment tools. Their objective results make it easier for consultants, regardless of their training, to identify athletes at risk for eating disorders and make the appropriate referrals:

• **Eating Attitudes Test** (EAT-26; Garner, Olmsted, Bohr, & Garfinkel, 1982). The EAT-26 is a 26-item self-report screening tool of eating disorder symptoms. A total score of 20 is recommended for referral for additional assessment by a trained clinician. This measure screens for extreme weight-control behaviors, which may be red flags indicating the need to meet with a qualified professional. The EAT-26 can be administered in individual or group settings by mental health professionals, school counselors, coaches, or others with an interest in screening and referral for additional evaluation for eating disorders. This measure has been used in a variety of cultures with male and female athletes.

- **Eating Disorders Examination Questionnaire** (EDE-Q; Fairburn & Beglin, 1994). The EDE-Q is a 41-item self-report questionnaire designed to evaluate the frequency of disordered eating behaviors over the past 38 days. It is different from the EAT-26 in that it evaluates eating behaviors and body dissatisfaction. The EDE-Q has been used in research with male and female athletes.
- **Female Athlete Screening Tool** (FAST; McNulty, Adams, Anderson, & Affenito, 2001; Robert-McComb & Mitchell, 2014). The FAST is a 33-item questionnaire developed to identify eating pathology and atypical exercise and eating behaviors in female athletes. In a small group of female athletes, subclinical scores were 77 to 94 and clinical scores were >94 (Robert-McComb & Mitchell, 2014).

Some researchers (e.g., Nagel et al., 2000) have argued that the use of general eating disorder assessments with athletes are inaccurate, leading to false negative or even false positive identification of eating disorders, such that athletes may appear more pathological than they actually are. For example, extreme levels of training, exercise, or nutrition by athletes may have little to do with manipulating weight or appearance (Thompson & Sherman, 2014) and may not reflect the emergence or presence of an eating disorder. While several athlete-specific screening tools have been developed, they typically have less established psychometric properties and may be based on outdated diagnostic criteria. Thus, it is recommended that consultants incorporate more than one screening tool when assessing athletes for eating disorders.

Need for Treatment

Because eating disorders present serious immediate and chronic health risks, including death, it is imperative that athletes who have been identified with eating disorders be referred for appropriate assessment and treatment as soon as a problem is detected (Schaffner & Buchanan, 2010; Sullivan, 2002). Early identification of symptoms is essential to the prognosis and treatment of eating disorders and determining if medical hospitalization is necessary to stabilize athletes should be one of the first determinations of treatment level and approach (Baum, 2013; Bratland-Sanda & Sundgot-Borgen, 2013; Pearson & Rivers, 2006). Additionally, timely referral for assessment of symptoms and diagnosis will help determine the level of care and treatment needs of athletes. Once assessed, the duration and severity of eating disorder symptomatology, including athlete's overall clinical and social picture in addition to weight and medical status, will dictate the level of care to which they should be referred (American Psychiatric Association, 2010). The degree of perceived support as well as existing comorbid psychiatric disorders are also important to consider when making decisions about treatment level, setting, and approach (American Psychiatric Association, 2010; Baum, 2013).

Levels of care guidelines are outlined by the American Psychiatric Association (2010) and take into consideration the frequency and severity of psychological, medical, and behavioral symptoms as well as environmental needs when determining the appropriate treatment setting. Levels of care for eating disorders (from least to most restrictive) include outpatient (level 1), intensive outpatient (level 2), partial hospitalization (level 3), residential treatment (level 4), and inpatient hospitalization (level 5). Medical stability plays a large role in determining level of care especially at levels 4 and 5 where more intensive medical monitoring is necessary.

Athlete-specific Barriers to Treatment

Stigma is a common barrier to treatment for many people with mental health concerns, but this stigma might be higher for athletes and more specifically for athletes with eating disorders (de Bruin, 2017). Athletes often perceive the stigma about mental health issues to be in conflict with their athletic identity, and thus can struggle to disclose problematic eating behaviors (Papathomas & Lavallee, 2010). Additionally, concern about how a diagnosis of an eating disorder may negatively impact training and competitive opportunities may also prevent athletes from seeking help.

Additionally, there are several barriers to the identification of eating disorders in athletes that are unique to the sports environment and context. For example, treatment might be delayed due to difficulty in identifying symptoms as they can be masked by attitudes and behaviors that are normative and valued in the athletic environment (Sherman & Thompson, 2001). At times, coaches and athletes might not consider the dietary and exercise behaviors to be problematic or indicative of an eating disorder within the context of the sport (Bar, Cassin, &

Dionne, 2016), particularly if athletes of concern are performing well and contributing to the success of their team. As such, coaches may feel conflicted about placing the health and well-being ahead of their own needs and the competitive goals of the team. Other times, symptoms of disordered eating or an eating disorder might go unnoticed, or even encouraged, by coaches if performance continues to be maintained (Pearson & Rivers, 2006). Furthermore, gender stereotypes, stigma, and the different ways that eating disorders present in male athletes (i.e., drive for leanness or muscle mass rather than drive for thinness) might inhibit male athletes from seeking treatment for eating disorders and contribute to the lack of identification of eating disorders in male athletes (Bratland-Sanda & Sundgot-Borgen, 2013; de Bruin, 2017).

Considerations and Challenges

Treatment for eating disorders can be challenging for other reasons as well. Often the entrenched behaviors and patterns, denial and low motivation for change, and resistance to treatment as well as the complexity of medical and psychological issues are common treatment challenges encountered by therapists (Baum, 2013; Fassino & Abbate-Daga, 2013). These themes can also be present and even more significant when working with athletes due to the unique cultural aspects of sports (Sherman & Thompson, 2001).

Of the themes that emerge from the literature, issues with management of exercise, nutritional support, and return to sport are commonly cited challenges that are unique to treating athletes with an eating disorder (de Bruin, 2017; Plateau, Arcelus, Leung, & Meyer, 2017). Relatedly, athletes might also be concerned about weight gain and body image in treatment as it relates to optimal performance in their sport (Sherman & Thompson, 2001). Other themes that present in treatment as reported by female athletes who received treatment for eating disorders have included loss of athletic identity and ambivalence about involvement of coaches in treatment (Papathomas & Lavallee, 2010; Plateau et al., 2017; Sherman & Thompson, 2001). In studies surveying athlete's experience of treatment, athletes have also stated that they often feel misunderstood in therapy and question the relevance of treatment if it is not connected to athletic identity or the sport context (de Bruin, 2017; Papathomas & Lavallee, 2010; Plateau et al., 2017; Sherman & Thompson, 2001). Therefore, it is recommended that athletes be referred to treatment providers who are trained in both the treatment of eating disorders and familiar with issues that are specific to athletes (Hildebrandt, 2005; Papathomas & Lavallee, 2010; Sherman & Thompson, 2001).

A common question that arises in the treatment of eating disorders with athletes is if participation in sport or exercise can continue when athletes are symptomatic (Sherman & Thompson, 2001). Most of the literature confirms that this determination is based on diagnosis and medical status and suggests that athletes with a diagnosis of anorexia nervosa do not exercise, train, or compete until symptoms have resolved (Sherman & Thompson, 2001). If athletes are allowed to continue to participate and compete, it is recommended that minimum criteria to maintain participation (i.e., weight status, progress in treatment, caloric intake) and frequency, intensity, and duration of the exercise be clearly discussed with and agreed upon by athletes and their support team (Sherman & Thompson, 2001). Treatment goals can also encourage athletes to exercise autonomy in making the decision to continue participating on their own (Sherman & Thompson, 2001).

Using or integrating exercise into treatment can also be challenging, especially if exercise contributed to the development of an eating disorder. However, with athletes, Baum (2013) also proposes that exercise can be used as a therapeutic tool. Returning to play can provide motivation for these athletes to engage in treatment and overcome symptoms as well as maintaining social support via the team and coaches (Baum, 2013; Sherman & Thompson, 2001). Currently, there are no specific criteria for determining when or if return to exercise or sport is beneficial or harmful for athletes in treatment for an eating disorder, and it is recommended that guidelines be developed to aid in this determination the treatment process (Bratland-Sanda & Sundgot-Borgen, 2013).

Prevention of Eating Disorders among Athletes

While treatment options are available, prevention efforts to reduce the rate or onset of eating disorders in specific populations such as athletes is essential (Bratland-Sanda & Sundgot-Borgen, 2013; de Bruin, 2017; National Eating Disorders Association, 2018; Pearson & Rivers, 2006). General prevention approaches are varied and can include a universal or primary educational approach for larger groups, selective prevention to target groups that are at risk of developing eating disorders, or targeted prevention for groups at high risk (Bar et al., 2016; National Eating Disorder Association, 2018). More research on the efficacy of prevention programs, especially with athletes, is needed, but preliminary research suggests that selective, interactive, and multimodal approaches and a group format, particularly targeting high-risk athletes, are showing promise in the ability to reduce risk factors associated with eating disorders (Bar et al., 2016; Pearson & Rivers, 2006). Two of the more researched prevention programs for athletes include the cognitive-dissonance-based *Female Athlete Body Project* (Becker, McDaniel, Bull, Powell, & McIntyre, 2012) and the *Bodies in Motion* program focused on developing healthy body image and eating behaviors among female athletes (Voelker & Petrie, 2017). Intervention and consultation can and should occur at multiple levels, including coaches, trainers, teams, and athletes. Studies suggest that coaches be educated and made aware of the signs and symptoms of eating disorders, and address any concerns with the athlete immediately (Bratland-Sanda & Sundgot-Borgen, 2013; Pearson & Rivers, 2006).

Treatment Approaches

Overall, a multidisciplinary team approach to treatment is essential to effectively address and manage the physical, medical, psychological, and nutritional symptoms that might be present (Walsh, Wheat, & Freund, 2000). The team approach is specifically recommended for treating children and adolescents with eating disorders (American Psychiatric Association, 2010). This team of professionals can include a psychiatrist, psychologist or therapist, dietitian, and physician as well as members of the "sport management team" such as coaches, athletic trainers, or strength and conditioning coaches (Sherman & Thompson, 2001). The physician plays an important role at the outset of treatment in determining the level of care necessary for the athlete (Walsh et al., 2000). The dietitian also plays a central role in the treatment goals for athletes with both AN and BN as this support is needed to normalize eating habits and restore or maintain healthy weight status (Yager et al., 2012).

Including coaches in the process can be challenging because of their roles and relationships with athletes, their position within the sports organization, their focus on results, and the authority that they exert over athletes' roles on the team. Thus, determining if and how the coach is to be involved and informed in the athlete's treatment should be a collective discussion with athletes and also with respect to athletes' rights to privacy and confidentiality. Likewise, determining if and how to involve teammates in the athlete's treatment can be considered if sustaining this contact will help their sense of athletic identity and the degree of social support they may receive as a beneficial part of their overall treatment program.

The involvement of any member of the sport management team should be collaboratively decided between athletes and their therapist and must be of clear therapeutic benefit to the athletes (Sherman & Thompson, 2001). Similar to the recommendations that the therapist be well-versed in sport culture, so too should the other treatment providers. Overall, the coordination of care and communication between providers and support persons is essential to the effective treatment of eating disorders, especially when the treatment is occurring in the outpatient setting or when athletes shift between levels of care (American Psychiatric Association, 2010).

Lastly, evidence-based treatment models for eating disorders can include cognitive therapy (CT), cognitive-behavioral therapy (CBT), interpersonal therapy (IPT), family therapy, pharmacotherapy, and relapse prevention models (Yager et al., 2012). CBT has been shown to be one of the most effective treatment approaches for bulimia nervosa (BN) and binge-eating disorder (Pearson & Rivers, 2006; Schaffner & Buchanan, 2010; Walsh et al., 2000). For children and adolescents with eating disorders being treated on an outpatient basis, family therapy has also been found to be effective (American Psychiatric Association, 2010; Yager et al., 2012). More specifically, the Maudsley approach to family-based treatment has been found to be effective for adolescents with AN (Schaffner & Buchanan, 2010). This approach incorporates the parents of the child or adolescent into the treatment approach where the parents are active participants in engaging in family sessions and the progression of treatment from weight restoration to returning control over eating to the adolescent and encouraging healthy behaviors. For a more comprehensive summary of evidence-based treatments for eating disorders, Walsh et al. (2000) provide a table that summarizes recent studies on supported treatment approaches for AN and BN.

Summary

- Disordered eating and eating disorders is an area of significant concerns among mental health practitioners who work with athletes in sports in which aesthetics and weight are related to performance and results.
- Disordered eating and eating disorders exist on a continuum, including abnormal eating and weight-control behaviors such as restricted food intake, binge eating and purging behaviors, and other compensatory behaviors such as excessive or compulsive exercise, and laxative and diuretic abuse.
- Eating disorder diagnoses from the DSM-5 include, but are not limited to, anorexia nervosa (AN), bulimia nervosa (BN), binge eating disorder (BED), and avoidance-restrictive food intake disorder (ARFID).
- Eating disorders such as AN and BN may be more prevalent among athletes than nonathletes, and in female as compared to male athletes, particularly in aesthetic and lean sports such as gymnastics, cross country running, and figure skating versus controls and higher rates of eating disorders may be found in elite versus recreational athletes.
- The veneer of nutrition, fueling for competition, and healthy eating may, in fact, mask an eating disorder. Several "good athlete" traits, such as perfectionism and overcompliance, are similar to traits found among people with AN and may be valued and reinforced by coaches, trainers, and teammates.
- Consultants must be sensitive to disordered eating and potential eating disorders, particularly in sports that encourage them and in athletes whose unhealthy practices may be covered by a façade of being "model" athletes.
- Both sports governing bodies and sports medicine groups advocate for screening of eating disorders during the preparticipation evaluation and periodically thereafter, though there is no consensus about how this should be done or which screening tools should be used.
- There are a variety of measures that have been found to be effective assessment tools and able to be administered by both trained and untrained professionals.
- Because eating disorders are serious and often chronic or fatal conditions, it is imperative that athletes be referred for appropriate assessment and treatment as soon as a problem is detected.
- The duration and severity of eating disorder symptomatology, including athlete's overall clinical and social picture in addition to weight and medical status, will dictate the level of care to which they should be referred.
- Stigma is a common barrier to treatment for many people with mental health concerns, but this stigma might be higher for athletes and more specifically for athletes with eating disorders.
- Often the entrenched behaviors and patterns, denial and low motivation for change, resistance to treatment as well as the complexity of medical and psychological issues are common treatment challenges encountered by therapists.
- It is recommended that athletes be referred to treatment providers who are trained in both the treatment of eating disorders and familiar with issues that are specific to athletes.
- While treatment options are available, prevention efforts to reduce the rate or onset of eating disorders in specific populations such as athletes is essential.
- A multidisciplinary team approach to treatment is essential to effectively address and manage the physical, medical, psychological, and nutritional symptoms that might be present.
- Evidence-based practice models for eating disorders can include cognitive therapy (CT), cognitive-behavioral therapy (CBT), interpersonal therapy (IPT), family therapy, pharmacotherapy, and relapse prevention models.

References

Academy for Eating Disorders. (2016). *Eating disorders: A guide to medical care*, 3rd ed. Reston, VA: Academy for Eating Disorders.

American Psychiatric Association. (2010). *Practice guidelines for the treatment of patients with eating disorders*, 3rd ed. Arlington, VA: American Psychiatric Association.

American Psychological Association (2013). *Diagnostic and statistical manual of mental disorders*, 5th ed. Washington, DC: American Psychological Association.

Bar, R. J., Cassin, S. E., & Dionne, M. M. (2016). Eating disorder prevention initiatives for athletes: A review. *European Journal of Sport Science, 16*(3), 325–335.

Baum, A. L. (2013). (2013). Eating disorders in athletes. In D. A. Baron, C. L. Reardon, & S. H. Baron (Eds.), *Clinical sports psychiatry: An international perspective*. Chichester: Wiley.

Becker, C. B., McDaniel, L., Bull, S., Powell, M., & McIntyre, K. (2012). Can we reduce eating disorder risk factors in female college athletes? A randomized exploratory investigation of two peer-led interventions. *Body Image, 9*(1), 31–42.

Bonci, C. M., Bonci, L. J., Granger, L. R., Johnson, C. L., Malina, R. M., Milne, L. W., Ryan, R. R., & Vanderbunt, E. M. (2008). National Athletic Trainers' Association position statement: Preventing, detecting, and managing disordered eating in athletes. *Journal of Athletic Training, 43*, 80–108.

Bratland-Sanda, S., & Sundgot-Borgen, J. (2013). Eating disorders in athletes: Overview of prevalence, risk factors and recommendations for prevention and treatment. *European Journal of Sport Science, 13*(5), 499–508.

de Bruin, A. P. (2017). Athletes with eating disorder symptomatology, a specific population with specific needs. *Current Opinion in Psychology, 16*, 148–153.

Fairburn, C.G., & Beglin, S.J. (1994). Assessment of eating disorder psychopathology: Interview or self-report questionnaire? *International Journal of Eating Disorders, 16*, 363–370.

Fassino, S. & Abbate-Daga, G. (2013). Resistance to treatment in eating disorders: A critical challenge. *BMC Psychiatry, 13*, 282. doi: 10.1186/1471-244X-13-282

Garner, D.M., Olmsted, M.P., Bohr, Y., & Garfinkel, P.E. (1982). The Eating Attitudes Test: Psychometric features and clinical correlates. *Psychological Medicine, 12*, 871–878.

Hildebrandt, T. B. (2005, January 1). A Review of Eating Disorders in Athletes. *Journal of Applied School Psychology, 21*(2), 145–167.

IOC. (2009). The International Olympic Committee (IOC) consensus statement on periodic health evaluation of elite athletes. *British Journal of Sports Medicine, 43*(9). doi: 10.1136/bjsm.2009.064394

Johnson, F., & Wardle, J. (2005). Dietary restraint, body dissatisfaction, and psychological distress: A prospective analysis. *Journal of Abnormal Psychology, 114*, 119–125.

Knapp, J., Aerni, G., & Anderson, J. (2014). Eating disorders in female athletes: Use of screening tools. *Current Sports Medicine Reports, 13*, 214–218.

Maron, B. J., & Pelliccia, A. (2006). The heart of trained athletes: Cardiac remodeling and the risks of sports, including sudden death. *Circulation, 114*, 1633–1644.

McNulty, K.Y., Adams, C.H., Anderson, J.M., & Affenito, S.G. (2001). Development and validation of a screening tool to identify eating disorders in female athletes. *Journal of the American Dietetic Association, 101*, 886–892.

Mitchell, J. J., & Robert-McComb, J. J. (2014). Screening for disordered eating and eating disorders in female athletes. In J. J. Robert-McComb, R. L. Norman, & M. Zumwalt (Eds.), *The active female: Health issues across the lifespan* (pp. 191–206). New York, NY: Springer.

Nagel, D.L., Black, D.R., Leverenz, L.J., & Coster, D.C. (2000). Evaluation of a screening test for female college athletes with eating disorders and disordered eating. *Journal of Athletic Training, 35*, 431–440.

National Eating Disorder Association. (2018). Prevention. Retrieved from www.nationaleatingdisorders.org/learn/general-information/prevention

Nattiv, A., Loucks, A.B., Manore, M. M., Sanborn, C. F., Sundgot-Borgen, J., & Waren, M. P. (2007). American College of Sports Medicine. The female athlete triad. *Medicine and Science in Sports and Exercise, 39*, 1867–1882.

Papathomas, A. & Lavallee, D. (2010) Athlete experiences of disordered eating in sport. *Qualitative Research in Sport and Exercise, 2*(3), 354–370.

Pearson, F. C., & Rivers, T. C. (2006). Eating disorders in female college athletes: Risk factors, prevention, and treatment. *College Student Affairs Journal, 26*(1), 30–44.

Plateau, C. R., Arcelus, J., Leung, N., & Meyer, C. (2017). Female athlete experiences of seeking and receiving treatment for an eating disorder. *Eating Disorders, 25*(3), 273–277.

Pope, Z., Gao, Y., Bolter, N., & Pritchard, M. (2014). Validity and reliability of eating disorder assessments used with athletes: A review. *Journal of Sport and Health Science, 8*, 1–11.

Robert-McComb, J. J. & Cisneros, A. (2014). The female athletic triad: Disordered eating, amenorrhea, and osteoporosis. In J. J. Robert-McComb, R.L. Norman, & M. Zumwalt (Eds.), *The active female: Health issues across the lifespan* (pp. 177–189). New York, NY: Springer.

Schaffner, A. D., & Buchanan, L. P. (2010). Evidence-based practices in outpatient treatment for eating disorders. *International Journal of Behavioral Consultation and Therapy, 6*(1), 35–44. doi:http://dx.doi.org.tcsedsystem.idm.oclc.org/10.1037/h0100896

Sherman, R. T., & Thompson, R. A. (2001). Athletes and disordered eating: Four major issues for the professional psychologist. *Professional Psychology: Research and Practice, 32*(1), 27–33. doi: 10.1037/0735-7028.32.1.27

Sullivan, P. F. (2002). Course and outcome of Anorexia Nervosa and Bulimia Nervosa. In C.G. Fairburn & K.D. Brownell (Eds.), *Eating Disorders and Obesity: A comprehensive Handbook*, 2nd ed. (pp. 226–230). New York, NY: Guilford Press.

Sundgot-Borgen, J., & Torstveit, M. K. (2004). Prevalence of eating disorders in elite athletes is higher than in the general population. *Clinical Journal of Sport Medicine, 14,* 25–32.

Thome, J., & Espelage, D. (2004). Relations among exercise, coping, disordered eating, and psychological health among college students. *Eating Behaviors, 4,* 337–351.

Thompson, R.A., & Sherman, R. (1999). "Good athlete" traits and characteristics of anorexia nervosa: Are they similar? *Eating Disorders: The Journal of Treatment and Prevention, 7,* 181–190.

Thompson, R. A. & Sherman, R. (2014). *Psychology of Sport and Exercise, 15,* 729–734.

Torstveit, M. K., Rosenvinge, J. H., & Sundgot-Borgen, J. (2008). Prevalence of eating disorders and the predictive power of risk models in female elite athletes: A controlled study. *Scandinavian Journal of Medicine and Science in Sports, 18,* 108–118.

Voelker, D. & Petrie, T. (2017). Bodies in motion: An evaluation of a program to support positive body image in female collegiate athletes. Retrieved from www.ncaa.org/sites/default/files/2017RES_NCAAGrant-FinalReportExtension-VoelkerPetrie-FINAL_20171106.pdf (accessed May 25, 2018).

Walsh, J. M. E., Wheat, M. E., & Freund, K. (2000). Detection, evaluation, and treatment of Eating Disorders: The role of the primary care physician. *Journal of General Internal Medicine, 15*(8), 577–590.

Yager, J., Devlin, M. J., Halmi, K. A., Herzog, D. B., Mitchell III, J. E., Powers, P, & Zerbe, K. J. (2012). *Guideline watch (August 2012): Practice guideline for the treatment of patients with eating disorders,* 3rd ed. Washington, DC: American Psychiatric Association.

SUBSTANCE USE

Kathy Pruzan

Substance use and abuse is a serious clinical issue across the general population. The 12-month prevalence rate for drug use disorders is just under 4% and lifetime prevalence is 9.9% (Grant et al., 2016). These numbers increase to 14 and 29% for alcohol use disorder. Recent research has demonstrated that athletes may be at risk for using substances at higher rates than non-athletes (Donohue et al., 2013). Unfortunately, rates of treatment for substance-use disorders for the general population fall woefully short of what would be hoped for, with just under 25% of those who meet criteria for a substance-use disorder seeking treatment in their lifetime (Grant et al., 2016). Taken together, these data suggest that substance use and abuse may be under-reported (Brisola-Santos et al., 2016), under-assessed, and/or under-treated among athlete populations.

The DSM-V provided an update on substance-related diagnoses. Changes included removing the abuse vs. dependence distinction and instead providing eleven criteria related to misuse of the substance.

1. Taking the substance in larger amounts or for longer than you're meant to.
2. Wanting to cut down or stop using the substance but not managing to.
3. Spending a lot of time getting, using, or recovering from use of the substance.
4. Cravings and urges to use the substance.
5. Not managing to do what you should at work, home, or school because of substance use.
6. Continuing to use, even when it causes problems in relationships.
7. Giving up important social, occupational, or recreational activities because of substance use.
8. Using substances again and again, even when it puts you in danger.
9. Continuing to use, even when you know you have a physical or psychological problem that could have been caused or made worse by the substance.
10. Needing more of the substance to get the effect you want (tolerance).
11. Development of withdrawal symptoms, which can be relieved by taking more of the substance.

Individuals can be diagnosed with a substance-specific disorder across a range of severities: Mild corresponding to 2–3 positive criteria, moderate corresponding to 4–5 positive criteria, and severe corresponding to 6 or more criteria met (American Psychiatric Association, 2013). DSM-V parameters can therefore result in two individuals with very similar profiles of actual substance use (for example, two individuals drinking 30 standard drinks per week) having different DSM-V diagnoses related to their substance use.

Theory and Research

Risk factors for substance-related disorders include both those of genetic and environmental origins. Estimates for genetic loading related to substance use disorders range from 40% to 70% (US Department of Health and Human Services, 2016). This increased genetic risk can include temperamental factors, such as sensation-seeking (Foulds, Boden, Newton-Howes, Mulder, & Horwood, 2017), which can be particularly relevant for athletes (Schroth, 1995). Environmental risk factors include an early environment where substance use or abuse was common and, also particularly relevant to athletes, association with peers who use substances (US Department of Health and Human Services, 2016). Conversely, protective factors include strong family, social connections, and societal ties, a feeling of control over successes and failures, and emotional factors such as hopefulness and emotional resilience (US Department of Health and Human Services, 2016).

Athlete-specific Factors

Considerable data suggest that athletes are at higher risk for misuse of at least certain substances, particularly alcohol (Nelson & Wechsler, 2001; Turrisi et al., 2007). Caucasian, male athletes seem to be at substantially higher risk for alcohol (Nelson & Wechsler, 2001) and marijuana use (Buckman et al., 2011). Athletes of both genders in US college settings report higher rates of binge drinking and alcohol-related consequences than their non-athlete peers (Nelson & Wechsler, 2001). In contrast, there is some evidence to suggest that athletic participation in high school might be protective against illicit drug use (Kwan et al., 2014). This may be due, in part, to increased adult supervision, exposure to adult role models, and less free time to be exposed to and engage in high-risk behaviors such as substance use. Additionally, some limited data suggest that athletes on team sports are more prone to alcohol use, whereas athletes participating in individual sports (snowboarding, skiing, kayaking) may be more likely to report marijuana use (Brisola-Santos et al., 2016). At the same time, these divergent findings may also be due to differences in the cultures of the sports themselves rather than their categorization as individual or team sports.

Additionally, internal factors such as sensation-seeking may explain some observed differences, for example, athletes higher in sensation-seeking (i.e., those who participate in sports such as snowboarding, skiing, and kayaking) are more likely to use marijuana (Buckman et al., 2011). Increased substance use and use-related consequences are linked with use as an effort to cope with stress and other life challenges, which is the case for both athletes and non-athletes (Doumas, 2013).

Misperceptions of normative use can also be a risk factor for increased and/or problematic use of substances. An environment rife with and supportive of substance use is a risk factor for substance use disorders (US Department of Health and Human Services, 2016). A feedback loop may occur among teams or athlete peer groups where members see or know that their peers are drinking, drink to be accepted and to have positive team/peer experiences (Zhou & Heim, 2016), and also overestimate the amount that peers are drinking (Turrisi et al., 2007). This pattern can create a feedback loop that encourages a culture of substance use within that athletic cohort.

Finally, injuries play a role in risk for substance misuse among athletes. For example, Cottler et al. (2011) found that 71% of retired NFL players surveyed misused opiates during their careers and 7% reported currently using. Pain during a playing career increased the odds of current use. Data indicate that the risk of opiate abuse increases following an initial pain management opiate prescription of longer than five days (Shah, Hayes, & Martin, 2017). There is also some evidence to suggest a higher prevalence of opioid misuse among athletes as compared with non-athletes in college, with injured male athletes being at the highest risk to misuse prescription opioids (Ford et al., 2017).

Athletes who sustain concussions are also at risk for substance use and abuse (Zuckerman et al., 2015). Consultants should be aware of the potential increased risk of substance misuse subsequent to a concussion. Concussion status has been found to predict number of drinks per outing in both athlete and non-athlete populations, with those who suffered concussions drinking more per occasion (Alcock, Gallant, & Good, 2018). One hypothesis for this relationship is that physiological under-arousal following a concussion leads to increased risk-taking behaviors.

Performance Enhancement vs. Substance Abuse

An important consideration in examining the use and misuse of substances among athletes is whether substances are used to enhance performance or in a manner consistent with a diagnosis of a substance-abuse disorder. This distinction has implications for treatment recommendations and this review focuses primarily on treatments for substance-abuse issues. Studies of the intersection of performance enhancement, pain management, and substance abuse are limited by small sample sizes and few athlete-specific studies. This is an important area of consideration due to the pull for both higher levels of performance and injury/pain management among athlete populations.

Though substances may be used for performance enhancement without tipping into substance abuse, performance enhancement-based use may be a starting point or risk factor for future abuse. There is evidence to suggest that athletes using performance-enhancing substances (PES) are more likely to use and misuse other substances as well (Buckman, Farris, & Yusko, 2013) because the fitness gains and improved performances reinforce the value of PES use. The researchers found that, among a sample of male NCAA athletes, those who reported PES use (3.1% of total) reported more use of other substances than did their non-PES-using peers. This included more frequent and heavier alcohol use and alcohol-related consequences. They were also more likely to use other substances with purported performance-enhancing properties that were not on a banned substances list. Concernedly, athletes also endorse athletic performance as a primary motive for initial off-prescription use of stimulants (Gallucci & Martin, 2015).

Practical Implications

Because of its profound immediate and long-term physical and psychological impact of substance use, misuse, and abuse on athletes, consultants must be sensitive to their presence in athletes' lives and teams' cultures. The ability of consultants to recognize, identify, and take action in response to indications of substance use is essential to the mental and physical health of the athletes with whom they work.

Assessment

Substance use should be included in any clinical intake and assessment with athletes, as they may be likely to omit or under-report (Brisola-Santos et al., 2016). As noted above, the DSM-V provides eleven criteria, which clients can be asked on a per-substance basis, as a screening option related to use or abuse of substances (American Psychiatric Association, 2013). Consideration should be given to other comorbid diagnoses that might contribute to or result from substance use or abuse.

One important concern in assessment and treatment is clarification about confidentiality and who will receive the results of any assessment. For example, will the athlete's team or institution receive results? As consultants explore the presence of substance use with athletes, they should be clear on athletes' rights to privacy to encourage honest responses and ensure proper treatment if appropriate. Particularly for consultants without the education, training, and experience to formally assess substance use and abuse, structured means of assessment can offer more comfort and clarity in determining the presence of substance issues. The objective data that come from the following formal screening tools can provide unambiguous information that can help consultants decide whether further assessment, treatment, or referral would be appropriate.

- **Alcohol, Smoking and Substance Involvement Screening Test** (ASSIST): A clinical interview rubric developed by the WHO (World Health Organization, 2008). Its length may preclude use in many settings, but it is a comprehensive guide for screening of substances and provides significant information about the sequelae of use of a variety of substances for the consultant's reference.
- **Alcohol Use Disorders Identification Test** (AUDIT): A 10-item measure developed as a screening by the World Health Organization to screen for excessive drinking. The AUDIT was developed to be sensitive to a broader range of problems related to alcohol use, in contrast to measures that tend to capture those

at the more intense end of the spectrum of problematic use (Saunders, Aasland, Babor, De La Fuente, & Grant, 1993). Clinician-administered and self-report versions are available online at www.drugabuse.gov/sites/default/files/files/AUDIT.pdf

- **CAGE-AID**: The CAGE-AID is an adaptation of the CAGE questionnaire which includes screening for substances other than alcohol (Brown & Rounds, 1995). It is a four-item screener, with one or more positive answers suggesting need for additional assessment. It is available online at www.integration.samhsa.gov/images/res/CAGEAID.pdf.
- **Timeline Follow-Back** (TLFB): A one-month Timeline Follow-Back (TLFB) has been found to be a reliable self-report measure of alcohol (Sobell & Sobell, 1992) and drug use (Hjorthoj, Hjorthoj, & Nordentoft, 2012) in substance abusing populations. The TLFB can be administered via paper and pencil or electronic calendar, and through clinical interview or client report. It provides a helpful prompt and timeline for a snapshot of clients' recent substance use and can be used to inquire about other substances in addition to alcohol. Available online at www.nova.edu/gsc/forms/timeline-followback-forms.html

Prevention

Personalized feedback and goal-setting are important components of both prevention and treatment efforts (Donohue et al., 2016). Evidence indicates that effective programs are aimed at both risk and protective factors at the individual, family, and community levels (Donohue et al., 2016). Prevention approaches can be universal (for everyone in a population), selected (targeted to those of at-risk groups), or indicated (for at-risk individuals) (Donohue et al., 2016). The latter of these categories has overlap with treatments and will be addressed below.

Universal prevention options may be most scalable and applicable to athletic team contexts. One evidence-based option is the Life Skills Training program, initially developed for schools (Botvin, Griffin, & Williams, 2015). Extensive information about it, including additional studies on evidence, is available at www.lifeskillstraining.com. The Life Skills Training approach has been recognized by a variety of health and governmental organizations including the National Institute on Drug Abuse and the Centers for Disease Control and Prevention (Griffin & Botvin, 2010). It trains teens in resistance skills, developing self-management and coping skills, and aims to build resilience while navigating developmental tasks. Providers attend a one and a half day workshop and materials include an instructor's manual. It was developed as a 30-session program over 3 years. Findings indicate 52% fewer daily substance users in the prevention condition vs controls in a high school population (Botvin, Griffin, & Williams, 2015). While no studies exist expanding this to athletic populations, it provides a user-friendly, structured option that could be adapted for high school and college athlete populations.

Evidence-Based Treatments

Athletes, particularly at more competitive levels, likely have a team of coaches, trainers, medical providers, and sport psychology consultants that can be harnessed to aid in efforts toward healthier substance behaviors. This support should include thorough assessment and treatment of any comorbid psychiatric conditions. In addition to specific techniques of change described below, consultants must also build a therapeutic alliance, enhance hopefulness, and convey accurate empathy of athletes' circumstances which are essential components of all evidence-based approaches for substance-abuse treatment (McGovern & Carroll, 2003).

Motivational Interviewing

Motivational interviewing (MI) involves eliciting clients' own reasons for making changes to substance use and aiding in developing a discrepancy between the current circumstances and clients' ideal circumstances, values, and goals (Miller & Rollnick, 1991). Consultants can use open-ended questions, reflections, and summary statements to reinforce athletes' healthy "change-talk" while selectively discouraging unhealthy "sustain-talk" that could maintain the status-quo of substance use. MI specifically targets resolving ambivalence about substance use. It can therefore be used with abstinence, moderation, or harm-reduction goals.

Findings across studies suggest that the strength of clients' language related to commitment to change predicts future abstinence from substances (Hettema, Steele, & Miller, 2005). MI dovetails nicely with consultants' roles in helping athletes improve performance in sport, which can be a significant motivator toward changing harmful behaviors, such as substance use, that might impact sport performance. However, like all the treatment approaches discussed here, MI should only be used if consultants are appropriately trained in addressing substance use and abuse.

Cognitive-Behavioral Therapy

CBT approaches have been found to be effective across a range of substance use disorders (Carroll & Onken, 2005). They are often grounded in a functional analysis of the client's substance use which provides an understanding of problematic use behaviors within a psychosocial context. CBT includes identifying high-risk contexts, internal mood states, and social circumstances that impact substance use. Additionally, CBT providers teach relapse prevention and coping skills (Carroll & Onken, 2005), as well as helping clients with goal-setting (Donohue, Pitts, Gavrilova, Ayarza, & Cintron, 2013). This approach also overlaps nicely with the work that properly trained consultants are already doing with athletes in their efforts to enhance sports performance

Community Reinforcement Approach

The community reinforcement approach (CRA) is a behavioral treatment which can be combined with elements of CBT. CRA focuses on increasing rewards that individuals receive from non-using behaviors and lifestyles and selectively non-reinforcing substance use, and ideally does this by recruiting significant others from clients' lives to participate as well (Meyers, Smith, Serna, & Belon, 2013). It has been effectively used with a wide range of populations including adolescents (Godley, Smith, Passetti, & Subramaniam, 2014) and in schools (Hunter, Godley, & Godley, 2014) and its principles could be applied in sports settings.

Community Reinforcement and Family Training

Community reinforcement and family training (CRAFT) is an approach for working with concerned loved ones when a substance user is not yet open to treatment (Smith, Meyers, & Milford, 2002). It is a CBT-based approach focusing on helping concerned others implement positive reinforcement for non-use, allow negative consequences of use to occur, engage in self-care, implement new communication skills for more effective communication, and look for motivational hooks that might help the substance user be open to treatment. It is an important option for consultants to be aware of as family members, coaches, or teammates may be the first to come to the consultant with concerns about an athlete's substance use.

Contingency Management

Systematic reinforcement of abstinence is linked with positive outcomes across a variety of substances including cocaine (Higgins et al., 1993), opiates (Silverman et al., 1996), and marijuana (Budney, Moore, Rocha, and Higgins, 2006). Grounded in behavioral-learning principles, rewards are offered on a predetermined schedule for toxicology test-demonstrated abstinence of the target substance(s). Teams in particular may have a number of windows of opportunity for providing additional reinforcement for healthier substance-use behaviors, either by the individual or the team as a whole.

Pharmacotherapies

Though an exhaustive review of pharmacotherapies for substance misuse is outside the scope of this section, it is important for consultants to be aware that there are several evidence-based options available. These are typically substance-specific and referral to an addiction psychiatrist familiar with athletes is ideal so as to help navigate any necessary eligibility-related therapeutic-use exemptions as well as to educate the athlete, family, and team. Some of the medication options must be taken daily and therefore monitoring by a supportive other increases adherence and effectiveness (McGovern & Carroll, 2003).

Athlete-Specific Intervention

Donohue and colleagues have developed a modification of Family Behavior Therapy (FBT; Donohue & Allen, 2011; Donohue & Azrin, 2011) for work with athletes (Donohue et al., 2013). This approach brings supportive significant others identified by the athlete into the therapy to help reinforce positive changes to substance use. Typically involving 12–20 outpatient sessions, clients participate in crafting a treatment plan from a menu of options in eight intervention areas such as treatment planning, goals and rewards, and self-control (Donohue et al., 2013). The authors modified FBT for work with athletes to address athlete-specific issues and to help increase engagement and retention. Examples of such adjustments are sessions being held the athletic facility to support attendance and being led by staff who are part of the athlete's sports-support team and institution. Additionally, video-conferencing of supportive others (e.g., parents) is offered to increase the likelihood of family engagement. Motivational techniques akin to MI are used throughout the treatment program. It then focuses on CBT techniques such as functional analysis of use, identifying and managing triggers, and enhancing reinforcement and relationship positivity with the family member.

The authors performed a clinical trial with 201 NCAA athletes randomly assigned to an abbreviated version of the modified FBT or to a wait-list control (Donohue et al., 2016). Athletes in the experimental condition engaged with a brief assessment of alcohol use followed by personalized goal development, contingency management, and a one-hour meeting with their supportive other present. Sessions occurred with a performance coach and supportive others could be video- or teleconferenced into sessions. Athletes received personalized feedback about their alcohol use, consequences related to sport performance were identified and then goals were developed. Supportive others were asked to reinforce goal achievement. Results of the study indicated that those in the experimental condition reduced their alcohol consumption over the two-month period of study, as evidenced by statistically significant reductions in scores between baseline and two months. The authors found the same results when sessions occurred in individual (athlete plus their supportive other) and group formats (several athletes and their supportive others together). Both versions of Donohue's FBT approach for athletes provide a framework for helping reduce substance use in athletes which can be used as either prevention or intervention after discovery of problematic use.

Summary

- Substance use and abuse is a relevant clinical issue across the general population and recent research has demonstrated athletes may be at risk for using substances at higher rates than non-athletes.
- The DSM-V provides eleven criteria related to misuse of the substance and clients can be diagnosed with a substance-specific disorder across a range of severities.
- Risk factors for substance-related disorders include both those of genetic (e.g., sensation seeking) and environmental origins (family history of substance abuse).
- An environment ripe with and supportive of substance use, such as a sports team, and the presence of injuries, are risk factors for substance use disorders.
- An important consideration in examining the use and misuse of substances among athletes is whether substances are used to enhance performance enhancement or in a manner consistent with a diagnosis of a substance-abuse disorder.
- Because of its profound immediate and long-term physical and psychological impact of substance use, misuse, and abuse on athletes, consultants must be sensitive to their presence in athletes' lives and teams' cultures.
- Substance use should be included in any clinical intake and assessment with athletes, as they may be likely to omit or under-report.
- Particularly for consultants without the education, training, and experience to formally assess substance use and abuse, structured means of assessment can offer more comfort and clarity in determining the presence of substance issues.
- Evidence-based treatments for substance-use disorders include motivational interviewing, cognitive-behavioral therapy, community reinforcement approach, community reinforcement approach with family training, contingency management, pharmacotherapies, and athlete-specific interventions.

References

Alcock, B., Gallant, C., & Good, D. (2018). The relationship between concussion and alcohol consumption among university athletes. *Addictive Behaviors Reports*, 7, 58–64. doi: 10.1016/j.abrep.2018.02.001

American Psychiatric Association. (2013). *Diagnostic and statistical manual of mental disorders* (5th ed.). Washington, DC: American Psychiatric Association.

Botvin, G. J., Griffin, K. W., & Williams, C. (2015). Preventing daily substance use among high school students using a cognitive-behavioral competence enhancement approach. *World Journal of Preventive Medicine*, 3, 48–53.

Brisola-Santos, M. B. et al. (2016). Prevalence and correlates of cannabis use among athletes—A systematic review. *The American Journal On Addictions*, 25, 518–528. doi: 10.1111/ajad.12425

Brown, R. L. & Rounds, L. A. (1995). Conjoint screening questionnaires for alcohol and other drug abuse: Criterion validity in a primary care practice. *Wisconsin Medical Journal*, 94, 135–140.

Buckman, J. F., Farris, S. G., & Yusko, D. A. (2013). A national study of substance use behaviors among NCAA male athletes who use banned performance enhancing substances. *Drug and Alcohol Dependence*, 131, 50–55.

Buckman, J. F., Yusko, D. A., Farris, S. G., White, H. R., & Pandina, R. J. (2011). Risk of marijuana use in male and female college student athletes and nonathletes. *Journal of Studies on Alcohol and Drugs*, 72, 586–591.

Budney, A. J., Moore, B. A., Rocha, H. L., & Higgins, S. T. (2006). Clinical trial of abstinence-based vouchers and cognitive-behavioral therapy for cannabis dependence. *Journal of Consulting and Clinical Psychology*, 74, 307–316.

Carroll, K. M. & Onken, L. S. (2005). Behavioral therapies for drug abuse. *American Journal of Psychiatry*, 162, 1452–1460. doi: 10.1176/appi.ajp.162.8.1452

Cottler, L. B., Ben Abdallah, A., Cummings, S. M., Barr, J., Banks, R., & Forchheimer, R. (2011). Injury, pain, and prescription opioid use among former National Football League (NFL) players. *Drug and Alcohol Dependence*, 116, 188–194. doi: 10.1016/j.drugalcdep.2010.12.003

Donohue, B. & Allen, D. A. (2011). *Treating adult substance abuse using family behavior therapy: A step-by-step approach*. New York, NY: John Wiley & Sons, Inc.

Donohue, B. & Azrin, N. H. (2011). *Treating adolescent substance abuse using family behavior therapy: A step-by-step approach*. New York, NY: John Wiley & Sons, Inc.

Donohue, B., Loughran, T., Pitts, M., Gavrilova, Y., Chow, G. M., Soto-Nevarez, A., & Schubert, K. (2016). Preliminary development of a brief intervention to prevent alcohol misuse and enhance sport performance in collegiate athletes. *Journal of Drug Abuse*, 2, 1–9.

Donohue, B., Pitts, M., Gavrilova, Y., Ayarza, A., & Cintron, K. I. (2013). A culturally sensitive approach to treating substance abuse in athletes using evidence-supported methods. *Journal of Clinical Sport Psychology*, 7, 98–119.

Doumas, D. M. (2013). Alcohol-related consequences among intercollegiate student athletes: The role of drinking motives. *Journal of Addictions & Offender Counseling*, 34, 51–64. doi: 10.1002/j.2161-1874.2013.00014.x

Ford, J. A., Pomykacz, C., Veliz, P., McCabe, S. E., & Boyd, C. J. (2017). Sports involvement, injury history, and non-medical use of prescription opioids among college students: An analysis with a national sample. *The American Journal on Addictions*, 27, 15–22.

Foulds, J. A., Boden, J. M., Newton-Howes, G. M., Mulder, R. T., & Horwood, L. J. (2017). The role of novelty seeking as a predictor of substance use disorder outcomes in early adulthood. *Addiction*, 112, 1629–1637.

Gallucci, A. R., & Martin, R. J. (2015). Misuse of prescription stimulant medication in a sample of college students: Examining differences between varsity athletes and non-athletes. *Addictive Behaviors*, 51, 44–50.

Godley, S. H., Smith, J. E., Passetti, L. L., & Subramaniam, G. (2014). The adolescent community reinforcement approach (A-CRA) as a model paradigm for the management of adolescents with substance use disorders and co-occurring psychiatric disorders. *Substance Abuse*, 35, 352–363. doi: 10.1080/08897077.2014.936993

Grant, B. F., et al. (2016). Epidemiology of DSM-5 drug use disorder: Results from the national epidemiological survey on alcohol and related conditions-III. *JAMA Psychiatry*, 73, 39–47.

Griffin, K. W. & Botvin, G.J. (2010). Evidence-based interventions for preventing substance use disorders in adolescents. *Child and Adolescent Psychiatric Clinics of North America*, 19, 505–526. doi: 10.1016/j.chc.2010.03.005.

Hettema, J., Steele, J., & Miller, W. R. (2005). Motivational interviewing. *Annual Review of Clinical Psychology*, 1, 91–111. doi:10.1146/annurev.clinpsy.1.102803.143833

Higgins, S. T., Budney, A. J., Bickel, W. K., Hughes, J. R., Foerg, F. E., & Badger, G. J. (1993). Achieving cocaine abstinence with a behavioral approach. *American Journal of Psychiatry*, 150, 763–769.

Hjorthoj, C. R., Hjorthoj, A. R., & Nordentoft, M. (2012). Validity of Timeline Follow-Back for self-reported use of cannabis and other illicit substances: Systematic review and meta-analysis. *Addictive Behaviors*, 37, 225–233. doi:10.1016/j.addbeh.2011.11025

Hunter, B. D., Godley, M. D., & Godley, S. H. (2014). Feasibility of implementing the adolescent community reinforcement approach in school settings for adolescents with substance use disorders. *Advances in School Mental Health Promotion*, 7, 105–122. doi: 10.1080/1754730X.2014.888224

Kwan, M., Bobko, S., Faulkner, G., Donnelly, P., & Cairney, J. (2014). Sport participation and alcohol and illicit drug use in adolescents and young adults: A systematic review of longitudinal studies. *Addictive Behaviors, 39*, 497–506.

McGovern, M. P. & Carroll, K. M. (2003). Evidence-based practices for substance use disorders. *Psychiatric Clinics of North America, 26*, 991–1010. doi: 10.1016/S0193-953X(03)00073-X.

Meyers, R. J., Smith, J. E., Serna, B., & Belon, K. E. (2013). Community reinforcement approaches: CRA and CRAFT. In P. M. Miller et al. (Eds.), *Comprehensive addictive behaviors and disorders, vol.3: Interventions for addiction.* San Diego, CA: Elsevier Academic Press.

Miller, W. R. & Rollnick, S. (1991). Motivational interviewing. New York, NY: Guilford.

Nelson, T. F. & Wechsler, H. (2001). Alcohol and college athletes. *Medicine & Science in Sports & Exercise, 33*, 43–47.

Saunders, J. B., Aasland, O. G., Babor, T. F., De La Fuente, J. R., & Grant, M. (1993). Development of the Alcohol Use Disorders Identification Test (AUDIT): WHO collaborative project on early detection of persons with harmful alcohol consumption—II. *Addiction, 88*, 791–804.

Schroth, M. L. (1995). A comparison of sensation seeking among different groups of athletes and nonathletes. *Personality and Individual Differences, 18*, 219–222. doi: 10.1016/0191-88669(94)00144-H

Shah A., Hayes C. J., & Martin B. C. (2017). Characteristics of Initial Prescription Episodes and Likelihood of Long-Term Opioid Use—United States, 2006–2015. *Morbidity and Mortality Weekly Report, 66*, 265–269.

Silverman, K., Wong, C. J., Higgins, S. T., Brooner, R. K., Montoya, I. D., Contoreggi, C. et al. (1996). Increasing opiate abstinence through voucher-based reinforcement therapy. *Drug and Alcohol Dependence, 41*, 157–165.

Smith, J. E., Meyers, R. J., & Milford, J. L. (2002). The community reinforcement approach. In R. Hester & W. Miller's (Eds.), *Handbook of alcoholism treatment approaches: Effective alternatives*, 3rd ed. New York, NY: Allyn & Bacon.

Sobell, L. C. & Sobell, M. B. (1992). Timeline follow-back: A technique for assessing self-reported alcohol consumption. In R. Z. Litten, & J. Allen (Eds.), *Measuring alcohol consumption: Psychosocial and biological methods* (pp. 41–72). New Jersey: Humana Press.

Turrisi, R., Mastroleo, N. R., Mallett, K. A., Larimer, M. E., & Kilmer, J. R. (2007). Examination of the mediational influences of peer norms, environmental influences, and parent communications on heavy drinking in athletes and nonathletes. *Psychology of Addictive Behaviors, 21*, 453–461.

US Department of Health and Human Services. (2016, November). *Facing addiction in America: The surgeon general's report on alcohol, drugs, and health, Executive summary.* Washington, DC: US Department of Health and Human Services

World Health Organization. (2008). The ASSIST project: Alcohol, Smoking, and Substance Involvement Screening Test. Retrieved from www.who.int/substance_abuse/activities/assist/en/

Zhou, J. & Heim, D. (2016). A qualitative exploration of alcohol use among student sportspeople: A social identity perspective. *European Journal of Social Psychology, 46*, 581–594. http://dx.doi.org/10.1002/ejsp.2195

Zuckerman, S. L., Kerr, Z. Y., Yengo-Kahn, A., Wasserman, E., Covassin, T., & Solomon, G. S. (2015). Epidemiology of sports-related concussion in NCAA athletes from 2009-2010 to 2013-2014: Incidence, recurrence, and mechanisms. *The American Journal of Sports Medicine, 43*, 2654–2662. doi: 19,1177.0363546515599634

SEXUAL ABUSE

Joan Steidinger

The acknowledgement of sexual harassment and abuse within the sports community has finally occurred. With the guilty verdict of Dr. Larry Nassar for sexually assaulting more than 150 gymnasts, the issue is no longer sport's dirty little secret that so many knew about. Nassar was a physician for USA Gymnastics and the Michigan State University gymnastics teams. The documented allegations of abuse against him date back to 1996, yet no action was taken until September, 2016 even though a significant abuse report was filed with the USOC in 2015 (Perez, 2018). Now, the sporting world realizes what many have known for years: Sexual misconduct is widespread at levels of many sports. It is estimated that between 2% and 8% of minor-age athletic children suffer sexual abuse and the vast majority are girls (Institut National Santé Publique, 2012). Moreover, Athletes who report sexual harassment and/ or abuse need to be believed and supported. Frequently, athletes are often hesitant to report sexual misconduct because they are afraid of the perpetrator who usually has a position of authority and often has control over their sports lives and futures. As such, athletes who in the past haven't reported this mistreatment must be encouraged to step forward. In a letter written by former Olympic gold medalist and president of Champion Women Nancy Hogshead-Makar and signed by hundreds of elite athletes, the letter reads: "Research shows that the more elite the athlete, the more likely they are to be sexually abused by someone within their own entourage" (Ladika, 2017).

Research on the issue of sexual abuse began in the mid-1980s (Crosset, 1986; Lackey, 1990; Lenskyj, 1992; Holman, 1995; Brackenridge & Kirby, 1997) when most female athletes who alleged sexual abuse were not believed.

In a 2008 report (Brackenridge et al., 2008), the authors found that 2% to 22% of youth were victimized in sport by mostly of male coaches, teachers, and instructors (98%) ranging in age from 16–63. Brackenridge further found that one-third were married with children. In the most recent 2017 International Olympic Committee (IOC) consensus statement, the IOC suggests even higher prevalence rates in sexual harassment extending from 19% to 92% while sexual abuse extends from 2% to 49%. The most vulnerable athletes to sexual abuse are LGBTQ and disabled athletes (Freeman, 2018). They go on to report: "Athlete reports indicate that sexual abuse can occur in the locker room, (the coaches office), the playing field, trips away, the coaches' home and/or car and social events, especially where alcohol is involved" (Mountjoy et al., 2016). What complicates matters is there are a number of sports that involve highly physical and violent behaviors often participated in by perpetrators, seen in such sports as ice hockey, wrestling, rugby, and others. These sports, as all violent sports, open the door for sexually abusive behaviors by male athletes.

The first step in gaining an understanding of sexual misconduct is to establish a shared definition of what it is. Sexual harassment is defined as the unwanted sexual advances of a person in a position of power in the form of verbal suggestions and/or behavioral actions. Taking it one step further, sexual assault/abuse is described as actual direct unwanted sexual contact including rape. Some of the features of sexual harassment and abuse include inappropriate use of authority, intimidation, threats, engaging in behavior against the wishes of the victim, and taking advantage of their position of authority and influence. Rape, Abuse, & Incest National Network (RAINN) defines sexual assault as referring to "sexual contact or behavior that occurs without explicit consent of the victim" (RAINN, 2018, p. 12). Some forms of sexual assault include:

- attempted rape;
- fondling or unwanted sexual touching;
- forcing a victim to perform sexual acts, such as oral sex or perpetrator's body; and
- penetration of the victim's body, also known as rape (RAINN, 2018, p. 12).

Theory and Research

In the United States, there are two kinds of sexual harassment: Quid Pro Quo and Hostile Environment (Fasting, Chroni, & Knorre, 2014). A Quid Pro Quo sports situation occurs when a coach or other authority figure (e.g., physician, administrator, trainer) provides special advantages or removes players from certain roles depending on whether the athletes comply with or reject their sexual advances. For example, a volleyball player was pulled out of her starting position when she refused to accept the sexual advances of her coach. In a Hostile Environment, the authority figure's behavior is so extreme that an athlete's ability to perform is compromised. For example, a female runner that was initially seen by a consultant for performance issues eventually opened up and talked about the sexual abuse that she had suffered by a coach. This occurred just three years previously but had gone on for over a year. She talked about how race results had declined during that period and how her coach showed anger and disappointment in her by yelling and screaming in front of others. He would then coax her back into the sexual abuse by using her performance as a way that she could make it up to him. In a Hostile Environment, the coach's behavior may also impact other players on the team or the team as a whole. In the case of the female runner, she described getting special treatment by the coach and other team members acting resentful toward her. In either type of abuse, the victim may decide to leave or change sports, skip training, or struggle with the concentration and focus (Institut National Santé Publique, 2012).

Sexual harassment and abuse in sports occurs with both female (41%) and male athletes (29%), although it is more prevalent with female athletes (Leahy, 2011). It is common that the power differential between authority figure and athlete is an essential and common denominator for all perpetrators. The perpetrators target the most vulnerable athletes who look to those in positions of power to provide friendship, guidance, and support. When this trust is broken, the results are often devastating, as was evidenced from the many testimonials of the gymnasts whom Larry Nassar abused.

Sexual harassment and abuse in sport has its roots during the Cold War and after the passage of Title IX. During this period, many young women entered competitive sports in high school and college. More often than not, they were coached more by men than women. Despite increased sexual harassment and abuse complaints during the 1990s, they were often not addressed by high schools, colleges, and universities led by men and/or brushed aside despite police reports in many instances. For example, as early as 1964, 14-year-old swimmer Diana Nyad's high school coach started a three-year recurring pattern of sexual assault. At that time, there were no laws in effect requiring the investigation of sexual assault; Nyad's high school was not legally bound to take any action. She eventually shared her abuse with her best friend when she was 21 only to learn that she was also sexually abused by the coach. At that time, they reported the sexual abuse to the principal of their high school who subsequently fired the coach. Despite this action, he moved on to a coaching position at a college and eventually coached at the Olympic level. With the advent of the #MeToo movement, Nyad finally felt at liberty to write a story about her abuse that was reported in the *New York Times* (Nyad, 2017). Despite having named her abuser many times in public, he suffered no consequences until after his death in 2014 despite many complaints by other female athletes. Not until 1978 were laws passed to protect the victims of sexual harassment and abuse, though this legislation didn't prevent the continued widespread sexual misconduct by coaches at many levels of sport that we frequently read about today.

Sexual misconduct occurs in all sports and at all levels with an even greater risk with elite athletes (Marks, Mountjoy, & Marcus, 2012). The manipulation by coaches of their athletes' (referred to as grooming) runs to great extremes in the behaviors and methods they employ to perpetrate and cover up the harassment and abuse. Brackenridge and Fasting (2005) addressed what they called the "process of grooming (for sex harassment and/or abuse) in sport" which has been used to describe the varied means by which authority figures prepare athletes to be sexually abused. Over time, the coach establishes trust and dependence from the athlete and begins to break down barriers of what is appropriate and what is not. Such treatment, which is often complimentary and ingratiating, can involve not only the athlete but their parents who feel flattered and fortunate to have their child's coach providing such attention.

In a later study by Fasting & Brackenridge (2009), the researchers classified a sport typology of coaches who sexual harass and abuse female athletes (Fasting & Brackenridge, 2009). The typology was developed through extensive interviews conducted of 19 female elite athletes who had faced sexual harassment by their coaches. The sport typology consisted of three main types:

- The Flirting-Charming Coach acts charming by joking around, flirting, and eventually making attempts to make physical contact with the athlete.
- The Seductive Coach often uses words then attempts to lay his hands upon the athlete.
- The Authoritarian coach acts in a domineering and controlling manner aimed at encouraging obedience and passivity on the part of female athletes.

Perpetrators, such as Nassar, generally cause their victims to feel powerless. They also create an alliance and a sense of intimacy or establish power with threats by using phrases such as "our special secret," "this is our special time together," "you will be humiliated," or "don't tell anyone or something bad will happen," respectively. The victims experience fear, doubt, uncertainty, shock, shame, guilt, self-blame, low self-esteem, hopelessness, depression, and anger. As Brackenridge et al. (2008) have described: "The intrinsic power dynamics within the coach–athlete relationship inevitably opens that relationship to abuse and enables coercion strategies to be used." The range of strategies employed by such perpetrators reflects the differing capacities for control, intimidation, and coercion that they exploit for sexual means.

Research has demonstrated that, until recently, colleges, universities, national governing bodies, and the USOC have not only been reluctant but often refused to investigate complaints, and even covered up allegations involving star athletes and leading coaches (Ladika, 2017). Even when such allegations are adjudicated in court, judges have handed down seemingly lenient sentences for sexual crimes committed by male athletes. Case in point involved the rape of an unconscious woman by a Stanford swimmer who was given a sentence of only six months after his conviction and released after three months.

Within many sporting organizations, the resistance to talking about and dealing with sexual harassment and abuse continues because of the negative ramifications of making such news public. As recently as 2016, Ken Starr, the president of Baylor University, failed to act on sexual abuse allegations against Baylor football players. When the story came out in the press, his lack of action led to his resignation along with those of the AD and head football coach. At the same time, as a number of ongoing cases in sports, including taekwondo, figure skating, swimming, volleyball, judo, and speed skating indicate, as well as the rise of the #MeToo movement and other cases currently being judged in other parts of our culture, allegations of sexual misconduct are now being taken more seriously.

Practical Implications

The indications of sexual abuse among victims are many and varied. SafeSport (www.safesport.org), a not-for-profit organization established to promote respect for athletes and to prevent and respond ethically to sexual misconduct in sports, identify five signs of abuse:

- loss of excitement for sport and competition;
- avoiding practice;
- wanting to stay away from certain individuals (e.g., coach, trainer, administrator);
- unexpected mood shifts; and
- desire to change teams despite good friends on team.

The USOC has recently partnered with SafeSport to educate the sports community about sexual misconduct, set guidelines of appropriate and inappropriate behavior, offer certification of SafeSport education for all stakeholders in sports, and to provide victims with the means to safely report sexual misconduct. The SafeSport mission "is to make athlete well-being the centerpiece of our nation's sports culture. All athletes deserve to participate in sports free from bullying, hazing, sexual misconduct or any emotional or physical abuse." As another part of this movement toward protecting athletes, Nancy Hogshead-Makar (three-time Olympic medalist and attorney) established Champion Women in 2015 to provide legal advocacy for girls and women in sports.

Primary advice to consultants who are not appropriately trained to treat sexual abuse victims is to immediately refer these athletes to licensed clinicians who have extensive training in these issues as well as sport psychology. There are often other complicated clinical issues that these athletes face. As this section has discussed, there are a myriad of symptoms that might be indicative of sexual abuse. Several examples include declining performance, depression, anxiety, withdrawal from teammates, and others previously mentioned.

The responsibility of consultants is to provide support and get the athletes the help they need. Generally, sexual abuse does not emerge in a first interview, yet as consultants develop a relationship of trust it may emerge. If consultants are working with an athlete who wants legal advice, they should contact Champion Women, (championwomen.org), Safe to Compete for children & teens (National Center for Missing & Exploited Children) at SafeToCompete@ncmec.org or www.safetocompete.org, or US Center for SafeSport at www.safesport.org/who-we-are.

Summary

- The acknowledgement of sexual harassment and abuse within the sports community has finally emerged with the guilty verdict of Dr. Larry Nassar for sexually assaulting more than 150 gymnasts.
- Athlete reports indicate that sexual abuse can occur in the locker room (the coaches' office), the playing field, trips away, the coaches' home and/or car, and social events, especially where alcohol is involved.
- Sexual harassment is defined as the unwanted sexual advances of a person in a position of power in the form of verbal suggestions and/or behavioral actions and sexual assault/abuse is described as actual direct unwanted sexual contact, including rape.
- There are two types of sexual harassment: Quid Pro Quo occurs when a coach or other authority figure provides special advantages or removes players from certain roles depending on whether the athletes comply with or reject their sexual advances, and in a Hostile Environment, the authority figure's behavior is so extreme that an athlete's ability to perform is compromised.
- Sexual misconduct in sports occurs with both female and male athletes, although it is more prevalent with female athletes and it is common that the power differential between authority figure and athlete is an essential and common denominator for all perpetrators.
- Sexual harassment and abuse in sport has its roots during the Cold War and after the passage of Title IX when many young women entered competitive sports in high school and college and they were coached more by men than women.
- Researchers classified a sport typology of coaches who sexual harass and abuse female athletes which include three main types: The Flirting-Charming Coach acts charming by joking around, flirting, and eventually making attempts to make physical contact with the athlete, the Seductive Coach often uses words then

attempts to lay his hands upon the athlete. the Authoritarian coach acts in a domineering and controlling manner aimed at encouraging obedience and passivity on the part of female athletes.

- Research has demonstrate that, until recently, colleges, universities, national governing bodies, and the USOC have not only been reluctant but often refused to investigate complaints, and even covered up allegations involving star athletes and leading coaches.
- Within many sporting organizations, the resistance to talking about and dealing with sexual harassment and abuse continues because of the negative ramifications of making such news public.
- Safe Sport, a not-for-profit organization established to promote respect for athletes and to prevent and respond ethically to sexual misconduct in sports, identify five signs of abuse: Loss of excitement for sport and competition, avoiding practice, wanting to stay away from certain individuals (e.g., coach, trainer, administrator), unexpected mood shifts, and a desire to change teams despite good friends on team.
- The USOC has recently partnered with SafeSport to educate the sports community about sexual misconduct, set guidelines of appropriate and inappropriate behavior, offer certification of SafeSport education for all stakeholders in sports, and to provide victims with the means to safely report sexual misconduct.

References

Brackenridge, C., Bishop, D., Moussali, S. and Tapp, J. (2008). The characteristics of sexual abuse in sport: A multidimensional scaling analysis of events described in media reports. *International Journal of Sport and Exercise Psychology, 6*(4), 385–406.

Brackenridge, C. & Fasting, K. (2005). The grooming process in sport: Narrative of sexual harassment and abuse. *The British Sociological Association, 13*(1), 33–52.

Brackenridge, C., & Kirby, S. (1997). Playing safe: Assessing the risk of sexual abuse to elite child athletes. *International Review for the Sociology of Sport, 32*(4), 407–418.

Crosset, T. (1986). Male coach/female athlete relationships. Paper presented at Coaching Female Top Level Athletes, Norwegian Confederation of Sport Conference, Norway, November 15–16.

Fasting, K., & Brackenridge, C. (2009). Coaches, sexual harassment and education. *Sport, Education, and Society Journal, 14*(1), 21–35.

Fasting, K., Chroni, S. & Knorre, N. (2014). The experiences of sexual harassment in sport education among European female sport science students. *Sport, Education and Society, 19*, 2.

Freeman, H. (2018). How was Larry Nassar able to abuse so many gymnasts for so long? *The Guardian*, January 26.

Holman, M. (1995) Female and male athletes' accounts and meanings of sexual harassment in Canadian interuniversity athletics. PhD thesis, University of Windsor, Ontario, Canada.

Institut National Santé Publique. (2012). Media kit of sexual assault. Retrieved from www.inspq.qc.ca/en/sexual-assault/understanding/perpetrators

Lackey, D. (1990). Sexual harassment in sport. *The Physical Educator, 47*(2), 22–26.

Ladika, S. (2017). Sports and sexual assault: Can colleges and pro leagues curb abuse by athletes? *CQ Press*, April 28. Retrieved from http://library.cqpress.com/cqresearcher/document.php?id=cqresrre2017042800

Leahy, T. (2011). Sexual abuse in sport. Retrieved from www.humankinetics.com/excerpts/excerpts/sexualabuseinsport-excerpt

Marks, S., Mountjoy, M., & Marcus, M. (2012). Sexual harassment and abuse in sport: the role of the team doctor. *British Journal of Sports Medicine, 46*, 905–908.

Mountjoy, M., Brackenridge, C., Arrington, M., Blauwet, C., Carska-Sheppard, A., Fasting, K., Kirby, S. Leahy, T., Marks, S., Martin, K., Starr, K., Anne, T., & Budgett, R. (2016). The IOC Consensus Statement: harassment and abuse (non-accidental violence) in sport. *British Journal of Sports Medicine*, April 26, p. 1020. Retrieved from https://hub.olympic.org/athlete365/wp-content/uploads/2017/11/IOC_Consensus_Statement_Harassment_and_abuse_in_sport__2016_.pdf

Nyad, D. (2017). Diana Nyad: My life after sexual assault. *New York Times*, November 7. Retrieved from www.nytimes.com/2017/11/09/opinion/diana-nyad-sexual-assault.html

Perez, A. J. (2018). USOC, USA Gymnastics, MSU responding to congress over the Larry Nassar case. *USA Today*, February 14.

RAINN. (2018). Sexual assault. Retrieved from www.rainn.org/articles/sexual-assault

PART III
Athlete Environment

9
COACHES

Introduction

Jim Taylor

Athletes cannot achieve their sports goals alone. Rather, they have behind them a variety of support including parents, coaches, fitness trainers, sports medicine staff, nutritionists, equipment technicians, sports scientists, and mental trainers. Of this group, coaches may play the most fundamental role in athletic development and in determining how far athletes climb the competitive ladder. This impact is so powerful because coaches are most involved in developing the many aspects of sports performance that are essential for athletic success. Most apparently, they teach the foundational technical and tactical skills that allow athletes to perform effectively in their sport. Regardless of the sport, examples of these skills include body position, stance, balance, sport-specific movement patterns, tracking of relevant objects (e.g., ball or puck), assessing opponents, decision making, and style of play. Additionally, this influence on athletes broadens significantly in most sports where coaches wear many hats including most of the roles of the support team just described.

Perhaps foremost among those roles that coaches assume in supporting their athletes is that of mental trainer. It is no surprise to anyone in the sports world that most great coaches are also great intuitive psychologists. In fact, most of what they do with athletes has a significant psychological element to it including many of the areas described in Chapters 1–4. For example, coaches are instrumental in:

- instilling healthy attitudes and removing unhealthy obstacles;
- motivating athletes;
- building their confidence;
- helping them focus in training;
- getting them fired up or calmed down before a competition;
- managing their emotions during the inevitable highs and lows of the sports season; and
- creating a positive team culture.

Given this wide and deep influence that coaches have on athletes, well beyond the roles and responsibilities that most people associate with coaching, consultants can play an important role in educating coaches on how to maximize their psychological impact on the athletes with whom they work.

This chapter will explore some of the most central aspects of the psychology of coaching. The goal of which is for consultants to provide coaches with the psychological, emotional, and interpersonal insights, information, and tools they need at several levels. First, to be the most effective coaches they can be in fulfilling their roles as teachers of technique and tactics. Second, to create a positive environment for in which athletes thrive athletically and personally. Third, provide athletes with the tools to fully develop themselves technically and tactically in their sport, one key component of this, in the technology-driven world in which sports now reside, is how to maximize the value of video in their coaching efforts, Fourth, because coaches are people too, to offer coaches the means to manage the stress they experience in their professional and personal lives. Fifth, to develop the most positive and healthy relationships with their athletes. Finally, to show coaches how to effectively integrate mental training into their overall athlete development.

OPTIMAL SPORT COACHING

Zach Brandon

Mental toughness (Loehr, 1986) has become one of the most commonly used terms among coaches to describe what separates great from good athletes. Yes, top athletes are innately talented, well-conditioned, and highly skilled. But it is their readiness mentally, however, that distinguishes the winners from the also-rans. The development of mental toughness in their athletes is particularly striking for coaches in today's sports climate given the immense pressures imposed on them to produce results, whether they coach at the junior level, collegiately, or in the Olympic or professional ranks. These pressures are magnified through the media's emphasis on winning at every level and the pedestals on which successful coaches are now placed by fans and the media. Adding to this burden, society generates a competitive narrative (Douglas & Carless, 2006) for coaches whose approaches are ever-evolving and chaotic in nature (Lyle, 2002; Rynne, Mallett, & Tinning, 2006) and whose impact on their athletes' and teams' performances may not be as strong as many believe. Numerous contextual factors contribute to the complexity of sport coaches' roles and performances (Lyle, 2002), which highlights the need for consultants to help them maximize the level of their own performances as well as provide them with the means to get the most out of their athletes mentally and competitively.

Theory and Research

As sport coaching continues to grow and evolve as a profession, there is an increasing responsibility to establish and regulate the standards of the occupation; however, this remains impossible without a consensus understanding of effective practice (Lyle, 2002). Part of this challenge is due to the inconsistent terminology that has been documented in the coaching science literature. These terms include, but are not limited to, *coaching effectiveness* (Côté & Gilbert, 2009; Flett, Sackett, & Camiré, 2017; Horn, 2008), *coaching excellence* (Côté, Young, North, & Duffy, 2007), *good coaching* (Lyle, 2002), and *great coaching* (Becker, 2009). Synthesizing these various descriptions into one singular definition is far too lengthy of an endeavor for the purposes of this section.

Understanding Optimal Sport Coaching

Côté & Gilbert's (2009) comprehensive definition of coaching effectiveness will be used as the guiding framework for optimal sport coaching; however, it is valuable to deconstruct some of the consistent practices (antecedents) across optimal sport coaches. They proposed that coaching effectiveness be defined as "the consistent application of integrated professional, interpersonal, and intrapersonal knowledge to improve athletes' competence, confidence, connection, and character in specific coaching contexts" (Côté & Gilbert, 2009, p. 316). A considerable amount of attention has been given to exploring the antecedents of effective coaching within the sport literature. One thing that is clear is that coaching is more than just developing physical and technical skills and teaching the sport's Xs and Os. Several desirable actions have also been identified for effective coaches (Côté & Gilbert, 2009):

- engaging participants;
- fostering a mastery-oriented motivational climate;
- promoting fun and play;
- utilizing an athlete-centered approach;
- encouraging positive social interactions; and
- focusing on fundamental skill development.

Côté and Gilbert (2009) also suggest that coaching effectiveness represents a blend of three interacting components including coaching contexts (e.g., performance demands, developmental stages), coaches' knowledge (i.e., professional, interpersonal, and intrapersonal), and athletes' outcomes (i.e., competence, confidence, connection, and character). Côté et al. (2007) provide further support for the role of context when they identified differences in coaching excellence across four categories that varied by competitive contexts (participation coaches vs. performance coaches) and the stages of individual development (i.e., sampling, recreational, specializing, or investment years). Participation coaching is characterized as less intensive with more short-term objectives focusing on the athlete's participation satisfaction. Alternatively, performance coaching is more progressive and rigorous with greater specificity in practice design to help athletes achieve both short- and long-term goals. From a developmental standpoint, it is imperative that coaches consider and align their competencies to the needs of their athletes according to their age and stage of development. Côté (1999) created the Developmental Model of Sport Participation (DMSP) which highlighted deliberate play and deliberate practice as key variables that influence the transition between sampling, specializing, and investment years. For example, the sampling phase consists of greater amounts of deliberate play and less deliberate practice; the specializing phase contains equal amounts of deliberate play and deliberate practice; and the investment phase demonstrates greater amounts of deliberate practice and less deliberate play. These sport participation phases start in early childhood (approximately age six) and continue into late adolescence (age 18). Coaches who are able to understand these developmental stages will be better prepared to adjust their coaching styles and training environments to meet the unique needs of their athletes.

Abraham and colleagues (2006) expanded on the requisite knowledge base for coaches by recommending that they understand athletes, techniques and tactics of their respective sport, and pedagogical principles (e.g., learning processes). Finally, according to Flett and colleagues, the process of "effective coaching involves a complex set of behaviors and characteristics that nurture technical, tactical, psychomotor, and psychosocial growth in athletes" (Flett et al., 2017, p. 166). Irrespective of sporting context (recreational, developmental, elite), effective coaching is distinguished by several common areas: skillful pedagogy and communication; thoughtful and action-oriented philosophies; meaningful and caring relationships to maximize athletes' holistic needs; and fostering an intrinsically motivating and process/mastery-oriented environment (Flett et al., 2017). Although optimal sport coaching is often linked with wins and losses, the aforementioned evidence highlights the significance of coaches who value the person first, which enables them to thrive on and off the field.

Coach Influence on Personal Development

Optimal sport coaches are charged with developing people as much as they are with developing athletes. In addition to helping their athletes optimize performance, coaches are expected to play a critical role in their psychosocial development (Horn, 2008; Nichols, Pettee, & Ainsworth, 2007), which is consistent with coaches' own beliefs and expectations (Gould, Chung, Smith, & White, 2006). As seen through a societal lens, sport is often viewed as a vehicle for participants to learn valuable life lessons and skills. In youth settings, sport can be used as a means to facilitate several developmental outcomes including identity development, personal exploration, initiative, improved cognitive and physical skills, cultivating social connections, teamwork, and social skills (Hansen, Larson, & Dworkin, 2003). Irrespective of athletes' developmental needs (e.g., age, physical maturity, commitment to sport, competitive level), effective coaches should focus on enhancing athletes' outcomes across the four Cs (competence, confidence, connection, character/caring; Côté et al., 2010; Jelicic et al., 2007).

Encouraging Mental Training

One way consultants can assist coaches in developing the four Cs is through helping them foster mental training in their athletes. The review of research addressing the antecedents and consequences of optimal coaching illuminates the role coaches have in influencing psychological outcomes in their athletes, most notably those related to mental readiness to perform their best, maximizing their enjoyment in their sport, and achieving their sports goals.

Despite acknowledgement of its impact on athletic success, previous studies have found that coaches lack an essential understanding of how to teach mental training to their athletes and teams. Gould and colleagues (1987) indicated that 82% of coaches rated mental toughness as the most important mental attribute in determining wrestling success, but only 9% of coaches interviewed felt they were successful in teaching or changing mental toughness in their athletes. More recent studies illustrate that coaches believe they can significantly influence their athletes' mental toughness by designing difficult physical practices, building confidence, and encouraging mental skill development (Driska et al., 2012; Weinberg, Butt, & Culp, 2011). Given the shared interest in developing mentally prepared athletes between sport coaches and consultants, it is worthwhile to explore strategies that consultants can employ to "teach coaches how to teach" specific mental muscles (e.g., motivation, confidence, focus) and tools (e.g., imagery, routines, self-talk).

There are several reasons why it may be valuable for consultants to teach coaches how to implement mental training with their athletes and teams. Consultants can leverage coaches to reinforce the value of mental training (McCann, 2014), which is critical due to coaches' impact on shaping athletes' attitudes toward mental training services (Zakrajsek & Zizzi, 2007) as well as coaches' daily contact with them. In addition, enhancing mental toughness is often a collaborative process between coaches and consultants (Weinberg, Freysinger, & Mellano, 2018) involving information sharing and an integrated plan for practice and refinement of mental training (Winter & Collins, 2015). Recently, Anthony and colleagues (2018) demonstrated how a coach-targeted education program could be used to increase the frequency of mentally tough behaviors in elite athletes. The preceding studies provide further support for why consultants should assist coaches with integrating mental training into their coaching practice, but the question still remains as to how.

Practical Implications

The "why" and "what" of the optimal sport coaching has now been established. The following section will explore the "how" in which practical information and tools are offered that consultants can share with coaches to encourage them to engage in optimal sport coaching with their athletes and teams.

Define Mental Muscles and Exercises

Despite the fact that most coaches express clearly the importance of mental training for athletic success, few coaches understand the behaviors that underpin this relationship. Consultants can play a key role in turning this belief into practice by helping coaches to identify and define the essential mental muscles and exercises that they can use with their athletes. This clarity on the part of coaches would enable athletes to gain a similar attitude toward and understanding of mental training (Bell, Hardy, & Beattie, 2013). Consultants can teach coaches how to develop athletes mentally with their practical application in practice and competitive settings. For example, if coaches are interested in building confidence in their athletes, then consultants can show them how to include confidence exercises, such as positive body language and self-talk, in their daily practices. Consultants can further assist with this process by identifying situations in training where coaches can reinforce and praise these behaviors such as between drills or conditioning sets. The mental muscles and mental exercises described in Chapters 1–4 can be used as guides for consultants to educate coaches about mental training.

With key mental training muscles and exercises defined, consultants can then show coaches how to incorporate mental training on and off the field. Coaches have the ability to reinforce the practice and refinement of mental training during conditioning and sport training rather than simply focusing on the physical, technical, and tactical aspects of the sport. Consultants can show coaches how to incorporate mental training into practice to strengthen motivation, confidence, intensity, and focus with the use of positive self-talk, imagery, breathing, routines, and other mental exercises. This inclusion demonstrates to athletes the value that coaches place on mental training. It also allows athletes to gain immediate feedback on the impact that mental training can have on practice and, by extension, competitive performances.

Fostering the Four Cs

Coaching practices aimed at developing the four Cs (competence, confidence, connection, character/caring) require coaches to possess a high degree of contextual intelligence, which can be defined as "more than 'knowing what' to do; it is 'knowing how' to get it done" (Brown, 2002, p. 26). Consultants play at important role in this process by helping coaches identify the appropriate strategies and techniques to employ for their athletes based on their competitive context and developmental stage. For example, consultants can help increase participation coaches' awareness of quantity and quality of feedback, which is an important contributor to children and adolescents' perceptions of competence (Weiss, Ebbeck, Horn, & 1999). This period of sport participation is marked by increases in peer comparison, thus coaches play a critical role in helping athletes form a healthy perspective of their abilities through promotion-oriented feedback, confirming and reinforcing desirable behaviors (Carpentier & Mageau, 2013), and performance feedback that emphasizes the way in which athletes execute a skill (Gilbert, 2016). To increase perceived competence in older athletes (young-to-late adolescents and adults), coaches need to increase the frequency of deliberate practice which requires athletes to utilize key mental muscles, such as confidence, and focus with more regularity (Côté et al., 2010). This phase is also a good time to start introducing mental training to manage the rigors of deliberate practice and enhance overall performance.

As mentioned earlier in this chapter, optimal sport coaches can significantly influence various life skills in their athletes in addition to their on-field performance. A fundamental outcome to strive for in sport participation is the development of positive and meaningful relationships through connection between teammates, coaches, family, community, and others. Consultants can assist coaches in this development by strengthening team cohesion with team-building and communication exercises (see Chapter 10). They can also provide further support by leading and facilitating parent education seminars on pertinent topics given the significant influence parents have on children's lives (Siegler, DeLoache, & Eisenberg, 2003). Additionally, they may guide coaches on asking effective questions to help them get to know their players on a deeper and more meaningful level. One strategy for this would be to empower coaches to co-facilitate mental training sessions and openly share their experiences on a topic in a discussion with their team. The shared dialogue will help foster greater closeness and mutual trust, which has been linked to enhanced team performance at higher levels (Dirks, 2002).

When it comes to building character and mutual trust, coaches should deliberately model the compassion, integrity, and ethical behavior that they expect to see from their players. Coaches cannot assume that their job title is enough for establishing trust and, instead, must continuously foster it through communication and consistency in coaching behavior. For example, a coach's inability to follow through on a promise, or losing control of their emotions in a specific situation, will likely lead to players doing the same. Thus, it is imperative that consultants help coaches continuously reflect on their coaching practices to raise their awareness and teach them how to use the same mental tools that they ask of their players.

Practice What They Preach

A reoccurring theme echoed at conferences in sport psychology and within the literature is the importance of consultants "practicing what you preach" by applying mental training in their own personal and athletic endeavors (Fifer, Henschen, Gould, & Ravizza, 2008). The same rule of thumb should be applied to coaches. As previously mentioned, sport coaches are performers (Giges, Petitpas, & Vernacchia, 2004) and, like their athletes, must exhibit a variety of mental attributes (e.g., composure, confidence, resilience) to help themselves perform optimally and consistently. One of the best ways to get comfortable teaching mental training to athletes is for coaches to practice them in their own lives. Mental training can help increase coaches' self-awareness and assist them in strengthening the mental muscles that will help them perform their very best. Consultants can support coaches in this process by providing tools and feedback so coaches can practice what they preach.

Summary

- Mental toughness (Loehr, 1986) has become one of the most commonly used terms among coaches to describe what separates great from good athletes.
- The acceptance and popularity of mental training in sport and recognition of its importance is increasing among coaches, but few possess the declarative (the "why") or procedural (the "how") knowledge to effectively teach this aspect of sports performance to athletes.
- Sports programs at every level of the competitive ladder struggle to provide their athletes with mental training that matches the sophistication and quality of their conditioning and sport training.

- Four barriers limit coaches' ability to offer quality mental training to their athletes: few resources to learn from, no programs to follow, not a programmatic priority, and time.
- Part of this challenge is due to the inconsistent terminology that has been documented in the coaching science literature. These terms include, but are not limited to coaching effectiveness, coaching excellence, good coaching, and great coaching.
- Several desirable actions have been identified for effective coaches which includes engaging participants, fostering a mastery-oriented motivational climate, promoting fun and play, utilizing an athlete-centered approach, encouraging positive social interactions, and focusing on fundamental skill development.
- The process of "effective coaching involves a complex set of behaviors and characteristics that nurture technical, tactical, psychomotor, and psychosocial growth in athletes."
- Optimal sport coaches are in the business of developing people as much as they are about building athletes and, as such, coaches are expected to play a critical role in their psychosocial development.
- Irrespective of athletes' developmental needs (e.g., age, physical maturity, commitment to sport, competitive level), effective coaches should focus on enhancing athletes' outcomes across the four Cs (competence, confidence, connection, character/caring).
- One way consultants can assist coaches in developing the four Cs is through helping them foster mental training in their athletes.
- Consultants can play a key role in turning this belief into practice by helping coaches to identify and define the essential mental muscles and exercises that they can use with their athletes.
- Consultants can show coaches how to incorporate mental training into practice to strengthen motivation, confidence, intensity, and focus with the use of positive self-talk, imagery, breathing, routines, and other mental exercises.
- Consultants are integral for increasing coaches' awareness of feedback and behavior, especially given their influence on athlete's perceived competence and character.
- Consultants should encourage coaches to be involved and facilitators in mental training sessions to help them foster closeness and trust with their athletes.
- One of the best ways to get comfortable teaching mental training to athletes is for coaches to practice them in their own lives.

References

Abraham, A., Collins, D., & Martindale, R. (2006). The coaching schematic: Validation through expert coach consensus. *Journal of Sports Sciences, 24*(6), 549–564.

Anthony, D. R., Gordon, S., Gucciardi, D. F., & Dawson, B. (2018). Adapting a behavioral coaching framework for mental toughness development. *Journal of Sport Psychology in Action, 9*(1), 32–50.

Becker, A. J. (2009). It's not what they do, it's how they do it: Athlete experiences of great coaching. *International Journal of Sports Science & Coaching, 4*(1), 93–119.

Bell, J. J., Hardy, L., & Beattie, S. (2013). Enhancing mental toughness and performance under pressure in elite young cricketers: A 2-year longitudinal intervention. *Sport, Exercise, and Performance Psychology, 2*(4), 281.

Brown, C. (2002). A model for developing contextual intelligence (CI). *Association for the Advancement of Applied Sport Psychology—2002 conference proceedings* (pp. 26–27). Denton, TX: RonJon Publishing

Carpentier, J., & Mageau, G. A. (2013). When change-oriented feedback enhances motivation, well-being and performance: A look at autonomy-supportive feedback in sport. *Psychology of Sport and Exercise, 14*(3), 423–435.

Côté, J. (1999). The influence of the family in the development of talent in sport. *The Sport Psychologist, 13*(4), 395–417.

Côté, J., Bruner, M., Erickson, K., Strachan, L., & Fraser-Thomas, J. (2010). Athlete development and coaching. In J. Lyle, & Cushion. (Eds.), *Sports coaching: Professionalization and practice* (pp. 63–84). Edinburgh: Churchill Livingstone Elsevier.

Côté, J., & Gilbert, W. (2009). An integrative definition of coaching effectiveness and expertise. *International journal of sports science & coaching, 4*(3), 307–323.

Côté, J., Young, B., North, J., & Duffy, P. (2007). Towards a definition of excellence in sport coaching. *International journal of coaching science, 1*(1), 3–17.

Dirks, K. T. (2002). Trust in leadership and team performance: Evidence from NCAA basketball. *Journal of Applied Psychology, 85*(6), 1004–1012.

Douglas, K., & Carless, D. (2006). Performance, discovery, and relational narratives among women professional tournament golfers. *Women in sport and physical activity journal, 15*(2), 14–27.

Driska, A. P., Kamphoff, C., & Armentrout, S. M. (2012). Elite swimming coaches' perceptions of mental toughness. *The Sport Psychologist, 26*(2), 186–206.

Fifer, A., Henschen, K., Gould, D., & Ravizza, K. (2008). What works when working with athletes. *The Sport Psychologist, 22*(3), 356–377.

Flett, M. R., Sackett, S. C., & Camiré, M. (2017). Understanding effective coaching: Antecedents and consequences. In R. Thelwell, C. Harwood, & I. Greenlees (Eds.), *The Psychology of Sports Coaching: Research and Practice* (pp. 156–169). London: Routledge.

Giges, B., Petitpas, A. J., & Vernacchia, R. A. (2004). Helping coaches meet their own needs: Challenges for the sport psychology consultant. *The Sport Psychologist, 18*(4), 430–444.

Gilbert, W. (2016). *Coaching better every season: A year-round system for athlete development and program success.* Champaign, IL: Human Kinetics.

Gould, D., Chung, Y., Smith, P., & White, J. (2006). Future directions in coaching life skills: Understanding high school coaches' views and needs. *Athletic Insight, 8*(3), 28–38.

Gould, D., Hodge, K., Peterson, K., & Petlichkoff, L. (1987). Psychological foundations of coaching: Similarities and differences among intercollegiate wrestling coaches. *The Sport Psychologist, 1*(4), 293–308.

Hansen, D. M., Larson, R. W., & Dworkin, J. B. (2003). What adolescents learn in organized youth activities: A survey of self-reported developmental experiences. *Journal of Research on Adolescence, 13*(1), 25–55.

Horn, T. S. (2008). Coaching effectiveness in the sport domain. In T. S. Horn (Ed.), *Advances in sport psychology,* 3rd ed. (pp. 239–267). Champaign, IL: Human Kinetics.

Jelicic, H., Bobek, D. L., Phelps, E., Lerner, R. M., & Lerner, J. V. (2007). Using positive youth development to predict contribution and risk behaviours in early adolescence: findings form the first two waves of the 4-H study of positive youth development. *International Journal of Behavioural Development, 31,* 263–273.

Loehr, J. E. (1986). *Mental toughness training for sports: Achieving athletic excellence.* Lexington, MA: Stephen Greene Press.

Lyle, J. (2002). *Sports coaching concepts: A framework for coaches' behavior.* London: Routledge.

McCann, S. (2014, summer). So you'd like a sport psychology consultant to work with your team? Three key lessons learned from Olympic teams. Retrieved from www.teamusa.org/About-the-USOC/Athlete-Development/Coaching-Education/Coach-E-Magazine

Nichols, J. F., Pettee, K. K., & Ainsworth, B. E. (2007). Physiological and metabolic dimensions of girls' physical activity in the Tucker Center Research Report: Developing physical active girls: An evidence-based multidisciplinary approach. Retrieved from http://hdl.handle.net/11299/48566.

Rynne, S. B., Mallett, C. J., & Tinning, R. (2006). High performance sport coaching: Institutes of sport as sites for learning. *International Journal of Sports Science & Coaching, 1*(3), 223–234.

Siegler, R. S., DeLoache, J. S., & Eisenberg, N. (2003). *How children develop.* Macmillan.

Weinberg, R., Butt, J., & Culp, B. (2011). Coaches' views of mental toughness and how it is built. *International journal of sport and exercise psychology, 9*(2), 156–172.

Weinberg, R., Freysinger, V., & Mellano, K. (2018). How can coaches build mental toughness? Views from sport psychologists. *Journal of Sport Psychology in Action, 9*(1), 1–10.

Weiss, M. R., Ebbeck, V., & Horn, T. S. (1999). Children's self-perceptions and sources of physical competence information: A cluster analysis. *Journal of Sport and Exercise Psychology, 19*(1), 52–70.

Winter, S., & Collins, D. (2015). Why do we do what we do?. *Journal of Applied Sport Psychology, 27*(1), 35–51.

Zakrajsek, R. A., & Zizzi, S. J. (2007). Factors influencing track and swimming coaches' intentions to use sport psychology services. *Athletic Insight: The Online Journal of Sport Psychology, 9*(2), 1–21.

COACH–ATHLETE RELATIONSHIP

Debi Corbatto

A dyadic affiliation is one in which two people's goals, actions, and emotions are symbiotic (Kelley, Berscheid, Christensen, Harvey, Huston, Levinger, & Peterson, 1983). The coach–athlete relationship in sport is an example of such a unique, interdependent bond. Athletes are immersed in an environment that their coaches co-create (Corbatto, 2018) and their relationship may be the most important in terms of athletes' abilities to perform their best, enjoy their sports experiences, and accomplish their sports goals. The importance of studying this relationship has taken on critical significance as recent events have uncovered significant issues facing the sports community relative to harmful relationships of coaches and athletes, such as the former USA gymnastics team physician found guilty of sexual assault of Olympic athletes (Hobson, 2018). Verbal, emotional or even physical abuse of athletes deters athletes from continued participation in sport (Women's Sports Foundation, 2016). Overarching problems surrounding the coach–athlete relationship include coach–athlete conflict, the power differential, physical and sexual abuse, and lack of appropriate support (Stirling & Kerr, 2009). These issues drive the call for significant research to complement anecdotal understanding of this powerful dyadic affiliation as well as interventions to ensure positive and healthy coach–athlete relationships.

Theory and Research

Athletes establish relationships with coaches to leverage their knowledge and experience of their sport, to learn the wide range of skills necessary to perform in their sport, to understand how to perform well in competitions, to gain psychological, emotional, and practical support, and, ultimately, to help them achieve their sports goals. Coaches are in the relationship to impart their know-how to help athletes develop within and outside the sports world, and to gain meaning and fulfillment as they guide athletes toward their sports dreams and goals. Both coaches and athletes share the goal of achieving personal success and satisfaction (Jowett & Nezlek, 2012). The interdependence of the coach–athlete relationship makes this relationship unique (Rusbult, Kumashiro, Coolsen, & Kirchner, 2004). Without the other party, neither can reach their goals.

A recent study by Vierimaa, Bruner, and Côté (2018) confirms the importance of the social interaction of the coach–athlete relationship to sports training and performance. This research affirmed the concept that the group of athletes that engaged in more frequent sport communication with their coaches had high perceptions of confidence, connection and character, all considered to be positive behaviors in athletics. These results highlight the significance of a contextual relationship between the coach and athlete during sport development.

Although the role of athletes has been extensively examined as an individual experience, coaches' influence on athletes and the social aspects of sports would suggest the value in studying the sports in relational terms as well. In fact, sports are inherently a social undertaking (Maguire, 2011) and athletes interact closely with their coaches in many capacities. The coach–athlete social dyad has been demonstrated to be one type of teacher-student affiliation (Bloom, Crumpton, & Anderson, 1999). The help-seeking/help-giving environment reflects this coaching behavior as a form of self-regulated learning (Karabenick & Dembo, 2011) and sport coaches can be instrumental in supporting athletes' self-regulatory habits (Kitsantas, Kavussanu, Corbatto, & van de Pol, 2018). There is also support for coaches as influential parties in the development of athletes' efficacy beliefs (Saville & Bray, 2016). For example, relation-inferred self-efficacy (RISE) has been shown to relate to improved effort, persistence, and optimum performances in athletes (Beauchamp, Jackson, & Morton, 2012; Feltz, Short, & Sullivan, 2008). Relation-inferred self-efficacy is a part of a framework presented by Lent & Lopez (2002) in which individuals who work alongside others (i.e., athlete/coach) have their efficacy beliefs (Bandura, 1986) influenced by those in their partnership. The complete relational efficacy framework presented by these researchers includes self-efficacy, other efficacy, and relation-inferred self-efficacy (RISE).

Importance of Coach–Athlete Relationships

When athletes and their coaches are working in a positive interdependent dyadic relationship, both benefit in many ways (Coe & Mason, 1988) including effective communication and conflict resolution, increased commitment, greater confidence, and enhanced practice and competitive performances. At the same time, incompatibility or conflict in the coach–athlete dyad can cause the relationship to fail (Jowett & Cockerill, 2002) and this failure can have negative effects on athletes and coaches' stress levels, self-assurance, motivation, self-esteem, and sport performance (Jowett, 2003). These dysfunctional situations detract from flow (Swann, Keegan, Piggott, & Crust, 2012) while a sense of control, concentration, automaticity, and enjoyment of the experience has been reported as necessary for peak performances and flow to occur (Swann et al., 2012; Krane & Williams, 2015). One recent example is the 2015/2016 coaching crisis suffered by the Sacramento Kings. Growing discontent and lack of engagement between the players and their coaches resulted in a demoralized team and a losing streak (Stein, 2016). The team leadership recognized the issue between the coaches and athletes and sought ways to solve this problem. They eventually replaced several members of the coaching staff in an attempt to turn around the team's performance (Redford, 2016).

We can also look at successful coach–athlete relationships such as that of the New England Patriots' Bill Belichick and Tom Brady, its head coach and star quarterback, respectively. They have a strong professional rapport and hold each other accountable for high-level performance (MacMullan, 2014). They have worked together for almost 20 years and have earned multiple Super Bowl championships. Their relationship demonstrates the outcomes that can come from a positive collaboration between athletes and their trusted coaches. The powerful Belichick–Brady relationship adds anecdotal support to the awareness that a sports dyad with a trusting relationship, positive relational self-efficacy, and a healthy help-seeking/help-giving environment can have remarkable performance outcomes for athletes, teams, and coaches.

Models of Coach–Athlete Relationships

Jowett

Jowett and her colleagues (Jowett, 2003; Jowett & Clark-Carter, 2006; Jowett & Cockerill, 2002, 2003; Jowett & Meek, 2000; Jowett & Ntoumanis, 2004) have leveraged social exchange and interdependence theories to explore the coach–athlete relationship. The constructs of their theory, called the 3 Cs model, are:

- Closeness: How the athlete and coach describe the values, beliefs, and emotions, such as respect and trust, that surround their relationship.
- Commitment: The intention of both parties in the athletic dyad to maintain the relationship over time.
- Complementarity: The cooperation, readiness, and responsiveness of the coach and athlete toward each other.

The strength of the relationship and the relational and sport benefits between the dyadic partners is thought to rise as each construct of the model increases.

Jackson

Jackson and his colleagues (Jackson, Grove & Beauchamp, 2010) have extended the 3 Cs framework in developing the Relation-Inferred Self-Efficacy (RISE) model which takes interdependence theory and applies its constructs to the coach–athlete relationship. Relation-inferred self-efficacy refers to the feelings of competence that athletes gain from knowing that their coaches have confidence in their abilities. This work in the sport context demonstrates that both internally generated self-efficacy and relation-inferred self-efficacy play roles in the successful coach–athlete dyad (Jackson et al., 2010). In particular, Jackson's research demonstrates that when athletes perceive a high degree of confidence in their coaches' capabilities, increased commitment by both athletes and coaches result.

Vallerand

Vallerand and his colleagues (Vallerand, 1997; Vallerand & Rousseau, 2001; Mageau & Vallerand, 2003) present a motivational model of the coach–athlete dyad that proposes that coaching behaviors nurture athletes' intrinsic motivation, such as an inherent desire to tackle a challenge and self-determined extrinsic motivation, such as placing a high value on a team goal. Vallerand stresses the roles that coaches play in the support of the autonomy of athletes to encourage both types of motivation (Deci & Ryan, 1985). This autonomy-supportive role emphasizes the coaches respecting the athletes' perspectives and feelings while providing them with choices, active participation in decision making, and minimizing pressure and demands on them. This model demonstrates that autonomy-supportive coaching has a strong positive impact on athletes' motivations which are important precursors to sustained effort and quality performance.

Other Areas of Research

In addition to the models just described, two other areas of research have been receiving attention as important contributors to effective coach–athlete relationships.

Trust

In recent work on the dynamics of elite coach–athlete dyads related to high-level performance, Corbatto (2016, 2018) highlights the importance of trust in the relationship. Trust is conceptualized as having confidence in someone, feeling safe with them, and knowing that person can be counted on to act in their best interests. Athletes trust their coaches in several key areas:

- athletes' general health and well-being;
- the coaches' knowledge and experience to advance their athletic development; and
- care and concern for them.

Without this deep and broad trust that athletes have toward their coaches, athletes would be unable to focus effectively on or commit themselves fully to their sports efforts.

Thriving

Thriving in sport has been defined as the sustained high-level performance and well-being of the participant (Brown, Arnold, Reid, & Roberts, 2017a). Thriving athletes display certain patterns of coach-driven relational support such as verbal reinforcement and affirmations to improve athlete confidence. Brown, Arnold, Standage, and Fletcher (2017b) demonstrated that, although coaches and athletes work together to improve performance and achieve sports goals, athletes' personal attributes and psychological capabilities are paramount to thriving in their sport experience. In this new area of research, it is suggested that the concept of thriving can not only positively predict athletic performance, but may actually result in improved or higher performance levels (Brown et al., 2017a). With this in mind, it is suggested that, to facilitate the experience of the athletes, coaches should consider strategies such as those provided in the Practical Implications section below that can influence both performance and well-being to support athletes' efforts (Barker, Jones, & Greenlees, 2010).

Practical Implications

The coach–athlete relationship is instrumental in improving many aspects of sports performance as well as serving as an important vehicle for both personal and social development (Johnson, Garing, Oliphant, Roberts, 2016; Vierimaa et al., 2018). Consultants can play an important role in helping both coaches and athletes take ownership of their place in the relationship and show them what they can do to strengthen it to the benefit of both.

Drawing on the models discussed in "Theory and Research" above, Mageau & Vallerand (2003) describe seven areas that a coach can use to strengthen their relationships with their athletes and, by extension, athletes' efforts and performances: To strengthen the working relationship, the coach can practice and role play strategies with consultants to hone language such as providing choices within specific rules and limits and offering reasons for any tasks, rules, or limits. Consultants can emphasize coaching language such as: "During our workout today, we will be working on low impact activities to limit your physical load. Would you prefer to work on spot shooting or free throws today?"

In addition, consultants can work with coaches on being open and acknowledging the athletes' perspectives and feelings: "I know you are disappointed with the results of the match yesterday, but it is over, and we will move on to next week's match now." Emotional intelligence in a coach, specifically the ability to discern, understand, and help regulate their own emotions as well as that of their athletes is particularly important as the potential for athletes' emotions to impact performance has been clearly demonstrated (Montse, Ragline & Hanin, 2017). Coaches routinely teach tactical skills in their sport but are less well versed in the mentorship aspect of dealing with emotions. Consultants can work with coaches develop their emotional intelligence.

Coaches may also benefit from an exploration of the benefits of allowing athletes to participate in their sport development to build commitment to their practice and competitive regimens. For example, dialogue between a coach and athletes might be, "For those of you interested, I am putting some voluntary workouts on the board for this offseason as a way to get ahead for next season." Participation in sports, as it moves from the novice to elite level, relies on hours of focused practice. As disciplined practices aren't always enjoyable to athletes, relying on both internal motivations, as well as self-determined external motivators, is a way to encourage behavioral compliance (Mageau & Vallerand, 2003).

Controlling behaviors in coaching should be limited. Controlling behaviors are those that endorse only the coach's ways of thinking, feeling, or behaving and ignore athletes' perspectives (Deci & Ryan, 1985). When athletes must ignore their own values and give up their autonomy to appease a coach, this constitutes psychological control. This control is sometimes expressed by coaches in the form of guilt-inducing criticisms and controlling statements and is a threat to the coach–athlete relationship. Consultants can work with coaches on avoiding language such as "You did great today, just as expected," or "Keep it up, you can do even better tomorrow" and help them refine autonomy-supportive comments such as, "What a great shot" or "When you move your feet like that, it is really hard to catch you". Likewise, feedback should be modified to focus on behaviors that are under the athletes' control rather than to exert control. "Keep it up and I might put you in the game next week," should be replaced with the simple but powerful endorsement to "Keep up the hard work!" Controlling statements or guilt-inducing criticisms sabotage athletes' intrinsic motivation and enjoyment of their sport.

Consultants should work with coaches on preventing ego-involvement from taking place in their athletes. As sport is fundamentally a reward-driven activity, coaches would benefit from finding ways to translate rewards and winning into a less ego-focused accomplishment by emphasizing the growth that the rewards represent. Language such as, "We are proud to have seen so much growth in the team this year; this trophy is a direct result of your efforts and progress, and you should all be proud of that." When athletes are overly ego driven, it has a negative impact on internal motivation and the ability to react constructively to negative outcomes (Nicholls, 1989). By working with coaches on creating an ego-neutral environment, athletes' self-esteem won't constantly be on the line with each win or loss.

Consultants can also improve coach–athlete relationships by showing coaches how to build and maintain trust with their athletes. Coaches must recognize the role that trust plays in athletes' abilities to give their best efforts and perform at a high level in competitions (Corbatto, 2018). Trust is a mutual relationship with three facets: institutional (athletes can rely on their team for support), cognitive (demonstrated coaching knowledge to develop athletes), and emotional (coach providing support through the highs and lows of athletes' lives). These areas of trust can be developed in the coach–athlete dyadic relationship.

Consultants can work with coaches to develop strategies to address each of these areas. In the area of institutional trust, coaches might ask their athletes what their needs and goals are and how they like to be coached. This approach helps to establish a personal and trusting relationship with each individual athlete. In addition to receiving trust from athletes, coaches can show trust in them by placing positive and realistic expectations on them and challenging and supporting them to be their best using techniques previously discussed in the motivational model of the coach–athlete relationship (Mageau & Vallerand, 2003).

In addition, supporting the cognitive area of trust, coaches can help athletes to be completely prepared to perform their best in practice and competitions. This means that every athlete on the team is important and needs to have the mentorship and coaching of the team leader. When athletes are ignored, they feel that the trust between coaches and athletes is broken.

Finally, the emotional support provided by a coach is critical to establishing trust. Consultants can help coaches to understand and treat athletes as people, not just players, by demonstrating commitment, caring, and confidence in them on and off the field of play. This requires that coaches and athletes communicate openly and genuinely with each other.

Consultants can also leverage the coach–athlete relationship by encouraging coaches to promote the concept of thriving in sport. Thriving allows for the growth of the internal motivators that keep athletes engaged over long periods of time in focused practice as well as improving the individual performances of athletes (Brown et al., 2017b). This area of athletic development can be developed using positive verbal reinforcement and performance feedback to increase athlete confidence and recognition of personal ability after both positive and negative experiences. In addition, consultants can use an assortment of psychological-needs support tools to improve the identified facilitators of thriving including focus exercises, relaxation and mindfulness, confidence builders, helping coaches establish an optimal support environment (e.g., coaches, family, teammates), and developing interventions around athletes' overall health and well-being. Work by consultants involving around motivation, autonomy, competence, and social relationships can also improve the ability of athletes to thrive in the competitive sport environment.

Sharing these recommendations with coaches and exploring ways in which they can best implemented in their relationships with athletes is an important role for consultants to play as a member of a team. Effective coaching is defined as "the consistent application of integrated professional, interpersonal, and intrapersonal knowledge to improve athletes' competence, confidence, connection, and character in specific coaching contexts" (Côté & Gilbert, 2009, p. 316). Consultants can assist athletes and coaches in strengthening their relationship with the end result being both enhance performance and improved well-being of both athletes and coaches.

Summary

- The coach–athlete relationship in sport is an example of a dyadic affiliation is one in which two people's goals, actions, and emotions are interdependent.
- Athletes are immersed in an environment that their coaches co-create and their relationship may be the most important in terms of athletes' abilities to perform their best, enjoy their sports experiences, and accomplish their sports goals.
- Coaches are in the relationship to impart knowledge and experience, and to care for athletes as they strive to reach their potential.
- When athletes and their coaches are working in a positive interdependent dyadic relationship, impressive outcomes can be obtained, but when there is incompatibility the relationship can fail and have a negative impact on athletes' efforts and performances.
- One model of the coach–athlete relationship suggests that closeness, commitment, and complementarity are most essential for healthy outcomes.
- Relation-inferred self-efficacy refers to the feelings of competence that athletes gain from knowing that their coaches have confidence in their abilities.
- A motivational model of the coach–athlete dyad which proposes that coaching behaviors nurture athletes' intrinsic motivation and self-determined extrinsic motivation.
- Trust is conceptualized as having confidence in someone, feeling safe with them, and knowing that person can be counted on to act in their best interests, and plays a key role in the coach–athlete relationship.
- Coaches have a significant impact on whether athletes thrive on and off the field of play.
- Consultants can play an important role in helping both coaches and athletes to take ownership of their place in the relationship and show them what they can do to strengthen it to the benefit of both coaches and athletes.

References

Bandura, A. (1986). *Social foundations of thought and action: A social cognitive theory.* Englewood Cliffs, NJ: Prentice-Hall.

Barker, J. B., Jones, M. V., & Greenlees, I. (2010). Assessing the immediate and maintained effects of hypnosis on self-efficacy and soccer wall-volley performance. *Journal of Sport & Exercise Psychology, 32,* 243–352. doi: 10.1123/jsep.32.2.243

Beauchamp, M. R., Jackson, B., & Morton, K. L. (2012). Efficacy beliefs and human performance: From independent action to interpersonal functioning. In S. Murphy (Ed.), *The Oxford handbook of sport and performance psychology* (pp. 273–293). New York, NY: Oxford University Press.

Bloom, G. A., Crumpton, R., & Anderson, J. E. (1999). A systematic observation study of the teaching behaviors of an expert basketball coach. *Sport Psychologist, 13,* 157–170.

Brown, D. J., Arnold, R., Reid, T., & Roberts, G. (2017a). A qualitative exploration of thriving in elite sport. *Journal of Applied Sport Psychology, 30*(2), 129–149. doi:10.1080/10413200.2017.1354339

Brown, D. J., Arnold, R., Standage, M., & Fletcher, D. (2017b). Thriving on pressure: A factor mixture analysis of sport performers' responses to competitive encounters. *Journal of Sport & Exercise Psychology, 39,* 423–437. doi: 10.1123/jsep.2016-0293

Coe, S., & Mason, N. (1988). *The Olympians: A quest for gold: Triumphs, heroes & legends.* London: Pavilion.

Corbatto, D. B. (2016, August). Perceptions of trust: Precursor of flow in elite sport. Poster session presented at the annual meeting of the American Psychological Association, Denver CO.

Corbatto, D. B (2018). Trust as a precursor to flow: A social cognitive view of flow in elite coach/athlete dyads. Doctoral dissertation. Available from ProQuest Dissertations and Theses database.

Côté, J., & Gilbert, W. (2009). An integrative definition of coaching effectiveness and expertise. *International Journal of Sport Science and Coaching, 4,* 307–323.

Deci, E. L., & Ryan, R. M. (1985). *Intrinsic motivation and self-determination in human behavior.* New York, NY: Plenum.

Feltz, D. L., Short, S. E., & Sullivan P. J. (2008). *Self-efficacy in sport*. Champaign, IL: Human Kinetics.

Hobson, W. (2018). Larry Nassar, former USA Gymnastics doctor, sentenced to 40-175 year for sex crimes. *The Washington Post*, January 24. Retrieved from www.washingtonpost.com/sports/olympics/larry-nassar-former-usa-gymnastics-doctor-due-to-be-sentenced-for-sex-crimes/2018/01/24/9acc22f8-0115-11e8-8acf-ad2991367d9d_story.html?utm_term=.710eb33f3c13

Jackson, B., Grove, J., & Beauchamp, M. (2010). Relational efficacy beliefs and relationship quality within coach–athlete dyads. *Journal of Social and Personal Relationships, 27*(8), 1035–1050. doi: 10.1177/0265407510378123

Johnson, K. E., Garing, J. H., Oliphant, J. A., & Roberts, D. K. (2016). Promoting positive youth development through sport: Continuing education opportunities for coaches and future directions for health promotion of athletes. *Journal of Adolescent Health, 58*(2) (supplement), S86–S87. doi: 10.1016/j.jadohealth.2015.10.185.

Jowett, S. (2003). When the honeymoon is over: A case study of a coach–athlete dyad in crisis. *Sport Psychologist, 17*, 444–460.

Jowett, S. & Clark-Carter, D. (2006). Perceptions of empathic accuracy and assumed similarity in the coach–athlete relationship. *British Journal of Social Psychology, 45*, 617–637. doi:10.1348/014466605x58609

Jowett, S., & Cockerill, I. M. (2002). Incompatibility in the coach–athlete relationship. In I. M. Cockerill (Ed.), *Solutions in sport psychology* (pp. 16–31). London: Thomson.

Jowett, S., & Cockerill I. M. (2003). Olympic medalists' perspective of the athlete–coach relationship. *Psychology of Sport and Exercise 4*(4), 313–331. doi:10.1016/S1469-0292(02)00011-0

Jowett, S., & Meek, G. A. (2000). The coach–athlete relationship in married couples; An exploratory content analysis. *The Sport Psychologist, 14*, 157–175.

Jowett, S., & Nezlek, J. (2012). Relationship interdependence and satisfaction with important outcomes in coach–athlete dyads. *Journal of Social and Personal Relationships, 29*(3), 287–301. doi: 10.1177/0265407511420980

Jowett, S., & Ntoumanis, N. (2004). The Coach–athlete Relationship Questionnaire (CART-Q): Development and initial validation. *Scandinavian Journal of Medicine and Science in Sports, 14*, 245–257.

Karabenick, S. A., & Dembo, M. H. (2011). Understanding and facilitating self-regulated help seeking. *New Directions for Teaching and Learning, 126*, 33–43. doi: 10.1002/tl.442

Kelley, H. H., Berscheid, E., Christensen, A., Harvey, J. H., Huston, T. L., Levinger, G. Peterson, D. R. (1983). Analyzing close relationships. In *Close Relationships* (Vol. 20, pp. 20–67). New York, NY: W. H. Freeman and Company.

Kitsantas, A., Kavussanu, M., Corbatto, D. B., & van de Pol, P.K.C. (2018). Self-regulation in athletes, a social cognitive perspective. In D. H. Schunk & J. A. Greene (Eds.), *Handbook of self-regulation of learning and performance*, 2nd ed. (pp. 194–207). New York, NY: Routledge.

Krane, V., & Williams, J. M. (2015). Psychological characteristics of peak performance. In J. M. Williams & V. Krane (Ed.), *Applied sport psychology: Personal growth to peak performance*, 7th ed. (pp. 159–175). New York, NY: McGraw-Hill.

Lent, R., & Lopez, F. (2002). Cognitive ties that bind: A tripartite view of efficacy beliefs in growth-promoting relationships. *Journal of Social and Clinical Psychology, 21*(3), 256–286. doi:10.1521/jscp.21.3.256.22535

MacMullan, J. (2014, January 16). A chemistry forged by triumph, failure. Retrieved from http://espn.go.com/boston/nfl/story/_/id/10305320/tom-brady-bill-belichick-chemistry-forged-success-failure

Mageau, G., & Vallerand, R. J. (2003). The coach–athlete relationship: A motivational model. *Journal of Sports Sciences, 21*, 883–904. doi: 10.1080/0264041031000140374

Maguire, J. A. (2011) Power and global sport: zones of prestige, emulation and resistance. *Sport in Society, 14*(7–8), 1010–1026. doi: 10.1080/17430437.2011.603555

Montse, C. Ruiz, J., Raglin, S., & Hanin, Y. L. (2017) The individual zones of optimal functioning (IZOF) model (1978–2014): Historical overview of its development and use. *International Journal of Sport and Exercise Psychology, 15*(1), 41–63. doi: 10.1080/1612197X.2015.1041545

Nicholls, J. G. (1989). *The competitive ethos and democratic education*. Cambridge, MA, Harvard University Press.

Redford, P. (2016, February 26). The Sacramento Kings found a few new ways to make their season even more of a joke. Retrieved from http://deadspin.com/the-sacramento-kings-found-a-few-new-ways-to-make-their-1767236617

Rusbult, C. E., Kumashiro, M., Coolsen, M. K., & Kirchner, J. L. (2004). Interdependence, closeness, and relationships. In D. Mashek & A. Aron (Eds.), *Handbook of closeness and intimacy* (pp. 137–161). Mahwah, NJ: Lawrence Erlbaum Associates.

Saville, P. D., & Bray, S. (2016). Athlete's perceptions of coaching behavior, relation-inferred self-efficacy (RISE), and self-efficacy in youth sport. *Journal of Applied Sport Psychology, 28*, 1–13. doi: 10.1080/10413200.2015.1052890

Stein, M. (2016, February 9). Sources: Kings planning to fire coach George Karl in coming days. Retrieved from http://espn.go.com/nba/story/_/id/14744059/sacramento-kings-planning-fire-coach-george-karl-coming-days

Stirling, A. E., & Kerr, G. A. (2009) Abused athletes' perceptions of the coach–athlete relationship, *Sport in Society, 12*(2), 227–239. doi: 10.1080/17430430802591019

Swann, C., Keegan, R. J., Piggott, D., & Crust, L. (2012). A systematic review of the experience, occurrence, and controllability of flow states in elite sport. *Psychology of Sport and Exercise, 13*(6), 807–819. doi: 10.1016/j.psychsport.2012.05.006

Vallerand, R. J. (1997). Toward a hierarchical model of intrinsic and extrinsic motivation. *Advances in Experimental Social Psychology, 29*, 271–360. doi: 10.1016/S0065-2601(08)60019-2

Vallerand, R. J., & Rousseau, F. L. (2001). Intrinsic and extrinsic motivation in sport and exercise: A review using the hierarchical model of intrinsic and extrinsic motivation. In R. N. Singer, H. A. Hausenblas, & C. M. Janesse (Eds.), *Handbook of sport psychology*, 2nd ed. (pp. 389–416). New York, NY: Wiley.

Vierimaa, M., Bruner, M. W., & Côté, A. J. (2018). Positive youth development and observed athlete behavior in recreational sport. *PLoS ONE*, *13*(1):e0191936. doi: 10.1371/journal.pone.0191936

Women's Sports Foundation. (2016). Addressing the issue of verbal, physical and psychological abuse of athletes. Retrieved from file:///C:/Users/Debi/Downloads/addressing-the-issue-of-verbal-physical-and-psychological-abuse-of-athletes-the-foundation-position_final.pdf

SKILL ACQUISITION

Derrek Fallor and Jim Taylor

At the heart of what makes the best athletes in the world in any sport great is their ability to learn, perfect, and execute a sport-specific set of motor skills that allows them to perform their best consistently, effectively, and successfully in the most important competitions of their lives. Specifically defined, a skill is an action or task directed toward achieving a specific goal. A motor skill is a defined set of voluntary and coordinated physical movements the purpose of which is to achieve a particular task goal (Magill, 2011). Examples of motor skills include a tennis or golf swing, a triple axel in figure skating, or a back handspring in gymnastics.

The acquisition of these skills and the accompanying expertise in sports is a complex and contextualized process that is impacted by the athletes themselves, their coaches, the environment in which they practice, and other support staff involved with the development of athletes including conditioning personnel, nutritionists, sports medicine staff, and sport psychologists and mental trainers. For coaches to help athletes develop their sport skills fully, they must understand motor learning theory, neurophysiology, psychological contributors to skill acquisition, and the environment in which athletes learn these skills.

Theory and Research

The science of skill acquisition has a long history of inquiry. Specifically, over the last five decades, research into the science of movement and motor learning has burgeoned across the various sub groups (Button & Farrow, 2012). Researchers have identified key stages of how athletes learn new skills and the important contributors to how fully and quickly the skills are acquired.

Motor Learning Principles

Experts in skill acquisition (Ericsson & Pool, 2016) hold the belief that athletes are made and not born. In other words, genetic gifts are less important than the effort that athletes expend in learning and mastering sport skills. While the importance of practice is widely acknowledged for skill acquisition in sports, not all forms of practice have equal value in helping athletes develop the skills needed to perform effectively and consistently in competition. Hall & Magill (1995) uncovered two key findings: a blocked practice session produces more immediate learning of a skill and a randomized practice schedule produces a higher retention of a skill over time. Blocked practice occurs when a learner performs the same skill over and over with little to no variance in repetitions in order to lock in a specific movement pattern. Examples include a basketball player shooting 50 free throws in a row, a sprinter repetitively working on starts, or a soccer player serving 20 corner kicks to the goalkeeper. Conversely, a randomized practice schedule exists when multiple skills are to be executed in one training session (Ruiz-Amengual & Ruiz-Pérez, 2014). An example of this type of practice can be illustrated by a tennis player working on her first serve, backhand return of serve, and volleys or net play all in the same training session. As noted by Kim et al. (2017), random practice, while characterized by relatively slow initial performance during training, is more effective for supporting long-term retention and execution of the practiced skills. Further, the important contribution of their present work is the demonstration that a learner with a history of high contextual interference practice will see a positive influence on the learning of skills not contained in the original bout of random practice.

Ericsson & Pool (2016) suggest using a deliberate and purposeful practice structure that incorporates four important elements (as discussed in Chapter 5):

1. Well-defined and specific goals.
2. Be focused.
3. Receive appropriate and timely feedback.
4. Must get out of their comfort zone.

The ability of athletes to effectively apply their skills during the high-pressure environment of competition is likely to be the factor that differentiates successful athletes from those who are less successful. Therefore, a key challenge for coaches and consultants working to help athletes develop their sports skills is to ensure that athletes are exposed to efficient blocked practice sessions early in the learning phase followed by randomized practice sessions later on to help athletes retain and transfer their new skills across a variety of challenges they experience in their sport.

Athlete–Environment Relationship

Multiple models have been developed that focus on the athlete–environment relationship as crucial to understanding skill acquisition for athletes. *Dynamic systems theory* suggests that skill acquisition occurs for athletes where movement is produced through the interaction of multiple subsystems within the person, task, and environment (Thelen, 1989). Athletes are not machines where motor learning and skill acquisition occur in a predictable linear path. The basic premise is that athletes are complex dynamic systems, constrained by their morphological, physiological, psychological and biomechanical factors, the demands of the task or skill to be executed, and the environment where they train and compete. As an example of how Dynamic systems theory affects skill execution, consider the soccer player learning to acquire and perform a dribbling move. First, he learns the move while dealing with personal fitness level, fatigue, and field conditions, among other subsystems. Next, the player must understand when the correct tactical time is to use the move against a defender, in this way considering the environment. Finally, the player will choose to use the move in a game based their confidence and on the location of the defender in relation to that opponent's teammates, location on field, score, and internal physiological feelings such as fatigue levels.

Ecological dynamics theory is another model that examines the interaction of the athlete with the environment. It proposes that the relationship between athletes and the environment involves how a person takes in information, makes a decision, and applies a consistent performance action by adapting to the changing tasks in sport (Davids et al., 2013). In other words, although trained athletes most often perform skills and action patterns through predictable movements in controlled environments like scripted practice, skilled performers are not locked into rigidly stable solutions (e.g., technical, tactical), but rather vary their behaviors based on competitive demands. Successful performers adapt their actions to dynamically shifting environments that characterize competitive sport including score, type of defense, conditions, and time remaining. This flexibility is based on the current environmental conditions and task demands, thus the ecological system affects the skill execution (Araújo et al., 2007). For example, a point guard in basketball who has been perfecting the execution of a bounce pass into the high post, brings the ball across half court and would like to make this type of entry pass to the team's center at the free throw line. However, the point guard notices that the center is better at catching chest passes. Thus, the point guard elects to throw a chest pass as that is the skill which is most likely to produce a positive pass completion.

A third way to view the relationship of athlete to environment as it affects skill acquisition is through the *bioecological model*. This model posits that coaches and consultants interact with athletes whose personal experiences, skills, and attributes have been shaped by the sociocultural constraints that surround them (Ueharaa et al., 2014). In general terms, the bioecological model conceives human development as function of the interaction between nature and nurture (Krebs, 2009). For example, in Brazil, soccer is woven into the fabric of its society differently than in many other parts of the world, so it could be suggested by this model of motor learning, that Brazilians are raised with the understanding that soccer expertise is not only desired but also acquirable through training. A young Brazilian player might be more open to learning a specific soccer skill than a youth from a part of the world where soccer is not such a significant part of their culture or lives.

Using these three skill acquisition models, consultants can analyze the contextual forces surrounding athletes as well as the sociocultural constraints leading to skill development in certain populations. They can then show athletes how to leverage the information that is most helpful in developing relevant sports skills and applying them to their practice and competitive performances.

Practical Implications

The discussion so far supports the notion that physical practice is not the only tool that coaches have to facilitate skill acquisition in their athletes. Instead, they can also use a variety of psychological, interpersonal, and contextual tools to help athletes develop their skills. According to Williams and Hodges (2005), while the classical, prescriptive instructional approaches to teaching skills are likely to produce faster performance gains initially, they may result in less efficient and reliable performances in the long term.

The findings of the studies described above with respect to the factors affecting skill acquisition share important implications for coaches working with athletes in their skill development and in the contributions that consultants can make to athlete development and individual and team performance. Because coaches may not be familiar with these nuances of sport skill learning, consultants are in an excellent position to partner with coaches in two ways that will benefit the athletes with whom they work. First, consultants can collaborate with coaches in identifying the key psychological, interpersonal, and contextual contributors to an optimal learning environment in which athletes can develop their skills. Second, consultants can educate coaches on specific approaches and tools that they can incorporate into their daily practice regimens that will encourage skill acquisition. Third, consultants can encourage coaches to consider the sociocultural factors surrounding athletes that may enhance or detract from their ability to acquire and perform certain technical and tactical skills in sport. In this process, consultants work to identify which strategies may be most effective to pair with physical practice to achieve maximum gains in skills and the commensurate increases in performance during training and competitions.

Innate vs. Learned

Wulf and Lewthwaite (2009) indicated that motor learning can be affected by whether learners believe that a skill can be learned or is more dependent on innate ability. They found instructions suggesting a skill reflecting an inborn talent resulted in less effective learning than did instructions that portrayed a task as an acquirable skill. Based on the above research, coaches and consultants can introduce skills in ways that encourage athletes to believe that their ability to develop the skills depends more on effort, focus, and persistence (which are controllable) than innate ability (which is outside their control). This attitude that is fostered in athletes by coaches and consultants can increase athletes' motivation, confidence, and perseverance as they initiate and progress through the stages of skill acquisition.

Mental Toughness

An additional consideration for athletes during the skill acquisition phase is that of mental toughness. Mental toughness is considered one of the main characteristics contributing to athletic success (Jones et al., 2007). Jones and colleagues (2002) defined mental toughness as follows:

> Having the natural or developed psychological edge that enables you to, generally, cope better than your opponents with the many demands (competition, training, lifestyle) that sport places on a performer and, specifically, be more consistent and better than your opponents in remaining determined, focused, confident, and in control under pressure.
>
> (Jones et al., 2002, p. 16)

Moradi, Mousavi, and Amirtash (2013) reported that subjects assessed to possess high mental toughness (via the MTQ-48) outperformed, in both skill acquisition and skill retention, those rated as having low mental toughness. Moreover, they found the group with higher mental toughness scores not only produced better basketball passing results (as compared to subjects with lower scores), but also retained their newly learned passing skills at a high level even after a break in learning.

Consultants can foster mental toughness through a variety of methods. Based on findings from Weinberg et al. (2016), consultants and coaches can build mental toughness by being thoughtful and purposeful both in how they think about athletes (i.e., be instructive and encouraging, foster autonomy, see them as individuals) and their staff (i.e., be multidimensional and educate), as well as what they do (i.e., create adversity and at the same time teach mental tools). Additionally, Crust and Azadi (2010) found significant positive correlations between mental toughness, mental imagery, and goal-setting. Finally, Mattie and Munroe-Chandler (2012) investigated the relationship between mental toughness and mental imagery. The results showed that mental imagery could significantly predict mental toughness in athletes; specifically, sophisticated motivational imagery proved to be the strongest predictor of all aspects of mental toughness. In this way, mental imagery is one of the key approaches to improving mental toughness (see Chapter 4 for more on mental imagery). Based on previously noted research, skill acquisition may be improved through mental toughness training by consultants and coaches given that this set of attributes allows athletes to persevere through difficult circumstances, ultimately leading to successful skill execution outcomes. Mental toughness can be viewed as a critical component of maximizing the performances of athletes since its subset of attributes promote a state of mind that enhances performance.

Goal-Setting

Goal-setting and self-regulation (Zimmerman & Kitsantas 1996) were found to have positive effects on skill learning for novices. Barnett and Stanicek (2013) found goal-setting to significantly improve performance of novice archers over the course of a ten-week study. However, Holt, Kinchin, & Clarke (2015) found that goal-setting alone was not enough to promote practice effort or significant learning in young soccer players. Recently, Zetou, Papacharisis, & Mountaki (2017) noted that goal-setting alone did not produce performance improvement in skills during the course of a season. Given the mixture of results, goal-setting by itself may not be a significant factor in improving skill acquisition across a variety of ages, genders, and abilities of athletes. Thus, it is important to consider the findings of Toering et al. (2011) where self-regulated players displayed behaviors which indicated that they create optimal learning conditions, are aware of their abilities and inabilities, take responsibility and initiative, are focused, and are prepared for practice. Similarly, as noted by Bartulovic, Young & Baker (2017), those athletes who demonstrated higher scores in the self-regulation learning processes were more frequently found in the elite and less-elite group compared to recreationally competitive athletes.

Given this information, consultants can work with both athletes and coaches in establishing realistic goals for acquiring particular sports skills (see SMARTER goal guidelines discussed in Chapter 3) and pair those goals with solid self-regulated behaviors of the athletes during training.

Focus

Research on the importance of focus in skill acquisition has consistently demonstrated that an external focus can enhance motor skill learning and performance more than an internal focus (Wulf, 2013). Additionally, Wulf notes a high skill level is associated with accuracy, consistency, and reliability in achieving the movement goal (i.e., effectiveness), as well as fluent and economical movement executions as evidenced by the investment of relatively little physical and mental effort (i.e., efficiency). An external focus of attention speeds up the learning process so that a higher skill level characterized by both increased effectiveness and efficiency is achieved sooner. An internal focus is associated more with kinesthetic feelings of athletes' bodies in relation to equipment or competition surface and can provide too much stimulus in one aspect of skill acquisition rather than an effective focus on the whole skill.

Results from Roshandel, Taheri, and Moghadam (2017) revealed that young learners benefit from instructions that relied on an external focus and internal focus in the same manner. However, adults benefited from more from externally focused instructions. The majority of studies on focus and skill acquisition suggest that, other than novices, learners' attention should be directed externally toward the skill being executed physically instead of toward bodily movements. For example, sprinters working on starts out of the blocks are often told to stay low for the first few strides. An internal focus would involve their attention to how much bend there is at the waist, the ducking of their head, and overall concentration on keeping their body parts all relatively close to the ground. In contrast, an external focus would involve sprinters exploding out of the blocks while directing all of their energy to going forward rather than up. Focusing on bending over (internal focus) could negatively affect balance and stride pattern. Focusing externally on driving forward simplifies the thinking and allows for more efficient movement. A meta-analysis of this research evaluating results from 57 studies (Tan, Lai, & Huang, 2012) supported the conclusion in which almost 75% of the studies found that skill acquisition was enhanced more by an external focus compared to an internal focus. Given this impact, consultants can share with coaches and athletes the mental tools that can improve focus and facilitate learning including keywords, mental imagery, video modeling of self and others, centering, and breathing.

Pre-performance Routines

Combinations of mental-training tools have been studied in terms of their influence on skill acquisition in sports. One such combination is called a pre-performance routine (PPR). A pre-performance routine is defined as a fixed series of motor and psychological activities performed prior to executing a motor skill such as throwing, catching, or kicking a ball (Lidor & Singer, 2003) with the goal of optimizing preparation. Perry and Katz (2015) concluded that athletes who were instructed to perform a PPR, whether it included both motor and mental techniques or motor techniques alone, performed more accurately in all phases of skill development: acquisition, retention, and transfer as compared with those who were provided with only technical instruction. Additionally, those who learned a preparatory routine that included motor and mental components executed sport skills more accurately than the participants in the control group or those who learned only a motor preparatory routine. As noted by Perry and Katz (2015), these findings support previous research that mental and motor pre-performance routine improves accuracy of skills, especially in closed-paced skills.

Pre-performance routines can be composed of a variety of physical and psychological tools that are aimed at maximally preparing athletes to focus on and expend effort toward the acquisition of new sports skills. Examples of helpful tools include:

- physical warm-up;
- static physical rehearsal of the skill;
- breathing;
- intensity regulation (either decrease or increase, depending on the type and stage of skill);
- mental imagery;
- focus keywords; and
- positive and motivating self-talk.

Video Modeling

Video modeling involves having athletes watch expert performers execute the skills they are attempting to learn. This technique, which is a form of mental imagery, has been shown to improve the rate and accuracy of acquiring a skill in two recent studies. Nahid, Zahra & Elham (2013) discovered that when learners watched film of a skill being performed by experts, their ability to learn the skill themselves exceeded a control group that was only given verbal instruction on a skill. They noted that to help learners focus on helpful aspects of the skill while viewing videos, coaches or consultants can give verbal cues that direct their attention to useful elements of the skill being demonstrated in the video.

Consultants can improve the value of video modeling by having coaches and athletes follow several guidelines:

- Have athletes watch video models who are physically like them (e.g., body proportions, muscle mass).
- Focus on successful models (what they do right), not failing models (what they do wrong).
- Take in the entire image rather than analyzing and focusing on minutiae.
- Combine video models with video of the athletes themselves performing as a means of integrating the positive images of the video models into their own performances.
- Immediately after viewing a video model, athletes should use mental imagery to incorporate the skill into their own performances.

Mental Imagery

Mental imagery appears to be effective in producing improvements in skill acquisition. In a landmark study by Maring (1990), it was determined that mental practice (i.e., imagery) combined with physical practice led to the best skill acquisition outcomes. In a similar manner, Waskiewicz and Zajac (2001) found that mental imagery combined with physical practice allowed for better skill outcomes than just physical practice alone. They also found that mental practice created a higher rate of skill acquisition in the early stages of learning as long as the learner clearly understood the task requirements.

Nyber et al. (2006) concluded that physical and mental practice are associated with partially distinct regions (motor vs. visual) of the brain and that, by activating these different brain regions, athletes can facilitate learning. Applying both physical and mental practice methods also improved motor flexibility with new tasks. Additionally, the findings of Kim, Frank and Schack (2017) revealed that sport skills improved through both action observation (subjects watching experts perform a skill) and motor imagery training (subjects using imagery to perform mental repetitions of a skill) as compared to physical practice alone. A visual demonstration is most effective when athletes are first learning the specific pattern of movement, but verbal instruction may be most beneficial to when the movement has already been acquired and simply needs to be performed faster or with more precision (Williams & Ford, 2009).

Consultants can help coaches and athletes to gain the many benefits of mental imagery in several ways. First, consultants can educate them about why and how imagery works. Second, they can show athletes how they can use imagery during practice, away from the field of play, and before and during competitions to enhance skill acquisition, retention, transfer, and consistency. Third, consultants can demonstrate ways in which coaches can incorporate imagery into their daily practices, for example, as part of their pre-performance routine, before a drill aimed at teaching a new skill, and at the end of practice as a part of cool-down and recovery.

Feedback

Feedback to athletes has proven to have an impact on their ability to effectively learn and perform a physical task, depending on the type of feedback given. Badami, Kohestani, and Taghian (2011) indicate that feedback following effective execution resulted in more effective learning than feedback after poor execution. Chiviacowsky and Drews (2016) confirmed that timely positive feedback provided to the athletes influences their self-efficacy and motor learning on a task. In their study, participants seemed to be sensitive to feedback informing them as to whether their performance got better or worse over time, with consequences on their perceptions of competence and learning. Both results highlight the important role of feedback for motor learning as it carries an important motivational function.

Consultants can help coaches become better teachers by educating them about different aspects of feedback in the process of skill acquisition. Key areas related to improving the quality of feedback include:

- timing (when it is given);
- quantity (how much is given);
- valence (how positive or negative it is);
- specificity (how detailed it is); and
- modality (whether verbal, visual, or kinesthetic).

Consultants also help athletes to be better receivers of feedback. Clearly, feedback from coaches has little value if it isn't processed, understood, connected to the skill, and remembered by athletes when practiced. Consultants can show athletes simple tools they can use to better absorb and use coach feedback:

- Look at the coach.
- Block out external (e.g., other athletes talking nearby) and internal (e.g., self-criticism) distractions.
- Give self-feedback before receiving coach feedback.
- Reflect back what the coach said.
- Ask questions for clarity of understanding.
- Use imagery to ingrain the feedback into the next execution.

- Demonstrate the feedback physically.
- Create a keyword as a reminder of the feedback during execution.

Practice Environment

The practice environment is an underappreciated and often neglected contributor to skill acquisition (Williams & Ford, 2009). The setting in which athletes practice skills can have a significant impact on their ability to focus on and persist as skills are practiced and learned. A skill acquisition method which can be employed by coaches and consultants, that combines aspects of both the drill (contextualized training) and the games approaches, is the *guided discovery* technique. This strategy can be used to create practice environments that foster enhanced learning of sports skills. Smeeton et al. (2005) found that guided discovery methods are recommended for expediency in learning and resilience under pressure. Using this method, coaches and consultants can establish a drill or practice pattern and then use questions to guide or shape the athletes' learning and thus influence subsequent performance attempts. Effective questions are those that direct the athletes' focus to a particular aspect of the skilled performance, either the decision-making process or the technical aspects of a particular movement or skill execution (Brewer, 2017).

Consultants can help coaches to create these positive learning environments as part of athletes' guided discovery experiences. Key practice-setting strategies for coaches include the following:

- Express confidence in their athletes related to learning sports skills.
- Establish expectations of quality, determination, patience, and persistence.
- Build a supportive team culture.
- Welcome athlete input and feedback.
- Explain the skill-acquisition progression to enhance familiarity, predictability, and control.
- Ensure a focused and distraction-free environment.
- Begin skill acquisition in a simple environment.
- Focus on only one element of the skill at a time.
- Increase the complexity of the environment as the skill is acquired (e.g., include other athletes, introduce other skills, add adverse conditions).
- As the skill is mastered, incorporate it into broader practice goals.
- Ultimately, practice the skill in a simulated competition.

Summary

- At the heart of what makes the best athletes in the world in any sport great is their ability to learn, perfect, and execute a sport-specific set of motor skills that allows them to perform their best consistently, effectively, and successfully in the most important competitions of their lives.
- A motor skill is a defined set of voluntary and coordinated physical movements the purpose of which is to achieve a particular task goal; examples of motor skills in sports include a tennis or golf swing, a triple axel in figure skating, or a back handspring in gymnastics.
- The acquisition of these skills and the accompanying expertise in sports (or other activities such as music and dance) is a complex and contextualized process that is impacted by the athlete themselves, the environment in which they practice, their coaches, and other support staff involved with the development of athletes including conditioning personnel, nutritionists, sports medicine staff, and sport psychologists and mental trainers.
- While the importance of practice is widely acknowledged in all sports, not all forms of practice have equal value in helping athletes develop the skills needed to perform effectively and consistently during competition.
- A deliberate and purposeful practice structure that incorporates four key elements is most effective: well-defined and specific goals, be focused, receive appropriate and timely feedback, and must get out of their comfort zone.
- A key challenge for coaches and consultants working to help athletes develop their sports skills is to ensure that are organized with efficient blocked practice sessions early in the learning phase followed by randomized

practice sessions later to help athletes retain and transfer their new skills across a variety of challenges they experience in their sport.

- Factors that relate to the athlete–environment relationship as crucial to understanding skill acquisition for athletes include aspects of the person, task, and environment, how athletes process the skill, and sociocultural influences.
- There is support the notion that physical practice is not the only tool that coaches have to facilitate skill acquisition in their athletes; instead, they can also use a variety of psychological, interpersonal, and contextual tools to help athletes develop their skills.
- Because coaches may not be familiar with these nuances of sport skill learning, consultants are in an excellent position to partner with coaches in two ways that will benefits the athletes with whom they work.
- Key areas in which consultants can help coaches and athletes in skill acquisition include developing mental toughness, goal-setting, focus, pre-performance routines, video, modeling, mental imagery, coach feedback, and developing positive practice environments.

References

Araújo, D., Davids, K., & Passos, P. (2007). Ecological validity, representative design and correspondence between experimental task constraints and behavioral settings. *Ecological Psychology, 19*, 69–78.

Badami, R., Kohestani, S., & Taghian, F. (2011). Feedback on more accurate trials enhances learning of sport skills. *World Applied Sciences Journal, 13*, 537–540.

Barnett, M. L., & Stanicek, J. A. (2013). Effects of goal setting on achievement in archery. *Research Quarterly: American Alliance for Health, Physical Education, Recreation and Dance, 50*(3), 328–332.

Bartulovic, D., Young, B. W., & Baker, J. (2017). Self-regulated learning predicts skill group differences in developing athletes. *Psychology of Sport and Exercise, 31*: 61–69.

Brewer, C. (2017). *Athlete movement skills: Training for sport performance.* Champaign, IL. Human Kinetics.

Button, C., & Farrow, D. (2012). Working in the field (Southern Hemisphere). In N. J. Hodges & A. M. Williams (Eds.), *Skill acquisition in sport* (pp. 376–380). London: Routledge.

Chiviacowsky, S., & Drews, R. (2016). Temporal-comparative feedback affects motor learning. *Journal of Motor Learning and Development, 4*, 208–218.

Crust, L., & Azadi, K. (2010). Mental toughness and athletes' use of psychological strategies. *European Journal of Sport Science, 10*, 43–51.

Davids, K., Araújo, D., Vilar, L., Renshaw, I., & Pinder, R. (2013). An ecological dynamics approach to skill acquisition: Implications for development of talent in sport. *Talent Development and Excellence, 5*(1), 21–34.

Ericsson, A., & Pool, R. (2016). *Peak: Secrets from the new science of expertise.* New York, NY. Houghton Mifflin Harcourt Publishing Company.

Hall, K. G., & Magill, R. A. (1995). Variability of practice and contextual interference in motor skill learning. *Journal of Motor Behavior, 27*(4), 299–309.

Holt, J. E., Kinchin, G. D., & Clarke, G. (2015). Effects of peer-assessed feedback, goal-setting and a group contingency on performance and learning by 10–12-year-old academy soccer players. *Physical Education and Sport Pedagogy, 17*(3), 231–250.

Jones, G., Hanton, S., & Connaughton, D. (2002). What is this thing called mental toughness? An investigation of elite sport performers. *Journal of Applied Sport Psychology, 14*(3), 205–218.

Jones, G., Hanton, S., & Connaughton, D. (2007). A framework of mental toughness in the world's best performers. *Sport Psychologist, 21*, 243–264.

Kim, T., Frank, C., & Schack, T. (2017). A systematic investigation of the effect of action observation training and motor imagery training on the development of mental representation structure and skill performance. *Frontiers of Human Neuroscience, 11*, 499–512.

Krebs, R. J. 2009. Bronfenbrenner's bioecological theory of human development and the process of development of sports talent. *International Journal of Sport Psychology, 40*(1), 108–135.

Lidor, R., & Singer, R. N. (2003). Pre-performance routines in self-paced tasks: Developmental And educational considerations. In R. Lidor & K. P. Henschen (Eds.), *The psychology of team sports* (pp. 69–98). Morgantown, WV: Fitness Information Technology.

Magill, R. A. (2011). *Motor learning and control: Concepts and applications.* New York, NY: McGraw-Hill.

Maring, J. R. (1990). Effects of mental practice on rate of skill acquisition. *Physical Therapy, 4.*

Mattie, P., & Munroe-Chandler, K. J. (2012). Examining the relationship between mental toughness and imagery use. *Journal of Applied Sport Psychology, 24*, 144–156.

Moradi, J., Mousavi, M. V., & Amirtash, A. M. (2013). The role of mental toughness in acquisition and retention of a sports skill. *European Journal of Experimental Biology, 3*(6), 438–442.

Nahid, S., Zahra, N. R., & Elham, A. (2013). Effects of video modeling on skill acquisition in learning the handball shot. *European Journal of Experimental Biology*, 3(2), 214–218.

Nyber, L., Ericksson, J., Larsson, A., & Marklund, P. (2006). Learning by doing versus learning by thinking: An fMRI study of motor and mental training. *Neuropsychologia*, 44(5), 711–717.

Perry I. S., & Katz, Y. J. (2015). Pre-performance routines, accuracy in athletic performance and self-control. *Athens Journal of Sports*, 2, 137–152.

Roshandel, S., Taheri, H. & Moghadam, A. (2017). Do children benefit from external focus of attention as much as adults? A motor learning study. *Modern Applied Science*, 11(7).

Ruiz-Amengual, A. & Ruiz-Pérez, L. M. (2014). Random practice and sport motor learning. *Revista Iberoamericana de Psicologia del Ejercicio y el Deporte*, 9, 123–142.

Smeeton, N. J., Williams, M. A., Hodges, N. J., & Ward, P. (2005). The relative effectiveness of various instructional approaches in developing anticipation skill. *Journal of Experimental Psychology*, 11(2): 98–110.

Tan, J., Lai, Q., & Huang, Z. (2012). A meta-analysis on the effects of attentional focus on motor learning. *Journal of Beijing University of Physical Education*, 35(4), 80–87, 110.

Thelen, E. (1989). The (re)discovery of motor development: Learning new things from an old field. *Developmental Psychology*, 25(6), 946–949.

Toering, T., Elferink-Gemser, M., Jordet, G. Jorna, C., Pepping, G., & Visscher, C. (2011). Self-Regulation of practice behavior among elite youth soccer players. *Journal of Applied Sport Psychology*, 23(1), 11–128.

Ueharaa, L., Buttona, C., Falcousa, M., & Davids, K. (2014). Contextualized skill acquisition research: a new framework to study the development of sport expertise. *Physical Education and Sport Pedagogy*.

Waskiewicz, Z., & Zajac, A. (2001). The Imagery and Motor Skills Acquisition. *Biology of Sport*, 18(1), 2–14.

Weinberg, R., Freysinger, V., & Mellano, K. (2016). How can coaches build mental toughness? Views from sport psychologists. *Journal of Sport Psychology in Action*, 9, 1–10.

Williams M. A., & Ford, P. R. (2009). Promoting a skills-based agenda in Olympic sports: the role of skill-acquisition specialists. *Journal of Sports Science*, 13, 1381–1392.

Williams, M. A., and Hodges, N. J. (2005). Practice, instruction and skill acquisition in soccer: Challenging tradition. *Journal of Sport Sciences*, 6, 637–650.

Wulf, G., She, C., & Lewthwaite, R. (2009). Motor skill learning and performance: A review of influential factors. *Medical education*, 44, 75–78.

Wulf, G. (2013). Attentional focus and motor learning: A review of 15 years. *International Review of Sport and Exercise Psychology*, 6(1), 77104. doi: 10.1080/1750984X.2012.723728

Zetou, L., Papacharisis, V., & Mountaki, F. (2017) The effects of goal-setting interventions on three volleyball skills: A single-subject design, *International Journal of Performance Analysis in Sport*, 8(3), 79–95.

Zimmerman, B., & Kitsantas, A. (1996). Self-regulated learning of a motoric skill: The role of goal setting and self-monitoring. *Journal of Applied Sport Psychology*, 8(1).

VIDEO

Brandon Orr and Jim Taylor

The use of video as a tool for athlete development is well entrenched in some sports, such as football, basketball, gymnastics, and soccer, but is still growing in its use in other sports (Boyer, Miltenberger, Batsche, & Fogel, 2009; Harle & Vickers, 2001; McGinnis, 2000). With new technology evolving at a rapid rate and new platforms (e.g., Hudl, SkyCoach) becoming more accessible in terms of cost and ease of use, coaches at every level of sport will have the ability to leverage video as a valuable means of helping athletes improve many aspects of their sports performances.

As the sayings go, "seeing is believing" and "images don't lie"; therein lies the power of video. The use of video in any setting is rooted in its ability to provide objective feedback on a wide range of physical, biomechanical, technical, tactical, team, and even psychological parameters. Its fundamental purpose is to offer clear and unambiguous information as a means of offering athletes corrective measures in the contributors to sports performance that were just mentioned.

At the same time, video as a tool is currently limited by a lack of grounded theory and evidence-based practices surrounding the inclusion of its use by coaches to advance athlete development. Because it is driven primarily by the "boots on the ground" experiences of coaches and technology companies that see a potential market for its products, rather than sound scientific inquiry, there is a lack of clarity on why video is beneficial, in what areas it can have a demonstrable impact, and how its value can be maximized.

To provide some clarity, this section will explore the use of video both outside of and within sports. It will also offer recommendations for how consultants can help coaches optimize its value in their work with athletes (Groom, Cushion, & Nelson, 2011).

Theory and Research

As with many aspects of sport, the use of various approaches and strategies by coaches began outside of sport in, for example, education, business, and medicine. The same holds true for video. An exploration of how video has been used in other settings will inform how coaches can use video to help their athletes to take full advantage of their practice opportunities with the ultimate goal of performing their best in competition.

Video Use in Outside of Sport

The use of video outside of sports for behavior modification and improvement has been documented in a variety of areas including communication skills and youth classroom behaviors (Ives, Straub, & Shelley, 2002). Most commonly, the use of video in this context involves showing a student video of their disruptive behavior and then coupling this with excerpts from the classroom environment of this same student engaging in adaptive and productive behavior in the classroom (Dowrick, 1991). This approach allows students to observe themselves demonstrating desired behaviors in the learning setting as a means of self-modeling (Dowrick, 1991, 1999). It also serves to allow the student's self-image to increase by observing their own competency to engage in appropriate and desired behaviors.

Video Use in Sport

Seeing the benefits of video use in education, researchers hypothesized a similar benefit in sports for helping athletes use videoed past performances to improve their skills within a new training or competition setting, and eliciting successful sport behaviors within the presence of anxiety (Dowrick, 1999; Ives et al., 2002). With advances in technology, it is becoming easier and more efficient to record, edit, and share videos for use in athlete development (Ives et al., 2002). It is now possible to shot, edit (if necessary), and review videos of practice or competitions as a means of providing coaches and athletes with a concise visual representation of the performances soon after they are completed. Video can be used by coaches to reveal both proper and incorrect aspects of technique, positioning, tactics, and the overall quality of individual and team performances (Groom, Cushion, & Nelson, 2011; Ives et al., 2002; Nelson, Potrac, & Groom, 2014).

Rymal, Martini, and Ste-Marie (2010) conducted a qualitative study investigating the ways in which video feedback helped athletes' self-regulation during performance. Results indicated that, by viewing video of their own performances, athletes were more likely and better able to understand and imagine the correct execution of skills. Effective skill breakdown on video was helpful in identifying shortcomings and errors with the aim of using that information to improve the skill. The participants also reported that the use of video review led them to feel more confident with regard to skill acquisition and retention. Finally, video review allowed athletes to engage in more objective and accurate self-evaluation including comparing current with previous performances to measure skill and performance progress.

A study by Ste-Marie, Vertes, Rymal, and Martini (2011) linked video feedback directly to improved performance such that gymnasts who viewed video of their performances throughout the competitive season produced significantly higher beam scores in competition than those gymnasts who did not use video review. Interestingly, the authors found no difference in objectively assessed self-efficacy between the two experimental groups. At the same time, follow-up interviews indicated that those who used video review felt more efficacious and attributed video review to increases in performance outcomes. One benefit of this approach is that as athletes are provided the opportunity to review their physical performance in training and competition coupled with active coaching on behalf of their coach, the time to skill acquisition is reduced given that the use of video reduced the number of practice sessions necessary for the athlete to acquire competency in performing a difficult skill (Boyer et al., 2009). It could be speculated that seeing frequent and successful images of themselves improved the gymnasts' confidence and focus, resulting in more committed and assertive performances on the beam.

While the use of video for sport performance enhancement within sport psychology is scant, there are examples arguing for the efficacy of the use of video for improving skill acquisition and sport performance: In Rickli and Smith (1980), the use of video was shown to improve skill and performance within tennis players on their service game. Hazen, Johnstone, Martin, and Srikameswaran (1990) found that the use of video resulted in improvements in swimmer stroke technique and performance. Lastly, Harle and Vickers (2001) reported that the use of video improved free throw performance and accuracy;

Practical Implications

Video allows coaches and athletes to overcome two barriers to athlete development. First, both coaches' and athletes' determinations of success in practice or competitions can be limited by their subjective evaluations based on their recall and interpretation of the performance. Incomplete memory, inaccurate recall, cognitive biases, and self-protection can result in divergent perceptions on the part of coaches and athletes. Second, because sports are outcome focused, both coaches and athletes may incorrectly or unfairly judge a performance based on its outcome; athletes may execute skills correctly, perform well overall, and still lose. In both cases, video mitigates these shortcomings and offers information about athlete performances that are observable and verifiable. This objectivity provides coaches and athletes with a shared reality from which to evaluate and learn from the sports performance.

Consultants can play a role in promoting the use of video review for both athletes and coaches. Specifically, consultants can educate coaches and athletes on the best practices for video use. Central to this approach is coaches considering how best to present video (e.g., focus on specific skills or overall performance), which video to present (e.g., practice vs. competition), to whom they would present the video (e.g., individually vs. team), and what the targeted purpose is (e.g., skill acquisition, team performance, confidence building). In addition, consultants can work in tandem with coaches to evaluate athletes' responses to video and customize video use to the specific needs and goals of individual athletes.

Performance Criteria in Video Analysis

An important consideration is for coaches to identify specific goals and desired outcomes when using video in athlete development. Moreover, to ensure clarity of purpose, athletes would also benefit from coaches providing an identified criterion of success that can range from the proper execution of a skill in isolation, the successful execution in the context of a complete or coordinated performance, or achievement of a particular competitive statistic or score due to the effective completion of a skill or sequence of skills (Hughes & Bartlett, 2004; Hughes & Franks, 2004). Additionally, because successful competitive outcomes are grounded in effective execution of technical, tactical, team, and psychological skills that are observable on video, having coaches define the particular skills they are interested in before a video session would help athletes to focus specifically on what coaches want them to (Liebermann & Franks, 2004).

Sports are complex activities with many contributors to performance and success. Moreover, that complexity can be reflected in the video of athlete and team performance. Without clarity of purpose, coaches can get bogged down in a morass of feedback to their athletes. In turn, athletes can feel overwhelmed by all of the things to watch, evaluate, and work on in a practice or competitive video. Consultants can help coaches to clearly communicate the purpose that they and their athletes will be working toward.

The nature of sport necessitates that the ultimate goal is winning. At the same time, there are many steps that must be taken and many areas that must be focused on to arrive at that destination. As a result, the value of video can be facilitated when smaller performance goals, indicators, and outcomes are established related to skill acquisition, task mastery, and personal bests. Performance goals that are chosen by coaches can depend on the type of sport, athletes' stage of development, time of year, and current level of performance (Hughes & Bartlett, 2004). Specific contributors to deciding on the performance goals can also include whether the sport is objective (e.g., basketball, football, golf) or subjective (gymnastics, figure skating, and diving). Whether the sport is individual (e.g., archery, ski racing) or team (e.g., water polo, lacrosse) or self-referenced (e.g., swimming, running) or confrontational (e.g., tennis, boxing).

In approaching coaches' video use with athletes, the first step involves coaches establishing clear goals about the value of the video session, in other words, how video will help athletes improve. These goals will provide both athletes and coaches with a shared and aligned purpose and a common starting point for examining the video. Research has suggested that reasonable performance goals can include most aspects of athletic performance including technical, tactical, physical, mental, and competitive (Groom & Cushion, 2004; Hughes & Bartlett, 2004; Lyle, 2002).

Performance indicators refer to the specific aspects of performance that will be the focus of the video. Examples might include body position, sport-specific movement patterns, overt expressions of confidence or intensity, tactical execution, and competitive statistics. With these markers clearly identified, both coaches and athletes will be able to focus on and address these particular performance indicators more effectively.

Performance outcomes indicate the ultimate results that would come from the video analysis. With an identifiable outcome established, coaches and athletes can "reverse engineer" their video use to approach the videoed performance with the expressed goal of achieving the specified outcome. When grounded in a clear set of goals, performance indicators, and outcomes, video can be a powerful tool for coaches and athletes to gain the most out of their practice and competitive experiences and to counter the reliability issues tied to subjective performance analysis on the part of coach and athlete.

Technical and Tactical Skill Acquisition

Video in skill acquisition is termed self-modeling and can be used in two ways: positive self-review and feedforward (Dowrick, 1991). Positive self-review involves recording individuals' best performances (i.e., highlight reels), editing the videos so as to eliminate any mistakes from the segments, and then allowing individuals to review their successful performance as models for their future efforts. Positive self-review can be used by athletes to identify and replicate effective technique and tactics, well-coordinated team efforts, and psychological and emotional practices that facilitate successful performances. In addition to using video to highlight the positive aspects of behavior and performance, it can also play a corrective role as well. With video, athletes can view errors in their efforts and use that information to make beneficial corrections.

Feedforward involves piecing together videos of basic skills that, once put together in the proper order, show individuals completing a skill they have not yet attempted or successfully executed. This method offers people correct and sequential information that they can then apply to their learning new skills or sport-specific patterns. The value of feedforward lies in offering people a clear understanding of what they must do for the effective execution of skills. It also is beneficial in instilling them with an initial sense of confidence in their ability to learn the new skills. Overall, the use of video in the learning process can serve a variety of functions: clarifying goals or outcomes, demonstrating positive images, correcting errors, reminding of previous competence in performance, and establishing the ability to complete new skills (Ives et al., 2002).

As has been demonstrated above, video can be a valuable tool for coaches in helping their athletes to develop the technical and tactical acumen necessary for success in their sport. At the same time, as with many aspects of athlete development, the benefits that athletes gain from video analysis depend on how coaches use it in their video sessions.

Common Mistakes

There is a tendency among coaches and athletes alike to focus on mistakes when watching video. This emphasis seems to make sense because if athletes watch their mistakes, they can learn from and correct them. And certainly some focus on errors is important for their correction in terms of both recognition and understanding. At the same time, when coaches show mistakes repeatedly to athletes, the perceptions, feelings, and images of the mistakes are ingrained, much like when athletes physically practice poor technique or tactics, they become habit in their mind and muscles.

Video offers coaches and athletes the ability to deconstruct technique and tactics so precisely and to focus on the minutiae of the videoed performances. Though there is a place for such nuanced analyses, this detailed approach can present two potential problems if used excessively. First, video analysis becomes an intellectual exercise that occurs in the mind when it should be a kinesthetic exercise that occurs in the body. Second, athletes miss out on the benefits of absorbing the "gestalt" of the video, that is, allowing the thinking part of the mind to turn itself off and enabling the unconscious mind and body to absorb the images and feelings that can then be reproduced during physical practice.

A final mistake that coaches can make is to conduct group sessions in which athletes watch video of their teammates. Though there can be some value in watching other athletes perform (e.g., peer modeling, learning from others' successes and errors), repeated viewing of other athletes can contaminate the images and feelings of the observing athlete as they attempt to internalize proper execution.

Rules of Video Watching

Consultants can help both coaches and athletes to use their video sessions to their maximum benefit. In addition to educating them about the common mistakes that they may be making, consultants can also introduce a few basic guidelines to allow coaches and athletes to get the most out of their video viewing.

Coaches and athletes can get bogged down in "thinking" too much about their video performances (i.e., analyzing, critiquing, judging). At the same time, after athletes have gained an understanding of their mistakes and how to correct them, coaches can encourage them to widen their focus and incorporate the corrections into the technical and tactical images and feelings they want to experience in their sport. In other words, athletes can allow the images from the videos to flow into their minds without unnecessary thought and into their bodies where the visual and kinesthetic information most needs to reside.

For many coaches, a primary purpose of video is to identify and correct mistakes and there is value in that. At the same time, as mentioned above, too much imagery of athletes' mistakes can actually cause them to ingrain those negative images. As a result, it is recommended that coaches ensure that their athletes watching at least 75 percent "highlight" videos of successful performances and to intermix the corrective and ideal performances to further support the blending of the corrective images into successful images. Coaches can use video in this more productive way when doing video analysis for error correction, initial technical or tactical development, inclusion of new technique and tactics into broader sports execution, fine tuning of specific skills, and overall practice and competitive performances.

Video as Mental Training

Video can have a significant impact on athletes beyond their sport skill development. In fact, video can offer benefits to athletes in their mental training as well. Consultants can show coaches how to leverage video feedback to strengthen their athletes' mental muscles and develop the tools in their mental toolboxes (see Chapters 3 and 4).

Motivation

Video can be a useful means for coaches to inspire and motivate their athletes. Several video strategies can bolster motivation in athletes. One of the most motivating aspects of sports occurs when athletes gain an understanding of why they are struggling with poor performance. Video enables coaches to provide clear feedback about what athletes need to do to improve. This knowledge provides a sense of control, hope, confidence, and determination, all of which will motivate athletes to continue to pursue their goals with vigor (O'Donoghue, 2006).

Athlete motivation is also bolstered by seeing the clear and unambiguous evidence that they are improving. Video enables coaches to show athletes directly of progress they are making in their sports effort which will buttress their ongoing efforts.

Additionally, motivation is rewarded when athletes demonstrate successful performances, whether acquisition of a new skill or an excellent result in a competition. Again, video offers athletes incontrovertible evidence of their successes, thus encouraging them to continue to work hard in their efforts.

Confidence

Another way in which video can be a valuable mental tool is for coaches to use it to boost their athletes' confidence. When coaches focus the preponderance of their attention on videos of successful performances rather than on mistakes, they are giving their athletes objective evidence of their capabilities. These clear successes further reinforce athletes' beliefs in their competence and their ability to achieve their sports goals.

Focus

As discussed in Chapter 3, the ability to focus effectively over the duration of a sports performance is essential for success. Video can offer several ways in which athletes can improve their focus in practice and competitions. First, coaches can point out times during a videoed performance in which athletes become distracted; for example, by a bad call or a competitive setback. Coaches can use these videoed situations with their athletes as teachable moments about the importance of maintaining or regaining focus. Second, coaches can also highlight and, in doing so, reinforce sustained focus or the effective reestablishment of focus during a videoed performance. Third, the simple act of watching a video without distraction strengthens athletes' focus "muscle" which will then help them focus when they are performing in their sport.

Mental Imagery

One thing that coaches don't often realize is that video is an external form of mental imagery. The power of video can be augmented by incorporating mental imagery into coaches' video sessions with their athletes. Consultants can offer the following suggestions for how coaches can make imagery a part of their video analyses:

- Coaches can have their athletes watch a performance of themselves on video.
- They can then identify what the athletes did well, what mistakes they made, and how to correct it.
- Then, instead of simply asking athletes if they understand, coaches can have them immediately close their eyes and see and feel themselves performing while incorporating the correction into their imagery.

Combining video and imagery strengthens the value of video by helping athletes translate those external images into internally generated images and feelings. Just like when athletes do mental imagery, watching video can help them to produce psychological and physiological states (e.g., increased confidence, elevated intensity, narrowed focus) that allow them to reenact their practice and competitive experiences. In this way, they can better understand what their ideal performance states are and then use that information to replicate those states in their mental imagery and actual sports experiences.

Video and Critical Moments

The ultimate test of athlete development is their ability to successfully execute in their sport physically, technically, tactically, and mentally when it matters most. These "critical moments" can include:

- important competitions;
- key competitive situations;
- high-pressure scenarios;
- when successful execution of technique or tactics is vital;
- during shifts in momentum;
- when behind;
- when holding a small lead; and
- when time is running out.

These critical moments demonstrate how well athletes have learned what they need to learn, to what degree those skills are being executed in the context of an overall performance, and how far they are in their progress toward their goals. Coaches can use video of these critical moments, whether successful or not, to highlight improvement, point out areas in need of continued work, or exceptional execution. In turn, athletes can share with their coaches their own insights into what went well and what didn't, and why the performance turned out as it did. This dialogue provides both coaches and athletes with useful information to guide their practice planning and programs that will lead to consistently successful performances in those critical moments.

Summary

- The use of video as a tool for athlete development is well entrenched in some sports, but, with new technology evolving rapidly and new platforms becoming more accessible in terms of cost and usability, coaches at every level of sport will have the ability to leverage video as a valuable means of helping athletes improve many aspects of their sports performances.
- The use of video in any setting is rooted in its ability to provide objective feedback on a wide range of physical, biomechanical, technical, tactical, team, and even psychological parameters.
- The effectiveness of video has been used as positive self-review and feedforward both outside of and within sports.
- Positive self-review can be used by athletes to identify replicate effective technique and tactics, well-coordinated team efforts, and psychological and emotional practices that facilitate successful performances.
- Video can play a corrective role in which athletes can view errors in their efforts and use that information to make beneficial corrections.
- Feedforward involves piecing together videos of basic skills that, once put together in the proper order, show individuals completing a skill they have not yet attempted or successfully executed.
- Research indicated that, by viewing video of their own performances, athletes were more likely and better able to understand and imagine the correct execution of skills.
- Coaches can consider how best to present the video, which video to present (e.g., practice vs. competition), to whom they would present the video (e.g., individually vs. team), and what the targeted purpose is (e.g., skill acquisition, team performance, confidence building).
- The effective use of video begins with establishing clear performance goals and indicators.
- Without clear goals, coaches can get bogged down in a morass of feedback to their athletes and athletes can feel overwhelmed by all of the things to watch, evaluate, and work in a practice or competitive video.
- A common mistake coaches make in using video is to focus too much on their athletes' errors and on the details of videoed performances.
- Coaches can increase the value of video by focusing on successful performances and to absorb the overall videoed performances.
- Video can strengthen mental muscles including motivation, confidence, and focus, and mental tools such as mental imagery.
- Video review of "critical moments" in competitions can provide teachable moments of both successful and error-ridden efforts.

References

Boyer, E., Miltenberger, R. G., Batsche, C., & Fogel, V. (2009). Video modeling by experts with video feedback to enhance gymnastics skills. *Journal of Applied Behavior Analysis, 42*(4), 855–860.

Dowrick, P. W. (1991). *Practical guide to using video in the behavioral sciences.* Oxford: Wiley.

Dowrick, P. W. (1999). A review of self modeling and related interventions. *Applied & Preventive Psychology, 8,* 23–29.

Groom, R., & Cushion, C. (2004). Coaches perceptions of the use of video analysis: A case study. *Insight, 7*(3).

Groom, R., Cushion, C., & Nelson, L. (2011). The delivery of video-based performance analysis by England youth soccer coaches: Towards a grounded theory. *Journal of Applied Sport Psychology, 23,* 16–32.

Harle, S. K., & Vickers, J. N. (2001). Training quick eye improves accuracy in the basketball free throw. *The Sport Psychologist, 15,* 289–305.

Hazen, A., Johnstone, C., Martin, G. L., & Srikameswaran (1990). A videotaping feedback package for improving skills of youth competitive swimmers. *The Sport Psychologist, 4,* 213–227.

Hughes, M. D., & Bartlett, R. M. (2004). The use of performance indicators in performance analysis. In M. Hughes & I. M. Franks (Eds.), *Notational analysis of sport: Systems for better coaching and performance in sport,* 2nd ed. London: Routledge.

Hughes, M., & Franks, I. M. (2004). *Notational analysis of sport: Systems for better coaching and performance in sport,* 2nd ed. London: Routledge.

Ives, J. C., Straub, W. F., & Shelley, G. A. (2002). Enhancing athletic performance using digital video in consulting. *Journal of Applied Sport Psychology, 14*(3), 237–245.

Liebermann, D. G., & Franks, I. M. (2004). The use of feedback-based technology. In M. Hughes & I. M. Franks (Eds.), *Notational analysis of sport: Systems for better coaching and performance in sport,* 2nd ed. London: Routledge.

Lyle, J. (2002). *Sports coaching concepts : a framework for coaches' behaviour.* London: Routledge.

McGinnis, P. M. (2000). Video technology for coaches. *Track Coach, 152*(Summer), 4857–4862.

Nelson, L. J., Potrac, P., & Groom, R. (2014). Receiving video-based feedback in elite ice-hockey: a player's perspective. *Sport, Education and Society, 19*(1), 19–40.

O'Donoghue, P. (2006). The use of feedback videos in sport. *International Journal of Performance Analysis in Sport, 6*(2), 1–14.

Rickli, R., & Smith, G. (1980). Videotape feedback effects on tennis serving form. *Perceptual and Motor Skills, 50*(3), 895–901.

Rymal, A. M., Martini, R., & Ste-Marie, D. M. (2010). Self-regulatory processes employed during self-modeling: A qualitative analysis. *The Sport Psychologist, 24*(1), 1–15.

Ste-Marie, D. M., Vertes, K., Rymal, A. M., & Martini, R. (2011). Feedforward self-modeling enhances skill acquisition in children learning trampoline skills. *Frontiers in Psychology, 2*, 155.

COACH STRESS

Stiliani "Ani" Chroni

Coaching athletes and teams is complex and demanding. Coaches at many levels and in many sports can feel tremendous pressure to be successful in a job that is on the line too often. Coaching is a profession that can appear inherently insecure because it is usually an easier calculus to fire coaches than athletes (Fletcher & Scott, 2010) and this instability and uncertainty can be a cause of stress. Coaches experience a wide range of stressors as the multidimensional demands of their jobs expose them to organizational, performance, and personal stressors. For coaches to remain healthy, motivated, effective, and happy, these stressors must be recognized and addressed in a timely manner.

When coaches enter their profession, few know that their lives will be stressful. For instance, some elite athletes who transit to coaching right after retirement are not prepared for how demanding coaching is (Chroni, Pettersen, & Dieffenbach, in press). Most coaches choose coaching for the love of the sport, the desire to invest in their sport and athlete growth, or the desire to achieve. As they gain experience, they learn to normalize the work load and the pressures that go with the job (see Chroni, Abrahamsen, & Hemmestad, 2016). Regardless of why they start coaching or how prepared they are, if the stress that coaches feel is significant and persistent, it takes a toll on them, both on and off the field of play, and can create substantial strain on their well-being, motivation, life and work satisfaction, physical and mental health, and may lead to burnout and as well as the desire to leave coaching altogether (Kelley, 1994; Olusoga, Butt, Maynard, & Hays, 2010; Rosenberg, 2013). Addressing stress both proactively and reactively is essential because research (e.g., Frey, 2007; Lastella et al., 2017; Olusoga et al., 2010) has shown that the effectiveness of coaches in their multiple roles can be hindered by stress in many ways including:

- focus and decision-making;
- leadership;
- ability to maintain healthy relationships with athletes, other coaches, administrators, parents, and other stakeholders;
- managing the logistics of running a sports organization; and
- damage to their lives away from the sport.

Moreover, unhealthy or unmanaged stress also impacts those with whom coaches interact, most noticeably, it is perceived by the athletes and can influence both the athlete-coach relationship as well as the athletes' performances (Thelwell, Wagstaff, Chapman, & Kenttä, 2017; Thelwell, Wagstaff, Rayner et al., 2017).

Theory and Research

Stress is considered here as "an ongoing process that involves individuals transacting with their environments, making appraisals of the situations they find themselves in, and endeavoring to cope with any issues that may arise" (Fletcher, Hanton, & Mellalieu, 2008, p. 329). Research on coach stress is limited compared to that on athlete stress (Norris, Didymus, & Kaiseler, 2017; Olusoga, Butt, Hays, & Maynard, 2009). This research has been informed by different theories and models of stress:

- Transactional Stress Theory (TST; Lazarus & Folkman, 1987): Stress is a systematic reciprocal process between the person and the environment appraised by the person.
- Cognitive–Motivational–Relational Model (CMRT, Lazarus, 1999): Emphasizes the role of emotions in the person-environment stress transactions.
- Meta-Model of Stress (MMS; Fletcher, Hanton, & Mellalieu, 2006): Focuses on the relationships between stressors, perceptions, appraisals, and coping, together with subsequent responses (positive or negative), feeling states, and outcomes which are influenced by "various personal and situational characteristics.
- Cognitive Activation Theory of Stress (CATS; Ursin & Eriksen, 2004): Knowing the type of stressor is less important than knowing whether the person believes that he or she can deal with it.

Understanding these models gives consultants explicit areas where they can intervene when working with stressed coaches.

Additionally, considering that a great deal of our understanding of coach stress comes from research exploring coach burnout, with stress acting as a mediator of burnout, the Cognitive-Affective Model of Stress and Burnout (CAMSB; Smith, 1986) and Kelley's Model of Coach Stress and Burnout (MCSB; Kelley, 1994; Kelley, Eklund, & Ritter-Taylor, 1999; Kelley & Gill, 1993) can also inform consultants' understanding of coach stress. In Smith's CAMSB work, personality variables affect burnout indirectly through the cognitive appraisal of stress. In demanding occasions, individuals consider their sport participation's benefits and costs and compare these with expectations they hold for the activity as well as with how attractive alternative activities are. Stress occurs when a person experiences an imbalance between the demands of the activity, and their own coping resources and perceives the demands as threatening. As such, perception is critical to whether a stressful experience is regarded negatively which also presents an area in which consultants can intervene by modifying coaches' perceptions of the stress. If the stress is frequent and prolonged, burnout might result. Kelley et al.'s (1999) model takes the role of personality variables identified by Smith a step further by acknowledging that personal and situational variables can also have a direct impact on burnout.

Early research (e.g., Kroll & Gundersheim, 1982; Sullivan & Nasham, 1993; Taylor, 1992) identified a number of factors that cause or mediate stress among coaches:

- role ambiguity;
- role conflict;
- pressure to win;
- lack free-time;
- work overload;
- low pay;
- conflict with athletes, parents, and fans;
- player recruitment;
- time away from family; and
- dealing with media.

The majority of these early studies were quantitative in nature. However, in the last decade, there has been a shift toward qualitative research that has supported and enriched the previous findings and our understanding of coach stress.

Frey (2007) was one of the first researchers to explore coach stress among American collegiate coaches employing a qualitative approach. Frey identified multiple sources of stress, such as lack of control over athletes and communication with them, recruiting, and the perceived excessive pressure from their many responsibilities and roles. In her work, she also looked into coaches' responses to stress which were perceived either as negative (e.g., problems on focusing, tension, change on body language, etc.) or positive in nature (e.g., increase awareness, better future preparation, motivation, etc.). To cope with stressors, the collegiate coaches:

- focused on factors within their control, such as the training process rather than the outcome of the competition (problem-focused coping strategies);
- relied on social support, sport psychologists' aid and visualization (emotional-focusing strategies); and
- used behavioral strategies including exercise, reading, and massaging.

For some, but not all, as coaches gained experience, their experience of stress diminished. Since Frey's work, a number of studies have been conducted, mostly focused on looking at the stress experiences of elite coaches in a number of sports (Potts, Didymus, & Kaiseler, 2018). This more recent research (Chroni et al., 2016; Chroni, Diakaki, Perkos, Hassandra, & Schoen, 2013; Didymus, 2017; Frey, 2007; Knight, Reade, Selzler, & Rodgers, 2013; Olusoga et al., 2009; 2010; Potts et al., 2018) has revealed other common causes of stress among coaches. Adding both depth and nuance to the quantitative research described above, the portrait that these findings paint is one of coaches having too many roles and responsibilities and too few resources to manage them effectively and for an extended period in timely manner:

- lack of control over athletes;
- communication difficulties with athletes;
- team selection;
- athlete health;
- athlete and team performance;
- competitive preparation and performance;
- coaches' own performances;
- team organization and administration;
- coaching lifestyle;
- team culture;
- ambiguous and unclear expectations and evaluation criteria;
- isolation and loneliness and isolation; and
- lack of social support.

As Norris et al. (2017) summarized in a recent systematic review, coaches experience an excess of stressors related to their own performances, athlete and team performances, intrapersonal, interpersonal, organizational, and contextual forces, many of which are outside of their control. The sheer number and diversity of these stressors reflect the complex and intersecting nature of coach stress. And the price coaches often pay should act as additional impetus for researchers to further study this phenomenon and for consultants to find ways to mitigate the persistent presence of stress that negatively impacts coaches at every level of their professional and personal lives.

Practical Implications

How coaches cope with these stressors is an equally complex phenomenon. In response to the diverse array of stressors that coaches experience, they employ an equally varied coping toolbox that serves different needs, goals, and functions including strategies that focus on appraisal, emotions, problem solving, avoidance, and approach (Norris et al., 2017). Overall, coping methods that are problem-focused, emotion-focused, and involve social support are the means of coping used most by coaches (see Didymus, 2017; Durand-Bush, Collins, & McNeill, 2012; Frey, 2007; Olusoga et al., 2009, 2010; Thelwell, Weston, & Greenlees, 2010). A vital role that consultants can play is to work with coaches to incorporate these strategies into both prevention and intervention of stress. To make traditional coping classifications more understandable and useable, Didymus (2017) suggested taking advantage of the 12 categories of stress coping offered by Skinner, Edge, Altmann, and Sherwood (2003; p. 245) and adding some additional categories:

- problem solving (find solutions to stress);
- information seeking (gain additional knowledge);
- helplessness (find limits of actions);
- escape (avoid stressful environments);
- self-reliance (relieve stress on their own);
- support seeking (use available social resources);
- delegation (find limits of resources);
- isolation (withdraw from unsupportive context);
- accommodation (flexibly adjust preferences to options);

- negotiation (find new options);
- role changes (alter their responsibilities);
- submission (give up preferences);
- negotiation (attempt to lessen stress through compromise);
- support seeking (actively pursue support);
- dyadic coping (collaborating with others); and
- opposition (resist stress).

Each of these general approaches to coping with stress can be leveraged by consultants to help coaches as they confront the inevitable stressors in their profession. Which ones that are selected depend on an examination of the interaction of coach, stressor, resources, and context.

Prior to discussing the specific practical strategies that consultants can draw the current research on coach stress and coping, it is worth considering how consultants can effectively introduce them to coaches. Coaches, as a general observation, are not always open to being coached by anyone who approaches them, even with best of intentions. When it comes to enhancing coaching practices, recent literature suggests that the feedback mechanisms coaches use are few and many are informal such as peer or athlete networks and other support systems (Nash, Sproule, & Horton, 2017). It is helpful if consultants are already a part of coaches' existing network; for example, they have a long-standing working relationship or on staff with the organization that employs the coaches. In the absence of a direct connection with coaches, indirect contact may be helpful in "getting inside the door" in the form of professional development courses, communities of practice, mentors, and successful colleagues successful colleagues, mentors, conferences, professional development courses, and online resources (Bertram, Culver, & Gilbert, 2016; Knowles, Borrie, & Telfer, 2005; McQuade & Nash, 2015; Nash, 2004). Ideally, coaches come to consultants willingly because they recognize that they have a problem with stress. Alternatively, valued members of coaches' networks can stage an "intervention" in which coaches are confronted with their struggles, the impact of their stress on others in the professional and personal lives, and encouraged to seek out support from a trusted consultant.

General Approaches to Coach Stress Coping

Before consultants use specific strategies with coaches to prevent or reduce their stress, there are several general approaches to stress coping that have been found to be effective. These methods involve broad ways of thinking and evaluating stress as a means of mitigating it. For example, one study by Chroni et al. (2016) explored the ways in which successful Norwegian national team coaches appraised stressors as challenges rather than threats. Their findings indicated that coping can be facilitated with three preventive steps.

Flexible Mindset

Coaches with a flexible mindset, as compared to a fixed mindset, were better able to handle the pressures and adversity (Chroni et al., 2016) that could lead to unmanageable stress. According to Dweck (2007), individuals with a flexible mindset endorse the belief that basic qualities can be cultivated through effort, which equips them with abundant desire to learn, tendency to embrace challenges, to persist in the face of setbacks, to see effort as the way to mastery, to learn from criticism, and to find lessons and inspiration in the success of others. Those with a fixed mindset believe that basic qualities of the person are rigid, thus see little room for change and growth. Based on the work of Dweck (2007), this finding suggests that when coaches have a flexible mindset, they:

- freely recognize and take ownership of their struggles with stress;
- see challenges instead of threats;
- are willing to seek help;
- are open to feedback;
- can adapt their perspectives and attitudes in a healthier direction; and
- are able to implement selected stress coping strategies.

Consultants can encourage a more flexible mindset by showing coaches the impact it will have their stress, the relief it can provide, and the positive influence it can have on their professional and personal lives.

Preparation

The research by Chroni et al. (2016) also demonstrated the value of preparation as a means of preventing stress. When coaches are prepared for the many challenges they face, familiarity, predictability, and control are enhanced, all essential perceptions for reducing stress. Consultants can assist coaches in several ways to maximize how prepared they are:

- Identify the numerous responsibilities coaches have and, in doing so, break down what seems overwhelming to more manageable chunks.
- Prioritize and re-prioritize their responsibilities and take those of low importance "off their plates."
- Increase their resources by seeking out support and delegating responsibilities, thus reducing the load they carry.
- Organize and fulfill those responsibilities as completely and as efficiently as possible.
- Identify and prepare for unexpected occurrences.

Reflection

Coaches can learn to recognize and respond more effectively to stress through the practice of reflection, both self-reflection and reflection through others (Chroni et al., 2016). Self-reflection refers to considering experiences, appraisals, decisions, and actions as a means of increasing awareness and fostering greater understanding of how those experiences impact lives (Anderson, Knowles, & Gilbourne, 2004; Knowles et al., 2005). Self-reflection is discussed in the coaching literature as a highly beneficial tool for coach education, development, and success (Côté & Gilbert, 2009; Nash et al., 2017). Consultants can guide the coaches in the practice of self-reflection of their stressors, and their reactions to them, as a tool for gaining insights into the stressors with the goal of either removing or reducing their impact on them in the future.

Consultants can help coaches to develop a process of systematic self-reflection by using, for example, Whitehead and colleagues' Think Aloud framework (2015, 2016), a stepwise technique that facilitates reflection-in-action and delayed reflection-on-action or Gibbs (1988) six-stage reflective cycle:

1. **Description:** Depict the stressful situation in detail.
2. **Feelings:** Express the emotions associated with the stressor.
3. **Evaluation:** Objectively assess what approaches to the stressor may work and which ones may not.
4. **Analysis:** Identify the key issues.
5. **Conclusions:** Draw inferences from the self-reflection to determine options for future action.
6. **Action:** Choose the best course of action, make a plan, and commit to taking action.

These three general approaches of flexible mindset, preparation, and reflection coalesce to have a significant impact on coaches' confidence in themselves and their perceptions of their ability to effectively cope with their stress (Chroni et al., 2016). This confidence develops through self-awareness and deliberate action (both a by-product of self-reflection) which leads to improved stress appraisal when the same or similar stressor are re-encountered as well as more effective coping. For instance, consultants can guide coaches in the practice of self-reflection of their coping practices, as a tool for gaining insight into their strengths with the goal of repeating the coping practice in the future and enhancing their confidence in dealing with stressors. The more confident coaches are, the less stress they will experience and the more capable they will be to cope effectively with the stress they do experience. This chain of events can then be revisited, reinforced, and reused repeatedly to create a virtuous cycle of learning, increasing confidence and competence related to coping with stress.

In addition to the benefits of self-reflection, coaches can also gain value from the reflections of other coaches who are either role models or peers. Because all coaches "play" fundamentally the same game, peers bring a level of credibility, practical knowledge, and experience that consultants don't often have. Observing or listening to how other coaches cope with stress acts as a mirror for their own struggles with stress and also provides lessons and tools that will expand the stressed coaches' coping repertoires. Moreover, not only does this practice offer practical coping strategies, it also offers coaches mutually beneficial support that has been found to be one of the most effective means of relieving stress (see Crocker, 1992; Cutrona, & Russell, 1990; Rees & Hardy, 2000). Consultants can facilitate these learning opportunities by organizing communities of practice, coaches' workshops, mentorship programs, peer groups, and "shadowing" opportunities in which early-career coaches follow and observe veteran coaches in real time in real coaching settings (see Bertram et al., 2016; Garner & Hill, 2017).

Organizational Influences

Coaches rarely work alone or in a vacuum; rather, they are usually a part of an organization, whether a sports club, collegiate program, or national or professional team. Given coaches' place in a larger and more complex organizational structure, it is reasonable to assume that much of the stress they experience arises out of tension that occurs in their roles and responsibilities within the sports organization. Power struggles among team personnel, undefined or conflicting roles, rigid hierarchy, and job uncertainty are often associated with a stress-filled organizational culture. As such, consultants who work in a sport organization must pay close attention to its culture and its impact on stress among its stakeholders.

Research has shown that the absence of hierarchy, clear roles and responsibilities, and a development-, rather than an outcome-oriented, organizational culture were key assets for Norwegian national teams in supporting and nurturing the coaches' work experiences (Chroni et al., 2016, Chroni, Abrahamsen, Skille, & Hemmestad, 2019; Skille & Chroni, 2018). Norwegian coaches spoke of their federations as being actively supportive, helping them to improve in the job, while giving them the opportunity to develop athletes over time.

The research has also found that giving coaches job security and continuity, opportunities to grow in their roles while providing them with time to develop themselves as well as their athletes, the necessary resources (human, logistical, and financial) to be successful in their jobs, and support for reflection and detailed planning are associated with job satisfaction, performance, and effective stress coping. Skille and Chroni (2018) concluded that a healthy organizational culture can empower coaches to appraise stressors as less threatening and to learn from them to produce better coping in the future. Consultants can work with sports organizations to (Chroni et al., 2019):

- Consciously and proactively develop cultures that nurture the healthy development of its coaches and athletes.
- Support coaches by, for example, acting as buffers against stressors such as fans and the media.
- Build strong and supportive relationships with its coaches.
- Establish open lines of communication between coaches and other organizational stakeholders.
- Encourage healthy work-life balance.

Specific Strategies for Coach Stress Coping

In addition to the broad approaches to coach stress coping that were described above as a means of preventing or mitigating stress, there are specific and active steps that coaches can take, including:

- accepting adversity, pressures, and stressors as an inevitable aspect of coaching (and life) that can be out of coaches' control;
- identifying coaches' most common stressors;
- recognizing when and where stressors are not dealt with and stress occurs; and
- shifting focus away from the stressor and onto finding solutions for the stress.

Moreover, coaches can consider four paths in addressing their stress in four ways. First, they can relieve the cause of the stress (e.g., eliminate or minimize stressors by delegating responsibility, preparing differently or re-evaluating what's at stake). Second, coaches can alter their perceptions of a stressor (e.g., learn to see the benefits than can be gained rather what can be lost, see an important upcoming game as a challenge rather than a threat). Third, coaches can treat the symptoms of the stress (e.g., meditation, biofeedback, exercise, music, reading, family time, get more sleep). Lastly, they can add a variety of general (e.g., manage time and energy, have healthy outlets, build a social support network), physical (e.g., breathing, muscle relaxation, yoga), and mental (e.g., positive thinking, mindfulness, imagery) tools to their stress toolboxes that can be useful in effectively addressing their stress.

Because a section of Chapter 7 already explores stress in depth and coach stress isn't fundamentally different than athlete stress, it would be redundant to examine stress in detail here. Readers are encouraged to revisit the "Stress" section of Chapter 7 through the lens of coaches and apply its ideas and methods to the specific demands of coach stress and coping.

Summary

- Coaches experience a wide range of stressors as the multidimensional job demands expose them to stressors associated with organizational, performance, interpersonal, intrapersonal, and contextual matters.
- The stress that coaches feel is significant and persistent, its toll on them both on and off the field of play can create substantial strain on their well-being, their motivation, life and work satisfaction, physical and mental health, and may lead to burnout and the need to leave coaching altogether.
- Addressing stress proactively and reactively is essential because the effectiveness of coaches in their multiple roles can be hindered by stress in many ways, including their focus and decision-making, leadership, ability to maintain healthy relationships with athletes, other coaches, administrators, parents, and other stakeholders, managing the logistics of running a sports organization, not to mention hurting their lives away from the sport.
- Research has identified a number of factors that cause or mediate stress among coaches: lack of control over athletes, communication with athletes, team selection, athlete health, competition and preparation for it, athlete, team, and own performance, team organization and administration, coaching lifestyle, team culture, unclear expectations and evaluation criteria, job insecurity, loneliness, and lack of social support.
- In response to the diverse array of stressors that coaches experience, they employ an equally varied coping toolbox that serves different needs, goals, and functions including strategies that focus on appraisal, emotions, problem solving, avoidance, and approach.
- A vital role that consultants can play is to work with coaches to incorporate effective approaches and strategies into both prevention and intervention of stress.
- General approaches that consultants can introduce to coaches include having a flexible mindset, being prepared, engaging in reflection, and addressing organizational causes of stress.
- Consultants can show coaches how to implement the many approaches and strategies detailed in the "Stress" section of Chapter 7.

References

Anderson, A., Knowles, Z., & Gilbourne, D. (2004) Reflective practice for applied sport psychologists: A review of concepts, models, practical implications and thoughts on dissemination, *The Sport Psychologist*, *18*, 188–201.

Bertram, R., Culver, D., & Gilbert, W. (2016). Creating value in a sport coach community of practice: A collaborative inquiry. *International Sport Coaching Journal*, *3*, 2–16. doi: 10.1123/iscj.2014-0122

Chroni, S., Abrahamsen, F., & Hemmestad, L. (2016). To be the eye within the storm, I am challenged not stressed. *Journal of Applied Sport Psychology*, *28*, 257–273. doi: 10.1080/10413200.2015.1113449

Chroni, S., Abrahamsen, F., Skille, E. Å., & Hemmestad, L. (2019). Sport federation officials' practices and national team coaches' stress. *International Sport Coaching Journal*. Manuscript submitted for publication.

Chroni, S., Diakaki, E., Perkos, S., Hassandra, M., & Schoen, C. (2013). What stresses coaches in competition and training? An exploratory inquiry. *International Journal of Coaching Science*, *7*, 25–39.

Chroni, S., Pettersen, S., & Dieffenbach, K. (in press). From athlete-to-coach: Understanding the transition beyond the change of title. *Sport in Society*.

Côté, J., & Gilbert, W. (2009). An integrative definition of coaching effectiveness and expertise. *International Journal of Sports Science & Coaching*, *4*(3), 307–323. doi: 10.1260/174795409789623892

Crocker, P. R. E. (1992). Managing stress by competitive athletes: Ways of coping. *International Journal of Sport Psychology*, *23*, 161–175.

Cutrona, C. E., & Russell, D. W. (1990). Type of social support and specific stress: Toward a theory of optimal matching. In B. R. Sarason, I. G. Sarason & G. R. Pierce (Eds.), *Social support: An interactional view* (pp. 319–366). New York, NY: Wiley.

Didymus, F. F. (2017). Olympic and international level sports coaches' experiences of stressors, appraisals, and coping. *Qualitative Research in Sport, Exercise and Health, 9*, 214–232. doi: 10.1080/2159676X.2016.1261364

Durand-Bush, N., Collins, J., & McNeill, K. (2012). Women coaches' experiences of stress and self-regulation: A multiple case study. *International Journal of Coaching Science, 6*(2), 21–43.

Dweck, C. S. (2007). *Mindset: The New Psychology of Success.* New York, NY: Random House Ballantine.

Fletcher, D., Hanton, S., & Mellalieu, S. D. (2006). An organizational stress review: Conceptual and theoretical issues in competitive sport. In S. Hanton & S. D. Mellalieu (Eds.), *Literature reviews in sport psychology,* 1st ed. (pp. 321–374). New York, NY: Nova Science Publishers.

Fletcher, D., Hanton, S., & Mellalieu, S. D. (2008). *An organizational stress review: Conceptual and theoretical issues in competitive sport.* New York, NY: Nova Science Publishers.

Fletcher, D. & Scott, M. (2010). Psychological stress in sports coaches: A review of concepts, research, and practice. *Journal of Sport Sciences, 28*(2), 127–137.

Frey, M. (2007). College coaches' experiences with stress: "problem solvers" have problems, too. *The Sport Psychologist, 21*(1), 38–57.

Garner P., & Hill, D. M. (2017). Cultivating a community of practice to enable coach development in Alpine ski coaches. *International Sport Coaching Journal, 4*(1), 63–75

Gibbs, G. (1988). *Learning by doing: A guide to teaching and learning methods.* Oxford: Oxford Brookes University, Further Education Unit.

Kelley, B. C. (1994). A model of stress and burnout in collegiate coaches: Effects of gender and time of season. *Research Quarterly for Exercise and Sport, 65*, 48–58. doi: 10.1080/02701367.1994.10762207.

Kelley, B. C., Eklund, R. C., & Ritter-Taylor, M. (1999). Stress and burnout among collegiate tennis coaches. *Journal of Sport and Exercise Psychology, 21*, 113–130.

Kelley, B. C., & Gill, D. L. (1993). An examination of personal/situational variables, stress appraisal, and burnout in collegiate teacher-coaches. *Research Quarterly for Exercise and Sport, 64*, 94–102.

Knight, C. J., Reade, I. L., Selzler, A. M., & Rodgers, W. M. (2013). Personal and situational factors influencing coaches' perceptions of stress. *Journal of Sports Sciences, 31*, 1054–1063. doi: 10.1080/02640414.2012.759659

Knowles, Z., Borrie, A., & Telfer, H. (2005). Towards the reflective sports coach: Issues of context, education and application. *Ergonomics, 48*, 11–14, 1711–1720. doi: 10.1080/00140130500101288

Kroll, W., & Gundersheim, J. (1982). Stress factors in coaching. *Coaching Science Update, 23*, 47–49.

Lastella, M., Roach, G. D., Halson, S. L. Gore, C. J., Garvican-Lewis, L. A., & Sargnt, C. (2017). Sleep at a helm: A case study of how a head coach sleeps compared to his team. *International Journal of Sports Science & Coaching, 12*(6), 782–789. doi: 10.1177/1747954117738882

Lazarus, R. S. (1999). *Stress and emotion: A new synthesis.* New York, NY: Springer.

Lazarus, R. S., & Folkman, S. (1987). Transactional theory and research on emotions and coping. *European Journal of Personality, 1*, 141–169. doi: 10.1002/per.2410010304.

McQuade, S., & Nash, C. (2015). The role of coach developer in supporting and guiding coach learning. *International Sport Coaching Journal, 2*, 339–346. doi: http://dx.doi.org/10.1123/iscj.2015-0059

Nash, C. (2004). Development of a mentoring system within coaching practice. *Journal of Hospitality, Leisure, Sport and Tourism Education, 2*, 36–47. doi: 10.3794/johlste.22.37

Nash, C., Sproule, J., & Horton, P. (2017). Feedback for coaches: Who coaches the coach? *International Journal for Sports Science & Coaching, 12*, 92–102. doi: 10.1177/1747954116684390

Norris, L. A., Didymus F. F., & Kaiseler, M. (2017). Stressors, coping, and well-being among sports coaches: A systematic review. *Psychology of Sport and Exercise, 33*, 93–112. doi: 10.1016/j.psychsport.2017.08.005

Olusoga, P., Butt, J., Hays, K. & Maynard, I. (2009). Stress in elite sport coaching: Identifying stressors. *Journal of Applied Sport Psychology, 21*, 442–459. doi: 10.1080/10413200903222921

Olusoga, P., Butt, J., Maynard, I., & Hays, K. (2010). Stress and coping: A study of world class coaches. *Journal of Applied Sport Psychology, 22*, 274–293. doi: 10.1080/10413201003760968

Potts, A. J., Didymus, F. F., & Kaiseler, M. (2018): Exploring stressors and coping among volunteer, part-time and full-time sports coaches. *Qualitative Research in Sport, Exercise and Health, 11*, 46–68. doi: 10.1080/2159676X.2018.1457562

Rees, T., & Hardy, L. (2000). An examination of the social support experiences of high level sports performers. *The Sport Psychologist, 14*, 327–347.

Rosenberg, M. (2013, November). Pressure, stress make coaching hazardous to your health. *Sports Illustrated Online.* Retrieved from www.si.com/nfl/2013/11/15/coaches-health-stress

Skille, E. Å, & Chroni, S. (2018). Norwegian sports federations' organizational culture and national team success. *International Journal of Sport Policy and Politics, 10*(2), 321–333. doi: 10.1080/19406940.2018.1425733

Skinner, E. A., Edge, K., Altman, J., & Sherwood, H. (2003). Searching for the structure of coping: A review and critique of category systems for classifying ways of coping. *Psychological Bulletin, 129*, 216–269. doi: 10.1037/0033-2909.129.2.216.

Smith, R. E. (1986). Toward a cognitive-affective model of athletic burnout. *Journal of Sport Psychology*, *8*, 35–50.

Sullivan, P. A., & Nasham, H. W. (1993). The 1992 United States Olympic Team sport coaches: Satisfactions and concerns. *Applied Research in Coaching and Athletics Annual*, *1993*, 1–14.

Taylor, J. (1992). Coaches are people too: An applied model of stress management for sport coaches. *Journal of Applied Sport Psychology*, *4*, 27–50.

Thelwell, R. C., Wagstaff, C. R. D., Chapman, M. T., & Kenttä, G. (2017). Examining coaches' perceptions of how their stress influences the coach–athlete relationship. *Journal of Sports Sciences*, *35*, 1928–1939. doi: 10.1080/02640414.2016.1241422

Thelwell, R. C., Wagstaff, C. R. D., Rayner, A., Chapman, M., & Barker, J. (2017). Exploring athletes' perceptions of coach stress in elite sport environments. *Journal of Sports Sciences*, *35*, 44–55. doi: 10.1080/02640414.2016.1154979

Thelwell, R. C., Weston, N. J., & Greenlees, I. A. (2010). Coping with stressors in elite sport: A coach perspective. *European Journal of Sport Science*, *10*, 243–253. doi: 10.1080/17461390903353390.

Ursin, H., & Eriksen, H. R. (2004). The cognitive activation theory of stress. *Psychoneuroendocrinology*, *29*, 567–592. doi:10.1016/S0306-4530(03)00091-X

Whitehead, A., Cropley, B., Huntley, T., Miles, A., Quayle, L., & Knowles, Z. (2016). 'Think aloud': Toward a framework to facilitate reflective practice amongst rugby league coaches. *International Sport Coaching Journal*, *3*(3), 269–286. doi:10.1123/iscj.2016-0021

Whitehead, A. E., Taylor, J. A., & Polman, R. (2015). Examination of the suitability of collecting in event cognitive processes using Think Aloud protocol in golf. *Frontiers in Psychology*, *6*, 1083. doi:10.3389/fpsyg.2015.01083

INTEGRATING MENTAL TRAINING INTO OVERALL ATHLETE DEVELOPMENT

Jim Taylor and Brandon Orr

The legendary New York Yankee and noted malapropist, Yogi Berra, once famously said, "Baseball is 90 percent mental and the other half is physical." This statement clearly lacked logical and mathematical accuracy. At the same time, it does seem to reflect the attitude that most coaches hold about the importance of the mind in athletic performance. However, as the exploration of how consultants can help coaches to integrate mental training into overall athlete development begins, a key question to ask is whether coaches' actions support or belie their beliefs about mental training.

To answer that question, one of this section's authors has conducted an informal decades-long survey in which he asked coaches in many sports and at many levels of sport how important the mind is to athletic success compared to the physical and technical aspects of sport. In sum, few of the coaches surveyed believed that the mental side of sports was less important and the vast majority stated that it was as or more important.

Though consultants can appreciate this powerful affirmation of the value of the mind to sports success, few would argue that it is actually the case. Athletes may have the best prepared minds possible, but if they don't have the requisite physical fitness and technical skills necessary to engage in their sport, they will have little opportunity to experience success. For athletes to perform their best, they must leverage fully the physical, technical, and mental aspects of their sport. Given this conclusion, coaches, athletes, and consultants alike would undoubted agree that the mind is a vital contributor to athletic performance that is also underappreciated and insufficiently used.

How Committed are Coaches to Mental Training?

A second part of the survey just described involved asking coaches how much time they devote to conditioning or sport training their athletes. For coaches who are involved in long-term athlete development, their estimate typically ranged from two to six hours a day. When they are asked how much time is committed to mental training, their answer is usually next to none. Though coaches do mental things with their athletes, for example, they motivate them, build their confidence, help them to focus, and much more, this is not, by definition, mental training any more than a couple of kids kicking a soccer ball around is soccer training. Coaches readily admit that the money, resources, time, and energy they dedicate to mental training pales in comparison to their commitment to the physical and technical aspects of their sport.

Obstacles to Mental Training Acceptance and Adoption

Coaches at every level of the competitive ladder struggle to provide their athletes with mental training that matches the sophistication and quality of their conditioning and sport training. Some programs bring in sport psychologists or mental trainers periodically to fill in this gap, but such an approach lacks the structure and consistency that is needed to have a significant impact on athletes. The absence of complete buy-in of mental training isn't due to coaches' lack of interest, appreciation, or the value it can bring to athletes. Instead, there are a variety of historical, perceptual, and institutional obstacles that have slowed the full adoption of mental training into overall athlete development.

Old Coaching Attitudes

Though sport psychology has been a field of study for more than 100 years, it has not been a traditional part of how coaches train athletes in most sports. Old coaching attitudes, habits, and methods die hard and new approaches to improving athletic performance are not easily accepted. Perhaps it will take a new generation of coaches who have been exposed to mental training as athletes and then in their coaches' education for the tide to turn toward wider acceptance and use of mental training with athletes. Consultants can have a significant impact on this transition by making mental training easy to understand and use by coaches.

No Clear Evidence of Need

The reality is that the best athletes in the world have done well without formal mental training. They simply developed mental capabilities through their own training and competitive experiences. In contrast, there has likely not ever been a successful athlete who didn't have a rigorous conditioning or technical program that they followed (at least not in the last 40 years). As a result, the need for structured mental training may not be perceived as great by coaches. Yet, for every successful athlete who develops mentally on their own, there are many more who are equally talented and motivated to become successful, but need help in developing their mental capabilities. Consultants can show coaches the mental attributes that successful athletes possess and demonstrate how those qualities can be proactively and fully developed in all of their athletes.

Lack of Concreteness

Most aspects of sport are, by their very nature, tangible. Coaches and athletes can readily see the areas in need of improvement physically and technically, for example, amount of weight lifted in the gym or technical problems revealed on video. They can also clearly see improvements in the physical and technical aspects of sports performance. The mental side of sport, however, is not so easily seen, quantified, or measured. It's harder to gauge where athletes are in different aspects of their mental preparation, what areas they need to work on, and any improvement that is made mentally. As a result, the mental side of sport holds a certain unknowable quality and mystery that can be daunting for coaches that makes it harder for them to wrap their arms around. Moreover, they see the mental training as qualitatively different than conditioning and sport training. Because they can't directly see, feel, or measure the mind, it's much less clear how to train the mind. Moreover, far beyond sports, coaches know the difficulty that goes into making changes to the way people think, feel, behave, and perform. It is the responsibility of consultants to educate coaches on how to make the mind more accessible and the show coaches how to train and change the mind.

Guilt by Association

Sport psychology can suffer from "guilt by association" with the broader field of clinical psychology that still carries the stigma that only mentally ill people or those with psychological problems seek professional help. This perception, however inaccurate, can prevent coaches and athletes from seeing mental preparation for what it is, namely, an essential contributor to sports performance that must be developed proactively. This fear can also scare athletes away from getting mental training help when it is needed. This negative association is why the term "mental training" is used in *CASP* instead of sport psychology. Additionally, consultants can help to alter this perception by designing and implementing mental training in much the same way as conditioning and sport training are.

Few Resources to Learn From

The recognition of the importance of mental training is increasing among coaches, but few possess the specific "what" and "how" knowledge to effectively teach this aspect of sports performance to athletes. There is little doubt coaches do what they can to nurture the mental development of their athletes as much as possible. Yet, as any coach knows, gaining knowledge by trial and error isn't an efficient or effective way to learn any sports skills. Coaches certainly wouldn't use this approach with conditioning or sport training. Yet, that is the way most coaches learn about mental training. There are simply few structured means by which they can gain not only clear and understandable information about mental training, but, more importantly, useful and practical tools that they could apply with their athletes. It is the job of consultants to educate coaches about the what and the how of mental training.

No Program to Follow

Compare mental training to physical or technical training. Every organization at every level of sport has clearly defined conditioning protocols and technical progressions they use with their athletes. Moreover, these structures are woven into the fabric of their overall athlete development regimens. Additionally, the internet offers a plethora of conditioning programs that can guide coaches in the creation of effective physical training programs.

Though there is also a wealth of information online about mental training, coaches would be hard pressed to find that information in an organized format that they can put into practice with their athletes. Information is one thing, useable programs are another. One of the most important roles that consultants can play is to provide coaches with a programmatic approach to mental training.

Not an Organizational Priority

Another major obstacle to implementing an effective mental training regimen is that, despite its professed importance, it rarely is a priority in sports programs. Running a sports organization takes energy, time, and money. Moreover, all three are in limited supply. Effective mental training requires a commitment from the leadership to allocate sufficient resources to create and maintain a viable program. Unfortunately, in the real world of limited budgets, teams have to prioritize what they are going to offer their athletes. And, however much coaches will say that mental training is important, it is always the last thing to be considered and the first thing to be dropped. Without organizational support, as expressed in professional development education, money, staffing, and scheduling, it's not surprising that coaches don't integrate it into their overall training with their athletes. To remove this obstacle, consultants have to be a combination of mental training evangelist and salesperson, offering coaches a compelling rationale for and a practical means to invest in mental training.

Time!

Time (or lack thereof) is the single biggest obstacle for coaches in making mental training an integral part of athlete development in sports. Coaches have many responsibilities that include training and competitive planning and scheduling, travel, equipment, athlete management, and dealing with parents, not to mention the actual coaching of the athletes. Consultants can help coaches to find the time and assume some of the responsibilities of mental training with their athletes.

Why Isn't Mental Training Treated the Same as Physical and Technical Training?

This question has been a source of consternation and frustration for every consultant who works with athletes, coaches, and teams. If everyone agrees that the mind is so important, why doesn't it have equal status in sports? Mental training clearly does have a place in most sports. Sport psychologists and mental trainers are employed by professional, Olympic, and collegiate athletes and teams. Many youth sports programs have consultants involved in some capacity as well.

At the same time, in comparison to the staffing, resources, time, and money dedicated to other aspects of sports performance, mental training is certainly not treated with the same level of respect and commitment. It goes without saying that competitive sports programs at every level have full-time coaches for conditioning and sport-specific skills, yet relatively few, even at the highest level of sport, have full-time sport psychologists or mental trainers on staff. Furthermore, when mental training is available to athletes, what is offered is substantially different from the regimented conditioning programs and sport-specific training programs that athletes are accustomed to.

To fully understand why this divergence exists in sports, it will be useful to, first, examine what enables conditioning and sport development to be effective. Then, there will be a discussion of the ways in which consultants can position mental training so that it is perceived and received in the same way by coaches and athletes alike. Five key elements emerge.

Comprehensive

Conditioning and sport training programs address more than a few areas of athletic performance. Instead, they prepare athletes *comprehensively*, meaning they make certain that every aspects of sports performance is fully developed. For example, conditioning regimens train strength, endurance, agility, and mobility. Sport training programs improve body position, skills, movement patterns, and tactics.

Structured

When coaches train their athletes in the gym or out on the practice field, they don't just do a random set of exercises or drills. Rather, they bring a *structured* program that will progressively lead their athletes to the highest level of fitness and skill. In each case, athletes follow a clearly defined path in their sports development and toward their sports goals.

Consistent

Athletes also don't just do conditioning or sport training periodically. What enables athletes to fully develop themselves in their sport is that they train *consistently*. By day, week, month, and year, coaches have their athletes regularly commit time and energy to their conditioning and sport efforts.

Developmentally Appropriate

Coaches provide conditioning and sport training opportunities that are developmentally appropriate, meaning the specific components of the regimens meet the immediate physical and technical needs of their athletes based on age, physical development, technical progress, and competitive level. Mental training must also be offered to athletes in a developmentally appropriate way depending on their psychological, intellectual, and emotional maturity and their current practice and competitive needs. For example, coaches may emphasize basic mental muscles, such as motivation, confidence, and focus (see Chapter 3) with younger athletes while addressing more sophisticated mental areas, including perfectionism, fear of failure, and expectations (see Chapter 2) with older athletes.

Periodized

One of the most important developments in athlete development in the past few decades has been the use of *periodization* in both conditioning and sport training. This concept involves focusing on different aspects of training at different times in the off-season and competitive season. For example, it is common to engage in high-intensity and high-volume conditioning early in the off-season to build a foundation of strength and then shift to lower volume and intensity with more of an emphasis on agility and mobility as the competitive season approaches. Similarly, early in the off-season, the focus is usually on learning or refining fundamental technical and tactical skills and then moving to incorporating those skills into overall sports performance, within a tactical framework and in competitive preparation as the competitive season grows near.

Personalized

The nature of athlete development dictates that most athletes need to follow the same development trajectory in their conditioning, technique, and tactics. At the same time, as they develop, coaches must create *personalized* programs to focus on each athlete's specific needs, goals, and stages of development. This personalized approach ensures that athletes develop as fully and quickly as they are capable of given their current level of long-term development.

As any experienced consultant knows, these six criteria are usually absent in the efforts at mental preparation that coaches offer their athletes. An essential step for consultants in incorporating mental training into coaches' overall development of their athletes is to create a mental training program that is built on the same six criteria that will bring it to the same level of engagement as conditioning and sport training. Consultants can accomplish this task by:

- creating a mental performance framework that provides structure to mental training;
- designing a mental training program with clear organization and process; or
- integrating mental training into practices and competitive preparations.

Goals for Incorporating Mental Training into Overall Athlete Development

To begin the process of making mental training an integral part of the overall athlete development program provided by coaches, consultants can establish a series of tangible goals that that a sports program can accomplish.

- Educate coaches about what it takes mentally for athletes to achieve their sports goals.
- Provide the means to proactively train the mind in a comprehensive, structured, developmentally appropriate, consistent, periodized, and personalized way.
- Incorporate mental training into all aspects of the athlete development program.

Periodized Mental Training

The more mental training can look and feel like conditioning and sport training, the more coaches and athletes will buy into its value. One way to increase this similarity, while also offering athletes a more effective program, is for mental training to be periodized based on the place it is in the preparation and competitive calendar for a sport. As part of the mental performance framework developed by consultants, they can indicate what mental aspects of mental training (e.g., attitudes, obstacles, muscles, and tools; see Chapters 1–4) are most appropriately offered at any given point in the season.

It is the responsibility of consultants to develop periodized mental training plans for the sports programs with whom they work. There is no clearly defined or widely accepted periodization plan for mental training, though Balague (2000) suggests three categories of mental areas that can guide the periodization process: foundational (e.g., motivation, confidence), performance (e.g., focus, intensity), and facilitative (e.g., relaxation, self-talk, imagery). Several pieces of information can be used in making this determination. First, consultants can examine the attitudes, obstacles, mental muscles, and mental tools described in Chapters 1–4 (as well as other mental areas that they deem important), leverage their own professional experiences, and create a progression that makes the most intuitive sense to them.

Second, consultants can look at the requirements of the sport. For instance, is it a sport requiring sustained effort (e.g., running, cycling), highly technical needing intense focus (e.g., golf, archery), or very physical (e.g., football, wrestling)? Additional aspects of the sport that should be a part of the periodized planning process include the nature and duration of performances (e.g., one short performance, a series of short performances, an extended performance), whether it is objective (e.g., time or distance) or subjective (e.g., judged), and whether it is an individual or team sport.

Third, they can consider the demands of the particular phase of the season the athletes or teams are in and consider which mental areas are most appropriate. For example, motivation may be most needed during a period of intense physical conditioning and focus may be most appropriate during a phase of dedicated technical development.

Fourth, consultants can collaborate with the coaches in examining the preparation and competitive calendars to find the best times to incorporate various aspects of mental training into them. For example, during the preparatory phase, imagery could emphasize learning and ingraining new technical skills and establishing competitive routines. As the competitive season approaches, imagery sessions could focus on pre-competitive preparations and overall high-quality performances.

Finally, and importantly, consultants must assess and structure an appropriately periodized regimen of mental training around the needs and goals of the athletes with whom they work. For instance, consultants who work with young athletes early in the preparation phase who lack confidence could focus on positive self-talk and successful imagery. In turn, periodized mental training for elite athletes preparing for an international competition could emphasize competitive planning, performance rehearsal of the important event, and identifying and training ideal attitudes.

Delivery of Mental Training

Because time and personnel are in limited supply in any sports organization, coaches must be cognizant of how mental training will be delivered to their athletes in a way that is both effective and efficient. Thanks to technology, it's now possible to provide mental training in more creative and flexible ways that ever before. Consultants can play a central role in offering mental training in ways that best meet the needs, goals, and schedules of the athletes and teams they work with:

- coaches' education;
- delivered by coaches or consultants in person;
- during practice or away from sport;
- online courses;
- team Skype sessions;
- YouTube videos; and
- 1:1 consultations.

Integrating Mental Training into Overall Athlete Development

The final stage of this process involves working with coaches on ways in which mental training can be put into action and fully integrated into athletes' practice and competitive preparations. This discussion could comprise an entire book, so this section will provide only a framework for doing so rather than offering specific and concrete ideas for every aspect of mental training.

During Practice

A variety of mental muscles (see Chapter 3) can be strengthened by incorporating them into conditioning sessions and sport practices. For example, depending on the nature of what is being worked on, mental muscles can be used in the following ways:

- **Motivation:** Athletes can ensure that they fully committed to give their best effort before practice performance.
- **Confidence:** Athletes can be encouraged to be confident before difficult practice experiences.
- **Intensity:** Athletes can be shown how to raise or lower intensity based on the type of practice performance they are engaging in.
- **Focus:** Athletes can make a conscious effort to narrow their focus onto the task at hand in practice.

Mental exercises and tools (see Chapter 4) can be used by coaches and athletes in practice to both strengthen mental muscles and improve the quality of practice time. For instance, the following exercises and tools can be used in practice:

- **Music:** Athletes can listen to their favorite music before practice to generate positive emotions, motivate them to work hard, and to block out distractions.
- **Goal-setting:** Just before beginning practice, athletes can set or review the goals they want to achieve that day.
- **Mindfulness:** Before practice begins, athletes can center and focus themselves in the present and the task that lies ahead.
- **Imagery:** Before working on a new technical skill, athletes can imagine themselves performing the skill correctly, thus narrowing focus, increasing confidence, and priming the mind and body for its execution.
- **Self-talk:** Particularly before attempting a new or challenging skill, athletes can repeat positive statements as a means of building their confidence and persistence.
- **Routines:** Athletes can develop pre-practice and during practice routines that optimally prepare them for every practice and every exercise and drill during practice.
- **Breathing:** Athletes can incorporate deliberate breathing into their preparation for practice exercises and drills as well as during practice performances.

Additionally, the approaches and strategies discussed in Chapter 5, including quality, consistency, experimentation, athletes training like they compete, and psychological recovery from training and competition, offer coaches and athletes ways to improve the quality of athletes' practice efforts and better prepare them for competitions.

In all cases described above, mental training can be conducted by consultants alongside the coaching staff or implemented by the coaches themselves. Additionally, there will be a period of adjustment with both coaches and athletes to the inclusion of mental training in their overall athlete development. At the same time, with time and consistent application, mental training with transition from something new and different to simply what coaches and athletes do to get the most out of their sports efforts.

Away from Sport

Mental training doesn't just happen during practices. The time that athletes spend away from their sport can also be used to strengthen the mind. Fortunately, given the busy schedules that most athletes have, mental training away from sport only requires a small commitment of time each day and can be done almost anywhere. This mental training can be led by coaches or consultants or left to the athletes themselves to do on their own.

Goal-setting

At the beginning of a new preparation period, athletes can complete a detailed goal-setting plan establishing where they want to go that season and how they will get there. Athletes can best accomplish goal-setting in collaboration with coaches who know the athletes well in terms of their level of development, strengths and areas in need of improvement, and expected trajectory for the coming season. Subsequently, athletes can review, evaluate, and update their goals periodically during the preparation and competitive season to keep their efforts on track to accomplishing their goals.

Mindfulness

This tool can be beneficial to many aspects of athletes' lives beyond sports including school, personally, and socially (see Chapter 4). Mindfulness can be used to improve focus, control emotions, manage stress, develop empathy and self-compassion, increase body awareness, lessen intruding thoughts, and reduce anxiety.

Mental Imagery

Mental imagery is one of the most important mental exercises that athletes can use away from their sport to improve their efforts in their sport. As noted in Chapter 4, a structured and consistent mental imagery program can help athletes develop themselves in every aspect of their sports performances.

Self-talk

What athletes say to themselves away from their sport and about themselves, whether positive or negative, will impact them in their sport. Self-talk can inspire or deflate, build or hurt confidence, raise or lower intensity, or focus or distract. Additionally, what athletes say to themselves and, in turn, how they feel about themselves as people, will influence what they think and feel when they're practicing and competing. Moreover, self-talk is an exercise and that athletes become good at, whether nourishing or critical. Self-talk away from sport gives athletes opportunities to practice being positive which will also translate into their sport.

Music

Many athletes not only use music in their sport, but are also avid listeners in their daily lives. In this way, the more athletes listen to music that makes them feel good, the more deeply they will associate it with positive thoughts, emotions, and physical sensations. In doing so, they will be better able to replicate those positive states in their sport to enhance their practice and competitive efforts.

Competitive Preparations

Mental training should be an integral part of every athlete's competitive preparations. Though athletes have always done mental things to get themselves ready to compete, as with physical, technical, and tactical preparation, the more mental training can be done in a structured and consistent way, the more they will be prepared to perform their best when it matters most. To avoid redundancy of what has just been discussed, all of the mental muscles discussed in Chapter 3 and mental exercises and tools described in Chapter 4 can be incorporated into athletes' pre-competitive routines aimed at total preparation for optimal performance in competition. Consultants can, first, help athletes to identify the mental areas they most need to address in their routines. Then, they can show athletes the mental exercises and tools that they can incorporate into their routines. Finally, consultants can work with athletes in developing a personalized pre-competitive routine that will maximally prepare them to perform their best in competition.

Summary

- The vast majority of coaches believe that the mental side of sports is as or more important than its physical and technical counterparts.
- For athletes to perform their best, they must leverage fully the physical, technical, and mental aspects of their sport and consultants, coaches, and athletes would agree that the mind is a vital part of athletic performance puzzle that is also underappreciated and insufficiently used.
- Coaches readily admit that the money, resources, time, and energy they dedicate to mental training pales in comparison to their commitment to the physical and technical aspects of their sport.
- There are a variety of obstacles that have slowed the full adoption of mental training into overall athlete development including old coaching attitudes, not always clear evidence of need, lack on concreteness in

mental training, negative associations with psychology, few resources to learn from, no programs to follow, not an organizational priority, and lack of time.

- Mental training should be treated like physical conditioning and sport training which are comprehensive, organized, developmentally appropriate, consistent, periodized, and personalized.
- Goals for integrating mental training into overall athlete development include educating coaches about its value, aligning mental training with the above six criteria, and actively incorporating mental training into practice and competitive efforts.
- One way to align mental training with other contributors to sports performance is for mental training to be periodized based on the requirements of the sport, the demands of the stage of the season, and the needs and goals of athletes.
- Delivery of mental training programs can occur through coaches' education, during practice or away from sport, through online courses, Skype sessions, YouTube videos, and in individual sessions.
- The mental muscles, mental exercises and tools, and training suggestions offered in Chapters 3–5 can be integrated into overall athlete development during practice, away from sport, and in athletes' pre-competitive preparations.

Reference

Balague, G. (2000). Periodization of psychological skills training. *Journal of Science and Medicine in Sport*, 3(3), 230–237.

10

TEAM

Introduction

Jim Taylor

As the well-known saying from the Greek philosopher, Aristotle, goes, "The whole is greater than the sum of its parts." This notion suggests that the functional or performance effectiveness of a group involves more than the effectiveness of its individual members. Rather, when the members of a group work together, the result is a higher level of functioning and performance that could not be achieved by simply adding together the efforts of its individual members.

This understanding of a group has particular relevance for sports that involve teams. Team sports can mean that team performance is simply an aggregate of individual performances (e.g., golf, archery, tennis) or it can involve team members working together to perform (e.g., soccer, baseball, basketball). In both cases, how a team functions and performances is impacted by more than simply how team members perform, individually or collectively, on the field of play. To the contrary, teams are influenced by intrapersonal, interpersonal, and cultural dynamics that shape how the team gathers, establishes, and evolves.

This process results in a team culture that is based in several key elements. First, a set of values, attitudes, and norms of behavior emerge. Second, the team culture must be embraced by its members. Third, team members must unify their efforts around agreed-upon and shared goals. Fourth, team members must prioritize those team goals above their own individual aspirations. Finally, each team member must understand their individual roles and responsibilities with the team's functioning and performance efforts.

Within the overarching rubric of team culture, two other components play an important role in how effective teams are. Team cohesion refers to the "glue" that holds a team together when either internal (e.g., selfishness, jealousy) or external (e.g., losing, criticism from others) forces attempt to disrupt the team culture. Team communication involves the quality of the interactions that occur between team members and how conflict is resolved.

An essential intention of this chapter is to demonstrate that a team culture shouldn't be left to chance or trial-and-error in its development. Rather, it should be created proactively and deliberately based on the coaching staff's vision of how it can function and perform at its best. This vision then becomes the guiding light for the values, attitudes, and norms that are established within a team. The strength of any team is based on the individual member's commitment to the team's vision, the development of a positive team culture, the ability of team members to work together effectively toward their shared goals, and well team members are able to communicate and resolve conflicts.

This chapter will explore the systems involved in building a high-functioning and high-performing team. In addition to reviewing the essential theory and research for the three areas of team functioning introduced above, consultants will be offered practical means by which they can collaborate with coaches and team members to help them to coalesce around a collective set of values, attitudes, and norms with the expressed goal of performing their best collectively and achieving the results they want.

TEAM CULTURE

Justin Foster and Lauren Tashman

A team's culture is simply "the way things work around here" (Kaplan, Dollar, Melian, Van Durme, & Wong, 2016, p. 1). In his book *The Culture Code*, Daniel Coyle (2018) defined it as, "a set of living relationships working toward a shared goal." It reflects the identity of the team and acts as a guidepost for how that identity is expressed in action. As Coyle states, "culture isn't something you are. It's something you do." According to Schein (1984), culture is:

> the pattern of basic assumptions that a given group has invented, discovered, or developed in learning to cope with its problems of external adaptation and internal integration, and that have worked well enough to be considered valid, and therefore to be taught to new members as the correct way to perceive, think, and feel in relation to those problems.
>
> *(Schein, 1984, p. 3)*

A team's culture, then, is the foundation for everything that a team is, values, and believes, as well as how it functions, interacts, and performs.

The consulting firm Deloitte (Kaplan, Dollar, Melian, Van Durme, & Wong, 2016) provides a more succinct definition, stating that culture "includes the values, beliefs, behaviors, artifacts, and reward systems that influence people's behavior on a day-to-day basis." (p. 1). This is consistent with Schein's proposition that there are three interacting levels of organizational culture:

1. **Basic assumptions:** The invisible underlying beliefs of the individuals and groups that they may take for granted and not be consciously aware of, but act as a guide for the attention, perspective, and responses of the team;
2. **Values:** The espoused beliefs that govern group behavior that are hard to observe directly but indicate the team's wants and priorities; and
3. **Artifacts and creations:** The observable environment of the organization including public documents, stories, charters, workspace layout, and visible/audible behavior patterns of the group that describe what the team does and how they do it, but may not clearly link to the underlying why.

Taking these different perspectives into consideration, team culture is composed of:

- vision;
- values;
- attitudes;
- expectations and goals; and
- norms and standards of behavior.

Why Culture Matters

Team culture impacts every aspect of an organization. It has implications for the attitudes, perceptions, behaviors, and emotional responses of the members of the team as well as the overall climate of the team (Aarons & Sawitzky, 2006). Team culture sets the tone for the team's priorities, the decisions that are made, and how its members interact and perform. Thus, the team culture defines the environment of the team. For example, is the environment relaxed or intense? Do team members work effectively together or is there unaddressed or unresolved conflict? Does the team emphasize relationships or results? Does the team make improvement or winning the priority?

In a broad sense, culture can be constructive (i.e., characterized by supportiveness, individuality, and positive approaches to relationships and tasks) or defensive (i.e., promote conformity, submissiveness, and self-protection) (Aarons & Sawitsky, 2006). Janssen (2014) proposed a model outlining eight types of team cultures representative of the emphasis that is placed on relationships or results:

- **Corrosive:** Low emphasis on both results and relationships creating a dysfunctional culture characterized by selfishness, negativity, distrust, lack of respect, apathy and conflict creating an inability to get on the same page or work towards a common goal.
- **Country club:** Greater emphasis on relationships and results characterized by a focus on status and appearance that fosters superficial relationships a lack of accountability, and preference for leisure over winning.
- **Congenial:** High emphasis on relationships and little to no focus on results creating a commitment to fostering and sustaining harmonious relationships and positive interactions.
- **Comfortable:** Equal yet moderate emphasis on relationships and results supporting the maintenance of a safe, comfortable, and content environment.
- **Competitive:** High emphasis on results and only moderate emphasis on relationships that creates a focus on competing both within and outside of team and stifles the ability of team members to bond and work together.
- **Cutthroat:** Results take precedence over all else including relationships representative of the prioritization of talent and winning over character and team dynamic.
- **Constructive:** High emphasis on both results and relationships that fosters a healthy team dynamic and often successful performance but lacks full commitment in both areas.
- **Championship:** Unrelentingly high emphasis on both results and relationships characterized by trust, accountability, deep and connected relationships, vulnerability, honesty, respect, valued contributions by all members, a clear mission and goals, high standards, and a commitment to excellence.

Thus, consultants working with a team on culture necessitates helping them to develop both effective relationships (e.g., social cohesion, trust) and the ability to work together to achieve shared outcome goals (e.g., task cohesion, team coordination).

Theory and Research

To date, most research on team culture has emerged from the corporate world while little empirical research exists examining the role of team culture on individual or team sports performance. However, the research available can provide some useful insights for sport organizations. For example, according to Kotter and Heskett (1992), a strong culture has nearly two-thirds lower-turnover rate (13.9%) compared to organizations with a poor culture (48.4%). This difference affects the retention of personnel and the stability of staff at every level of a team including front office, coaches, support staff, and athletes. Culture also impacts revenue. A longitudinal study that followed more than 200 companies for a ten-year period found that those with a strong culture experienced an increase in net revenue of 765% compared to those with poor cultures (Gordon & DiTomaso, 1992). This finding has economic relevance for sport teams, particularly collegiate and professional teams that rely heavily on revenue.

Finally, team culture influences performance. Heskett (2012) found that as much as half of the performance differential between organizations can be attributed to culture. This finding has been supported anecdotally in sport. For example, when taking over the Ohio State University football program, Urban Meyer observed that training the right behaviors wouldn't stick if the culture doesn't support it (Meyer & Coffey, 2015). The culture, he realized, is the foundation that a team's strategy, skill, and effort are built upon. Moreover, the legendary San Francisco 49ers coach, Bill Walsh, summarized the impact of culture this way: "The culture precedes positive results. It doesn't get tacked on as an afterthought on your way to the victory stand" (Janssen, 2014, p. 5).

Additionally, in an article about Google's Project Aristotle, its study of team effectiveness (Duhigg, 2016), five elements were found to be associated with a healthy team culture and high effectiveness:

- **Psychological safety:** an environment in which team members feel comfortable being vulnerable and taking risks.
- **Dependability:** team members have high standards and hold themselves accountable to the team.
- **Structure and clarity:** team members understand what is expected of them and how to meet those expectations (i.e., roles, goals, and plans).
- **Meaning:** team members have a sense of personally meaningful purpose in their participation.
- **Impact:** team members know their contributions matter not only to the success of the team but also to society and the creation of change.

Moreover, the study revealed that psychological safety involved (1) conversational turn-taking, everyone on the team feels comfortable and has the opportunity to share their perspective, and (2) social sensitivity, team members tune in to nonverbal cues that may indicate how team members are feeling. More broadly, Google's research (Rozovsky, 2015) confirmed the importance of team norms and identified.

The results of these and other studies examining team culture demonstrate strongly that culture is a prerequisite to optimal team functioning, relationships, and performance. Moreover, the above taxonomies can provide consultants with a structure for both assessing a team culture and developing a plan for creating a healthy culture based on their vision, needs, and goals.

Practical Implications

Consultants and team cultures have a reciprocal relationship. First, consultants' ability to work effectively with coaches and athletes is influenced by team culture. Providing mental training to a team is dependent on their having a culture of innovation, openness to change and personal growth, and the pursuit of excellence. In turn, consultants can help shape the team culture in which they work by helping teams to proactively develop the culture that best meets their vision, needs, and goals. Thus, consultants would be wise to include team culture in their initial assessment of a team and to making the development of a team culture a centerpiece of the services that they offer.

Consultants should also be sensitive to the fact that the most painstakingly constructed team cultures may not turn out as intended because not every contributor to a team culture can be controlled. A team may be more than the sum of its parts, but, at the same time, its parts, namely, its team members and other stakeholders, have an impact on its culture. And all stakeholders (e.g., team members, coaches, administrators, boosters, fans, media) bring to a team unique attributes (e.g., personalities, beliefs, values, goals) that may or may not be positive or mesh with the culture that is sought. According to Bronfenbrenner (1992), there are layers of systems/ environments surrounding individuals that will affect their development. If this notion is extended to teams, it can be assumed that the various levels of systems within and outside of the organization will play a role in both individual and team performance, as well as the consultant's role, experience, and impact. For example, in collegiate sport, the athletic department, university administration, conference, division, city, and state are examples of systems that can have implications for the team and its culture.

Additionally, team cultures can be deeply entrenched in an organization, but that doesn't necessarily mean they are effective (Schein, 1984). Teams can either build a culture by default or by design. If team culture isn't intentionally designed, a default culture is created as a result of factors such as the personalities of the team members, leadership style, past performance, institutional history, lack of awareness for the need for culture change, ingrained cultural habits, and agendas that have prevailed over time. This is especially true in more stagnant organizations that may characterize their culture by the phrase, "the way we've always done it."

In contrast, organizations that have intentionally designed their team culture can often point to a deliberate process by which the team considered who they are, why they exist, what they stand for, and what they do as well as the impact of these on team, functioning, relationships, and performance. Designed cultures often have a documented vision statement, core values, code of conduct, team goals, or a set of key principles. Further, in the most effective team cultures, these elements are not just words documented or displayed somewhere or conversations that were once had. Instead, they are attitudes, beliefs, and behaviors that are both embedded in and expressed by team members in their daily team activities. At the same time, the degree to which those within the organization embrace the team culture and use it to drive what they do and how they do it varies greatly from team to team and also from team member to team member.

Overall, in helping to shape a team culture, consultants must first focus on understanding the type of culture that currently exists. They may, for example, use the six team cultures described by Janssen (2014) to see what culture a team currently demonstrates. Next, they can collaborate with the relevant stakeholders to identify the fundamental vision, values, attitudes, norms, and goals that would be the foundation of a new team culture. Then, consultants can create a process for establishing those areas within the team and create buy-in and commitment among its stakeholders, most notably, the coaching staff and athletes.

In the process of helping a team develop an effective culture, there may be a tendency on the part of consultants to want to "do things" at a practical level with the teams they work with that can have an immediate, albeit potentially short term, impact on team functioning and performance. In some cases, this may be the role that consultants have been asked to play in their team role, Instead, it would be incumbent on them to begin this process by having the team take a "deep dive" into the foundational aspects of team culture that have been described thus far to ensure the development of and commitment to both quality relationships and high standards for performance. Not only will these proactive steps get everyone on the team on the "same page," but the process of building a team brick by brick from the foundation up creates lasting trust and the ability and willingness to work together when it matters most (e.g., leading up to a big competition).

Interestingly, the connections and trust that are engendered in this process are not solely psychological, but actually produce biochemical changes. For example, Zak (2017a) suggested that a direct relationship exists between oxytocin levels and the degree of trust that people feel toward one another. In sport, Pepping and Timmermans (2012) proposed that oxytocin plays a role in emotional contagion (i.e., spread of emotions and moods) on a sports team impacting both social emotions (e.g., empathy, trust, cooperation, envy) and social perception (e.g., emotion recognition and gaze behavior) that ultimately impact team performance. Zak (2017b) recommended eight strategies leaders can use to create a culture of trust:

1. recognize excellence publicly when it happens;
2. induce "challenge stress" on the team using difficult but attainable goals;
3. empower team member autonomy in designing the environment;
4. allow stakeholders autonomy in how they approach their roles;
5. engage in frequent communication;
6. intentionally build relationships;
7. support personal growth; and
8. demonstrate vulnerability.

Building a High-performing Team Culture

Whether a team wants to initiate a new culture or reshape an existing culture, the authors recommend five stages that teams must accomplish:

- Phase 1: Assess the Current Culture
- Phase 2: Establish the New Culture
- Phase 3: Implement the Culture
- Phase 4: Sustain the Culture
- Phase 5: Re-align or Change the Culture

Consultants and the teams they work with must also recognize that a team culture isn't a static entity or a final product. Rather, it is an ongoing work in progress in which the process of developing and inculcating a team culture must be periodically revisited, re-assessed, and revised to meet the changing needs, priorities, and goals of new personnel, sport changes, level of competitiveness, and broader cultural changes. As the intentional design or redesign of a team culture progresses toward implementation, consultants should regularly check in on how well daily actions by the team alignment with the desired culture and continue to refine the understanding of what the culture looks like in action. Then, periodically, consultants can help teams to re-evaluate, re-align, or evolve their culture. Fundamental to this entire process is that consultants provide stakeholders with a rationale for a certain team culture, educate them about its components, offer them procedures and strategies for building the team culture, and, importantly, ensure complete buy-in and ownership of the team culture.

Phase 1: Assess the Current Culture

To help a team build, modify, or re-establish its culture, consultants must begin by assessing its current culture. For a team to function, interact, and perform to its capabilities and sustain that level over time, it is essential that the culture be clearly defined, bought into, and lived by all of its stakeholders. Consultants can help the team conduct an analysis of its culture and the structures and processes that support it.

In this way, consultants first become "cultural anthropologists" to uncover where the team currently is and where they want or need to be. According to Steiner's model of group productivity (Steiner, 1972), faulty group processes (i.e., losses in potential due to motivation and coordination) will determine the alignment or discrepancy between a group's potential and its actual performance. If a team has a problematic culture or is not reaching its real or perceived potential, consultants need to determine where the problems or challenges might lie relative to the factors and concepts discussed in this chapter.

There is no one-size-fits-all process for assessing the culture of teams. According to Schein (1984), four approaches in combination can be useful for assessing the current team culture:

1. analyzing the process by which new members are brought on board;
2. taking a multimodal approach (e.g., reviewing documents, observing team functioning) to analyzing the team's history;
3. conducting interviews with key stakeholders (e.g., "culture creators or carriers") to analyze beliefs, values, processes, environment, goals, and outcomes; and
4. jointly exploring with team members the basic assumptions underlying the culture.

As a part of the assessment, consultants may also consider using objective assessments to evaluate key factors that have implications for culture, such as motivational climate, coach leadership, coach-athlete relationship, trust, collective efficacy, organizational commitment, athlete satisfaction, and team resilience.

Thus, when working with a team on building their culture, consultants can use a myriad of qualitative and quantitative methods of assessment. For example, quantitative approaches such as questionnaires (e.g., Collective Efficacy Questionnaire, Short, Sullivan, & Feltz, 2005; Group Environment Questionnaire, Whitton & Fletcher, 2014) or performance profiling done as a team (e.g., Dale & Wrisberg, 1996) can be used to assess various facets of team environment and dynamic. Qualitative approaches, such as focus groups and one-on-one conversations, can also be very informative. This more informal approach enables consultants to ask follow-up questions and allow others to share their experiences based on another team member's comment. More formal approaches, such as social network analysis (Lusher, Robins, & Kremer, 2010) can also be useful.

How consultants choose to assess the team's culture should align with the needs and goals of the team and the intervention style of the individual consultants. Ultimately, consultants should seek to understand the experiences, values, perceptions, attitudes, norms, interpersonal dynamics, tensions, and roles of the team members. Then, the findings should be shared with relevant stakeholders for feedback to determine the most appropriate way forward.

Phase 2: Establish the New Culture

Once the assessment has been completed and the team has an agreed-upon sense of the type of culture that currently exists, and clarity on the culture they want for the future, consultants can begin to put that plan into action. But, before implementation begins and as the new culture is rooted in the team, consultants can set the team up for success by assisting it in building psychological safety (Duhigg, 2016) and quality connections that are going to be needed throughout this process as well as impact their ability to implement their new culture through cooperation and collaboration (Coyle, 2018). When a team has psychological safety, its members are more likely to share similar beliefs about the team, trust one another, and be committed to the team above themselves as individuals (Edmondson, 1999; Edmondson & Lei, 2014). Teams whose behavior reinforces this sense of safety improve at a greater rate than those who don't because they are willing to stretch their comfort zones, own their mistakes, and collectively find solutions rather than protecting their egos (Edmondson 1999; Edmondson & Lei, 2014). A team's sense of trust and safety will impact their ability to build an effective team culture.

The process of taking a team culture from the whiteboard to reality involves three phases:

- core component 1—purpose;
- core component 2—values; and
- core component 3—standards.

Core Component 1—Purpose

High-performing cultures are driven by a deep purpose, a compelling vision, and a collective goal. Consistent with this notion, Valée and Bloom (2016) found that the first key to building a championship culture was enacting the clear vision that drives a team forward. Some teams may focus more on a mission (something they aim to accomplish, such as a league championship) while others may choose to focus on a more expansive vision (a future state of the organization or world). For example, the Chicago Cubs' vision is "to change the world through the game of baseball" (Lifrak, 2015).

Many organizations have a mission, vision, or goal statement. However, leaders and team members within the organization often have a difficult time operationalizing what they mean on a daily basis. This disconnection leaves coaches and athletes unsure of how the purpose expressed in the mission, vision, or goal statements impacts their daily decisions and actions. When this occurs, a useful exercise is for consultants to ask team members what it would look like if they were living out the purpose on a daily basis. For example, they could ask, "How do you know when team members are or are not acting according to the team's purpose?" Or, "How do you know when the team is fulfilling their purpose?" These and other questions can help make the purpose more concrete and actionable to individuals at every level of the team.

Core Component 2—Values

A culture is the enacting of agreed-upon underlying and espoused values (i.e., beliefs and principles that guide a team in every aspect of its functioning including daily operations, interactions, and performance). Therefore, a values-based approach should be used to establish the new team culture. This process can begin in several ways, for example, by providing a list of potential core values or using questions that prompt the exploration of individual and group values (e.g., If you achieved your ultimate goal as a team, what would you have done or not done along the way that would have been critical to that success?; What is an "ideal" team in your mind and what does it do or not do that makes it ideal?). The following questions can be used to select and evaluate team values: Who are we? What is most important to us? Who do we want to be? Recently, Cotterill (2013) recommended the following five-stage approach for creating team values:

1. establish clear goals for the team;
2. brainstorm the values that would enable the accomplishment of those goals;
3. discuss those identified in step two to choose team values;
4. prioritize the selected values; and
5. elicit team agreement on the adoption of the values and the use of them to drive team actions.

Keep in mind that the values chosen and the wording used for them should demonstrate what is unique about the team rather than generic or category values or words (Yohn, 2018). Additionally, the values should not be ethereal concepts, but rather able to be translated into daily value-driven action. Further, consultants should encourage organizations to strive for what Hodgkinson (1996) referred to as "principle values" (i.e., those that have been derived through extensive critical reflection and embody important ideals that will not be compromised) in comparison to consensus (i.e., what others have chosen), consequence (i.e., if-then considerations that prioritize outcome over process), or preference (i.e., likes or desires based on affect or emotion) values.

This exploration should be a multi-phased process that is not rushed. Further, while the coaches and staff members should have a substantial role in creating the team culture, it is recommended that the athletes also be provided with the opportunity to be a part of the process because their commitment to the team's values will ultimately determine whether the values take hold and are fully embraced. Additionally, alignment of both informal and formal leaders is important (Cole & Martin, 2018). For example, consultants might start the process with the coaches, bring the discussion to team leaders among the athletes, then create a discussion among both coaches and leaders, before it is brought to the entire team for consensus. Values can mean different things to different people; thus, operationalization of the values is important (Hodgkinson, 1996). Therefore, a final process for this phase should include consultants facilitating the team in getting on the same page by collectively defining their values in relevant terms.

As an illustration of this essential aspect of developing a team culture, when Mike Krzyzewski became the head coach of USA Basketball, he knew he needed to set an intentional culture centered on selflessness and unity. Leading up to the 2008 Olympic Games in Beijing, China, "Coach K" invited his influential captains to partner with him in leading the team in identifying their core values which would be the basis for how they conducted themselves as a team: (1) no excuses, (2) great defense, (3) communication, (4) trust, (5) collective responsibility, (6) care, (7) respect, (8) intelligence, (9) poise, (10) flexibility, (11) unselfishness, (12) aggressiveness, (13) enthusiasm, (14) performance, and (15) pride. The number of values identified will vary from team to team, however given the limits of memory and attention, a smaller number may be more effective.

Core Component 3—Standards

This final part of the establishing a team culture involves turning the values just identified into a living entity that guides the team's daily actions by translating those values into accepted standards of behavior. The goal is to identify "keystone behaviors" that are the critical, meaningful, observable, and repeatable patterns that will most aid the team in achieving its vision and goals (Hull, 2017). Standards should be established for both on and off field contexts including team and community interactions, and practice and competitive performances.

For example, Dabo Swinney, head coach of the Clemson Tigers football team, has distilled their team's values and standards into fifteen "Team Commandments":

1. Go to class and be engaged.
2. Be a good citizen.
3. Great effort all the time.
4. Work ethic: nobody works harder.
5. Decide to be successful (choice).
6. Expect to be successful (mentality).
7. Clemson football is 60 minutes, or as long as it takes to finish.
8. Toughness! Mental and physical.
9. Maintain a positive attitude no matter what the circumstances.
10. Never lose faith.
11. Do everything with passion and enthusiasm.
12. Don't expect more from a teammate than you're willing to give.
13. Have a genuine appreciation for each other's role.
14. Be coachable. Learn to handle criticism.
15. Have fun!

As with identifying values, ownership of the standards by the entire team can be encouraged by allowing all members to participate in determining them. These behaviors should be stated in a simple, clear, and objective fashion. Further, it can be helpful to specify what it looks like to fall short of, meet, and exceed each standard to facilitate accountability to facilitate clear understanding and accountability as well as ensure everyone is on the same page.

Phase 3: Implement the Culture

The purpose, values, and standards are the foundation of a team culture, but they will have little value if they are not reinforced (Cole & Martin, 2018; Schroeder, 2010). Reinforcement by and for coaches and team members must occur early and often in the implementation of a new culture (e.g., every day checking on alignment to culture) to ensure full adoption and then periodically as the team's purpose, values, and standards become internalized and woven into the fabric of a team's daily functioning and performance (e.g., end of each week or at selected time points throughout a season). This can be done informally (e.g., as part of end-of-day debriefs) or more formally (e.g., a brief self-assessment completed by each team member). Individual accountability is important, but team accountability can also be useful by, for example, using accountability partners that every few days provide feedback on culture alignment (i.e., what they saw out of each other that represented being aligned or not with the values and standards). Further, Cole and Martin (2018) found that having a short, simple overarching theme that captures the team's core values each day as well as daily rituals are useful for helping teams to successfully implement values and standards. Additionally, teams can strengthen the buy-in of team members into their culture by incorporating other rituals (e.g., player awards) and artifacts (e.g., signs in the locker room, hashtags in social media) that serve as reminders of the values and reinforce their daily use in team activities. This part of the process is essential given the discussion above about oxytocin and its implications for emotional contagion and team performance, but also given what science has uncovered about the impact of mirror neurons and the role they play in our modeling of others, learning, and transmission of emotions (Iacoboni, 2009). Further, ongoing efforts to build psychological safety and trust among team members is necessary for this level of transparency and accountability to be realized (Edmondson & Lei, 2014).

Phase 4: Sustain the Culture

In the world of sport, the "game" is always changing. There are new team members, successes and setbacks in performance within and across seasons, new rules and goals to accomplish, and a whole host of other issues that teams must navigate that can impact team culture. Over time, teams will need to continue to work on team culture including various aspects of both task cohesion (i.e., working together to achieve results) and social cohesion (i.e., quality relationships, trust, and connection).

Each member of a team needs to feel a sense of belonging, meaning, and contribution for a culture to operate effectively. Consultants can work with coaches and team members to identify ways in which everyone can feel that they are an integral part of the team. For example, strategies for identifying and valuing contribution include frequent recognition of outstanding contributions to the team, both tangible and otherwise, shared team responsibilities, and connecting individual efforts with accomplishment of team goals (Lencioni, 2002). To enhance connection and social cohesion, consultants can assist the team in fostering a sense of belonging. According to Coyle (2018), belonging cues (e.g., subtle verbal and nonverbal messages) signal a sense of investment in each other, a willingness to accept and embrace individuality of team members, and demonstrate a commitment to each other now and in the future. From an evolutionary standpoint, the members of a group will always be on the "lookout" for belonging cues when interacting with each other to get a sense of the level of safety of the group. When a sense of safety is felt, individuals will shift into "connection mode" (Coyle, 2018). Getting these signals once isn't enough; thus, from a team perspective, they must be intentionally and continually transmitted and reinforced by all members of the team. To enhance individual meaning, consultants can, for example, assist team members in the identification and sharing of personal values and the development of role clarity.

Consultants can also help teams to support and sustain their team culture by providing regular opportunities for discussion and reflection on how the team is doing (e.g., alignment to culture, adhering to standards of behavior, working together towards goals) and use that information to continually deepen and evolve the team culture. For every team, each new season brings new goals, people, changes, and challenges, so agility and adaptability are essential for a team culture to remain strong and resilient. For example, working with a team that is striving to win a first national championship may bring different challenges than working with a team that is striving to achieve a repeat. As a general approach, consultants may find it useful to help the team highlight their "keys to success" and standout performances that reflect the optimal culture in action. These can serve as benchmarks for regular reflection and evaluation. Consultants can also use more specific reflection frameworks in team sessions such as:

- Bright (what is going well), blurry (what is inconsistent), blind (what is not working or hasn't been discussed).
- What, so what, now what.
- Well, better/different, learned, (next).
- Start, stop, continue, change.

Phase 5: Re-align or Change the Culture

Over time, a team may lose sight of its culture or need to engage in an intentional change as a result of an ineffective or stagnant culture. For example, the stability of team members (i.e., high turnover of members or excessive stability), complacency or conflict that can arise as a result of the paradox of success, or the changing landscape of the performance domain (e.g., reinstatement of a sport back into the Olympics) may necessitate the re-evaluation, re-design, or evolution of the team culture. Re-alignment may mean refocusing the team back onto its culture or creating a change in a culture that is no longer proving to be effective for the team or is dysfunctional. It is important for both consultants and members of the team to be aware that this may not be a smooth or comfortable process and may elicit resistance from team members depending on the factors that led to the need for change (Schein, 1984). Thus, consultants engaging in this process with teams should be competent in conflict resolution and change management.

If a change in the team culture is warranted, Schroeder (2010) identified three phases to guide this process:

- **Unfreezing:** Illuminating the current culture and exposing the flaws in it.
- **Cognitive restructuring:** Creating a mindset shift and identifying a new vision supported by new values and assumptions.
- **Refreezing:** Implementing the new culture and adopting artifacts that will help in this process.

Unfreezing requires that evidence be provided to aid the team members in understanding that the culture needs to be changed. In sport, coaches have found that losing serves as a powerful form of "data" needed to unfreeze from an old culture and winning serves as the impetus for refreezing to the new culture (Schroeder, 2010). However, a team may need to undergo culture change or evolution despite "success" requiring the use of other "data" during the unfreezing process. Further, from the team's past successful and unsuccessful experiences, values, relationships, practices, and strategies should be identified and serve as a guide for team-member recruitment, behavioral reinforcement, and the teaching of the values to those on the team. One of the best-known examples of intentional team culture re-design is that of the New Zealand All Blacks rugby teams, for decades the dominant team in the world. Spurred by an incident that occurred after a loss in 2004, the new culture began with the notion of "better people make better All Blacks" (Hodge, Henry, & Smith, 2014) and led to the identification of a new set of values that drive the new team culture.

Summary

- A team culture is the foundation for everything that a team is, values, and believes, as well as how it functions, interacts, and performs.
- A team culture is grounded in a team's vision, values, and standards of behavior.
- Research from the corporate world demonstrates that team culture impacts retention, revenue, and performance.
- Five elements have been found to be associated with a healthy team culture and optimal performance: psychological safety, dependability, structure and clarity, meaning, and impact.
- Consultants would be wise to include team culture in their initial assessment of a team and to make the development of a team culture a centerpiece of the services that they offer.
- Organizations that have intentionally designed their team culture can often point to some clarity and consistency surrounding who they are, why they exist, what they stand for, and what they do as well as the impact of these on performance.
- Consultants can help the team take a "deep dive" into the foundational aspects of team culture to ensure the development of and commitment to both quality relationships and high standards for performance (i.e., championship culture).
- Five phases of building high-performing teams include assessing the current culture, establishing the new culture through the identification of purpose, values, and standards, implementation of the culture, sustaining the culture, and re-aligning or changing the culture as needed.

References

Aarons, G. A., & Sawitsky, A. C. (2006). Organizational climate partially mediates the effect of culture on work attitudes and staff turnover in mental health services. *Administration and Policy Mental Health and Mental Health Services, 33*(3), 289–301.

Bronfenbrenner, U. (1992). Ecological systems theory. In R. Vasta (Ed.), *Six theories of child development: Revised formulations and current issues* (pp. 187–249). London: Jessica Kingsley Publishers.

Cole, J., & Martin, A. J. (2018). Developing a winning sport team culture: organizational culture in theory and practice. *Sport in Society, 21*(8), 1204–1222. doi: doi: 10.1080/17430437.2018.1442197

Cotterill, S. (2013). *Team psychology in sports: Theory and practice.* New York, NY: Routledge.

Coyle, D. (2018). *The culture code: The secrets of highly successful groups.* New York, NY: Random House.

Dale, G. A., & Wrisberg, C. A. (1996). The use of a performance profiling technique in a team setting: Getting the athletes and coach on the "same page." *The Sport Psychologist, 10,* 261–277.

Duhigg, C. (2016, February 25). What Google learned from its quest to build the perfect team. *The New York Times.* Retrieved from www.nytimes.com/2016/02/28/magazine/what-google-learned-from-its-quest-to-build-the-perfect-team.html

Edmondson, A. (1999). Psychological Safety and Learning Behavior in Work Teams. *Administrative Science Quarterly, 44*(2), 350–383.

Edmondson, A. & Lei, Z. (2014). Psychological safety: The history, renaissance, and future of an interpersonal construct. *Annual Review of Organizational Psychology and Organizational Behavior, 1,* 23–43.

Gordon, G. & DiTomaso, N. (1992). Predicting corporate performance from organizational culture. *Journal of Management Studies, 29,* 783–798.

Heskett, J. (2012). *The culture cycle: How to shape the unseen force that transforms performance.* Hoboken, NJ: FT Press.

Hodge, K., Henry, G., & Smith, W. (2014). A case study of excellence in elite sport: Motivational climate in a world champion team. *The Sport Psychologist, 28,* 60–74.

Hodgkinson, C. (1996). *Administrative philosophy: Values and motives in administrative life.* New York, NY: State University of New York Press.

Hull, K. (2017, May). *Getting to the critical few behaviors that can drive cultural change.* Strategy+Business.

Iacoboni, M. (2009). *Mirroring people: the science of empathy and how we connect with others.* New York, NY: Picador.

Janssen, J. (2014). *How to build and sustain a championship culture.* Cary, NC: Winning The Mental Game.

Kaplan, M., Dollar, B., Melian, V., Van Durme, Y., Wong, J. (2016, February 29). Shape culture drive strategy. Retrieved from www2.deloitte.com/insights/us/en/focus/human-capital-trends/2016/impact-of-culture-on-business-strategy.html

Kotter, J. P., and Heskett, J. L. (1992). *Corporate Culture and Performance.* New York, NY: Free Press.

Lencioni, P. (2002). *The five dysfunctions of a team: A leadership fable.* San Francisco, CA: Jossey-Bass.

Lifrak, J. (Director of Mental Training). (2015, October 5). The High Performance Mindset [Audio podcast]. Retrieved from https://thehighperformancemindset.com/chicago-cubs-director-of-mental-training-talks-winning-mindset-big-dreams-josh-lifrak

Lusher, D., Robins, G., & Kremer, P. (2010). The application of social network analysis to team sports. *Measurement in Physical Education and Exercise Science, 14*(4), 211–224.

Meyer, U., & Coffey W. (2015). *Above the line: Lessons in leadership and life from a championship program.* New York, NY: Penguin Books.

Pepping, G.-J., & Timmermans, E. J. (2012). Oxytocin and the biopsychology of performance in team sports. *The Scientific World Journal, 2012,* 1–10.

Rozovksy, J. (2015) The five keys to a successful Google team. *Re:Work.* Retrieved from: https://rework.withgoogle.com/blog/five-keys-to-a-successful-google-team/

Schein, E. H. (1984). Coming to a new awareness of organizational culture. *Sloan Management Review, 25*(2), 3–16.

Schroeder, P. J. (2010). Changing team culture: the perspectives of ten successful head coaches. *Journal of Sport Behavior, 33*(1), 63–88.

Short, S. E., Sullivan, P., & Feltz, D. (2005). Development and preliminary validation of the collective efficacy questionnaire for sports. *Measurement in Physical Education and Exercise Science, 9*(3): 181–202.

Steiner, I. D. (1972). *Group process and productivity.* New York, NY: Academic Press.

Valée, C. N., & Bloom, G. A. (2016). Four keys to building a championship culture. *International Sport Coaching Journal, 3,* 170–177.

Whitton, S. M., & Fletcher, R. B. (2014). The group environment questionnaire: A multilevel confirmatory factor analysis. *Small Group Research, 45*(1), 68–88.

Yohn, D. L. (2018, February). Ban these 5 words from your corporate values statement. *Harvard Business Review.*

Zak, P. J. (2017a, January–February). The neuroscience of trust. *Harvard Business Review.*

Zak, P. J. (2017b). *Trust factor: The science of creating high-performance companies.* New York, NY: American Management Association.

TEAM COHESION

Jim Taylor and Brandon Orr

The importance of team cohesion and its relationship to team functioning and performance is well established anecdotally and empirically (Carron & Eys, 2012; Eys, Patterson, Loughead, & Carron, 2006; Eys & Kim, 2017).

In general, the research indicates that the more cohesive the team, the better team members get along and the more successful the team performs. At the same time, team cohesion can be thought of as an end result, not a process. From this perspective, an argument can be made that there should be more emphasis placed on team building as it involves the process by which team cohesion is achieved (McEwan & Beauchamp, 2014). The intent here is not to diminish the importance of team cohesion, but rather to frame the position that team building should be the priority over team cohesion for consultants because of its practical value in improving team functioning and performance. The framework for consultants is established by defining team cohesion and team building, understanding the research both outside of and within sports, and providing actionable team-building strategies that will increase team cohesion.

Theory and Research

Outside of sports, Gross and Martin (1952) defined team cohesion as the collective struggle against allowing factors from outside a group to disrupt group function and the degree to which a group can withstand outside pressure. This definition, however, fails to account for the fact that the disruption of a given group can also come from within. Festinger, Schacter, and Back (1963) defined team cohesion as the nexus of all elements causing not only group member attraction, but also factors influencing the decision of members to stay in the group.

Carron and Eys's (2012) characterize cohesion as the strength of bonds among group members. A more applied definition emerged from McEwan and Beauchamp (2014) where team cohesion results from from specific behaviors that teams engage in (e.g., communication, mutual sharing, goal-setting).

As with any group setting, team dynamics (i.e., culture, cohesion, and communication) play a significant role in impacting not only the outcomes of team efforts, but also the manner in which those outcomes are pursued and achieved. How individual team members engage with teammates and fulfill their roles and responsibilities influence the quality of team functioning, interactions, and performance. This interplay between the individual and the team is the framework for cohesion representing one of the most important elements of any team (Severt & Estrada, 2015). As such, it is no surprise that cohesion is one of the most expansive bodies of research within sport psychology and one of the most influential contributors to team success (for an authoritative review of the literature on cohesion in sport, see Carron & Eys, 2012).

Cohesion is conceptualized as the degree to which a group is united in its commitment to achieved shared goals and how connected group members feel to one another. Simply put, group cohesion involves how well its members are able to "stick together" in the face of internal conflict, opposing external forces, and variation in team performance relative to their goals (Severt & Estrada, 2015). Two types of cohesion can be identified: *Task cohesion* refers to the collective commitment that a group had to accomplishing relevant tasks in pursuit of shared goals, while *social cohesion* involves the emotional connections that members have to the group. Later research has supported this categorization (Loughead & Bloom, 2013; Severt & Estrada, 2015). Additionally, Beal, Cohen, Burke, and McLendon (2003) offered a third component of cohesion, group pride, which has been identified to play a meaningful role in the development of cohesion. Group pride is defined as members of a team exhibiting attraction to the values and standards the team represents and experiencing fulfillment in the status and prestige team membership affords them. According to Beal et al. (2003), group pride occurs when team members are able to set aside their individual needs for the greater good of the team realizing that "the team is more important than the sum of its parts" (p. 7). Researchers also suggest that group pride cultivates an enduring desire for the team to remain intact and high functioning in spite of turnover by individual members of the team (Mullen & Copper, 1994).

Perceptions of cohesion by team members have been shown to have a direct impact on the behaviors and performance outcomes of sport teams (Eys & Kim, 2017). The importance of cohesion within sport is evident in the shear volume of research on how and why components of the construct of cohesion impact individual performance and individual and team functioning, relationships, and performance (for a full review, see Eys & Brawley, 2018). For the purposes of this section, cohesion will be examined within the dimensions of task and social cohesion and how these individually and respectively interact at the individual and group levels to influence team performance and sport outcome (Carron, Widmeyer, & Brawley, 1985; Eys & Brawley, 2018).

Task Cohesion

Considerable research has demonstrated the impact of task cohesion on many aspects of team performance. For example, increases in task cohesion among team members has been reported to allow them to view team failures with a process orientation which results in a more positive adaptive response to setbacks and failure and subsequent increased persistence (Shapcott & Carron, 2010). In addition, greater task cohesion within a team predicts a more positive interpretation of and behavioral response to pre-competition and competition anxiety (Wolf, Eys, & Kleinert, 2015).

Social Cohesion

A similar relationship between social cohesion and team performance has also been found. For instance, strong social cohesion in a team is related to greater attraction and adherence to team roles and tasks resulting in greater prosocial behavior demonstrated among teammates (Bruner, Boardley, & Coté, 2014). Interestingly, this same social cohesion promotes greater antisocial behavior towards opponents, highlighting the vexing nature of cohesion's impact on team function and behavior (Bruner et al., 2014; Eys & Brawley, 2018).

Additional research has explored the relationship between the two types of cohesion and their cumulative impact on team functioning and performance in an effort to decipher whether one has a more favorable effect on teams (Carron & Eys, 2012; Eys & Brawley, 2018). Representative of this line of inquiry, Jacob and Carron (1998) reported that greater task cohesion promoted less emphasis on social standing among team members, thus improving team functioning and performance. Overall, the extant findings suggest that task cohesion has a greater effect on team functioning and performance than does social cohesion, while social cohesion has the benefit of strengthening connections between team members and increasing enjoyment in athletes' participation in team activities.

Team Cohesion and Coaches

Not surprisingly, coaches have a significant impact on cohesion in a team. Research shows that athletes report greater perceptions of cohesion when playing for coaches who infuse task-oriented language and instruction into their motivational climate while also exuding greater social support for their athletes through positive feedback (Jowett & Chaundy, 2004; Vincer & Loughead, 2010). Similarly, coaches who use a task-centered approach produce greater task and social cohesion among their athletes (Eys et al., 2013; Horn, Byrd, Martin, & Young, 2012). In contrast, coaches who emphasize an ego-involving motivational climate reduce task and social cohesion among team members (McLaren, Eys, & Murray, 2015).

Gender Interactions with Cohesion in Sport

Of particular note is the manner in which sport literature has reported differences in the the way cohesion develops and drives team performance among male and female athletes (Eys et al., 2015). Specifically in female teams, cohesion develops first and then serves to positively influence team functioning. However, the opposite is true of male teams where performance develops first from which cohesion then follows. Furthermore, Eys et al. (2015) suggest that cohesion on the whole develops more quickly in male teams.

Negative Impact of Cohesion on Performance

The multidimensional nature of cohesion and the manner in which task and social cohesion interact in their impact on performance produces different effects on team functioning and performance when one type of cohesion is more salient than the other within a team. Specifically, when social cohesion on a team is high and task cohesion is low, team members report being less likely to critique key members' performance when needed. Moreover, social issues become of greater importance than task concerns and team members who do not adhere to shared group values become ostracized (Hardy, Eys, & Carron, 2005; Rovio, Eskola, Kozub, Duda, & Lintunen, 2009).

Practical Implications

Born out of the sentiment that team cohesion is too narrow a focus (McEwan & Beauchamp, 2014), there is a need for consultants to direct their intervention efforts to focus on team building as a means to the end of enhanced team cohesion and improved team performance. Loughead and Bloom (2013) note two protocols for consultants within team building:

1. **indirectly**, in which consultants facilitate team building by working with the coaching staff who will then implement the team-building protocols, and
2. **directly**, in which consultants facilitate team building by working in concert with the coaches and athletes.

There is no one established model or formula for team building, but consultants would be well served to base approaches to team building off of the specific team for whom they are consulting (Martin, Carron & Burke, 2009). The intention is not to present this material as though it is a formulaic system for team building; nor should it be received as a proposed system for a "canned approach" (Yukelson, 1997, p. 86). Instead, consultants should use the information that is offered below and design a team-building program that meets the unique culture, values, needs, and goals of the teams with whom they work (Yukelson, 1997).

Task Cohesion

As noted previously, there is strong evidence for the important role that task cohesion plays in team building and performance (Dunlop, Falk, & Beauchamp, 2013; Eys et al., 2006; Wolf et al., 2015). An essential finding is that task cohesion acts as a motivator in enhancing individual and team performance (Shapcott & Carron, 2010; Wolf et al., 2015). As such, consultants would do well to establish task-oriented interventions geared towards highlighting the value of task-oriented team climate. Several strategies have been found to build task cohesion in teams.

Consultants can lay the foundation for high task cohesion in a team by, first, working with coaches and athletes to establish clarity on their individual and collective roles and responsibilities in three areas (Carron & Eys, 2012). Role identifiability is defined by team members' understanding of what is expected of them (Kahn, Wolfe, Quinn, Snoek, & Rosenthal, 1964). For individual performance within a team setting to increase, it is paramount that each member be clear on what their role is and the specific tasks attached to that role. When these systems are not clear, both the individual and the team are in a state of role ambiguity that can have a negative effect on team functioning and performance (Cunningham & Eys, 2007). Using football as an example, there are specific roles each player is asked to fulfill such as starter, substitute player, special teams player, or scout team. Role identifiability also plays a critical role in the execution of team performance. Continuing to use football as an example, on any given play, there are eleven members who have identified specific tasks they must complete successfully for the team performance to also be successful (e.g., blocking, running routes).

Once roles within a team have been identified, the next component is for team members to accept the role they are being asked to play within the team. The degree of acceptance of team members' roles will be based on several factors: (1) how much the role aligns with their individual goals, (2) whether they are willing to subjugate their individual goals for the team's goals, and (3) how well other members of the team, including both coaches and teammates, effectively communicate the value of that role to overall team functioning and performance. Athletes report that the largest variable negatively impacting roles in sport is a lack of clear communication from the role designator who is most often the coach (Eys, Carron, Bray & Beauchamp, 2005). Consultants can have an impact on role acceptance by clearly describing the value of each member's role and encouraging coaches to regularly praise athletes for accepting and fulfilling their roles (Cunningham & Eys, 2007).

The ultimate success of a team in terms of both functioning and performance depends on how well its members can execute their roles. Role execution involves, first, team members gaining an understanding of precisely what those roles entail in terms of specific tasks they must engage in and how to perform them. Next, team members must learn and practice those tasks until they are effectively performed. Finally, they must execute those tasks successfully in competition.

Consultants can enhance the effectiveness of task cohesion by encouraging coaches to adopt a motivational climate that is task-oriented (i.e., emphasis on the successful completion of identified tasks) rather than ego-oriented (e.g., emphasis on doing tasks better than others (Carron & Eys, 2012; Eys, Jewitt, Evans, Wolf, Bruner, & Loughead, 2013). Research has shown that teams that foster a task-oriented motivational climate are reported to have greater task and social cohesion while also improving performance and reducing performance-related anxiety (Eys et al., 2013; Kingston & Hardy, 1997; Thelwell & Maynard, 2003).

Second, team members, or members of subgroups within a team (e.g., offensive linemen in football, infielders in baseball or softball, goalies in soccer), can collaborate to *establish goals* for the tasks they are responsible for. This collective effort pulls individual team members together around a shared set of goals that all are motivated to achieve and must work together to achieve.

Third, allowing team members to be a *part of the decision-making process* in selecting tasks in which they have roles. This approach has the effect of increasing ownership and commitment among team members toward those tasks. In turn, members will individually and collectively feel more motivated to complete the tasks they have chosen successfully.

Fourth, creating opportunities for *problem solving* among team members can provide solutions to team functioning and performance difficulties that arise in practice and competitive situations. This strategy has two benefits. It offers solutions that may not have been thought of otherwise. And the act of collaborating gives team members the chance to build social cohesion. A general framework for problem solving can involve team members having to complete a task or solve a problem in a way that includes the identification of roles, identified tasks for that role, and expectations for how that role is to be fulfilled.

These strategies can be used in many aspects of functioning and performance. Consultants can use them in conjunction with physical conditioning, sport training, video analysis, and mental training. Additionally, these approaches can be applied in psychoeducation, mutual sharing and disclosure, peer support, and shared accountability to a team's vision, values, standards, and expectations.

Social Cohesion

Though the research suggests that social cohesion should play a subordinate role in relation to task cohesion due to its lesser impact on team performance, social cohesion should by no means be ignored by consultants (Carron, Colman, Wheeler, & Stevens, 2002; Eys, Ritchie, Little, Slade, & Oddson, 2008; Filho, Dobersek, Gershgoren, Becker, & Tennenbaum, 2014; Jacob & Carron, 1998). To the contrary, though social cohesion may not directly influence team performance, it certainly has a meaningful effect on the enjoyment that members of a team experience, which may, indirectly, improve individual and team performance. There are a variety of tools that consultants can use to build social cohesion with a team.

One noted approach is personal disclosure and mutual sharing (PDMS). PDMS involves providing opportunities for team members to share experiences, thoughts, and feelings about their sport and non-sport lives. This practice deepens relationships, builds trust, encourages vulnerability and healthy risk-taking, and offers team members both catharsis and support, all of which will increase social cohesion. Dunn and Holt (2004) and Holt and Dunn (2006) operationalized this approach within a team setting by having individual members share meaningful personal stories prior to a major competition within the team's championship season. Pain and Harwood (2009) argued in favor of a less-elementary approach by incorporating multiple theme-focused sessions of PDMS into team building surrounding various aspects of team performance including goal-setting, positive thinking, and emotional regulation. Regardless of the approach to PDMS instituted by the consultants, athletes engaging in these practices, especially before major competitions, reported feeling a greater social bond characterized by increased trust, shared collective bond to team outcomes, and normalization of pre-competitive anxiety among members leading up to "big games" (Windsor, Barker, & McCarthy, 2011).

Similar PDMS sessions can be valuable after competitions as a means of debriefing the team's performance, allowing team members to "ventilate," acknowledging successful individual contributions, and problem solving difficulties that arise during the competitions. The sessions described by Pain and Harwood also involved inclusion of coaches in the PDMS sessions which was found to strengthen social cohesion between the coaching staff and team members.

Social cohesion can also be strengthened by having the tasks that team members engage in require cooperation, trust, and teamwork. When team members have a shared vision, common goals, and like each other, they will feel connected with their teammates, associate positive emotions with their team experiences, and work together effectively.

Another useful way to build social cohesion is through non-sport interactions among team members. Activities outside of sport allow team members to see each other in different roles where diverse personality styles and other competencies may be showcased. This approach enables team members to see their teammates as more than just athletes, but also as people with wide-ranging interests and capabilities. These added components of who team members are beyond the field of play provide a depth and breadth of "personness" that that can strengthen relationships and augment social cohesion among athletes within a team.

Mental Training for Team Building

The ultimate success of any team lies in its ability to perform its best when it counts the most. To that end, teams subject their athletes to intense conditioning and sport training to ensure that they possess the requisite physical, technical, and tactical capabilities to execute their roles maximally in competition. Mental training is also now used as an essential means of helping athletes and teams perform at their highest levels consistently. Though not often considered in this light, mental training can also be a powerful means of team building and, specifically, in developing both task and social cohesion.

As research has clearly demonstrated, many types of mental training, such as goal-setting, imagery, self-talk, intensity control, and emotional regulation, can result in improved skill acquisition and better competitive performances (Durand, Bush, & Salmela, 2002). In other words, mental exercises and tools can be used to help team members optimally perform their assigned roles and responsibilities which, in turn, can build task cohesion.

Similarly, many aspects of mental training can used to improve social cohesion. Any mental training that is done collectively can create shared experiences, build trust, establish stronger bonds, and result in the ultimate influence on social cohesion, namely, successful performances in competition. Examples of mental training that can facilitate social cohesion include team goal-setting, group mental imagery sessions, pre-competitive team routines, group relaxation, and emotional support.

Summary

- Team cohesion can be thought of as an end result, an argument can be made that there is should be more emphasis placed on team building as it involves the process by which team cohesion is achieve.
- Team cohesion refers to the degree to which individual members share a commitment to a common goal and how close they feel to one another.
- Research has demonstrated three components of team cohesion: task, social, and group pride.
- Task cohesion refers to the collective commitment that a team has to accomplishing relevant tasks in pursuit of shared goals.
- Social cohesion involves the emotional connections that members have to the team.
- Group pride is defined as members of a team exhibiting attraction to the values and standards the team represents and experiencing fulfillment in the status and prestige team membership affords them.
- Consultants would be well served to ask what specific team-building interventions will encourage team cohesion and, by extension, team functioning and performance.
- Strategies for building task cohesion include team members collaborating to establish goals for the tasks they are responsible for, including team members in decision making, and allowing team members to be a part of problem solving.
- Though social cohesion may not directly influence team performance, it does have a meaningful effect on the overall experience and enjoyment that members of a team experience.
- Personal disclosure and mutual sharing (PDMS) involves providing opportunities for team members to share experiences, thoughts, and feelings about their sport and non-sport lives which practice deepens relationships, builds trust, encourages vulnerability and healthy risk-taking, and offers team members both catharsis and support.
- Mental training can be a powerful means of team building and, specifically, in developing both task and social cohesion.

References

Beal, D. J., Cohen, R. R., Burke, M. J., & McLendon C. L. (2003). Cohesion and performance in groups: A meta-analytic clarification of construct relations. *Journal of Applied Sport Psychology, 88*, 989–1004.

Bruner, M. W., Boardley, I. D., & Côté, J. (2014). Social identity and prosocial and antisocial behavior in youth sport. *Psychology of Sport and Exercise, 15*(1), 56–64. doi: 10.1016/j.psychsport.2013.09.003

Carron, A. V., Colman, M. M., Wheeler, J., & Stevens, D. (2002). Cohesion and performance in sport: A meta-analysis. *Journal of Sport & Exercise Psychology, 24*, 168–188.

Carron, A. V., & Eys, M. A. (2012). *Group dynamics in sport*. Fitness Information Technology.

Carron, A. V., Widmeyer, W. N., & Brawley, L. R. (1985). The development of an instrument to assess cohesion in sport teams: The group environment questionnaire. *Journal of Sport Psychology, 7*(3), 244–266. doi: 10.1123/jsp.7.3.244

Cunningham, I. J., & Eys, M. A. (2007). Role ambiguity and intra-team communication in interdependent sport teams. *Journal of Applied Social Psychology, 37*(10), 2220–2237.

Dunlop, W. L., Falk, C. F., & Beauchamp, M. R. (2013). How dynamic are exercise group dynamics? Examining changes in cohesion within class-based exercise programs. *Health Psychology, 32*(12), 1240–1243. doi: 10.1037/a0030412

Durand-Bush, N., & Salmela, J. H. (2002). The development and maintenance of expert athletic performance: Perceptions of World and Olympic champions. *Journal of Applied Sport Psychology, 14*(3), 154–171.

Eys, M. A., & Brawley, L. R. (2018). Reflections on cohesion research with sport and exercise groups. *Social Personality Psychology Compass, 12*(4), 1–15.

Eys, M. A., Carron, A. V., Bray, S. R., & Beauchamp, M. R. (2005). The relationship between role ambiguity and intention to return the following season. *Journal of Applied Sport Psychology, 17*(3), 255–261.

Eys, M. A., Evans, M. B., Martin, L. J., Ohlert, J., Wolf, S. A., Van Brussel, M., & Steins, C. (2015). Cohesion and performance for male and female sport teams. *The Sport Psychologist, 29*, 97–109.

Eys, M. A., Jewitt, E., Evans, M. B., Wolf, S., Bruner, M. W., & Loughead, T. M. (2013). Coach-Initiated motivational climate and cohesion in youth sport. *Research Quarterly for Exercise and Sport, 84*(3), 373–383. doi: 10.1080/02701367.2013.814909

Eys, M., & Kim, J. (2017, June 28). *Team building and group cohesion in the context of sport and performance psychology (vol. 1)*. Oxford: Oxford University Press.

Eys, M. A., Patterson, M. M., Loughead, T. M., & Carron, A. V. (2006). Team building in sport. In D. Hackfort, J. L. Duda, & R. Lidor (Eds.), *Handbook of research in applied sport and exercise psychology: International perspectives* (pp. 219–231). Morgantown, WV: Fitness Information Technology.

Eys, M. A., Ritchie, S., Little, J., Slade, H., & Oddson, B. (2008). Leadership status congruency and cohesion in outdoor expedition groups. *Journal of Experimental Education, 30*, 78–94.

Festinger, L. (1950). Informal social communication. *Psychological Review, 57*, 271–282.

Festinger, L., Schachter, S., & Back, K. W. (1963). *Social pressures in informal groups: A study of human factors in housing*. Stanford CA: Stanford University Press.

Filho, E., Dobersek, U., Gershgoren, L., Becker, B., & Tennenbaum, G. (2014). The cohesion-performance relationship in sport: A 10-year retrospective meta-analysis. *Sport Sciences for Health, 10*, 165–177.

Gross, N., & Martin, W. E. (1952). On group cohesiveness. *American Journal of Sociology, 57*(6), 546–564. doi: 10.1086/221041

Hardy, J., Eys, M. A., & Carron A. V. (2005). Exploring the potential disadvantages of high cohesion in sports teams. *Small Group Research, 36*, 166–189.

Holt, N. L., & Dunn, J. G. H. (2006). Guidelines for delivering personal-disclosure mutual-sharing team building Interventions. *The Sport Psychologist, 20*(3), 348–367. doi: 10.1123/tsp.20.3.348

Horn T. S., Byrd, M., Martin, E., & Young, C. (2012). Perceived motivational climate and team cohesion in adolescent athletes. *Sport Science Review, 21*, 25–49.

Jacob, C. S., & Carron, A. V. (1998). The association between status and cohesion in sport teams. *Journal of Sports Sciences, 16*, 187–198.

Jowett, S., & Chaundy, V. (2004). An investigation into the impact of coach leadership and coach-athlete relationship on group cohesion. *Group Dynamics: Research, Theory, & Practice, 8*, 302–311.

Kahn, R. L., Wolfe, D. M., Quinn, R. P., Snoek, J. D., & Rosenthal, R. A. (1964). Organizational Stress: Studies in Role Conflict and Ambiguity. *Administrative Science Quarterly, 10*(1), 470. doi: 10.2307/2391654

Kingston, K. M., & Hardy, L. (1997). Effects of different types of goals on processes that support performance. *The Sport Psychologist, 11*(3), 277–293. doi: 10.1123/tsp.11.3.277

Loughead, T. M., & Bloom, G. A. (2013). Team cohesion in sport: Critical overview and implications for team building. In Paul Potrac, Wade Gilbert, & Jim Denison (Eds.), *Routledge Handbook of Sports Coaching* (pp. 345–356). New York, NY: Routledge.

Martin, L., Carron, A. V., & Burke, S. M. (2009). Team building interventions in sport: A meta-analysis. *Sport & Exercise Psychology Review, 5*, 3–18.

McEwan, D., & Beauchamp, M. R. (2014). Teamwork in sport: a theoretical and integrative review. *International Review of Sport and Exercise Psychology, 7*(1), 229–250. doi: 10.1080/1750984X.2014.932423

McLaren, C. D., Eys, M. A., & Murray, R. A. (2015). A coach-initiated motivational climate intervention and athletes' perceptions of group cohesion in youth sport. *Sport, Exercise, and Performance Psychology, 4*(2), 113–126. doi: 10.1037/spy0000026

Mikalachki, 1969

Mullen, B., & Copper, C. (1994). The relationship between group cohesiveness and performance: An integration. *Psychological Bulletin, 115*(2), 210–227.

Pain, M., & Harwood, C. (2009). Team building through mutual sharing and open discussion of team functioning. *The Sport Psychologist, 23*(4), 523–542. doi: 10.1123/tsp.23.4.523

Rovio, E., Eskola, S. A., Duda, J. L., & Lintunen, T. (2009). Can high group cohesion be harmful? A case study of a junior ice-hockey team. *Small Group Research, 40,* 421–435.

Severt, J. B., & Estrada, A. X. (2015). On the function and structure of group cohesion. In E. Salas, W. B. Vessey, & A. X. Estrada (Eds.), *Team cohesion: Advances in psychological theory, methods and practice* (pp. 3–24). Bingley: Emerald Publishing.

Shapcott, K. M., & Carron, A. V. (2010). Development and validation of a team attributional style questionnaire. *Group Dynamics: Theory, Research, and Practice, 14*(2), 93–113. doi: 10.1037/a0018252

Thelwell, R. C., & Maynard, I. W. (2003). The effects of a mental skills package on "repeatable good performance" in cricketers. *Psychology of Sport and Exercise, 4,* 377–396. doi: 10.1016/S1469-0292(02)00036-5

Vincer, D. J. E., & Loughead, T. M. (2010). The relationship between athlete leadership behaviors and cohesion in team sports. *The Sport Psychologist, 24,* 448–467.

Windsor, P., Barker, J., & McCarthy, P. (2011). Doing sport psychology: Personal-disclosure mutual-sharing in professional soccer. *The Sport Psychologist, 25,* 94–114.

Wolf, S. A., Eys, M. A., & Kleinert, J. (2015). Predictors of the precompetitive anxiety response: Relative impact and prospects for anxiety regulation. *International Journal of Sport and Exercise Psychology, 13*(4), 344–358. doi: 10.1080/1612197X.2014.982676

Yukelson, D. (1997). Principles of effective team building interventions in sport: A direct services approach at Penn State University. *Journal of Applied Sport Psychology, 9*(1), 73–96.

TEAM COMMUNICATION

Amanda Myhrberg and Jim Taylor

Consider the importance of communication at every level and in every function of a sports team. It is vital to all aspects of team functioning, interactions, and performance. Communication is required to express the team culture, establish relationships, teach new skills in practice, and perform effectively in competition. Effective communication:

- offers clarity and understanding;
- leads to empathy and trust;
- identifies problems and provides solutions;
- facilitates decision making;
- enhances skill acquisition;
- ensures coordinated effort;
- resolves conflict; and
- allows for successful team performances.

Most basically, communication involves the sharing and exchange of information, ideas, and emotions (Kim, Magnusen, & Andrew, 2016). It can occur through several forms of media including spoken or written words, voice inflection, facial expression, emotional tone, and body language. Imagine the execution of an offensive play in football. The quarterback verbally communicates a pass play in the huddle. He may call an audible in response to the defensive formation. He calls the snap count. As the play unfolds, the quarterback communicates messages with his eyes to both his receivers and his opponents. He does a pump fake. He turns his body in one direction while pointing in another direction. The quarterback makes eye contact with various receivers. Finally, he launches the ball through the air. If the ball is caught, he congratulates his teammates. If the throw is incomplete, he may provide encouragement and corrective feedback. Without all these methods of communication, team success would be impossible. In sum, without communication, a team would cease to be a team.

Despite its obvious importance to team functioning and performance, communication is not typically seen as a priority that deserves time, energy, and resources to maximize its value. It is often not even seen as a tool that can enhance performance. Much like breathing, it happens frequently and automatically and, as a result, conscious attention or thought is rarely given to it, except when a communication problem, such as a misunderstanding or conflict, arises.

Consultants can play an important role is ensuring that teams appreciate the power of effective communication and the dangers of poor communication, engage with it in a deliberate way, and actively train its members to use communication in ways that optimize its value. From administration to its coaching staff to its members, consultants can offer teams practical ways to improve the quality of their communications to reduce and resolve conflict when it arises.

Theory and Research

Communications within teams is characterized as interpersonal communication involving at least two people engaged in a meaningful exchange of information (Bell & Riol, 2017; Weinberg & Gould, 2011). Interpersonal communication starts with one person who decides to send a message. They then encode it, meaning they choose the way it will be sent (e.g., verbally or nonverbally), and send the message with the intention that it will be accurately understood by the receiver. Next, the recipient receives and decodes the message; in doing so, establishes their understanding of the message. Finally, the receiver selects an appropriate response to the initial message and conveys it in some form to the original sender. This chain of communications initiates a feedback loop until all relevant information is transmitted between the two parties (Yukelson, 2006). Essential to effective communication is that, regardless of the medium that is used, the message that is received is understood in a way that aligns with the intention behind the message that is sent.

Verbal messages have been found to be the most direct and effective form of communication because most words have a shared and agreed-upon meaning, thus reducing the chances of ambiguity or misinterpretation. In turn, nonverbal communication is more amorphous and, as a result, more prone to misunderstanding. This divergence is important because research indicates that nonverbal messages, for all their relative uncertainty, are less in our conscious control, yet convey 50–70 percent of the information that is communicated (Mouratidis, Lens, & Vansteenkiste, 2010; Weinberg & Gould, 2011).

Shared Mental Models

In an ideal world, communications between two or more people would work seamlessly, meaning the messages that are sent are the same messages that are received, and all messages would be conveyed without ambiguity, confusion, or misinterpretation. However, in the real world, some communication breakdowns are inevitable for several reasons. First, senders and receivers each have their own unique perceptual, interpretive, and analytical filters, based on their genetic make-ups, past experiences, biases, and preconceived notions, that can result in a disconnect between message sent and message received. Second, people have varied capabilities for encoding and articulating information, ideas, and emotions. Similarly, people have a range of capacities for decoding and understanding the messages that are sent. Third, depending on the tone of the messages, they may be garbled due to hesitancy to communicate the message (e.g., with criticism) or muddled in their conveyance by strong emotions (e.g., anger). In all cases, these breakdowns in communication can have a significant impact on individual team members and overall team functioning, interactions, and performance (Rasker, Post, & Schraagen, 2000).

The construct of a *shared mental model* can be a helpful tool in minimizing communication breakdowns and strengthening the effectiveness of communications within a team. Shared mental models consist of a collective understanding of how a system composed of a group of people work. They involve an agreed-upon set of intentions, needs, knowledge, procedures, and vocabulary. They also create a cognitive framework (i.e., a way of thinking) that helps to predict understand, and coordinate individual and team behavior (Eccles & Tenenbaum, 2004).

From a team perspective, a shared mental model encompasses a team's values, attitudes, goals, and standards of behavior that comprise its team culture. In a sense, a shared mental model allows team members to "think alike" and, as a result, makes communication more clear, understandable, and aligned. A shared mental model leads to more effective communication because team members see and interpret their world in a similar manner. Giske, Rodahl, and Hoigaard (2015) investigated the existence and development of a shared mental model in elite ice hockey and handball players and found that shared mental models do exist at the elite level.

With a common view of the world, misinterpretations and misunderstandings are less likely, thus the potential for conflict is reduced. A key benefit of this shared mental model is a stronger team culture, greater task and social cohesion, and a greater sense of connectedness among team members. Establishing shared mental models also allows individuals on a team to predict behavior during moments where lengthy communication might not be possible (e.g., middle of a game) (Blickensderfer & Reynolds, 2010; Lim & Klein, 2006). Researchers have found that certain types of feedback help in the development of shared mental models: self-correction and performance monitoring (Rasker et al., 2000). Self-correction is viewed as a process that occurs after the task is completed. With self-correction, team members engage in reflection of the past events, correcting errors, discussing strategies, and planning for the next time. By doing this, team members correct their team attitudes, cognitions, and behaviors without outside intervention (Rasker et al., 2000). Performance monitoring is when members of the team are capable of giving, seeking, and receiving feedback related to the execution of a task.

Communication and Team Development

Tuckman's four stages of group development describe the journey needed for a group of individuals to become a team: forming, storming, norming, and performing (Tuckman, 1965; Tuckman & Jensen, 1977). Communication plays a vital role in each stage. The *forming* stage is characterized by new team members getting to know each other. Interactions tend to be polite and cautious and relationships remain at a superficial level. Initial goals and tasks are established, but team efforts begin slowly and build toward greater coordination. This stage is best served for teams to communicate openly about identity, culture, values, attitudes, standards of behavior, and goals. It also allows teams to establish communication as an essential component of its structures and processes. In doing so, a shared mental model of communication is an important factor becomes woven into the fabric of the team (Tuckman & Jensen, 1977).

Next, teams move to the *storming* stage in which members gain greater understanding of their individual needs and what will be required of them to become an integral part of the team. Conflicts often arise as team members find, by choice or selection, their role in a team and what tasks they must assume. They also begin to figure out how to work collectively rather than independently. Emotions are heightened, equal parts facilitative and disruptive due to the changes that are occurring within the team as it gels. Storming also involves establishing defined expectations of its team members as limits are challenged and shaped according to the emerging team culture. Effective communication can minimize the negative impact of this stage by providing a means of increasing trust and reducing conflict.

In fact, teams that embrace conflict and learn to resolve disagreements in a healthy manner end up stronger. Additionally, experiencing conflict within a team has been shown to encourage communication and build trust (Bradley, Anderson, Baur, & Klotz, 2015). Tekleab, Quigley, and Tesluk (2009) wanted to investigate how a team navigates conflict, works together, and eventually develops into an effective team. Results from the study demonstrated that managing conflict in earlier stages increased overall team cohesion and effectiveness (Tekleab et al., 2009).

As team formation develops, it moves into the *norming* stage in which intimacy is established and cooperation between team members develops. When communication is emphasized from the initial stages of this process, team members are more united around a common vision and develop a shared mental model. Due to greater mutual understanding and respect, there is an acceptance of individual differences, and members feel like an integral and valued part of the team. Having effective communication leads to greater social and task cohesion (Bradley et al., 2015).

Lastly, teams that are well formed and capable move toward the *performing* stage of Tuckman's stages of group development (Tuckman, 1965; Tuckman & Jensen, 1977). In the performing stage. team members can direct their energies toward collaboratively executing their identified tasks and pursuing their specified goals.

By this time, team members have the motivation, knowledge, and skills to perform their individual and team tasks successfully. In the performing stage, communication is important for both maintaining high-quality effort and further developing as team members and as a team overall. Additionally, clear and effective communication encourages commitment to team goals, facilitates the quality and efficiency of individual and team practice and competitive performance, and produces sound problem solving and decision making.

Practical Implications

Communication is a skill that develops with practice. As a result, consultants can provide teams with the values, attitudes, and tools to enable and encourage effective communication. There are two key areas that consultants can teach teams: Communication skills and conflict resolution strategies.

Facilitating Team Communication

Establishing effective communication within a team begins with coaches and how they communicate with their fellow coaches and their athletes. Coaches show the team how communication is prioritized, why it is important, and how it is used to enhance team functioning and team performance.

Create a Culture of Communication

The development of effective communication begins by having coaches create a team culture in which communication plays a vital role. It begins by being woven into the fabric of the culture as an essential value that sets the tone for its use among the team. This foundation is then operationalized in the standards of behavior that team members are expected to uphold related to communication and, at a hands-on level, how communication is used and incorporated into the practices, routines, and interactions of daily team life.

Model Communication

The most powerful way that coaches can encourage their team to adopt effective communication is through modeling of good communication behaviors. When coaches use the approaches and strategies that will be described below, team members get the message that communication is important. Also, by observing coaches, it also conveys to team members specific ways for them to communicate with teammates. Consultants can work with coaches at two levels: first, to help them to better understand how they communicate and identify their communication strengths (e.g., explanations of correct technique) and areas in need of improvement (e.g., messages of anger or frustration); and, second, to instruct them in ways to improve their communication skills.

Communication Techniques

As noted earlier, effective communication at the most basic level is about sending and receiving a message. Implementing good communication techniques can be an art as well as a science. There are empirically tested strategies, but it is also important to remember there will be individual differences when working with teams and individuals (Gustafsson, Lindholm, & Sikstrom, 2013). Consultants can provide the means by which teams can formally learn and practice these communication skills (Gustafsson et al., 2013; Weinberg & Gould, 2011; Yukleson, 2006):

- Understand who the message is for to judge how the message will be received and to shape the best possible message for the recipient.
- Start from a position of mutual respect and shared purpose.
- Be honest and open.

- Take ownership of messages by using "I" statements (e.g., "I feel that . . .") rather than "You" statements (e.g., "You did that . . .") which are often blaming or accusatory.
- If the communication is important, rehearse it to ensure clarity of message.
- Be aware of the emotions that might be brought into a communication and how they might alter your message.
- If the communication is in person, be aware of body language to ensure that it aligns with the message.
- Because effective communication is interactive, make listening a priority so that the message that is sent is accurately received.
- See feedback as a means of being and doing better rather than a criticism or personal attack.
- If the communication is sensitive, focus on the positives (e.g., what is good) rather than the negatives (e.g., what is bad).
- Deliberately choose a form of communication (e.g., in-person, phone, text, email) that will maximize the chances of the message is received effectively.

Team Conflict

An inevitable part of any team is that conflicts will arise among team members. Conflict can be thought of as an intense disagreement about a topic of importance to those involved for which an immediate solution is not forthcoming (Laios & Tzetzis, 2005). Researchers have identified four types of conflicts (Bradley et al., 2015; De Dreu & Weingart, 2003; De Wit, Greer, & Jehn, 2012; Mohd, Omar, & Asri, 2016; Tekleab et al., 2009):

- task conflicts (e.g., differing goals or approaches);
- relationship conflicts (e.g., dislike, jealousy);
- process conflicts (e.g., leadership, roles); and
- status conflicts (e.g., power, competition).

Within these four broad categories, common team conflicts include:

- lack of communication;
- misunderstandings;
- personality differences;
- competing goals;
- lack of role ambiguity or acceptance;
- differing opinions;
- ego investment;
- power struggles;
- strong emotions;
- personal agendas;
- uncertainty;
- competitive stress;
- intrateam competition for available positions; and
- ups and downs of individual and team performance.

Conflict can be potentially harmful to both individual and team functioning, relationships, and performance. Individual effects include a loss of motivation, stress, distancing from team members, a decrease in individual performance. The impact of conflict on a team includes reduced, ineffective, or damaging communication, loss of respect and trust, a loss of team confidence, a decline in collaboration, and poor team performance (De Dreu & Weingart, 2003).

At the same time, conflict can be beneficial to both individual team members and the team as a whole (Bradley et al., 2015):

- acts as a wake-up call for the need for change;
- identifies unproductive or inefficient processes;

- reveals useful new ideas;
- expresses team member needs;
- encourages tolerance, flexibility, and compromise;
- provides opportunities to improve communication skills;
- teaches self-awareness;
- resolution improves morale;
- indicates problems;
- offers solutions;
- improves performance; and
- supports personal growth.

Preventing Conflict

The best way to deal with conflicts is to prevent them from occurring. Consultants can suggest approaches and strategies in every aspect of team functioning that will reduce the chances of conflicts arising. This intervention begins with team culture in which, as described above, communication is considered an important value and team members are shown effective ways of communicating. Conflict resolution is further strengthened by having consultants proactively teach the communication skills described above. Coaches and team members are encouraged to be honest, give constructive feedback, and set team goals at the beginning of the season to ensure buy-in (Wachsmuth, Jowett, & Harwood, 2017).

Task conflict can be reduced by establishing task clarity and improving individual and shared task execution among team members. Relationship conflict can be mitigated by building trust, fostering open communication, and encouraging friendships and interdependence. Process conflict can be lessened by ensuring role clarity and acceptance and setting clear procedures for all aspects of team functioning. Finally, status conflict can be eased by ensuring respect among all team members, nurturing collaborative rather than competitive goals, and recognizing the contributions of every team member to team success. Additionally, the adoption of standards of behavior that address expectations of team members, team interactions, general team rules, and how team members should behave can have an overall positive effect on preventing team conflict.

Resolving Conflicts

Consultants can provide approaches and strategies to prevent conflicts from arising within a team, but the very nature of team sports means that conflicts will emerge despite those efforts. It is not a matter of whether conflicts will occur, but rather how the individuals involved and the team as a whole respond to them. Consultants can also play a key role in showing teams how to approach and react to conflict among its members and, in some cases, act as objective mediator who helps to broker a positive resolution.

Before specific strategies are discussed, consultants can shape conflict resolution by the attitudes that team members have about conflict. Conflict can be uncomfortable and, typically, people often prefer to avoid rather than confront it. Unfortunately, conflicts that are ignored on the surface, often fester underneath, causing the conflict to grow in size and intensity. Consultants can encourage teams to embrace conflicts and to address them head on as early as possible to prevent them from escalating or spreading. This approach tends to reduce the pressure and tension associated with conflicts by allowing them to be expressed and resolved immediately rather than being left suppressed and unresolved by the involved parties.

Another "setting the stage" strategy for resolving conflicts involves having everyone caught up in a conflict stepping away from the situation that caused it and taking a break. This tactic allows the conflicted team members to gain emotional distance from the conflict, calm down, and then to return to the situation more relaxed, rational, and open to finding a resolution. During this separation, those involved can actively relax their body with deep breathing, meditation, or exercise. They can also "vent" their concerns to another team member thus allowing them to release some of their pent-up emotions.

If some sort of mediation is needed, the consultant, coach, or team captain can also meet with the team members who are having the conflict separately to understand it and come to some consensus on how best to move forward to resolution. It should also be decided whether the conflict is best addressed privately or in the presence of the team. Once the stage has been set for resolution of the conflict and the conflicted parties meet, a variety of other strategies can be used (Dizon, 2018; Dontigney, 2018; Semczuk, 2017):

- Set ground rules emphasizing mutual respect, calmness, an openness to understand the other person's perspective, and the shared desire to resolve the conflict to everyone's satisfaction.
- Get to the real issue underlying the conflict.
- Don't make assumptions.
- Focus on the problem, not the person.
- Focus on the present.
- Start with shared goals.
- Focus on solutions rather than problems.
- Use "I" statements when expressing what you think and feel.
- Listen as much as talk and don't interrupt.
- Seek out win–win.
- Be willing to compromise.

If handled properly, using the strategies described above, conflict can be a valuable contributor to team development in several ways. It can affirm team culture, strengthen team cohesion, reinvigorate team values, and model healthy team behavior.

Summary

- Communication is required to express the team culture, establish relationships, teach new skills in practice, and perform effectively in competition.
- Communication involves the sharing and exchange of information, ideas, and emotions, and can occur through several forms of media including spoken or written words, voice inflection, facial expression, emotional tone, and body language.
- Consultants can play an important role in ensuring that teams appreciate the power of effective communication and the dangers of poor communication, engage with it in a deliberate and formal way, and actively train its members to use communication in ways that optimize its value.
- Essential to effective communication is that, regardless of the medium that is used, the message that is received is understood in a way that aligns with the intention behind the message that is sent.
- Verbal messages have been found to be the most direct and effective form of communication because most words have a shared and agreed-upon meaning, thus reducing the chances of ambiguity or misinterpretation.
- In an ideal world, communications between two or more people work seamlessly, meaning the messages that are sent are the same messages that are received, and all messages would be conveyed without ambiguity, confusion, or misinterpretation; however, in the real world, some communication breakdowns are inevitable.
- Shared mental models involve a collective understanding of how a system composed of a group of people work and involves an agreed-upon set of intentions, needs, knowledge, procedures, and vocabulary.
- Communication plays an important role in Tuckman's four stages of group development outline the journey needed for a group of individuals to become a team: forming, storming, norming, and performing.
- Consultants can provide teams with the values, attitudes, and tools to enable and encourage effective communication.
- Establishing effective communication within a team begins with coaches and how they communicate with the team. Including creating a culture of communication, modeling effective communication, and teaching athletes useful communication techniques.
- Four types of team conflict have been identified: task, relationship, process, and status.
- Conflict can be potentially harmful to both individual and team functioning, relationships, and performance, yet it can also provide benefits to teams.

- The best way to deal with conflicts is to prevent them from occurring. Consultants can suggest approaches and strategies in every aspect of team functioning that will reduce the chances of conflicts arising.
- Though consultants can provide approaches and strategies to prevent conflicts from arising within a team, the very nature of team sports means that conflicts will emerge despite those efforts and consultants can shape conflict resolution by the attitudes that team members have about conflict.

References

Bell, R., & Riol, C. F. (2017). The impact of cross-cultural communication on collective efficacy in NCAA basketball teams. *International Journal of Cross Cultural Management, 17*(2), 175–195.

Blickensderfer, E. L., & Reynolds, R. (2010). Shared expectations and implicit coordination in tennis doubles teams. *Journal of Applied Sport Psychology, 22*, 486–499.

Bradley, B. H., Anderson, H. J., Baur, J. E., & Klotz, A. C. (2015). When conflict helps: Integrating evidence for beneficial conflict in groups and teams under three perspectives. *Group Dynamics: Theory, Research, & Practice, 19*(4), 243–272.

De Dreu, C. K., & Weingart, L. R. (2003). Task versus relationship conflict, team performance, and team member satisfaction: a meta-analysis. *Journal of Applied Psychology, 88*(4), 741.

De Wit, F. R., Greer, L. L., & Jehn, K. A. (2012). The paradox of intragroup conflict: a meta-analysis. *Journal of Applied Psychology, 97*(2), 360.

Dizon, A. (2018). Top 25 workplace conflict resolution strategies from the pros. Retrieved from https://fitsmallbusiness.com/workplace-conflict-resolution-strategies (accessed December 14, 2018).

Dontigney, E. (2018). 5 conflict management strategies. Retrieved from https://smallbusiness.chron.com/5-conflict-management-strategies-16131.html (accessed December 14, 2018).

Eccles, D., & Tenenbaum, G. (2004). Why an expert team is more than a team of experts: A social-cognitive conceptualization of team coordination and communication in sport. *Journal of Sport & Exercise Psychology, 26*, 542–560.

Giske, R., Rodahl, S. E., & Hoigaard, R. (2015). Shared mental task models in elite ice hockey and handball teams: Does it exist and how does the coach intervene to make an impact. *Journal of Applied Sport Psychology, 27*, 20–34.

Gustafsson Senden, M., Lindholm, T., & Sikstrom, S. (2013). Selection bias in choice of words: Evalutations of "I" and "we" differ between contexts, but "they" are always worse. *Journal of Language and Social Psychology, 33*(1), 49–67.

Kim, S., Magnusen, M. J., & Andrew, D. P. S. (2016). Divided we fall: Examining the relationship between horizontal communication and team commitment via team cohesion. *International Journal of Sports Science & Coaching, 11*(5), 625–636.

Lim, B. C., & Klein, K. J. (2006). Team mental models and team performance: A field study of the effects of team mental model similarity and accuracy. *Journal of Organizational Behavior, 27*(4), 403–418.

Mohd, I. H., Omar, M. K., & Asri, T. N. T. (2016). Organizational conflict: The effects on team effectiveness in a Malaysian statutory body. *The European Proceedings of Social & Behavioural Sciences, 165*, 572–576.

Mouratidis, A., Lens, W., & Vansteenkiste, M. (2010). How you provide corrective feedback makes all the difference: The motivating role of communicating in an autonomy-supporting way. *Journal of Sport and Exercise Psychology, 32*, 619–637.

Rasker, P. C., Post, W. M., & Schraagen, J. M. C. (2000). Effects of two types of intra-team feedback on developing a shared mental model in command and control teams. *Ergonomics, 43*(8), 1167–1189.

Semczuk, N. (2017). The 10 most effective conflict resolution strategies. Retrieved from https://thedigitalprojectmanager.com/10-effective-conflict-resolution-strategies (accessed December 14, 2018).

Tekleab, A. G., Quigley, N. R., & Tesluk, P. E. (2009). A longitudinal study of team conflict, conflict management, cohesion, and team effectiveness. *Group and Organization Management, 34*, 170–205.

Tuckman, B. W. (1965). Developmental sequence in small groups. *Psychological Bulletin, 63*(6), 384.

Tuckman, B. W., & Jensen, M. A. C. (1977). Stages of small-group development revisited. *Group & Organization Studies, 2*(4), 419–427.

Wachsmuth, S., Jowett, S., & Harwood, C.G. (2017). Conflict among athletes and their coaches: What is the theory and research so far? *International Review of Sport and Exercise Psychology, 10*(1), 84–107.

Weinberg, R.S., & Gould, D. (Eds.). (2011). *Foundations of sport and exercise psychology*, 5th ed. Champaign, IL: Human Kinetics.

Yukelson, D. (2006). Communicating effectively. In J. M. Williams (Ed.), *Applied sport psychology: Personal growth to peak performance* (pp. 174–191). New York, NY: McGraw-Hill Higher Education.

11

PARENTS

Introduction

Jim Taylor

Sports can be a wonderful part of raising healthy children. Parents who expose their children to sports at a young age are not only providing their children with experiences that have immediate advantages, but also lifelong value in many aspects of their lives. Regardless of the sports in which they participate or the level they attain, sports offer children a wide range of life-affirming benefits that will serve them well throughout their childhoods and into adulthood:

- **Physical health:** exercise, fitness, vitality, and mastery of their bodies.
- **Mental health:** self-identity, self-esteem, goals, passions, commitment, confidence, focus, discipline, and resilience, just to name a few.
- **Social:** teamwork, cooperation, communication, conflict, relationships, mentorships, shared family experiences.
- **Play:** learn, practice, and ingrain essential physical, personal, and social skills in preparation for adulthood.
- **Fun:** touches children in ways that create joy.

A Changing Youth Sports Culture

Unfortunately, the value of youth sports that was just described in previous generations are losing their place in a youth sports culture that has changed significantly in the 21st century. This shift in the purpose and focus of youth sports over the last several decades is not only preventing children from benefiting from sports participation, but, for many, sports may incur harm to their athletic, personal, and social development. This new youth sports landscape has been due to changes that have been occurring due predominantly to the infusion of money into sports, turning it into "Big Sport" in which the goal is now about making money at every level of sport. Moreover, the allure of wealth and fame that comes from athletic success, by parents and children alike, has distorted youth sports into something that, in some ways, is unrecognizable from what it was 50 years ago.

This new youth sports culture has resulted in the emergence of a new kind of sport parent for whom the goal of sports has shifted from the many benefits described above to preparing their children for athletic greatness. It has also created a new industry—what is referred to as the "youth sport-industrial complex"—that has caused the professional of youth sports. This new direction is aimed at fulfilling the needs of this new generation of sport parents and making money for those who are perpetuating this new culture including youth sports leagues, teams, schools, coaches, and private trainers.

This new youth sports culture, which has made early specialization and results its central tenets, is having the cumulative effect of hurting young athletes in several ways. The focus on results from teams, coaches, and parents has become the principal message that young athletes receive in their sports participation. In turn, they can't help but internalize this preoccupation with results. This emphasis brings expectations and pressure which can lead to fear of failure and debilitating performance anxiety. The ultimate outcome is an unpleasant and unfulfilling sports experience which often ends with children leaving youth sports because it's no longer fun and is too stressful.

Good Intentions

All parents *want* what best for their children in their sports participation. But, the reality is that those good intentions don't always translate into *doing* what's best for their children. Some parents have fallen prey to the unhealthy youth sports culture as a result of the pressures they feel from this youth sports culture, youth teams, coaches, and other parents. At the same time, the vast majority of parents have their children's best interests at heart, but simply don't have the perspective, information, and tools to create a life-affirming sports experience for their children.

Before this shift in the youth sport culture occurred, most of the forces involved, including coaches, teams, and parents, supported children's healthy involvement in sports. But now, because of the dramatic and unhealthy changes that have happened to the youth sports culture, the role of parents in guiding their children's sports participation has taken on new importance. In other words, parents need to counteract the negative messages of today's youth sports culture to ensure that their children are playing sports for healthy reasons. These responsibilities include:

- examining their own intentions about their children's sports participation;
- emphasizing the healthy reasons and benefits of youth sports;
- advocating for their children to ensure a healthy sports experience;
- shielding their children from the harmful youth sports culture;
- challenging the current youth sports culture to reexamine its priorities; and
- being a role model for why children participate in sports.

The goal for every sport parent is to ensure that their children have the most positive and healthy sports experience possible. This objective means that their immediate sports participation is healthy, fun, and rewarding. In the long run, this goal involves parents putting children in a sports environment that allows them to develop the physical, personal, and social skills that will enable them to achieve their sports goals and positively impact their lives for years to come.

Consultants can play another important role when working with a team by developing a parent education program that will support the healthy development of young athletes. One-on-one consultations, group workshops, and collaborating with teams and parents to create a parent "contract" are just a few of the ways in which consultants can help ensure that parents develop and maintain healthy perspectives and attitudes about their children's sports participation.

IMPACT OF PARENTS ON YOUNG ATHLETES

Christopher Stanley and Jim Taylor

The National Council of Youth Sports (2008) survey reported approximately 60 million children are involved in some form of organized youth sport each year. Moreover, 44 million of these youth participate in more than one sport. These statistics suggest that youth sports are viewed by parents as valuable experiences for their children. Organized youth sports are characterized by: (1) adult supervision and leadership; (2) an emphasis on skill building; and (3) an element of structure (Eccles, Barber, Stone, & Hunt, 2003). Participation in organized youth sports has been linked with a variety of psychosocial benefits including enhanced self-esteem, academic achievement, and leadership skills (Bohnert & Garber, 2007; Stanley & Bohnert, 2011). When coupled with the physical health benefits sports involvement offers, it is understandably a popular outlet for children (and their parents) to pursue.

Parents play a vital role in organized youth sports as volunteer coaches, managers, and administrators. Additionally, parents are involved in governance, planning, finances, and travel of youth sports. This parental involvement continues in different forms as young athletes climb the competitive ladder with elite teams, off-season camps, private coaching, and college recruitment (Ryan, Groves, & Schneider, 2007). Given this level of engagement by parents, an exploration into the impact that parents can have on their young athletes, both positive and negative, is warranted. Moreover, an essential part of this discussion involves how consultants can help parents provide a nurturing sports environment in which their children can participate that will foster their healthy athletic and personal development.

Theory and Research

A variety of theories clarify parental impact on their children's development, originating in the broader disciplines of family systems, social learning, and cognitive development. Seminal theorists have long asserted the importance of social interactions and processes in cognitive and socioemotional development (e.g., Bandura, 1973; Bronfenbrenner, 1979; Vygotsky, 1962). Notably, critical interactions which facilitate dialogue and transmission of messages may occur in the context of sport. Whether these experiences are unorganized (e.g., backyard ball games) or organized (e.g., youth leagues), they often create an "arena" in which children and adults interact, collaborate, play, and learn.

A *family systems* perspective may aid in clarifying how parents impact young athletes' thoughts, emotions, and behaviors in athletic contexts. Specifically, a principle tenet of family systems theory is that each family group is an important element of the larger group system (e.g., teams, leagues, and youth-sport culture), and all members are interdependent upon one another, and also responsive to the forces that arise in the environment. Additionally, systems theory is useful in clarifying family dynamics, communication patterns, and boundaries within and outside of the family (Rothbaum, Rosen, Ujiie, & Uchida, 2002). A systems perspective fits nicely within youth sport contexts as parents and young athletes are often mutually reliant upon one another to participate and perform in a sport and concurrently reliant upon others residing within larger sports systems (e.g., coaches, teammates).

According to *social learning* theory, young athletes mimic behaviors related to sports based on observations and vicarious experiences (Bandura, 1973). Parents serve as salient role models for young athletes in the context of being coaches themselves, by personally participating in sports, or in the many roles parents play in youth sports. In doing so, parents offer a model of sport to their children that includes values, attitudes, beliefs, and behaviors that may be healthy or harmful. Such scenarios are certainly evident in many youth sport leagues and camps.

An extension of Vygotsky's (1962) theory involving the *zone of proximal development* (ZPD) is the notion of *guided participation*, which is a "process and system of involvement of individuals with others, as they communicate and engage in shared activities" (Rogoff, Mistry, Göncü, & Mosier, 1993, p. 6). In sport contexts, guided participation involves parents providing the opportunities for many fundamental experiences including an introduction to sports as well as increased participation and commitment as children mature. Guided participation may be explicit, as evident when parents transmit clear messages during practice (e.g., instruction) or competitions (e.g., rules). It may also be implicit, as when children observe their parents in different roles in their sport. The youth sport arena provides countless illustrations of the interactional nature of ZPD and guided participation. Parents find themselves intimately involved in all aspects of their children's sports participation including broad activities such as coaching, managing, and fundraising as well as specific activities such as introducing them to coaches and teammates, taking their children to practices and competitions, prompting them to follow rules, and showing them how to be good sports. Taken together, there are broad theoretical underpinnings and significant empirical support for parental impact upon children's athletic lives.

The sport literature is replete with studies and other writings demonstrating that parents are critical agents in facilitating sport initiation, enjoyment, and adherence in developing athletes (e.g., Crane & Temple, 2015; Fredricks & Eccles, 2004; Gagné, Ryan, & Bargmann, 2003; O'Sullivan, 2014). Researchers and authors have examined socialization, social support, enjoyment, satisfaction, motivation, and sport specialization as they impact the youth sport experience (e.g., Curran, Hill, Hall, & Jowett, 2015; Dorsch, Smith, & Dotterer, 2016; Evans et al., 2017; Jayanthi et al., 2013; Hoyle & Leff, 1997; Pugliese & Tinsley, 2007).

In many ways, parental involvement in sport may be viewed as a process of *socialization* for their children. Broadly, socialization processes include explicit messages and knowledge as well as social support, which are transmitted from parents to their children. Forms of socialization and support include observational learning and instrumental support. The latter form of instrumental support is evident in observable actions (e.g., team registration assistance, transportation to practice, co-participation) and related tangible items (e.g., payment of fees, purchase of equipment) which otherwise facilitate sport involvement and development (Duncan, Duncan, & Stycker 2005). There is a large body of scientific evidence that parental socialization extends to physical activity and sport, as parents socialize children into sport by exposing them to the athletic environment and teaching and demonstrating relevant skills (Hemery, 1986; Pugliese & Tinsley, 2007).

Along these lines, the *expectancy-value* model (Eccles et al., 1983) was originally formulated to clarify socialization effects and has been applied specifically to sport (Fredricks & Eccles, 2004). According to this model, expectation of success and task value are deemed as particularly important for children's motivation, behavior, and adherence related to sport involvement. According to Fredricks and Eccles (2004), a child's *expectation of success* may be impacted by their self-concept of their abilities alongside the perception of the task difficulty. Moreover, *task value* is composed of four key components: (a) intrinsic value (i.e., enjoyment derived from participation), (b) utility value (e.g., how participation relates to future goals), (c) attainment value (i.e., perceived importance of performing well), and (d) costs (perceived potential negative aspects of participation). According to this model, key "socializers," including parents, facilitate participation and enhance motivation by not only helping to provide sport experiences (akin to instrumental support) but also be helping interpret the experiences by offering messages related to their likelihood of success and the positives values and benefits of participation (Fredricks & Eccles, 2004). Together, parents are important figures in socializing their children into sport.

Parental Involvement

The level of enjoyment derived from sport is a critical determinant of sport participation, motivation, and adherence for young athletes. Research has consistently corroborated the notion that young athletes with parents who offer an appropriate quantity and quality of support are more likely to enjoy the sport and are less likely to drop out (e.g., Crane & Temple, 2015; Fredricks & Eccles, 2004; Martens, 1978; Sacks, Tenenbaum, & Pargman, 2006). Specifically, parents who contribute warmth, positive affect, and support a mastery climate create an enjoyable atmosphere for young athletes (Dorsch et al., 2016). Thus, an appropriate type and degree of parental involvement is critical for children's healthy sports experiences.

A fundamental way by which to ascertain parental impact upon young athletes is to determine their intensity of involvement. Hellstedt (1987) originally described parental involvement on a continuum, ranging from under-involvement to over-involvement. For athletes with under-involved parents, there may be a lack of connection between parents, their children, and the sport. These athletes may feel unsupported, that their sports participation isn't valued by their parents, and, at an extreme, that they aren't worthy of their parents' attention and support. These athletes often turn to their teammates, coaches, and others in their sport for support (e.g., encouragement, advice, and emotional support). In fact, the sport and team context may offer a sense of caring, support, and belonging for these children that is not otherwise realized in the family environment (Sacks et al., 2006).

On the other end of the continuum, for athletes of over-involved parents, there may be a deep enmeshment of family and sports with parents being highly invested psychologically, emotionally, financially, and practically, with activities and schedules centered around sport. The children are often acutely aware of how invested one or more of their parents are in their athletic lives as expressed by their emotions, expectations, and involvement.

Over-involved parenting styles in sport may be akin to *helicopter parenting* (also referred to as Little League parenting, stage parenting, and tiger parenting) which consists of excessive ego investment by parents, extreme control over children's lives, and high demands and expectations based on results (LeMoyne & Buchanan, 2011). Helicopter parents of young athletes are often overly intrusive, for example, talking about their sports constantly, dictating their schedules, coaching them outside of team practices, and assuming responsibilities that should be the athlete's. Certain types of over-involvement may become particularly problematic as children mature and enter adolescence (Schiffrin et al., 2014) as they attempt to gain independence and control over their own sports lives. Padilla-Walker and Nelson (2012) describe helicopter parenting as a unique pattern which may or may not be high on nurturance and support, but also high on control (behavioral or emotional) and low on granting autonomy. While considerable research suggests parental involvement in children's lives is beneficial, too much involvement, to the point of inhibiting healthy development and enjoyment, may be problematic.

The degree and intensity of support that parents give to their young athletes can impact the amount of *pressure* that children feel to participate, perform, and succeed. Even parents with the best of intentions may unwittingly be subjecting their young athletes to significant pressure to accomplish goals established by their parents and not disappoint them. *Support* to participate and improve is focused on the needs and goals of children, perceived as positive, and associated with adaptive outcomes for young athletes (e.g., enjoyment, autonomy). In contrast, *pressure* is about the needs and goals of the parents, focused on producing successful results, and related to maladaptive outcomes. A high-pressure environment created by parents can be threatening and stressful to children, laden with conflict and negative affect, and otherwise negatively associated with enjoyment (Dorsch et al., 2016).

Between these two extremes of under- and over-involvement lies a moderate level of involvement, whereby parents support the needs and goals of their children and offer essential emotional and instrumental support, but do not otherwise exert undue pressure to succeed, win, or pursue a particular athletic trajectory (Sacks et al., 2006). This level of involvement appears to be linked with better outcomes in terms of enjoyment and satisfaction in sport, and adherence to sport involvement (Wuerth, Lee, & Alfermann, 2004).

In line with the notion that a moderate level of involvement is preferable, it may be challenging to create an environment in which parents are involved, but not adding undue pressures. In such a situation, it may be useful to examine the *types* of interactions which occur between parents and their young athletes. For instance, offering praise and emotional support are less likely to be perceived as forms of pressure from parents by athletes. However, directive behavior which interferes with children's autonomy in their sport may be experienced as pressure (Sacks et al., 2006; Wuerth, Lee, & Alfermann, 2004). It can be a particularly pressurized situation when such directive (and corrective) behavior, communication, and attention heightens after mistakes, poor performances, or losses. Such a scenario often is viewed when parents offer (whether discretely or noisily) advice during a practice or competition. Although often with the intent of being supportive, such behavior generally is thought to be detrimental (Sacks et al., 2006).

Sport Specialization

An area which has received considerable attention in recent years is sport specialization, particularly at increasingly younger ages of athletes Specialization is characterized as intense, year-round (eight or more months per year) commitment to a single sport to the exclusion of other sports (Jayanthi et al., 2013). Early in children's sports participation, parents play a significant role in deciding which sports their children engage in, how often and how seriously they are involved in a sport, and whether their children participate in several sports or commit to one sport. The current youth-sport culture has led parents to believe that early specialization is a competitive advantage and a requirement for later success in a sport. These messages are amplified by the prominence of Olympic and professional athletes who began their sports lives at a very young age (e.g., LeBron James, Simone Biles, Michael Phelps, Tiger Woods).

However, the preponderance of opinion from sport professionals (e.g., coaches, sports medicine physicians, athletic trainers, pediatricians, and consultants) and findings from sport researchers does not support the notion that early sport specialization offers any long-term competitive benefits. To the contrary, it appears to be linked to higher rates of injury, burnout, and drop out (Buckley et al., 2017; Di Fiori et al., 2013). Accordingly, the recommendation of sports experts is for parents to encourage their children to sample a variety of sports, take each season one at a time, develop overall athleticism, and for parents to then "follow their children's lead" with decisions about specialization and a deeper commitment to one sport rather than making irreversible and unilateral decisions regarding their level of participation (Sacks et al., 2006). With this diversified and measured approach, children are allowed to fully experience sport(s), develop a greater sense of autonomy around their sports participation, enjoy the process of developing a broad array of sport skills, and perhaps find a passion and desire to commit to one sport at some point in their athletic lives.

Practical Implications

Consultants are in a unique position to have a positive impact on parents' perspective on and involvement in their children's athletic lives. For consultants who work one-on-one with athletes, they likely have a trusted relationship with parents, giving them the opportunity to provide direct and honest feedback about how parents can best support their young athletes. For consultants who are embedded in teams, essential services they can provide include discrete parent education workshops, ongoing parent training curricula, and written materials (e.g., articles, blog posts) that focus on relevant topics for parents. These approaches provide parents with an awareness of the influence that they have on their children in their athletic lives, whether positive or negative, and offer practical insights, information, and tools they can use to be the best sport parents they can be.

Entire books have been written on sport parenting (e.g., O'Sullivan, 2014; Taylor, 2018), so what is offered below in terms of practical implications for consultants will be an overview of what are believed to be some of the most important lessons that consultants may employ in their work with youth athletes and their parents.

How Involved Are Parents?

Given the research that shows the divergence in experiences between parents who maintain a healthy balance of involvement in their children's sport endeavors as compared to overly involved parents (e.g., Crane & Temple, 2015), an important point of intervention for consultants is to help parents evaluate how involved they are in their children's athletic lives (Sacks et al., 2006; Taylor, 2018). Some of the observable "red flags" of over-involvement by parents include:

- Parents seem more interested in the sport than their children.
- Micromanaging their children's athletic lives.
- Placing their happiness on their children's performances.
- While all parents understandably enjoy seeing their children succeed, are there seemingly excessive (in intensity or duration) positive or negative emotional displays based solely on their children's athletic performances?
- Losing perspective on why their children participate in sports (e.g., it's about fame and fortune rather than fun, skill development, and life lessons).
- Overemphasis on results, rather than skill improvement, enjoyment, and value.
- Trying to rush children's athletic development.
- Pushing children to specialize in a sport that they're not interested in, continue pushing a sport the child no longer seems to enjoy, or have explicitly stated they no longer enjoy.
- Parents experiencing and expressing emotions before and after a competition that are excessive or out of control (e.g., anxiety before a competition; anger following a loss).
- Related to the above, observable instances or patterns of negative interactions with their children, their coaches, or other parents.

Consultants can encourage and create opportunities for reflection and recognition on the part of parents related to their respective level of involvement. This will help them identify what healthy involvement is, and thereafter, the consultant may offer recommendations on how to achieve it.

Healthy Participation Begins with Values

The values that parents hold about their children's sports participation play a vital role in all aspects of their athletic and personal development (Fredricks & Eccles, 2004). As such, the values that parents have and those that their children embrace about their sports involvement influence their priorities and goals, how much they enjoy sports, their level of commitment, and act as road signs in dictating the direction their athletic lives take.

Determining what values parents want to instill in their children as they enter sports should be grounded in what they want their children to get out of sports. Using this measure of the healthiness of a sports value, consultants can then ask parents: "Will this value help your children become the athletes and, more importantly, the people you want them to become?" With these criteria, here is a list of values that will support a healthy sports experience:

- work ethic;
- pursuit of personal excellence;
- love of sport;
- fun;
- being a good sport;
- gratitude;
- humility;
- teamwork;
- perseverance; and
- physical health.

In contrast, there are values that are associated with unhealthy sports participation:

- winning is the ultimate goal;
- win at any cost;
- bravado;
- selfishness; and
- pursuit of fame and fortune.

Consultants can help parents recognize how they may verbally and nonverbally transmit such value-laden messages to their children. In addition, consultants can help parents understand the divergent influence that healthy and unhealthy values have on their children in terms of their motivation, enjoyment, and performance, and guide parents in adopting those that are positive and affirming of their children's sports participation.

Healthy Attitudes

The attitudes that children develop about their sports participation act as the foundation upon which positive sports experiences are based, both in terms of enjoyment and success. The attitudes that children adopt usually come from those held by their parents. Five attitudes that are essential to healthy sports involvement include:

- Self-esteem based on feeling loved, secure, and competent, not on results.
- Defining success as children giving their best effort and failure as valuable lessons to learn from rather than judgments on their value as people.
- Risk-taking (and accepting that risks don't always work out) is essential for enjoyment, fulfillment, and success in sports.
- Mistakes are a natural, necessary, and valuable part of sports and life.
- Adversity is essential to children achieving their sports goals because only by experiencing adversity will they develop the skills necessary to overcome challenges in the future.

Setting Healthy Expectations for Young Athletes

Setting expectations for their children is an essential responsibility of being a sport parent. Expectations communicate messages to young athletes about what's important to parents and establish a standard toward which children can strive. Expectations can be double-edged swords though. They can be a tremendous benefit to children's athletic and personal development or they can be heavy burdens that crush their motivation for and enjoyment of their sport. The impact that expectations have on children depends on the type of expectations parents set for them.

There are two types of expectations that parents should *not* set for their children. *Ability expectations* are those in which children get the message that parents expect them to achieve a certain result because of their natural ability, "We expect you to win because you're the most talented athlete out there." The problem with these messages is that children have no control over their athletic ability; they are genetically endowed with a certain amount and all they can do is maximize whatever ability they are given.

Parents also shouldn't set *outcome expectations* in which the message is that their children must produce a certain result—"We expect you to win this match." The problem is that, again, children are asked to meet an expectation over which they may not have control. They might perform well, but still not meet their parents' outcome expectations because other competitors performed better than they did.

Instead of the focus on results, parents should help their children establish *effort expectations* over which they have control and that actually motivate them to do what it takes to achieve the outcomes parents want. Consultants can encourage parents to think about what their children need to do to be successful (e.g., commitment, positive attitude, hard work, focus, good technique) and establish expectations about doing those things.

Parent and Child Responsibilities in Sports

For children to have great sports experiences, which include essential elements such as having fun, developing essential life skills, and achieving their goals, both parents and their children must understand and fulfill their respective responsibilities and those responsibilities alone. Taylor's (2018) *Law of Family Responsibilities* states that if family members fulfill their own responsibilities and do not assume others', then young athletes will have positive sports experiences, increase their chances of achieving their athletic goals, and develop into healthy, mature, and successful people. However, problems arise when parents take on the responsibilities of their children who are not allowed to be accountable on their own. This usurping of responsibilities results in parents taking ownership of sports away from their children which ends up interfering with, rather than fostering, positive and healthy athletic experiences for them. Consultants can help parents to understand the different responsibilities that they and their young athletes have and how to ensure that each assumes their own and avoids the others'.

Send the Right Messages

Whether parents realize it or not, children are being constantly bombarded by messages about their sports participation from coaches, teammates, the youth-sports culture, and parents themselves. Unfortunately, parents can no longer assume that their young athletes will receive healthy messages from the first three above. Unfortunately, as discussed earlier in this chapter, the youth-sports culture is toxic in many ways and subsequently many coaches, other young athletes, and other parents have fallen victim to it. In doing so, they become unwitting conveyors of unhealthy messages. As a result, it is essential for parents to ensure that they are not also complicit in these harmful messages and, even more importantly, are sending messages that will counter those from outside of their family. Though there are many positive messages that parents can send to their young athletes, there are several core messages that consultants can help parents to understand, embrace, and express in relation to their children in sports (Taylor, 2018):

- Have fun.
- Give your best effort.
- Be a good sport.
- Support your teammates.
- Listen to your coaches.
- Mistakes and failure are actually good as they are part of the learning process.
- If you win, it's icing on the cake.
- We love you no matter what!

The above messages are usually communicated by parents verbally to their children. At the same time, parents send messages in other ways that are equally powerful, through their emotions and actions. Consultants can show parents how they express themselves in their children's athletic lives that can also convey healthy messages (Taylor, 2018):

- showing interest in their children's sports participation;
- expressing love and affection;
- assisting in establishing appropriate goals;
- offering tangible, instrumental support (e.g., paying for their sports participation, buying them the necessary equipment, getting them to practice, attending competitions);
- providing frequent encouragement;
- staying positive and calm during competitions;
- being supportive after failures; and
- providing a nourishing perspective about the importance of sports in their lives.

Summary

- Parents play a vital role in organized youth sports as volunteer coaches, managers, and administrators as well as in governance, planning, finances, and travel.
- Given this level of engagement by parents, an exploration into the impact that parents can have on their young athletes, both positive and negative, is warranted.
- An essential part of this discussion involves how consultants can help parents provide a nurturing sports environment in which their children can participate that will foster their healthy athletic and personal development.
- A principle tenet of family systems theory is that each family group is an important element of the larger group system (e.g., teams, leagues, and youth-sport culture) and all members are interdependent upon one another.
- According to social learning theory, young athletes mimic behaviors related to sports based upon observations and vicarious experiences, of which parents serve as salient role models for young athletes.
- Guided participation involves parents providing the opportunities for many fundamental sports experiences including an introduction to sports as well as increased participation and commitment.
- Research shows that parents are critical agents in facilitating sport initiation, enjoyment, and adherence in developing athletes in addition to socialization and social support, enjoyment, satisfaction, and motivation in sports.
- The degree and intensity of support that parents give to their young athletes can impact the amount of *pressure* that children feel to participate, perform, and succeed.
- Specialization is characterized as intense, year-round (eight or more months per year) of commitment to a single sport to the exclusion of other sports.
- Early in children's sports participation, parents play a significant role in deciding which sports their children engage in, how often and how seriously they are involved in a sport, and whether their children participate in several sports or commit to one sport.
- The preponderance of opinion from sport professionals and findings from sport researchers argue that early sport specialization does not offer long-term competitive benefits and, to the contrary, is linked to higher rates of injury, burnout, and drop out.
- Consultants are in a unique position to have a positive impact on parents' involvement in their children's athletic lives, whether working one-on-one with athletes or in a team setting.
- Consultants can provide parents with awareness of the messages that they send to their children in their athletic lives, whether positive or negative, and offer practical insights, information, and tools they can use to be the best sport parents they can be.
- Key areas in which parents can have a positive impact on their young athletes include the degree of involvement they have, the values and attitudes they bring to their children's sports participation, the expectations they set for their children, the responsibilities that parents and children have in sports, and an awareness of the messages they send to their children.

References

Bandura, A. (1973). *Social learning theory*. New York, NY: General Learning Press.

Bohnert, A. M., & Garber, J. (2007). Prospective relations between organized activity participation and psychopathology during adolescence. *Journal of Abnormal Child Psychology*, *35*, 1021–1033. doi: 10.1007/s10802-007-9152-1.

Bronfenbrenner, U. (1979). Toward an experimental ecology of human development. *American Psychologist, 32,* 513–531. doi: 10.1037/0003-066X.32.7.513.

Buckley, P. S., Bishop, M., Kane, P., Ciccoti, M. C., Selverian, S., Exume, D., Emper, W., Freedman, K. B., Hammoud, S., Cohen, S. B., & Ciccitt, M. G. (2017). Early single-sport specialization: A survey of 3090 high school, collegiate, and professional athletes. The *Orthopaedic Journal of Sports Medicine, 5,* 1–7. doi: 10.1177/2325967117703944.

Crane, J., & Temple, V. (2015) A systematic review of dropout from organized sport among children and youth. *European Physical Education Review, 21,* 114–131. doi: 10.1177/1356336X14555294.

Curran, T., Hill, A. O., Hall, H. K., & Jowett, G. E. (2015). Relationships between the coach-created motivational climate and athlete engagement in youth sport. *Journal of Sport and Exercise Psychology, 37,* 193–198. doi: 10.1123/jsep.2014-0203

Di Fiori, J. P., Benjami, H. J., Brenner, J. S., Gregory, A., Jayanthi, N., Landray, G. L., & Luke, A. (2013). Overuse injuries and burnout in youth sports: A position statement from the American Medical Society for Sports Medicine. *British Journal of Sports Medicine, 48,* 287–288. doi: 10.1136/bjsports-2013-093299.

Dorsch, T. E., Smith, A. L., & Dotterer, A. M. (2016). Individual, relationship, and context factors associated with parent support and pressure in organized youth sport. *Psychology of Sport and Exercise, 23,* 132–141. doi: 10.1016/j.psychsport.2015.12.003.

Duncan, S. C., Duncan, T. E., & Stycker, L. A. (2005). Sources and types of social support in youth physical activity. *Health Psychology, 24,* 3–10. doi: 10.1037/0278-6133.24.1.3.

Eccles, J. S., Barber, B. L., Stone, M. and Hunt, J. (2003), Extracurricular activities and adolescent development. *Journal of Social Issues, 59,* 865–889. doi:10.1046/j.0022-4537.2003.00095.

Evans, M. B., Allan, V., Erickson, K., Martin, L. J., Budziszerwski, R., & Côté, J. (2017). Are all sport activities equal? A systematic review of how youth psychosocial experiences vary across differing sport activities. *British Journal of Sports Medicine, 51,* 169–176. doi: 10.1136/bjsports-2016-096725.

Fredricks, J. A., & Eccles, J. S. (2004). Parental Influences on Youth Involvement in Sports. In M. R. Weiss (Ed.), *Developmental sport and exercise psychology: A lifespan perspective* (pp. 145–164). Morgantown, WV: Fitness Information Technology.

Gagné, M., Ryan, R. M., & Bargmann, K. (2003). Autonomy support and need satisfaction in the motivation and well-being of gymnasts. *Journal of Applied Sport Psychology, 15,* 372–390.

Hellstedt, J. C. (1987). The coach–parent–athlete relationship. *The Sport Psychologist, 1,* 151–160.

Hemery, D. (1986). *The pursuit of sporting excellence: A study of sport's highest achievers.* London: Willow Books Collins.

Hoyle, R. H., & Leff, S. S. (1997). The role of parental involvement in youth sport participation and performance. *Adolescence, 32,* 233–243.

Jayanthi, N. A., Pinkham, C., Dugas, L., Patrick, B., & Labella, C. (2013). Sports specialization in young athletes: Evidence-based recommendations. *Sports Health, 5,* 251–257. doi: 10.1177/1941738112464626.

LeMoyne, T., & Buchanan, T. (2011). Does "hovering" matter? Helicopter parenting and its effect on well-being. *Sociological Spectrum, 31,* 399–418. doi: 10.1080/02732173.2011.574038.

Martens, R. (Ed.) (1978). *Joy and sadness in children's sports.* Champaign, IL: Human Kinetics.

National Council of Youth Sport. (2008). *Report on trends and participation in organized youth sport.* Atlanta, GA: National Council of Youth Sport. Retrieved from www.ncys.org/pdfs/2008/2008-ncys-market-research-report.pdf.

O'Sullivan, J. (2014). *Changing the game: The parent's guide to raising happy, high-performing athletes and giving youth sports back to our kids.* New York, NY: Morgan James Publishing.

Padilla-Walker. L. M., & Nelson, L. J. (2012). Black hawk down?: Establishing helicopter parenting as a distinct construct from other forms of parental control during emerging adulthood. *Journal of Adolescence, 35,* 1177–1190. doi:10.1016/j.adolescence.2012.03.007.

Pugliese, J., & Tinsley, B. (2007). Parental socialization of child and adolescent physical activity: A meta-analysis. *Journal of Family Psychology, 21,* 331–343. doi:10.1037/0893-3200.21.3.331.

Rogoff, B., Mistry, J., Göncü, A., & Mosier, C. (1993). Guided participation in cultural activity by toddlers and caregivers. *Monographs for the Society for Research in Child Development, 58,* 1–179. doi: 10.2307/1166109.

Rothbaum, F., Rosen, K., Ujiie,T., & Uchida, N. (2002). Family systems theory, attachment theory, and culture. *Family Process, 41,* 328–350.

Ryan, C.J., Groves, D., & Schneider, D. (2007). A study of factors that influence high school athletes to choose a college or university, and model for the development of player decisions. *College Student Journal, 41,* 532–539.

Sacks, D. N., Tenenbaum, G, & Pargman, D. (2006). Providing sport psychology services to families. In J. Dosil (Ed.), *The Sport Psychologists Handbook* (pp. 39–61). West Sussex, England: John Wiley and Sons.

Schiffrin, H. H., Liss, M., Miles-McLean, H., Geary, K. A., Erchull, M. J., & Tashner, T. (2014). Helping of hovering? The effects of helicopter parenting on college students' well-being. *Journal of Child and Family Studies, 23,* 549–557. doi: 10.1007/s10826-013-9716-3.

Stanley, C. T., & Bohnert. A. (2011). The moderating influence of organized activities on the relations between body mass and psychosocial adjustment in adolescents. *North American Journal of Psychology, 13,* 201–218.

Taylor, J. (2018). *Raising young athletes.* Lanham, MD: Rowman & Littlefield.

Vygotsky, L. S. (1962). *Thought and language*. In E. Haufman & G. Vakar (Eds. & Trans.). New York, NY: MIT Press and Wiley (original work published 1934).

Wuerth, S., Lee, M. J., & Alfermann, D. (2004). Parental involvement and athletes' careers in youth sport. *Psychology of Sport and Exercise*, *5*, 21–33. doi: 10.1016/S1469-0292(02)-00047.

DOS AND DON'TS OF SPORT PARENTING

Lindsey Hamilton and Jim Taylor

The benefits that young people derive from participating in sport cannot be overstated. Of equal importance is the influence that parental figures can have on children's sports experiences. As previously mentioned in the chapter, parents can influence young athletes' enjoyment, commitment to, and performances in their sports lives. Most parents want to appropriately support their children by communicating directly and indirectly in ways that will nurture their children's development as both athletes and as people. Yet, parents may lack the knowledge and tools to express their love, support, and good intentions to effectively facilitate their children's healthy athletic development. When this occurs, consultants can play a meaningful role in helping parents to understand what will encourage and what will discourage healthy sports experiences for their children.

Theory and Research

Sport parenting expertise does not simply focus on achieving desired athletic outcomes for children. Optimal sport parenting is revealed through a level of engagement that increases the likelihood that young athletes will enjoy their sports participation, achieve their athletic goals, and experience positive developmental and psychosocial growth (Harwood & Knight, 2015). In the pursuit of healthy sport parenting, Harwood and Knight (2015) assert that, to best support their children, sport parents should have an understanding of both why they want their children participating in sport and, in turn, why their children want to participate in sport. Consultants should encourage sport parents to engage in conversations with their young athletes on these questions, as well as other attitudes, benefits, and behaviors that stem from this foundation. For example, if parents are primarily focused on their children learning life lessons through sport, they will likely speak to their children differently and reinforce different sport values compared to parents who are focused on results and possess a "winning at all costs" attitude. Furthermore, if parents' motivations and values for sport participation align with those of their children, they are more likely to support their children in the ways their children want to be supported (Knight & Holt, 2014). If not, children might interpret well-intended offerings of support and encouragement from the parents as pressure-filled or disinterested (Goodman & James, 2017). Having an enhanced awareness around parental motivations and those of their children initiates best practice for youth sport parents. Consultants can help both parties effectively navigate these conversations.

Another competency of expert sport parents that Harwood and Knight (2015) espouse is that they adapt their level of involvement to the various stages of their children's sports participation. Côté's (1999) developmental model of sports engagement is a widely recognized framework in which he identifies three stages of sports involvement and talent development: sampling, specializing, and investing. Each stage offers a new role, area of emphasis, and behaviors for parents to engage in or avoid to best support the growth and development of their children as athletes and as people. Consultants who understand these stages of youth-sport and psychosocial development will be better positioned to guide the parents with whom they work to engage in more productive interactions with their young athletes.

Sampling

Children's optimal entry into youth sports begins in the *sampling* stage. Typically occurring during the ages of 6–12, these years are characterized by a broad exploration of sport in general (Côté, 1999). During this time, parents serve as the provider of sport. It is their responsibility to cultivate an interest in sports for their children, provide the tangible and financial resources for them to experience sports, and, in some cases, introduce their children to the rules and technical aspects of sports as a coach. It is not important which sports children choose, but that they are able to sample a wide range (Côté, 1999) to help them find one or more that they want to continue.

In the sampling stage, parents should emphasize fun and learning above all else. By focusing on the process of participation rather than goal attainment or winning, parents are able to reinforce the values of participation and improvement through sports. Consultants can help parents reinforce these values by offering them a set of questions to facilitate conversations with their children related to their sports lives:

1. **What was fun about sport today?** Asking such a question reinforces fun as a primary value of sport participation. It also helps to ask an open-ended form of the question to elicit more conversation.
2. **What did you learn today?** Asking children what they learned emphasizes the process of development instead of the outcome. Try to avoid questions about performance, comparison with others, or winning.
3. **What new things did you try today?** Exploration is an essential component of the sampling stage. Asking children about new things they tried highlights the importance of experimentation. Questions regarding new skills or positions in sports or even about new sports, in general, are good ways to start.

In the sampling stage, parents should be encouraging active participation of their children in a wide variety of sports, seeking out environments that prioritize intentional play, and reinforcing the principles of fun, process orientation, and experimentation. Additionally, because parents' view of how they see their children influences the behaviors through which they support them (Côté, 1999), it is important to see children through a productive lens. Consultants can guide parents to avoid the temptation to see their children as talented or not, as this can lead to behaviors that pigeonhole them into a specific perception about themselves as athletes. Instead, consultants should help parents see their children as learners, as ever-evolving and continually progressing athletes who grow and develop through sports (Côté, Baker, & Abernethy, 2007).

Specializing

Through the sampling stage, children begin to cultivate a more focused interest in specific sports. This demonstrates the progression into the *specializing* stage, which generally occurs between the ages of 13–15 (Côté, 1999). The specializing stage is characterized by a commitment to one or two sports through a focus of both committed practice and intentional play (Côté, 1999). While skill development becomes a more powerful factor in young athletes' engagement, enjoyment remains a central theme for participation. For parents, their role transitions from provider of sport to managers and supporters. It is here that parents often find themselves helping their children to manage their sports experiences (Horn, 2011) in terms of equipment, scheduling, and other practical aspects of their sports participation. Parents also guide their children in the new psychological and emotional aspects of sport including effort, enjoyment, and the role of sport in the formation of their self-identities.

Effort

With the increased attention on training and specializing, it can be easy for the conversation in sport to focus on the outcome. However, in this period of development, it is important for parents to maintain an emphasis on the effort young athletes give in their sports experience. Praising moments where children worked hard or persisted in the face of challenges are great ways to highlight the value of effort. Suggested statements that consultants can share with parents include:

*   "I saw you work really hard in practice today!"
*   "You were in a tough situation today, but pushed through it!"
*   "Your commitment to improving is really paying off. Keep it up!"

Enjoyment

While sport participation is supposed to be fun, an increased focus on performance at this stage can detract from the focus on and experience of enjoyment in sports. Increased conditioning, more challenging drills, and greater competitive demands can present experiences of failure, mistakes, and setbacks, all of which can cause frustration, disappointment, and other ill feelings that may reduce children's enjoyment of their sport. Consultants should remind parents to shift the conversation with their children to finding overall enjoyment and fulfillment of the experience as athletes and place less emphasis on the fun they may experience at any one point in time. Questions or statements that consultants can suggest to parents include:

- "I know that situation wasn't easy to get through, but you did it! How are you better prepared now to compete next time?"
- "I understand you might be frustrated that the game didn't go your way. What did you learn from today's tough loss?"
- "Challenges are a sometimes-unpleasant part of sports, but it can feel so good to keep at it and overcome them."

Holistic Identity

While young athletes may be specializing in one or two sports, their self-identities should still be broad based (e.g., as a sibling, student, friend) rather than narrowly focused on being an athlete. During this stage, consultants can help parents emphasize the holistic achievements of their children by highlighting development in other areas of their life as well. Doing so reinforces to their children that they are more than just athletes; they also possess many skills, interests, and goals in other areas that can be sources of meaning, fulfillment, and joy as well.

There are a wide range of circumstances that offer opportunities for parents to support their young athletes and reinforce efforts, enjoyment, and identity (Elliott & Drummond, 2017). Consultants can discuss and role-play specific scenarios with parents to arm them with the skills to support their children toward success.

Before training and competitions, consultants can help parents frame conversations with their children about their goals and effort, and avoid the trap of focusing on the outcome. While sport is often a win-or-lose endeavor, ultimate success comes from being able to focus on the process that leads to winning, not on the victory itself. Praising enjoyment, preparation, effort, persistence, and resilience are strategies that are far more beneficial. Additionally, young athletes appreciate when their parents are familiar with the sport they participate in (Harwood & Knight, 2015), so consultants should encourage parents to learn more about their children's sports, for example, their star athletes and teams, as well as rules and strategies. However, consultants should make it clear to parents that this is not an invitation to coach the tactical or technical aspects of the game, as this role is the responsibility of their children's coaches. Instead, consultants can clarify with parents that such knowledge is simply an expression of interest in and support for their children's athletic pursuits.

During competitions, young athletes tend to interpret their parents' responses to performances as more negative than parents perceive their own reactions to be, and athletes deem these perceived negative reactions as the least helpful for their performances (Goodman & James, 2017). As such, consultants can help parents be mindful of the verbal and nonverbal messages they send to their children during competitions. Many children are still looking for validation from important others and how parents conduct themselves on the sidelines can send powerful messages, either healthy or otherwise, that impact young athletes' competitive enjoyment, effort, and performances. Consultants can help parents to become aware of what emotions they may be communicating during competitions that their children see. For example, consultants can teach parents ways to remain relaxed, open, and positive during competitions. Children love to know their parents are interested in and enjoying themselves at their competitions. Additionally, consultants can let parents know that it is acceptable and encouraged to cheer for all children on the team and opposing teams, not just their own. This behavior provides a powerful role-modeling opportunity on valuing teammates and the success of others. Cheering after moments of great effort also demonstrates valuing the process more than the outcome.

After a tough loss, emotions can be powerful. Sadness, disappointment, and frustration are common feelings experienced by both parents and their young athletes (Knight, Berrow, & Harwood, 2017). As a role model during these difficult experiences, parents can position themselves successfully to be calm and positive after a poor performance or defeat. This demeanor sets a potent example to children for how to react to a loss. As guides, parents can prepare to have supportive conversations with their children after a disappointing competition ends. Moments of loss are demanding for everyone, including parents, so consultants can encourage them to collect themselves emotionally before their children approach them to clear their minds in preparation for the discussion to come. Consultants can help the parents understand that it is healthy for children to feel unpleasant emotions after a disappointing performance and parents should avoid the temptation to assuage, placate, or distract from those emotions. In addition, consultants can remind parents that they do not have to have all the answers. Being a willing ear or shoulder to cry on can be some of the best "medicine" after a loss. When children are ready, parents can begin to engage them in a conversation about the competition, offer a comforting perspective, and share potential lessons learned from the defeat.

Investing

According to Côté (1999), when children decide to make a significant commitment to and investment in one sport, they will progress to the stage of *investing*. This stage usually occurs after the age of 15 and is typified by committing to achieve an elite level in a sport. In this vein, young athletes will focus their time on more deliberate practice and intense play (Côté, 1999).

As young athletes increase their investment in their sports lives, parents should gradually divest themselves of their investment. Children's shift toward greater autonomy in their sport also provides the opportunity for parents to create separation between their children's results and parents' investment in those results. It is not uncommon for parents to feel that their children's results are a reflection of their capabilities as parents (Horn, 2011), resulting in their self-identity and self-worth becoming overly invested in their young athletes' results. This is understandable given the significant investments of money, time, and energy that parents make in helping their children to achieve their athletic goals. If this investment becomes too large, then parents will likely impose expectations and pressure on their young athletes and, in doing so, hurt rather than support their children.

Consultants can help parents understand their investment in their children and enable them to see if they are placing their own self-worth or happiness on their young athletes' shoulders. While families expend many resources and much family time on youth sports (Dunn, Dorsch, King, & Rothlisberger, 2016), it is essential that parents maintain their own sense of self through their marriage, career, avocations, or other avenues. A healthy sense of self creates the best foundation from which parents can act in their children's best interests rather than their own.

The parents' role during the investing stage progresses into more of a mentor and cheerleader. While still assuming practical responsibilities such as finances, scheduling, and travel, and providing emotional support to their young athletes, the primary responsibilities of skill development and competitive preparation lay in the hands of sport experts including coaches, conditioning specialists, nutritionists, and mental coaches. Respecting the roles and responsibilities of others, including coaches, teammates, and other sport-performance professionals, builds trust, reduces role confusion in the young athletes, and allows parents to be a safe haven from which their children can explore their sports participation more deeply.

Over the course of these developmental stages, parental involvement transitions from having a leading and controlling role to one that is more following, advisory, and supportive. It is important for parents to allow their children to gain increasing ownership of their sports experience as they invest more of themselves and have the maturity and tools to take on more responsibilities. Allowing this separation to occur accomplishes two important objectives. First, it allows children to have greater autonomy in their sport experience as they develop both athletically and personally. Second, giving young athletes the freedom to gain ownership and make decisions regarding their sports experience while also taking responsibility for it can enhance their motivation and sense of self-efficacy (Ryan & Deci, 2000). To achieve this, consultants can help parents avoid micromanaging their young athletes in this stage once they demonstrate the ability to assume many logistical responsibilities. For example, packing and carrying their competition bags is one form of micromanaging that strips children of an opportunity to become self-sufficient for the future. Moreover, while parents badgering, harassing, or guilting young athletes into doing extra physical conditioning or watching and analyzing video tends to be more common at this stage, such behaviors present an authoritarian parenting style that is generally poorly received and lacks effectiveness (Lauer, Gould, Roman, & Pierce, 2010).

The most successful parents in this stage serve as mentors when their children solicit advice or other feedback on a given situation. They also can be supporters who provide emotional sustenance during the challenging times that are inevitable in sports. Consultants can help parents understand that any feedback provided to their young athletes should focus on their emotional experiences in their sport and avoid any technical or tactical discussions, which are best left to coaches. When parents need to offer unsolicited mentorship, consultants can help parents process that need and its relative value by arming them with these three questions:

1. **Does this need to be said?** It is not uncommon for parents to have thoughts or reactions to their children's sports experiences; however, parents want to be sure that addressing them is in the best interest of their young athletes rather than fulfilling some personal need. If it diminishes their children's sports experiences, sense of self, or isn't positive role modeling, parents should be encouraged to keep it to themselves.
2. **Does this need to be said by me?** If a conversation needs to be had, is the parent the best person to address it? Anything that is related to practice or competitive performances, for example, technique, tactics, or equipment, it is best left unsaid by the parents. Coaches are best suited for those topics. There are also times when teammates sharing a message is far more powerful than when it comes from a parent.
3. **Does this need to be said by me right now?** Consultants should help parents be mindful of the timing of conversations. For example, right after a performance might not always be the best time. Consultants should remind parents that paying attention to the emotional state of their young athletes, recognizing who else is around to hear, and assessing the receptivity of their children for feedback can increase the likelihood that they will receive the intended message well.

Parents can use these three questions as litmus tests for what, when, and how to offer feedback to their children relative to their sports experiences.

Overall, consultants can help parents see that, by the time they arrive at the investing stage, they should be taking more of an advisory role while their children gain full ownership of their athletic lives. By helping the parents maintain a healthy perspective about their children's sports participation, consultants can support parents through the many challenges they face and, ultimately, provide their young athletes with the best opportunity of finding both enjoyment and success in their sport and developing the life tools that will enable them to thrive outside of the sports world.

Practical Implications

This section thus far has introduced some key theoretical and empirical concepts as well as some general ways for consultants to approach working with sport parents. But, as the saying goes, being a sport parent isn't a spectator sport. And, in addition to developing an understanding of what it takes to be a sport parent, they also want clear guidelines and tools for what they should and shouldn't do with their young athletes and the sports world in which they are deeply involved. To that end, the remainder of this section will describe practical dos and don'ts that parents can apply to themselves, other parents, coaches, and their children that will enable them to be the best sport parents they are capable of being (Taylor, 2018).

- **Do for themselves:**

  o Get vicarious pleasure from their children's sports participation.
  o Enjoy themselves at competitions.
  o Be positive and calm when watching their children compete.
  o Have a life of their own outside of their children's sports.

- **Do with other parents:**

  o Make friends with other parents at competitions.
  o Volunteer as much as possible.
  o Police their own ranks to ensure that all parents behave appropriately.

- **Do with coaches:**

  o Leave the coaching to the coaches because they are the experts.
  o Give coaches any support they need to help them do their jobs better.
  o Communicate with coaches about their children.

  o   Inform coaches of relevant issues at home that might affect their children in practice and at competitions.
  o   Make coaches their allies.

- **Do for their children:**

  o   Provide guidance for their children.
  o   Assist them in setting realistic goals in their sports.
  o   Emphasize fun, skill development and other benefits of sports, and downplay results.
  o   Show interest in their children's sports lives.
  o   Provide regular encouragement and always be positive and supportive.
  o   Provide a healthy perspective about success and failure.
  o   Emphasize process and reward effort rather than results.
  o   Intervene if their children's behavior is unacceptable in practice or at competitions.
  o   Understand that their children may need a break from sports occasionally because sports are physically demanding and life is busy.
  o   Give their children space when needing to figure things out on their own.
  o   Keep a sense of humor because if parents are having fun, their children will more likely as well.
  o   Give their children unconditional love no matter how they perform.

- **Don't for themselves:**

  o   Base their self-esteem and ego on their children's success in sports.
  o   Care too much about how their children perform.
  o   Lose perspective about the importance of their children's sports participation.

- **Don't with other parents:**

  o   Make enemies of other parents.
  o   Talk *about* others in the sports community, talk *with* them.

- **Don't with coaches:**

  o   Interfere with their coaching during practice and competitions.
  o   Work at cross purposes with their children's coaches.

- **Don't for their children:**

  o   Ask their children to talk with them immediately after a competition.
  o   Show negative emotions while attending competitions.
  o   Make their children feel guilty for the time, energy, and money they are spending and the sacrifices they are making for their children's athletic lives.
  o   Think of their children's sport as an investment for which they expect a "fame and fortune" return.
  o   Live out their own dreams through their children's sport.
  o   Compare their children's progress with that of other children.
  o   Badger, harass, use sarcasm, threaten, or use fear to motivate their children.
  o   Expect anything from their children except their best effort, good behavior, and expressions of gratitude.
  o   Expect their children to get anything more from their sport than fun, physical fitness, mastery and love of a lifetime sport, and transferable life skills.
  o   Ever do anything that will cause them to think less of themselves or of their parents!

Summary

- Most parents want to appropriately support their children by speaking and acting in ways that will help their children's development as both athletes and as people.
- Yet, parents may lack the knowledge and tools to express their love, support, and good intentions with the goal of effectively facilitate their children's athletic development.

- Consultants can play a significant role in supporting parents in understanding what will encourage and will discourage healthy sports experiences for their children.
- Optimal sport parenting is revealed through a level of engagement that increases the likelihood that young athletes will enjoy their sports experiences, reach their sporting potential, and experience positive developmental and psychosocial growth.
- Theorists posit three stages of youth sport participation and development: sampling, specializing, and investing.
- In the sampling stage, parents should be encouraging active participation of their children in a wide variety of sports, seeking out environments that prioritize intentional play, and reinforcing the principles of fun, process orientation, and experimentation.
- The specializing stage is characterized by a commitment to one or two sports through a focus of both intentional practice and play.
- The investing stage is typified by young athletes committing to achieve an elite level in a sport.
- Parents want clear guidelines of dos and don'ts with themselves, other parents, coaches, and their young athletes.

References

Côté, J. (1999). The influence of the family in the development of talent in sport. *The Sport Psychologist, 13,* 395–417.

Côté, J., Baker, J., & Abernethy B. (2007). Practice to play in the development of sport expertise. In Eklund, R. & Tenenbaum, G. (Eds.), *Handbook of sport psychology* (pp. 184–202). Hoboken, NJ: Wiley.

Dunn, C. R., Dorsch, T. E., King, M. Q., & Rothlisberger, K. J. (2016). The impact of family financial investment on perceived parent pressure and child enjoyment and commitment in organized youth sport. *Family Relations, 65,* 287–299.

Elliott, S. K., & Drummond, M. J. N. (2017). During play, the break, and the drive home: The meaning of parental verbal behavior in youth sport. *Leisure Studies, 36,* 645–656.

Goodman, M., & James, I. A. (2017). Parental involvement in young footballers' development: A comparison of the opinions of children and their parents. *Sport & Exercise Psychology Review, 13,* 2–8.

Harwood, C. G., & Knight, C. J. (2015). Parenting in youth sport: A position paper on parenting expertise. *Psychology of Sport and Exercise, 16,* 24–35.

Horn, T. S. (2011). Enhancing coach-parent relationships in youth sports: Increasing harmony and minimizing hassle [A commentary]. *International Journal of Sports Sciences & Coaching, 6,* 27–31.

Knight, C. J., & Holt, N. L. (2014). Parenting in youth tennis: Understanding and enhancing children's experiences. *Psychology of Sport and Exercise, 15,* 155–164.

Knight, C. J., Berrow, S. R., & Harwood, C. G. (2017). Parenting in sport. *Current Opinion in Psychology, 16,* 93–97.

Lauer, L., Gould, D., Roman, N., & Pierce, M. (2010). Parental behaviors that affect junior tennis player development. *Psychology of Sport & Exercise, 11,* 487–496.

Ryan, R. M., & Deci, E. L. (2000). Self-determination theory and the facilitation of intrinsic motivations, social development, and well-being. *American Psychologist, 55,* 68–78.

Taylor, J. (2018). *Raising young athletes.* Lanham, MD: Rowman & Littlefield.

SPORT PARENT EDUCATION

Michael Q. King, Travis E. Dorsch, and Jim Taylor

The majority of American youth engage in organized sport at some point over the course of their development into adulthood (Jellineck & Durant, 2004; Sports & Fitness Industry Association, 2016), and sport is the most common extracurricular activity for youth across the developed world (Hulteen, Smith, Morgan, Barnett, Hallal et al., 2017). Parents exhibit a range of involvement behaviors in an effort to facilitate this participation, and have become increasingly involved over time (American Academy of Pediatrics, 2000). In many cases, this comes in the form of increased family resources being devoted to the youth sport experience, leading to potentially deleterious effects on parent involvement and children's outcomes (see Dunn, Dorsch, King, & Rothlisberger, 2016).

Theory and Research

Youth sport, particularly as it is structured in much of the Western world, would not exist without the involvement of parents. Parent involvement is integral to children's participation, as it is parents who organize, administer, and evaluate their children's youth sport experiences. Behind the scenes, parents serve as travel agents, launderers, nutritionists, chauffeurs, and psychologists. In assessing parents' role in youth sport, contemporary researchers have focused on: (a) the influence of parental involvement on children, (b) factors influencing parent involvement, and (c) the strategies developed by parents to facilitate their involvement in their children's sport (Knight, Berrow, & Harwood, 2017). In addressing the third of these areas, the purpose of this section is to highlight how parent education in organized youth sport can be a powerful means to maximizing the sports experiences of young athletes. To this end, the section will describe one evidence-based parent-education program's development, implementation, and assessment, and share practical considerations that consultants can use to develop parent education programming in the youth sports in which they work.

Parental involvement in youth sport is important as it has the potential to shape the experience that children have as they develop in sport (Holt, 2008). Despite this knowledge, researchers and practitioners have been slow to develop evidence-based parent education programs in the context of youth sport. This is not to say efforts to enhance parent behavior in youth sport are not happening (see Harwood & Knight, 2015). For example, efforts to improve sideline behavior of parents can be found in the United States and abroad (e.g., behavior contracts, "Silent Saturdays," posted signs at venues encouraging good behavior). While well-intentioned and potentially helpful, these efforts represent little more than a "quick fix" as most of these efforts tend to be scattershot in their design and implementation and have not been based on or evaluated for their effectiveness scientifically.

Designing Evidence-based Parent Education

Parent involvement is especially salient at the earliest stages of youth sport, as parents hold the potential to positively and negatively influence children's early sports experiences and, by extension, how they come to view athletic participation in the future. Accordingly, researchers have sought to identify how parents can be most appropriately involved in their children's sport participation and how they can be supported in doing this. The most important aspect of designing evidence-based parent education in youth sport is translating the field's growing theoretical and research evidence base into practice.

Recognizing the need for evidence-based parent education in the context of youth sport, Dorsch, King, Dunn, Osai, and Tulane (2017) designed an evidence-based *Sport Parent Guide* for parents of youth sport participants. Initially, the research team conducted a comprehensive literature search across multiple disciplines (e.g., human development, family studies, interpersonal communication, sport psychology). Articles and texts pertaining to organized youth sport parenting were annotated to inform the evidence-based education program. This analysis yielded seven distinct categories based on previous research:

1. A review of *youth sport participation* and referenced research that illuminated the reasons for participation/drop out from sport (Babkes & Weiss, 1999; Fredricks & Eccles, 2005; Gould, Feltz, & Weiss, 1985).
2. A *developmental model* of participation in sport (see Côté, 1999; Côté, Baker, & Abernethy, 2007) that focused on the processes that youth athletes navigate as they develop in sport.
3. Current *participation rates* in sport and the likelihood of participation at elite levels (Aspen Institute, 2015; National Council of Youth Sport, 2008; National Federation of State High School Associations, 2014).
4. The importance of *communication* in sport and offered parents practical strategies to apply to their interactions with their athlete (Dorsch, Smith, Wilson, & McDonough, 2015; Gershgoren, Tenenbaum, Gershgoren, & Eklund, 2011; Knight & Holt, 2014).
5. The most effective strategies for *working with coaches* (Gould, Lauer, Rolo, Jannes, Pennisi, 2006; Hellstedt, 1987).
6. *Sport parent behavior* and discussed findings on positive practices for before, during, and after a sporting event (Dorsch et al., 2015; Stein, Raedeke, & Glenn, 1999; Wuerth, Lee, & Alfermann, 2004).
7. The intervention provided parents with tips and strategies for success and overall *positive sport parenting* (see Knight & Holt, 2014, for review).

Upon finalizing the guide, the authorship team used its contents to build a complementary *Sport Parent Seminar*. The *Guide* and *Seminar* were created to offer parents practical strategies to enhance their sport parenting. As such, the program was designed using a "strengths-based" rather than "deficit" approach.

Implementation

Families from nine U8 and U10 soccer teams in suburban Utah were recruited for participation. Both boys and girls were included in this study. Each team was assigned to one of three quasi-experimental conditions (full-implementation, partial-implementation, or non-implementation). Parents in the full-implementation group ($n = 18$) were provided with the *Guide* and took part in a face-to-face *Seminar* prior to the beginning of the season. Parents in the partial-implementation group ($n = 36$) were given a copy of the *Guide* and encouraged to read through it, but the research team did not did not otherwise interact with these parents. Parents in the non-implementation group ($n = 27$) served as a control and were therefore not provided with either educational resource.

Assessment

To assess the efficacy of the program, children completed surveys of multiple variables at pre- and post-season. Specifically, children were asked to provide their perceptions of parent support and pressure as well as warmth and conflict in the parent–child relationship. Furthermore, children reported on their own enjoyment, competence, and stress in sport. The authorship team then examined variance among the three conditions (full-implementation, partial-implementation, non-implementation) from pre- to post-season. Herein, we highlight a number of notable trends in the data, as reported by Dorsch and colleagues (2017).

Parent Involvement

Parents exposed to the *Guide* and *Seminar* were rated as significantly more supportive and less pressuring from pre- to post-season. There were significant group × time interactions in children's perceptions of parent support and pressure, with group membership explaining 21% and 32% of the variance, respectively. Interestingly, parents in the partial-implementation and non-implementation conditions were rated by their children as more pressuring from pre- to post-season, suggesting that parents (in the absence of any efforts at behavior mitigation) may actually demand more of the children over the course of a youth sport season.

Parent–Child Relationship

Parents exposed to the *Guide* and *Seminar* were rated as demonstrating significantly more warmth and less conflict in the parent–child relationship from pre- to post-season. There were significant group × time interactions in children's perceptions of parent support and pressure, with group membership explaining 16% and 11% of the variance, respectively. Interestingly, although parents in the partial-implementation condition were rated as demonstrating relatively little change in conflict, parents in the non-implementation condition were rated as more conflictive from pre- to post-season. This highlights the fact that parents (in the absence of targeted programming) may interact with their children in such a way that their children perceive more conflict in their relationship over the course of a youth sport season.

Children's Outcomes

Children whose parents were exposed to the *Guide* and *Seminar* rated sport as significantly more enjoyable, and themselves as significantly more competent and less stressed from pre- to post-season. There were significant group × time interactions for all three variables, with parents' group membership explaining 14%, 13%, and 20% of the variance, respectively. Children whose parents were in the non-implementation condition rated themselves as less competent and more stressed from pre- to post-season. These findings highlight an unfortunate status quo in youth sports: namely, that many children are having a neutral, if not negative, sports experience in many respects. This is unfortunate, given the many positive outcomes typically associated with organized youth sport.

Collectively, results from Dorsch and colleagues' pilot intervention highlight the potential for an increase in positive outcomes (i.e., parent support, parent–child warmth, child enjoyment, child competence) and a simultaneous decrease in negative outcomes (i.e., parent pressure, parent–child conflict, child stress) if parents are provided tools to optimize their involvement. These inferences should prove encouraging for key stakeholders (e.g., researchers, practitioners, administrators, coaches, parents, and athletes) seeking to improve the climate in youth sport.

Practical Implications

Efforts toward educating parents whose children are involved in sports build on previous work examining parenting behavior in organized youth sport (e.g., Hoyle & Leff, 1997; Leff & Hoyle, 1995; Stein et al., 1999) and demonstrate the potential for this type of translation to be pursued by researchers and practitioners across a range of youth sport contexts (i.e., recreational, competitive, elite). In combination with growing knowledge of best practices (see Harwood & Knight, 2015), the further development, implementation, and assessment of evidence-based programs will help to refine targeted approaches to working with parents in organized youth sport settings.

There are a number of considerations that should be made when consultants approach parent education efforts in youth sport. Perhaps most important, future efforts to provide sport parents with education should continue to be based in evidence-based practices (see Thrower, Harwood, & Spray, 2016, 2017). League directors and administrators should seek to avoid the temptation to implement quick-fixes; instead treating educational efforts as a way to enhance the overall culture of the league or team. Future efforts should also aim to become more accessible to populations that otherwise might not be able to take part in the programming due to time, distance, cost, or other constraints. Considerations for future work include the potential to use web-based curricula that could be accessed at parents' convenience. Such efforts that leverage modern technology are both cost-effective and time-efficient. A final consideration is related to the growing population of Americans who may not speak or understand English fluently. This limitation has the potential to alienate or otherwise limit parents whose children are involved in youth sports in their attempts to engage in any form of educational programming. By translating educational curricula, more parents would be served and there would also be a greater opportunity to assess a program's efficacy across a wider range of parent demographics. As an example, the curriculum created by Dorsch and colleagues (2017) has been translated into German and is in the process of being translated into Spanish.

For those seeking to implement their own intervention, a community case study carried out by Dorsch, King, Tulane, Osai, Dunn, and Carlsen (in press) illuminates what parents, coaches, and administrators feel would be the necessary components of a parent education program. Parents offered the feedback that any intervention should be cognizant of parents' demanding schedules. Some parents mentioned that during the children's practice may be an effective time for an intervention. Speaking more broadly, coaches spoke of their preference for such interventions at earlier stages and even expressed the idea that such intervention at the high school level would be "too late" (Dorsch et al., in press, p. 14). Administrators in this study urged for the intervention to be a positive experience for the parents and that it shouldn't be too time consuming. These findings align with work conducted with tennis parents in the United Kingdom (Thrower et al., 2016), and suggests that education should begin early and be ongoing over the course of development, so as not to inundate parents with ineffective and cumbersome one-time sessions.

As for the logistics of the actual delivery of an intervention, coaches specifically felt that the parent education program should be delivered by a third party rather than the coaching staff (Dorsch et al., in press). The stated preference was for a well-respected professional with expertise and experience (i.e., credibility) to implement the program. As was rightly noted by administrators, the program should be customized to the particular sport, developmental level of the children, and specific needs and goals of the parents (Dorsch et al., in press).

Developing a Sport Parent Education Program

Dorsch et al. (2017) offer a helpful framework from which consultants can draw from as they develop their own parent education program. Building on that general structure, the following section will provide more detailed guidance in how consultants can create their own unique parent education program that best provides a meaningful educational experience for the parents in the youth sports organizations with whom they work.

Needs and Goals Assessment

Though there are topics that will apply to most sport parent audiences, each youth sports programs has its own unique set of needs, goals, and challenges that must be considered when developing a sport parent education program. As a result, consultants are encouraged to immerse themselves in the youth sports program they are involved in as a means of gaining a broad and deep understanding of the organization's structure and processes, its parent population, the sport in which the children participate, and the level and goals of that sports involvement (e.g., introduction to sport, fun and skill development, competition, long-term athlete development). This knowledge can be gained by observing parents at practices and competitions, seeing the interactions they have with their athletes and the coaching staff, and interviewing key stakeholders in the organization. This information will inform consultants on what needs the organization has in wanting a structured parent education program, what "pain points" exist among the parents involved, and what goals it sees being accomplished with such a program.

Content

With a detailed picture of the youth sports organization completed, consultants can select what content should be included in the parent education program. These materials can be gathered based the prior experience of consultants in delivering such sport parent programming, reading the many books that have been written about sport parenting, exploration of the extant research on the topic, and other resources found on the internet. Common topics include child development, impact of sports on children, values, investment, goals, motivations, roles and responsibilities, messages to their children, relationships with coaches, and communication.

Curriculum

Once a range of content has been selected by consultants, they can decide how to incorporate it into an effective curriculum. This curriculum details what topic areas will be offered, the specific information that will be provided in those topic areas, the order in which it will be delivered, the length of the curriculum, and the amount of contact that consultants will have with their parent audience. An emphasis in consultants developing a sport parent education curriculum should be on what content will be most impactful to sport parents and how they will translate the information into meaningful changes in their attitudes, emotions, and behavior in their roles as parents of young athletes. Taylor (2016) provides an example of a robust curriculum that is packaged into a four-class course that he offers to youth sports organizations either in person or online.

Modes of Delivery

Good content and a carefully planned curriculum are essential starting points for an impactful sport parent education program. The next issue that must be addressed is the mode by which consultants will deliver the program. Time may be the most influential contributor to deciding how the program is offered. The reality of life for many parents is that they are very busy and simply don't have much discretionary time available to devote to being educated about their role as sport parents, however receptive they are to learning how they can best support their young athletes. An important part of the needs and goals assessment is for consultants to determine how much time the youth sports organization can devote to parent education.

Dorsch et al. (2017) have demonstrated that one seminar and even just having parents read a guide about how to be a better sport parent had a significant short-term effect on their behavior and how their children perceived them. At the same time, it seems reasonable to assume that a series of educational opportunities in which parents can learn more, become more engaged, and maintain awareness of their influence on their children would have a more meaningful and longer lasting impact.

In addition to frequency of contact with the youth sport organization's parent community, another question to be asked by consultants is how the curriculum can best be delivered to the widest audience. Certainly, in-person contact would seem to be the most effective mode of delivery. However, again due to time constraints, attendance may be lacking which, by definition, diminishes the impact of the program on the youth sport organization's parent community.

Thanks to the internet, delivery of information is now possible through several forms of media. Webinar platforms would allow consultants to reach a broader audience by offering remote participation to those who are unable to attend in person. Pre-recorded audio or video classes that allow parents to access the curriculum on-demand and participate at their own pace is another way to reach a wider audience (Taylor, 2016). Admittedly, one weakness of leveraging technology in this way is that the communication is unidirectional which may limit the audience's engagement and takeaway.

As demonstrated by Dorsch et al. (2017) and Taylor (2016), the creation and use of a written workbook can be used as a primary or supplemental means of curriculum delivery. Such a guide that leads readers through the curriculum can allow for another means of delivery that could be appreciated by those who are visual learning and who prefer reading as a mode of learning. A well-thought-out workbook that includes content descriptions and exercises would enable consultants to reach an even larger audience and keep participants in the sport parent education program engaged through another mode of delivery and for an even longer period. As noted by Dorsch et al. (2017), a workbook could be translated into other languages to meet the needs of those who are English as Second Language speakers.

Additionally, the curriculum of a sport parent education program could also be delivered primarily or as secondary sources through periodic online newsletters, blogs, and social media. This approach allows consultants to continually engage with their parent audience with regular postings that either support already discussed ideas or introduce new or timely ideas that would benefit a youth sports organization's parent community. Other benefits of using this type of online technology is that consultants' messages will likely be shared with an even broader audience and it further engages followers by allowing comments, likes, and shares.

Timing

With the content, structure, and means for delivering a robust sport parent education program in place, the last issue that consultants must consider is the timing of the program at several levels. First, when in the course of the season should the programming be delivered? As shown by Dorsch et al. (2017), just before the season begins is the ideal time to deliver the curriculum because, as the saying goes, "An ounce of prevention is worth a pound of cure." By offering the program before the season starts, parents are able to apply their new-found knowledge and insights from the first practice and competition.

Second, as discussed above, an essential challenge for consultants and youth sports organizations is deciding when to deliver the program that will maximize attendance, for example, during practices when parents might be watching, in the evening, or on weekends. In all likelihood, whenever the program is scheduled, some parents will be unable to attend due to conflicting responsibilities. As such, one option is for consultants to offer the program at different times so as to provide the opportunity for as many interested parents as possible to attend.

Finally, as noted previously, the impact on a youth sports organization's parent community will be greatest if the presence of the sport parent education program and its engagement with the parents is maintained throughout the season. If the program's curriculum involves multiple, connected workshops, then scheduling each "class" monthly will provide an ongoing registering on their radar screens. If the program's curriculum consists of a "one-off" workshop, consultants could increase its "shelf life" by scheduling periodic follow-up workshops or sport parent round table discussions and Q&As periodically throughout the season. If that level of time commitment isn't available, then consultants can maintain contact and influence with the parent community through online media.

Summary

- Youth sport is a nearly ubiquitous context that plays an important role in the development of millions of North American children.
- Parents, displaying a range of behaviors, play an important role in providing for and impacting the sport experience.
- As youth sport has increasingly become driven by adults, parent behavior has appeared to become more problematic in the context of sport.

- While many efforts exist to improve parent involvement and behaviors in youth sport, such efforts up to this point have not been based in research and have not been empirically tested.
- A recent pilot study displayed the ability that evidence-based parent education has to improve parent–child interactions and child's experience in sport.
- Future efforts should seek to find ways to utilize technology, reach out to diverse populations, and continue to be based in empirical findings.
- Consultants can use the following steps to develop a robust sport parent education program: conduct a needs and goals assessment, determine program content, develop a compelling curriculum, specify the modes of delivery, and establish the timing for the implementation of the program.

References

American Academy of Pediatrics. (2000). Intensive training and sports specialization in young athletes. *Pediatrics, 106,* 154–157.

Aspen Institute. (2015). *Sport for all, play for life: A playbook to get every kid in the game.* Washington, DC: Aspen Institute.

Babkes, M. L., & Weiss, M. R. (1999). Parental influence on children's cognitive and affective responses to competitive soccer participation. *Pediatric Exercise Science, 11,* 44–62.

Côté, J. (1999). The influence of the family in the development of talent in sport. *The Sport Psychologist, 13,* 395–417.

Côté, J., Baker, J. & Abernethy B. (2007). Practice to play in the development of sport expertise. In Eklund, R. & Tenenbaum, G. (Eds.), *Handbook of sport psychology* (pp. 184–202). Hoboken, NJ: Wiley.

Dorsch, T. E., King, M. Q., Dunn, C. R., Osai, K. V., & Tulane, S. (2017). The impact of evidence-based parent education in organized youth sport: A pilot study. *Journal of Applied Sport Psychology, 29,* 199–214.

Dorsch, T. E., King, M. Q., Tulane, S., Osai, K. V., Dunn, C. R., & Carlsen, C. P. (in press). Parent education in youth sport: A community case study of parents, coaches, and administrators. *Journal of Applied Sport Psychology.*

Dorsch, T. E., Smith, A. L., Wilson, S. R., & McDonough, M. H. (2015). Parent goals and verbal sideline behavior in organized youth sport. *Sport, Exercise, and Performance Psychology, 4,* 19–35. doi: 10.1037/spy0000025

Dunn, C. R., Dorsch, T. E., King, M. Q., & Rothlisberger, K. J. (2016). The impact of family financial investment on perceived parent pressure and child enjoyment and commitment in organized youth sport. *Family Relations, 65,* 287–299.

Fredricks, J. A., & Eccles, J. S. (2005). Family socialization, gender, and sport motivation and involvement. *Journal of Sport & Exercise Psychology, 27,* 3–31.

Gershgoren, L., Tenenbaum, G., Gershgoren, A., & Eklund, R. C. (2011). The effect of parental feed- back on young athletes' perceived motivational climate, goal involvement, goal orientation, and performance. *Psychology of Sport and Exercise, 12,* 481–489.

Gould, D., Feltz, D., & Weiss, M. (1985). Motives for participating in competitive youth swimming. *International Journal of Sport Psychology, 16,* 26–40.

Gould, D., Lauer, L., Rolo, C., Jannes, C., & Pennisi, N. (2006). Understanding the role parents play in tennis success: a national survey of junior tennis coaches. *British Journal of Sports Medicine, 40,* 632–636.

Harwood, C. G. & Knight, C. J. (2015). Parenting in youth sport: A position paper on parenting expertise. *Psychology of Sport and Exercise, 16,* 24–35.

Hellstedt, J. C. (1987). The coach/parent/athlete relationship. *The Sport Psychologist, 1,* 151–160. doi: 10.1123/tsp.1.2.151

Holt, N. L. (2008). *Positive youth development through sport.* New York, NY: Routledge.

Hoyle, R. H., & Leff, S. S. (1997). The role of parental involvement in youth sport participation and performance. *Adolescence, 32,* 233–243.

Hulteen, R. M., Smith, J. J., Morgan, P. J., Barnett, L. M., Hallal, P. C., Colyvas, K., & Lubans, D. R. (2017). Global participation in sport and leisure-time physical activities: A systematic review and meta-analysis. *Preventive medicine, 95,* 14–25.

Jellineck, M., & Durant, S. (2004). Parents and sports: Too much of a good thing? *Contemporary Pediatrics, 21,* 17–20.

Knight, C. J. & Holt, N. L. (2014). Parenting in youth tennis: Understanding and enhancing children's experiences. *Psychology of Sport and Exercise, 15,* 155–164.

Knight, C. J., Berrow, S. R., & Harwood, C. G. (2017). Parenting in sport. *Current Opinion in Psychology, 16,* 93–97.

Leff, S. S., & Hoyle, R. H. (1995). Young athletes' perceptions of parental support and pressure. *Journal of Youth and Adolescence, 24,* 187–203.

National Council of Youth Sport. (2008). *Report on trends and participation in organized youth sport.* Atlanta, GA: National Council of Youth Sport. Retrieved from www.ncys.org/pdfs/2008/2008-ncys-market-research-report.pdf.

National Federation of State High School Associations. (2014). High school athletics participation survey. Retrieved from www.nfhs.org/content.aspx?id=3282

Sports & Fitness Industry Association (2016). 2016 US trends in youth sports. Retrieved from www.sfia.org/reports/510_2016-U.S.-Trends-in-Team-Sports.

Stein, G. L., Raedeke, T. D., & Glenn, S. D. (1999). Children's perceptions of parent sports involvement: It's not how much, but to what degree that's important. *Journal of Sport Behavior, 22*, 591–601.

Taylor, J. (2016). Prime sport parenting 505: Raising successful and happy athletes. Retrieved from www.taylorprimeperformance.com/prime-sport-parenting-4-week-online-course

Thrower, S. N., Harwood, C. G., & Spray, C. M. (2016). Educating and supporting tennis parents: A grounded theory of parents' needs during childhood and early adolescence. *Sport, Exercise, and Performance Psychology, 5*, 107–124.

Thrower, S. N., Harwood, C. G., & Spray, C. M. (2017). Educating and supporting tennis parents: an action research study. *Qualitative Research in Sport, Exercise and Health, 9*, 600–618.

Wuerth, S., Lee, M. J., & Alfermann, D. (2004). Parental involvement and athletes' careers in youth sport. *Psychology of Sport and Exercise, 5*, 21–33. doi: 10.1016/S1469-0292(02)-00047

12

SPORTS ORGANIZATION

Introduction

Jim Taylor and Tim White

The composition of sports organizations at every level of sport is changing for several reasons. First, as the stakes for success grow greater, primarily in terms of profits, organizations from elite youth sports clubs to university athletic departments to professional teams, are seeking every competitive advantage available to them. Second, advances in the sports sciences have provided these organizations with knowledge, methods, and technology that can help their athletes to elevate the level of their performances. Today, valued high-performance professionals in the sports world include coaches with differing areas of technical, tactical, and performance competencies, physical conditioning specialists, sports medicine professionals, nutritionists, technologists, and, increasingly, sport psychology consultants or mental trainers. Additionally, for sports that involve equipment, such as sailing, bobsledding, and ski racing, scientists, designers, and engineers are also a part of the mix. These high-performance teams vary in their make-up depending on the type and level of sport in which the organizations, the vision of their leadership, their financial resources, and their structure and priorities. The expressed purpose of these gatherings of high-performance experts is to ensure that every contributor to sports performance is being addressed with the clear goal of giving their athletes the information and tools they need to maximally prepare themselves to perform their best and achieve competitive success.

As high-performance teams are assembled by sports organizations to support athlete and team performance, it is critical for its members to team to recognize the structure of the organization, their roles within that structure, and how they can build strong working relationships that facilitate collaborative efforts among numerous professionals, all in the name of supporting performance and well-being of its athletes. Because consultants' responsibilities may span many relevant aspects of athlete and team performance, including psychological, interpersonal, and organizational, they can play a vital role in ensuring that these high-performance teams, and the organizations of which they are a part, are themselves groups that are performing optimally through an understanding of effective roles and responsibilities, communication, and collaboration. This chapter explores these issues and the roles that consultants can play within three primary areas of a high-performance team: coaches and conditioning staff, the sports medicine staff, and the organization's management.

SPORT AND CONDITIONING COACHES

Zach Brandon

fundamental component of effective consulting involves consultants' ability to develop positive, trusting, and collaborative working relationships with the athletes they serve and those they work with to support the athletes. Historically, consultants have operated in the periphery whereby their access to athletes and teams was often less frequent compared to other staff such as sport coaches and strength and conditioning (S&C) coaches. Given the limited "facetime" that consultants often have with athletes and teams, it is imperative for them to form partnerships with other performance-related staff to ensure that the organization's needs and goals relative to its athletes are effectively met. To date, considerable attention has been given to exploring how relationships with coaches are an integral part of successful consulting (Andersen, 2000; Petitpas, Giges, & Danish, 1999; Fifer, Henschen, Gould, & Ravizza, 2008; Ravizza, 1988; Sharp & Hodge, 2011, 2013; Sharp, Hodge, & Danish, 2015). Sport coaches, in particular, have been labeled as "gatekeepers" for consultants hoping to gain entry into teams (Barker & Winter, 2014; Fifer et al., 2008), but the same could be said of S&C coaches given their daily interaction with athletes and the inherent buy-in that coaches and athletes have with physical conditioning. As the interest level and use of sport psychology and mental training services continues to grow, it is imperative that consultants understand how they can support, be supported by, and collaborate with both sport and S&C coaches.

Theory and Research

To develop the most integrative and effective mental training programs, consultants must understand what sport and S&C coaches do, need, expect, and want from their services. Recent growth within the field of sport psychology has been accompanied by a more thorough investigation of coaches' perceptions toward consultants. For example, Wrisberg and colleagues (2010) surveyed 815 NCAA Division I coaches and discovered that 88.8% were in favor of encouraging their athletes to see consultants for performance-related issues and another 77.5% would do the same for personal concerns. Additional support for services has been reported by coaches across a variety of domains including youth (Barker & Winter, 2014; Zakrajsek, Martin, & Zizzi, 2011), collegiate (Zakrajsek et al., 2013) and elite levels (Gould, Greenleaf, Guinan, & Chung, 2002). Despite ample support for sport psychology services, it should be noted that some have documented concerns toward the field, which have been linked to coaches' negative perceptions and limited knowledge, the challenge for consultants of integrating with players and coaches, lack of clarity in role and services, practical constraints, and the perceived value of consultant services (Pain & Harwood, 2004). Furthermore, Johnson and colleagues (2011) provided additional evidence that coaches' limited knowledge of sport psychology and mental training, consultants' inability to clearly define their services, and their difficulty in integrating into the team were significant barriers to entry. The insights gleaned from both positive and negative attitudes toward consultants is important for them to consider in order to mitigate common barriers such as coaches' lack of knowledge toward their services, coaches' belief that they can provide similar support, biases they might hold about sport psychology and mental training, and environmental constraints (e.g., space, time, and money) (Barker & Winter, 2014; Johnson et al., 2011; Pain & Harwood, 2004).

Despite ample evidence of coaches' views toward sport psychology and mental training, there is a dearth of information in the literature on other sport professionals' perceptions toward consultants. In fact, a recent review of sport psychology referenced no peer-reviewed articles examining how S&C coaches view consultants (Fortin-Guichard, Boudreault, Gagnon, & Trottier, 2018). The lack of attention toward S&C coaches in the literature is concerning given the importance of designing mental training programs that are systematically integrated into all aspects of athlete or team preparation including physical conditioning (Holliday et al., 2008; Reid, Stewart, & Thorne, 2004). The weight room, in particular, provides a great "laboratory" for athletes to engage in mental training in a controlled environment with a high volume of repetitions and varying levels of intensity. With this information in hand, consultants should consider how they can complement and support the services provided by S&C coaches. The value of collaborating with these professionals is essential given the current shifts in developing high-performance staffs within sports organizations.

Interdisciplinary collaboration has been recognized as a valuable service delivery model in sport, whereby experts from various disciplines can inform and enhance the services of other professionals. Collaboration has been defined as the "coming together of diverse interests and people to achieve a common purpose via interactions, information sharing, and the coordination of activities" (Jassawalla & Sashittal, 1998, p. 239). Collaboration is an essential practice among coaching staffs, which has been recommended for consultants as an effective framework for service delivery (Poczwardowski, Sherman, & Ravizza, 2004). Although not an exhaustive list, the benefits of interdisciplinary collaboration include (Gordin & Henschen, 1989):

- sharing and synthesizing information to create new knowledge;
- reinforcement and consistency of messaging to athletes;
- increased understanding of other disciplines;
- heightened awareness and appreciation for one's own discipline; and
- greater objectivity in approaching performance or training issues.

Despite the acknowledgement of several benefits of collaboration, there are potential challenges facing consultants operating within these teams. For example, Reid and colleagues (2004) highlighted the pivotal role consultants can have in maintaining the health and effectiveness of coaching staff. A primary difficulty for consultants is that they can serve as both a facilitator and participant within such staff, which is dependent on their ability to foster trusting relationships with other members in the group. In addition, they may be challenged by other service providers if there is a perceived imbalance of power among its members (Reid, Stewart, & Thorne, 2004). Other potential concerns for consultants include determining appropriate boundaries for confidentiality, varying levels of commitment among staff members, lack of role clarity, messaging inconsistencies, and differences in expectations and goals. Nevertheless, as the use of high-performance staffs continues to grow in sports organizations, consultants must understand their role and how to operate optimally as a member of the coaching staff.

Practical Implications

The following section outlines relevant considerations and practical approaches, methods, and strategies for consultants to follow in working with other coaches in a sports organization. Specifically, pertinent areas such as gaining entry, developing and maintaining trust, and integrating mental training into the services of other coaches are highlighted. Unless otherwise noted, the following considerations can be applied to working with both sport and S&C coaches. Recommendations will be derived from the existing literature as well as the author's personal experience operating within a coaching staff.

Gaining Entry

One of the most difficult challenges confronting consultants is their ability to gain entry and develop a working alliance with the coaches on staff. Ultimately, this process starts with the development and maintenance of a positive relationship between consultants and coaches. In most situations, the head coach of an athlete or team will be the first person consultants meet and must connect with (Ravizza, 1988). The quality of this consultant–coach relationship will greatly impact the effectiveness of the mental training program that is implemented due to coaches' influence on their athletes' willingness to buy into and take ownership of consultants' services (Fifer et al., 2008; Zakrajsek et al., 2013). Realistically, if coaches don't believe in mental training, the chance of consultants having success with athletes or teams is significantly diminished. With this in mind, consultants must demonstrate the following qualities which have been shown to strengthen relationships with clients: honesty, commitment, knowledge and expertise, and ethical behavior (Sharp, Hodge, & Danish, 2015).

Establishing Trust

Honest communication is essential for consultants to reflect an authentic version of themselves and build trust within the consultant–coach relationship. Sharp and Hodge (2013) conducted a case study involving consultants and sport coaches where one consultant expressed the importance of "not over-promising and under-delivering" (p. 319). Furthermore, some professionals have stressed the need for consultants to accurately define their roles, responsibilities, and boundaries for other coaches (Sharp & Hodge, 2011). The initial meeting with a coaching staff can have a significant impact on the consultant–coach relationship and is often where consultants should explain the mental training process rather than approach coaches with a "menu" of topics (Speed, Andersen, & Simons, 2005). Despite consultants' good intentions, a breakdown of potential mental training topics does not provide coaches with the most relevant information they are looking for such as "how" consultants are going to work with their athletes and what the "program" involves. A comprehensive understanding of the mental training program will foster consultants' trust with coaches, thus encouraging them to reinforce the messages conveyed by consultants to athletes and allow them to be collaborators and co-facilitators in their athletes' mental training. Trust can also be fostered by having consultants keep coaches informed of their work, which supports previous studies referencing coaches' interest in being involved in the mental training process (Haberl & McCann, 2012; Zakrajsek et al., 2013).

As mentioned previously, consultants often operate as a satellite service where the mental training program is separated from other aspects of an athlete's or team's training regimen. In these situations, consultants are not viewed as integral members of the coaching staff, which creates challenges for them in being seen as an integral part of the high-performance team and in weaving the mental training program into athletes' and teams' overall training regimens. Being present and accessible during training and competitions is one strategy that consultants can exhibit to reinforce their involvement in a program (Sharp, Hodge, & Danish, 2015). They can also collaborate with coaches to incorporate mental training into conditioning and sport training.

A greater presence within all aspects of the sport organization can also help foster trust between consultant and coaches by creating informal opportunities for both parties to discuss ideas and support one another. Several coaches have endorsed the value of consultants attending training and competitions (Sharp & Hodge, 2013), but it is also important to note that there can be exceptions. Initial meetings, when defining roles and boundaries, are an appropriate time to talk with the coaching staff about the expectation for attending events. Commitment to the program may also be showcased by consultants' willingness to be flexible and assist with responsibilities not directly related to mental training. For example, consultants may perform other duties such as assisting with setup and removal of equipment, facilitating a station during physical testing, or transporting athletes. These experiences are especially common among neophyte consultants who are often willing to complete any task that develops trust and demonstrates their value to a coaching staff (Collins, Evans-Jones, & O'Connor, 2013).

As seen by the recent modifications and increased rigor of the certification program developed by the Association for Applied Sport Psychology (AASP), consultants must possess competency across a variety of domains. It is not enough to simply have a basic understanding of the psychological principles that underlie performance excellence. As the field continues to expand and draw public attention, consultants will be evaluated by an increasingly higher standard. Several studies have already recognized the importance of consultants' knowledge from athletes' and coaches' perspectives (Anderson, Miles, Robinson, & Mahoney, 2004; Sharp & Hodge, 2013; Sharp, Hodge, & Danish, 2015) in addition to how it relates to gaining entry into a sports organization (Fifer et al., 2008; Ravizza, 1988). In particular, sport-specific knowledge is essential for consultants to develop in order to increase their contextual intelligence (Winter & Collins, 2015) and gain respect from coaches (Fifer et al., 2008; Zakrajsek et al., 2013). If consultants will be working in a sport of which they have no experience, an extensive self-study would be warranted that might include reading books, watching the sport on television, viewing videos of practices and competitions, and interviewing coaches in that sport outside of the organization they will be joining. Being able to understand and speak a sport's "language" will go a long way toward establishing credibility with coaches, athletes, and other members of the high-performance team. This competency will also allow consultants to develop an ideal mental training program that will meet the needs and goals of the organization and more readily incorporate their knowledge and skill sets into the team's overall athlete development program.

Another effective strategy for consultants to increase their sport-specific knowledge, as well as to build trust and rapport, is by asking questions. Posing questions can provide insight for consultants on the terminology used by coaches to teach technical or tactical skills. Increased awareness of this terminology will also strengthen consultants' ability to integrate their mental training program into a process that is meaningful and relevant to coaches, athletes, and teams (Fifer et al., 2008). The benefit of asking questions applies to other settings as well including the weight room. For example, it can be valuable for consultants to ask S&C coaches what mental challenges they see in their athletes while doing conditioning. Or consultants may ask how might the S&C coach incorporate a specific mental tool (e.g., breathing) into an exercise. These lines of inquiry invite S&C coaches to share how mental training may impact athletes' performances in the weight room, thereby "opening a door" for consultants to integrate their mental training program into the strength and conditioning regimen (Stutzman et al., 2017).

The growth of sport psychology and mental training as applied fields is accompanied by an increased need for consultants to engage in professional and ethical service delivery. In an investigation of NCAA Division I coaches' perceptions toward mental training services, one coach stated, "I think the first thing you'd want is that person to be of high moral character" (Zakrajsek et al., 2013, p. 261). Consistent ethical behavior is another catalyst for trust and respect in the consultant–coach relationship and it requires a high degree of contextual awareness. For example, consultants should be accountable for their behavior and mindful of situations where their professionalism may be called into question. These situations might include attempting to coach athletes on physical or technical skills within their sport, engaging in gossip regarding coaches or athletes, or breaking the confidentiality of an athlete. Each of these scenarios challenge consultants' abilities to maintain professional boundaries which, as discussed earlier, are a central tenet of effective consulting relationships (Sharp, Hodge, & Danish, 2015). To reduce the potential threats to consultants' professional integrity, they should familiarize themselves with the ethical guidelines that have been created by governing bodies such as AASP and the American Psychological Association (APA).

Integrating with the Coaching Staff

The final consideration for consultants in this section is understanding how they can integrate with and leverage the services of other coaches. Specific recommendations for integrating mental training into coaching are discussed in Chapter 9, therefore this section will focus on identifying a few tips for working with sport and S&C coaches. As mentioned previously, the weight room offers an ideal setting for athletes to strengthen their mental muscles and practice and refine the use of mental exercises and tools. Consultants are not the only ones who believe this as S&C coaches have acknowledged the value of using mental training during physical conditioning (Radcliffe, Comfort, & Fawcett, 2015). Radcliffe and colleagues (2015) interviewed 18 S&C coaches who identified specific mental muscles and exercises including goal-setting, self-talk, mental imagery, focus, intensity, and pre-performance routines as pertinent in the development of various desirable outcomes (e.g., building confidence, achieving ideal intensity, and learning new skills).

When it comes to collaborating with S&C coaches, the timing and setting of introducing mental training is important for consultants to consider (Stutzman et al., 2017). Prior to the start of a physical workout provides a great opportunity for consultants to work with S&C coaches to develop a physical and mental warmup for athletes to follow. During this period, athletes can build a routine that primes their bodies and minds using mental tools such as mental imagery, self-talk, and breathing. At the conclusion of a physical workout is another place where athletes can employ recovery-based mental strategies. For example, progressive muscle relaxation has been shown to be an effective mental tool for decreasing blood lactate concentration post exercise (Solberg et al., 2000).

Lastly, drawing from an experientially-informed practice, it may also be worthwhile for consultants and S&C coaches to brainstorm strategies for using mental training during workouts. Stutzman and colleagues (2017) implemented "Mental Toughness Mondays" with their S&C coach for a high school baseball program, which consisted of a five-week progression of mental challenges intertwined with physical exercises. Within these integrated sessions, athletes would participate in a high-intensity interval circuit led by the S&C coach, while being tasked in-between sets with completing a "mental challenge" designed to help them strengthen their mental muscles or use mental tools discussed earlier in the year. For example, at the conclusion of an exercise set, athletes would work with partners to stack hex nuts on a clipboard using chopsticks. Partners would alternate after each hex nut was stacked, however failure to stack a designated amount in 30 seconds resulted in both athletes having to complete another physical circuit. During the debrief of these sessions, consultants emphasized previously discussed mental tools such as purposeful breathing to remain calm and keywords to maintain focus on the task at hand. This example of integrating mental training into strength and conditioning sessions can be used in a similar manner with sport coaches as they work with athletes on technical and tactical aspects of their sport.

Summary

- A fundamental component of effective consulting involves consultants' ability to develop positive, trusting, and collaborative working relationships with the athletes they serve and those they work with to support the athletes.
- As the interest level and utilization of sport psychology and mental training services continues to grow, it is imperative that consultants understand how they can support, be supported by, and collaborate with both sport and S&C coaches.

- To develop the most integrative and effective mental training programs, consultants must understand what sport and S&C coaches do, need, expect, and want from their services.
- The weight room, in particular, provides a great "lab" for athletes to engage in mental training in a controlled environment with a high volume of repetitions and varying levels of intensity.
- Interdisciplinary collaboration has been recognized as a valuable service delivery model in sport whereby experts from various disciplines can inform and enhance the services of other professionals.
- As the utilization of high performance staffs continues to grow in sport organizations, consultants must understand their role and how to operate optimally as a member of these high-performance teams.
- The quality of the consultant–coach relationship will greatly impact the effectiveness of the mental training program that is implemented due to coaches' influence on their athletes' willingness to buy into and take ownership of consultants' services.
- Consultants must demonstrate the following qualities which have been shown to strengthen relationships with clients: honesty, commitment, knowledge and expertise, and ethical behavior.
- A comprehensive understanding of the mental training program will foster trust consultants' trust with coaches, thus encouraging them to reinforce the messaging proposed by consultants and allow them to be collaborators and co-facilitators in their athletes' mental training.
- Sport-specific knowledge is essential for consultants to develop in order to increase their contextual intelligence and gain respect from coaches.
- The growth of sport psychology as a field is accompanied by an increased need for consultants to engage in professional and ethical service delivery.
- Research found that strength and conditioning coaches who identified specific mental muscles and tools including goal-setting, self-talk, mental imagery, focus, intensity, and pre-performance routines as pertinent in the development of various desirable outcomes (e.g., building confidence, achieving ideal intensity, learning new skills).
- Integrating mental training into strength and conditioning sessions can be used in a similar manner with sport coaches as they work with athletes on technical and tactical aspects of their sport.

References

Andersen, M. B. (2000). *Doing sport psychology*. Champaign, IL: Human Kinetics.

Anderson, A., Miles, A., Robinson, P., & Mahoney, C. (2004). Evaluating the athlete's perception of the sport psychologist's effectiveness: What should we be assessing?. *Psychology of Sport and Exercise*, 5(3), 255–277.

Barker, S., & Winter, S. (2014). The practice of sport psychology: A youth coaches' perspective. *International Journal of Sports Science & Coaching*, 9(2), 379–392.

Collins, R., Evans-Jones, K., & O'Connor, H. L. (2013). Reflections on three neophyte sport and exercise psychologists' developing philosophies for practice. *The Sport Psychologist*, 27(4), 399–409.

Fifer, A., Henschen, K., Gould, D., & Ravizza, K. (2008). What works when working with athletes. *The Sport Psychologist*, 22(3), 356–377.

Fortin-Guichard, D., Boudreault, V., Gagnon, S., & Trottier, C. (2018). Experience, Effectiveness, and Perceptions Toward Sport Psychology Consultants: A Critical Review of Peer-Reviewed Articles. *Journal of Applied Sport Psychology*, 30(1), 3–22.

Gould, D., Greenleaf, C., Guinan, D., & Chung, Y. (2002). A survey of US Olympic coaches: Variables perceived to have influenced athlete performances and coach effectiveness. *The Sport Psychologist*, 16(3), 229–250.

Haberl, P., & McCann, S. (2012). Evaluating USOC sport psychology consultant effectiveness: A philosophical and practical imperative at the Olympic Games. *Journal of Sport Psychology in Action*, 3(2), 65–76.

Holliday, B., Burton, D., Sun, G., Hammermeister, J., Naylor, S., & Freigang, D. (2008). Building the better mental training mousetrap: Is periodization a more systematic approach to promoting performance excellence?. *Journal of Applied Sport Psychology*, 20(2), 199–219.

Jassawalla, A. R., & Sashittal, H. C. (1998). An examination of collaboration in high-technology new product development processes. *Journal of Product Innovation Management*, 15(3) 237–254.

Johnson, U., Andersson, K., & Fallby, J. (2011). Sport psychology consulting among Swedish premier soccer coaches. *International Journal of Sport and Exercise Psychology*, 9(4), 308–322.

Pain, M. A., & Harwood, C. G. (2004). Knowledge and perceptions of sport psychology within English soccer. *Journal of Sports Sciences*, 22(9), 813–826.

Petitpas, A. J., Giges, B., & Danish, S. J. (1999). The sport psychologist–athlete relationship: Implications for training. *The Sport Psychologist*, 13(3), 344–357.

Poczwardowski, A., Sherman, C. P., & Ravizza, K. (2004). Professional philosophy in the sport psychology service delivery: Building on theory and practice. *The Sport Psychologist, 18*(4), 445–463.

Radcliffe, J. N., Comfort, P., & Fawcett, T. (2015). Psychological strategies included by strength and conditioning coaches in applied strength and conditioning. *The Journal of Strength and Conditioning Research, 29*(9), 2641–2654.

Ravizza, K. (1988). Gaining entry with athletic personnel for season-long consulting. *The Sport Psychologist, 2*(3), 243–254.

Reid, C., Stewart, E., & Thorne, G. (2004). Multidisciplinary sport science teams in elite sport: Comprehensive servicing or conflict and confusion? *The Sport Psychologist, 18*(2), 204–217.

Sharp, L. A., & Hodge, K. (2011). Sport psychology consulting effectiveness: The sport psychology consultant's perspective. *Journal of Applied Sport Psychology, 23*(3), 360–376.

Sharp, L. A., & Hodge, K. (2013). Effective sport psychology consulting relationships: Two coach case studies. *The Sport Psychologist, 27*(4), 313–324.

Sharp, L. A., Hodge, K., & Danish, S. (2015). Ultimately it comes down to the relationship: Experienced consultants' views of effective sport psychology consulting. *The Sport Psychologist, 29*(4), 358–370.

Solberg, E. E., Ingjer, F., Holen, A., Sundgot-Borgen, J., Nilsson, S., & Holme, I. (2000). Stress reactivity to and recovery from a standardized exercise bout: A study of 31 runners practicing relaxation techniques. *British Journal of Sports Medicine, 34*(4), 268–272.

Speed, H. D., Andersen, M. B., & Simons, J. (2005). The selling or the telling of sport psychology: Presenting services to coaches. In M. B. Andersen (Ed.), *Sport psychology in practice.* Champaign, IL : Human Kinetics.

Stutzman, T., Brandon, Z.E., Wieland, A., Larsen, L. K., Hamilton, L., Andreoli, D. A., Ingalls, R., Morgan, T., Hesse, D., Da Silva, D., Smith, C., Simpson, D. (2017, October). Let's get physical: Utilizing strength & conditioning to train mental skills. Paper presented at Association for Applied Sport Psychology Conference, Orlando, FL.

Winter, S., & Collins, D. (2015). Why do we do, what we do? *Journal of Applied Sport Psychology, 27*(1), 35–51.

Wrisberg, C. A., Loberg, L. A., Simpson, D., Withycombe, J. L., & Reed, A. (2010). An exploratory investigation of NCAA Division-I coaches' support of sport psychology consultants and willingness to seek mental training services. *The Sport Psychologist, 24*(4), 489–503.

Zakrajsek, R. A., Martin, S. B., & Zizzi, S. J. (2011). American high school football coaches' attitudes toward sport psychology consultation and intentions to use sport psychology services. *International Journal of Sports Science & Coaching, 6*(3), 461–478.

Zakrajsek, R. A., Steinfeldt, J. A., Bodey, K. J., Martin, S. B., & Zizzi, S. J. (2013). NCAA Division I coaches' perceptions and preferred use of sport psychology services: A qualitative perspective. *The Sport Psychologist, 27*(3), 258–268.

SPORTS MEDICINE STAFF

Tim White

Within an organization, consultants are often part of a larger sports medicine team. The sports medicine team is composed of numerous professionals (Brukner & Khan, 2012; Prentice, 2006) who must work together to be most effective (Prentice, 2006). Collectively, this group facilitates the health, well-being, and sports performance of the athletes they serve. Understanding the structure and function of the sports medicine team and recognizing how consultants fit within their current organization is important so that they can maximize their value with individual athletes, teams, and organizations.

Sports Medicine Team

When describing how a sports medicine team is organized, proximity to the injured athlete and the relationship between the professional and the athlete recovering from injury are defining characteristics (Clement & Arvinen-Barrow, 2013). This emphasis on proximity and relationships, which are heavily influenced by professional roles and responsibilities, creates a primary and secondary sports medicine team. Typically, athletic trainers (also known as sports physiotherapists or athletic therapists outside the US), and team physicians (including general practitioners, sports medicine specialists, and orthopedic surgeons), are closest in proximity to athletes recovering from injury (Clement & Arvinen-Barrow, 2013; Prentice, 2006). Together, an injured athlete plus an athletic trainer and team physician make up the primary sports medicine team. This group is the most intimately involved in an athlete's recovery and return to sport. Other members of the sports medicine team who interact with recovering athletes less directly or less consistently are described as functioning in a secondary role and may include physical therapists, massage therapists, consultants, strength and conditioning specialists, nutritionists, sport coaches, chiropractors, and other specialists (i.e., exercise physiologists, biomechanists, orthotists; Brukner

& Khan, 2012; Clement & Arvinen-Barrow, 2013; Prentice, 2014). Although the proximity and frequency of interaction between injured athletes and those of the secondary sports medicine team are less than for the primary sports medicine team, their role can be equally important and influential on both the recovery experience and outcomes obtained by injured athletes.

Additionally, it is noted that many sports medicine team members traditionally function in roles related to performance enhancement (e.g., consultants, strength and conditioning specialists) while others typically function in roles related to injury diagnosis, management, and recovery (e.g., athletic trainers, team physicians). Despite these traditional delineations, professionals in either group can support and facilitate the work of professionals in the other group. Thus, consultants may primarily interact with healthy athletes for the purposes of performance enhancement but consultants may also serve a critical role in the support and enhancement of athletes striving for comprehensive recovery via their rehabilitation efforts.

As a member of a larger team charged with the rehabilitation and return to sport of injured athletes, and the performance enhancement of all athletes, it is critical for consultants to build relationships with those who also work to enhance athletic performance (e.g., sport coaches, strength and conditioning specialists, and nutritionists; see above section) as well as those who help athletes avoid and recover from injuries (e.g., athletic trainers and team physicians). The precise nature of these relationships within the sports medicine team may vary depending on the education, training, experience, certification, and licensure that consultants possess. Regardless of the nature of each relationship, a strong collaborative approach is critical for group success, which is ultimately measured by successful athlete outcomes and performances.

Within the standards of confidentiality—that is, the Health Insurance Portability and Accountability Act (HIPAA)—collaborating professionals can be a valuable source of information for consultants and, together, the sports medicine team can collectively assist athletes seeking comprehensive health, well-being, and performance excellence.

Professionals Relationships to Build

As the medically trained professionals who are most often present at team practices and competitions, athletic trainers function as the point person for injured athletes and regularly coordinate their care and rehabilitation with the rest of the sports medicine team. More often than not, they will address athletes' concerns; however, there are numerous instances that require athletic trainers to seek assistance from other members of the sports medicine team including consultants. Many athletic trainers are aware of the psychological aspects of injury and rehabilitation (Clement, Granquist, Arvinen-Barrow, 2013; Larson, Starkey, & Zaichkowsky, 1996) but do not feel adequately trained (Clement et al., 2013; Stiller-Ostrowski, & Hamson-Utley, 2010; Zakrajsek, Fisher, & Martin, 2017) or have sufficient time to effectively address this area of recovery. Thus, it is critical for consultants and athletic trainers to collaboratively address the physical *and* psychological aspects of rehabilitation and recovery. Not only can consultants support athletic trainers, but the opposite is true as well. Athletic trainers, operating within the guidelines of HIPAA, can be a beneficial source of information for consultants in their work in the psychological rehabilitation of the physical injury. As appropriate, athletic trainers and consultants can judiciously share information with each other that helps the other professional when working with a specific athlete. Examples of this type of collaboration include:

- Athletic trainers may provide information about an athlete's thoughts, emotions, and behaviors regarding their injury that may help consultants gain insight into any challenges they may face during their rehabilitation and return to sport.
- Consultants may learn that an athlete is concerned about their ability to fully recover and avoid re-injury. When this information is appropriately shared, athletic trainers can tailor their treatment plans, particularly the sport-specific activities, for that athlete.

An additional consideration regarding the relationship between consultants and athletic trainers is the fact that consultants may benefit from existing relationships between athletes and athletic trainers. Athletic trainers can be a strong referral source for consultants and may even provide a form of access to teams when consultants are looking to establish new connections.

If the sports medicine team employs a physical therapist on-site, many of the same principles regarding the relationship between consultants and athletic trainers apply to them as well. When physical therapists are offsite (such as a high school athlete being treated at a community clinic), the opportunity to communicate and support each other's work remains, however, it may take additional effort to contact and communicate with them. Regardless of their location, it is important to note that unlike athletic trainers, physical therapists do not attend practices or competitions. Also, physical therapists do not see the athletes they are treating on a daily basis like athletic trainers do. Due to these differences, their connection to individual athletes and teams is reduced and thus it is more difficult for consultants to gain access to athletes and teams through physical therapists.

For consultants who do not hold a license as a mental health provider it is important to establish a relationship with both the clinicians who focus on physical health (i.e., athletic trainers, team physicians) as well as licensed mental health professionals such as psychiatrists, psychologists, counselors, and/or clinical social workers. At a minimum, a consultant's referral network should include *at least* one psychiatrist and one of the other mental health clinicians just mentioned. These professionals contribute to athletes' comprehensive health and well-being, particularly when they present with concerns that are beyond the scope of practice for unlicensed consultants. Examples include, but are not limited to, eating disorders, depression, anxiety, trauma, and personality disorders. Unlicensed consultants must have and take advantage of these resources to avoid liability and malpractice, but more importantly, to ensure that the needs and best interests of their athletes are met.

Consultants who are also licensed as mental health providers should establish the same relationships within the sports medicine team previously described. Like unlicensed consultants, licensed mental health providers create a network of mental health professionals (i.e., psychiatrists, psychologists, etc.) around them. This gives licensed consultants a list of resources they can consult when facing challenging cases or situations in which another provider may have greater levels of experience or expertise.

When consultants are licensed mental health providers, there is potential for the relationships they have with professionals such as team physicians and nutritionist to be slightly different. Because licensed individuals are trained to treat mental health concerns such as depression, eating disorders, and other clinical diagnoses, it is probable they will discuss and co-manage these concerns with team physicians and other clinicians (e.g., nutritionist) as appropriate. This creates opportunities for additional interaction with these professionals that are less likely to occur for unlicensed consultants. Given the complexity of some mental health concerns, it is critical to ensure that athletes are cared for by a team of professionals who can collectively promote their health, safety, and well-being. For example, athletes presenting with disordered eating may benefit from the collective care of a team physician, nutritionist, and mental health provider who has training and experience with disordered eating in athletes. If comorbid conditions such as anxiety or depression are present and warrant the use of prescription medication, a psychiatrist is an appropriate addition to this group of professionals. Unlicensed consultants and others may provide secondary care and support and are encouraged to seek the guidance of the providers primarily responsible for the treatment plan.

A final professional within the sports medicine team that bears mentioning are strength and conditioning specialists. These individuals are addressed in other sections of this chapter, therefore the discussion of this relationship is isolated to their involvement with an athlete who is preparing to return to sport participation during the latter stages of rehabilitation. In this situation, with appropriate release of information documentation, consultants may provide relevant information about the athlete to strength and conditioning specialists and vice versa.

It is worth reiterating that as consultants communicate with other members of the sports medicine team, they must ensure confidentiality standards are met. In addition, discussion of athletes should be limited to pertinent information necessary for the sports medicine team members directly involved in their care so they may effectively assist the individuals being discussed.

As part of this emphasis on confidentiality, consultants should have a release of information form athletes can sign should they wish for the consultant to speak to other members of the sports medicine team, their sport coaches, or any other individual the athlete may designate. This form should also offer athletes the ability to designate which details consultants may discuss and with whom. Taking these measures is not only ethical practice, they ensure privacy and confidentiality, enhance understanding and transparency between consultants and athletes, and provide consultants with an added layer of protection from legal claims.

Why Build These Relationships?

While the answer to this question may seem obvious, it is important to consider the empirical evidence supporting these connections. From the perspective of those within the sports medicine team who focus on performance enhancement, countless studies have demonstrated the relationship between mental preparation and athletic performance. For sports medicine team members concerned with rehabilitation from injury, there is also an observable connection between athletes' mental states and their general approach toward treatment and rehabilitation and recovery outcomes (Arvinen-Barrow & Walker, 2013; Clement, Arvinen-Barrow, & Fetty, 2015; Podlog & Eklund, 2006; Tracey, 2003; Walker, Thatcher, & Lavallee, 2007; Wiese-Bjornstal, Smith, Shaffer, & Morrey, 1998). This research demonstrates the mind-body connection in a setting outside of traditional sports performance. Consultants can assist athletes, team physicians, and athletic trainers by encouraging them to perceive their rehabilitation and recovery experience as an alternative form of performance that has its own objective measures and sources of evaluation.

Additionally, preventing injuries is an objective consultants can collaboratively approach with professionals such as athletic trainers, strength and conditioning specialists, exercise physiologists, and sport coaches. Several studies have identified the relationship between an athlete's mental state and their risk for injury (Gledhill, Forsdyke, & Murray, 2018; Ivarsson, Johnson, Andersen, Tranaeus, Stenling, & Lindwall, 2017; Singh & Conroy, 2017). Consultants who are aware of relevant mental states (e.g., stress; Ivarsson et al., 2017; Singh & Conroy, 2017) can share this information with athletic trainers, coaches, and strength and conditioning specialist for planning athletes' training activities. Consultants can also influence injury risk by teaching athletes strategies used to reach a mental state associated with lower risk for injury. Examples include stress coping skills, relaxation techniques, and focusing tools.

Having made these suggestions, consultants must be sure to address these considerations in a collaborative fashion, particularly when adjustments to training plans are being discussed. This is critical to reducing potential conflict among professionals as well as athletes they support. Ultimately, sports performance and recovery from injury are significantly more complex than engaging in rehabilitation exercises or executing physical skills. Relevant professionals addressing the numerous facets of injury rehabilitation and athletic performance are needed to maximize athletes' efforts and the outcomes they obtain. These professionals must effectively communicate and collectively work toward a common goal to maximize their professional success and ultimately position the athletes they serve to optimize their athletic performances.

Roles and Responsibilities when Injury Occurs

The previous sections illustrated the types of relationships consultants have within the sports medicine team. A discussion regarding consultants' roles and responsibilities at the time of athletic injury is now warranted. Numerous professionals have varying degrees of education, training, and experience regarding injury rehabilitation and it is critical for consultants to understand their own capabilities and limitations, and which professionals are capable of and responsible for the diverse range of activities involved in the rehabilitation of an injury and athletes' subsequent return to sport (Arvinen-Barrow & Clement, 2017).

Athletic Trainers

Within a sports medicine team, athletic trainers often function as the point person responsible for directing and coordinating the day-to-day care and rehabilitation of injured athletes. Additionally, athletic trainers regularly implement treatment plans and make decisions regarding when and how to incorporate other sports medicine team members into the rehabilitation process.

Athletic trainers and other therapists are becoming increasingly aware of the psychological component of athletic injury (Arvinen-Barrow, Hemmings, Weigand, Becker, & Booth, 2007; Clement et al., 2013; Larson et al., 1996; Zakrajsek et al., 2017). With this increased awareness, consultants are being identified as important members of the sports medicine team (Arvinen-Barrow & Clement, 2015). These authors further note that athletic trainers believe that having better access to consultants can improve comprehensive care for injured athletes. This finding reiterates the importance of building strong relationships with athletic trainers.

Although these positive perceptions are encouraging, it should also be noted that athletic trainers view the mental aspect of injury and rehabilitation as part of their responsibilities (National Athletic Trainers' Association, 2011). Specifically, the competency standards outlined by the National Athletic Trainers' Association (2011) state athletic trainers should have the ability to describe and implement mental strategies and interventions such as goal-setting, mental imagery, positive self-talk, and relaxation/anxiety reduction. Thus, there is an overlap in some of the mental approaches that are common practice for consultants.

However, consultants remain the experts in this area and serve as excellent sources of collaboration. A collaborative approach allows consultants to provide greater levels of detail and variety for athletes using specific mental strategies within their recovery plan. Furthermore, consultants can guide injured athletes through more advanced interventions that extend beyond the scope of practice or competency of athletic trainers. Additionally, given that athletic trainers are busy addressing the physical aspects of athletes' rehabilitations, consultants can play a practical role of taking on responsibilities for which athletic trainers don't have the time to focus on.

Adding value to consultants is the fact that not all athletic trainers believe it is their role to provide mental interventions and instead will refer injured athletes to consultants for the purposes of mental recovery after injury (Cormier & Zizzi, 2015). Another benefit for consultants who are also licensed mental health providers is that the athletic training competencies also include statements regarding their role in identifying individuals displaying signs and symptoms of various mental health concerns and subsequently making a referral to a qualified mental health provider (National Athletic Trainers' Association, 2011).

Promoting the role of consultants also comes in the form of the perceived insufficient training and proficiency in effectively implementing mental training among athletic trainers and other sports medicine practitioners (Clement et al., 2013; Zakrajsek et al., 2017). Students studying athletic training and physical therapy in the US, or physiotherapy around the world, receive different levels of education and training in the psychological factors associated with athletic injury, rehabilitation, and recovery (Arvinen-Barrow, Penny, Hemmings, & Corr, 2010; Harris, 2005; Hinderliter & Cardinal, 2007; Kolt & Anderson, 2004; Taylor & Taylor 1997). According to Arvinen-Barrow et al. (2010), skills such as mental imagery and relaxation techniques are often misunderstood by athletic trainers and physical therapists. Clement et al. (2013) supplements these findings by noting that relaxation techniques, mental imagery, and emotional control strategies are least commonly used by athletic trainers.

The statistics around sport psychology education and training for athletic trainers and other rehabilitation professionals provide insights into their use and comfort level with such interventions. Interestingly, many of the mental strategies used by certified athletic trainers (Clement et al., 2013; Zakrajsek et al., 2017) are more subtle and less overt. Zakrajsek et al. (2017) revealed that the interventions used by athletic trainers, including self-talk, arousal/anxiety management, and visualization, were least commonly implemented (less than 50% of the time), while more subtle methods such as normalizing the recovery process, goal-setting, reassurance, and connecting rehabilitation to sport skills were incorporated more than 50% of the time. These approaches are in line with the suggestions provided by Arvinen-Barrow, Massey, and Hemmings (2014) in their study of professional athletes' perceptions of the role of athletic trainers in addressing the mental components of recovery. The participants in their study noted a preference for athletic trainers to use subtle psychological interventions throughout the recovery process and avoid explicit intervention strategies aimed at the psychological components of healing.

A final, yet critical, role within the mental component of injury recovery that athletic trainers often fulfill is providing social support. Social support is a key component to rehabilitation (Podlog, Dimmock, & Miller, 2011) and athletic trainers providing social support have been identified as having the greatest influence on injured athletes' rehabilitation and well-being (Clement & Shannon, 2011). Furthermore, this study found that injured athletes were more satisfied with the social support provided by their athletic trainer when compared to the social support received from coaches and teammates.

Consultants

When exploring the composition of the sports medicine team, 86% of consultants indicated they should be a part of the primary sports medicine team along with the injured athletes, athletic trainers, sport coaches, and strength and conditioning specialists (Arvinen-Barrow & Clement, 2017). Within this perspective, it is noted by consultants that the injured athletes should be at the center of the care team.

Despite these findings, it is not consistent practice for consultants to be part of the primary sports medicine team (Arvinen-Barrow & Clement, 2015, 2017). This current reality should not discourage consultants as it is believed that they are gaining access to injured athletes and the sports medicine setting (Arvinen-Barrow & Clement, 2017). Furthermore, the field of sport psychology is growing but an athletic trainer's access to consultants remains limited (Clement et al., 2013; Hamson-Utley, Martin, & Walters, 2008; Hemmings, & Povey, 2002; Roh & Perna, 2000). This represents a significant opportunity for consultants to further their contribution to comprehensive and holistic health care initiatives for athletes.

Fortunately for consultants, athletic trainers and other sports medicine professionals believe mental training is effective and can facilitate the recovery of an injured athlete (Hamson-Utley et al., 2008). Research by Zakrajsek, Martin, and Wrisberg (2016) supports the idea that as consultants become more accessible, athletic trainers will increasingly refer and incorporate consultants into their work in the care of injured athletes.

Consultants can increase their contributions within sports medicine settings by providing quality services that athletes and teams deem valuable. This may seem overly simplified and obvious, however, athletic trainers who have high-quality experiences when collaborating with consultants are more likely to encourage injured athletes to work with a consultant again in the future (Zakrajsek et al., 2016). In addition, athletic trainers have identified consultants' expertise related to managing anxiety, regulating other emotions, improving coping skills, reducing return to sport participation concerns, and building confidence as areas of interest (Zakrajsek et al., 2016). Thus, consultants may want to develop specific proficiency in approaches and strategies directly related to these areas.

Adding to the possibilities for consultants to expand their roles and involvement in the sports medicine team is the opportunity to augment the knowledge of athletic trainers. Similar to the idea that many sport coaches have a basic understanding of a related field like strength and conditioning, many athletic trainers have a basic recognition of mental factors associated with injury and rehabilitation. Consultants are capable of providing additional professional education that can increase the likelihood that appropriate action is taken by those who act as primary care providers for injured athletes (Zakrajsek et al., 2017). In addition, consultants may normalize the mental aspects (e.g., thoughts, emotions) of recovery from injury for athletes similar to the way athletic trainers normalize the physical aspects of recovery. Finally, consultants can address individual athlete needs extending beyond the scope of practice for athletic trainers. Continued efforts to educate others regarding the competencies, proficiencies, and scope of practice existing for licensed and unlicensed consultants are critical to expanding the field as well as the roles of consultants within the sports medicine team.

Another consideration regarding consultants' participation in the recovery efforts of injured athletes relates to motivation for returning to sport participation. Similar to addressing motivation by asking *why* an athlete participates in sport, consultants can help athletes increase their understanding of their reasons for committing to and completing a rehabilitation regimen. For many athletes, the answer to the question "why?" is simple: return to their sport to continue the pursuit of their goals. However, not every athlete has that opportunity (e.g., high school or college senior who sustains a season-ending injury and will not play at the next level of sport; Ardern, Webster, Taylor, & Feller, 2011). These athletes should receive particular attention and assistance in identifying a specific reason for rehabilitation adherence and full recovery.

Regardless of athletes' options for resuming competitive sport participation after an injury, it is critical for self-motivation toward rehabilitation to exist. Self-motivation was identified as the personal factor most commonly associated with rehabilitation adherence (Spetch & Kolt, 2001). Thus, athletes need tangible reasons for devoting effort, energy, and time to a rehabilitation program. Helping injured athletes explore their values and motivations in relation to their sport as well as life outside of sport is a critical role consultants can fill that can directly influence injured athletes' motivations as well as the rehabilitation experience and outcomes they obtain.

Consultants can also contribute to the sports medicine team by offering their assessment of athletes' psychological readiness to return to sport, in terms of both practice and competition. Athletic trainers often use physical assessments (e.g., strength tests, stability tests, etc.) to help them determine athletes' physical readiness to resume their sport participation. However, recovery is not isolated solely to physical parameters. Psychological recovery needs to be considered when making return-to-sport decisions and the concept of psychological readiness has received noticeable attention recently (Ardern, Taylor, Feller, & Webster 2013; Ardern, Taylor, Feller, Whitehead, & Webster, 2013; Burland, Toonstra, Werner, Mattacola, Howell, & Howard, 2018; Forsdyke, Gledhill, & Ardern, 2016; Glazer, 2009; Monahan, 2018; Podlog, Banham, Wadey, & Hannon, 2015; Werner, Burland, Mattacola, Toonstra, English, & Howard, 2018). Consultants can assist athletic trainers and team physicians with this decision by using a combination of conversations with recovering athletes, observing them as they perform sport-specific movements in rehabilitation and practice settings, and administering psychometric assessments. Of the psychometric assessments that exist, consultants may want to consider employing one or more of the following:

- Injury-Psychological Readiness to Return to Sport (I-PRRS) Scale (Glazer, 2009).
- Shoulder Instability-Return to Sport After Injury (SIRSI; Gerometta, Klouche, Herman, Lefevre, Bohu, 2017).
- ACL-Return to Sport After Injury (ACL-RSI; Webster, Feller, Lambros, 2008).
- Rehabilitation Overadherence Questionnaire (Podlog, Gao, Kenow, Kleinert, Granquist, Newton, Hannon, 2013).
- Profile of Mood States – Adolescent (POMS-A; Terry, Lane, Lane, & Keohane, 1999). Note that this measure has been validated for adult populations as well (Terry, Lane, & Fogarty, 2003).
- Tampa Scale of Kinesiophobia (TSK; Miller, Kori & Todd, 1991).
- Re-Injury Anxiety Inventory (RIAI; Walker, Thatcher, & Lavallee, 2010).
- Knee Self-Efficacy Scale (K-SES; Thomeé, Wahrborg, Borjesson, Thomeé, Eriksson, & Karlsson, 2006).
- Athlete Fear Avoidance Questionnaire (Dover & Amar, 2015).

Consultants contributing to this aspect of returning to sport will provide the sports medicine team and the coaching staff with additional information that will enable them to make the best decisions that will result in athletes' safe and complete return to their sport.

Lastly, consultants can contribute to sports medicine teams by participating in events such as pre-season health screenings, tryouts, and performance testing. Most collegiate and professional organizations complete some form of pre-participation exam at the beginning of the year (or season) and aim to gather a comprehensive view of athletes' current health status and readiness for sport participation. As mental health considerations are increasingly recognized and acknowledged in the athletic community, consultants, particularly those with clinical training, may contribute to the comprehensiveness of these exams. Various surveys, mental health history questionnaires, and psychometric measures may be used to gather information regarding the past and present mental health status of athletes in a similar manner used by athletic trainers and team physicians in gathering information about athletes' physical health. When conducting these assessments, consultants must consider their scope of practice, what information is most appropriate for them to gather, and what steps need to be taken to ensure confidentiality is maintained. Consultants are encouraged to collaborate with other mental health providers (as appropriate) as well as the professional charged with directing the sports medicine team (often a team physician) to determine if, and how, they should participate in the various assessment and testing protocols that are becoming a routine part of elite-team selection and preparation.

Athletes

According to Arvinen-Barrow et al. (2015), 27% of athletes will use mental training (e.g., goal-setting, positive self-talk, relaxation, and mental imagery) during their recovery. Curiously, of those using mental training, very few learn the specific strategies, or how to apply them, from consultants. Other individuals sharing these principles with injured athletes include athletic trainers, physical therapists, coaches, and family members (Arvinen-Barrow et al., 2015).

This finding is surprising, particularly considering that consultants are ideally suited to implement mental training. However, it must be recognized that the field of sport psychology remains underused and, as a result, access to consultants may be limited. Despite this current state, consultants should not be discouraged. Arvinen-Barrow et al. (2015) suggest that athletes using mental training as part of their rehabilitations may not directly learn these tools from others. Instead, they may be learning how to *apply* mental strategies they have previously used within their athletic performance to support and enhance their recovery efforts. Thus, the potential for consultants to expand their reach is reiterated.

As a final thought regarding roles, members of the sports medicine team are encouraged to discuss, identify, and formalize a general list of responsibilities and functions for each professional as a part of their job description. This approach establishes these critical delineations *before* an athlete sustains an injury and reduces the likelihood of confusion and conflict among professionals. Ultimately, this role clarity provides each professional with the opportunity to identify the expertise they offer to injured athletes while also determining other resources and forms of support that exist. Naturally, various injuries, athletes, and situations will require flexibility and adjustments; however, having a general sense of roles and responsibilities will position the sports medicine team to function optimally when supporting injured athletes.

Summary

- Within a sports organization, consultants are often part of a larger sports medicine team.
- Understanding the structure and function of the sports medicine team and recognizing how consultants fit within their current organization is important so that they can maximize their value with individual athletes, teams, and organizations.
- An injured athlete plus an athletic trainer and team physician make up the primary sports medicine team that is the most intimately involved in an athlete's recovery and return to sport.
- Other members of the sports medicine team who function in a secondary role may include physical therapists, massage therapists, consultants, strength and conditioning specialists, nutritionists, sport coaches, chiropractors, and other specialists (i.e., exercise physiologists, biomechanists, and orthotists).
- It is critical for consultants to build relationships with those who also work to enhance athletic performance (e.g., sport coaches, strength and conditioning specialists, and nutritionists) as well as those who help athletes avoid and recover from injuries (e.g., athletic trainers and team physicians).
- Consultants and athletic trainers should work collaboratively to address the physical *and* psychological aspects of rehabilitation and recovery.
- For consultants who do not hold a license as a mental health provider it is important to establish a relationship with licensed mental health professionals such as psychiatrists, psychologists, counselors, and/or clinical social workers.
- Consultants can assist athletes, team physicians, and athletic trainers by encouraging them to perceive their rehabilitation and recovery experience as an alternative form of performance that has its own objective measures and sources of evaluation.
- Preventing injuries is an objective consultants can collaboratively approach with professionals such as athletic trainers, strength and conditioning specialists, exercise physiologists, and sport coaches.
- Athletic trainers regularly implement treatment plans and make decisions regarding when and how to incorporate other sports medicine team members into the rehabilitation process.
- Consultants can contribute to the sports medicine team by offering their assessment of athletes' psychological readiness to return to sport, in terms of both practice and competition.
- Athletic trainers have identified consultants' expertise related to managing anxiety, regulating other emotions, improving coping skills, reducing return to sport participation concerns, and building confidence as areas of interest.

References

Ardern, C. L., Taylor, N. F., Feller, J. A., & Webster, K. E. (2013). A systematic review of the psychological factors associated with returning to sport following injury. *British Journal of Sports Medicine, 47*, 1120–1126.

Ardern, C. L., Taylor, N. F., Feller, J. A., Whitehead, T. S., & Webster, K. E. (2013). Psychological responses matter in returning to preinjury level of sport after anterior cruciate ligament reconstruction surgery. *The American Journal of Sports Medicine, 41*(7), 1549–1558.

Ardern, C. L., Webster, K. E., Taylor, N. F., & Feller, J. A. (2011). Return to sport following anterior cruciate ligament reconstruction surgery: A systematic review and meta-analysis of the state of play. *British Journal of Sports Medicine, 45*(7), 596–606.

Arvinen-Barrow, M., & Clement, D. (2015). A preliminary investigation into athletic trainers' views and experiences of a multidisciplinary team approach to sports injury rehabilitation. *Athletic Training and Sports Health Care, 7*(3), 97–107.

Arvinen-Barrow, M., & Clement, D. (2017). Preliminary investigation into sport and exercise psychology consultants' views and experiences of an interprofessional care team approach to sport injury rehabilitation. *Journal of Interprofessional Care, 31*(1), 66–74

Arvinen-Barrow, M., Clement, D., Hamson-Utley, J. J., Zakrajsek, R. A., Lee, S. M., Kamphoff, C., . . . & Martin, S. B (2015). Athletes' use of mental skills during sport injury rehabilitation. *Journal of Sport Rehabilitation, 24*(2), 189–197.

Arvinen-Barrow, M., Hemmings, B., Weigand, D., Becker, C., & Booth, L. (2007). Views of chartered physiotherapists on the psychological content of their practice: a follow-up survey in the UK. *Journal of Sport Rehabilitation, 16*(2), 111–121.

Arvinen-Barrow, M., Massey, W. V., & Hemmings, B. (2014). Role of sport medicine professionals in addressing psychosocial aspects of sport-injury rehabilitation: Professional athletes' views. *Journal of Athletic Training, 49*(6), 764–772.

Arvinen-Barrow, M., Penny, G., Hemmings, B., & Corr, S. (2010). UK chartered physiotherapists' personal experiences in using psychological interventions with injured athletes: An interpretive phenomenological analysis. *Psychology of Sport and Exercise, 11*, 58–66.

Arvinen-Barrow, M., & Walker, N. (2013). Introduction to the psychology of sport injuries. In M. Arvinen-Barrow, & N. Walker (Eds.), *The psychology of sport injury and rehabilitation* (pp. 2–5). New York, NY: Routledge.

Brukner, P., & Khan, K. (2012). *Brukner & Khan's Clinical Sports medicine*, 4th ed. North Ryde, Australia: McGraw-Hill.

Burland, J. P., Toonstra, J., Werner, J. L., Mattacola, C. G., Howell, D. M., & Howard, J. S. (2018). Decision to return to sport after anterior cruciate ligament reconstruction, Part I: A qualitative investigation of psychosocial factors. *Journal of Athletic Training*, *53*(5), 452–463.

Clement, D., & Arvinen-Barrow, M. (2013). Sports medicine team influences in psychological rehabilitation: A multidisciplinary approach. In M. Arvinen-Barrow, & N. Walker (Eds.), *The psychology of sport injury and rehabilitation* (pp. 156–170). New York, NY: Routledge.

Clement, D., Arvinen-Barrow, M., & Fetty, T. (2015). Psychological Responses during different phases of sport-injury rehabilitation: A qualitative study. *Journal of Athletic Training*, *50*(1), 95–104.

Clement, D., Granquist, M. D., Arvinen-Barrow, M. M. (2013). Psychosocial aspects of athletic injuries as perceived by athletic trainers. *Journal of Athletic Training*, *48*(4), 512–521.

Clement, D., & Shannon, V. R. (2011). Injured athletes' perceptions about social support. *Journal of Sport Rehabilitation*, *20*(4), 457–470.

Cormier, M. L., & Zizzi, S. J. (2015). Athletic trainers' skills in identifying and managing athletes experiencing psychological distress. *Journal of Athletic Training*, *50*, 1267–1276.

Dover, G., & Amar, V. (2015). Development and validation of the athlete fear avoidance questionnaire. *Journal of Athletic Training*, *50*(6), 634–642.

Forsdyke, D., Gledhill, A., & Ardern, C. (2016). Psychological readiness to return to sport: three key elements to help the practitioner decide whether the athlete is REALLY ready? *British Journal of Sports Medicine*, *51*(7), 555–556.

Gerometta, A., Klouche, S., Herman, S., Lefevre, N., & Bohu, Y. (2017). The Shoulder Instability-Return to Sport after Injury (SIRSI): a valid and reproducible scale to quantify psychological readiness to return to sport after traumatic shoulder instability. *Knee Surgery, Sports Traumatology, Arthroscopy*, *26*(1), 203–211.

Glazer, D. D. (2009). Development and preliminary validation of the Injury-Psychological Readiness to Return to Sport (I-PRRS) scale. *Journal of Athletic Training*, *44*(2), 185–189.

Gledhill, A., Forsdyke, D., & Murray, E. (2018). Psychological intervention used to reduce sports injuries: A systematic review of real-world effectiveness. *British Journal of Sports Medicine*, *52*, 967–971.

Hamson-Utley, J. J., Martin, S., & Walters, J. (2008). Athletic trainers' and physical therapists' perceptions of the effectiveness of psychological skills within sport injury rehabilitation programs. *Journal of Athletic Training*, *43*(3), 258–264.

Harris, L. (2005). Perceptions and attitudes of athletic training students toward a course addressing psychological issues in rehabilitation. *Journal of Allied Health*, *34*(2), 101–109.

Hemmings, B., & Povey, L. (2002). Views of chartered physiotherapists on the psychological content of their practice: a preliminary study in the United Kingdom. *British journal of sports medicine*, *36*(1), 61–64.

Hinderliter, C. J., & Cardinal, B. J. (2007). Psychological rehabilitation for recovery from injury: the SCRAPE approach. *Athletic Therapy Today*, *12*(6), 36–38.

Ivarsson, A., Johnson, U., Andersen, M., Tranaeus, U., Stenling, A., & Lindwall, M. (2017). Psychosocial factors and sport injuries: Meta-analyses for prediction and prevention. *Sports Medicine*, *47*(2), 353–365.

Kolt, G. S., & Andersen, M. B. (Eds.). (2004). *Psychology in the physical and manual therapies*. Philadelphia, PA: Churchill Livingstone.

Larson, G. A., Starkey, C., & Zaichkowsky, L. D. (1996). Psychological aspects of athletic injuries as perceived by athletic trainers. *The Sport Psychologist*, *10*(1), 37–47.

Miller, R. P., Kori, S. H., & Todd, D. D. (1991). The Tampa Scale: A measure of kinesiophobia. *The Clinical Journal of Pain*, *7*(1), 51.

Monahan, A. C. (2018). Psychological readiness of athletes to return to play following injury. Retrieved from https://digitalcommons.georgiasouthern.edu/etd/1736.

National Athletic Trainers' Association. (2011). *Athletic training educational competencies*, 5th ed. Dallas, TX: National Athletic Trainers' Association.

Podlog, L., Banham, S. M., Wadey, R., & Hannon, J. C. (2015). Psychological readiness to return to competitive sport following injury: a qualitative study. *The Sport Psychologist*, *29*(1), 1–14.

Podlog, L., Dimmock, J., & Miller, J. (2011). A review of return to sport concerns following injury rehabilitation: practitioner strategies for enhancing recovery outcomes. *Physical Therapy in Sport*, *12*(1), 36–42.

Podlog, L., & Eklund, R. (2006). A longitudinal investigation of competitive athletes' return to sport following serious injury. *Journal of Applied Sport Psychology*, *18*(1), 44–68.

Podlog, L., Gao, Z., Kenow, L., Kleinert, J., Granquist, M., Newton, M., & Hannon, J. (2013). Injury rehabilitation overadherence: Preliminary scale validation and relationships with athletic identity and self-presentation concerns. *Journal of Athletic Training*, *48*(3), 372–381.

Prentice, W. E. (2006). *Arnheim's principles of athletic training: A competency-based approach*, 12th ed. New York, NY: McGraw-Hill.

Prentice W. E. (2014). Arnheim's principles of athletic training: A competency-based approach, 15th ed. New York, NY: McGraw-Hill.

Roh, J. L. C., & Perna, F. M. (2000). Psychology/counseling: a universal competency in athletic training. *Journal of Athletic Training, 35*(4), 458.

Singh, H., & Conroy, D. E. (2017). Systematic review of stress-related injury vulnerability in athletic and occupational contexts. *Psychology of Sport and Exercise, 33,* 37–44.

Spetch, L., & Kolt, G. (2001). Adherence to sport injury rehabilitation: Implications for sports medicine providers and researchers. *Physical Therapy in Sport, 2,* 80–90.

Stiller-Ostrowski, J. L., & Hamson-Utley J. J. (2010). Athletic trainers' educational satisfaction and technique use within the psychosocial intervention and referral content area. *Athletic Training Education Journal, 5*(1), 4–11.

Taylor, J., & Taylor, S. (1997). *Psychological approaches to sports injury rehabilitation.* Gaithersburg, MD: Aspen.

Terry, P. C., Lane, A. M., & Fogarty, G. J. (2003). Construct validity of the Profile of Mood States: Adolescents for use with adults. *Psychology of Sport and Exercise, 4*(2), 125–139.

Terry, P. C., Lane, A. M., Lane, H. J., & Keohane, L. (1999). Development and validation of a mood measure for adolescents. *Journal of Sports Sciences, 17*(11), 861–872.

Thomeé, P., Wahrborg, P., Borjesson, M., Thomeé, R., Eriksson, B. I., & Karlsson, J. (2006). A new instrument for measuring self-efficacy in patients with an anterior cruciate ligament injury. *Scandinavian Journal of Medicine & Science in Sports, 16*(3), 181–187.

Tracey, J. (2003). The emotional responses to the injury and rehabilitation process. *Journal of Applied Sport Psychology, 15*(4), 279–293.

Walker, N., Thatcher, J., & Lavallee, D. (2007). Psychological responses to injury in competitive sport: A critical review. *The Journal of the Royal Society for the Promotion of Health, 127*(4), 174–180.

Walker, N., Thatcher, J., & Lavallee, D. (2010). A preliminary development of the Re-Injury Anxiety Inventory (RIAI). *Physical Therapy in Sport, 11*(1), 23–29.

Webster, K. E., Feller, J. A., & Lambros, C. (2008). Development and preliminary validation of a scale to measure the psychological impact of returning to sport following anterior cruciate ligament reconstruction surgery. *Physical Therapy in Sport, 9*(1), 9–15.

Werner, J. L., Burland, J. P., Mattacola, C. G., Toonstra, J., English, R. A., & Howard, J. S. (2018). Decision to return to sport participation after anterior cruciate ligament reconstruction, part II: Self-reported and functional performance outcomes. *Journal of Athletic Training, 53*(5), 464–474.

Wiese-Bjornstal, D., Smith, A., Shaffer, S., & Morrey, M. (1998). An integrated model of response to sport injury: Psychological and sociological dynamics. *Journal of Applied Sport Psychology, 10*(1), 46–69.

Zakrajsek, R., Fisher, L., & Martin, S. (2017). Certified athletic trainers' understanding and use of sport psychology in their practice. *Journal of Applied Sport Psychology, 29*(2), 215–233.

Zakrajsek, R. A., Martin, S. B., & Wrisberg, C. A. (2016). National Collegiate Athletic Association Division I certified athletic trainers' perceptions of the benefits of sport psychology services. *Journal of Athletic Training, 51*(5), 398–405.

TEAM MANAGEMENT

Charlie Maher and Jim Taylor

The inclusion of sport psychology and mental training programs in sports organizations is an increasingly important area in which consultants can provide athletes and teams with an essential piece of the sports performance puzzle. As noted in the Introduction, given the demands of sports organizations to meet the performance and personal needs of its athletes and the pressures on those organizations to succeed, mental training is becoming an integral part of their operations, particularly at the collegiate, Olympic, and professional levels.

As discussed earlier in this chapter, consultants are typically a part of a high-performance team that includes sport coaches, strength and conditioning coaches, athletic trainers, team physicians, nutritionists, and other sports-performance specialists. Yet, despite the growth in the operations of such teams, theory, research, and practical experiences about how to consult with key stakeholders in sports organizations related to implementing mental training programs in collaboration with an organization's management has been largely unexamined in the sport psychology literature. Mental training, when managed with a premium being placed on structure, process, and mutual accountability, will be a valuable asset to sports organizations now and in the future, so an in-depth of understanding of how consultants work with its management is essential.

This section will explore how consultants can collaborate with a sports organization's management on the design and implementation of mental training services. In this regard, collaboration of this nature will be considered as reflecting in where consultants reside in a team's structure and how mental training is implemented in the larger rubric of the high-performance teams.

Theory and Research

There is a vast literature that has examined how consulting is integrated into a range of organizations outside of sports (Driskell, Salas, & Driskell, 2018; Salas, Tannenbaum, Cohen, & Latham, 2015; Zaccaro, Marks, & DeChurch, 2012). Theory and research that has relevance for the work of consulting as part of high-performance teams in sports organizations can be found in studies and naturalistic investigations that have occurred in the military (McChrystal, 2015), business (Katzenbach & Smith, 2001), commercial aviation (Salmon, Stanton, Gibbon, Jenkins, & Walker, 2010), education (Driskell, Salas, & Driskell, 2018), and human services (Kozlowski, Grand, Beard, & Pearce, 2015).

Within these contexts, research on consulting with organizations has focused on the process of team development, resolving conflict among team members, committing to a unified process (Shuffle & Carter, 2018), and the pursuit of mutual accountability among team members (Katzenbach & Smith, 2001). In the sport psychology domain, some research has been conducted on consulting with multidisciplinary teams in elite sport settings (Reid, Stewart, & Thorne, 2004). In all of these areas, several themes are apparent that have relevance for this section: (1) the importance of team structure (purpose and design); (2) the necessity of a clear process for working together as a team (procedures and implementation); (3) the task of collaboration (communication and integration); and (4) and the challenge of mutual accountability (roles and responsibilities). In this regard, research strongly suggests that consultants have opportunities to take the lead in ensuring that an organization's management and its high-performance team of which they are a member have clear goals and an explicit process by which team members work together for the common good of athletes. Relatedly, consultants can use their expertise and experience to educate an organization's leadership about key elements of effective teamwork.

Practical Implications

The information presented in the remainder of this section is intended to guide consultants in how to partner with the management of sports organization for the establishment and continued development of mental training programs for their athletes.

It is important to note here, however, that, due to the dearth of research in this area, the guidelines that will be presented are based on the combined 60 years of experience of the authors in working within corporate, military, educational, and sports organizations. At the same time, the recommendations that are offered have been influenced by theory and research on consulting in organizations that were introduced above.

The guidelines are organized into sequential stages that approximate the process that consultants would proceed through when working with a sports organization:

1. Identify the client.
2. Assess the context.
3. Clarify team structure.
4. Review team operations.
5. Provide feedback.

Identify the Client

As is the case with any type of consultation with sports organizations, identifying the client is a necessary first step in the process. This determination is important because who precisely the client is may not be clear in many sports organizations. Depending on its level, scope, and goals, clients might include team owners, team leadership, sports medicine staff, coaching staff, or athletes.

The identification of the client for the provision of mental training services enables consultants to address several key areas that are relevant for offering the highest quality services to a sports organization. First and foremost, this clarity ensure that consultants behave in the most professional ethical way possible. This concern includes issues of confidentiality and disclosure, financial compensation, decision making, autonomy, and whose interests are prioritized.

Second, this stage allows consultants to explore with the identified client what their specific needs and goals are, how they can be best met, and obstacles that may exist. In this regard, the following are actual examples of the needs and goals of sports organizations drawn from the professional experiences of the authors of this section:

- Assess and address the mental health needs of its athletes and coaching staff.
- Assess the mental performance needs of its athletes.
- Design and implement an integrated mental training program for its athletes.
- Offer psychological insights as part of the draft and recruiting evaluation team.
- Collaborate with other members of the organization's high-performance team to support the physical, mental, and technical development of its athletes.
- Design and implement a process for team development.
- Evaluate the current status and future direction of mental training services within the organization.

The identification of the client and their expressed needs for mental training services allows consultants to establish an agreement with sports organizations that will address their needs and goals while also allowing for ethical professional behavior and providing safeguards for the athletes and staff who would be the recipients of these services.

Assess the Context

Once the client for consultants' services in the sports organization has been established and needs, goals, roles and responsibilities, and direct reports have been specified, the next phase for consultants is to assess the organizational context within which they will be embedded. Context assessment of this kind will provide consultants with information about how to best build relationships within the organization and how to optimize the services they provide as members of the high-performance team.

A context assessment can occur primarily by means of interviews of relevant stakeholders, observations, and informal information gathering. Toward that end, twelve factors can be used as the basis for the assessment by consultants:

- **Values:** Are the values espoused by the organization aligned with those of the consultant?
- **Ethics:** Will the organization allow the consultant to work in an ethical manner?
- **Goals:** Do the goals of the organization align with those of the consultant?
- **Understanding:** Does the organization have a clear understanding of what mental training is, how it can benefit its athletes, and how it can be effectively implemented?
- **Resources:** Does the organization have the financial and human resources to commit to a comprehensive mental training program?
- **Timing:** In the overall operations and evolution of the organization, is now the right time to introduce a mental training program?
- **Collaboration:** Does the organization's management believe that high-performances services are best delivered in a collaborative and integrated way?
- **Buy-in:** Is there buy-in and commitment to a mental training program at all levels of the organization?
- **Resistance:** Is there anyone in the organization who may resist or undermine efforts to establish a mental training program and, if so, why?
- **Obstacles:** Are there any structural obstacles (e.g., facilities, equipment) to implementing a mental training program?
- **Time:** Is there time in the relevant schedules within the organization to implement the mental training program?
- **Benefits:** Do the stakeholders see the value of mental training within the overall context of the organization?

Clarify Team Structure

During this phase of exploring the viability of embedding a mental training program, the attention of consultants shifts to clarifying the structure of the organization and the high-performance team of which they will be a member. Team structure involves determining the extent to which the following elements of an organization are present and conducive to implementing a mental training program and integrating it into the structure of the high-performance team and the organization as a whole:

- **Purpose:** This statement details the rationale for the mental training program within the high-performance team and the overall organization.
- **Service delivery goals:** These goals establish clear outcomes and the processes for achieving them for each component of a mental training program including assessment, intervention, and evaluation and how the high-performance team expects to coordinate their efforts to assure that quality and effective services will be provided.
- **Communication:** This element of organizational structure determines the procedures for how consultants are to communicate with athletes, high-performance team colleagues, and management.
- **Organization contact information:** A listing of the names and contact information of every member of the organization including athletes, coaches, sports medicine staff, management, and other stakeholders.
- **Reporting relationships:** This information identifies who will be the consultant's direct report within the organization's leadership as well as other individuals who will be involved in the coordination of service delivery for the athletes.
- **Mutual accountability:** This agreement will specify who the consultant will be accountable to within the high-performance team and the organization's leadership to ensure adherence to the purpose and goals that were established above.
- **Budget:** This component will provide a budget that delineates the funding and its sources within the organization and the costs of the mental training program and how they will be accounted and paid for.
- **Program evaluation:** This procedure provides a formal structure and process for assessing the effectiveness of the mental training program with input from all stakeholders.

Review Team Operations

Operations refers to the specific processes by which an organization and its many functions work. Operations can refer to finance, marketing, sales, research and development, human resources, sports medicine, coaching, and the high-performance team. More specifically, it also includes those procedures by which consultants deliver the mental training services as well as the means by which athletes can seek out individual services. During this stage, consultants can use the following indicators in reviewing team operations (using actual examples):

1. Determine if there are principles that have been documented which guide the organization in how it functions.

   a. Vision, mission, and goals.
   b. Collaboration and integration.
   c. Use evidence in organizational decisions.
   d. Transparency.

2. Consider the ground rules that help members to work with one another.

   a. Everyone has a voice.
   b. Prioritize the athletes, their needs, and the tasks at hand.
   c. Be nonjudgmental with one another.
   d. Leave egos and self-serving interests at the door.

3. Find out how the organization makes decisions.

   a. Defined decision-making process.
   b. Cross-organizational input.
   c. Consensus building and buy-in.
   d. Nature and scope of work plans and agendas.
   e. Collaboration on program plans.
   f. Data collection and record keeping.

4. Determine in what ways the organization answers the following questions on a regular basis.

   a. Which athletes have been provided mental training services?
   b. How have these services been provided?
   c. Who was involved in the delivery of the mental training services?
   d. What benefits have accrued to athletes through their participation in the mental training program?
   e. What are the next steps for the continued development of mental training program?

Provide Feedback

The stages that have been described above will provide consultants with a range of information about the structure and operation of a sports organization and its high-performance team. Within this context, this current stage allows consultants to provide feedback to the client. This feedback may be provided verbally as well as in written form, depending on the agreement that consultants have with the organization.

1. The extent to which the structure of the organization is clear and documented with respect to the following:

   a. Clarity of organizational purpose and goals.
   b. The extent to which the organization has a process which they implement in a consistent manner.
   c. The professional qualifications and credentials of staff members.
   d. The degree to which the organization manifests mutual accountability.
   e. Whether there is a plan or procedure for evaluation within the organization.

2. The current strong points of the organization and why.
3. The current aspects of the organization that appear to be limiting itself from realizing its purpose and attaining its goals.
4. Action steps for continued development and improvement of the organization.

   The successful design and implementation of a comprehensive mental training program within a sports organization begins well before consultants start to work with its athletes. To set the stage for the effective delivery of services, consultants should engage in in-depth due diligence as a means of gaining an across-the-board understanding of an organization's foundation, structures, processes, and relationships. Only by establishing a detailed knowledge base of the inner workings of an organization can consultants be sure that they are in a position to offer it the highest-quality mental training services possible that is embraced and supported by all levels of the organization, with the ultimate goal of helping the athletes, and the organization as a whole, achieve its goals.

Summary

- Given the demands of sports organizations to meet the performance and personal needs of its competitive athletes and the pressures on those organizations to succeed, mental training is becoming an integral part of their operations, particularly at the collegiate, Olympic, and professional levels.
- Despite the growing use of mental training in sports organizations, theory, research, and practical experiences about how to consult with key stakeholders in sports organizations related to the management of mental training have been largely unexamined in the literature.

- Theory and research that has relevance for the work of consulting as part of high-performance teams in sports organizations can be found in studies and naturalistic investigations that have occurred in the military, business, commercial aviation, education, and human services.
- Research on consulting with organizations has focused on the process of team development, resolving conflict between and among team members, committing to a unified process, and the pursuit of mutual accountability among team members.
- The guidelines for collaborating with an organization's management are organized into sequential stages that approximate the process that consultants would proceed through.
- Identifying the client is a necessary first step because may be many possible clients within a sports organization including: team owners, team leadership, sports medicine staff, coaching staff, or athletes.
- Assessing the organizational context within which mental training services will be embedded is the next stage including issues such as values, ethics, goals, resources, timing, buy-in, resistance, obstacles, and benefits.
- Clarifying the organizational structure involves identifying structure, service delivery goals, communication, contact information, reporting relationships, mutual accountability, budget, and program evaluation.
- Operations refers the specific processes by which an organization and its many functions work including finance, marketing, sales, research and development, human resources, sports medicine, coaching, and the high-performance team. This final stage allows consultants to provide feedback to the organization in relation to all aspects of its functioning and performance.

References

Driskell, J. E., Salas, E., & Driskell, T. (2018). Foundations of teamwork and collaboration. *American Psychologist, 73*(4), 334–348.

Katzenbach, J. R., & Smith, D. (2001). *The discipline of teams*. New York, NY: Wiley.

Kozlowski, S. W. J., Grand, J. A., Beard, S. K., & Pearce, M. (2015) Teams, teamwork, and team effectiveness: Implications for human services integration. In D. A. Boehm-Davis, F. T. Druse, & J. D. Lee (Eds.), *APA handbook of human services integration* (ch. 34). Washington, DC: American Psychological Association.

Kozlowski, S. W. J., & Chao, G. T. (2018). Unpacking team dynamics and emergent phenomena: Challenges, conceptual advances, and innovative methods. *American Psychologist, 73*(4), 576–592.

McChrystal, S. (2015). *Team of teams*. New York, NY: Penguin.

Reid, C., Stewart, E., & Thomas, G., Multidisciplinary sport sciences teams in elite sport: Comprehensive servicing or conflict and confusion. (2004). *The Sport Psychologist, 18*, 204–217.

Salas, S. I., Tannenbaum, D., Cohen, D., & Latham, G. (Eds.). (2015). *Developing and enhancing high-performance teams: Evidence-based practices and advice*. San Francisco, CA: Jossey-Bass.

Salmon, P. M., Stanton, N. A., Gibbon, A. C. Jenkins, D. P., & Walker, G. H. (2010). *Human factors methods and sport science*. New York, NY: CRC Press.

Taylor, J. (Ed.). (2015) *Professional practice development for sport and performance psychology*. Morgantown, VA.: FIT Publishing.

Zaccaro, S. J., Marks, M. A., & DeChurch, L. (2012). *Multiteam systems: An organization form for dynamic and complex environments*. Abingdon: Routledge.

INDEX

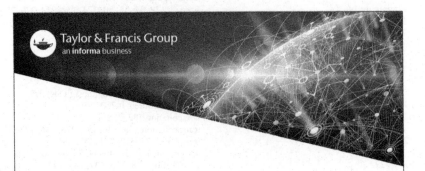